PRAISE FOR

Celebrate Your Divinity

"All who thirst for genuine meaning behind life and explanation of greater reality will find what they are looking for in Orest Bedrij's book *Celebrate Your Divinity*. Many contemporary 'theories of everything' conclude with an all-encompassing particle or astronomic singularity. This book covers the unfinished terrain, showing a mathematical unity behind the physics, and how such discoveries relate to our deepest sensibilities about God, the All-in-All, and the world.

The book weaves also together many vistas of history and recent sociopolitical events with this arcane matter. It shows the reader where humanity must go, and provides material suggestions on simple approaches they can use to improve life's quality at any immediate moment . . . His guidance is a wonderful steppingstone toward a fulfilled life."

—**Prof. Stephen Modell**, MD, MS, Director Research, Genetic Policy, University of Michigan

"This is a visionary work of monumental proportions; a masterpiece of man's highest thoughts and insights. Orest Bedrij has trodden where most dare not. He has had the courage to visit and deliberate in the great disciplines and then to reap the harvest of the world's greatest minds—minds from those at the dawn of the understanding of man's consciousness to those at the forefront of today's level of understanding. Just as so many of the great minds before us, in their flashes of inspiration, Bedrij has seen the thread of new unity among the fruits of the disciplines of science, philosophy, religion, mathematics, bringing them under one brillian   ith us all. This work will bring to us a   bring

D1157962

inspiration to those seeking new and deeper insights into reality. It will encourage these pioneers of human thought to move ever boldly forward."

—**Prof. Peter Kotzer**, President of
Washington Natural Philosophy Institute

"The ideas in this book bring to our civilization a new basis for optimism, a sense of the achievability of sanity. Orest Bedrij delivers to his readers a guide for living which supplements that greatest of guidebooks written for all mankind almost 2000 years ago. The beauty of the writings and the clarity of thinking raised my level of consciousness. I felt cleansed and elevated with new hope. With this book on our bedside table, our sleep can be filled with the wisdom of one of today's great thinkers."

—**Jen Eddy**, Poet, Artist and Spiritual Teacher

"This profound book holds sacred insights sought by the scientists, saints, and prophets throughout history and reveals to us who we truly are, and our interconnectedness with all of creation and the Creator."

—**Charles O. Bubar**, President of The International
Institute for Educational Excellence, Inc.

"This is the book to keep beside your bed and read often. Behind Orest Bedrij's words is the voice of a man who demonstrates the ultimate reality of "One" through science and personal experience. I know of no one else today who could do such a magnificent job in integrating ancient wisdom into an overall non-fragmentary worldview—while inspiring his readers at the same time. The liberal use of quotations from enlightened leaders of humanity today and in the past beautifully demonstrate our evolving human awareness of "I." This book is not just for scientists or the "spiritually" focused; it is for all intelligent open minds and souls who are truth seekers."

—**LaUna Huffines**, Author, *Healing Yourself with Light;*
Bridge of Light: Tools of Light for Spiritual Transformation

"In the midst of guns and glamour, and the ascendant loss of life in the name of serving them, here is a manual for raising the human dimension and struggle to its cosmic significance. Its encyclopedic scope and depth are the product of a lifetime of dedicated study. Orest Bedrij brings fresh light to the Divine disguised in time, the pecking order of Graces, the evolutionary adventure, and located in the Heart of God. He picks his grapes in bunches, harvests clusters—not solitary fruits—and always has hold of the stems.

The book turns out to be a brilliant translation of the insight of contemporary mathematical physics, into the coinage of everyday parlance. This is no bedside novel to nurture sleep, but a wake-up call on the rim of disaster. It is not addressed to the faint of heart or to those with tired minds, but a summons to *know* what it is to *be* fully human, and *do* now what is invited, yes, required of us. Thank Bedrij for blowing a clear, clean, warning signal. It is born of his deepest optimism about the human venture, rooted in his contagious religious and scientific outlook. *Sersum Corda*! *Up Hearts*!"

> —**Dr. Glenn A. Olds**, Former President of Kent State University, US Ambassador to the UN Economic and Social Counsel

"I found this to be a book of revelation about our own divinity and the principle *above* the laws of nature. As such, it is the greatest book of revelations since the Holy Bible."

> —**Dr. Clancy McKenzie**, MD, Author of *Delayed Post-traumatic Stress Disorders from Infancy*

Praise for Orest Bedrij's Previous Books

One

"I have not seen any recent book which encompasses a greater range of factual information nor does so under a more poetic guise than *One* . . . Quotes from the great religious writings of our own and other civilizations link it to the best thinking of all times and all ages."

> —**Prof. John Archibald Wheeler**, Princeton University

"Bedrij is a scientist, a businessman, a mystic. He writes with rare power about science and religion, mysticism and business . . . Beautifully written by a man of sheer intelligence."

> —**The Book Reader**, San Francisco, California

You

"This book is an important stepping-stone to a quantum jump in evolution, a world of Oneness which is in the making under our very eyes. May this book inspire leaders to catch up with the sages of our times who are revealing to us the fundamental Oneness of humanity and of all creation."

—**Dr. Robert Muller**, Chancellor of the United Nations University for Peace, Former Assistant Secretary General of the United Nations

"This very original book is both a work of science and mysticism . . . It will nourish both the mind and the spirit . . . a genuine contemporary spiritual anthology . . . with meditations that succeed each other like beads on a rosary."

—**Prof. Antoine Faivre**, Chair of Esoteric and Mystical Studies, University of Paris (Sorbonne)

CELEBRATE YOUR DIVINITY

The Nature of God and the Theory of Everything

CELEBRATE YOUR DIVINITY

The Nature of God and the Theory of Everything

Orest Bedrij

Xlibris

Copyright © 2005, 2007 by Orest Bedrij.

Library of Congress Control Number: 2005906221
ISBN 10:   Hardcover   1-4134-8172-8
                Softcover   1-4134-8171-X

ISBN 13:   Hardcover   978-1-4134-8172-3
                Softcover   978-1-4134-8171-6

Library of Congress Cataloging-in-Publication Data

Bedrij, Orest, 1933—
p. Celebrate Your Divinity: The Nature of God and the Theory of Everything / Orest
Bedrij. —2nd ed. cm.

Includes bibliographical references and index.
1. Absolute—The, nature, attributes. 2. God—The, science, religion, proof. 3. The
Theory of Everything—Physics, theology. 4. Zero—'1' in physics. 5. Life—Philosophy,
cosmic tales. 6. Science—The Unchanging. 7. Religion—Spirituality. 8.
Enlightenment—Cosmic consciousness. 9. Education—Unchanging facets. 10. One
and Many. 11. History—Political and religious atrocities. 12. Truth. 13. Freedom. 14.
Mind—Superconsciousness. 15. Slavery—Cosmic. 16. Time, space, and gravity—
Nature. 17. Evolution—Unchanging aspects. 18. Family. 19. Vacuum—Philosophy, attributes.

I. Title

Published in the United States by Xlibris, a strategic partner of Random House Ventures,
LLC, a subsidiary of Random House, Inc.

Printed and bound in the United States of America.
January 2007
Second Edition
10 9 8 7 6 5 4 3 2 1

To order additional copies of this book, contact:
Xlibris Corporation
1-888-795-4274
www.Xlibris.com
Orders@Xlibris.com
26217

For You
Boundless Love—the Light of the world.
You
Gazing forth from every face.
You
In Your splendor and glory.

CONTENTS

Pound of Cure * How Do You Tell People They Are Shining Like the Sun? * The Infinite Splendor within Each and Every One of Us * The Exhilarating Peace: Tasting a Fragrance from the Unmanifest Potentiality * See within God Himself: You Become Light * Sages' Glimpses of Unity: Our Hearts Should Do This More

Heart * Love is Sacred: Love Ceaselessly * A New Spirit of
Teamwork: Try to Do Things Right All the Time * The Cuisine
of the Heart: Mother's Love Is Indispensable for Babies *
Parenthood Requires Skills in Human Technology * Something
Is Not Kosher Here: You Cannot Legislate '1' * To Master
Love Is to Practice Love * Freedom Is Directly Related to the
Right Choice: Live Consciously in His Heart

Challenges by Truth: Avoid Problems via the Unchanging Knowledge * Acting in the Interest of the Human Family: A Treasure beyond Price * Cutting-Edge Science of the Future: The Principle *above* the Laws of Nature * No More Doubt about the End: We will Emerge Victorious and Thankful

PREFACE

You are a divine elephant with amnesia
Trying to live in an ant hole.
Sweetheart, O Sweetheart
You are God hiding from yourself.

—Hafiz

When I was a galactic cluster,
I did not understand;
When I was a mighty sequoia,
I did not grasp;
And when on my way I became an elderly woman,
I still did not know;
But, when I let the Life Triumphant, wisdom,
Beauty, truth, goodness, and boundless love of
Sacred teachings be my life,
I realized that I am, was,
And shall always be
The Absolute Reality.

—Orest Bedrij

O Infinite Splendor:
Celebrate Your Life, Celebrate Your Divinity

This groundbreaking work spotlights the most important matter in your life. It is an exhilarating story about God, you, and your Infinite Splendor. Its aim is to give you back your identity. Tens of thousands of individuals and mountains of peer-reviewed evidence support this finding. It will help you understand, love, and admire your infinite nature, leading to a richer and a more exuberant living. The majority of facts with which I shall deal are generally old, incontrovertible relevant, and familiar to most of us.

How would you like, in the spirit of universal incognito, to forget who you are and what you do and to emerge in a cosmic masquerade? Can the "Spirit of God" (the "theory of everything" or '1' in conventional physics), which is biblical in its formulation but the profound "Unchanging State" of the universe in its foundation, rediscover itself within us? Can scientific rigor, precision physics, inner traditions, religious insight, creative problem-solving, and education show us the road map to the heart of things, crack the infinite code across levels of knowledge, and expand "loving relations" among all of us? Can we find the strength and wisdom to carry the great torch of liberty, altruism, and appreciation on its next lap from an unconscious to a conscious growth or remembering?

Just think if it were possible to purify our consciousness ("Who is this I? What on earth am I here for?"), to live and love from the perspective of the "ultimate" or God, celebrate our splendor and divinity, in the "rough and tumble of the real world," as opposed to "the brilliance of the Ivory Tower," we would see the holiness in everyday life and build the golden alphabet of love, goodness, and abundance. With breathless grace we would have the skill to manage our destinies more effectively, the capacity to work miracles daily, and the gift to cheer up our hearts forever.

Among the many tantalizing "what ifs" of the Christ era (AD)— what if the high priests (Annas, Caiaphas, the Sanhedrin), and the teachers of the law, understood what Moses, Isaiah, Jesus, the Buddha, Niels Bohr, Erwin Schrödinger, David Bohm, Albert Einstein, Mother Teresa of Calcutta, John A. Wheeler, and the leading scientists in quantum theory understand today? What if the chief officials, scribes, and the elders of the people in their quest for truth, knowledge, and values understood the nature of God, the secret teachings of the Nazarene, and our Oneness: "all one in Christ Jesus" (Gal 3:28)? What would our human health, music in our minds, fragrance from our hearts, and planetary life be like today if Hitler, Stalin, Mao Ze-dong, husbands and wives, parents and children, employers and employees were encouraged to think of themselves as an absolute family and to call each other "brother" and "sister" who are "filled with the Spirit" of God (Eph 5:18), the wisdom, compassion, and happiness absolute?

My take is, the grand story today would be completely different. The quality of our life (freedom, peace, human dignity, health, cognition, communication, opportunities for individual and social flourishing) would be stunningly higher. There would be no Crucifixion, no Mel Gibson's *The Passion of the Christ*, no Inquisitions, no Crusades, no *Uncle Tom Cabin*, no white slave markets of Morocco, Algiers, Tunis, and Salé, no World War I, no World War II, no Hitler-Stalin-Mao Ze-dong death factories or Holocaust, no 9/11, no nuclear, biological, chemical, and conventional weapons, no jihad (a holy duty obligatory on Muslims to spread Islam by waging war), and no struggle against military Islam. We would have profound peace, unrestrained altruism, heartfelt freedom, great prosperity, and great happiness on earth.

For decades eminent scientist, their troubadours, and the most accomplished scholars of bold vision, daring, and boundless love from a variety of disciplines, knew about our connectedness with everyone and everything. Now you have the opportunity to peer into the minds of brilliance and examine what a galaxy of wisdom teachers, mothers, and fathers have attempted to answer for thousands of years. Now this information can find its way into all reaches of our humanity—help us recover our memory and become conscious of our identity, celebrate our life and our divinity.

'1': The Deepest Law of Nature
Unifies the Laws of the Large and the Small

The Unchanging State, '1' (where the fundamental laws of nature that were true yesterday are true today and will be true tomorrow), which transcends time, space, science, and religion is more than the "ultimate" ground from which all things originate and the basic unity at every point of cosmic order. It is a profoundly personalized experience related to your Infinite Splendor, and how the physics of God and "the unchanging nature of his purpose" (Heb 6:17) flourish in your being, our families, religion, and in science. Why are scientists incorporating God in their equations of physics?

Exhilarating, inspiring, and uplifting, '1' removes layers of mythmaking and casts a new light on this heart-stopping playground of God's masquerade—as us, the latest breakthroughs concerning the personal knowledge and experience of God's heartbeat within everything, the interdependence of our human family, and the common foundation that is *above* all laws of nature. Brimming with old and familiar facts about a priceless treasure, the frontiers of altruistic love, and the momentous principles that control the universe—propelling science, peace, freedom, and economy to one breakthrough after another. This book may be said to have more than eleven thousand corroborators. My sincerest appreciation and indebtedness to all of them and to you for reading this book: Thank you; I love you very much. You will see shortly why.

The evidence is consistent, awesome, and life transforming. You will find in the Notes and Bibliography elaboration, amplification, and strengthening of ideas that are presented in the book. It integrates this heart-to-heart love in each one of us as well as the most recent advances about you, your family, and the people you know through multidisciplinary approaches of books that changed the world and the cutting edge of science. They are for your eyes to see, for your ears to hear, for your mind to know, and your heart to experience. This cross-discipline and cross-sector corroboration produces a unified "theory of everything" (the Holy Grail of modern physics), the future of the universe, and recommends ways of accelerating our individual and social advancement. So that your heart can always be full of eternal joy and deep peace, the sort of pure happiness and gladness that no one can take away from *you*.

INTRODUCTION

Sing praises to God, sing praises:
Sing praises unto our King, sing praises.

—Psalms 47:6

An Exhilarating Experience: Why Tamper with Success?

Manuel Lisa, an Indian trader, accompanied by John Colter, a trapper and explorer, whose traveling party is thought to be the first white people to observe Yellowstone National Park, reported the spectacular thermal phenomena of thousands of erupting hot springs and mud volcanoes. No one believed the story. It was after others crossed the forty-fifth parallel, halfway between the North Pole and the equator, *observed, experienced,* and *verified* the broad, beautiful volcanic plateau, with its ten thousand geysers, steam vents, and oozing mud pots, rivers, fishes, Yellowstone Lake, Mammoth Hot Springs, majestic waterfalls, mountains, flowers, buffalo, elk, deer, moose, bears, and exquisite Old Faithful, that the Yellowstone experience became believable and accepted.

Similar to the Yellowstone explorers, men and women like you and I, throughout the short history of our wonderful planet, have observed, validated, and corroborated the Unchanging State that is *above* the laws of nature. In the wisdom traditions of the world's great cultures we term the Unchanging State as: the nature of God, the greatest good, absolute consciousness, or the secret of secrets.

In precision science, the Unchanging State is the Common Ground, the pre-quantum fact, the ordering principle of the universe, or the *foundational condition of nature* in which time, space, and the texture of reality are in pre-physical potentiality. Metaphorically, this state is like this page before any letters were printed on it, similar to a calculator set at *zero*. Observations of the Unchanging State have led to the endeavor

probabilities

25

of confirming, authenticating, and integrating knowledge into a demonstrable body of natural laws, values, and fundamental physical constants. Today, we characterize this branch of learning, concerning the Unchanging State, as *science*.

Albert Einstein, a towering intellectual gardener of ideas, wrestled for over thirty years with the realms of fields, gravitation, non-Euclidean geometries, and the quantum to develop his unified field theory; namely, a single theory to decipher all physical interactions. Einstein spoke and wrote of how we overvalue science when considered next to Reality. Still, it is our most prized possession; wrote Einstein, "One thing I have learned in a long life: that all our science, measured against reality, is primitive and childlike—and yet it is the most precious thing we have."

What do your deepest intuitions suggest about God and yourself? How is the nature of God manifested? Who does your thinking when you think? Are they identical? I found they are. Furthermore, I discovered that there are numerous methods through which a person can attain validation and enlightenment about their own nature and then deepen one's "realization" further. Additionally, I discovered that the nature of our common bond, human cognition, and goodness of heart, is much greater than generally recognized.

Several questions may well be asked. Given that the truth about our fundamental nature has been known for over three millennia, why has this truth and the study of the Unchanging State not diffused into the planetary appreciation in a more significant manner? Why isn't this news being shouted from the rooftops? Why is the Old Testament insight that "You are 'gods'; all are sons of the Most High ['1']" (Ps 82:6), not reflected in humanity's actions and social outcomes?

Perchance the Unchanging State notion is overly majestic and the human family is not ready to perceive such a grand initiative. Possibly, the Copenhagen interpretation of quantum theory, one of the most imposing structures in all physics, that the "observer and the observed are fundamentally one" has not percolated into the planetary realization. Perhaps Jesus' suggestions for enhancing individual and social flourishing and triumphs and Irenaeus' notion that "God the Logos became what we are, in order that we may become what He Himself is" has not been integrated into humanity's awareness. Perhaps all of these; perhaps none of these.

What has changed? The far-reaching nature of human potential, growth, and transformation was known prior to Darwin. Moses, the Buddha, Jesus, Newton, Darwin, and Einstein brought additional observations to the table. That is my aim here. Now we have new and more compelling evidence of how these insights relate to the Unchanging State, which gave us atoms, stars and planets, our cognition and worldviews about existence; now we have new and more scientific proof. Also, we are at a very crucial time in history. On the one hand, there are countless challenges, some of which are listed in part 2, chapter 10. On the other hand, the solutions to our challenges are coming of age.

Filled with the great joy, wisdom, courage, humor, and empathy of countless luminaries, this book embodies the development of humanity's thinking over the last five millennia. It addresses a multiplicity of relationships: how to live in our maze of the marketplace, how to learn to love beauty and gladness, experience the Holy Light within ourselves, follow our bliss. It suggests an answer to the questions: what is the unified "theory of everything," the future of the universe and cosmic history, and the secret teachings of Jesus. How to make music in our heart? How do we become conscious of who we are, enhance group interaction, and improve quality of our life?

You will marvel, as I did, at the joys and wonders in discovering the answers behind the shadows of Light and life, the alleviation of human suffering, and the advancing your own life and a universe of your own. You will learn how history is fashioned, its implications for us, and why the Emperor of Emperors ('1') has no clothes, and why a matrix of information and knowledge of the Unchanging State will give you and your loved ones the "hidden benefits," more personal liberty, and the improvement of human life and aspirations.

Synthesis of Corroborations:
A Convergence of Science and Spirit

Part 1 concentrates on the traditional historical evidence, from the great treasures of ancient and contemporary wisdom into the various aspects of the nature of God and its implications for us. Does God ('1', the Unchanging State) continue to take an active role in our destiny, or did participation end with the creation of the universe? Part 2 focuses on old and familiar scientific evidence and the latest breakthrough findings of the Unchanging State as a unifying explanation spanning every branch of science and technology, as well as economic, political, and social considerations based on these findings.

There is an absolute core or the Unchanging State to us all, despite the changes observed at the atomic, worldly, and cosmic levels. Albert Einstein points out: the unchanging obstructs nothing, pervades everything, is free from variableness and is "changeless and unmovable." In Christian tradition it was termed as "the unity of the Spirit" (Eph 4:3). Mystery schools and occult teachings signify the Unchanging State with "self-realization," "liberation," and "illumination."

With a bibliography of over six hundred references, the corroborations of cosmologists, physicists, and educators are linked with the validations of researchers and scholars of spiritual ways of thinking; joining the threads of science and symbolic expressions of metaphors and weaving them into a texture of nuanced tapestry. The objective is not to support any individual tradition or science. The purpose is to assist in building bridges, or to give a synthesis of cutting-edge interdisciplinary fields and new insights centering on the unchanging within everything. The goal is to deepen scientific inquiry into the Unchanging State, to reconcile humanity and the Eternal, and to transform information into experiential knowledge. In connecting knowledge of observable proofs in the empirical sciences with verifications of sacred traditions, you will see that all are corroborating the Unchanging State in merely different words.

Some of the researchers, verifiers, and educators of the Unchanging State were elevated to superhuman Olympian heights as holy beings, saints, and prophets, and were worshipped as divinities, goddesses, and extraordinary individuals. The Nobel Prize laureates, recipients of one of the most prestigious of all awards for intellectual eminence, decided by the Nobel Foundation at the Karolinska Institute and presented by the Royal Swedish Academy at the Stockholm Concert Center, have been honored with the elaborate prize-giving ceremonies to become scientific demigods.[1]

The initial prizes of the Unchanging State instituted by Alfred Nobel, the Swedish armament manufacturer, were for physics, chemistry, medicine, peace, and literature. Others were cruelly persecuted, treated as criminals, burned alive at the stake, or had their heads chopped off for "bizarre" stories relating their evidence of the

Unchanging State and our position in nature. If you wish to awaken within yourself a sense of dreadful awe and reverence for the very early Christian martyrs, visit the Appian Way catacombs and secret chapels leading out of ancient Rome. Saint Justin inscribed previous to his own martyrdom, "We are beheaded, we are crucified, thrown to wild beasts, burned, and put to every kind of torture. Everyone sees it."[2]

"Rabbi" ("teacher" of Scripture) Jesus of Nazareth (Yeshua, the Christ), one of the most compassionate and revered human beings who ever walked this planet, was not the only one to sustain the cruelties and gruesome loss of life. He was persecuted, tortured, and murdered for enabling us to appreciate our sense of worth, improving human cognition, and quality of life, and for revealing the embracing nature of the Unchanging State (Christ's Spirit, the nature of God) *in us*. Saint Cecilia, Kabir, Mansur, Paltu, Guru Amar Das, and many others were censored, tormented, or killed under the instigation of the high priests, scholars, or the radical fundamentalists of the day.

Insights into the Nature of Your Being:
All Tell the Same Story

There is a massive body of perennial corroboration, as well as innumerable archaeological finds and endless galleries of scientific books and validation, regarding the Unchanging State and our Infinite Splendor. Some of this evidence is mentioned in the book, Notes, and Bibliography. Other support, like the Nyingma Edition of the Tibetan Buddhist Canon and the Great Treasures of Ancient Teachings (755 volumes with 36,000 titles by 1,500 authors) and the Tao-tsang (1,476 works in 5,481 volumes) is awaiting translation into English.

These most beautiful orchids and timeless classics deepen our understanding of the Unchanging State and our Splendor. They show us how to live and as the Bhagavad Gita put it, "Know this Atman, unborn, undying, never ceasing, never beginning, deathless, birthless, unchanging for ever." They reiterate profound knowledge beyond our grandest notions of evidence that has changed the direction of history and of many lives. Excerpts characterize the embodiment of a deeply intense wisdom which glimpses into the central essence of both the unchanging and *you*—the organizing principle *above* the laws of science that is accepted within the scientific community for proposing, conducting, and reporting research.

gnostics / sanhedrin

Not long ago, most of these classics were censored, prohibited, misrepresented, burned, or lost. Most secret knowledge was communicated verbally and limited to small groups. Even when it appeared on paper, the meaning was frequently cryptic, as the Chinese stated, "the Tao that cannot be spoken," or as the Kabbalists put it, "this is sufficient for one who is enlightened," or "the enlightened one will understand." *Opposition to new knowledge, new learning, and new extensions of rights and freedom of thought and expression has emerged in all communities, small and large, in all parts of the world, during all periods of history.*

"Mind has waited for three billion years on this planet before composing its first string quartet," rhapsodized Freeman Dyson, professor of physics at the Institute for Advanced Study in Princeton. "It may have to wait for another three billion years before it spreads all over the galaxy. I do not expect that it will have to wait so long." These classics present a road map in the exhilarating voyage of human life, leading us all to our Highest Good, the state of being consciously unified with the Unchanging State. Currently we are unconsciously unified.

In ancient times, whether it was putting in place the calendar of seasons, plotting the course of heavenly bodies or measuring the Nile water level, determining the optimum planting and harvesting time in the fields, or cataloging restorative herbs, these efforts were, in most cases, initiated by the upper elite of priests and other high officials dedicated to the service or worship of a deity, holy beings, or nature itself. As particular subject matters acquired systematic depth and validity, some beliefs became verifiable facts. Knowledge and magical moments of experience advanced from the temples of faith, belief, and educated nobility, thus becoming a way of life and living truth in homes, schools, and communities. This was the case with one of the oldest of sciences, astronomy, which was essential for farming, creating calendars, and navigation. The same held true with medicine, education, biology, and mathematics.

Today, "the whole structure of our society does not correspond with the worldview of emerging scientific thought," said physicist and systems theorist Fritjof Capra. Erwin Schrödinger maintained that it takes approximately fifty years before a major scientific breakthrough enters the public consciousness—before the populace recognizes what science knows. In addition, we are facing revisions of the fundamental concepts of science by the Unchanging State, which is *above* and beyond the laws

30

of science, and is more drastic than those engendered by relativity, quantum mechanics, and particle physics. Now we can glimpse dimly into the grand structure of the Unchanging State; as Thomas Merton suggested, "It implies an awareness and acceptance of one's place in the whole; first, the whole of creation, then the whole plan of Redemption— to find oneself in the great mystery of fulfillment."

God's Involvement in History:
You Are Gazing Forth from Every Face

Please forgive my extensive use of citations, enumerations, references, and emphases, parenthetical remarks in quotes [], and accent by way of highlighting or italicizing significance attached to a meaning. There is no substitute for reading and understanding the original words. To make certain that what we say is remembered customarily in life we converse with emphasis. For example, two thousand years ago we did not have the breadth of cosmetics to emphasize some part of the "face" as the eyes or the cheekbones. My purpose, therefore, is to clarify, explain, simplify, and to harvest the "truth" in time and space that expresses ideas and emotion in significant forms through the elements of meaning, harmony, and ease of reading by various kinds of people—young and old, highly educated and less well educated, scientists, ministers, and laymen. Consequently, as an aid to comprehension, please make a note that all Bible (the collection of Jewish and Christian texts), Bhagavad Gita, Koran, Vedic, Islamic, and Upanishadic emphases are mine. I pray that this approach will lead into a fuller appreciation of the Unchanging State, God Almighty within us.

Each human being is unique. What resonates for one heart may not resonate for another. Experience shows the average person has to be informed several times before they see the point. There is a saying in the marketing business that an advertisement has to be seen no less than six times before a communication makes an impact. Reaching the potential buyer with the message is not the challenging part of marketing. What is challenging is getting consumers remember it and then act on it. These devices enable us to understand our human closeness with the Splendor of Light ('1'), to which all explanations and universal truths may be traceable. Each person will find parts of their own life revealed in this journey, and I would suggest reading it either in small chocolate-like doses or making it your main holiday reading. You will not be the same person afterward as before. That is the purpose of this book.

Using verifications of the empirical sciences and support from ancient and recent spiritual wisdom, we discover that all complex phenomena are produced by very simple rules. We learn that we have aspects or capacities not yet developed, that all of us are related, that there is no one else within "our robe" but the Infinite Splendor itself.

Albert Einstein reinforces this perennial wisdom of the world's spiritual traditions thusly: "A human being is a part of the whole, called by us the 'Universe' . . ." Yes, science has achieved a certain level of understanding of the Unchanging State, the nonfragmentary worldview. The Vedas, the ancient Aryan Scriptures and the earliest spiritual revelations of Indian literature, whose pages constitute six times the length of the Bible, gave birth to the idea of an ultimate explanation, beyond the ultimate explanation of traditional religion, "You are looking forth from every face." The Righteous One refined the unchanging concept, "You are the light of the world."

The evidence is compelling. The Unchanging State in mathematical physics, the Light of life in religion, having no explanation in terms of a deeper principle, is nearer to us than we are to ourselves. It has no political doctrine or manifesto and is the central principle of the universe. We are all one. "The kingdom of God ['1'] is near" (Lk 21:31), said Jesus. Our salvation is closer than we accept as true, wrote Saint Paul to the Romans. "The hour has come for you to wake up from your slumber, because our salvation is nearer now than when we first believed. The night [of who is this I?] is nearly over; the day [of the Unchanging State] is almost here" (Rom 13:11).

You Will Never Forget: The Beating of the Heart of God

On one hand, imagine a universe where everything is invisibly connected to everything else on a fantastically deep level, in a most fundamental sense if we are brothers and sisters to one another, members of a family, transcending time and space, being unconcerned with the color of skin or individual ideologies. On the other hand, it is an opportunity to experience your life, in the framework of the Impressionist light, color and inspiration in the arts, such as Handel's *Messiah*, Marc Chagall's series *Message Biblique*, and Thomas Mann's *Joseph and His Brothers*. The corroborations are irrefutable, elucidating, and gripping with the subtleties and elegance of a Stradivarius or a Gardini violin in a concert chamber. I invite you to a personal experience of the beating of the Heart of God, wherein everything is one and works together in crisp megapixel resolution. Come along on a spellbinding adventure of the greatest thinkers and their priceless gems. We owe them a great debt of gratitude after a job well done. They'll touch your soul, as they have touched mine. Make the Great Discovery for yourself about yourself, the meaning of life and your liberation. Renew your conscious connection with the Infinite Beauty, Inner Goodness, and Priceless Splendor within You. Journey. Ascertain. Marvel.

Advances in our civilization have always entailed the awareness of new universal principles, leading to breakthroughs in living, such as reverence to the family, the structure of DNA, and seeing a baby before it is born. Here, you will have the opportunity to understand how *you* can improve the nature of your personal universe, the richness of your life, serenity, and success. You will learn of its absolute simplicity, profundity, and naked magnificence of the One Principle ('1') that is behind everything which has come to pass and will ever take place in our universe. You will wonder why it took us so long to discover the treasure and why we sometimes do not work together in unity and harmony, as do the cells in our bodies and the galaxies and clusters of galaxies.

"We have found a strange footprint on the shores of the unknown," attested the twentieth century pioneer in the fields of relativity and cosmology (study of the largest-scale structure of the universe), Sir Arthur Eddington. "We have devised profound theories, one after another, to account for its origin. At last, we have succeeded in reconstructing the creature that made the footprint. And lo! It is our own."

For an egg to transform into a human, it must stop being an egg. Entry into the highest mode of living involves accessing our highest potential and nourishing our hungry souls. Ultimately, the keys of life are within us: keys to unleashing mighty forces that could be used for good or evil, for creating or destroying; keys to add brightness to the sun or glory to the Infinite Splendor within us.

As the human family gains more knowledge, our prejudices will diminish. Our unity, optimism, appreciation, and loving-kindness will increase. Our standard of living will improve. We will broaden and deepen our compassion, admiration, and happiness in our families, social institutions, schools, and governments. We will bring about more light into light, more compassion into compassion, more teamwork into teamwork, and more freedom into freedom. We will leave our world in a better state than we found it. We must accept the possibility, even the probability that the greatest era of humanity is about to begin. Such convergent reasoning has the potential to impact the general course of our immediate knowledge, national economies, general welfare, and the human disciplines. It can guarantee prosperity, deep peace, health, and happiness for those who practice how to know, learn, care, and make new science, medicine, and religion utterly different from the old. We see our lives yoked to the chariot of the unchanging.

"God speed the mark," wrote Ralph Waldo Emerson. Now, let us deal with the collective evidence leading to a new scientific renaissance, referred to in the idiom of our age as a "final theory." Let us enjoy the trail of light and concern of those spiritual and intellectual contributors upon whose broad shoulders millions have stood and who have enriched this book: Jesus the Christ, Moses, Shakyamuni Buddha, Lao-tzu, Holy Prophet Muhammad, Mahavira, Saint John, Saint Paul, Ramana Maharshi, Jetsun Milarepa, Jalal al-Din Rumi, Paramahamsa Yogananda, Socrates, Seneca, Cicero, Bayazid, Origen, Shankara, Saint Irenaeus, Gregory the Great, Saint Augustine, Moses Maimonides, Sarvepalli Radhakrishnan, Angela of Foligno, John of the Cross, Aldous Huxley, Ernest Rutherford, Enrico Fermi, Albert Einstein, Werner Heisenberg, Charles Darwin, Mother Teresa of Calcutta, Erwin Schrödinger, David Bohm, Max Planck, Niels Bohr, Richard Feynman, Georg Cantor, Paul Adrien Maurice Dirac, Galileo Galilei, Kurt Gödel, James Maxwell, George Santayana, William James, Alfred North Whitehead, Benedict de Spinoza, Teilhard de Chardin, Saint Teresa of Avila, Hildegard of Bingen, Elizabeth of Schoenau, Marie of Oigniens, Hadewijch, Mechthild of Magdeburg, Anandamayi Ma, Saint Thomas Aquinas, Meister Eckhart, Meher Baba, Mahatma Gandhi, Thomas Merton, Sathya Sai Baba, John von Neumann, Eugene P. Wigner, Hans Albrecht Bethe, John A. Wheeler, Steven Weinberg, Arthur Eddington, Isaac Newton, David Finkelstein, Sir Roger Penrose, Stephen W. Hawking, and other noted peers. They are a treasure! The theme is You—the Infinite Magician—playing hide-and-seek from Yourself!

34

PART 1

THE ULTIMATE JOY OF PARADISE— SEEING GOD FACE-TO-FACE

LIGHT OUT OF LIGHT

If you do not expect it,
You will not find the unexpected,
For it is hard to find and difficult.

—Heraclitus

At night prisoners are unaware of their prison,
At night kings are unaware of their majesty.

—Rumi

From ignorance we come to belief;
Through belief we achieve knowledge;
With knowledge we reach understanding.
Understanding in action is wisdom;
Wisdom in action is love;
Love in action is God manifest.

—Orest Bedrij

If you want others to be happy,
Practice compassion.
If you want to be happy,
Practice compassion.

—The Fourteenth Dalai Lama

1

WHERE IS GOD? WHO ARE WE, MY FRIEND?

Washington taught the world to know us,
Lincoln taught us to know ourselves.

—Donn Piatt, a Union soldier and journalist

Who'll Tell Me My Secret?

Would you enjoy a breathtaking hide-and-seek adventure, dressing yourself in masquerade costumes of whirling particles, clusters of galaxies, a gigantic sequoia, a beautiful sunrise, or captivating women? How many billions of years will it take us, in these constantly camouflaging appearances, to awaken to our fundamental identity? How many disguising masks and compassionate songs will it take to perceive the Greatest Wonder in the World, or the Infinite Beauty, Freedom, Wisdom, and Goodness in us?

In the course of this temporary unawareness of our true nature ("identity amnesia"), we may perhaps challenge our mind and heart with liberating questions. Who is the knower? What are we trying to know? Can I free myself from this loss of memory and function in the consciousness and the capability of the Infinite Splendor? How can I contribute to the world around me?

Why are we here? Can we cultivate the energy of life for health, generosity, happiness, inner peace, and longevity? What is the nature of God and its implications for the contemporary science, religion, and society? Can we translate the Eternal Wisdom into the common currency of knowledge, exuberance, and into reverence for the sanctity of our common humanity? How do we upgrade the sacrament of lovemaking to the beatific vision of Einstein's "cosmic religious feeling?" Broadly, can we find the solutions to problems before they actually become problems and, in so doing, advance humanity in awareness, freedom, happiness, and prosperity to greater heights? Do all of these questions point to a common yearning?

The distinguished seminal essayist with an extraordinary depth of poetic and philosophical insight, and the founder of American literary culture, Ralph Waldo Emerson (1803-1882) wrote,

> Who'll tell me my secret,
> The ages have kept?—
> I awaited the seer,
> While they slumbered and slept.[1]

Truth on Parade: Let Us Explore Together

Valéry Giscard d'Estaing (1926-present), former minister of finance and economy, one of the best in France's twentieth century history, was also a seven-year president of France. In the 1950s, German chancellor Konrad Adenauer and three Frenchmen, Jean Monnet, Robert Schuman and Valéry Giscard d'Estaing, originated and pursued the concept of what is now the European Union (EU). In 2002, Valéry Giscard d'Estaing chaired the EU's body drafting the constitutional arrangements for an enlarged, all-embracing twenty-first century EU. France's ex-president stated, "The world is unhappy. It is unhappy because it doesn't know where it is going and because it senses that if it knew, it would discover that it was heading for disaster."[2]

Going . . . going faster . . . but to where? In *Civilization,* Kenneth Clark shared his personal view of our direction:

> I have followed the ups and downs of civilization, historically trying to discover results as well as causes; well, obviously I can't do that any longer. We have no idea where we are going, and sweeping, confident articles on the future seem to me, intellectually, the most disreputable of all forms of public utterance. The scientists who are best qualified to talk have kept their mouths shut.[3]

Is the universe "pointless," as a most distinguished scholar, Steven Weinberg, once suggested, or is it "God's home," as the psalmist put forward? Is it possible that the reason is more basic, more fundamental?

Is it conceivable that even though the present is the most rapid and the most significant evolutionary period in human history, although science has grown with this advancement in power and prestige, deeply we don't understand what we are looking for?

Thomas Berry, in "The Universe Story," remarked that scientific research of the universe in the last four hundred years turn out to be detached from spiritual significance and value. Consistent with Berry, so far, the scientific community was not capable to appreciate the implication of its own attainment, nor recognize its effects. Perhaps we have been focusing on and refining the methods and processes while neglecting our primary goals; as Albert Einstein (1879-1955) stated: "Our age is characterized by perfecting the means, while confusing the goals."[4]

What are the answers in this subtle wonderland? Do today's adults and their children and grandchildren appreciate that they can play key roles in the formation of a global society in which the growth of each individual's capacities is the most important objective? Is life cruel, unyielding, and merciless, or is life incredibly precious, gorgeous, compassionate, and worthy of our deepest respect? Truth seekers, scholars, scientists, and laymen have raised this duality time and time again, within every country on our planet. Still, for most of us, the masquerade remains intact.

Yet, here and there, at various times in history, a small cluster of individuals forged through the haze into the very core of our Infinite Splendor. They "found a strange footprint on the shores of the unknown," as Arthur Eddington points out. They understood who they were and that the exceedingly precious nature of our existence is not to be exchanged for anything else. The first pioneers broke new ground in learning: how to leave behind the Stone Age violence and bloodshed, how to bring peace and prosperity, and how to experience love and to deal with other human challenges. They knew that cruelty breeds cruelty and violence begets violence. They realized that the cornerstone for planetary advancement must be anchored both in an *appreciation of human nature* and an *appreciation of the rest of nature.*

The first pioneers sacrificed their lives toward the same end. They found "The Way" (Lao-tzu; Acts 9:2, 19:9) to divine unity, universal responsibility, and the cultivation of life and human liberty through the advancement of human rights, unconditional love of humanity, goodwill, and empathy. They gave us a taste of how to wage war against evil without implementing evil devices, and of the pristine conditions of the universe before the beginning of the beginning, before the so-called big bang cosmology. They committed their lives to teamwork excellence and to the service of others. Above all, they lived in the ultimate joy of paradise— *working* with God face-to-face.

Lessons for All Times:
The Life of Humanity Is the Life of God

Dag Hammarskjöld (1905-1961), secretary-general of the United Nations (1953-1961), was one such extraordinary individual. He was a serious, exacting, and an impressive world diplomat who dedicated himself to the service and elevation of humanity to its eternal apogee by way of peace, holiness, freedom, and human connection. Hammarskjöld was very much a product of Swedish austerity, sense of duty, and few words. He deployed ascetic methods of lonely farmers and mountaineers in far away places to "purify his consciousness" and heighten his state of awareness and intellectual acuity. His Swedish austerity involved purity of life, rising above self, service-excellence, self-sacrifice, compassion, silence, and meditation. Hammarskjöld discovered the connection between external appearance and internal unassuming nature. "To have humility is to experience reality," said he.

Hammarskjöld is known by every Swede and remains a legendary figure in Sweden. He was aware of who he was. As an apostle to an intellectually oriented rising generation, he tried to ascend above wealth, power, fame, and pomp. He brought freedom of choice with a sense of responsibility, cooperation, peace, and liberty to nations. Similar to John Fitzgerald Kennedy (35th president of the U.S., 1917-1963) assassination in our country, most Swedes who were alive on the 17th of September, 1961, can tell you where they were when they learned of his death.

Despite his demanding banking and a stunningly successful political career, Hammarskjöld devoted himself to personal growth. In banking, at age thirty-one, he was undersecretary of state for financial affairs and at thirty-six, chairman of the board of governors of the National Bank of Sweden (1936-1945). In his political career, Hammarskjöld was vice chairman (1951) and chairman (1952) of the Swedish delegation to the UN, and then secretary-general until his passing. He had the conviction that "no man can properly do what he is called upon to do in his life unless he can learn to forget his ego and act as an instrument of God."[5] Hammarskjöld wrote,

> You are one ['1'] in God, and God is wholly in you, just as for you,
> He is wholly in all you meet. With this faith, in prayer you descend
> into yourself to meet the Other.[6]

Hammarskjöld used as his spiritual anchor the divine perfection of "the point of rest," or perpetual stillness:

> To have humility is to experience reality, not in relation to ourselves, but in its sacred independence. It is to see, judge, and act from the *point of rest* in ourselves. Then, how much disappears, and all that remains falls into place.
> In *the point of rest at the center of our being*, we encounter a world where all things are at rest in the same way. Then a tree becomes a mystery, a cloud a revelation, *each man a cosmos* of whose riches we can only catch glimpses. The life of simplicity is simple, but it opens to us a book in which we never get beyond the first syllable [emphasis by the author].[7]

For Hammarskjöld, a life of ascetic simplicity and mutual support was not an issue of having a few possessions, wearing patched robes, eating begged food, or living in a Himalayan or Tibetan cave. It takes a mind which is not engrossed in self (forget yourself—remember the good of other people), does not waste everyday moments on nonessentials, but is concerned with the spontaneity of action in a world of unity and purity, compassion, loving kindness, and service to others first.

Rabbi Abraham Joshua Heschel (1907-1972) was another special human being and a deeply astute, engaging thinker. He realized that "no one will live his life for him, no one will think his thoughts for him, or dream his dreams." He knew that each of us must build our life as if it were a great work of art. The essential attribute of being human is the recognition that *we are all brothers and sisters*. Heschel was a commanding voice in support of the plundered poor. To reflect on Heschel's voluminous writings, depth of insight, and righteous deeds is to peer into that rare, pure, and most perfect diamond of the human phenomenon: the very holy and wise.

Like Mother Teresa of Calcutta and Albert Einstein, Rabbi Heschel understood that "the deepest wisdom we can attain is to know that one's destiny is to aid, to serve" others. In the vein of his biblically prophetic ancestors, Heschel had the skill of harvesting purity with wisdom and grace. At this point, I would like to share with you Rabbi Heschel's philosophical and artistic pearls pertaining to *who this I is*:

> A person wakes up one day and maintains that he is a rooster. We do not know what he means, and assign him to the insane asylum.
>
> But when a person wakes up one day and maintains that he is a human being, we also do not know what he means.
>
> Assuming that the earth was endowed with psychic power, it would raise the question: Who is he—the strange intruder who clips my wings, who trims my gardens? He who cannot live without me and is not quite a part of me?[8]

Yes! Yes, held the kind Rabbi Heschel. You, too, can learn to shed failure and overcome disappointments to achieve a rich, satisfying life of deep peace and state of happiness. *The life of humanity is part of the life of God*: "How embarrassing for man to be the greatest miracle on earth and not to understand it! How embarrassing for man to live in the shadow of greatness and to ignore it, to be a contemporary of God and not sense it. Religion depends upon what man does with his ultimate embarrassment."[9]

In May 1961, President John F. Kennedy announced a challenge and made a public promise to land a man on the moon by the end of the decade. In 1969 the fulfillment of Kennedy's vision was achieved. Apollo 11 was launched on July 16, 1969, with Commander Neil A. Armstrong, command module pilot Michael Collins, and lunar module pilot Edwin "Buzz" Aldrin. The spacecraft, traveling 24,200 miles per hour, reached the moon on July 19, and the following day, at 10:56 p.m. EST, Armstrong took his left foot off the module footpad and placed it on the moon. The entire world heard Armstrong's legendary expression: "That's one small step for man, one giant leap for mankind."

"As the first astronauts traveled out into space and the Earth receded into the distance," wrote Peter Russell in his insightful book *The Global Brain*, "national boundaries began to lose their significance. These space pioneers no longer found themselves identifying with a particular country, class, or race but with humanity and the planet as a whole. Standing on the lunar surface, the astronauts saw what no human being had ever seen before: the great sphere that is Earth, four times as big and five times as bright as the moon itself.

"To Edgar Mitchel [U.S. astronaut, participant in the 1971 Apollo 14 mission, founder in 1973 of the Institute of Noetic Sciences, of Sausalito, California, a nonprofit educational, research, and membership organization committed to advancing the exploration of science by inquiry into consciousness and spirit], the sixth man to stand on the moon, this was a deeply moving experience, and he felt a strong connection to the planet. "It was a beautiful, harmonious, peaceful-looking planet, blue with white clouds, and one that gave you a deep sense . . . of home, of being, of identity. It is what I prefer to call instant global consciousness."

Mitchel observed that everyone who has been to the moon has had similar experiences. "Each man comes back with a feeling that he is no longer an American citizen—he is a planetary citizen."[10]

Russell Schweickart, U.S. astronaut, participant in the Apollo 9 mission, in 1969, equally experienced a profound change in his remembering, liberation, and enlightenment to that little spot out there. "You recognize that you are a piece of this total life [of the planet] . . . And when you come back there is a difference in that world now. There is a difference in that relationship between you and that planet and you and all those other forms of life on that planet, because you've had that kind of experience."[11]

Ralph Waldo Emerson, the prophet of that archetypal American compassion, freedom, value, and individualism, "riding on the ray of sight" to a point of beatific vision (the mystical *visio beatifica*) and cosmic religious feeling, stated:

> Profounder, profounder,
>   Man's spirit must dive;
> To his aye-rolling orbit
>   No goal will arrive;
> The heavens that now draw him
>   With sweetness untold,
> Once found,—for new heavens
>   He spurned the old.[12]

1.1

IMAGINE IT! IMAGINE YOUR CHILDHOOD

Why spend money on what is not bread,
And your labor on what does not satisfy

—Isaiah 55:2

When You're in a Hurricane, You Can't Buy Hurricane Insurance

Perhaps these firsthand personal experiences can be of help. It is a rather badly acted cosmic comedy about the masters of deception and the political choreography that would be difficult to top. They also illustrate how the purifying fires of our daily challenges can be a recovering memory pilgrimage to a higher quality of life, service-excellence, deep peace, and unity with our Infinite Splendor.

To put the subject matter in historical perspective and the crime against humanity, on the night of August 23, 1939, Joseph Stalin (1879-1953) signed the Nazi-Soviet Pact, which allied the USSR with Germany. In trade for Soviet neutrality, Adolf Hitler gave Stalin a free hand in Finland, Estonia, Latvia, and Eastern Poland (Western Ukraine now) where our family resided. A week later, September 1, 1939, World War II broke out. In superpower diplomacy, Russia and Germany jointly in the blitzkrieg started "liberating" parts of Europe: driving the suffering index off the scale; impoverishing its subjects; slaughtering them in the tens of millions.

Reminiscent of countless other children, I was overwhelmed, at age six, with the mindless promulgation of executions, political assassinations, torturing, religious murder, and genocide of brother against brother/sister perpetrated by the Bolsheviks and their Marxist teams. Acting both on orders and their own initiative, the communists beat women and men to

44

bloody pulps, mutilated their faces beyond recognition, and carried out endless numbers of grizzly massacres, as it is now done by China to the people of Tibet. My aunt identified her husband in the midst of over 10,000 bodies, by his shoes, three days after his kidnapping. The massacre was perpetrated on Beria's orders in Lviv, Western Ukraine, as the Red Army retreated. It was heartbreaking. My father was almost there.

Class hatred and class war were the rallying call and the battle cry of Marxism. This was a proclamation of glamorous visions and extermination at the highest level; it took so little to tip one's destiny. Mass killings, sadism, dispossession of personal belongings, and control over the press and radio were disseminated unalloyed by pretense. Karl Marx disapproved of private property, basic political freedoms, and the free market. He must have recognized that a market economy cannot work without a principled foundation; there must be an underpinning of integrity, freedom, and dependence. You have to rely, you have to trust people; you have to believe, you have to delegate.

Out of Step:
Brother against Brother—Blood Had Been Shed

The "enemies of the people" ("filth," "vermin," and "poisonous weeds," as Stalin and his trusted henchmen and assassins called us) were the enemies of Karl Marx's pie-in-the-sky vision for the communist economic and sociopolitical system, and therefore they were tortured during interrogations, murdered, or hauled away to the GULAG. No one came home after a show trial or the interrogation in Lubianka. The concentration camps at Vorkuta, Kolyma, Dalstroi, Barashevo, Butyrka, Chukotka, Karaganda, Krasnoyarsk, Nova Zemla, Norilsk, Nuksha, Pechora, Polyana, Potma, Ukhta, Unzha, Ust-Vym, Vladimir, Yakutia, Zubova, and so on were not the Soviet Union most prestigious addresses. These were some of the well-oiled death factories. The "central planners" (the NKVD—the secret police and forerunner of the KGB) had a quota of forced laborers, in "the liberation [osvobozhdeniye] of oppressed nations . . . and the struggle for full democracy [consolidated Socialism to full Communism]," as stated by Lenin.[13]

Vladimir Ilyich Ulyanov Lenin (1870-1924): Russian Communist revolutionary leader (Soviet premier, 1918-1924) and Leon (Leib Davidovich Bronstein) Trotsky (1979-1940), another Russian Communist revolutionary, were co-organizers of the Bolshevik revolution.

Interesting synchronicity: Lenin, Trotsky, Adolf Hitler, Sigmund Freud, Vasili Kandinsky (founder of abstract paining), Arnold Schönberg (atonal dissonance music) all lived in pre World War I Vienna.

Andrei Sakharow, Nobel Prize winner for physics, in his address "Peace, Progress, and Human Rights," in Oslo Norway thirty-five years later (1975), stated:

> Thousands of political prisoners in the Soviet Union are forced to wage a ceaseless struggle for their human dignity and their conviction against the "indoctrination machine," in fact against the very destruction of their souls . . .
>
> Worst of all is the hell that exists in the special psychiatric clinics in Dnieperopetrovsk, Sytshevk, Blagoveshensk, Kazan, Chermakovsk, Oriol, Leningrad, Tashkent . . .
>
> In the Soviet Union today many thousands of people are persecuted because of their conviction . . . for the sake of their religious beliefs and for their desire to bring their children up in the spirit of religion . . .

Time and again I went to sleep in fear. One did not know in the evening where one would be by the morning. A friend told my father that because we were attending church, we were branded as the "enemies of the people" and were thus dispensable. Marx claimed that religion was the "opiate of the masses," a means of repression for a privileged class protecting their prominence. The state maintained that the church and religion had no place in the affairs of the country and the people; neither did thinking academics, artists, lawyers, scientists, and writers.

From 9 to 12 p.m. I kept watch in the window; my mother had the 12 p.m. to 7 a.m. shift. My father did not participate in the lookout; he had to go to work in the morning. I was in school by 8 a.m. We had a plan. Should the livestock truck (used for the GULAG transports) come for us, I was to escape through the back window to our neighbor, who in turn would dispatch me to other people for safety. My parents wanted to rescue me from the extermination madness. Terror mastermind Lavrentij Beria, Stalin's commissar for internal affairs, the NKVD, was in charge of the GULAG empire.

It was considered a crime to be an individual in a classless, robotlike, society. Dehumanization of ordinary people, hunger torture, atrocities, and human rights abuses of the "liberated" to "full Communism" proceeded methodically, in the prison house of nations and races. On the other side of the Empire, the Bolshoi Ballet was performing *Swan Lake* in the Palace of Congresses, while the Empire's "men of power" (Malenkov, Molotov, Khrushchev, Bulganin, and Stalin's executioners who headed the security forces and secret police: Feliks Dzierzynski, Viacheslav Menzhinsky, Genrich Iagoda, Nikolai Ezhov, and Lavrentij Beria), well lubricated, passed the bottle frequently, were raising vodka toast after vodka toast, inside the Kremlin's walls to visiting comrades. The security forces and secret police at different times had different names: the Cheka (Extraordinary Commission), GPU and OGPU (State Political Directorate), NKVD (People's Commissariat of Internal Affairs), MVD (Ministry of Internal Affairs), MGB (Ministry of State Security), the KGB, and is now, with renewed life under Vladimir Putin, the Russian FSB.

What One Fool Can Do, Another Can

From 1942 to 1945, I experienced the invading boots of Adolf Hitler (1889-1945) and his Nazi (the National Socialist German Workers' Party) state upon the necks of the "liberated," the elimination of "critics," "undesirables," and "waste," through a collection of extermination camps and the Final Solution. Swastika banners, "Heil Hitler" pronouncements, the Third Reich films (motorcades, rallies, politicized journalism, self-congratulatory declarations by Gebels [Hitlers propaganda minister], mass agitation, Hitler going through a frenzy), coercion, and atrocities were customary. Nazi resisters were executed by hanging in the middle of the marketplace. Disease, hunger, and starvation were rife. Underworld criminal enterprises lured and slaughtered young people for sausage to sell at the market. Our family (my sister was four years old) was forced to flee our home and live transiently in ghettos, cattle cars, chicken sheds, and camps.

In the little Hungarian town of Satoraljaujhely we "holidayed" in a crowded Jewish ghetto under Hungarian sentry "protection" that worked with the Germans to prepare a freight train for a concentration camp. We had no clothing or food. Food rations in the detention camp were paltry. People traded their wedding rings, necklaces, and crosses for a loaf of bread with Hungarian sentries. We slept on the floor of a synagogue with beautiful windows. There was some straw on the floorboards. The British bombed at night. When the bombings took place, the Hungarian

Oh God, My God: Do You Have Any Small Children?

A similar soul-crushing suffering visited my future wife, Oksana. At age four she was hauled off with her great grandmother, her grandparents, and their two children, in a cattle train that had a hole in the floor for a toilet, to one of thousands of Soviet annihilation camps.[14] How is one to explain this? Oksana's great grandmother owned oil wells, which were taken and made part of the state holdings. The family was part of the "vampire to be destroyed," according to the economic planners. Her grandmother was tied with a rope while the Marxists kicked her. Their four-year-old, Oksana, jumped on top of her grandmother to protect her from the kicking. They finally stopped.

Oksana was placed in a "slow death" liquidation encampment, deprived of most aspects of ordinary life which could be recognized as human. Cold and famished, without father or mother, stomach rumbling with hunger in the bitter steppes of Kazakhstan, she lived in the Siberian arctic winter in an underground dugout, with "kiziaky" (dry dung) used for fire. To get a first-rate appreciation for the black deeds of the Kremlin, the GULAG empire, and the labor camp inmates (*zeki*, the "subhuman enemies of the people," as the Marxists called them), read Donald Rayfield's *Stalin and His Hangmen* and Aleksandr Solzhenitsyn's *The Gulag Archipelago*.

Three years later, Oksana was starving in the Nazi extermination camp at Dachau, Germany.[15] Oksana was fortunate to be saved, first, from the gas chambers and inferno in Dachau, and then, from Soviet (SMERSH) repatriation from Dachau to the GULAG. Her uncle (the grandparents' third son, who escaped the "permanent purge" of Russians en route to the GULAG) and stepfather were sent off to gas chambers at Auschwitz (German concentration camp in Poland, Oswiecim now) for the twentieth century version of the crucifixion.[16] You did not last long in Auschwitz. Both family members were asphyxiated and burned into ashes, three month after their arrest. The Germans sent their shoes home, less than one month apart. She still has the telegram from the Auschwitz authorities, which her mother gave her.

Truth and denunciations were irrelevant at this juncture. It injures a person's self-importance and awakens bitterness. In Hitler's way of thinking it was an efficient method of imposing Nazi standards on the rest of society, managing critics or those you did not like, similar to Carmelite nun and martyr for the Jewish-Catholic faith, Edith Stein (1891-1942). Stein, a renowned philosopher, educator, and a groundbreaking feminist scholar, is known these days in Roman Ca . circles as Saint Teresa Benedicta of the Cross. She died in Auschwitz gas chambers; her sister Rosa dying there on the same day.

These are memorable examples of the concepts of value of the "liberators" advocating individual freedom of action and expression, bound by unawareness of the Oneness of all, the sacred dimensions of life, and our essential divine nature. The rule of reason was the rule of the death squads, in the empires of the Holy Horror, the crimes of genocide, and the most grievous black deeds against the human family. There was no respect for life, education of its spiritual content, or the improvement of human life and hopes. Medical experiments, hunger, exhaustion, terror, fear, dehumanization of "enemies of the people," raping and looting were the guiding ethical principles and political correctness. Looting included the personal possessions from people's homes (clothes, watches, bicycles, books, herds of cattle), as well as national treasures of paintings, sculptures, art, coins, and icons. Even the topsoil was stripped from the land and taken out by trainloads.

One learns a great deal "living in the land of the shadow of death" (Is 9:2), the gratification of hate, government crime, and the forces of darkness. At first, I experienced inner suffering from the associated flashbacks, what is now called post-traumatic stress syndrome. Later, as an adolescent, I pondered and researched the despotism of Europe and Asia, the decline of free institutions, the growth of the state, the never-ending arming for future war, the Machiavellian credo that heads of state and social institutions can govern without the need for integrity or truthfulness. I became all too familiar with the idea of censorship, bookburning, and oftentimes their authors, thought control, and the glorification of the absurd. I witnessed the global ambitions of despotic leaders who enslaved Europe and Asia for much of the last century, and the hideous atrocities of these and other Hitler-Stalin-Mao Ze-dong death factories.[17]

Questions arose in my consciousness. Where is God in all this violence? Does God have any small children? Does the Great Unseen Power of the universe maintain an active part in our destiny, or did participation end with the creation of the universe? How legitimate are governments, corporate management, and social and religious institutions, if they do not conduct their business by the highest principles and values? How can people do this to people, culture, civilization, and scientific thought; human inhumanity to humanity—

wasted lives and futures? Grief stricken and in tears, others, as the deep pain caused by universal suffering beings. "What is history?" questions Abraham Heschel:

victories, and wars. So many dead. So many tears. So little
et. So many fears. And who could sit in judgment over the
victims of cruelty when their horror turns to hatred? Is it easy to
keep the horror of wickedness from turning into a hatred of the
wicked? The world is drenched in blood, and the guilt is endless.
Should not all hope be abandoned?[18]

From the Trail of Tears Came the Gift of Compassion

As a teenager I realized, what so many others had absolutely well
realized, that we all hurt, and this hurt—this wordless pain—can be
our common starting point and action to security, group and social
prosperity, gratitude, and kindness; force destroys enemies, but
forgiveness and loving-kindness turns enemies to friends. I understood,
like the Christ on the cross, from whom I drew my encouragement,
compassion, and guidance, that there is no future without
reconciliation, unconditional forgiveness, and absorption in life to the
fullest. One will kill oneself through grief, hatred, worry, and fear, as
recent studies on the relationship between immune system and negative
emotions have established. The expression one has in one's heart and
on one's heartwarming smile is far more important than the clothes,
gold, pearls, and diamonds one has on one's body.

After World War II, the Marshall Plan was set up to produce the
healing of Europe, including West Germany. This plan facilitated turning
a former enemy into an ally. President Jimmy Carter, through the Camp
David Accords, also strived to break the cycle of violence by drawing
together Anwar Sadat, the president of Egypt, with Prime Minister
Menachem Begin of Israel.

From the trail of tears came the gift of compassion for the afflicted
and for the spiritually neglected "liberators" united by lack of knowledge
of their own essential value and our fundamental kinship. From the
grace of compassion arose profound behavior and character overhaul, by
means of self-examination, self-education, equanimity, and courage; and
the resolve to do something that would empower change on lessening
conflict or aiding in the normalization of relations between states. Finding

a better path of advancement, expanding human cognition, creating freedom, abundance, happiness, and elevating the human family.

I became aware that as in mountaineering we can ascend to a higher view. From that view we can see and experience a new perspective. Also, I gradually realized that anyone could destroy; not everyone can build. The acid test: the difference between people rests in their ability to perceive or reason from the point of compassion, deep inner peace, recovering memory of their identity, and recollection of former existences (see chapter 23). Physical beauty cannot replace the beauty, character and wisdom within. Additionally, the politics of fear, intrusive government, class hatred, and self-absorption was a reality in our own midst; one can see it at work, in the Senate, or on TV.

Mahatma Gandhi (1869-1948), the gentle secular saint of India, once prayed, "I do not long for a kingdom nor for heaven nor for salvation. I long to lessen the suffering of the wretched." Yes, a compassionate heart is full of love; it always thinks about others, about helping them.

They Were All Proud as Hell of What They Had Done

Webster defines "evil" as that which produces harm, suffering, or injury, as evil deeds, life, or laws. Evil is a term for a lower sense of conscience and empathy for other people. That is, the inner sense of what is right or wrong in one's attitude or behavior, human awareness, and reasoning.

We all know: "Fools rush in where angels fear to tread." The human exterminators were blind to the fact that we together are human beings— "the light of the world" (Mt 5:14)—the Infinite Splendor, and as such owe respect to the sanctity of human life. The leaders and perpetrators at times were unconscious of their own magnificence, brilliant light, individual value, and that the human body is the temple of the Compassionate Love. Al Capone, the Unibomber, the Washington, D.C., sniper, Joseph Stalin, Mao Ze-dong, Chou En-lai, Adolf Hitler, etc., justified their antisocial acts even to themselves. Like many others in the history of humanity, from a cosmic perspective, *they did not know what they were doing; they have not "awakened" to their Infinite Splendor.* They destroyed human beings, based on their "values in use" and "values in exchange" principles. Behind the Communist and Nazi parties stood countless citizens.

Zbigniew Brzezinski, professor of American foreign policy at Johns Hopkins University and former national security advisor, in his superb book

Out of Control, wherein he described how 175 million people were slaughtered in the name of the "politics of organized insanity," states:

> Contrary to its promise, the twentieth century became mankind's most bloody and hateful century of hallucinatory politics and of monstrous killings. Cruelty was institutionalized to an unprecedented degree; lethality was organized on a mass production basis. The contrast between the scientific potential for good and the political evil that was actually unleashed is shocking. Never before in history was killing so globally pervasive, never before did it consume so many lives, never before was human annihilation pursued with such concentration of sustained effort on behalf of such arrogantly irrational goals.

1.2

DON'T KICK OVER THE BEEHIVE, IF YOU WANT TO GATHER HONEY

We make a life by how we serve.

—Orest Bedrij

A Moment of Decision: Motherhood and Apple Pie?

The fall of the Bastille prison in Paris, on July 14, 1789, which symbolized the old cruel and corrupt order, created a window of opportunity for new thinking in advancing humanity. Karl Marx (1818-1883), Friedrich Engels (1820-1895), Friedrich Nietzsche (1844-1900), Ludwig Feuerbach (1804-1872), and Sigmund Freud (1856-1939) were some of the leading thinkers and the key social human architects of the "new" worldview: its motherhood and apple pie. Their ideas provided the line of thinking for power-hungry individuals to gain power and stay in power. They precipitated the empires of organized insanity, well-oiled killing machines, modern-day slavery, and loss of life.

Karl (Heinrich) Marx, German economist, philosopher, social scientist, and revolutionary, and the German Socialist (in England) Friedrich Engels equipped Soviet Russia (Union of Soviet Socialist Republics and its satellites), China, Vietnam, North Korea, Cuba, and anywhere else it has been lived out, with the blueprints for hallucinatory politics and gruesome bloodshed. *The Communist Manifesto* was the most eminent Pandora's box pamphlet in the history of the Socialist movement. It was the Marxist's "bible of the working class," as it was officially characterized in a resolution of the International Working Men's Association.

nor prime ministers predicted the demise of the Soviet Union with Mikhail Gorbachev's *glasnost* (greater openness) and *perestroika* (restructuring), in 1991.

The Soviet Union and its Communist empire were defeated not on the battlefields of armor but on the battlegrounds of right-to-life thinking: freedom, peace, trust, and a better life for humanity. A similar chain-breaking panorama is awaiting Marx's class hatred philosophy in North Korea, Cuba, China, and other nations. The reason Marxism exists in these states at the moment is that the populace is not allowed to "vote with their feet." They are figuratively chained inside of their own countries. They cannot escape from these "Marxist Heavens."

When Abraham Lincoln issued the Emancipation Proclamation edict (January 1, 1863), to end the brutal reality of human slavery (which declared all slaves free in the secessionist Southern states), Karl Marx, working as a newspaper correspondent, mocked Lincoln's legal document as written by a third rate "pettifogging lawyer."

The British Act of 1807 outlawed the slave trade, fifty-six years prior to Lincoln's Emancipation Proclamation. It was followed up with the final emancipation of slaves in the British possessions in 1833, the year Lincoln was appointed postmaster of New Salem (Illinois) and Chopin wrote piano pieces (Etudes). Holland, Sweden, and France also passed antislave trade laws by the 1820s. History will note, Marx shackled humanity to the slave block; Father Abraham freed humanity from the slave block. Here is Honest Abe's answer to Marx's class hatred:

> You cannot strengthen the weak by weakening the strong.
> You cannot help the wage earner by pulling down the wage payer.
> You cannot further the brotherhood of man by encouraging class hatred.
> You cannot help the poor by destroying the rich.
> You cannot keep out of trouble by spending more than you earn.
> You cannot build character and courage by taking away man's initiative and independence.
> You cannot help men permanently by doing for them what they could and should do for themselves.

"Ownership society" is a Madison's Avenue maxim today. In his acceptance speech at the Republican National Convention in New York, president George W. Bush affirmed: "Ownership brings security, and dignity, and independence." Father Abraham, the rail-splitter, declared many moons ago, "Property is desirable, and is a positive good in the world. Let not him who is houseless pull down the house of another, but let him work diligently and build one for himself, thus by example assuring that his own shall be safe from violence when built."

The fall of the Bastille took place in 1789, and the fall of the Berlin Wall in 1989. Both gave hope for the oppressed. In 1999, facing the tenth anniversary of the collapse of the Berlin Wall, which was built to block escape from the "Marxist Heaven" of sufferings and injustices, the BBC (British Broadcasting Corporation), after conducting a series of polls, in somewhat colorful style of reporting announced the people's choice for the "greatest thinker" of the millennium. It was Karl Marx! Yes. Einstein, Newton and Darwin were the runners-up, respectively. In 2002 the NSF (National Science Foundation) also completed a survey. The NSF announced that at least 50 percent of the population did not know Earth travels around the sun.

The Biggest Realization: "I Have Been Looking for Myself"

Jalal al-Din Rumi or Maulana Rum (1207-1273) was a brilliant Persian scholar, judge, lover of literature, poet, academy head, and a virtuous man. The Sage of Rum was born in Balkh, Afghanistan, which was part of the Persian Empire. At the age of thirty-seven he met the nomadic dervish Shams of Tabriz, of whom Rumi said, "What I had thought of before as God, I met today in a human being." From this association came Rumi's transformation, recovering memory of his identity and spiritual enlightenment. Rumi realized that "when I was looking for God I HAVE BEEN LOOKING FOR MYSELF [emphasis mine]."

Comparable to Johann Wolfgang von Goethe in the German-speaking world, Taras Shevchenko in the Ukrainian-speaking community, and William Shakespeare in the English-speaking populace, Rumi holds undeniably a sympathetic place in the hearts of Middle Easterners. He equates the waging of war to children's games—children who are not aware of their unity and who have not left the "child's play" behind. Rumi wrote:

God said, "The world is a play, a children's game, and you are the children." God speaks the truth. If you haven't left the child's play, how can you be an adult [in consciousness of our unity]? Without purity of spirit, if you're still in the middle of lust and greed and other wantings, you're like children playing at sexual intercourse. They wrestle and rub together, but it's not sex! The same with the fightings of mankind. It's a squabble with play-swords. No purpose, totally futile. Like kids on hobbyhorses, soldiers claim to be riding.[19]

Jeremiah (650-570 BC), reformer, prophet, and author of one of the major prophetical writings of the Old Testament, nineteen centuries before Rumi, quoted God, saying, "My people are fools; they do not know me ['1']. They are senseless children; they have no understanding. They are skilled in doing evil; they know not how to do good" (Jer 4:22). Yes, declared Shams-ud-din Muhammad (Hafiz, 1320-1389), the deeply treasured poet of Persia, who lived at approximately the same time as Chaucer in England and a hundred years following Rumi, "We all sit in His orchestra, some play their fiddles, some wield their clubs. Tonight is worthy of music. Let's get loose with compassion, let's drown in the delicious ambience of love."[20]

Growth Expands Our Concept of God, Reminds Us of Our Essential Nature

There is an unmatched single-mindedness among the synoptic gospels (Matthew, Mark, and Luke) and the Gospel of John that "the kingdom of God" is the essence of Jesus' teachings, miracles, death, and resurrection, and the most important subject matter within his undertaking (Mt 4:17).[21] From Saint Luke we learn, "I must preach the good news of the kingdom of God to the other towns also, because that is why I was sent" (Lk 4:43).

The Compassionate One healed the sick without generic or name-brand blockbuster drugs, "gold standard" clinical trials to back this up, surgery, or the supplements, and demonstrated the life of Infinite Splendor through his wisdom, integrity, gentleness, fearlessness, forgiveness, service-excellence, and unconditional love. In total, the Gospels present over one hundred twenty accounts (Matthew fifty-four;

Mark twenty; Luke forty-three; John four) of the Beloved regarding "the kingdom of God," which is within our own being, making "the kingdom of light" and sharing "in the inheritance of the saints" (Col 1:12) his primary "mission statement" and one of the most momentous events in the social and political history of western civilization.

The Nazarene who shared insights and wisdom that would live forever in the collective memory, with the dedicated persistence advised searching for the kingdom and his righteousness to start with, as the principal purpose in our life: "Seek first his kingdom and his righteousness, and all these things will be given to you as well" (Mt 6:33). In our day language: Seek first the *Common Ground* (the Unchanging State), the Heart and Mind of Perfection, and everything else will be yours.

Rabbi Jesus stated, "the kingdom of God [comparable to the water for (water) waves] is near you" (Mk 1:15) and "within you" (Lk 17:21), suggesting an intimate relation of the kingdom to humanity, as the relationship between water and (water) waves, the harmonization between spirit and matter.

In a different parable he likened the kingdom to a mustard seed (Mt 13:3),[22] one of the smallest of all seeds. "A man takes it and plants it in the ground; after a while it grows up and becomes the biggest of all plants . . ." (Mk 4:31). Consider the "dimensionless point" (mustard seed), and the expansion of the universe from a single point or cosmic singularity.

Saint Paul proclaims, "the kingdom of God is not a matter of eating and drinking, but righteousness, peace and joy in the Holy Spirit" (Rom 14:17). In the Gospel of Saint John with Nicodemus, a leader of the Jews, who belonged to the party of the Pharisees (Jn 3:1-7), and other Pharisees (Lk 17:21), it is made clear that the kingdom of God, the Unchanging State, is within us.

We know that Siddhartha Gautama, Holy Sage of the Shakya Clan, like Jesus the Christ, had an air of wisdom, humility, loving-kindness, appreciation, and compassion for all. He addressed the nature of life, the nature of self, the nature of environment, and the nature of liberation. Similar to the Nazarene, Shakyamuni's priority was bringing to fruition the highest state of spiritual realization—to penetrate the veils of maya (illusion) and perceive the Heart and Mind of Perfection, or to become conscious what one is unconscious.

The enlightened perceives the Infinite Splendor in all beings and the Christ's kingdom "near you," "among you," and "within you." This is a state of being where every thought and act in life is a spiritual exercise, and *our reality is the thought of God manifest in human form.* Namely, Gautama set his monumental work and the highest goal for all beings on attaining complete liberation through the knowledge that one is not the body but rather absolute consciousness, or a Buddha (*videhamukti* in Hinduism). He pointed out: "In the search for truth there are certain questions that are not important. Of what material is the universe constructed? Is the universe eternal? Are there limits or not to the universe? . . . If a man were to postpone his search and practice for enlightenment until such questions were solved, he would die before he found the path."

Gautama amplified his priority with a story of a hunter who has been wounded by a venomous arrow. The doctor wants to remove the lethal arrow, but the patient declares, "The arrow shall not be pulled out until I know who the man is who shot me; to what family he belongs, if he is big, small, or of medium size; if his skin is black, brown, or yellow." Just as the hunter wounded by the poisonous arrow would have expired before he obtained his answers, so we have to postpone many of our questions and hasten to attain liberation in a timely manner. Namely, we have to achieve complete peace of mind, happiness, and the "great death" of ego, as soon as possible.

Albert Einstein, like the Christ and the Buddha, had a similar priority: to bring the true value of a human being to a state of consciousness in which she or he can come to realize that life is continuous, undivided. Einstein stated, "A human being is a part of the whole . . ." Furthermore, said he, "The true value of a human being is determined primarily by the measure and sense in which he has attained liberation from the self."[23]

As a matter of fact, our scientists by applying their human genius at that which is "first" or invariable are in reality building a realm of the Unchanging State—statements of timeless truths and liberation through science and technology. In focusing on the unchanging ('1'), scientists are making science more scientific.

Rumi gives his "number one" priority (referring to enlightenment) a lively air of duty, "You have a duty to perform. Do anything else, do any number of things, occupy your time fully, and yet, if you do not do this task; all your time will have been wasted."[24]

The Unexpected Universe: Brilliant Perspectives

Picture for a moment an orchestra playing your most beloved symphony, with ear-thrilling ease. Ah! Hear and feel the captivating music. Now, instead of allowing the musicians to perform your enchanting piece as a unit, isolate each player in a soundproof booth. Being skilled musicians, they will still execute each individual part flawlessly. Imagine having a remote control switch enabling you to choose, to tune in on each player individually. Because you know the symphony, you will be able to relate each individual part to the piece as a whole.

Visualize a situation in which a class of students, none of whom is familiar with your beloved symphony, is then invited to listen only to the violin theme, the flute, the tuba, the cymbals, the kettledrums, or the viola. Will they hear what you hear? How can they, if they do not know the piece?

Mathematician Atle Selberg, recipient of the Fields Medal for unearthing the Selberg trace formula, once stated: "There's no point going off to fight a battle if you haven't got a weapon to fight with." Our challenge and test resembles those who could not comprehend the Holy Symphony, which rings out: "God's temple is sacred, and *You are that temple*" (1 Cor 3:17). "You are God's field [of perception]. You are also God's building [house]" (1 Cor 3:9).

Can we do better? Can we remember what Jesus and the Buddha remembered about their identity? The kingdom of God—the ordering principle of the world—is where God is. And God is everywhere. The laws of physics are always the same (unchanging). They exist at every point of the universe.

We are not what we appear. Sometimes we do not realize that there is more than what we see, more than what we ordinarily know or understand. A few brief illustrations:

a) Our central nervous system utilizes roughly one trillion (yes, trillion with a *T*, 10^{12}) neurons, all joined in networks of profound sophistication. We do not manage these networks consciously. Who manages them and how do these networks do their job?

b) The rotation curves of swirling galaxies indicate most (perhaps more than 95 percent) of our strange cosmos (23 percent is unidentified "dark [a starless mass of spinning] matter," and a gigantic 73 percent is "dark energy") is hidden and therefore unknown. Yet many of us think that what we see (now determined to be four percent atoms) is all there is.

c) Each human offspring (fetus), still in the womb, is female (without regard for XX or XY chromosomes), for its first thirty-five days. On approximately the thirty-sixth day, the genetic encoding takes effect. Female constructions fade away and male constructions begin to form. Why the genetic switch from female (Eve) to male (Adam)? Why not a male fetus for its first thirty-five days of embryology?

d) A century ago, the incidence of all cancers in this country was about one in 150 people. Today the rate is one in three, and most likely will be one in two by 2050. Why? How can we cancer-proof our life?

From time to time, in the name of our convictions, we may believe that the individual participants in the orchestra of life comprise the total grandeur of the Symphony, and that the symphony belongs to us alone, as our personal monopoly. We may even build weapons of mass destruction or come to blows with each other, as exemplified by the countless men, women, and children who were victims of World War I, World War II, China, the Middle East turmoil, and the flattening of the World Trade Center and Pentagon bombings. This is the sad result of a lack of awareness of our true interconnected nature and our ultimate goal.

The Greatest Secret in the World in Different Terms

Axiom is a self-evident fact or a commonly acknowledged principle that requires no proof. A self-evident truth in literature, science, or mathematics is a universally accepted principle of unity. Without unity nothing can exist. When you walk, swim, or fly in an airplane, if the ground, water, or space, were not connected, you could not go from point to point or place to place. Unity is self-evident; unity does not require proof. If you understand unity, you will understand the Common Ground, God, and your Infinite Splendor in eternity.

Analogous to the water, which connects (water) waves or the marble, which connects form in a statue, there is a "sacred-space"—a connecting "zero-state" ('1') for all manifestations in the universe. We can equate this Common Ground to the "empty-space" that links one letter to another on this page, the empty-space between the frames of the film in a movie projector, or the empty-space between stars or the particles in an atom. *Light travels in empty-space.* The empty-space or connecting zero-state is the essence of every atom of matter. If there was no empty-space, you could not differentiate between things.

In the books of the Old Testament, the empty-space is symbolized with "the Spirit of the Lord": "The Spirit of the Lord fills the whole universe and holds all things together." Saint Luke, who has been customarily recognized as the author of the fifth book of the New Testament, the Acts of the Apostles, denoted the sacred-space with this passage, "He [the Spirit of the Lord] is not far from each one of us. For in him we live and move and have our being.'" (Acts 17:27-28). Rephrasing it: the empty-space is actually not far from any one of us; for in the empty-space of unbroken unity we live and move and have our being. Consider the sacred-space of unbroken unity very carefully. It will help you understand the nature of our own journey, the infinite coordinates of science, and the ultimate mystery you yourself shape.

Hafiz, whose wisdom, insight, and poetry were greatly admired by Ralph Waldo Emerson, Goethe, Pushkin, Turgenev, Carlyle, Hazrat Inayat Khan, and Garcia Lorca, presents the connecting state in his own way:

> Between your eye and this page I [the sacred-space, '1'] am standing.
> Between your ear and sound
> The Friend ['1'] has pitched a golden tent
> Your spirit walks through a thousand times a day . . .
> Each time you pass any object from within it I bow.[25]

The book of Judges (6:24) characterized Common Ground as "peace." The Hebrew word translated "peace," *shalom*, appears 250 times in the Bible. It is well worth repeating: just as (water) waves cannot separate themselves from water, we cannot separate ourselves from the Common Ground! The waves live, move, and dance in the water!

In effect, Gautama, Jesus, Rumi, and Einstein were suggesting in different words to "seek first" the sacred-space in the universe! "Search first" that which is constant, that which unifies, penetrates, and transforms knowledge, the natural sciences, philosophy, and mathematics. "Seek first" the kingdom of God (the fulcrum of consciousness) or the universe of the sacred-space, since it is prior to all other knowledge. *Seek first the water and you will find the waves!*

When Einstein declared, "Our age is characterized by perfecting the means, while confusing the goals," it means that our era is focusing on the (water) waves and not on the water. Just as in a loving union, where one can experience the "unity of life" shared by a husband and wife, the Common Ground can be in a roundabout way verified with instruments as that which is constant or invariable.

John Archibald Wheeler is one of the leading scientists in quantum theory. He terms the Common Ground or doorway as the "boundary of a boundary," that is, a mutual boundary of one wave with another wave, a shared boundary of one word with another word through empty-space on a page.

The British physicist and Nobel laureate Paul Dirac characterized the Common Ground as "nothingness" that is immaterial, undetectable and omnipresent, out of which all matter is created. David Finkelstein, head of the School of Physics at Georgia Institute of Technology, describes the connecting state as the "causal networks" in a general theory of the vacuum. The world-celebrated physicist and insightful thinker David Bohm identifies the connecting state as "implicate order," where everything is enfolded into everything and the properties of the parts can be grasped only from the dynamics of the totality.

The Copenhagenists, Niels Bohr of Denmark (founder of the standard Copenhagen interpretation of quantum mechanics), Werner Heisenberg of Germany (one of the great scientific minds of the twentieth century and discoverer of the uncertainty principle), and J. Robert Oppenheimer of the United States (one of the few Americans who learned quantum theory at the Copenhagen Institute from Bohr himself and the father of the atomic bomb) term the connecting zero-state as the "pre-quantum" fact. Isaac Newton christened the connecting state as the "absolute space." Albert Einstein represented the zero-state where "a human being is part of the whole" as "ether." He said the "ether" obstructs nothing, pervades everything, is free from variableness, and is "changeless and unmovable."

In Christian tradition the sacred-space, which possesses no substance, can be termed as the "unity of the Spirit" (Eph 4:5-6). When Jesus declared, "Seek first his kingdom and his righteousness . . ." in scientific parlance, it means: "Seek first that which is unchangeable, seek unity, seek freedom, seek peace." Additionally, stated Jesus, when you link up consciously with the kingdom of God, "your whole body will be full of light."[26] How truthful this is will be seen shortly.

Also, affirmed the Nazarene, "When that day [of conscious unity] comes, you will know that *I am in my Father, and that you are in me, just as I am in you*" (Jn 14:20); you will be experiencing, according to the Japanese, *kensho*. That is, you will be "seeing one's own true nature." You will realize that your neighbor is connected to you and her/his face is but your own. You will become conscious, similar to Rumi: "I have been looking for myself."

The Hindus depict the Common Ground as *samadhi* (the void or liberation). In Taoist vocabulary it is the Ultimate Tao and the absence of qualities perceivable by the senses. For Buddhists the Common Ground is *shunyata* (the void, the Absolute), *nirvana*, or the "Buddha Mind." In Sanskrit (the sacred language of Hinduism), the connecting state is "emptiness." The Zen expression for the zero-state is *satori*. Satori represents the same meaning as the Japanese word *kensho*; the two terms are often used synonymously. However, satori is a deeper level of enlightenment than kensho. Kensho is the initial enlightenment that needs first to be developed. For Judaism it is the Star of David. Sri Aurobindo called it the Supermind, Gurdjieff named it objective consciousness, and Richard Bucke labeled it cosmic consciousness. Mystery schools call it self-realization, liberation, and illumination.

In scientific language the connecting or the Unchanging State, its core values and inseparable web of relationships can be represented as the fundamental region of pre-physical potentiality, the field of potential action, or the unified theory of physics. Unless one is able to directly experience and verify the connecting zero-state "between your eyes and this page" or beyond all contents of consciousness, one cannot easily equate one's understanding with spiritual traditions, and also integrate her or his experience with science.

Give the Future a Warm Embrace

We know what happened in the name of religion to the Holy Ones who were killed for bringing forth the wisdom of life's "unity" and knowledge of the Unchanging State. We know what came to pass to Isaiah, John the Forerunner (the Baptist), the Apostolic Founders such as Saint

Stephen, Saint James the Elder, Saint James the Just (the Lord's brother, bishop of Jerusalem), Saint Peter, Saint Paul, and Saint Matthias. Yes, we know what happened to the Apostolic Fathers, for instance Saint Symeon, bishop of Jerusalem, Saint Clement I, the martyrs of Lyons and Vienne, and other saintly notables, such as Saint Polycarp, the Bishop of Smyrna, Saint Eustachius, Saint Symphorosa and her seven sons, Iman Hussein, Sarmad, Shams-i Tabrizi, and Inayat Shahid of Jhok. Their insights about unity of the universe, our Infinite Splendor, or the ageless "kingdom of heaven," appeared to be quite out of the ordinary to the religious, the academic thinking, and cults of their ages. These individuals experienced cruel persecutions, stoning, burning, martyrdom, and baptism of blood for making the "unity of the Spirit" and our birthright understandable.

In Egypt, Christian victims (in an effort to end the Christian sect) were beaten to death during the Diocletian persecution. Carthaginian theologian Quintus Tertullian (160-230), of North Africa, wrote, "If the Tiber reaches the walls, if the Nile does not rise to the fields, if the sky does not move or the earth does, if there is a famine, if there is plague, the cry is at once 'Christians to the lion!'" Recall that Greek philosopher and mathematician Pythagoras (circa 582-500 BC) with three hundred others was burnt to death. The Hebrew prophet Moses (circa fourteenth to thirteenth century BC) who liberated the Israelites out of Egypt and conveyed the Law during their nomadic years in the desert was almost stoned to death. "Why did you bring us up out of Egypt to make us and our children and livestock die of thirst?" protested those set free (Ex 17:3).

Can you and I, in concert, living in contemporary times, explore "new thinking" and pave "The Way" for more unity, freedom, peace, prosperity, and truth? Of course we can!

2

HUMANITY CRUCIFIED AND RISEN: HAPPINESS IS OUR RESPONSIBILITY

Thy brightness does consume all darkness,
Transforms the gloomy night to light.

—Johann Sebastian Bach

The Highest Principles for Our Aspirations

David Bohm (1917-1992), a seasoned physicist with penetrating mental acuity, wit, and a nonfragmentary worldview, was certain that matter and consciousness are one. Bohm had exceptional foresight and eloquence in pointing out the summits of the past in the world of learning. He developed new fields of science and was profoundly affected by his close contact with Albert Einstein and Jiddu Krishnamurti, one of the great philosophers of the last century. Bohm was acclaimed as one of the world's leading researchers of quantum theory and the "empty-space" in which all energy, gravity, force, and matter fields have *zero* strength. Bohm advanced knowledge by stretching our cosmic horizons to the great mystery of a new freedom. He wrote:

> A great deal of work has been done showing the inadequacy of old ideas, which merely permits a range of new facts to be fitted mathematically (comparable to what was done by Copernicus, Kepler, and others), but we have not yet freed ourselves thoroughly from the older order of thinking . . . ["The whole structure of our society does not correspond with the world view of emerging scientific thought," as Fritjof Capra stated earlier]. When we see

new basic differences, then (as happened with Newton) we will be able to perceive a new universal ratio or reason relating and unifying all the differences. This may ultimately carry us far beyond quantum theory and relativity as Newton's ideas went beyond those of Copernicus.[1]

Albert Einstein did not always follow the beaten track of other thinkers. His fertile mind contributed fundamentally to the understanding of mathematical laws underpinning the fabric of our universe, through special and general relativity theory, the Brownian movement theory, and the quantum photoelectric effect. Einstein challenged our understanding of the physical universe. He exhibited a luminosity of language and a profound grasp of the Holy Symphony. He was a prophet with deep compassion for biblical tradition and a vast awareness of cosmic identity. Einstein also contributed a Judeo-Christian point of view in addition to his more familiar perspectives on special relativity and general relativity. He rhapsodized:

> The highest principles for our aspirations and judgments are given to us in the Jewish-Christian religious tradition. [Where we do not think or act as though we were beings separated from the world or each other.] It is a very high goal which, with our weak powers, we can reach only very inadequately, but which gives a sure foundation to our aspirations and valuations. If one were to take that goal out of its religious form and look merely at its purely human side, one might state it perhaps thus: free and responsible development of the individual, so that he may place his powers freely and gladly in the service of all mankind.[2]

There is good reason for this, said Einstein:

> If one holds these high principles clearly before one's eyes, and compares them with the life and spirit of our times, then it appears glaringly that civilized mankind finds itself at present in grave danger. In the totalitarian states, it is the rulers themselves who strive actually to destroy that spirit of humanity. In less threatened parts, it is nationalism and intolerance, as well as the oppression of the individuals by economic means, which threaten to choke these most precious traditions.[3]

The Splendor of Light:
I Heard God Laughing and Crying

Much has been said and written about the greatest liberator of humanity and God in human flesh: "Christ's bringing the human race out of Hell," his profound work, his crucifixion with felons (two cohorts of Barabbas, where a holy man was more dangerous than a murderer) and the future consummation of the new creation. What I cover here is the tip of the iceberg, recreating the barest outline of his life, power, and incredible wisdom.

Jesus (b. 7 to 4 BC, d. AD 33),[4, 5] whose generosity of heart, life of unlimited compassion, and very name evoke joy, peace, and boundless love for many, was a towering altruistic servant and a keen healer of the sorrows of humanity. His Semitic name was Yeshua, meaning, "the Sacred Life, will save."[6] Isha was the name given to Jesus by Hindus, and it is the name of an Upanishad of the White Yajurveda. A good number of Indian works of the Upanishads begin with the Isha.

As acknowledged in the book of Matthew, Jesus was born during the rule of King Herod the Great, who died in 4 BC. We also know that Jesus and his parents escaped to Egypt when Herod ordered his soldiers to kill every male child two years old or younger. After the passing of Herod, Jesus and his family returned from Egypt to their home in southern Galilee. Most scholars calculate Jesus' birth to 6 BC, or possibly 7 BC. Various prophets and teachers of the Hebrew Scriptures[7] announced "God's imminent coming to lay bare the secrets of hearts," a continuous disclosure of eternal truth through the human form, to *reveal the divine disguise in us.*[8]

It is generally agreed that Isaiah (circa eight century BC) has played a central role in both Jewish and Christian tradition. In Christian liturgy and theology, the book of Isaiah every so often is termed the "Fifth Gospel." Isaiah points out: "God is with us (8:10) . . . and the whole earth is full of his glory,"[9] not only on Mt. Zion or the Temple in the city of Jerusalem, as was commonly recognized. In one of his remote viewing experiences, discussed in chapter 14, Isaiah was transported from his time frame to the dimension where "a young woman shall conceive and bear a son . . ." Isaiah stated:

> The people walking in the darkness have seen a great light;
> On those living in *the land of the shadow of death* a light has dawned.
> You have enlarged the nation and increased their joy . . .

71

You have shattered the yoke that burdens them,
The bar across their shoulders, the rod of their oppressor.
Every warrior's boot used in battle and every garment rolled in
blood
Will be destined for burning, will be fuel for the fire.
For to us a child is born, to us a son is given,
And the government will be on his shoulders.
And he will be called Wonderful Counselor,
Mighty God, Everlasting Father, Prince of Peace (9:2-6).

Approximately two centuries later, Shakyamuni Buddha (563-483 BC) in Digha Nikaya stated, "There will arise in the world a lord, a fully enlightened Buddha [a being of unconditional compassion and understanding] endowed with wisdom and conduct, enlightened and blessed, just as I am now. He will teach the dharma [the "Unchanging Principle" of the universe: the "theory of everything" or '1' in the laws of physics] and proclaim the holy in its fullness and purity" (26:25). According to Isaiah, "To open the eyes that are blind, to free captives [the Infinite Splendor] from prison and release from the dungeon those who sit in darkness" (42:7).

Jesus conveyed fundamental values ("look out for each other's interests . . . treat people the way you want people to treat you"[10]), advanced science ("You must shine among them like stars lighting up the sky, as you offer them the message of life" [Phil 2:15]), and elementary principles for building bridges of self-awareness and Being (the Sermon on the Mount [11]).

It should be noted that for the majority of humanity the birth of the "World honored One" in Bethlehem, six miles south of Jerusalem, over two thousand years ago, is a starting point for the calendar. For Buddhists the count time begins at 563 BC, the birth of the "Fully Awakened One" in India. For Islamic history (the Islamic Era, AH or Anno Hegirae) it marks the Prophet's flight from Mecca to Medina, 622 in the Western calendar. And in Rabbinic Judaism, 2000 was the year 5760 of the Hebrew calendar, computed as described in Genesis.

You Are Divine: Strive to Be Free

Jesus, a being of pure and boundless love, charity, and wisdom, delineated the subtleties of human liberty, personal responsibility, and the development of social skills to a primitive aspiring populace. Most of them could not identify with the fine points of our shared dependency, the edification of the whole body (1 Cor 13:8-13), and the great Oneness (the connectedness of everything to everything), harmonizing with nature, respect for the rights of women, the healing capacity of compassion, or the might of bonding, prayer and fasting. Even his apostles, including the most daring statements of Saint John and Saint Paul, quite do justice to the splendor of Absolute Infinity (Jn 1:1) that became conscious in Jesus.

The Nazarene was exceptionally adept at communicating timeless values and vision to his legion of brothers (the 120 or so believers in the year AD 30 (Acts 1:15): apostles, prophets, teachers, workers of miracles) and the public, who in Homer's allegorical words in the Odysseus voyage, "wanted to stay with the Lotus-Eaters and forget the way home." He underlined that it was our duty to seek for freedom, wisdom, happiness, and to labor for the union with God and for self-fulfillment. He yearned for the community to put this cutting-edge knowledge into practice. That is, you refine and perfect these higher values of compassion, inner peace, and bonding so that it, like walking, becomes second nature to you, and once you have that ability, you can react more freely when challenges arise. Instead of divide and destroy, this is unite and live; instead of discursive intellect and "I thinking," it is insight into depths of truth and "Thy will be done" thinking. A different way of stating it is that if you build on a solid foundation, you can adapt effortlessly to changing circumstances and live better.

It was a huge challenge, mind shift, and a culture shock for the religious authorities, who did not internalize these concepts of empathy, reconciliation, and forgiveness and whose role and power base was being tested. Jesus was transforming the laws of nature, of freedom, of requirements for entrance into God's kingdom, of union with God. Just as Copernicus' unbiblical heliocentric model of the universe placed in jeopardy the Earth-centered Ptolemaic theories of astronomy, so Jesus' principles, values, and tenets put in danger the walls, laws, and prevailing stability of the old official doctrines of theology. The Nazarene advanced a new paradigm of awareness: unity, forgiveness, purity of heart, caring for others, extraordinary patience, living in the present, a "there's no limit to what we can achieve" spiritually, as in, God is with us and within us (". . . you are gods" [Jn 10:34]).

In the Sermon on the Mount Jesus consoled not "to take life for life, eye for eye, tooth for tooth, hand for hand, foot for foot, burn for burn, wound for wound, bruise for bruise,"[12] as it was and is currently done in many parts of our planet. There is a "higher law" of mercy, goodness of heart, or compassion, suggested the Christ. "If someone strikes you on the right cheek, turn to him the other also . . . Love your enemies and pray for those who persecute you . . ." (Mt 5:38-48), for *we are One!*

People were urged to embody the pure altruism of "not for myself, but for the world I live," remembering always that the central sanctuary of the tabernacle (the Holy of Holies, our conscience or sense of right and wrong), which was banned to the community by the "thou shall not" of Mosaic doctrines of theology, was now open to the whole of the human family by the understanding of God's presence in them. They were reminded that there is no temple in New Jerusalem, but a realization of God's temple within the human family. For the Lord Almighty and the Christ is the temple (Rev 21:22); "WE ARE the temple of the living God" (2 Cor 6:16).

Bring to Mind Unity—Think Quantum Reality

Like in the days of Jesus of Nazareth, imagine today David Bohm, Carl Friedrich von Weizacker, Jeffrey Bub, Nick Herbert, Willis Harman, Karl Pribram, Paul Dirac, John von Neumann, Erwin Schrödinger, Niels Bohr, Werner Heisenberg, Max Born, John Stewart Bell, Basil Hiley, and John Archibald Wheeler on the steps of political power in Washington, London, Bonn, Moscow, Delhi, Beijing, and Tokyo advancing a new scientific truism. To help the system of navigating soft landing in the economy, they are explaining to the authorities the essential concepts in the foundations of quantum mechanics, the significance of the Copenhagen interpretation, and the "new scientific axiom" of economic (the 101 for businesses), social, political, religious, and personal life. The Copenhagen interpretation points toward the perennial wisdom ideal of the connectedness of everything to everything or a harmonious unity at every point of the universe: adjustment from the parts to the whole—change from the many to the One; not only the "objects" and "events" of the external universe, but also our internal, personal experiences.

In quantum physics, "one is led to a new notion of unbroken wholeness, which denies the classical analyzability of the world into separate and independently existing parts."[13] "Body and soul are not two substances but one. They are man becoming aware of himself in two different ways,"[14] said Carl Friedrich von Weizacker (1912-present), German nuclear physicist and philosopher of science. The unbroken wholeness stands for the "unity of the Spirit" in Christianity—or the Great Perfection in Buddhism. This event is known as quantum nonlocality or nonseparability. The manner we recognize the world is influenced by the contents of our consciousness.

In quantum theory, which most contemporary physicists acknowledge without qualification, the *observer* (the seer: *drig* in Sanskrit) and the *observed* (the seen, *drishya* in Sanskrit) are fundamentally One— (the Unchanging State, *chit* in Sanskrit). Specifically, nothing exists other than the Common Ground (i.e., the organizing principle of the universe). The Common Ground (i.e., the connecting zero-state, the water), which is reflected in the human mind (the wave, as Alfred North Whitehead, Meher Baba, Dag Hammarskjöld, David Bohm, and Hryhoryj Skovoroda realized) produces reality, which is encrypted (unfolded) into '1', making consciousness (decryption process), not substance or the ego-bound individual (the wave), a priori. The human being takes this reflection to be her/his own state of consciousness and thus slows down the unearthing of the Common Ground within her/himself.

Nick Herbert articulates in his masterfully written *Quantum Reality: Beyond the New Physics*, "The world is not objectively real but depends on the mind [decryption algorithm of the search engine] of the observer. The observer may be said to partially create the attributes he observes . . . A rainbow appears in a different place for each observer—in fact, each of your eyes sees a slightly different rainbow. Yet the rainbow is an objective phenomenon; it can be photographed."[15]

Jeffrey Bub studied physics with David Bohm at Birkbeck College and philosophy of science with Karl Popper at the London School of Economics. Bub published with Bohm a "hidden variable" dynamical reduction theory of quantum mechanics and helped sculpt the discussion on the foundational problems in quantum physics. In his illuminating book, *Interpreting the Quantum World*, which is a must reading for advanced students in philosophy of science, physics, and mathematics wishing to get up to speed on the present-day debate over the conceptual foundations of quantum mechanics, Bub states: "It seems that what there is depends in some essential way on how we look. We used to think of the physical universe as composed of separable systems with objective properties that change in certain ways under the action of forces. Now, the story goes, we see that the very notion of a system having a property in the absence of a specific interaction with a measuring instrument is untenable for quantum phenomena." Stanford's Willis Harman states, "We are all connected and all part of the whole." Additionally, "We are indeed cocreators of that world, and that ultimate cause is to be sought not in physical matter, but in mind, or consciousness."

Self-Awareness Is the Best Medicine

In order for us to emerge from our sleep (hunger for fame, regime of fear and worry), to realize the profound happiness that arises from the awareness of being one with God, that "you are one with me"—the Christ provided, similar to a capable mountaineering guide, live demonstrations, explanations, and cutting-edge wisdom. The Nazarene promoted the Old Testament principles of the heart. He quoted Deuteronomy 6:4, that "you should love the Lord your God with all your heart, all your soul and all your strength," and Leviticus 19:18, that "you should love your neighbor as yourself"[16]—for she/he is yourself.[17] "Whatever you did for one of the least of these brothers of mine, you did for me" (Mt 25:40). Reflect on these deep considerations. It can help you answer questions that humans have attempted to answer for thousands of years.

In the Dhammapada the Buddha presented our Oneness bond this way, "[When you] See yourself in others, then whom can you hurt? What harm can you do?" This was the Nazarene's prerequisite for attaining the perfection of insight into, and the realization of, the Absolute Splendor within us, a consciousness shift from the part to the Oneness of the whole, from the many to the One. That is, the awakening from our amnesia or incognito to consciousness of one's own Christ-nature: "that all of them may be one, Father, just as you are in me and I an in you" (Jn 17.21)—the complete enlightenment of a Buddha in Hinayana Buddhism.

Jesus elucidated concepts on the mastery of life, such as developing character, eliminating egocentricity and showing the meaningless of pointless ceremonials: "We do not put any trust in external ceremonies" (Phil 3:3). "God is Spirit," said the Christ. "And those who worship him must worship [live, make decisions, pursue professional success] in spirit and in truth [discovering clarity and balance in the midst of chaos]" (Jn 4:24). Worship in spirit and in truth would no longer take place on some mountain or in Jerusalem, but in the temple of the human being, for our "bodies are members of Christ himself" (1 Cor 6:15).

He demonstrated how to serve one another, how to help the needy, and how to achieve the sublime presence of harmony, altruistic love, wisdom, and never-ending joy. The Nazarene built up people's inner authority and empowered them to take responsibility for their own lives, to act as one intimately connected with His limitless heart ("I am the vine; you are the branches" Jn 15.5), and to change society as necessary. He made it possible to take advantage of our inner might through the self-surrender to the Highest Good within us: "Thy [quantum physicists' world of potentialities] will be done,"[18] or as Hafiz put it, "'Come dance with Me'. Come dance,"[19] to the tune of '1'. Namely, be in unity and harmony with the Infinite Splendor (interior Software or source code of '1') of the universe, and thus turn your existence into the happiness of heaven.[20]

In most cases, the masses could not fathom these deep insights and sophistication that are behind the general discursive reasoning and examples; like old eyes, they lack keenness to the states of knowledge. They are states of insight into depths of truth not explored by the thinking intellect. The populace focused not on the conceptual foundations and the advanced step-by-step knowledge of how "good may arise here," but on the "signs and wonders,"[21] the "lollipops" or miracles. The public noticed only extraordinary supernatural happenings: reality shifts, similar to switching channels on a TV. One should regard the totality of the profound significance behind the capacity to work miracles (such as making the blind see, the lame walk, the deaf hear, and resurrecting the dead) and the kind of advanced science facilitating them. That is to say, understanding how to create the technology of TV.

Each of us arrives into this life as a newborn requiring love, the cuisine of the heart, encouragement, and caring to survive. Not all of us receive these intimate delicacies. Yet, being in love with life (the sanctification of compassion) and experiencing peace and beauty are essential nutrients without which one cannot live. People did not realize, for instance, that the concept held by Jesus, Heschel, Einstein and Hammarskjöld of glad service to another (Good Samaritan [Lk 10:33], washing the feet of the apostles [Jn 13:14]), and devotion to peace, freedom, truth, forgiveness, chastity, compassion, the "feeling of deep union" and care for one another, in point of fact, produce reality transformation: i.e., miracles.

A miracle occurs when, through "the Way" of love, a baby is born. Lighting one candle with another, wireless e-mail, voice transmission through the telephones, digital cameras, fuel cells, flat-screen televisions, DVD recorders, computers, carbon 14 dating, e-commerce, currency futures, financial engineering, nanotechnology, the interbank markets, or whisking hundreds of people away in a jumbo jet can be termed miracles, when you do not understand the basic principles behind them. So the importance of bringing idealistic enthusiasm, cooperation, sincerity, and "Thy will be done" (alignment with the ultimate source code, "it thinking") into all aspects of our life, in Oneness and goodness of heart, even today, two thousand years later, is not always grasped. But when grasped, modern science will appear as prehistoric to future scientists as the science of Greek physicist Archimedes (287-212 BC) appears to us today.

Letting in the Light: The Truth Will Make You Free

One such revolutionary, 101, principle that the Christ advanced concerning the '1' is the intimate relationship between *truth, knowledge,* and *freedom*: "Know the truth, and the truth will make you free" (Jn 8:32). How do we know? What happens when we become deeply aware—when we understand the delicate fragrance of truth? What is the meaning of liberty?

When we know how to speak, read, and write we have more freedom; when we can see, hear, smell, taste, touch, feel, and understand we have more freedom.

Reflect on Jesus' profound words, "I was born and came into the world for this one purpose, to speak about the truth" (Jn 18:37), to expand understanding: to teach people how to fish for truth and knowledge. What are physicists conveying with equations of the laws of physics? They express the truth, the unchangeable laws of physics: the source code of '1'. Physicists add to the acquirement of foundational knowledge of the universe, with the equations of physics. In addition, as we heard earlier, "I must preach the good news of the kingdom of God ['1'] in other towns also, because that is why I was sent" (Lk 4:43). Here we see a link between the kingdom of God and truth: they are one and the same.

And the Roman governor Pontius Pilate's question: "What is truth?" Jesus was "silent" in his response. For me, it is a profoundly insightful way to exemplify truth, through means of the silence.

When we want to hear someone or something, we are silent; when we want to hear our inner voice, we are silent. Elijah encounters truth in a sound of sheer silence, "a still small voice" (1 Kgs 19:12). I don't think Pilate recognized truth's face through "the art of arts": the sound of silence. When the Buddha was asked about nirvana (Absolute Truth), the sage also remained silent.

I observe two types of truth: Absolute or Ultimate Truth (relates to our Infinite Splendor) and relative truth (relates to our daily experiences). In computer terms it indicates that there is a simple and elegant common source code (Common Ground, Absolute Truth, '1') for the universe, and there can be many computations or manifestations of the source code (relative truth) in the universe. Relative truth is the agreement of mind with Reality. In science it means that measurement and theory concur. The two see eye to eye. Brihad-Aranyaka Upanishad, considered "great" for its depth, characterizes the agreement of mind with Reality by way of a man who sees with his eyes. "When they say to a man who sees with his eyes, 'Have you seen?' and he says, 'I have seen,' that is the truth" (iv, 1, 4).

René Descartes (renowned French mathematician, philosopher, scientist, and founder of modern philosophy), Saint Augustine of Hippo (a towering intellect and one of the principal founders of the theology of Christianity), and Benedict de Spinoza (foremost rationalist philosopher) also acknowledged that truth is the agreement of mind with Reality. Likewise, Saint Thomas Aquinas (Italian philosopher, theologian, and logician, one of the most influential Roman Catholic thinkers of the medieval period), al-Hallaj (insightful thinker, writer, and teacher of Islamic mysticism [Sufism], and martyr of Baghdad) and Bodhidharma (the twenty—eight patriarch after Shakyamuni Buddha in the Indian lineage, a merciless debater, and the founder of Zen Buddhism) maintained that truth is the agreement of mind with Reality. When they say to you, "Have you seen it, have you heard it, have you touched it?" and you say, "I have seen it, I have heard it, I have touched it," that is the agreement of mind with Reality—the two are in accord.

Earlier, I have pointed out that analogously to water connecting (water) waves there is a connecting zero-state, a universal source code, which a variety of individuals have characterized by different names. In subsequent chapters, we shall see that the connecting zero-state is the Common Ground of the universe, never changes, pervades everywhere, is motionless, never becomes exhausted, and, as the world-renowned David Bohm characterized, is where everything, like in a hologram, is enfolded (encrypted) into everything. In part 2, the connecting zero-state and a common need to *take what we know one step further* will be addressed more fully. For now, let us consider the zero-state as it relates to the principle of truth and the agreement of mind with Reality.

The More Truth We Discover, the More Good We Will Uncover

Challenge: if everything is related to everything, or the "unity of the Spirit" is all pervading and unchanging, how does one explain a relationship between the changes we experience daily and the Unchanging State? How does one venture and explore "a land without a way" or "the gold of truth" of Edith Stein?

When we walk, read, write, or speak, our walking, reading, writing, or speaking is what creates change in our experience. Were it not for the Common Ground, we could never replicate a situation or repeat an experiment. The reason we can say, "Have you seen?" or "I have seen" is because truth is one, like water for waves or a personal computer (PC) that has fixed software. The type of waves we see in water or the calculations we obtain from a desktop PC, however, are relative, or can differ for each person.

Additionally, there is "manifest truth," as when we bring the light of knowledge of '1' to the surface or observe a "number" in a desktop PC display window, and there is *unmanifest truth,* as when we see a *zero* in a desktop PC display window. The "manifest truth" can be described as "relative truth," as length of your step:

Relative truth = Manifest reality = Waves in water = Thinking consciousness.

The *unmanifest truth*, the fundamental source code, or the ordering principle of the universe, can be defined as the Common Ground, or the Copenhagenists' pre-quantum fact, prior to walking:

Absolute Truth = Unmanifest Reality = No waves in water = At rest consciousness = '1'.

Relative truth is a subset of the Absolute Truth, as a house is a subset of our planet. Relative truth has "limits" or dimensions between points (the Alpha and the Omega in religion, the '1' and the '=' in physics), as in physical quantities, length of one's step, or the distance between the eyes in Michelangelo's marble sculpture *Madonna of the Stairs*.

Absolute Truth ('1') is that which is. It has neither limits nor dimensions; one can carve a limitless number of sculptures (*Moses*; *David*; *Victory*; *Palestrina Pieta*; *Rondanini Pieta*, etc.) out of one marble. In Rumi's words, "Earthly forms are only shadows of the Sun of the Truth—a cradle for babes, but too small to hold those who have grown to spiritual manhood."

Until now, the majority of scientists have been concentrating on relative or manifested truth. The foundational condition of nature, the Common Ground, has been generally below the radar of professional focus. Nonetheless, to characterize physical relationships, it is essential to recognize the pre-quantum "doorway"—the source code—between the dimensionless points in '1'. We must learn to grasp that *empty-space*—the "initial condition" ('1') and the "final condition" ('=') which keeps things (letters and words on this page, notes in music) apart and in equilibrium. The manifestations that come into being and the changes we experience daily, in '1', are due to our "thinking consciousness" scanning ("walking," decrypting the "infinite hologram": see the Nature of Time and the Nature of Space in part 2, chapter 6) the Common Ground of Truth.

"Plan your work, and work your plan" is an old and true adage. Truth manifests when a potentiality of the '1', becomes actualized or downloaded: i.e., visible and testable. Like chiseling out a face in marble, every time we have an insight into Truth, some slice of darkness drops away, some component of consciousness is transformed. The more truth we discover, the more good we'll eventually uncover.

Profound truths have been discovered abundantly, often out of the blue. However, our thinking consciousness, most of the time, is aware only of the relative truth, the manifest or observable universe. Yet we have the faculties, or the potential, to suspend discursive thought ("I thinking") and to tune into and *function* at the Absolute state ("Thy will be done," "it thinking") or the cosmic consciousness state. Similar to the pupil in one's eye, appearing in different modes or cinematographic focusing, our thinking consciousness and our Infinite Consciousness are of an identical essence. By shifting our thinking from activity to *rest* (from talking to listening), from relative truth to Elijah's "sound of sheer silence," one experiences the fresh fidelity to the complexity, breth, and immeasurable beauty of the crystal-clear Light and a progressive unfolding of the '1'.

Science is the orderly acquirement of knowledge by systematic means (experience and/or experiment). In reaching for the foundational condition of nature, Jesus characterized absolute consciousness or Truth as "God's will." By doing His will, by "dancing with me," as Hafiz verbalized, one is doing what is right. One is synchronizing to the internal groove of '1'. Einstein stated, "Reality ['1'] is the real business of physics." Winston Churchill declared, "Men occasionally stumble over the truth, but most pick themselves up and hurry off as if nothing had happened."

When we add numbers in the manner a computer would, we are doing what is right. When Michelangelo Buonarroti carved the marble *David* in the right sequence, he was doing what is right. When we discovered how to walk, talk, make fire and electricity, and how to transport people by ship, automobile, or airplane, we brought into light some aspects of the Highest Good. Whenever we have an insight into truth, some slice of darkness drops away, some component of consciousness is transformed. We are doing "God's will." Therefore, said the Christ, "If any one chooses to do God's will, he will find out whether my teaching comes from God or whether I speak on my own" (Jn 7:17).

Love the Truth with All Your Heart and All Your Power

The insight into the Highest Good, the Common Ground, is the foremost mandate in the search for the unchanging in science, the cultivation of wisdom, and the development of the spiritual life. For Buddhists it means direct knowledge of the Buddha Mind, or, in Maimonides, Pure Intellect ['1']. Knowing, gathering knowledge, loving, and uniting with Truth, as the first commandment suggests, is to love God with all of you:[22] "You must love the Lord your God ['1'] with all your heart, and with all your soul, and with all your strength, and with all your mind."[23] Equally, "Worship the Lord your God and serve only him ['1']!" (Mt 4:10).

Truth does not rely on show of hands. In scientific lingo it means *we must love and comply with that which is unchanging*, or we will get nowhere with our theory, experiment, or scientific method. In Christ's terminology, "Anyone who loves his father or mother more than me ['1'] is not worthy of me; anyone who loves his son or daughter more than me is not worthy of me; and any one who does not take his cross and follow me is not worthy of me" (Mt 10:37). Anyone who desires to fly a plane must abide by the ordering principle ('1') of the universe.

Abraham Lincoln verbalized it this way: "You may burn my body to ashes and scatter them to the winds of heaven; you may drag my soul down to the regions of darkness and despair to be tormented forever, but you will never get me to support a measure which I believe to be wrong—although by doing so I may accomplish what I believe to be right." In the Bhagavad Gita (Sanskrit: The Song of the Lord) we find, "Make Me ['1'] the ultimate goal of life (6.13)."[24] In Mother Teresa of Calcutta's lingua franca, "Let God work through you without consulting you." In Saint Paul's saying, the "Christ in you, the hope of glory."

We do not create or invent the Common Ground; we discover it— we come into attunement with Truth. In the same way, in a PC we do not generate or formulate the internal software of a PC; we download the information or make the unchanging potentiality visible. There are countless "faces of truth" that can be decrypted from '1', just as we can tap numerous relationships (2 x 3 = 6, 6 x 4 = 24) from a PC. We dive deep into that unfathomable ocean of truth in celebrating choice/ responsibility, sunrise/sunset, love letters sent by the wind, rain and snow, a free "private enterprise exchange economy," or deeper avenues of intimacy. Therein is a joyous serenity. Therein is freedom.

Your Thoughts and Understanding Come from Within

Our encounter with the quantum has taught us, however, that, like nibbling food, walking, or carving a marble sculpture, we gain knowledge of the Common Ground in bits, discrete steps, or "quantals." Similar to reading print on a page, we gain knowledge by integrating letters, words, or sentences between points of space. Can all Truth be known? Can we discover all mathematical structures, all "parallel universes" (multiverse), or human civilizations that exist somewhere else in space? Can we access all the mathematical permutations of which a PC is capable?

Kurt Friedrich Gödel (1906-1978) has impressed his audience in a variety of remarkable ways: as one of the world's greatest logicians, mathematicians, and eminent thinkers. Einstein sought out his friendship and considered Gödel an intellectual peer. With his incompleteness theorems, which represent an immense achievement for the human family, Gödel rejected the prospect of structuring a complete, consistent mathematical description of Reality. "For every consistent formalization of arithmetic, there exist arithmetic truths that are not provable within that formal system."

Gödel's theorem raises challenging questions. Can the full light of truth be finitely (mathematically) describable? What are the limits of thought and science? Can we ever fully understand the Old One ('1'), our planes of consciousness, or parallel universes located in an abstract realm of all possible states?

Gödel, to a degree, is correct. There are no limits on the number of faces one can carve out of a block of marble (Reality) that is infinite in all directions. In essence, mathematics cannot characterize all facets of infinity deploying finite data; we cannot decode all potentialities within '1' by means of manifestation. Namely, arithmetic, as a recognized formal system, is inadequate to prove its own consistency. Compared to the printing on this page, we cannot determine from English letters what the nature of Chinese characters will be.

However, to facilitate Gödel's complete and consistent mathematical description of Reality, we can reach the highest ultimate truth or the Common Ground via our consciousness at rest, the Buddhist "it thinking." The mind or "thinking consciousness," which is infinite and unlimited, has the capacity, by means of purity of heart and silence, to know '1' directly because the mind is the '1' in the disguise of manifestation—"the light of the world" of the Christ. (See "How Do We Know What We Know?" and "On-Demand Solutions," in chapter 14).

In other words, manifestation, which is purely a thought projection of our inner faculty (Antahkarana in Sanskrit), with which we reason, experience, and learn, has the potential for human perfection. Or as the Christ suggested, perfection of spirit: "You must be perfect ['1']—just as your Father in heaven is perfect" (Mt 5:48). To me it represents *complete focus on consistent excellence by a process of constant improvement*: "I am going to give them the very best I possibly can." For Toyota's bright and happy charman Hiroshi Okuda it stands for the "just-in-time" TPS (the Toyota Production System) car manufacturing of bringing parts together just as they are needed on the line. At the core of TPS is the relentless drive to eliminate waste (*muda*) and absolute concentration on consistent high quality by a method of continuous improvement (*kaizen*). For IBM's heartfelt chairman Thomas J. Watson Jr. it meant that, every new computer brought into the market must be ten times better for less money. In real terms, the quality, economy, and market penetration of today's Toyota cars and IBM computers is incomparable with those of the 1970s.

Origen (185-254) was the greatest mind before Constantine and one of the most prominent theologians and biblical scholars of the early Greek Church. In *Sermon on Leviticus* (5:2), Origen put it this way, "Understand that you yourself are another world in little, and have within yourself the sun and the moon, and also the stars." When one reads Max Tegmark's "Parallel Universes," in *Scientific American*, one gets a modern version of Origen's statement. "Parallel Universes" (Origen's "another world in little") is "not just a staple of science fiction, other universes are direct implication of cosmological observations," says Tegmark.

Leviticus is the third book of the Pentateuch (the first five books of the Bible: Genesis, Exodus, Leviticus, Numbers, Deuteronomy). In Leviticus the Christ's suggestion is reworded: "You shall be holy for I am holy" (Lev 11:44). Then, said Rumi, the "essence and its deepest secrets are open and manifest to the eyes of the perfect." That is, since everything is here and now ('1'), the human mind, when properly developed, is capable of attaining a full knowledge of everything. As the waters of a lake must be clear and still to reflect your face, so the mind must be purified and tranquil to reflect the essence of life.

To experience '1' directly, the thinking consciousness has to shift into the connecting sacred-space, which is discussed in part 2, chapter 6. The mind must be purified and stilled so that absolute consciousness is free from any overlay. In Sanskrit it means reaching the "nirbita-samadhi" state, in which all thought waves have been switched off or, as Dag Hammarskjöld stated, at "the point of rest." For Buddhists it is the realization of emptiness or absolute voidness. Similar to Origen, the Buddha stated, "I declare to you that within this body . . . you can find the world, and the origin of the world, and the end of the world, and the path . . . to all the goals." He is right.

Acharya Shankara (788-822) was a penetrating thinker and one of the greatest sages of the Hindu tradition. His name means "he who brings blessings." Shankara systematized the basic ideas of the Upanishads and the Bhagavad Gita. He made commentaries on the twelve principal Upanishads which are regarded the oldest portion of the Vedas. He also wrote explanations of the Bhagavad Gita, as summarized in his *Viveka-Chudamani*, often translated as "The Crest-Jewel of Wisdom." Shankara exhibited great wisdom, practical altruism (goodwill and service, benevolence and loving-kindness, unlimited love and compassion), and holiness. He was regarded as an incarnation of Shiva, the third divinity in the Hindu trinity. Shankara maintained that the Atman, pure consciousness or one's Infinite Ground, is identical with Brahman, or the Absolute Infinity. Addressing the Formless Infinity, Shankara, like Rumi, confirmed that through pure silence or illumination the Infinite Light could be experienced and characterized; *you* are "That" Infinite Light:

> Supreme, beyond the power of speech [finite manifestation] to express, [however] Brahman ['1', "white" space on the page] may yet be apprehended by the eye of pure illumination [the superconscious state, Elijah's "sound of sheer silence"]. Pure, absolute and eternal Reality—such is Brahman and "Thou art That" (*Tat tvam asi*). Meditate upon this truth within your consciousness.

"That" refers to the Unchanging Absolute. "Thou art That" or "That thou art" means the Infinite Ground is in essence one with yourself, or, according to Hafiz, "Flushing love and God out into the open."

Lao-tzu (Laozi, circa sixth century BC, China) was a contemporary of Confucius (they met briefly several times), the Lord Mahavira, and Siddharta Gautama. Lao-tzu was an archivist (librarian) for the state of Chou. He is credited with writing the slim volume *Tao Te Ching* (Classic of the Way and Its Power), consisting of a little over five thousand Chinese characters. Of all the great wisdom teachings about the nature of '1' that I had the opportunity to study, the *Tao Te Ching* is by far the most profound—the most penetrating writings in the literature of the unchanging—and the most enlightening. Lao-tzu's magical narrative, as taut and gripping as any thriller, contains ethical, political, cosmological, psychological, linguistic, metaphysical, and epistemological elucidations of the '1', all under a single cover.

Lao-tzu characterized Tao or the Way as the cosmic void (modern physicists vacuum or the lowest energy state; the Christ's Spirit) from which all manifestations materialize and to which they return, such that the fundamental nature of all manifestations is this emptiness—this "nothing." Addressing Kurt Gödel's theorem, similar to Shankara and Rumi, Lao-tzu suggested that "nothing" really matters:

> Without going out-of-doors, one may know all under heaven; without peering through a window, one may know the Way ['1'] of heaven. The farther one goes, the less one knows. For this reason, the sage knows without journeying, understands without looking, accomplishes without acting.[25]

Advancing beyond the stage where our reason is of any avail (i.e., reaching complete peace of mind, pure consciousness)—the search for David Bohm's new universal order—is of singular importance to aspirants throughout the world. The simpler the truth, the more comprehensive and the more fundamental it is. The search for self-knowledge moves a person ever deeper into a direct realization of inner silence, levels of consciousness and actual experiential knowledge. Jalal al-Din Rumi observed in *Masnavi* (*Spiritual Couplets*) that "he who has not tasted does not know."

The Here and Now: Validate through Direct Experience

In science we view the agreement of mind with Reality; this proof of testing is the inseparability of measurement with theory. Darkness is illuminated through verification of physical laws, wherein theory and experiment agree. To understand the ultimate meaning of truth, our predecessors believed that we must be able to assimilate, validate, and corroborate Reality as it is, not as it might appear through speculation, a filter, or an optical illusion. "Test everything," said the remarkable Paul to the Thessalonians (1 Thess 5:21). And, as the great electrodynamics unifier

James Clerk Maxwell declared, experiment must be the judge. Bodhidharma (470-543) and al-Hallaj (858-922), like our scientists, took their cue from everyday experience. Bodhidharma advised his constituency to validate through direct personal experience the essence of truth and the most sublime revelation of the Shakyamuni Buddha.[26]

Al-Hallaj recommended validation of all spiritual truth through actual experiential knowledge. Al-Hallaj's suggestion was a very innovative contribution to Muslim spiritual life. Similar to Jesus, Bodhidharma, al-Hallaj, Saint Paul and Maxwell, Sir Karl Raimund Popper, leader of modern philosophy of science, suggested verification by experience. Popper stated:

> But I shall certainly admit a system as empirical or scientific only if it is capable of being tested by experience . . . In other words: I shall not require of a scientific system that it shall be capable of being singled out, once and for all, in a positive sense: but I shall require that its logical form shall be such that it can be singled out, by means of empirical tests, in a negative sense: it must be possible for an empirical scientific system to be refuted by experience.[27]

Galileo Galilei (1564-1642), Italian astronomer, physicist and mathematician, was one of the leading thinkers in the history of Western science. His uncaged way of thinking, in turning old answers to more profound questions while propelling the birth of rigorous science, taught: "The knowledge of a single fact, acquired through a discovery of its causes, prepares the mind to understand and ascertain other facts, without need of recourse to experiments, precisely as in the present case, where by argumentation alone the author proves with certainty that the maximum range occurs when the elevation is forty-five degrees."[28]

To verify is to unify, to bring together new truth with old truth. To unify is to know; to know is to be free. The simple fact of knowing that it is painful to place a bare hand on a red-hot stove means more freedom from suffering than not knowing. Therefore, to achieve higher levels of emancipation, justice, and the dignity of human life, the future of human society will require the organized acquisition of knowledge and education of that knowledge, making unlimited freedom the realization of our Infinite Splendor. The fruits we produce determine whether we understand the truth or are subject to error. If we decide to place our hands on a hot stove, then our immediate knowledge of hot stoves is obviously incomplete.

Numerous truth seekers possessing equivalent tools and verifiable processes have obtained identical results. These intellectual gardeners of natural laws considered keeping truth alive as a very holy, and at times very risky, calling. Marilyn Wilhelm, penetrating thinker, educational pioneer, and distinguished administrator and scholar, wrote, "Their profound insight into the problems of human existence and the question of right and wrong, and their intuitive solutions to the problems and the questions of right or wrong, have been verified by recent breakthroughs in brain research and medicine."[29]

Experiential knowledge is not intellectual knowledge; intellectual knowledge is not realization. Experience or inner communion ascertains realization. Of course, experience and realization in the ultimate sense, without sufficiently clearing and constantly purifying the consciousness, may cloud the water. Liberation comes when one rises above self-imposed boundaries—when we see perfection everywhere and enjoying every minute of our life. We experience the world as a means of expression of the highest values of life. We witness the birth of a new type of humanity.

Heraclitus (sixth to fifth century BC) wrote, "To men, some things are good and some are bad. But to God, all things are good and beautiful and just."[30]

The More You Know Yourself, the More You Know God

At every step of our self-imposed journey of personal self-discovery, there is always some subtle truth that we believe must be understood—some fine knot that we think must be untied, involving the continuous search for understanding of the inner nature of our Splendor and one's affinity with Absolute Infinity. Consequently, states the Lankavatara Sutra, "With the lamp of word and discrimination one must go beyond word and discrimination and enter upon the path of realization."[31]

Steven Weinberg was educated at Cornell, Copenhagen, and Princeton. He has taught at Columbia, Berkeley, MIT, Harvard and the University of Texas at Austin, where he holds the Josey Regental Chair of Science and is a member of the physics and astronomy departments. Blending scholarship with his own experience, his research has spanned from elementary particle physics and quantum field theory to astrophysics and cosmology. Weinberg has been honored with numerous awards and honorary doctoral degrees from a dozen of universities. He received the 1979 Nobel Prize in Physics, one of the most esteemed of all prizes for scientific excellence, for his contribution in unifying two of the fundamental forces in physics, where all interactions observed and every particle discovered can be elucidated by just four fundamental forces. Weinberg has also been honored with the 1991 National Medal of Science at the White House. He was an active participant in the Superconducting Super Collider project and is a member of a number of learned societies including the U.S. National Academy of Sciences, the American Academy of Arts and Sciences, the International Astronomical Union, the American Philosophical Society, and the Royal Society of London, one of the most ancient scholarly associations on earth. Weinberg points out:

> We search for universal truths about nature, and, when we find them, we attempt to explain them by showing how they can be deduced from deeper truths. Think of the space of scientific principles as being filled with arrows, pointing toward each principle and away from the others by which it is explained. These arrows of explanation have already revealed a remarkable pattern: they do not form separate disconnected clumps, representing independent sciences, and they do not wander aimlessly—rather they are all connected, and if followed backward they all seem to flow from a common starting point. This starting point [universal source code, '1'], to which all explanations may be traced, is what I mean by final theory.[32]

Additionally, as when you balance your checkbook or look at a photograph, truth must be grasped not as a sequential succession of particulars but together as a whole, from all angles and from all sides, as Gottfried Wilhelm von Leibniz (1646-1716), German philosopher and mathematician, asserted. Similar to the LSI (large-scale integration) of computer circuitry on a chip, truth is perceived by connecting propositions all at the same time, in parallel. René Descartes (1596-1650) wrote:

> If, after we have recognized intuitively a number of simple truths, we wish to draw any inference from them, it is useful to run them over in a continuous and uninterrupted act of thought, to reflect upon their relations to one another, and to grasp together distinctly a number of these propositions so far as possible at the same time. For this is the way of making our knowledge much more certain, and of greatly increasing the power of the mind.[33]

Simple truths lead to greater truths. They embrace our lives, give them meaning, and point to our connection with the rest of the cosmic play.

The journey into the Infinite Light transcends all borders. "It is a journey which has unfolded as it must within the horizon of personal self-consciousness," wrote the pilgrim of peace and enormous charisma, His Holiness John Paul II (Karol Wojtyla, 1920-2005) in his *Encyclical Letter to the Catholic Bishops of the World.* "The more human beings know reality and the world, the more they know themselves [as "God's home"] in their uniqueness, with the question of the meaning of things and of their very existence becoming ever more pressing."[34]

3

SETTING YOURSELF FREE: WORTH WORKING FOR

You are love, you are wisdom, you are humility,
You are endurance, you are rest, you are peace.
You are joy and gladness.

—Saint Francis of Assisi

Spiritual Gems of Great Value: Seeing One's Own True Nature

Consider the meaning of Jesus' words: once you *know the truth, the truth will set you free.* Similarly, the Upanishadic mantra "You are That," Socrates, as well as the inscription from the Temple of Apollo at Delphi, acknowledged, "Know thyself" (*Gnothi seauton*), who you really are at your foundation; you shall be free.

Free. Free from what? Free from the deterministic philosophies of history, whether they are the ancient type found in religious writings of the Old Testament or of Saint Augustine, which incline to make us the hand puppet of God or the newer version, which tends, in all its scientific diversity, to make us the marionette of nature? Free from the fear of the unknown regarding immediate knowledge of our sacred foundation, our individuality, and our potential? Free from incarceration in a human body and a camouflaged space-time environment, governed by fate, belief, and chance? What does freedom in the cosmic sense mean? In mathematical terms it means

Freedom = 1/Restriction; Restriction = 1/Freedom

Freedom entails the absence of restriction, limitation or hindrance. When freedom equals 100, restriction or constraint is 0.01; when freedom equals 10,000, constraint is 0.0001. In addition,

Ultimate Freedom ('1') = Ultimate Truth ('1') = Ultimate Responsibility ('1')

According to our present understanding, only God ('1') is free. Free from worry, crisis, regrets, fear, and other human challenges. Is it possible that the Prince of Peace is implying that we, too, can "be full of God," that when we understand the heart of the mystery, the secret teachings of Jesus, we shall then be free? That this is the Metamorphosis we must undergo?

Were we born to be in bondage? Will we enter the Land of Oneness, conscious growth and participation in God's splendor? Should we develop our boundless capabilities—find ourselves in the great unknown of completion? Can some seeds bring forth fruit a thousandfold?

What did Pope John Paul II mean when he dispatched his extraordinary *Encyclical Letter* stating: "The more we know reality and the world, the more we will know our true self, and of our connection with the meaning of things." What did the first Christians, who advanced ecumenism, a nonfragmentary worldview, and the Trinity concept, understand about salvation?

Alastair Logan studied the works of Saint Clement of Alexandria (about 153-217), a contemporary of the apostles, and a witness to their teachings, who was consecrated by Saint Peter. Logan presents difficult topics with a richness of meaning and a marvelous clarity:

> Salvation, then, is special knowledge of one's true self ["seeing one's own true nature" through samadhi, shunyata, or satori as quoted earlier], of one's kinship with the unknown transcendent God and of the true nature of the visible world . . . the knowledge [gnosis] of our origin, nature and destiny, a knowledge which tells Gnostics who they really are and frees them from their present state of ignorance and imprisonment in an alien body and a hostile world governed by Fate. Salvation is *gnosis* in this special sense and its cosmic and metaphysical implications are summed up most concisely in the Marcosian formula reproduced by [Saint] Irenaeus[1]:

The perfect redemption is said to be the knowledge of the ineffable Greatness [*in us*]. From ignorance both deficiency and passion arise; through "knowledge" will the entire substance derived from ignorance be destroyed. Therefore this "knowledge" is redemption of the inner man.[2]

The knowledge and experience of the Divine Presence in one's own being, this lifting of the veil and awakening of interconnected identity, each of us has experienced at least once in life. Heschel writes:

God is not always silent, and man is not always blind. In every man's life there are moments when there is a lifting of the veil at the horizon of the known, opening a sight of the eternal. Each of us has at least once in his life experienced the momentous reality of God. Each of us has once caught a glimpse of the beauty, peace, and power that flow through the souls of those who are devoted to Him. But such experiences are rare events. To some people they are like shooting stars, passing and unremembered. In others they kindle a light that is never quenched. The remembrance of that experience and the loyalty to the response of that moment are the forces that sustain our faith.[3]

Our awareness of "God in us" may be limited at this time, but it is more than we realize, said Heschel, "Man is more than what he is to himself. In his reason he may be limited, in his will he may be wicked, yet he stands in a relation to God which he may betray but not sever and which constitutes the essential meaning of life. He is the knot in which heaven and earth are interlaced."[4]

9/11: Adventure in Prejudice
Saul! Saul! Why Do You Persecute Yourself?

A very special girl works in our office. Her name is Julia, born in Frankfurt to a German mother and an American father. Julia studied in Germany and at Berkeley. She kindles Heschel's momentous glimpses—collegiality of beauty, peace, and happiness—that flow through her when she reaches out to those who need help.

Julia personally experiences the embodiments of love in her life through the joy of giving and a contact of the heart. During the day Julia works as an investment analyst and stockbroker, one block from the two World Trade Center (WTC) towers. The Twin Towers were recently razed to the ground, after two hijacked jumbo jets crashed into them. Julia witnessed from the street below people jumping out of the blazing 110-story Twin Tower in flames when Islamic fundamentalists, in a carefully planned jihad ("holy war") against the despised "infidels" (people who do not accept the Islamic faith or who violated the Islamic Holy Law), bombed the WTC. At day's end, on weekends and holidays Julia brings comfort to the homeless, food to the needy, helps the blind play baseball . . . Here are Julia's momentous glimpses and the spirit of colleagueship:

> I have been volunteering in New York City for over five years now and it gives me great joy, inspiration, and love. I do countless different activities. For example, feeding the homeless at different sites in Manhattan, such as Harlem, churches, walking shelter dogs and coaching mentally and physically disabled persons, and playing softball in Central Park with them. Even though all these activities are different in nature, they all make me feel the same thing: pure and simple happiness. I found that just a very simple and small gesture, such as a helping hand, a cheer, a smile, a nice word, supporting hug can have a great impact. These ordinary for the love of God events mean so much more for these people. It makes them happy; their faces glow with pure joy and happiness. This is also true for the dogs I walk. They are so grateful that somebody takes them out of their cages in the shelter and plays with them. Experiencing this—just one day at a time—makes me feel the same. It's like an infection. I feel "infected" by other people's pure and simple joy and happiness.

The plain truth is this: the Bible, for over two millennia, has been the basic text for Judaism and Christianity. It teaches that "We are one body with many parts" (1 Cor 12:12). The Vedas revere that "Human beings all are as head, arms, trunk, and legs unto one another." The Qur'anic doctrine of "the Unity of Allah" [the Arabic word for God] underscores the Oneness of all: "All creatures are members of the one family of God . . . To Allah belong the East and the West: whithersoever you turn, there is Allah's countenance . . . That man is a Muslim who never hurts anyone by word or deed, but who works for the benefit and happiness of God's creatures. Belief in God is to love one's fellowmen."[5] They all emphasize a state of awareness of one's identity with the Absolute and call attention to the Universal Brotherhood of all living beings. The world over, they forbid murdering of innocent people. They teach, *we are all partners in God* (Heb 3:14); life is sacred; a true lover of God has no room for hatred; love your neighbor:

> Thus we enjoin on you, thus do we say,
> Thus we believe, thus we proclaim to all:
> No living things should be slain anywhere,
> Nor ordered forcibly this way or that,
> Nor put in bonds, nor tortured any way,
> Or treated violently otherwise;
> *Because YOU ARE THAT SAME* which ye would slay,
> . . . *YOU ARE THAT SAME*;
> The selfsame life doth circulate in all.[6]

Yet, on September 11, 2001, at 8: 46 a.m., an entourage of mujahedin (Muslims who wage jihad [holy war as a sacred duty] against infidels), "in the name of Allah, Most Gracious, Most Merciful," carried out an indiscriminate slaughter against the United States, murdering innocent people in the Land of the Free. What right did these "soldiers of God" have to take life in the United States, Spain, and Russia? What right did Rabbi Saul, Hitler, Stalin, Mao Ze-dong, and Chou En-lai have to kill men and women? Thousands perished at Ground Zero.

You have heard of Rabbi Saul's fundamentalist life in Judaism, how intensely he persecuted the church of God and how he tried to destroy it (Gal 1:14). You remember how the fanatic Saul "was extremely zealous for the traditions of his fathers," and how this soldier of God made it his responsibility to hunt down and persecute "the followers of this Way [Christianity] to their death . . ." (Acts 22:4).

There Is No Place for Violence in the Qur'an

The "religious cream of the crop" of the al-Qaeda network (who are linked to mosques that profess conservative Wahhabi strain of Islam) utilizes the Holy Qur'an (or Koran, the Islamic divine book, analogous to the Christian Bible and Hebrew Torah) as the sacred source of their religious and "commit suicide" infallibility. This religious point of view is dominant in Saudi Arabia and advocates hatred against Christians,

Jews, Shiite Muslims, and even moderate Sunnis. They profess that if Muslims die in a jihad, in the praise to Allah, they are guaranteed a high place in the Most Forgiving, Most Forbearing heaven; it is their calling to slaughter infidels in America, where more than 90 percent of population is Christian. How can any rebellious person from any faith give reason for the politics of holocaust perpetrated in the name of religion, let alone consider a mass murder in the "Praise to Allah, the Cherisher and Sustainer of the Worlds"?

Jesus, the Buddha, and Muhammad, three majestic Lights, speak with one heart of love and healing to all of us:

> Why do you look at the speck of sawdust in your brother's eye and pay no attention to the plank in your own eye? How can you say to your brother, "Brother, let me take the speck out of your eye," when you yourself fail to see the plank in your own eye? (Lk 6:41).

Next, the Buddha in Dhammapada,

> Do not look at the faults of others, or what others have done or not done; observe what you yourself have done and have not done (4.7). [And in Udanavarga,] The faults of others are easier to see than one's own; the faults of others are easily seen, for they are sifted like chaff, but one's own faults are hard to see. This is like the cheat who hides his dice and shows the dice of his opponent, calling attention to the other's shortcomings, continually thinking of accusing him (27.1).

Then, Muhammad in the Holy Qur'an,

> Jesus was a true servant of Allah, to whom doth belong the dominion of the heavens and the earth: Glory and Power are His, and His alone . . . Then will Allah say: "O Jesus, son of Mary! Recount My favor to thee and thy mother. Behold! I strengthened thee with the Holy Spirit, so that thou didst speak to the people in childhood and maturity. Behold! I taught thee the Book and Wisdom, the Law and the Gospel . . . And thou healest those born blind, and the lepers, by My leave. And behold! Thou bringest forth the dead by My leave. And behold! I did restrain the Children of Israel from (violence to) thee when thou didst show them the clear signs" (5.109).

Compassion on the Tablets of Human Hearts

Reminiscent of Fascism, Marxism, and the Reign of Terror of Jacobin spirit, fanatic religious extremism is a bizarre sacrificial spectacle of a unique brand of human hatred, bloodshed, and spiritual retardation. Al-Qaeda, who crashed civilian aircraft full of innocent people into commercial and military symbols in the Home of the Brave, did a great deal more than Hitler, Stalin, and Mao Ze-dong. Hitler, Stalin, Mao Ze-dong, and those who killed for them waged war and murdered innocent populace in the name of Fascism and Marxism. Fanatic Islamic fundamentalists wage war and murder innocent people in the name of Allah, staining Muslim faith and Islamic nation-states.

"Qur'an" stands for "protect, save, and find peace." The word "Islam" has two meanings. It denotes "peace" or "surrender to the Allah" (surrender to God's will). "Muslim" means "one who has surrendered."

Al-Qaeda takes on the mantle of human bombs and feasts on an ideology of violence, persecution, and prays for death, commits crimes against God, the Purity of Faith (Al Ikhlas), the foundations of Islamic civilization, and the Holy Qur'an. They use the Muslim greeting, Salaam-o-Aleykum, meaning "peace be with you." They have forgotten that "all those who take the sword will perish by the sword" (Mt 26:52).

In the 1990s, Egypt's interior minister, on the subject of jihad in his own country, declared that the public should "be made aware that the killers who conduct violence against officials and innocent tourists are not Muslims. They do not practice any religion. There is nothing in the Koran that justifies such murder. These men are using Islam as a cover for their political goals."

The renowned sculptor Paul von Ringelheim, who resides a few blocks away from the WTC, with his eyes aglow and his heart alive to the right, stated to me, "So much talk of God, so little feeling of love for our fellow man is the flaw of religion. Man kills one another in the name of the true God while missing his message of love. If we all begin to love, this civilization would finally have meaning."

The Dhammapada, according to Sinhalese tradition, is an essence of sayings given by Gautama Buddha on some three hundred different occasions. The 426 verses on the basics of the Buddhist teaching are called "The Path of Dharma" (law, duty, justice, truth). Here is a thought for the jihadist bombers to consider: "Never by hates are hates extinguished; only by love may hate be changed to love and cease as hate—such is the Eternal Law" (1:5). Furthermore said the Buddha, "Overcome anger by love, overcome evil by good. Overcome the miser by giving, overcome the liar by truth" (17.3).[7] Five hundred years later Jesus, with incisive clarity, affirmed,

> Love your enemies, do good to those who hate you, bless those who curse you, pray for those who mistreat you. If someone strikes you on one cheek, turn to him the other also. If someone takes your cloak, do not stop him from taking your tunic. Give to everyone who asks you; and if anyone takes what belongs to you, do not demand it back. Do to others as you would have them do to you (Lk 6:27-31).

Love is infallible," remarked William Law (1686-1761), writer on actualization of human development through disciplined training, "it has no errors, for all errors are the want of love."[8] Saint Francis of Assisi, Italy (1181-1226), founder of the Franciscan order of men and women for the reform of the church, suggested a similar message, "Lord, make me an instrument of your peace. Where there is hatred, let me sow love; where there is injury, pardon; where there is doubt, faith; where there is despair, hope; where there is darkness, light; where there is sadness, joy."[9]

During the WTC/Pentagon/Flight 93 massacre, where over three thousand innocent people were mass-murdered, words cannot express the great heroism, group altruism, unlimited compassion, and goodness in action written "not on the tablets of stone but on tablets of human hearts" (2 Cor 3:3), in this Empire of Liberty, as Thomas Jefferson had called his new land. The pure and simple kindness, mutual aid, team spirit, and unconditional love (Heschel's "sight of the eternal") shone as hundreds of selfless firefighters, police, medical personnel, and people at large frantically searched for survivors in a time of tears and pain to save life.

This pure and simple solidarity was engraved in the excitement of rescue dogs when they found a living being under the massive rubble, and on the faces of nurses, doctors, and thousands of volunteers working endless hours to save lives. It was potently revealed when people were standing in lines all over America to donate their blood, when children were washing cars and selling lemonade to raise the green stuff for hungry children in Afghanistan, when the president of the United States, members of Congress, and our nation stood shoulder to shoulder, united—to protect life—to put an end to hatred and the insanity of violence. Heschel is correct: "In every man's life there are moments when there is a lifting of the veil at the horizon of the known, opening a sight of the eternal."[10]

In this never-to-be-forgotten September 11, 2001 event, mothers, fathers, and children who lost their loved ones, persons who prayed and rushed ("Let's roll") to prevent Flight 93 from reaching yet another target, firemen, policemen, and others giving their lives to save lives, all standing shoulder to shoulder to help in the WTC/Pentagon rescue, all sharing this grief have experienced the momentous reality of love in action in their lives. We cannot thank them enough for what they did. For them will always stand the message: You are loved. God bless you and your families for eternity.

"We have all been created for greater things," goes the heart Mother Teresa of Calcutta,

> to love and to be loved. Love is love—to love a person without any conditions, without any expectations. Works of love are works of peace and purity. Works of love are always a means of becoming closer to God, so the more we help each other, the more we really love God better by loving each other. Jesus very clearly said, "Love one another as I have loved you." Love in action [shining through good works] is what gives us grace. We pray, and if we are able to love with a whole heart, then we will see the need. Those who are unwanted, unloved, and uncared for become just a throwaway of society—that's why we must really make everybody feel wanted.[11]

Yes, we must love unconditionally. However, destruction to the Body must be defended against. We must be wide-awake, we must be vigilant, or pain, tears, and loss of life might visit us. *When an infection is destroying the body, white cells are obliged to go to work or the body will die.* Freedom, peace, and happiness require prudence, solutions, resolve, care, and accountability. A halt had to be put to the Hitler-Stalin death factories (Auschwitz, Sachenhausen, the GULAG Archipelago, and more). Unlimited love, boundless freedom, perseverance, justice, and never-ending vigilance carry into the present.

It All Starts with Trust

Every challenge, every obstacle, every dilemma, every crisis, every problem has a solution. The price of freedom is systematic pursuit of a solution through the unchanging. Adversity imparts a deep sense of courage and self-knowledge and expands insight into the essence of the unchanging in us. Similar to climbing the world's greatest mountain peaks, dealing with home and on-the-job challenges, bringing up children, trying to pay your bills or meet payroll when money is in short supply, or struggling to work your way out of the slums, adversity can be either terrifying or liberating. Adversity introduces us to ourselves and to God's attributes in us, each one of which expresses our absolute essence.

In my formative years, when I lived in the Empires of the Holy Horror and the most grievous crimes against the human family, my little glimpse into the lives of so many significant others enabled me to tackle a number of questions with a certain passion of its own. I chose to follow Jesus. Instead of being worried, or alarmed, I put my *trust in God* (Psalm 23). You can see this prompt on every coin and every dollar bill. To me it meant: remain peaceful and confident. Trust that the greatest good will be yours. Practice trust with effort and hard work to attain your objective. Be Christlike (increasingly reveal perfection in your actions). Do all your work in unconditional love and compassion. Lead an immaculate life, one day at a time. God will take care and provide in His own way.

Why? To receive a radio or a high-definition TV program, we have to tune into its frequency, the observer and the observed have to become one. To receive from God (to manifest highest-quality reality) more fully, we have to tune in to God's "power" ('1': the architecture or the source code of the universe) more fully. We have to become more Godlike. I found that simple joy and wonder in our hearts, service to one's fellow men and women, and outpourings of compassion and generosity heal the grief of violence, hunger, disease, and death. These qualities create inner peace and spiritual transcendence. By being in touch, by doing all our work in unqualified love, and compassion, by living an immaculate holy life, we expand our "unity of life" (altruistic) consciousness; we simultaneously reduce the authority of our everyday ego consciousness. We shift our point of view and decision-making from consciousness that has limits (selfish egoism) to consciousness without limits (group altruism,

'1'). We get a higher perspective, better solutions and quality of results. We come into contact with more happiness and more miracles in our life—we encounter God face-to-face.

The more I focused my thinking and actions on solutions to the adversity, the more I lent a hand and did good for others, the more inner bliss and equanimity I experienced inside of me. I learned that through the spirit of loving-kindness, purity of heart and deep peace the mind grows keener and sharper and we produce more solutions and miracles to our challenges. The more there was of God in me (very caring, very compassionate surrender to the Highest Good and altruism within a group), the more serendipitous and extraordinary phenomena I encountered in my life.

Immaculacy, Compassion, Freedom, and Peace Produce Miracles

Important: please read the next two paragraphs with care; try to make them a part of your awareness. Earlier, I mentioned that the masses saw unbelievable events in Jesus' miracles and that one should not discount the profound faculty behind the miracles—"the hidden benefit"—a kind of advanced science facilitating miracles.

What is a miracle but a shift in point of view in '1'—an embodiment called for and freed by the human fulcrum of consciousness, using the zero-state "doorway" of the Unchanging State; such as going from one room to another room through a "door" in a house, or one computation to another in a computer. Notice, Jesus called himself the door . . . the gate.

The zero-state "doorway," the fast lane, or "the hidden benefit," is an in-between, "transforming-state," which is an integral part of water, the house, or the empty-space. On this page, the fast lane, which unites letters, words, sentences and paragraphs, arises at the white (immaculate) space. The fast lane for matter and energy, in Einstein's famous equation, is neither matter nor energy but the encrypted Spirit (the immaculate empty-space) of the Unchanging State, which determines how the decryption (transformation) of matter into energy should take place! In a fast lane an electron leaps from "one orbit" of an atom to "another orbit," *without transitory space in between or time delay*.

In conventional physics, the connecting "doorway" or the common boundary for $E = mc^2$ is denoted by the equality '=' and the '1' (1 = E/

mc^2), to be discussed in more detail later. On the seesaw, the connecting "doorway" is the fulcrum. The manager behind miracles is the zero-state "doorway," the no man's land that is *above* and beyond the laws of nature, explained in chapter 33. In our life the zero-state fulcrum behind miracles is the inner peace, patience, righteousness, truth, compassion, freedom and confidence of the Highest Good ('1').

Unlike the Christ, the Buddha refused to perform miracles: heal the sick or the deprived of the sense of hearing. "I will not make you well," he would respond to the deaf and the blind, "but I can show you how to heal yourself." Then he would teach the science facilitating miracles. Consequently, to accept from God more fully, we have to tune in to God's zero-state "doorway" (Christ's Sermon on the Mount [Mt 5]); to make all our decisions based on the greatest good of all beings on earth. We have to put trust in the Highest Good, which some call the Mind and Heart of God, others term the reality of Christ's nature, or to borrow a phrase from frontier physics the "theory of everything."

Jesus of Nazareth taught: "*My power is strongest when you are weak*" (2 Cor 12:9), when you "empty yourself and be filled with the Holy Spirit ['1']." Namely, when your heart and mind shift to the connecting *zero-state* of what is the same as "least energy condition"—where you can go from any letter or word to any letter or word through the consciousness "doorway." For light to travel most effectively from one point to another point in the universe it must go through empty-space. In a calculator it is the starting point when all is set to *zero*. In our lives it is when we strive for perfection, allowing the Highest Good to be our good; permitting the immaculate life of Christ to be our life. It is when we let the Highest Wisdom to be our wisdom, and the Mind that created our universe, to be our mind. For Buddhists it is the Buddha Mind, and for Christians it is discerning Christ's presence ('1') *in themselves*: the Christ in you[12]—where you "have taken upon yourselves the qualities of Christ himself" (Gal 3:27).

Back to Square One: The Joy of Living Is the Art of Loving

Later in life, I realized that "miraculous phenomena" are as natural as shaking hands or walking with a baby. In going with the flow, all it takes is a deep *compassion, altruism,* and *equanimity* in our heart for the other person or the attracting situation. And, this state can be enhanced, advanced, and made more predictable and more profound through self-forgetfulness, immaculateness, and attentiveness to what really matters.

Cultivating this course of wisdom—doing my best every time, and addressing every moment with love, forgiveness, compassion, and intelligence, made my life richer, filled with peace and strength. I discovered that freedom, gladness, and treasured private rights are extraordinary and mathematically precise zero-state (sometimes called the "miracle zone," or zero-point field) in nature. Furthermore, the state of happiness and intoxication of union with God, like democracy, natural immunity, peace or personal liberty, is a continuous ascent "from glory to glory" (2 Cor 3:18).

A wonderful series of experiences and miraculous phenomena followed. Fear of adversity or loss of life stopped controlling my thoughts and actions. Self-centeredness, the buzz and the static of everyday events and worry gradually disappeared. The shift established new habit patterns: a break from attachment to the fruit of action and the awakening of the deeper self—Heschel's "a lifting of the veil at the horizon of the known, opening a sight of the eternal,"[13] occured. A long-term commitment to the perfection of virtue took place. The Christ and His wisdom (the Christ in me, me in Christ [2 Cor 13:5]) became the Light in my life.

In the beginning, many of Christ's teachings did not make sense to me: "keep yourself pure" (1 Tim 5:22); "keep yourself in training for godly life" (1 Tim 4:7); about settling of scores, such as "do not take revenge on someone who does you wrong" (Mt 5:39); or "love your enemies, do good to those who hate you, bless those who curse you, and pray for those who mistreat you" (Lk 6:27). They were strange, considering the environment I came from, worked, and lived in. However, I was convinced that Jesus had acted from some higher principle, which I did not understand. Accordingly, I followed His advice; he served me as a role model. Rumi once wrote that, "Whoever enters the Way without a guide will take a hundred years to travel a two-day journey."

I saw the Shining One in many very vivid and remarkable dreams. My wife Oksana did as well. The "unity of the Spirit"—essentially a state of awareness of one's identity with the Absolute—was revealed. At first, I saw my dreams present the Nazarene of Golgotha crucified and lifeless, the same way we see Him hanging on the cross today. These gifts of the Blessed Love in various settings and coincidences were very meaningful to me. His consecration, providence, and encouragement fortified me to overcome my pressure-filled years of daily challenges, "to put away childish things [in letting go of trivialities and "I thinking"]" (1 Cor 13:11), as Jesus, Rumi, and my parents advised. These heartening dreams and synchronistic events improved my day-to-day relationships, health and outlook. They enhanced my productivity and increased my earning power and happiness at work and home. My spiritual and corporate advancement both benefited.

As my struggling self tried to change for the better, my dreams of the Christ event also started to transform. The Holy Love on the cross became a *living, moving* and *suffering presence*, with the crown of thorny laurels on his bleeding head and face. In other dreams the Infinite One was watching over me, protecting me ("Know that all shall be well . . . behold, I am with you always"), as I walked the path of life.

In my daily home and corporate involvements I became aware that everything can work out smoothly and effortlessly when I focus on the "miracle zone" ("it thinking"): inner peace, goodness, compassion, and "Thy will be done." I realized that one who conquers self is greater than one who conquers thousands in war, and that we can do anything we set our mind to. *The more inner peace, integrity, compassion and "Thy will be done"* ('1', the skill to play the hand you're dealt, the ability to meet life's condition) *I could generate, the more miracles in my daily activities I would experience.*

Splendor beyond Words: Christ Gives Up the Cross

Then came a marvelous day for the extraordinary. *Christ came down off the cross.* It was very fast. The Blessed Holy Light was no longer shedding his blood, in pain, or mutilated. His face was full of serenity, loving-kindness, beauty, compassion, and goodwill. To me, he appeared brilliant, majestic, and the most miraculous and Perfect Love: blue/green eyes, blond-reddish hair, 5'11" to 6' tall, 165 to 170 pounds. The experience was more lucid, more engaging, and more stunning than what we regularly live through during the clearest of days.

Right after WWII, when I was twelve to fifteen years old, I lived a life of rugged simplicity and under the most austere conditions, without parents, with TB, in a Capuchin cloister in Innsbruck, Austria. There was a large cross with the Beloved crucified upon it. The Capuchin monks provided a free room, radiant smiles, encouragement, and friendliness for several war-torn boys who were attending school (gymnasium) outside the monastery. The significance of this cross to me is that when I had a need, as happened every day, I would go touch Christ's feet. What I asked of the Holy Love would happen. It was a spiritually important breakthrough for me. I had found a way to pure magic. As a child I encountered the potential of synchronistic events and everyday miracles and of experiencing the divine mystery. Later in life I became acutely aware that universal Omnipotence is within me, and that all humanity has that all-powerfulness within them.

After coming off the cross, the Christ started walking toward me through this long corridor of a monastery that I used to sweep for the monks for a bowl of odds and ends. They didn't have much; they shared what they had. Jesus reached me, put His arms around me, His face next to my face, His heart next to my heart, and hugged me. There was light-expanding peace and an overwhelming feeling of bliss throughout my whole being during and after our embrace. Words are inadequate to describe His goodness of heart, compassion, and peace: all-uplifting Light of light. That ineffable brightness of my heart's compassion and inexpressible happiness stayed with me for a long time.

Compassion or the pure bliss of Heavenly Banquet can't be known through words. It must be experienced. Later in life I learned how to bring and hold on all the more firmly to this luminous Light, how to bring this Pure Spiritual Heaven and the kindness of God into my daily experience.[14] I learned how to deepen and extend this luminous Light in my being. Einstein has referred to this ultimate joy of paradise, this beatific vision, as cosmic religious feeling.[15]

Next, as the Christ was hugging me, His living face changed to my neighbor's face with whom I worked at the IBM Research Laboratory. To me it meant: I love you immeasurably! "I am in each human being." The All-Pervading Light of lights and Unconditional Compassion are present in all forms of expression, at every point of the universe. This was an unforgettable experience and I would not exchange it for a trillion-dollar certified check.

"I am with you at all times" (Mt 28:20), said Jesus two thousand years ago. Krishna, an avatar of Vishnu, the second member of the Hindu Trinity, and one of the most revered of Hindu deities, in the Bhagavad

Gita, time after time states that he is seated in the heart of everyone. The All Highest Himself, the ordering principle of the universe, is everywhere and in everyone continually. In essence, the face of Christ's Father or that of the Mother of the Universe is but your own! Take a short break here; reflect on these last statements.

What a marvel; others made the same discovery. Ivan (Sergeyevich) Turgenev (1818-1883), Russian novelist, playwright, and poet, shared his dream:

> I saw myself, in dream, a youth, almost a boy, in a low-pitched wooden church. The slim wax candles gleamed, spots of red, before the old pictures of the saints.
>
> A ring of colored light encircled each tiny flame. Dark and dim it was in the church . . . But there stood before me many people. All fair-haired, peasant heads. From time to time they began swaying, falling, rising again, like the ripe ears of wheat, when the wind of summer passes in slow undulation over them.
>
> All at once some man came up from behind and stood beside me. I did not turn toward him; but at once I felt this man was Christ.
>
> Emotions, curiosity, awe overmastered me suddenly. I made an effort . . . And looked at my neighbor.
>
> A face like every one's, a face like all men's faces. The eyes looked a little upwards, quietly and intently. The lips closed, but not compressed; the upper lip, as it were, resting on the lower; a small beard parted in two. The hands folded and still. And the clothes on him like every one's.
>
> "What sort of Christ is this?" I thought. "Such an ordinary, ordinary man! It can't be!"
>
> I turned away. But I had hardly turned my eyes away from this ordinary man when I felt again that it really was none other than Christ standing beside me.
>
> Again I made an effort over myself . . . And again the same face, like all men's faces, the same everyday though unknown features.
>
> And suddenly my heart sank, and I came to myself. Only then I realized that just such a face—a face like all men's faces—is the face of Christ.[16]

In the letter to the Hebrews we read, "God left nothing that is not subject to him ['1']. Yet at present we do not see everything subject to him" (2:8). Saint Teresa of Avila (1515-1582), one of the most adored spiritual beings in history, in *Vida*, wrote,

> In the beginning it happened to me that I was ignorant of one thing—I did not know that *God was in all things* [emphasis added]: and when He seemed to me to be so near, I thought it impossible. Not to believe that He was present was not my power; for it seemed to me, as it were, evident that I felt there His very presence. Some unlearned men used to say to me that He was present only by His grace. I could not believe that, because, as I am saying, He seemed to me to be present Himself: so I was distressed. A most learned man, of the Order of the Glorious Patriarch St. Dominic, delivered me from this doubt; for he told me that He was present, and how He communed with us: this was a great comfort to me.

In the language of quantum physics: the observer (perceiver of truth) and the observed (perceiving truth) are fundamentally united. They achieve greatest stability when they are in the "ground state," the still point, '1', for this is the point of the miracle zone ("doorway," transformation) of unlimited potentiality.

Omnipotence Is Our Natural State

Furthermore, the closer we come to the '1' (fulcrum on the seesaw), the more order, unity, clarity, structure, gladness, abundance, wisdom, and love we experience. The farther we go from the '1', the more ambiguity, disorder (second law of thermodynamics), and pain we encounter. Suffering arises when our consecrated nature—our divine Omnipotence—is ascribed to a few select people but is denied to the rest of "sacred humanity." Jesus, the Buddha, Krishna, Emerson, and Einstein spoke about it and pointed beyond to a universal celebration of the human spirit.

Rebirth consists in the reschooling of our being so as to focus on life's Oneness and unchangeable as if atop the high-exposure Himalayas, while still in the mode of our daily living: family, marriage, intimacy, children, school, work, and pursuits. It means sacred commitment and progressive growth ("veil after veil will lift") in compassion, the unity of life, and deep peace. We free (resurrect) the Imprisoned Light, Infinite Splendor and Joy in ourselves. We see God face-to-face in our children, family, coworkers, fellow citizens, and our enemies. We live life passionately, make love with the whole of ourselves, and express our true nature in every action. The Christ points out, "Unless a man is born again [or "born from above"; also in verse 7], he cannot see the kingdom of God" [Jn 3:3]. We come to the realization that we are the sons and daughters of Infinite Love, climbing its majestic heights while in our daily life. Then we deepen this realization still further. We see the Light of lights, described in the Upanishads as "brighter than a thousand suns," face-to-face, not as an icon or a theoretical concept with no relation to reality. We create a conscious heaven within and without us, in which the Mind and Heart of God can live. As Saint Gregory of Nyssa stated in the *Life of Moses*, God, "who encompasses everything in Himself," took upon Himself *our* nature ("pitched his own tabernacle among us") in order to "restore us" to our "original" nature.[17] We dwell in deep peace and "unity of the Spirit": "I am in my Father, and you are in me, and am I in you" (Jn 14:20), which is beyond an external constitutional, dogmatic, and liturgical uniformity.

Love at First Sound: Christ Union

My wife Oksana observed many similar lucid dreams. In one such experience, she saw herself in church, in a gorgeous white wedding gown, her face stunning, getting married. Her bridegrooms were Jesus and me. Oksana thought this was mysterious. She was already wedded to me. Yet, she reasoned, "If this was all right for the Christ, it must be all right for me [her]."

Life has conversed with life in collective dreaming, opening breathtaking new vistas for us to explore, a kind of wonderful transfiguration. Oksana's spiritual marriage to the Shining One suggests that in a broader sense the wedding feast of the soul fuses and unites us consciously not only with our spouses but also to its Divine Source in the universe—the "life of the All." Namely, the universe can be viewed as God's "self-manifestation"—the revelation of God in manifest form: *God in me, me in God.*

By way of these and related events, both of us have found that our marriage is a sacred commitment and life—not merely a social contract. That marital growth includes spiritual, intellectual, emotional, and lovemaking intimacy that can help us live a more compassionate and kindhearted life. It establishes very caring patterns of communication, deep inner peace, strength to overcome adversity, and the apotheosis of immaculate drunkenness in the Beloved's delightful game: transparent bliss that permeates your whole being.

Through this incredible peace, inner freedom and happiness we realized who is the knower. We discover what many others have discovered. Our body, "our house of prayer," is a holy temple of Love (2 Cor 6:16), while the personal experience, value, and essence of the Life of God in daily living is compassion, selfless service, responsibility, freedom, justice, learning, and living together in One family of humanity.

Of course, the challenge is to leave the baggage of the past behind—to "rise above self," to increase intimacy and compassion, and to deepen our awareness day after day. This entails adopting an altruistic lifestyle—to each other, to our family, friends, and on the job—arousing highest ambitions, actualizing the importance of each moment. Every breath and every act can be a consecrated activity.

Growth in spiritual reverence and humility, the imitation of Christ's example, and sacredness of what we do should be integrated with passionate involvement in the daily affairs of the world. To the degree we deploy this personal "value in use" and "value in exchange" in our daily lives, this service-excellence, pure and impartial decision-making, and working for the positive, we manifest divine perfection in us—we create miracles. *Note*, on account of the invariance of the laws of physics, the invariance of vacuum, and the invariance of the universe, to be discussed in part 2, *our values and our actions generate our miracles and our personal universe.*

The Turning Point: Realization of the Organizing Principle

Certainly, when there is light, darkness disappears. It is no more. The formerly unknown becomes known. Our daily way of life, "our daily bread" ideally performed in selfless and compassionate service, is the shining light: "bringing about what we see, think, and experience." I now understood Albert Einstein, Dag Hammarskjöld, and Saint Paul's statements, that by virtue of our unity, compassion and service-excellence *we are sharing in an image of God.*

Namely, *God manifests himself through us.* For, "In him ['1'] we live and move and have our being" (Acts 17:28); "Christ ['1'] is all, Christ is in all!" (Col 3:11). I realized that just as water embraces waves, so God ('1') holds all of us in his arms. We ourselves are God's sacred temples, "God's home," and God's image lives in us (1 Cor 3:16). In the Holy Qur'an, the Chosen One of Allah, stated: "To Allah belong the East and the West: whithersoever you turn, there is Allah's countenance. For Allah is All-Embracing, All-Knowing" (2:115).

"Your real life is Christ ['1']" (Col 3:4), said Saint Paul, a founding architect of the Church, in his letter to the Colossians. '1' is an abbreviated mathematical representation, the unifying symbol in physics, of the ultimate organizing state behind the foundation of physical science and the cosmic field of creation. It is the law (algorithmic compression) *above* and behind the laws of science, explained more completely in part 2. '1' is a shorthand formula for *the initial condition of everything.*

Dante referred to it as *il riso del universo,* the joy that spins the universe. It is the great beginning from which emerged the cosmos and the first conditions of the universe's properties, both prior to form (or individuality) and pervading form. The symbol provides a single coherent framework, the Alpha and the Omega point, from which the entire universe around us and within all things and all physical constants (and we ourselves) can, in principle, be derived.[18]

Like the transition between night and day, life and death, and the seasons, '1' is the point of inversion, transformation, or fulcrum of consciousness at which things change. It is also a natural location for the "collapse of the wave function," the "quantum jump," and the "point of amplification." '1' transcends space and time and is the unitary state where all the information about the universe is preserved. It is changeless, self-identical essence with decentralized (zero) power. Again, for a tangible metaphor, '1' can be equated to the *white space of this page* while the letters of this writing compare to the manifestations of the universe.

Note, "metaphor" denotes the use of a symbol, word, or representation for an idea that it does not literally and exactly signify, suggesting a relationship to a common fabric of life or shared nature. In exact science, '1' signifies invariance (infinite code) in the physical laws that govern the universe. It is a scientific representation for the cosmic void in its ground state—radiation free empty-space, equivalently, vacuum, or potential (Absolute) infinity in all directions, from which the universe and atoms spring. '1' is also the biblical symbol for God. It is stillness, freedom, Spirit, and pure consciousness. It is ultimate dependability, accountability, simplicity, and profundity. '1' is the boundary between the classical and the quantum world that transforms physics and creates miracles.

Getting the Best out of Yourself as Everyday Ecstasy

The Light of lights is within my mother, my father, my sisters, my brothers, my children, my coworkers, that suffering one, and this happy one. We are one at the foundational level of reality. We all reflect and are dependent on each other. *Purity of heart, gladness, caring, service, and compassion are not only emotionally nourishing but bring to light, and thus awareness, our Oneness with others and all life, and at last the discovery of one's place in the whole.*

The source of happiness, the ubiquitous Love that has no elucidation in expressions of deeper principles, the '1', in scientific parlance is within all of us, everywhere, and in everything. I am you and you are me. At the invariable foundation of physics we are '1', or as Bayazid of Bistun put it, "I went from God to God, until they cried from me in me, 'O thou I!'" In the embrace of Perfect Love and passion for doing things rightly and as best I can do in the moment, comes a resurrected life of inner peace, courage, stamina, ecstasy of flow, clarity of the heart and mind, spiritual fortitude and action. The attitude or position I have come to assume is that, as a brother, I am to live with you, in you, and for you.

The truth of transforming pain and suffering into a steady stream of supportive relationships, joyful vitality and a life of daily celebration of the sacred has always existed. It requires:

- setting priorities
- establishing new habits
- systematic life cultivation
- a lifelong commitment to becoming a better person
- instilling goodness of heart and compassion into all aspects of daily experience
- demanding the best from oneself all the time

- finding deep inner peace within oneself
- enlightenment as to who we are
- selfless service
- teamwork excellence.

Education: Man Does Not Live by Bread Alone

John Archibald Wheeler, a world-renowned physicist, and one of the finest fundamental scholars of the moving frontier of science, was an associate and close friend of Einstein and Bohr. In 1939 Wheeler published, with Niels Bohr, the first paper to describe nuclear fission, in terms of quantum physics. In the 1940s he worked on the Manhattan Project, and in the 1950s Wheeler lent a hand in developing the hydrogen bomb. In 1965, he and Bryce DeWitt launched the field of quantum cosmology. Wheeler is a contributor to atomic, nuclear and elementary particle physics, relativity theory, cosmology, astrophysics, and ultimate reality. He is a member of the American and the National Academy of Sciences. The list goes on and on. Like all others who have had the pleasure of knowing John Wheeler, I treasure his wisdom. To Wheeler, Heschel's "moments when there is a lifting of the veil at the horizon" is Mother Teresa's "making everybody feel wanted," a labor of love for the benefit of society. His daily "spirit of colleagueship," bonding with students, and learning the real meaning of friendship in the search for more light at Princeton:

> There is no topic on which I would rather comment than the quality of colleagueship between undergraduates, graduate students, and junior and senior staff as I see it in the sciences at Princeton. A tie between young and old, between student and worker, a shared enthusiasm for searching out new truth and introducing it into the life stream of the body politic, this to me is what makes the spirit of a university.
>
> Some time ago, as a visitor was taking his leave, he said, "Princeton is a great place, but don't fool yourself, it's no university. No medical school, not even a law school. Chicago is a university," he went on, "and Harvard is a university, but not Princeton." His comment troubled me until I learned the historical meaning of the word "university" as it comes down to us from the Middle Ages.

That term, I found, has to do, not with subject matter or with buildings, but with people. A university groups together, not a certain specific number of departments of knowledge, but a certain variety of colleagues. To the medieval world the university of coppersmiths meant a lively organization composed of the beginners at working copper, plus apprentice coppersmiths, along with experienced workers and master craftsmen, all banded together for their mutual benefit and for the benefit of society. Similarly with the university of carpenters and the university of barbers—and so with the university of those who work with knowledge. Thus I learned what so many others had already perfectly well realized all the time: the university is an association of beginners in acquisition of learning, plus apprentices in the organization of knowledge, together with experienced workers and master researchers for truth.

If you agree that this definition of university continues to make sense today, then I must report that I do not know of any university at any time in any country where one can see this colleagueship more fully developed, nor a closer tie between underclassmen, graduate students, experienced staff members, and master scholars than here and now in the sciences at Princeton, where we are colleagues together in the search for understanding. Quality of colleagueship makes the spirit of this university and of every great university.[19]

To Wheeler's thinking one could add that we are all in a university, learning from and contributing to each other. Jaroslav Pelikan, a Sterling Professor Emeritus of History at Yale, perhaps the greatest of contemporary scholars of religion, and prolific author with forty-two honorary degrees, stated:

> The university has not discharged its moral and intellectual responsibility if, in its heroic achievements of attaining the possibility of putting bread on every table, it ignores the fundamental axiom, which may be biblical in its formulation but is universal in its authority, that man does not live by bread alone. The religions of humanity all have their special versions of that axiom, and both in its teaching and research the modern secular university often ignores these at its peril.[20]

4

BIRTH OF A NOTION: EXCITING POSSIBILITIES AHEAD

Silent night, holy night,
All is calm, all is bright . . .

—Josef Mohr

Amazing Find: Extraordinary Beauty

The Nag Hammadi library, unearthed in 1945 near the town of Nag Hammadi, in Upper Egypt, was slowly made accessible to select scholars (1956 and 1977) and then first published in 1978. It contains the Gospel of Thomas and a whole range of fifty-one other texts, with a total of over one thousand pages. Ricky Alan Mayotte, a lifelong student of the history of religion, offers this description about the Nag Hammadi discovery:

> The amazing discovery of these texts occurred in 1945 when an Arab peasant decided to dig for fertilizer near a huge boulder, near the town of Nag Hammadi in Upper Egypt. During his labor he uncovered a large earthenware jar. Thinking the jar could contain gold, he smashed it only to find a treasure of another sort. The jar contained thirteen ancient papyrus codices. A codex (plural: codices) is an ancient book . . .
>
> The codices found at Nag Hammadi have come to be known as The Nag Hammadi library. The fifty-two texts (tractates) contained within [some forty previously unknown] are written in Coptic, a common language in Egypt during the early Christian

Era, and had been translated from Greek about 1,500 years ago. It is possible that some of these Greek texts were written around the same time as the New Testament Gospels, or even earlier.[1]

The Gospel of Thomas brings to light a gold mine of knowledge and beauty of insights into early Judaism and the roots of Christianity and Islam. Researchers had long recognized that the Gospel of Thomas existed at some point in the initial Christian era. Three Greek fragments had been unearthed by British archeologists in an ancient rubbish mound at Oxyrhynchus, in Upper Egypt, and published at the beginning of the twentieth century. However, scholars cataloging the hundreds of bits and pieces had no way of linking them with the Gospel of Thomas, which was considered destroyed. It was not until the Nag Hammadi breakthrough that the Oxyrhynchus puzzle could be linked to the Gospel of Thomas. There are numerous points to be considered about the Gospel of Thomas. According to John Crossan:

> There may be at least two separate layers in it. One was composed by the fifties AD, possibly in Jerusalem, under the aegis of James' authority. After his martyrdom in AD 62, the collection and maybe also its community migrated to Syrian Edessa. There a second layer was added, possibly as early as the sixties or seventies, under the aegis of the Thomas authority.[2]

A great number of Jesus' sayings in the Gospel of Thomas have striking equivalence in each of the synoptic gospels and the Gospel of John. Other sayings are also known to occur in noncanonical gospels, such as the Gospel According to the Hebrews, and the Gospel of the Egyptians.

Mark and Luke were disciples of apostles, while Matthew and John were apostles. The Marcan gospel was written between AD 50 and 70; the Lucan gospel, most likely as early as 70, and possibly as late as AD 80-85; the Gospel of Matthew, as early as 70 to as late as AD 95; and the Gospel of John most scholars date to about AD 90-125.[3, 4] These gospels were chosen out of a large number of books which were in circulation. The selection took place in the second and third centuries by the management of the church as "canonical," a list of gospels permitted for communal reading in the Church's worship.

Other Christian writings of the Eastern Churches (the Acts of Thomas and in all probability the Book of Thomas, discovered as part of the Nag Hammadi library) have been accredited to the same apostle (Didymos Judas) Thomas. In the Syrian church (Judas) Thomas was recognized as the brother of Jesus who established the churches of the East, particularly of Edessa.

Neil Douglas-Klotz, internationally known scholar of religious studies, researcher, and student of the writings of Saint Thomas, who has been decoding the spiritual message of the Aramaic Jesus, declared, "Most scholars date the composition of the Gospel of Thomas in the first century AD. This makes it one of the oldest gospel texts in existence. [Furthermore], many scholars now consider that the Gospel of Thomas reflects a type of early Jewish Christian spirituality rather than later, corrupted form of 'orthodox' Christianity."[5, 6]

Note: the term "Christian" appears in Acts 11:26, 26:28 and 1 Peter 4:14-16. The expression has its root in the Greek word "Christ," meaning "anointed one" (Messiah) with an ending denoting "followers of" the Messiah. Cornelius Tacitus (56-120), Roman provincial governor of Asia, orator, and possibly the greatest historian who wrote in the Latin language, in *Annals* (15.44), dealing with the period 14-68, speaks of Christians as people despised for their evil activities. Suetonius (Gaius Suetonius Tranquillus, 69-122), Roman biographer and antiquarian, in *The Lives of the Caesars* (5.16), concerning the lives of the first eleven emperors, identifies Christians as "a new and evil superstition."

Jesus' disciples were first called Christians in Antioch. Saint Ignatius, bishop of Antioch in Syria, in his letter to the Magnesians, first used the word "Christianity" during a persecution of the Antioch church. The letter was written after Ignatius was put in chains, condemned to the wild beast in the Roman arena, and taken, along with others of the Antioch church, to Rome during the reign of the Roman emperor Trajan (98-117). Helmut Koester, member of the Coptic Gnostic Library Project of the Institute for Antiquity and Christianity at Claremont Graduate School in California, pointed out:

> If one considers the form and wording of the individual sayings in comparison with the form in which they are preserved in the New

Testament, the Gospel of Thomas almost always appears to have preserved a more original form of the traditional saying (in a few instances, where this is not the case, the Coptic translation seems to have been influenced by the translator's knowledge of the New Testament gospels), or presents versions which are independently based on more original forms. More original and shorter forms are especially evident in the parables of Thomas.[7]

Ocean of Wisdom: The Whole Is Harmonized

The sayings preserved in the Gospel of Thomas are of numerous types: Jesus speaking about himself, parables, commandments (rules for the community), wisdom sayings, teachings, proverbs, the Realm of Joy or Unknown Reality as something knowable, and revelations (prophecies). Following are two "secret sayings" of "Rabbuni," which in Aramaic means Master or Teacher, that Saint Thomas wrote:

> Jesus said, "I shall give you what no eye has seen and what no ear has heard and what no hand has touched and what has never occurred to the human mind . . . When you come to know yourselves [in the cosmic-conscious state], then you will become known, and you will realize that it is you who are the sons of the living Father." (17, 3)[8]

The Book of Thomas the Contender is the seventh treatise in Codex II of the Coptic Gnostic Library from Nag Hammadi. It is a question-and-answer discourse between the resurrected Jesus and his brother Judas Thomas. I highlight the issue of the special (secret) "knowledge of one's true self"—of *who one is*:

> You had already understood that I am knowledge of the truth. So while you accompany me, although you are uncomprehending, you have (in fact) already come to know, and you will be called "the one who knows himself." For he who has not known himself has known nothing, but he who has known himself has at the same time already achieved knowledge about the Depth of the All ['1']. So then, you, my brother Thomas, have beheld what is obscure to men, that is, that against which they ignorantly stumble.[9]

History makes many symbolic references to the discovery of the Infinite in the finite, the Absolute in the relative, the Unchanging in all that is changing, and the opposite, from the formed to the Unformed, from the mortal to the Immortal. Einstein, for example, said he feels "admiration of the illimitable superior Spirit who reveals Himself in the slight details we are able to perceive."

In the sacred texts of Brihad-Aranyaka Upanishad, which teaches the unconditional identity of God or Absolute Being with the soul of human beings. We read, "From the unreal lead me to the real, from darkness lead me to light, from death lead me to immortality."[10]

It's Time We Came out of the Cave to Enjoy Our Sacredness

"If I have seen farther, it is by standing on the shoulders of giants," stated Isaac Newton in a letter to Robert Hooke in 1676. There is a tremendous body of great literature concerning the Unchanging Absolute, the foundation of experiential knowledge and the experience of the Divine within the manifested world. The study of consciousness through meditative techniques and insights into planes of consciousness for the most part are unfamiliar to the West. To study the entirety of Buddhist or Taoist literature alone would require several human lifetimes. What we deal with in this work on aspects of '1' represents a microscopic morsel when compared with what is out there for us to enjoy.

To help booklovers find their way through the vast wisdom study of the "Unchanging Light," in chapter 21 I have listed works from China, India, Japan, Korea, and the Muslim world. We gather further insights and systematic presentations into the nature of God and facets of '1' through the prophet Moses, the Christ, Lao-tzu, Krishna, and Shakyamuni Buddha. Also, we find 220 Dead Sea scrolls, the Mishnah, the Hebrew Bible, the Bhagavad Gita, the Talmud, the Gospels, the Upanishads, the Rig-Veda, the Prajnaparamita-sutra and Brahma (Vedanta)—Sutra, the Dhammapada, the Qur'an, the Sunnah, the *Profound Teaching of the Natural Liberation through Contemplating the Mild and Fierce Buddha Deities*, the Ramayana, the Mahabharata, the Rubaiyat, the Ladder to Paradise, and Guru Granth Saheb.

In addition, landmark fruits are presented in: *The Early Church Fathers* (thirty-eight-volume collection of primary documents from the church's first 800 years), the *Philokalia* (five volumes), a collection of texts written between the fourth and fifteenth centuries by spiritual masters of the Eastern Christian tradition, compiled by Saint Nikodimos of the Holy Mountain of Athos (1749-1809) and Saint Makarios of Corinth (1731-1805). Also, the Nyingma Edition of the Tibetan Buddhist Canon, the Great Treasures of Ancient Teachings (755 volumes with 36,000 titles by 1,500 authors), and the Taoist canon, the Tao-tsang. The Tao-tsang consists of 1,476 works in 5,481 volumes.

Furthermore, the body of literature embraces the *Ching-te ch'uan-teng-lu* ("Record Concerning the Passing On of the Lamp, Composed in the Ching-te Period," a thirty-volume work, wherein six hundred Zen masters are recorded and more than one thousand Zen masters are mentioned), the Shobo-genzo, the Book of Mormon, and the *Classics of Western Spirituality: A Library of the Great Spiritual Masters* (104 volume series).

Additionally, we discover wisdom and insights of ancient and modern sages, including: Hildegard of Bingen, Bonaventure, George Washington Carver, Nicolas of Cusa, Daisetsu, Gejong Tenzin Gyatso (His Holiness the Fourteenth Dalai Lama), Aldous Huxley, Dogen Kigen, Frank Laubach, Robert Muller, Pope John Paul II, Walter and Lao Russell, Erwin Schrödinger, Hryhoryj Skovoroda, Francisco Suarez, Suzuki, Paramahamsa Yogananda, and many others.[11]

Historical evidence by itself is not always skillful guidance and convincing. Because these unfailingly enlightening thinkers and transformers of the perennial wisdom did not have modern scientific tools of high-precision measurement and corroboration, many of their notions, validations, and understandings concerning the "Unchanging Heart" of the universe, continue to be regarded as mere speculation. The Encyclopaedia Britannica states:

> There are moments in the history of all sciences when remarkable progress is made in a relatively short period of time. Such leaps in knowledge result in great part from two factors: one is the presence of a creative mind—a mind sufficiently perceptive and original to discard hitherto accepted ideas and formulate new hypotheses; the second is the technological ability to test the hypotheses by appropriate experiments. The most original and inquiring mind is severely limited without the proper tools to conduct an investigation;

conversely, the most sophisticated technological equipment cannot of itself yield insights into any scientific process. An example of the relationship between these two factors was the discovery of the cell. For hundreds of years there had been speculation concerning the basic structure of both plants and animals. Not until optical instruments were sufficiently developed to reveal cells, however, was it possible to formulate a general hypothesis, the cell theory that satisfactorily explained how plants and animals are organized.[12]

Inner or intuitive knowing, "it thinking," or becoming conscious of our identity allows us to know the unitary nature of all, or to observe the '1' directly. Inner knowing or remote thinking has advanced medicine, science and technology, mathematics, philosophy, art, music, the principles of human perfection, and the peace process. It has facilitated understanding the evolution of spiritual and moral capacities, the general thrust of modern physics, biological evolution, and the interrelationships among human liberty, virtue, society, beauty, goodness, and truth. Intuitive solutions have enhanced appreciation of worldly letters and books, the special knowledge of the inner nature of Truth, and our timeless unity.

Inner knowing involves getting in step (synchronizing), similar to tuning your radio or TV, with the unchanging. It entails the art of silence, peace and mindfulness. Practicing mindfulness means to be consciously aware and one with what we are doing, i.e., driving, walking and breathing. It requires assuming the attitude of "pure observation." Mindfulness facilitates bringing the mind to a state of inner peace, love, and Oneness. In the Gospel of Thomas, Jesus refers to this state as turning "into a single one." He said:

> When you make the two one [when you hush your mind, you create Oneness], and when [by practicing mindfulness] you make the inner as the outer and the outer as the inner and the above as the below, and when you make the male and the female into a single one [they become a single life] . . . then shall you enter (the kingdom [23]).

Notice, "*then shall you enter*" the kingdom of God. In general, this means being calm and peaceful, alert, having a grasp for the subtle *clues*

(Archimedes'[13] discovery of the principle of water displacement), testing conjectures, and seeing the old state of affairs in new ways. From the mathematical physics point of view it means the '1' state is the state in which all modes are unexcited, and the zero-point field is in its ground state. In a bank account, the more zeros we have behind a number, the bigger the bank account; in inner knowing or remote viewing, the more inner peace, compassion, and Oneness we experience the better the quality of our inner knowing.

Consider This: Every Life Is Precious

A mirror image of God ('1') is seen in all creation. It is reflected in all acts of service. One of the most selfless servers and passionate lovers of all time, Agnes Gonxha Bojaxhiu, is known to us as Mother Teresa of Calcutta (1910-1997). She was the recipient in 1973 of the Templeton Prize and in 1979 of the Nobel Peace Prize for her exceptional life of undaunted courage, genius for sincerity, great kindness and compassion. The Templeton Prize (about $1 million) is bestowed for Progress toward Research or Discoveries about Spiritual Realities. The Nobel committee wrote that she "promotes peace in the most fundamental manner: by her confirmation of the inviolability of human dignity." Her very caring altruism—to make the world a holier place—replaced human abortion with human adoption:

> I always ask doctors at hospitals in India never to kill an unborn child. If there is no one who wants it, I'll take it.
>
> I see God in the eyes of every child—every unwanted child is welcomed by us. We then find homes for these children through adoption.
>
> You know, people worry all the time about innocent children being killed in wars, and they try to prevent this. But what hope is there in stopping it if mothers kill their own children? Every life is precious to God, whatever the circumstances.[14]

In her triumph of amity, Mother Teresa and her staff of compassionate nuns care for hundreds of thousands of needy, deprived and sick people. It is said they treated 186,000 victims of leprosy and 22,000 forsaken, dying, and destitute individuals. They fed 126,000 hungry and homeless persons in seventy-one countries. *Silence* (Moku-funi in Japanese Zen), shared Mother Teresa, was at the very core of her everyday life. At the point of silence she could listen to God giving her strength to move mountains, to direct her tireless work and to bring her closer to God:

> I always begin my prayer in silence, for it is in the silence of the heart that God speaks. God is the friend of silence—we need to listen to God because it's not what we say but what He says to us and through us that matters. Prayer feeds the soul—as blood is to the body, prayer is to the soul—and it brings you closer to God. It also gives you a clean and pure heart. *A clean heart can see God,* can speak to God, and can *see the love of God in others.* When you have a clean heart it means you are open and honest with God, you are not hiding anything from Him, and this lets Him take what He wants from you.
>
> If you are searching for God and do not know where to begin, learn to pray and take the trouble to pray every day. You can pray anytime, anywhere. You do not have to be in a chapel or a church. You can pray at work—work doesn't have to stop prayer and prayer doesn't have to stop work [emphasis mine].[15]

The Savior of Mothers:
An Ounce of Prevention Is Worth a Pound of Cure

Dr. Ignaz Philip Semmelweis (1818-1865) is known as "the Savior of Mothers" for his unearthing of the source of puerperal fever and inauguration of antiseptic prophylaxis, thereby initiating a new era in medical science. Puerperal fever is a bacterial infection of the endometrium, taking place in women after childbirth or abortion, typically as the effect of unsterile obstetric practices.

While working as an assistant at an obstetric clinic in Vienna, Austria, Semmelweis observed that the women in the underprivileged area, there because of poverty, illegitimacy, or obstetrical complications, had maternal mortality rates higher than the women in the privileged area or those who delivered at home, a result of childbed fever or puerperal infection. Semmelweis noticed that among women in the underprivileged area of the hospital, the mortality rate from childbed fever was two or three times higher than those in the privileged area. Physicians were of the opinion that this was on account of poor ventilation and overcrowding, and reconciled themselves to the belief that the illness was unpreventable.

When contemplating the question in silence, Semmelweis had intuitive insight that doctors and students who came directly from the dissecting room to the maternity ward carried the infection from mothers who died of the disease to healthy mothers. He also become aware of the fact that those doctors washed their hands less frequently in the underprivileged area of the hospital, which in turn added to the swell of puerperal fever. Physicians prided themselves with the status symbol of "Bloody Hands"; they were not afraid of blood.

It should be noted that from a historical standpoint, Semmelweis was a Johnny-come-lately by a millennium or two. The ancient Tibetans prohibited touching or doing autopsy on persons they deemed to be dead of an infectious disease. They carried bodies on long poles to avoid direct physical contact with infected tissue. Also, archeological evidence of ancient cultures indicates that not only the maternal mortality but also the infant mortality was high. In ancient Israel the infant mortality rate was as high as fifty percent.

Semmelweis publicly disagreed with the customary lifestyle of not washing hands rule before each examination during labor or performing delivery. He suggested a cleaning-of-hands procedure in a solution of chlorinated lime. Now doctors wash their hands, use gloves, and sterilize their instruments. As they deployed these measures, the fatality rates plunged drastically, and in March and August of 1848, no woman died from childbirth in his division. While the younger doctors in Vienna realized the implication of Semmelweis' finding and assisted him, the medical establishment, including his superior, failed to comprehend the hand-washing suggestion. They opposed the hand washing "ritual" and persecuted him. In 1849 Semmelweis was fired from his post at the clinic. He submitted an application for a teaching job at the University of Vienna midwifery department but was rejected. Now Semmelweis was out of work and wageless.

Serendipity is a gift and triumphs when explored: in every misfortune there is a fortune. In 1850 Semmelweis went to Saint Rochus Hospital in Pest, now part of Budapest, Hungary, where an epidemic of puerperal fever raged. His sterile surgical procedures swiftly cut the loss of life. In 1855 Semmelweis was appointed professor of obstetrics at the University of Pest. Two years later his discovery was accepted in Hungary, with the government ordering the introduction of Semmelweis' hand-washing method. The entrenched "scholars of medicine" in Vienna still remained hostile toward Semmelweis' findings, and the editor of the *Wiener Medizinische Wochenschrift* deeply pessimistic about the hand washing procedure recorded that it was time to stop the nonsense about the chlorine hand wash.

In the dark ages of medicine, how many lives and how much ink has been wasted on debates among the protagonists and antagonists of washing hands or preventive lifestyle in conventional medicine is anyone's guess. For some people it was hard to open their mind—to penetrate the collective amnesia. However today, one hundred fifty years later, try to deliver a baby in Vienna without washing your hands or wearing gloves. It's crime. You might be jobless and put away.

Jacob Burckhardt (1818-1897) has been characterized "the most civilized historian of the nineteenth century," and he was, indeed, one of the best historians of art and culture of his time. Whereas Semmelweis focused his intuitive reflections on saving mothers, Burckhardt focused on the nature and reciprocal interactions of the state, religion, and culture of Europe in the nineteenth century. Like Abraham Lincoln, Burckhardt, with a grace and elegance that many aspire to, denounced human bondage and listened to the views of others. He maintained, like Mother Teresa, that *contemplation and reflection are the keys to insight and reasoning* into the nature of man and history. Using this approach, Burckhardt generated insights through his explorations of antiquity, the Renaissance, and Europe. His *Reflections on History* describes, "The totalitarian direction that history could take" in Europe—and which history, in fact, did take in the twentieth century—the horrors and atrocities of totalitarian governments and world war.

How Do You Tell People They Are Shining Like the Sun?

Thomas Merton (1915-1968), born in Prades, France, became a Trappist monk, spiritual seeker, teacher, and hardened social activist. In the vein of Dag Hammarskjöld, Erwin Schrödinger, Saint Tulsidasa, and other illuminated notables, Merton used the depth of his goodness, not his outer form, to purify his consciousness and intellectual acuity. Like the research scientist who is more concerned with foundations than applications, Merton became more involved in spiritual profit and the imitation of the Christ, to whom all things are one, rather than elegance of style and external observances.

Important Distinguishing Note: a scientist desires to "qualify experiments with qualities of the Unchanging State," through observation and testing of the laws of nature. The illuminated spiritual seeker desires to "qualify experience with qualities of the Unchanging State," through "direct realization" and conscious experience of '1'. In physical terms, a scientist measures manifestation (length of a step, size of the shoe) between points or infinities: specifically, the start of measurement ('1' in the laws of physics) and the end of measurement (length between steps, gap between empty points or "boundaries" of the shoe, '=' in the laws of physics). This is explained more fully in part 2. The illuminated spiritual seeker strives to stay put at the connecting zero-state or the pre-quantum fact of '1'.

A scientist is profoundly concerned about scientific integrity: experiments and published results must be consistent, trustworthy and reliable. The illuminated spiritual seeker is even more deeply concerned than the scientist about the impeccable integrity and truthfulness of his or her assertion. A scientist may or may not *believe* in life after death; the illuminated spiritual seeker *knows* that she or he is timeless, that there is no death, only a change of form, and that not being truthful encompasses serious consequences.

Analogous to the writing on this page, a scientist gives attention to words (like relationships between letters [*a, b, c,* . . . and *z* order], cataloging the meaning of letters in words [dictionary]). The illuminated spiritual seeker gives attention to the unelaborated zero-state empty gap connecting the lettering or print, such as these attributes of the empty interval: freedom, peace, purity, and the ordering principle. In both cases one is dealing with the manifest (lettering) and unmanifest, dimensionless qualities of the Unchanging State.

In real life, the dark blue bird or the green parrot, the flowers, the trees, the clouds, the galaxies, the old man wobbling with a cane are manifested qualities of the Unchanging Principle of the universe. The empty-space between them is the unmanifest part of the Unchanging State, or the Great Perfection of the Buddhist. '1' pervades from the atom through the Milky Way (with a corona diameter of six hundred thousand light-years and one hundred billion stars in its galaxy), to billions of galaxies all the way to the cosmic scale of the universe and beyond. Reflect on this note. It can help you understand the difference between manifest and unmanifest, between medicine and miracles. Merton probed the spiritual depths, the dimensionless qualities of the Unchanging State. He was an extraordinary spring of encouragement and spiritual illumination: his mind and heart were uncaged. In silence he found vistas of our own "infinite possibilities." Merton wrote about silence, to "become silent, the ultimate perfect emptiness to attain perfect emptiness," and his search for God's face reflected in all his experiences. In 1968, Merton, with Jimpa Rinpoche, Father Sherburne and Harold Talbott, visited Chartral Rinpoche near Bagdogra. In his personal journal Merton wrote, "We started talking about *dzogchen* ['1', the foundation out of which phenomena emerge and the most secret teaching of Shakyamuni Buddha. Dzogchen is the deepest state of consciousness; beyond space and time] and direct realization [the process of finding our true self] and soon saw that we agreed very well [that there is no substitute for direct experience]":

> We must have talked for two hours or more, covering all sorts of grounds, mostly around about the idea of dzogchen, but also talking in some points of Christian doctrine compared with Buddhist: dharmakaya [the unity of Buddha with everything existing; the "unity of the Spirit" in Christianity]—the Risen Christ, suffering, compassion for all creatures, motives for "helping others" [for bringing spiritual voyagers through the labyrinths of mind], all leading back to dzogchen, the ultimate emptiness, the unity of shunyata [absolute voidness] and karuna [compassion], going "beyond the dharmakaya" [the unity of the Buddha with everything existing] and "beyond God" to the ultimate perfect emptiness [the "unity of the Spirit"; union without ceasing with God].[16]

Merton had vigor; he had charisma, and he was committed to creating unity. In Merton's social, political, and personal commentaries he turned purity of heart, inner silence, and stillness into new insights and awareness:

> I have the immense joy of being man, a member of the race in which God Himself became incarnate. As if the sorrows and

stupidities of the human condition could overwhelm me now that I realize what we all are. If only everybody could realize this! But it cannot be explained [others have been persecuted, executed and burned alive at the stake for explaining it]. There is no way of telling people they are all walking around shining like the sun.[17]

The Infinite Splendor within Each and Every One of Us

The exploration for complete peace of mind and perception into the deepest, the unmanifest, structure of the universe (Christ's kingdom of God, Shakyamuni Buddha's dzogchen or nirvana, Weinberg's final theory) or our experience of the Infinite Splendor within us is not all that uncommon in our day. It cuts across countries and cultures. It encompasses a variety of forms—some ordinary, such as Archimedes, Semmelweis, and some extraordinary, such as Emerson, Heschel, Schrödinger, Hammarskjöld, Merton, and Mother Teresa. One such personal experience sheds light on the conception of the essential unity of all and the shining, greater than the sun, of the Absolute Light within us.

It was a very peaceful and quiet evening. I was sitting in our living room. Daylight became twilight and then turned into night. I continued to "dwell in peace" and deep gratitude amid the music of silence and the reverence of the Unchanging in us. As time moved onward, the street lamp in front of our house lit up. Its light broke the darkness of the room. I remained absorbed in stillness, striving to advance deeper and deeper into peace ("rest with God" [Heb 4:11]).

All of a sudden, in vein of French impressionist Claude Oscar Monet's (1840-1926) painting *Impression: Sunrise,* 1872, where the horizon has vanished and sky, water, buildings, ships, and reflections have merged with their surroundings—melting into them, with the sunrise dominating the painting—everything in my being dissolved into the crystal-clear transparency and empty-space field. Like Monet's *Sunrise*, the blazing Light (where the intensity of our sun appears relatively nil) connected what lay outside and its inner content into a state of complete peace. The blazing Light resembled the empty-space between you and the sky, or the cosmic void that links electrons, planets, and galactic systems. I felt weightless as though I had no body and at one with the universe and the self-luminosity of all things. There was no physical I, only the clear Light consciousness of the Infinite Splendor and transparent stillness without borders within me. Like when one is in love, human language reaches its limit when it tries to express the experience of the empty-space Light.

At some point I found myself asking the question: "Why am I experiencing this?" From within the Light I heard, "Because you are a part of it all, for all is Light and thus love. And you are Light and thus love too. We are One." Later, searching through the Bible and other Sacred Scriptures, I sought to find each and every passage that spoke of the holy Light, the ocean of peace and the splendor of freedom. I wanted to learn of others who discovered what I had found.

The Exhilarating Peace:
Tasting a Fragrance from the Unmanifest Potentiality

At countless other times, in my daily exercises, as I surrendered to higher heights of silent peace and stillness, "where soul and spirit meet, to where joints and marrow come together ['1']" (Heb 4:12), my consciousness would stop making reflections and projections of the world. My awareness would became clear and free from any overlay, or impulse of creation, merging in the Infinite Splendor. It would melt away into the Infinite Light of absolute peace as transparent as clear glass or diamond. The Light (a zero-point field of potential action without boundary and separability) is more transparent than the empty-space we customarily observe between objects. What would come to the forefront is a state of very pure awareness and very lucid joy that is behind customary consciousness, the Light of lights and Peace of peace that supports and is the core of everything seen and experienced. At that state of awareness there is no me without you, or you without me, because you are me and we are all one.

The merging into the Infinite Peace beyond peace or "free of thought" (pre-thought) state can be compared to a calm lake or a pre-physical potentiality in the physics of the vacuum, while the discriminating state resembles a lake where there are waves, like when the restless consciousness spins out an endless web of creations. In the clear Light state, when we shift our consciousness to silent stillness, the multiplicities of forms vanish, while in the discriminating state, when we shift our consciousness to thinking, the universe comes into being. I realized, what so many others had in the past realized, that the transparent Light is the Common Ground of our Being without desire or any content other than pure awareness, pure peace, pure freedom, or love itself. It is the unmanifest and it is the imperishable sphere of the Holy of Holies. Heaven, or "the kingdom of God" in the Bible, is not a location in the eastern or the western part of the cosmos but rather it is a priori reference or a transparent state of consciousness, which pervades the universe.

All exists in the transparent Light of awareness, and the transparent Light state exists in all. God's presence or the exhilarating Peace is everywhere! Like water for waves, *in stillness we can tune into that presence. In stillness we become the clear Light of peace.* I understood that the principle of the a priori behind phenomena is formless, without boundaries and "latent in us." I recognized my identity with this cosmic infinity and grace.

The Infinite Light is a dimensionless foundation where all of our laws of science, like waves in an ocean, emanate from and fade away to. It contains, in itself, not only our universe, but also a multiplicity of other universes, realities, and infinities. What are generally termed manifestations or fundamental physical constants of nature take various forms or values as we the observer, the Infinite Magician (atom, human, galaxy, universe) change our point of view (quantum fluctuation), with respect to scale of distance, or time of the history of the cosmos. I experienced heart-exploding freedom, peace, and knowledge: the central message of all practicing religions is the same; the fundamental message of all sciences is the same.

Similar to seeing, hearing, smelling, touching, or tasting, different people, sciences, religions, or nations, are relaying the same fundamental message through a different spectrum, another point of view. Our physical differences and perceptions of experience, our personal devotion to ideals and aspirations for Truth, or our likes and dislikes, are perceived and expressed by each one of us dependent on our level of growth. By limiting ourselves to any one single observation of the Common Ground, we are shortchanging ourselves.

There are numerous passageways in Sagarmatha, for the people of Nepal (Chomolungma for the Tibetans) National Park, the highest national park in the world and covering 470 square miles, up the Mount Everest (the goddess of the heavens for the people of Nepal, 29,021 ft.), but all roads converge to a single summit, the tallest thing there is. All roads are God's roads. The goal of any religion is to make the "learner" independent of religion but dependent on truth. The aim of any educator is to make the student independent of, rather than dependent on, the teacher.

That (the transparent Light, '**1**') which is ever the same is unchangeable and unmoving. The religion's God, the physicist's magic vacuum prior to the definition of any metrical structure, the Highest Good, and the clear Light of basic awareness all converge. The outer life of God has an essentially human form. My consciousness perceived the eternal Spirit of our Infinite Splendor and the profoundest reality of the universe. To borrow from the Upanishads, "Thou art that," or through the prophet Moses and the children of Israel, "I am that I am."

See within God Himself: You Become Light

While at one with the Light of lights and Peace of peace, I was aware that each one of us is linked to everyone else through the clear Light, like the waves of water through water. All is in the clear Light of love, and the clear Light of love is in all. *God is wholly in me, and I am wholly in God.* In honoring life, I honor myself. When in a silent and peaceful state, like still water in a clear lake, I can see that "I am that clear Light of bliss," that the deepest reality of the present is infinite and within everyone. It is the ocean of the silent freedom, the silent knowing, the silent serving, and silent heaven in everyone and everything that emanates from this stillness, this selfless compassion and, simultaneously, our universe.

The Acts of the Apostles records a period of approximately thirty-years after Jesus' death, resurrection and ascension. Luke wrote Acts as a continuation to the Gospel of Luke for the book market. He points out: God "is not far from each one of us. 'For in him we live and move and have our being'" (Acts17:27-28).

Through these and similar experiences into the clear Light of peace and Freedom of freedoms, I observed the Formless Infinity and unity between the fundamental structure of our surroundings (matter, knowledge, infinities, symmetry in linear and nonlinear mathematical physics, and the cosmos) and the "Nameless One."[18] I realized that every piece of matter is absolute consciousness, emptiness (in which all thought waves and impulses of creation have subsided and all duality is extinguished), Light (which is unchanging, uncreated, indestructible), and love. Wisdom, knowledge, and harmony are accessible at every point of the cosmos; the fundamental composition of the world is enfolded into '1', at every point in the universe.

The Prince of Life used the Aramaic word "Abba" (Mk 14:36), meaning "my father" or "the father," as another way to address "Our Father . . ." (Mt 6:9), the Infinite Wisdom of the Worlds, or the inexpressible potential that is *dormant in us*. Therefore, Abba is within you, Abba is within me—Abba is within all (Rom 8:15; Gal 4:6). He is the Light ('1') we *scan* (see the Nature of Time and the Nature of Space in part 2, chapter 6) to detect what we observe, in the ever-moving self-aware universe of continuous entertainment ("Your kingdom come" [Mt 6:10; Lk 11:2]). I understood that unconnected objects and life do not exist. Everything is sagaciously related, like letters, words, and thoughts on paper; all is wit, thought, and reflection of the clear Light of lights and transparent Peace of peace in disguise.

Now I was faced with these challenges: Do I cover up my find, like the French scholar Blaise Pascal did in 1654, or do I share my experiences with others? When Pascal died in 1662, people discovered a little slip of paper sewed into the lining of his jacket. The little slip contained the precious testimony of an experience Pascal had undergone.

How do I integrate the deep meaning of the Scriptures and science through my own experience? How do I put on a rigorous footing and formulate a general hypothesis of my experiences in the realization of the true nature of phenomena, in which diversity comes to rest? How do I incorporate the meaning and wonder of one's luminous state and consciousness-created universe with mathematics and high-precision measurements in scientific inquiry? How do I fully test and verify this hypothesis through experiments of science?

Sages' Glimpses of Unity:
Our Hearts Should Do This More

Subramuniya, who, by silencing his desires and cravings learned that contact with "the center of this blazing avalanche of light" did not have to wait until the afterlife, shares:

> When you unfold spiritually on the path, you discover what it is
> that you know, although you cannot easily explain it. At first you

feel light shining within you. You may think it is only an illusion, yet you will find as you move into a quiet area of your mind you can *see* the light again and again. It becomes brighter and brighter. You will begin to wonder what is in the center of the light . . .

As you release desires and cravings through daily meditation, *the external mind releases its hold on your awareness* and you dive deeper, fearlessly, into *the center of this blazing avalanche of light beyond form and formlessness*. And as you come back into the mind, you see the mind for what it is, and you see the mind for what it is not . . .

As you come out of that samadhi [a state of consciousness in which mind becomes silent and you recognize as Rumi did, "I have been looking for myself"—I am the eternal, imperishable Absolute; the supreme principle of the world in Vedanta], you realize you are the spirit, *the life force of all.* You become the spirit consciously, if you could say spirit has consciousness. *You are That* spirit in every living soul [emphasis added].[19]

Ibn al-Farid, thirteenth century Spanish-born poet of Sufism, was a contemporary of the great Andalusian sage, Ibn 'Arabi. Ibn al-Farid's spontaneity, purity of expression, and kind-heartedness lift up the reader's heart. He articulates Subramuniya's "you are the spirit, the life force of all" in the words: "Everything you see is the action of the One" ['1'].[20] And, "I knew for sure that we are really One, and the sobriety of union restored the notion of separation, and my whole being was a tongue to speak, an eye to see, an ear to hear, and a hand to seize."[21]

Hafiz, who relentlessly persuades our hearts to dance, to synchronize with '1', stated, "At night if I feel divine loneliness, I tear the doors of Love's mansion and wrestle God onto the floor. He becomes so pleased with Hafiz and says, 'Our hearts should do this more.'"[22]

In the epistle of Paul to the Romans we read that we must become that which *we are*: "All who are led by the Spirit of God are *sons of God* [described in the Upanishads as aditi, the sons of the Infinite Ground] . . . *we are children of God*. But if we are children, *we are* heirs as well: heirs of God, *heirs with Christ*, if only we suffer with him so as to be glorified with him" (Rom 8:14-17).

Saint Symeon the New Theologian (9491022) moved inside of himself to change his vision of himself. He wrote, "I became light in the night":

As I was meditating, Master, on these things, suddenly You appeared from above, much greater than the sun, and You shone brilliantly from the heavens down into my heart . . . But, while I was there surrounded by darkness, You appeared as light, illuminating me completely from your total light. And I became light in the night.[23]

Paramhamsa (Swami Muktananda, 1909-83) was so attuned to the Light of lights that he did not have to meditate or contemplate in the "classic" sense to observe the "Unchanging Being." Muktananda, whom I met, would behold in all conditions that "this entire world, in which we live, is a play of the self-luminous Universal Spirit." Muktananda's view is similar to Lao-tzu's characterization of the Tao ('1', "the Way"), the Greek concept of the Logos, the Hindu Brahman-Atman (Eternal Happiness, absolute consciousness) from which all nature proceeds and returns, and the Nahuas, the native peoples of Mesoamerica from the High Central Plateau of what is now Mexico, concept for *Teotl* (the single, all-encompassing, animating force of the universe).[24] Muktananda goes on to write:

I see the soft conscious mass of light trembling delicately and shining in all conditions—whether I am eating, drinking, or bathing. It surrounds me even during sleep . . . Thou art That—is, in fact, my own Self—vibrating subtly within me . . . The universe belongs to you. You are its Soul. Different levels of manifestations arise from you. They are your own forms. You are perfect in your aspect as the indwelling Universal Spirit. Remain continuously aware that the universe is your own splendid glory.[25]

Everything in the cosmos is bustling and full of life. The Eternal Happiness belongs to all of us. Is it time to end the cover-up and to touch it with the deepest part of us?

5

DEEP SECRETS IN CODE LANGUAGE

The laws of nature are in code. The job of
the scientist is to crack the cosmic code,
and therefore reveal the secrets of the universe.

—Paul Davies

Garments Protect Your Body: The Absolute Is Hidden

Heinz Pagels, the great conciliator and old hand for his immaculate
scholarship, in his profound book *The Cosmic Code,* wrote:

> Although the idea that the universe has an order that is governed
> by natural laws that are not immediately apparent to the senses is
> very ancient, it is only in the last three hundred years that we have
> discovered a method for uncovering the hidden order—the
> scientific-experimental method. So powerful is this method that
> virtually everything scientists know about the natural world comes
> from it. What they find is that the architecture [the ordering
> principle, the universal software] of the universe is indeed built
> according to invisible universal rules, what I call the cosmic [source]
> code—the building code of the Demiurge.[1]

A number of our predecessors recognized that each one of us has the
strength and capability to reach or experience the invisible God: the
Absolute Infinity, where in all places order, stability, and harmony reigns.
They realized that by shifting from thinking consciousness or
manifestation to absolute or cosmic consciousness, through a purity of
heart, compassion, and a peace of mind, one could reach the Unchanging

State, the concealed universal code. Also, they became conscious that the cosmic code of the vastness beyond is reflected in our mind, giving rise to zero state consciousness, which in turn projects the visible universe. The ancients held that foundational knowledge (our unity) should not be too readily accessible to the undeserving. Some quantum physicists embrace a comparable view in science. Cesareo Bandera, in *The Sacred Game*, stated, "Ultimate truth has very often been forbidden truth, truth that must be surrounded and protected from discovery by the most formidable sacred taboos."

The Infinite Splendor has been clad in the strangest of garments in Scripture: literal, allegorical, philosophical, tropological (moral), homiletic, and the inner mystical sense or the soul of the Bible. For instance, the name Jerusalem appears 804 times in the database of the *Zondervan NIV Exhaustive Concordance* to the Bible. It has a wide range of biblical meanings: "The Holy City where stands the sacred Temple of the Most High God," the house of worship, the city of destiny (our ultimate destination), the "city of peace," the human soul and our Spiritual Home. Similarly, "neighbor" is someone living close, the member of social unit, the friend, and the lover. In Tantric symbolism, eroticism, even though "repugnant to both reason and common sense," has frequently been employed to keep under wraps the innermost essence of truth.

From the New Testament (Gospels, Acts of the Apostles, Revelations) it is known that the Christ, the apostles, and the Apostolic Fathers did not discuss openly or place in writing the essence of the Invisible Order, of God's word (1 Cor 3:2). It was not to be given to those who were not adequately ready, such as the unconverted (heathen) to the Life of Sanctity. They could be more harmed than helped from the wisdom of Scripture. The deeper meaning (*hyponoia*) than what its words seem to suggest was concealed beneath the attire of fables, myths, and paintings, as allegories or with allegorical subjects, needing patient excavation and decoding to uncover, at least partly, its richness of value. This was an old formula among Greeks and the early poets.

Today, as in the days of the Nazarene, the underlying spiritual meaning of the Christ and his ministry escapes the majority of the people. We read the Bible; in the most cases we do not understand its profound meaning. If the Bible lovers and the scientific community understood our foundational Oneness or Einstein's unity, we would have another world. You will see why.

In the deep love of marriage we experience tantalizing clues, intense feelings of unity, and references to "the special knowledge of one's real self." The clues point the way to "finding one's life"—to "the forbidden fruit" of the "tree of life and knowledge" and the process of "knowing" each other. This fundamental wisdom represents the true intimacy of the soul of one with another and was taught by the Jewish teachers of the Law, Greek and Latin scholars, as well as by the Christ and the apostles.[2]

We know that Pythagoras of Samos, Socrates of Athens, Shariputra and Mahamaudgalyayana of India, Saint John the Baptist and Jesus of Judea, al-Hallaj of Iraq, Suhrawardi of Syria, Yoshida Shoin of Japan, Saint Agatha of Sicily, and Saint Agnes of Rome were treated as criminals and put to death. For personal safety reasons the ancient sages and scriptwriters concealed the most intimate secrets of our nature in the symbolic mask of delicately textured parables, clandestine codes, and metaphors. This underground code language was widely used the world over in scholarly groups and amongst people of literary and philosophical bent. Many times, "forbidden knowledge" was entrusted to verbal communication, not to writing, as in the case of extremely subtle mystical truths, or first principles of nature.

The Sacred Pearls Were Kept for the Elect

Professor Manlio Simonetti teaches at the University of Rome and the "Augustinianum," the Patristic Institute in Rome. In his *Biblical Interpretation in the Early Church* he gives a historical introduction to patristic exegesis, the most characteristic element of Christian learning in the earliest centuries, "the allegorical interpretations of the sacred text," and "the need for a deeper understanding of the significance of the Christ and his ministry in relation to Jewish tradition." Addressing Saint Clement of Alexandria, Simonetti states:

> Indeed, neither the prophets nor Our Lord himself expressed the divine mysteries in a simple way, which would be accessible to all, but they spoke in parables [allegories] as the apostles themselves declared (Matthew 13:34).
>
> There were various reasons for this: to encourage the more zealous to sustained and skillful research, and because those who are not sufficiently prepared would receive more injury than help from a knowledge of Scripture. The sacred mysteries are reserved for the elect;

those predestined for this "gnosis." This explains the characteristic use of the parable-style in Scripture (*Strom.* VI 15:124).[3]

"In our literature," states *The New American Bible*, "we possess this literary form in the Negro spirituals; for example, 'Let My People Go'. The slaves sang it in their wooden plantation churches: 'Tell de Pharaoh [the "boss man" of the plantation] to let my people go.'"[4]

The Ukrainian philosopher Hryhoryj Skovoroda (1722-1794) was a contemporary of the East Prussian philosopher Immanuel Kant (1724-1804), and the great *maskil* (Ps 52-55) and "Jewish Socrates" Moses Mendelssohn (1729-86). Skovoroda's evolving spirit of ecumenical understanding and influence extended to other Slavic countries. He was commonly acknowledged as the "Ukrainian Socrates." Skovoroda was a keen scholar of the Bible, which he constantly carried. He valued the Socratic tenet "Know thyself," the realization of one's true nature as the state of unbounded love, so much that he taught it everywhere he went.

According to Skovoroda, each human is a miniature representation of the universe (little world, microcosm) *projecting* (reflecting) from the Absolute the enormous universe (macrocosm) *within oneself*. In effect, each point of pure consciousness is projecting itself as an outer expression or universe. Dag Hammarskjöld, Emerson, Meher Baba, Ramanuja, G.W.F. Hegel, F.W.J. Schelling, Kitaro Nishida, Alfred North Whitehead, Swami Ramakrishna, and Yogananda held comparable views. Their cosmos is an expansion of the '1' (external self-projection of the universal software) and all its activities are Absolute's movements.

Human beings, in most cases, are unaware that their consciousness is projecting itself as an outer manifestation. In order to better appreciate the universe, Skovoroda maintained, similar to Jesus in the Gospel of Thomas, Shankara, Aurobindo, and others, one must first know oneself. Addressing parables, fables and the great book of God, Skovoroda wrote:

> My friend! Do not disregard fables! Fables and parables are one and the same. Do not estimate one's worth by his purse—judge justly! Fable is bad and stupid when it does not contain the grain of truth in its ugly and ridiculous crust; it then resembles an empty nut . . . Sometimes the pearl is hidden in a heap of trash . . . This interesting and complex mode of writing used to be normal with the most revered ancient sages.

The sun and the queen of all planets is the Bible with its mysterious images, parables, and similes. It is sculpted from clay that, once breathed by the spirit of life, hides the wisdom of everything that is mortal.[5]

Symbolic code language can be an endless resource of learning, peeling away deeper layers of the ultimate truth en route to greater and greater understanding. The following reference to symbolic code language is found in the Hebrew Sefer ha-zohar (The Book of Splendor), the classic work of Jewish mysticism, and considered to be one of the greatest expressions of the Kabbalah:

> Woe to the man who sees in Torah ["Law": traditionally called the "five books of Moses"—Moses received the Torah at Mount Sinai"] only simple recitals and ordinary words! Because, if in truth it contains only these, we would even today be able to compose a Torah much more worthy of admiration. But it is not so. Each word of the Torah contains an elevated meaning and sublime mystery . . . The recitals of the Torah are the vestments of the Torah. Woe to him who takes this vestment for the Torah itself . . . The simple take notice of the garments or recitals of the Torah alone. They know no other thing. They see not that which is concealed under the vestment. The more instructed men do not pay attention to the vestment but to the body which it envelopes.[6]

The Zohar, a noteworthy mystical commentary, assembled by Moses de Leon in Spain, at the end of the thirteenth century, can scarcely be read without a teacher who is a member of the Oral Torah. Ponder the subtle hint of the Beloved: "There is something here, I tell you, greater than the Temple [of Jerusalem or Mt. Gerizim]. If you really knew what this scripture means" (Mt 12:6). Samaritans considered Mt. Gerizim as the dwelling place of God, while the Jews of Palestine regarded Mt. Zion and the temple in Jerusalem as the place where Israel had the favor of God's special earthly presence.

What does the Nazarene mean: "There is something greater than the temple here?" What transcendent secret and elevated meaning is concealed under this (Mt 12:6) vestment?

Milk for Babies Solid Food for Grown-Ups

Growth comes in both baby steps and giant leaps. Why were babies (common folk, "without any experience in the matter of right and wrong" [Heb 5:13]), in the kindergarten of the spiritual school, fed with "milk" and with baby talk of parables, allegories, and the elementary knowledge about the Spirit of God, and the more knowledgeable ("who have trained and used their tastes to know the difference between good and evil" [Heb 5:14]) with solid food: the "meat" of the secret of secrets (1 Cor 3:2)?

Why did Jesus suggest vigilance in daily life with the heathen (unconverted to the life of altruistic love), advocating not "to cast pearls before swine" (1 Cor 13:12)? When will solid food, the Gospel's (Eph 6:19) and the Holy Qur'an's secret ("Everywhere you turn, there is Allah's face" [2:115]), be brought to our table?

Reflect on Christ's previous words: "I shall give you what no eye has seen and what no ear has heard and what no hand has touched and what has never occurred to the human mind . . ." In Paul's First Letter to the Corinthians we find a similar statement: "No eye has seen, no ear has heard, no mind has conceived what God has prepared for those who love him" (1 Cor 2:9). There are many options. Can we narrow the range of choice?

Religion Can Be Deadly: Who Did This to Us?

Al-Hallaj[7] was the summum bonum of unbounded love, a spiritual engine of great intellectual breadth, and a teacher of Sufism. Reminiscent of Saint John the Baptist, Jesus, and his apostles, al-Hallaj called people to Infinite Life: continuing personal sanctification, love and compassion, and the realization of one's true nature: a return of the memory of wholeness. Being a saintly man, he would prefer to feed the black dog at his side, "the image of his lower nature," than eat the food himself. Al-Hallaj performed numerous miracles (creating delightful food in the middle of the desert, and so forth) and tried to spiritually revitalize the Muslim's warring empire of the caliphs, the foremost military and economic power in the world.

Al-Hallaj emphasized the need for self-purification, universal brotherhood, and recommended systematic studies of consciousness and "validation through direct personal experience." He maintained that Allah, the Lord and Sustainer of the Worlds, is in everyone and everywhere, including the barbarian infidels, as they were called then. We read in the Holy Qur'an, "To Allah belong the East and the West: anywhere you turn, there is Allah's face." (2:115). The bolt from the blue, the one that shook up the religious and prevailing authorities of Baghdad was the "exchanging of acts" idea.[8] Al-Hallaj recommended that instead of performing the holy pilgrimage to Mecca, which he visited three times, it is better to shelter orphans, feed them, dress them, and make them happy, just as sixteen centuries before him, Isaiah advanced, "Seek justice, encourage the oppressed. Defend the cause of the fatherless, plead the case of the widow" (1:17).

"He [al-Hallaj] declared," wrote Annemarie Schimmel, a very penetrating scholar into the mystical reach of Islam, "that God is visible in every trace of His creation, and although the common folk, the blind and dumb, animal-like [from which there was nothing to learn and little even to be imported, except slaves and raw material], do not recognize Him, the mystic drinks not a single drop of water without discovering His vision in the cup."[9]

The governing elite and the doctors of the Islamic Holy Law (with tragic ability of vision), similar to the teachers of the Law during the time of the Christ, who "nailed him to the cross for claiming to be the Son of God" (Jn 19:6-12), were incapable of understanding the profound *unity of being* concept, and that we are all children of God. Al-Hallaj's sanctity, purity, and the spreading of that knowledge became dangerous to the stagnant religious and political will of Baghdad, in their quest for wealth and power. Al-Hallaj was arrested, his hands and feet were cut off, his body crucified, burned, and his ashes scattered in the Tigris.

Al-Hallaj's parting words were like those of the Christ on the cross (Lk 23:34). At the place of execution, reciting a religious poem about dying in love and reaching a new, higher life in union with God, the goodbye words appear: "They do not know what they do, but they should have known it."

Anyone Can Destroy; Not Everyone Can Build?

Around three hundred-years later, Suhrawardi[10] (1153-1191), Persian Muslim saint and "master of illumination," founder of the School of

Illumination (*ishraq*), maintained that at the heart of the divinely revealed traditions of wisdom, there is one universal truth, one Absolute Order, '1'. Material bodies (Einstein's mass) are constituent of light (Einstein's energy); the nature of the universe is pure Light, and the ultimate cause of all things (the ultimate Light—the Necessary Being [*wajib al-wujud*]) is the Light of lights. Suhrawardi, like al-Hallaj, was a genius in his line. He maintained that there is no substitute for direct experience, comparable to our scientific-experimental method.

Suhrawardi argued that the validity of the Principle of Priority (knowing the truth—observing the world and the self as they really are, free of the masks of illusion) could be verified through direct personal experience and spiritual illumination of the intellect. That is simple. However, this type of wisdom was inconsistent to the religious authorities accustomed to despise and kill the infidel barbarians beyond the frontiers of Islamic civilization. They were unable to grasp Suhrawardi's depth and majesty of insight.

What did they do to him? The religious opposition asked the reigning sultan Saladin the Great, Syrian commander and Sultan of Egypt, to have Suhrawardi's head chopped off for advocating heretical ideas, ideas at variance with the orthodox doctrine. It was done. The interesting part, from the Jewish perspective, Jesus was also advancing heretical ideas.

Approximately three hundred years before al-Hallaj (640), Caliph Omar destroyed by fire the great library of Alexandria, where Saint Clement and Origen earlier taught as pioneers in biblical learning and Christian values. Omar's reason for burning over 500,000 papyrus scrolls: if the books agreed with the Qur'an, they were useless, if not, they were harmful and ready for total destruction. After Alexandrian destruction Egypt virtually vanishes from Christian church history.

A Partial Truth Is Not a Whole Truth: Mujahedin, Why Do You Kill Yourself?

"Muslims often have the feeling that history has somehow betrayed them," states David Landers, of Harvard University, in Bernard Lewis' book review, *What Went Wrong: The Clash Between Islam and Modernity in the Middle East*. A number of Muslims (military Islam) aim to bring God's message to all mankind in the world. Yes, but do these Muslims understand what God's message is? It is to love your neighbor as yourself, for God is in your neighbor! The best-known examples of the World Islamic Front message, going round the frontiers of Islam, are West Africa, Bosnia, Chechnya, Kashmir, Kosovo, Palestine, southern Philippines, Sinkiang, Sudan, Timor, USA (WTC/Pentagon/Flight 93), and the like.

The conscience of the American nation has been deeply touched by the barbarous behavior of the mujahedin butchery and a religion claiming absolute truth. Roughly twelve hundred fifty days before the "blessed conquest of New York and Washington," as the Madrid bombers called it, in February 23, 1998, Usama bin Laden in *Al-Quds al 'Arabi*, an Arabic newspaper published in London, had proclaimed a jihad in the name of the World Islamic Front,

> Kill Americans and their allies, both civil and military . . . By God's leave, we call on every Muslim who believes in God and hopes for reward to *obey God's command* [my emphasis] to kill the Americans and plunder their possessions wherever he finds them and whenever he can. Likewise we call on the Muslim ulema [the body of scholars and learned men who are authorities on Muslim religion and law] and leaders and youth and soldiers to launch attacks against the armies of the American devils and against those who are allied with them from among the helpers of Satan . . ."

Not long ago it was Hitler who called on the German people to exterminate Jews, Poles, Ukrainians, Russians, Czechs, French, conscientious objectors, gypsies, and so on. Karl Marx had a similar class hatred and class war rallying call, with his *The Communist Manifesto* and *Das Kapital*. Now it is Usama bin Laden and his xenophobic circle of the World Islamic Front jihadists.

The post-9/11 era isn't only the U.S. challenge, it is other people's challenge, and it is a challenge for Muslims, who claim absolute truth, and who are not open to a dialogue and new views of understanding. Can a partial truth be a whole truth? Is that what God wants Muslims to do: destroy rather than build? Kill non-Muslims of the world? If Muslims believe in God and "you shall not kill" of the Ten Commandments, Muslims should realize that the future of humanity depends on the cooperation between people that work hand-in-hand.

Mahamaudgalyayana was one of the ten great disciples of the Shakyamuni Buddha. The lord Mahavira had eleven disciples. The Christ had twelve disciples. Mahamaudgalyayana came into the Buddhist community simultaneously with his childhood friend, Shariputra, who was noted for his supernatural abilities. Their images, similar to Christ's disciples in the Western tradition (i.e., Saint John, the disciple, whom Jesus loved, sitting next to Jesus on the Passover supper [Jn 13:23]), are regularly found in Buddhist monasteries next to that of the Buddha. Opponents of Christianity murdered apostles after the Christ. Opponents of Buddhism murdered both Mahamaudgalyayana and Shariputra prior to the departing of the Buddha.

Eight years preceding the passing away of Shakyamuni Buddha, Devadatta, Gautama's cousin, like Judas, was a part of a group of seekers who gathered around a teacher in order to attain spiritual realization. Devadatta battled for rigorous renunciation and mortification, condemning the Buddha for living a pampered life. A similar accusation was made against the Compassionate One and his disciples (Mt 11:19; Lk 5:33).

What Devadatta did not realize, what the members of the Jewish council did not understand, is that following asceticism and the direct encounter of God comes a more profound level of enlightenment—a realization of the Absolute presence within oneself, the flowering of goodness, and teaching others how to heal or how to find God for oneself. With the help of the king of Magadha (Ajatasattu), Devadatta devised a plan to murder the "Silent Sage of the Shakyas." There were three assassination attempts on the Buddha's life.

"Religion often considers spiritual life as made up of renunciation and mortification," writes Sri Aurobindo (1872-1950), one of the world's leading scholars and spiritual leaders. He adds:

> Religion thus becomes a force that discourages life, and it cannot, therefore, be a true law and guide for life.
>
> But here comes in an ambiguity which brings in a deeper source of divergence. For by spirituality religion seems often to mean something remote from earthly life, different from it, hostile to it. It seems to condemn the pursuit of earthly aims as a trend opposed to the turn to a spiritual life and the hopes of man on earth as an illusion or a vanity incompatible with the hopes of man

in heaven. The spirit then becomes something aloof which man can only reach by throwing away the life of his lower members. Either he must abandon this nether life after a certain point, when it has served its purpose, or must persistently discourage, mortify, and kill it. If that be the true sense of religion, then obviously religion has no positive message for human society in the proper field of social effort, hope, and aspiration or for the individual in any of the lower members of his being.[11]

The Living Waters from Our Secret Garden: Illuminates and Enlightens

In Christian tradition, illumination (the light of higher consciousness) and enlightenment (the kingdom of heaven or cosmic sense) are considered a third stage of our progress toward the Infinite One, coming after purification and awakening.[12] In other traditions, such as Hinduism and Buddhism, the ascetical practices of self-discipline, moral strictness and sanctity are the means to the "supreme reality." That is, through self-discipline and sanctity of life one is opening the door to the living waters from our inner garden; a human being is capable of realizing—the Buddha nature *within us*, or experiencing Einstein's cosmic religious feeling.

For Japanese people of Jichin's period (1155-1225) the way of poetry, through the poetic ideal of rare beauty, simplicity, purity, eloquence and few words, was the means to Buddhist enlightenment. And for the Japanese sage Suzuki Shosan's (1579-1655) economically productive work, which is reminiscent of Dag Hammarskjöld's, Mahatma Gandhi's, and Robert Muller's notions of self-discipline in selfless pursuit of one's occupation ("inner-worldly asceticism"); one's work becomes spiritual practice, rebirth and the simultaneous attainment of enlightenment. The Dalai Lama put it this way: "We are visitors on this planet . . . during this period we must try to do something useful with our lives."

Let us go back to Socrates (470-399 BC) and the fatal hemlock this martyr was forced to drink. In Athens, the condemned person "drank the hemlock" within twenty-four hours after the death verdict, in most cases. Why was this practitioner of righteousness and "morally the purest" promulgator of the idea of "know thyself," prosecuted for irreligion and "impiety"? Socrates was indicted on two counts: "Corruption of the young" and "neglect of the [many] gods whom the city worships and of the practice of religious novelties."

Plato (428-348 BC) was one of the greatest of philosophical writers and the founder of the Academy in Athens, an institute for the systematic pursuit of philosophical and scientific research. In *The Seventh Letter*, Plato stated that Socrates was "all glorious within," and "the most upright man of that day."

Marcus Tullius Cicero (106-143 BC), a Roman statesman, scholar, orator, lawyer, and writer, whose productivity and variety of topics were amazing, and who explored the ultimate destiny of the human soul, said Socrates "brought down philosophy from heaven to earth"—to the corrosion of the moral values in Athens.

Perhaps Socrates' outlook was too controversial, suggesting something very dangerous about the primordial principle of the universe, to the "slaves of *gnosis*." He was telling something that would free the youth of their day from their ignorance "about the Depth of the All." This appeared to disagree with the Athenian traditional viewpoint of honoring the many gods whom the city worshiped. Socrates, similar to Jesus, held himself responsible for his assignment from God to make his fellowmen know themselves. He was more than ready to die rather than to neglect his assignment.

Why is it so overwhelmingly dangerous to know one's self? What does it mean "to find one's life"? How long must we keep our minds shut about the ultimate source of all understanding, the foundations of physical and spiritual science? Why is the self-knowledge of our origin, nature, and destiny considered to be such a "special knowledge"? Should the key to salvation and "redemption of the inner man" be so remote? What does Saint Irenaeus' symbolic terminology denote: "The perfect redemption is said to be the knowledge of the ineffable Greatness"? What did Jesus mean when he stated, "The one who knows himself . . . has at the same time already achieved knowledge about the Depth of the All'; and, "then you will become known, and you will realize that it is *you* who are the sons of the living Father."

Why is it that the Socratic maxim to "know thyself" was the first aim of philosophy and the steppingstone with the religious geniuses and sages of antiquity? Why does the knowledge of ineffable Greatness of the All release us from ignorance? Why does knowing this Truth set us free? To use Jesus' words,

Brother Thomas, while you have time in the world, listen to me and I will reveal to you the things you have pondered in your mind.

Now since it has been said that you are my twin and true companion, examine yourself that you may understand who you are, in what way you exist, and how you will come to be. Since you are called my brother, it is not fitting [for a brother] that you be ignorant of yourself.[13]

Dear Reader, at this point I suggest that you lay aside this book for a day or two while you think, reflect and consider quietly: "Examine yourself that you may *understand who you are*, in what way you exist, and how you will come to be." Allow your inner voice to guide you in your silent illumination. Mull over, contemplate and deliberate on why it is undignified to keep truth alive: to know "Who the knower is?" and to be in ownership of final universal principles?

Treasure is where one finds it. You find your real self by attuning yourself to the '1'. When you do it, you will have the answer. You will discover what many others have discovered.[14]

After the execution of Socrates by the democrats in 399 BC, Plato taught the doctrines of Socrates and of Parmenides, who maintained, "All is one," and only one. Namely, the multiplicity of existence is but an appearance of a single eternal reality ("being"). In *Timaeus* Plato wrote, "To find out the Maker and Father of this universe is difficult, and, when found, it is impossible to declare Him to all."[15]

No One Can Learn Until One Is Ready to Learn

Milton Friedman, the Nobel Prize winning economist, is renowned for outstanding analytical powers and technical virtuosity. In *Capitalism & Freedom*, he shows another striking example:

From 1933 to the outbreak of World War II, [Winston] Churchill was not permitted to talk over the British radio, which was, of course, a government monopoly administered by the British Broadcasting Corporation. Here was a leading citizen of his country, a Member of Parliament, a former cabinet minister, a man who was desperately trying by every device possible to persuade his countrymen to take steps to ward off the menace of Hitler's Germany. He was not permitted to talk over the radio to the British people because the BBC was a government monopoly and his position was too "controversial."[16]

Physics and Society is a quarterly newsletter of the Forum, a division of the American Physical Society. The Forum publishes articles, book reviews, letters, and commentary on the affairs of physics and the physics community. The newsletter contains news of the Forum and provides the medium through which Physical Society members exchange ideas. Dean Abrahamson, based on his thirty-years of personal experience doing public education work on atomic energy, wrote a commentary, "So You Want To Become A Critic." He stated:

> A critic is defined as one who publicly expresses disagreement with established policy or dogma [as Semmelweis did with washing hands before delivery; Socrates; al-Hallaj; Suhrawardi; Churchill; and the Christ]. A critic must be prepared for attempts to be discredited, intimidated, co-opted, and, or, fired. Attempting to discredit is a routine part of the agenda for dealing with a critic, be it relating to atomic energy, drug or tobacco testing, or most other issues . . . e.g., investigations into the critic's personal life looking for scandal, setting the critic up with a honey trap or some such, alleging that the critic is not really interested in anything other than personal fame or financial gain, the list goes on . . . get his or her funding cut, assert pressure on officials at his or her university, muck around with the critic's credit rating . . . [17]

In Mao Ze-dong's China, Hitler's Germany, Stalin's Russia, Amin's Africa, and Hussein's Iraq, a more severe level of censorship and intrusion for dealing with a critic have been applied: death. It is evident that "the son of the man" was conscious of human makeup. Jesus advised, "Do not give what is holy to dogs or toss your pearls before swine. They will trample them underfoot, at best, and perhaps even tear you to shreds" (Mt 7:6). "Indeed," articulated the Holy Emancipator, "Not everyone can accept [digest/assimilate] this teaching, but only those to whom it has been given . . . The one who can accept this should accept it" (Mt 19:11-12). Yes,

You have been given the secret of the kingdom of God [which is within and without you]. But the others, who are on the outside [the inner circle], it is all presented in parables [baby fables, allegories], so that they will look intently and not see, listen carefully and not understand (Mk 4:11).

In the houses of prayer, churches, temples, synagogues, mosques, educational institutions, corporations and governments, the allegorical storytelling and parables about "the kingdom of God" are at the heart of religious, economic, political, social, philosophical, scientific and cultural inspirations and continuity. Deeper, fundamental spiritual meaning, the "meat" of the Bible or the Holy Qur'an, is not recognized, eluding the majority of people.

"No man can learn what he has not preparation for learning, however near to his eyes is the object," declares Emerson. He adds:

> A chemist may tell his most precious secrets to a carpenter, and he shall be never the wiser—the secrets he would not utter to a chemist for an estate. God screens us evermore from premature ideas. Our eyes are holden that we cannot see things that stare us in the face, until the hour arrives when the mind is ripened; then we behold them, and the time when we saw them not is like a dream.[18]

The Jewish philosopher, jurist, physician, and leading medieval thinker, Moses Maimonides (Rabbi Moses ben Maimon, 1135-1204), the foremost Talmudist of the Middle Ages, wrote a most penetrating commentary on the Mishna, the compilation of oral laws assembled about AD 200 and forming the basic element of the Talmud. This monumental compendium in Jewish law, spanning the earliest times to the third century, corroborates the Galilean and the Hebrew *Book of Splendor*, "Every time that you find in our books a tale, the reality of which seems impossible, a story which is repugnant to both reason and common sense, then be sure that the tale contains a profound allegory veiling a deeply mysterious truth; and the greater the absurdity of the letter, the deeper the wisdom of the spirit."[19]

Saint Jerome (342-420), one of the great Fathers in the Church of Western Europe, knew Greek, Aramaic and the Old Hebrew languages. In 382, Pope Damasus entrusted Saint Jerome with the preparation of the first Latin translation of the complete Bible. His translation, called Vulgate, has been accepted and used as an authorized version of the Roman Catholic Church. Addressing the translation of Genesis, Saint Jerome expounded: "The most difficult and most obscure of the holy books, Genesis contains as many secrets as words concealing many things even under each word."[20] Jesus', Saint Clement's, Saint Jerome's, and Maimonides' viewpoints are widely echoed in the writings of Origen, Irenaeus, Gregory of Nyssa, Bishop Papias, Justin the philosopher and martyr, Ambrose, and others.

A Deeper Spiritual Sense: Ever the Quest

Origen, the Alexandrian genius, had a profound knowledge of the Bible, theologically mature and a prolific exponent of the Scriptures. Origen extended the space in the Christian exegesis (critical research, explanation and interpretation) of Scripture in both form and issue. He made biblical hermeneutics, the principles of biblical exegesis—the knowledge of Scriptural interpretation—into a coherent methodology and science. His most important lifework was about the Greek Old Testament and the elucidation of the whole Bible.

Preceding Origen, exegetes focused on only some Old Testament books (Genesis, Exodus, Psalms, Isaiah, and little else). Origen, by comparison, delved into the whole of Scripture (Books of Wisdom [Ecclesiastes, Job], Joshua, and Judges, etc.): twelve books just for the first chapters of Genesis. He wrote thirty-three books for the Gospel According to John, some of which are preserved in Munich, and other texts on the Old and New Testaments, such as the annotations on Saint Matthew, which can be found in Trinity College, Cambridge. Origen composed scholarly expositions for the *advanced practicing and spiritually aware* (not the uninitiated who were given "milk"—fables, "lollipops," and parables). These are Christian commentaries on individual parts or books.

Case in point: in *On Prayer*, written in AD 233, preserved in one manuscript at Cambridge, Origen developed the Lord's Prayer, affirming that the highest prayer is "unity of the Spirit"—an elevation of the soul over the material universe to a *union* ("worship in spirit and truth," Jn 4:24) with the All.[21] This Unchanging State the Buddhists describe as the blissful uncreated void (*Ku*) or nirvana, and it is the all-embracing First Principle from which all appearances arise, discussed in more detail in part 2. The Hindus recognize this state of consciousness in which mental activity ceases as a total absorption in the object of meditation, union with the Absolute, or samadhi.[22] In physics, the concept of the void state is known as the empty-space, vacuum, "pre-space" or the implicate order. Saint Paul, elucidating *union* with the superconscious state (God is Spirit [Jn 4:24]) stated, "he who unites himself with the Lord [the '1'] is one with him in spirit" (1 Cor 6:17).

How many of us know the way into the innermost heart of God's presence, the kingdom of Light? How many people understand what becoming *one* spirit with the Highest Good means? In Oneness, which Whitehead expressed as the "seamless coat of the universe," there is no boundary between the Old One and us: "God is in us" (Is 7:14) consciously, as water is in a wave.

Spirit (Hebrew *ruah*; Greek *pneuma*) in the symbolic words of the Bible, stands for wind as well as breath. The English expression "spirit" is merely the Anglicized version of the Latin expression for breath (*spiritus*). You cannot grip wind with your hand nor see it with your eyes. In the language of Sanskrit, it is emptiness that is boundless and always exists, only is not recognized. Breath is a "mini-wind" with life-giving qualities. The spirit exemplified by the prophets is invisible, immaterial and the essence of Reality. "One Spirit" is the conscious experience of the unity with the "One Mind" says Wonhyo, the outstanding seminal philosopher and spiritual practitioner in the history of Korean philosophy. The unified state has many metaphors: two rooms becoming one, a lake or river emptying into an ocean. It is essentially a state of deep inner peace—stillness of the mind and awareness of one's identity with the Unchanging State.

Sri Aurobindo stated, "As the individual advances spiritually, he finds himself more and more united with the collectivity and the All."[23] Thus, to be "in Christ" (Rom 8:1) is the same as to be in "the Spirit of God" (Rom 8:9). It is an experience of the unified nature of the world with the '1': "I am in my Father, and *you in me*, and *I in you*" (Jn 14:20). "I am He," declare the sages of India.

"If orthodoxy were a matter of intention," states the Encyclopaedia Britannica, "no theologian could be more orthodox than Origen, none more devoted to the cause of Christian faith. His natural temper is world denying and even illiberal. The saintliness of his life is reflected in the insight of his commentaries and the sometimes quite passionate devotion of his homilies."[24]

Getting to the Absolute Treasure: Cherishing the Infinite Order

Commenting on the literal interpretation of the Bible, Origen provides, like the Hubble Space Telescope, a spectacular picture:

> What man of sense will agree with the statement that the first, second, and third days in which the evening is named and the morning were without sun, moon, and stars, and the first day without heaven? What man is found such an idiot as to suppose that God planted trees in Paradise, in Eden, like a husbandman, and planted therein the tree of life, perceptible to the eyes and senses, which gave life to the eater thereof; and another tree which gave to the eater thereof knowledge of good and evil? I believe that every man must hold these things for images, under which the hidden sense lays concealed.[25]

And in *Selecta in Psalmos, Patrologia Graeca XII,* Origen provides additional details, "The Holy Scriptures are like houses with many, many rooms, and outside each door lies a key; but it is not the right one. To find the right keys that will open the doors, that is the great and arduous task."[26]

Consider the following quote from Manlio Simonetti, "Origen treats as a traditional article of faith, the belief that Scripture, over and above the literal sense ["milk"], has a deeper spiritual sense ["meat"], which escapes the majority of people. Moreover, the difficulty in penetrating this sense was actually intended by the Holy Spirit to prevent profound truths from being too readily available to those unworthy of them, people who would not know how to appreciate them, since they would have been attained without any effort."[27] Simonetti states:

> The difficulty in understanding fully the meaning of God's Word thus lies in the fact that its deeper, essential, and spiritual meaning is concealed beneath the literal expression which covers it, and clothes it like a veil, a garment, or a body. This difficulty has caused many to stop at the level of the external, "fleshy" sense, and they fall into error; *the literal meaning though not itself mistaken does not represent the ultimate goal of Scripture* [emphasis added], but serves

rather as an educative *starting-point* which points the reader to an awareness of a deeper meaning. If this awareness remains defective, error results—as with the Jews, who limited themselves to a merely material observance of the Law; or with the Gnostics, who took the anthropomorphism of the Old Testament at face value, as do many of the less educated in the Church.[28]

Teachings Tailored to Fit the Level of the Student

Clement of Alexandria was a seasoned teacher of his distinguished successor in the Alexandrian school, Origen. Saint Jerome spoke of Clement as the most learned of all the ancients; Saint Theodore declared, "He surpassed all others, and was a holy man." Saint Cyril of Alexandria called him "a man admirably learned and skillful, and one that searched to the depths all the learning of the Greeks, with an exactness rarely attained." Eusebius praised Clement as an "incomparable master of Christian philosophy."

The Stromata, or *Miscellanies,* one of three great works by Clement, is among the most valuable remains of Christian antiquity. He discusses "higher knowledge" and "the perfecting of the saints for the work of the ministry, for the edifying of the body of Christ." Following is what Clement said about disclosing the secret things, as in the case of the Pure One (Christ's casting "pearls before swine," Simonetti's "deeper meaning"):

> The Lord did not hinder from doing good while keeping the Sabbath, but allowed us to communicate of those divine mysteries, and of that holy light, to those who are able to receive them. *He did not certainly disclose to the many what did not belong to the many, but to the few to whom He knew that they belonged,* who were capable of receiving and being molded according to them. But *secret things are entrusted to speech, not to writing, as is the case with God* [emphasis mine].[29]

Publishers of the *Stromata* have included these "Elucidations" to Clement's doctrine:

> Early Christians, according to Clement, taught to all alike . . . But, in the presence of the heathen, they remembered our Lord's words,

and were careful not "to cast pearls before swine." Like Saint Paul before Felix, they "reasoned of righteousness, temperance, and judgment to come," when dealing with men who knew not God, preaching Christ to them in a practical way. In their instructions to the churches, they were able to say with the same apostle, I am pure from the blood of all men, for I have not shunned to declare unto you all the counsel of God." Yet, even in the Church, they fed babes with milk, and the more intelligent with meat of God's word.[30]

William Law stated that it is up to us to "Begin to search and dig in your own field for this pearl of eternity that lies hidden in it; it cannot cost you too much, nor can you buy it too dear, for it is all; and when you have found it you will know that all which you have sold or given away for it is as mere a nothing as a bubble upon the water."[31]

Feel the deep love . . . "walk as children of light" (Eph 5:8).

6

WE CAN'T IMPROVE ON GOD:
WE ARE MEANT TO REVEAL HIM IN US

Dear children, let us not love with
words or tongue but with actions and in truth

—1 John 3:18

All Life Is Sacred: Let the World Enjoy Your Light

The founders of Buddhism, Christianity, Confucianism, Hinduism, Islam, Jainism, Judaism, Shinto, Taoism, and Zoroastrianism might wonder what has happened to the principles and the sacred values (compassion, peace, freedom, humility, and happiness, where all human beings are viewed as a unity, with no nation existing for itself alone) they had stood for. Why the fragmentation? Why don't the different economic, political, social, scientific, and religious communities, of the global village, "sing" from the same Oneness page? Why are the relationships between the various groups less than brotherly and sisterly, in particular, when *we are the colors of the same One Light*? The Spirit of God (the Common Ground: '1') of the three Abrahamic religions (Judaism, Christianity, and Islam) is the Spirit of God of Buddhism, Taoism, Hinduism, Shamanism, Zoroastrianism, and indigenous religions; all humanity's history is His affair; all holy books, all scientific verifications, are only road maps of the sacred-space.

Christianity is the world's largest religion, with 1.9 billion followers worldwide. Consistent with a current estimate (*World Christian Encyclopedia*) there are no less than thirty-four thousand different Christian denominations. The creeds vary significantly and are in many cases

155

incompatible. Today, many "accredited religions" assume that theirs is the only "true religion," declared Sri Aurobindo, the great contemporary sage of India. Many denominations—including Anglican, Assemblies of God, Baptist, Brethren, Catholics, Christian Reformed, Church of Christ, Jehovah's Witnesses, Lutheran, Mennonite, Methodist, Mormons, Nazarene, Pentecostals, Presbyterian, Seventh-Day Adventists, Wesleyan and other churches—seem to imply that only their flock will be saved.

Islam is the world's second largest religion. The world's 1.3 billion Muslims regard the Holy Qur'an, which is the same length as the New Testament and comprises 114 chapters that include approximately 6,200 verses, to be the final statement of Allah and the only way of life—i.e., surrender to Allah and find peace. Yet, there is no peace within Islam, nor man's obedience and submission to God alone, as the Holy Qur'an instructs. The sectarian schisms between Sunnis Muslims, Shias Muslims, Wahhabi Islam, apostates (the rulers of the Islamic countries), and infidels have caused coreligionists to slaughter each other for the last thirteen hundred years or so.

"Holy War":
Doing God and Humanity Great Disservice

As you know, on September 11, 2001, radical Islamists in a jihad attacked the United States. Three years later, we see three hundred thirty people die in Beslan school, Southern Russia, and one hundred ninety one commuters slaughtered in Madrid, Spain. Afghanistan, Bali, Egypt, Iraq, Israel, Europe, Pakistan, and others around the globe are under attack by a religious caliphate. Radical and Jihad destroyers of modern secular society maintain the "defense of Allah" justifies almost any action (the "pen," the "tongue," or the "sword"), no matter how extreme.

For example, recently one could see on the TV Nick Berg, 26, from the Philadelphia suburb of West Chester, who went to Iraq to help rebuild the infrastructure. He stated: "My name is Nick Berg, my father's name is Michael, my mother's name is Suzanne. I have a brother and sister . . ." A moment later a scream sounded as the militant Islamists cut his head off, shouting "Allahu Akbar!" or "God is Great." Then, the masked defenders of Allah held Berg's head out before the camera.

The Muslim doctors of the Holy Law and the radical fundamentalists that take life, enslave women, and instruct in schools and mosques to hate, persecute, and kill the infidels are no different from atheistic governments that made their case in comparably appalling ways. According to Islamic fundamentalists, those dying in a jihad are martyrs who rise right away to Djanna ("garden of Allah"—eternal paradise of the Islamic religion), where the "saved" sip fine wine, dine on delicious food and have gorgeous virgins satisfy the carnal desires prohibited in earthy life. All Muslims will eventually reach the Promised Land; no infidel, nevertheless, could ever enjoy the presence of Allah.

If the warring against each other is to be successful we must understand, address, and reconcile the root of causes: the validity of jihadis faith, the emancipation of Muslim women, commitment and religious education of hatred and killing. Similarly, Buddhists, Hindus and Jews and their ever-proliferating sects and subsects appear to indicate a rigidity of dogmatism, elitism and even intolerance of other views. Clearly, no evidence of bias here.

The path is not the goal; we can too easily get attached to a particular path. Sri Ramakrishna (1836-1886), one of India's leading teachers and saints, followed the path of Hinduism, Islam, Christianity, and God-intoxication of other traditions. In his visions (remote viewings) he saw Jesus, Muhammad, and the "limitless, infinite, effulgent ocean of spirit ['1']." From his studies, experiences, and revelations, Ramakrishna came to the conclusion that all religions are in essence one and the same and *all are true.* Similar to the Buddha, Mother Teresa of Calcutta, Hammarskjöld, Einstein, and Jesus, Ramakrishna perceived the essential unity of all in everyone and everything. God can be realized through different paths, said Ramakrishna, "Some people indulge in quarrels, saying, 'One cannot attain anything unless one worships our Krishna,' or 'nothing can be gained without the worship of Kali, our Divine Mother,' or 'One cannot be saved without accepting the Christian religion.' This is pure dogmatism. The dogmatist says, 'My religion alone is true, and the religions of others are false.' This is a bad attitude. God can be reached by different paths."[1]

Your God Is Our God: Encourage Scientific Literacy

Every religion has to a smaller or larger degree suffered and made others suffer by inflicting the view that others are not on the right path while they themselves are. While it is absolutely correct that what the eye sees is true for the eye, what the ear hears is true for the ear, what the nose smells is true for the nose, what the tongue tastes is true for the tongue, and what the hand touches is true for the hand, where would one be if one had only one sense? Yes, just one sense! Is that enough for you? The account of "the first, only, and true" religion, philosophy, and science, is as breathtaking as humanity's upward climb that leads to perfection. Our quest is so genuine, our need so great, and our find so valuable that nothing in the world is more essential than our spiritual advancement, or, as we heard from Jesus, "Seek first his kingdom and his righteousness, and all these things will be given to you as well" (Mt 6:33).

Once I heard a wonderful story about two beggars. One was blind, the other without legs. Their respective families dropped them off at the marketplace in the morning and picked them up at night. In the morning they were in the shade; in the afternoon the sun was scorching them. They could not relocate. The blind man did not know where the shade was; the one without legs could not move about. Shoplifters helped themselves to what was in their hats. They had an insight: let the one without the legs sit on the back of the one with legs. Now they were no longer incapacitated. Between them they had a pair of eyes and legs. Now they decided to work together not as beggars, but by selling goods at the bazaar. Because their partnership prospered, they could get married and have families and a happier life.

The clothes we wear, the food we eat, the electricity, the telephones or computers we use, the magazines we read, the automobiles we drive, or the airplanes in which we fly are a result of literally hundreds of thousands of people's contributions to what we enjoy. We all know what happened to the poor and downtrodden when the communists cut them off with the Berlin Wall from the rest of the planet. It will take years to get them back in phase with the balance of the human family. Must we keep the spiritual Berlin Wall between religions, science and nations?

Saint Clement of Alexandria expressed the essential *unity of all truth* with the words, "The river of truth is one." Christ's ('1') unity of all things is the call of the human race to enter into the "Greatest Miracle on Earth," to share our unity of Being, Freedom and Love. We can't improve on God! Together we will build a better future. Historian Arnold Toynbee stated:

> I was brought up in the belief that my religion held the key to the
> mystery of existence, but I have come back to the belief that this

key is not held by my ancestral religion exclusively. Since this is the religion in which I have been brought up, my own earliest approach to the mystery will always lie along this path. But this need not prevent me from also realizing that there are other paths, which are for people bred in other traditions.[2]

Hafiz exemplified, with the "Lousy at Math" parable, how some dissect the Indivisible One:

Once a group of thieves stole a rare diamond larger than a goose egg. Its value could have easily bought one thousand horses and two thousand acres of the most fertile land in Shiraz [where Hafiz was born and lived virtually all his life]. The thieves got drunk that night to celebrate their great haul. But during the course of the evening the effects of the liquor and their mistrust of each other grew to such an extent they decided to divide the stone into pieces. Of course then the Priceless became lost. Most everyone is lousy at math and does that to God—dissects the Indivisible One, by thinking, saying, "This is my Beloved, he looks like this and acts like that, how could that moron over there really be God?[3]

The Heart of the Gospels:
"There Is No Division in the Body"

Let us go back to the essence and spirit of the founders of religions. Because we live in the West I will touch briefly on Christianity. The leading causes of the rapid growth of Christianity are to be found in the immaculate life of its founder, the truth and self-evidencing primacy of His message, and its renewing and purifying effect on the knowledge and the brotherly love of humanity.

"Christianity is the imitation of Christ," declared Saint Basil. "Christ appeared," stated Saint Augustine of Hippo (354-430), modern Souk-Ahras in Algier, "to the men of the decrepit, decaying world, that while all around them was withering away, they might through Him receive new, youthful life." The unknown author of the "Epistola ad Diognetum," in the early part of the second century, recorded:

The Christians . . . dwell in the Grecian or barbarian cities, as the case may be; they follow the usage of the country in dress, food, and the other affairs of life. Yet they present a wonderful and confessedly paradoxical conduct . . . They marry, like others; they have children, but they do not cast away their offspring. They have the table in common, but not wives. They are in the flesh, but do not lust after the flesh. They live upon the earth, but are citizens of heaven. They obey the existing laws, and excel the laws by their lives. They love all, and are persecuted by all.[4]

It appears as if neither persecutions nor death could extinguish the stream of immense love for the whole of humanity and the apostolic conviction of the Christians. It is estimated that approximately one hundred thousand Christians, throughout the Roman Empire, were slaughtered for their way of life.[5] Schaff, in the *History of the Christian Church*, recorded:

Eusebius [bishop of Caesarea in Palestine since 315, died 340; secret friend, adviser, and eulogist of Constantine the Great; "the father of church history," "the Christian Herodotus"] was a witness of this persecution in Caesarea, Tyre, and Egypt, and saw, with his own eyes, as he tells us, the houses of prayer razed to the ground, the Holy Scriptures committed to the flames on the market places, the pastors hunted, tortured, and torn to pieces in the amphitheatre. Even the wild beasts, he says, not without rhetorical exaggeration, at last refused to attack the Christians, as if they had assumed the part of men in place of the heathen Romans; the bloody swords became dull and shattered; the executioners grew weary, and had to relieve each other, but the Christians sang hymns of praise and thanksgiving in honor of Almighty God, even to their latest breath.[6]

The Edict of Milan (313), by Roman emperor Constantine the Great (280-337), ended the imperial persecution, torture, and killing of Christians and extended freedom and state support of the martyred Church, resulting in a great expansion of Christianity. The central idea in spreading Christianity (from Jesus to Constantine AD 30-312) was the "unity of the Spirit" ("I am in my Father, and that you in me, just as I am in you" [Jn 14:20]) and the "unity of divine service" (the washing of feet example: "The greatest among you must be the servant of all."). Christ's profound wisdom became the Christian "mystery" teachings for the assemblies of the primitive faithful, the world of pagan antiquity and those less educated in spiritual matters.

The implementation of the Christian message was by means of the imitation of Christ, the "experience of living by Christ's principles." Christianity ("Christianismos") stood for "essence" of the Absolute Splendor ('1'), sign of *God's glory in humanity*. To be called Christian (Acts 11:26; 26:28) meant that a person who lives by Christ's principles was aware that the Spirit of Unity and of God rests in them (1 Pt 4:14-16). The Spirit of Unity related to "the interdependence of the human race," the shift from the part to the Oneness of the whole, as "one body with many parts," and the celebration of the Christ mystery in *us*!

For example, to survive, we need air, water, and food; they are our lifelines to life. To think differently is childish. To not know that we are "one body with many parts" is meant not reveal Him in us. This includes everyone, not merely those who call themselves Christian. It was understandable that the kingdom of God ['1'] is within us (Lk 17:21), along with a growing appreciation of our Oneness and therefore, *one had to accept one's responsibility to each other, and responsibility for each other's welfare*. Our interdependency, working together as One, and responsibility to care for one another and creation in love, respect, forgiveness, and gratitude was presented by way of numerous teachings and the development of cultural, economic, and social skills. Here is an example from Saint Paul's First Letter to the Corinthians:

> For Christ ['1': the Spirit of God] is like a single body, which has many parts; it is still one body, even though it is made up of different parts [similar to a watch, automobile or an airplane with many parts] . . .
>
> For the [human] body [like a mechanical body] itself is not made up of only one part, but of many parts. If the foot [Indian] were to say, "Because I am not a hand [Arab], I don't belong to the body," that would not make it stop being a part of the body. And if the ear [American] were to say, "Because I am not an eye [Chinese], I don't belong to the body," that would not make it stop being a part of the body. If the whole body were just an eye [Chinese], how could it hear? And if it were only ear [American], how could it smell [French]? . . .
>
> So then, the eye [Chinese] cannot say to the hand [Arab], "I don't need you!" Nor can the head [British] say to the foot [Indian], "Well, I don't need you!" [Imagine a functional human being without legs or a head.] On the contrary; we cannot get along

without the parts of the body that seem to be weaker, and those parts that we think aren't worth very much are the ones which we treat with greater care; while the parts of the body which don't look very nice receive special attention, which the more beautiful parts of our body do not need . . .

And so *there is no division in the body* [Hafiz's dissection of the Indivisible One], but *all its different parts have the same concern for one another* [they work together and help each other as one]. If one part on the body suffers, all the other parts suffer with it; if one part is praised, all the other parts share its happiness.

All of you, then, are Christ's body, and each one is a part of it. (1 Cor 12:12-27).

The Core of Christianity: Unity of the Spirit

The "unity of the Spirit," interdependency of all things, and the concern for one another were presented by the early Church teachings and explained by the active revelatory principle of the Eternal existing even before the creation of the world, that is, before the first three minutes of the big bang, the modern theory of the origin of the universe.[7] In the Gospel of John we read, "Before the world was created, the Word [the sacred space] already existed." Namely, Augustine's "changeless light" existed before the so-called big bang. "He was with God, and he was *the same* as God" (Jn 1:1).

In the second, as inspiring people to the "acquirement of knowledge" ("know the truth, and the truth will make you free" [Jn 8:32]), holiness, and Christlike immaculate life of compassion, peace, service-excellence, harmony, and happiness. Expressly, "steering them to that higher knowledge of the things of God [within them], to which those only who devote themselves assiduously to spiritual, moral, and intellectual culture can attain."[8]

It was absolute to the Apostolic Fathers (i.e., the Christian thinkers of the late first and early second centuries) that a common essence of Christianity was the "unity of the Spirit" and the "unity of divine service" just as it is absolute to scientists today that the essence of science is the unity and interdependence of the laws of nature and the laws working as one. The Apostolic Fathers recognized, that without the "unity of the

Spirit" and the "unity of divine service," there is no Christianity, as Jesus taught. That is, the Christianity *of* Christ rather than the Christianity *about* the Christ; essentially, what keeps faith alive is experiential realization of God's spirit within us. *Without being Christlike there is no basis to call oneself a Christian.* It's like declaring, "I am airline pilot, and I play in a symphony orchestra," and collecting disability benefits for being legally blind and deaf.

Every Christian must not only believe in Christ; "Every Christian must be Christ himself," stated German physician and mystical poet Angelus Silesius (Johann Scheffler, 1624-1677). "On account of Him [Jesus]," declared Origen, "there have come to be many Christs in the world, even all who, like Him, loved righteousness and hated iniquity." Yes, said the Nazarene, life does have a purpose; to attain and express perfection, "You must be perfect—just as your Father in heaven is perfect" (Mt 5:48). Christians were reminded:

> I may be able to speak the language of men and even of angels, but if I have not love, my speech is no more than a noisy gong or a clanging bell. I may have the gift of inspired preaching; I may have all knowledge and understand all secrets; I may have all the faith needed to move mountains—but if I have not love, I am nothing. I may give away everything I have, and even give up my body to be burned—but if I have not love, it does me no good.
>
> Love is patient, love is kind. It does not envy, it does not boast, it is not proud. It is not rude, it is not self-seeking, it is not easily angered, it keeps no record of wrongs. Love does not delight in evil but rejoices with the truth. It always protects, always trusts, always hopes, always perseveres.
>
> Love never fails. There are inspired messages, but they are temporary; there are gifts of speaking, but they will cease; there is knowledge, but it will pass. For our gifts of knowledge and our inspired messages are only partial; but when what is perfect comes [the realization that we are one body—that "I have been looking for myself"] then what is partial will disappear (1 Cor 13:1-10).

As time went on, however, through gradual development of additional doctrine by the Christian leadership has come, by and large, innovative ways of interpreting the "unity of the Spirit" to heathen (the paganism of Greece and Rome).[9] Also, resolution of theological disputes over the centuries has produced both seismic shifts and diluted practices of the Christ's teachings of our Oneness, *our essential divine nature*, and that we are meant to *reveal Him in us* ("be perfect . . ."). Namely, the Christian leadership bowed to a severely watered-down grasp of the unity of all things and Christ's values, or as we read from Neil Douglas-Klotz, the "corrupted form of orthodox Christianity."

"Very often the accredited religions have opposed progress and sided with the forces of obscurity and oppression," stated Sri Aurobindo:

> And it has needed a denial, a revolt of the oppressed human mind and heart, to correct these errors and set religion right. This would not have been so if religion were the true and sufficient guide of the whole of human life . . . We must observe the root of this evil, which is not in true religion itself, but in its infra-rational parts, not in spiritual faith and aspiration, but in our ignorant human confusion of religion with a particular creed, sect, cult, religious society or church . . .
>
> The whole root of the historic insufficiency of religion as a guide and control of human society lies there. Churches and creeds have, for example, stood violently in the way of philosophy and science, burned a Giordano Bruno, imprisoned a Galileo, and so generally misconducted themselves in this matter that philosophy and science had in self-defense to turn upon religion and rend her to pieces in order to get a free field for their legitimate development."[10]

Beyond Chutzpah:
Beyond Absolute Audacity and Imprudence

Earlier I cited atheistic regimes of genocide and the unbridled addiction to power as practiced by the Nazis and Communists in the name of "liberation of oppressed nations": "have slaughtered them in a rage that reaches to heaven" (2 Ch 28:9). In the innovative ways of revealing the "unity of the Spirit," we learn that translation, publishing, or the ownership of a translation of Scripture in a vernacular language was a crime punishable by death.

William Tyndale (1494-1536) translated the New Testament into everyday English. His translation was modern, clear, and with unmatched narrative intensity. Tyndale phraseology became the basis of the King James Version of the New Testament. Tyndale was arrested, condemned for revealing the forbidden text, taken to the stake, strangled by the hangman, and burned.

In 1421, Archbishop Arundel wrote to pope John XXIII, "This pestilent and wretched John Wyclif, of cursed memory, that son of the old serpent . . . endeavoured by every means to attack the faith sacred doctrine of Holy Church, devising—to fill up the measure of his malice— the expedient of a new translation into the mother tongue." Wyclif (1320-1384), a master at Balliol College in Oxford, rested peacefully until 1424, when his bones were dug up, burned, and dumped into the River Swift, for his translation of Scripture into the everyday English.

We see a Europe soaked in the blood of countless religious wars. Under the flag of Protestant Christianity, armed forces assault Catholic neighborhoods, butchering populace, burning communities, houses of worship, and raping women. Also, we witness Catholic soldiers doing a similar thing to Protestant sanctuaries and faithful. We meet the vicars of Christ leading armies into battle, crusades against the Muslim powers at Edessa, Antioch, Tripoli, and Jerusalem, the burning of books, such as Islamic, rabbinic, and Talmudic, and the employment of force and control to secure ecclesiastical unity.

We witness the Inquisition (medieval, Roman, and Spanish); people condemned by the Inquisition were burned. We see the indulgence money payments (the fast track to heaven), where the offenders pay for their crime, as an accepted way to raise funds for capital projects. We notice utilization of torture, witch burning, and confiscation of property, exile, and loss of civil rights as weapons. We observe repression of the scientific spirit (the orderly acquirement of knowledge) and burning alive those who were charged with heresy "in direct violation of the principles and practice of Christ and apostles, and in basic confusion of the spiritual nature of the kingdom of heaven."[11] Millions perished through the division within Christianity, religiously motivated wars, and inquisitorial procedures. Christians imposed comparable penalties on anyone who did not conform to their view, doctrine or principle, as had atheistic regimes and Nero before them. Philip Schaff wrote,

> Skeptical writers have endeavored to diminish its moral effect by pointing to the fiendish and hellish scenes of the papal crusades against the Albigenses and Waldenses, the Parisian massacre of the

Huguenots, the Spanish Inquisition, and other persecutions more recent date . . . the Diocletian persecution was a mere shadow as compared with the persecution of the Protestants in the Netherlands by the Duke of Alva in the service of Spanish bigotry and despotism . . . the number of Protestants who were executed by the Spaniards in a single province and a single reign far exceeds that of the primitive martyrs in the space of three centuries and of the Roman empire.[12]

"If religion has failed," declared Sri Aurobindo, "it is because it has confused the essential with the adventitious. True religion is spiritual religion [to think of others before ourselves], it is a seeking after God, the opening of the deepest life of the soul to the indwelling God, the eternal Omnipresence [within us]."[13] Annie Besant put it this way, "Poor indeed is that religion that cannot yield to men and women inspiration which shall aid them in their upward climbing to the light."

"In the realm of theology, shallowness is treason,"[14] confirmed Abraham Heschel. Although there is a warmer wind blowing around us these days (Pope John Paul II, Mother Teresa of Calcutta, Peter Roche de Coppens, Robert Muller, Teilhard de Chardin), the "unity of the Spirit" and the Oneness teachings that were fundamental for the heart of Christianity, in the birth of the Church, for majority of Christians is alien history. Christians do not realize that Christ (the unchanging) lives in every human being, and that these teachings are not simply relics that one is meant to know about, but they are connected to our own daily lives: *we are meant to reveal Him in us.* The majority of Christians do not understand the "experience" of one body with many parts, as Saint Paul verbalized, or that "A human being is a part of the whole," as Einstein articulated.

We Are All Called to Perfection

The saints and pristine spirits of the apostolic and the post-apostolic age took, and continue to take, Christ's profound principles to heart, "to acquire 'spiritual senses,' which allow one to perceive, through communion in Christ and the Holy Spirit, the One who is beyond creation." Namely, directly experience, live, and work in the "unity of the Spirit" and the "I am that I am" of Exodus, and a realization of the Christ of boundless Majesty in every human being.

The pursuit of excellence and the formation and development of Christian character is realized by daily living a consecrated Christian life,[15] or "the imitation of Christ," as described by Saint Basil. For instance, in order to gain new insights and inspiration or perform miracles, sanctity of life, inner peace, and a life of perfection have to be at the bedrock of one's daily existence. We all remember the prophet Moses was in such a state of holiness when his face glowed with God's glory.

John White, internationally known researcher, scholar, and author in the field of consciousness and human development, in his magnificent book, *What is Enlightenment?* states,

> [Saint] Teresa [of Avila] finds the order Mount Carmel hopelessly corrupt; its friars and nuns blind to reality [unawareness regarding our divine identity], indifferent to the obligations of the cloistered life. She is moved by the spirit to leave her convent and begin, in abject poverty, the foundation of new houses where the most austere and exalted life of contemplation shall be led. She enters upon this task to the accompaniment of an almost universal mockery. Mysteriously, as she proceeds, novices of the spiritual life appear and cluster around her. They come into existence, one knows not how, in the least favorable of atmospheres, but one and all are salted with the Teresian salt. They receive the infection of her abundant vitality; embrace eagerly and joyously the heroic life of the Reform. In the end, every city in Spain has within it Teresa's spiritual children: a whole order of contemplatives as truly of her as if they were indeed her sons and daughters in the flesh.[16]

In contrast, the greater part of Western Christendom demonstrated a particular propensity to stress the Outer Teachings (suitable for communication to the emergent humanity) and the theoretical basis or didactic encounter with life's Oneness. The Inner Teachings (more advanced knowledge) and the experiential "unity of the Spirit" that connects us all as members of One Body are not broadening humanity's horizon and expanding its world. It is easier to lecture than it is to get people engaged by creating a close-knit community, the education of the heart, building relationships, and touching the sacred-spaces of our soul. The average became abstract, incorporating literal interpretation (Manlio Simonetti's "starting point") of the Old and New Testament. In other words, sermon *about* miracles and the historical Christ versus living a life *of* direct personal experience in the "unity of the Spirit" that binds us all together into one essence of God as noted by Paul, in a letter to the Ephesians,

> Be completely humble and gentle; be patient, bearing with one another in love. Make every effort to keep the unity of the Spirit through the bond of peace. There is one body and one Spirit ['1'], just as you were called to one hope when you were called [that you may become one body and one Spirit], one Lord, one faith, one baptism; one God and Father of all, who is over all *through all and in all* (Eph 4:5-6).

In the Bhagavad Gita we discover another view of the same notion, "When you have thus learned the truth, you will know that *all living beings are but part of Me* [God in all]—and that *they are in Me* [and all in God], and are Mine" (4.35). The great saint and soul-stirring poet of Gujarat in India, Narasimha Mehta, expressed the Oneness state thusly,

> You alone are in the Universe
> Appearing in numerous forms,
> In the body you are the vital breath,
> You are the Light that makes light visible,
> In the void you are the Word . . .
> The forms may be many, but the substance is the same.

How do we swim without getting into water? How do we heal the 1000-year-old schism between Eastern and Western Christianity? How do we experience compassion, beauty, happiness, or the love of our children with our minds and not our hearts? How do we repair the immeasurable damage done to the molesting children, parents, and society by the teachers of the world and the privileged custodians of our spiritual deliverance?

"The more we tolerate ineffective teachers, the more our teachers will be ineffective," declared the California governor Arnold Schwarzenegger, when he started his offensive to raise teacher quality in the country's largest education system. The lecture-versus-the-personal-experience debate on the "unity of the Spirit" has correlates in modern physical science. Steven Weinberg was required to give testimony before Congress on the Superconducting Super Collider (SSC). Rather than "sitting at my desk or at some café table, I manipulate mathematical expressions and feel like Faust playing with his pentagrams before Mephistopheles arrives,"[17] he far preferred experimenting with the SSC in the discovery of the "final theory."

Hold On to Your Hat: Follow the Spirit

The "essence of Christianity" was thus dramatically torn asunder, writes the Encyclopaedia Britannica:

> The unity of life and teachings that was determinative for the essence of Christianity in the early church was thus not maintained for long. Because the development of doctrine along the lines of "true" and "false" religion involved relationships with numerous heretical groups and external critics, the earlier and less rigid concept of unity was displaced by a tendency toward uniformity in the theological definitions of orthodox church doctrines . . . and theology became increasingly detached from its original relationship to liturgy and ethics.[18]

Is there a need for a deeper understanding and application of the essence ("milk" to "meat") of Christ's unity and interdependence of life and the education of the heart? Can Christians, Buddhists, Hebrews, Hindus, Muslims, Taoists, Zen, *and* science be spiritual and material beneficiaries of the infinite treasures of the "unity of the Spirit" of religion or the Common Ground of science?

Can the "unity of the Spirit," that the Christ symbolized with bread and wine at the Last Supper and celebrated as the Eucharist by Christians, and the apostolic message in the personal experience of the One River of Life in All, be consciously ours? What was the Christ trying to convey? "How terrible for you, teachers of the law [concerning the Unity of God, '1', Jn 8:30]! You have kept the key that opens the door to the house of learning; you yourselves will not go in [to the inner peace which is within you], and you stop those who are trying to go in!" (Lk 11:52; Mt 23:13).

169

There is a shred of comfort in the emergence of the reign of the Infinite Splendor in us. We are all members of One Body, now manifesting as the universe. Reassurance is slowly percolating down through all branches of science and many spiritual centers of the unchanging nature of '1'—of our living unity. Summoning us to a life of service-excellence and a surrender of our whole being to perfection— perfection to the beauty, the truth, and every deed of our lives as God's self-revelation.

What Marvel! What Wonder!
The Infinite Splendor within Us

Men and women have perceived and/or personally experienced Absolute Presence from the time of Abraham to the present day. The phases have stretched from pagan idol worship of many gods to monotheism of "the One God" in Judaism, Hinduism, Buddhism, Christianity, Islam, onward to classical philosophy, the Reformation, the Enlightenment, the modern age of skepticism, and the "final theory" of physics.

We often hear, "To see is to believe." Yet, when sight is united with our senses of taste, smell, touch, and hearing, our understanding becomes even more inclusive, more credible, and more instantaneous of the moment. Meanwhile, each of us has something to add that is full of life and full of action by way of clarity to make the "picture" more comprehensive, more perfect and complete. For this reason, I have attempted integrating, like letters forming words and words producing sentences, faith-based and scholarly approaches of similar content as well as depth. To enhance these findings and to give them meaning, I have incorporated verification of the invariance through the underlying physical laws, the fundamental physical constants, and spectral line support in astrophysics, mathematical laws and computer-assisted proofs. Corroboration of the '1' also took place through firsthand personal experiences and recognition of the unchanging behind collective meaning, values, and proportions.

The essential teachings of all cultures, age after age, race after race, are the same and invaluable. Although they differ in their religious practices, like different scientific experiments that test the same laws of physics, the various faiths in essence are not dissimilar. They are all united in their commitment to the right and soundness of their Scriptures as God's Word in written form. They believe that it contains the heavenly response to the deepest needs of human race, that it sheds exclusive light on our life, and that it sets forth the way to our never-ending happiness. At the heartbeat of all the traditions, there is one common truth in its completeness—one idea, as the Greeks and Rudolph Steiner characterized, or as stated by the Upanishads:

> The One God hidden in all living beings,
> The Living Witness biding in all hearts—
> The Wise who seek and find Him in them-Self,
> To them, the None Else, is Eternal Joy.
> The all-pervading Inner Self of all,
> Who from His Formlessness creates all Forms—
> The wise who see that One within them-Self,
> To them alone belongs Eternal Joy . . .
> The Colorless, who from His secret store
> Exhaustless, countless colors draws, to paint,
> Efface, repaint the worlds upon the face
> Of empty-space with Mystic Potency—
> May He endow us with the lucid mind![19]

Or Sufi writings,

> What marvel! That a Being [like white light] colorless
> [When through a prism] Displays a hundred thousand hues, tints,
>   shades!
> What wonder! That being void of form
> Enrobes in forms beyond all numbering!—
> May we behold Him in all hues and forms!
> Yet lifts to every name an answering head,
> The name of Him who is the changeless One
> Amidst the changing many, and within
> Whose oneness all this many is confined,
> May we begin our loving work of peace.[20]

British poet Francis Thompson (1859-1907) wrote,

> O world invisible we view thee
> O world intangible, we touch thee
> O world unknowable, we know thee
> Inapprehensible, we clutch thee.[21]

'1': All-Inclusive Name; Do You Have a Favorite?

As the bees integrate honey from the nectar of different flowers, so integrating the spiritual validations with scientific evidence, placing one upon another in verification after verification, we arrive at an amalgam of the one single fundamental concept: the '1'.[22, 23] The result is a cumulative body of knowledge far more reliable and thorough than if any one of them is taken individually: Buddhism, Christianity, Confucianism, Taoism (Laotsism), Islam, Jainism, Judaism, Shintoism, Sikhism, Vedism, Zoroastrianism (Parsism), the Community of Christ, the agnostic, and the scientific.

The majestic "Glory and Presence of God" or "the kingdom of heaven" as religions have called it and the Eternal Nature of human identity have been recognized throughout the centuries. They go by many different names, metaphors, and characterizations:[24]

1. "I am who I am," "I will be what I will be" (Moses, Ex 3:14)
2. The Most High (*El-Shaddai*), YHWH (Lord), the Lord Almighty, Compassion, the kingdom of the Lord (the Bible)
3. The Unchanging, Void, the Source of the Universe (Lao-tzu)
4. The Principle of Priority (a priori) (Confucius, Aristotle)
5. The Principle of Non-violence (Confucius)
6. The Great Perfection, Primordial Awareness, Emptiness, Mind of Intuition, the Unchanging, Nirvana (Gautama Buddha)
7. The Father (Krishna Chaitanya)
8. The Unity of Knowledge (Deuteronomy, Isaiah, Jeremiah, and Ezekiel)
9. God Almighty, the kingdom of the Father, Mustard Seed (Jesus the Christ)
10. The Ultimate Value (Job, Saint John)
11. The Teotl (Nahuas: the native peoples of Mesoamerica)
12. Allah (Muhammad)
13. Ein Sof (Kabbalists)
14. The Divine Life, Eternal Nature (William Law)
15. The Absolute Ground (Huxley)
16. The Reason, Reality (Einstein)
17. The Ultimate Ground (Whitehead)
18. The Ultimate Reality (Horvath)

19. The *Seeing Into the Nature of One's Being* (Suzuki)
20. The Final Theory; the Final Law of Nature (Weinberg)
21. The Unified Theory of Physics; the Mind of God (Hawking)
22. The Theory of Everything (John D. Barrow)
23. The Cosmic Code (Heinz Pagels)
24. The Law of Life (John Templeton), and
25. '1': The Unchanging State, the Connecting Zero-State, the Absolute Space, the Mother and the Father of the Universe, the Clear Light, the a priori Awareness, He Who Is Absolute Over All in Heaven and on Earth, Infinite Splendor. (Bedrij)

The list can easily be lengthened. All of these ascriptions essentially point to the same one sacred-space that permeates human thinking—one central principle of the universe.

Infinite Ascent: All Roads Lead to God

My experiences into the foundations of physical science, the essential Oneness of the human family, as well as the core self of the person, are shared insights. Others throughout history have reached similar states of understanding: to see God as God sees. But what is the key that will unlock this basic secret—the Final Principle of all reality and the ultimate explanation of the mind of God?

1. How do we infinitize a single life, discern the unchanging Common Ground in all that is changing, and characterize the infinite principle of the universe?
2. How do we symbolize the infinite in the finite, the absolute in the relative?
3. How do we integrate, incorporating physics and measurements, the experience of unity with the idea of the Absolute Infinity that is beyond all categories of time, space, and the texture of reality, deploying verified equations of time, space, and causality?
4. How can we characterize and manipulate mathematical expressions of confirmed scientific formulas, infinities, touching on everything that was, is, and will ever be in the universe, linking them with the Unfathomable One and the infinite code?

5. How can we validate the infinity of potential possibilities "about the Depth of the All," or specify all phenomena at one go with symbols of physics?

6. Finally, how can we test the unified theory of All and the Good News of the Highest Good in science?

The journey into the infinite coordinates of science, out of which everything in the universe emerges, is uncompromisingly demanding. Philosophers, such as Pythagoras, Plato, Aristotle, Montaigne, Descartes, Spinoza, Hume, Kant, and others, wrestled with reconciling the ultimate and the transient—God and man. Einstein invested a good part of his life to a search for the so-called unified field theory that would marry James Clerk Maxwell's theory of electromagnetism with the general theory of relativity and Einstein's theory of gravitation. Steven Weinberg (University of Texas at Austin), Stephen Hawking (University of Cambridge), Richard Feynman (California Institute of Technology [CalTech]), Edward Witten (Princeton University), Michael Green (Queen Mary College, London), John Schwarz (CalTech), and others were looking for rational explanations of the present generation of a "final theory."

When I began my search into unlocking the tantalizing mystery of the foundational infinities of physical science, I met Jesus in a dream. He was full of radiant compassion, incredible goodness, and selfless love. This encounter was of much longer duration than the encounter in Innsbruck, Austria. The Christ extended his hand to me, as if I were to follow Him. I did. Following Him, we arrived at a bench in a garden. We sat down. In this dream I was across from the Beloved face-to-face, feeling uneasy for taking His precious time.

Jesus looked at me and said: "If you really love me, as you say you do, will you do this for me?" The Compassionate One did not articulate what he wanted me to do. I had to discover it for myself. However, the Christ enlarged my point of view and the perspective, "If you do it . . ."— He let me know the end result . . . Both "today and tomorrow!"

This experience intensified my daily self-cultivation and advancement for the perfection of everything (Mt 5:48), or, as Saint Gregory restated, "the only perfection available to men in this life is to be found in continued progress [transforming our nature] toward perfection." From Matthew I remembered, "the gate [to perfection, infinities] is narrow and the road is hard that leads to life and there are few that find it" (Mt 7:13). It established a need for a better point of view and refinement of the heart. I realized that I must improve my physical and spiritual life if I wanted to have a better appreciation of what the Christ wanted me to do. This led to successively higher perspectives and grasping, by insight, a fundamental set of rules, in my personal garden.

Initially, it was as if I were traveling through a fog filled swamp at night. As I wadded hip deep in the murky waters of the cryptic code of different views of understanding and symbolism describing the nature of God, what is the core of humanity, and the basic laws of science and its many fundamental principles and processes, all strived for my attention. It took years of research and discussion regarding the substance of the wording and the exact way of putting them into mathematical language, infinities, and English. It entailed in this case how to view God, science, and ourselves; the importance of knowledge and understanding, why does science and spirituality matter, principles of symmetry, order and chaos; the cosmic distance scale and electromagnetic processes in space; dynamics and masses of astronomical bodies and particles; the Lamb shift, Lagrangian formalism, nuclear physics, particle physics and general relativity; quantum processes in physics and astrophysics, and the principle of least action.

The challenge was to elucidate the processes involved in the interaction of light with matter at the atomic level, in astrochemistry (chemistry in stars), and in astrobiology (what is the recipe for life?). It concerned cosmic structures, distance ladder, galaxies, galaxy clusters, and sponge structure; radiation and spectra, the frequency distributions, spectra emitted by ensembles, and radiation by accelerated point charge. It related to the evolution of the astronomical ideas of the Egyptian and Mesopotamian philosophers and of the Greek period. It entailed the golden age of astronomy with Copernicus, Galileo, Kepler, and Newton. It involved modern theories of cosmology, Einstein's principle of relativity, the zero-point energy vacuum fluctuations of the EM field, the Einstein-Podolsky-Rosen (EPR) paradox, the test of Bell inequalities, and concepts of plasma and space physics; the physics of neutron star interiors, quantum mechanics, and black holes in binaries and galactic nuclei.

It called for Heisenberg's uncertainty principle, Erwin Schrödinger's wave mechanics, gravitation, and general constants and units; the big bang model, its problems, as well as its usefulness, stellar evolution, equilibrium and stability; diverse string theories, the essence of which neutrons and protons are suspected to be built and atoms. It included molecules and spectra; the anthropic principle; the theory of orbits and the weak nuclear force; mathematical infinities in the atom and toward the edge of the universe, and more. All called for agreement with our collective experience and reduction observation to mathematical language. It seemed at any moment that the bottom would drop away. Would I be faced with struggling to stay afloat?

But then, again, what began to grow stronger and stronger was the awareness of that infinite Omnipotence within me. I knew that I had that Omnipotent power to do anything. It was the Omnipresent power of Jesus, the Buddha, and others who lived out their values, a conviction that soon my feet would be on dry land, that I would find a simple a priori principle, the law of laws that fulfilled all of these requirements.

As time went on, I no longer faced a marshland of speculation, with galaxies of theories and infinities rushing toward each other in my mind's eye. Instead, I was seated at my desk surrounded by mounds of books. I leafed through volume after volume, extracting relevant information, confirmed knowledge, standards, and verified physical equations.

Each established fact, every corroborated formula with a singular meaning, outlined another unity, a new infinity. Every fact was a witness to the Common Ground of the Formless Infinity, filled with the Infinite Order, representing different ways of characterizing the same underlying foundation. Each was a segment of completeness, drawn from an infinite sequence of a more refined class of observations. Each was a "liberated image," a microcosm of the whole and a part of the One cosmology, suggesting that Reality is organized on a rigorous economy and a precise invariant (infinite) footing. Furthermore, this insight suggested that deliberate, wide-awake, conscious life is a fundamental feature of the universe. I understood: to articulate a challenge is more fundamental than to elucidate it. I decided to go back to the commonality of symbols, infinities, and return to the relationship of connectedness behind the infinite code.

The Vital Spark Opens Our Wings

The pivotal moment came when I realized that in the task of organizing and recording my observations of infinities it was not necessary to forsake religion and the writings of the Buddha, the Christ, Lao-tzu, Krishna,

Muhammad, Moses, Guru Nanak, Shankara, and Vyasa, for science and the writings of Galileo, Newton, Leibniz, Lavoisier, Faraday, Planck, Rutherford, Bohr, Fermi, Bethe, Einstein, Kepler, Maxwell, Darwin, Mendeleev, Pauli, Schrödinger, Watson, and Crick. Or anyone else, such as Archipenko, Bach, Beethoven, Botticelli, Calder, Matisse, Miro, Mondrian, Mozart, Michelangelo, Picasso, Rembrandt, Raphael, Roden, Titian, Vinci, Shakespeare, Goethe, Luther, and Adam Smith, to mention only a few.

Each personage, their insights, and work resembled a traveler with a camera, although through a dark glass. I saw that each individual's delimited understanding was necessary, like "a line in the spectrum of light," or a plucked sense in the full range of senses of our body, to a full view of comprehensive "beauty and truth." That is, *if the universe is to be understood, the parts of the universe must be connected into a single, unifying foundation of physical principles around which the universe, both human and physical, revolves.* I also understood that the ordering principle of all reality is not only the Infinite Source and the Common Ground of our own being, but also the cause of its destruction. The neighbor is truly the self, for each is the Absolute Infinity at the core: "In thyself know thy friend, in thyself know thy enemy."

My years turned into tens of years. The walls and floor of my study became filled with volumes of long-established evidence, symbolic formulas, infinities, and subtle clues and prompts: ancient, medieval, modern. As an aide to linking verification with verification in this activity, I went about with a large ball of string, making connections from one side of the room to another, from one "liberated image" (fact/symbol/equation/infinity) to another. I attempted to integrate in a single account the evidence obtained from different fields of explanatory perspective. The room came to be transformed into a vast inner web, a genetic code of stringed reality and mathematical conceptions of infinities.

With a careful daily routine and very selective use of time, I was trying to simplify and systematize this storehouse of knowledge while attempting to support my work with rigorous scientific protocol in the expanding circle of potentialities. I was preparing myself for a capstone of insight into all these observations, classifications, and terminologies, to pass beyond the manifested framework to an ultimate framework: for the imminent moment when an integrated key of a final explanation would emerge.

The connections seemed limitless. It took years to grasp the "inner meaning" of the concepts I was exploring and to unfold their various partial meanings and the relationships between them. Each meaning displayed its own set of elementary laws and successively higher degrees of universality and infinities. The facts of given discipline entities have an outer embodiment with an inner symbolism and a rationale for this existence, as if coming into the world for a naturally evolved reason. The variety of meanings, which the facts represent, fit together into a single emerging whole called *coherent domain* with a *hierarchical structure of infinities*. The scientific correlate of this hierarchical structure is a ladder of more and more refined physical laws pointing toward the central core, the Absolute Infinity, behind the universe. A similar hierarchical structure exists within levels in the Scriptures: the most important part (seed) is enclosed in a shell; the baby lies in a manger. To know the central principle is to know that which is unchanging, infinite, in us; it is to live your love.

7

SEEK GOD'S FACE: A CHILD'S STORY DECODED

Christ could be born
a thousand times in Galilee—
but all in vain until He is born in me.

—Angelus Silesius

The Adam and Eve Parable

In earlier decades, great danger and harm was done by a poorly understood truth in the wrong hands. Currently, great danger exists in the harm done by a truth not recognized at all. Science has bestowed the machines of war and a power on humanity which it has not yet learned to handle. Dealing with the violent and bare-knuckled risks (see part 2, chapter 10) has become the task of the new millennium.

Most of us are aware that the lessons of the past have been found to be reasonable secure lessons for advancing into the unknown future. We are also aware of our common challenges: hunger, violence at home and on the streets, the mind-destroying drug addiction, the stockpiling of conventional, chemical, biological, and nuclear weapons, HIV/AIDS, the crisis of ethics in corporate America, global income gaps, economic conflicts, jihad, the struggle for human acceptance, the arbitrary abuse of individuals and groups in the name of national emergency or security, global warming, and the many crises in our system of values. Hitler rose to power on the basis of Article 48 of the Weimar Constitution, the emergency article, which gave practically limitless power at the altar of national security, as presented earlier in *Mein Kampf*. We are witnesses to an escalation of thousands of complex national and international challenges taking place today.

Will the full light of truth, the "cosmic cover-up" of space-time camouflaging and the concealment of a spiritual universe, modern physicists the lowest energy state, be made known? Will we be helped to be all that we can be: free people, self-reliant, and aware of our interdependence, caring for others and ourselves more effectively?

In speaking of the direct encounter with the Light of God, Muktananda articulates, "All this, indeed, is the Absolute . . . God pervades everywhere . . . This universe is a true image of the Supreme Reality."[1] Thirteen hundred years earlier, the Holy Prophet Muhammad (570-632) declared in the Holy Qur'an: "Everywhere you turn, there is Allah's face. For Allah is All-embracing, All-Knowing" (2:115). All is of one essence, but in various states and forms—in various-sized containers. In the spiritual verse, "Wherever you turn, there is the face of God."

Understanding the vacuum state or the zero-point field, is the basis to understanding God, the "theory of everything," and all creation. As will be seen in part 2, all manifestations in the universe are *different number of vacuum states*—different aspects of '1'. In physical terms, it can be stated that all are various conditions of the pregnant emptiness of the physical vacuum underlying all phenomena. As DNA, atoms, elements and the human body have preexisting "software programs" or "cosmic music grooves," so the laws of physics, and all life have a similar modus operandi. We, the observer, have freedom of choice to select what "cosmic music" we want to listen to.

Recall the Socratic maxim "Know thyself." The Beloved enlightened his brother in the Gospel of Thomas, "Whoever knows the All but fails (to know) himself lacks everything" (65). The great value of self-knowledge is not only that it will help us to leap beyond theoretical speculations, beyond the hot big bang cosmology, but that it will lead to the practical removal of obstacles in our inner sanctum. It is service-excellence, teambuilding, helping those in need, and spiritual happiness, which, according to the insights of thinkers and sages, are the very purpose of our existence. Moses, Zoroaster, Lao-tzu, the Buddha, Krishna, Confucius, and Yeshua wanted us to achieve peace, a feeling of great joy in our hearts, and a more abundant life.

"Know the truth [about the Sacred Unity and about yourself], and the truth will make you free" (Jn 8:32). The Bhagavad Gita expressed, "Destroy with the shining lamp of knowledge the darkness born of ignorance" (10:11). Daniel Boorstin, the great historian and author of

The Discoverers and *The Creators,* stated: "The greatest obstacle to discovery is not ignorance—it is the illusion of knowledge."

The Adam and Eve parable is one of many eloquent symbolic passages in the Hebrew (Old Testament) Bible. It contains profound metaphors that cut across the Jewish and Christian boundaries, through which the hidden sense of our nature is camouflaged. That is, there are traditions comparable to the Adam and Eve biblical exegesis that are comprehensive enough to assist as the basis of such a study. Mine beneath this surface, and we find a surprising mesh of roots. Before proceeding further, let us study the Adam and Eve allegory in Genesis:

1. Out of the ground the Lord God made various trees grow . . . with the *tree of life* in the *middle of the garden* and the *tree of knowledge* of good and bad (Gen 2:9).

2. The Lord God gave man this order: "You are free to eat from any of the trees of the garden, except the *tree of knowledge* of good and bad. From that tree you shall not eat; the moment you eat from it you are surely doomed to die" (Gen 2:16).

3. But the serpent said to the woman: "You certainly will not die! No, God knows well that the moment you eat of it *you will be like gods* who know what is good and what is bad." The woman saw that the tree was good for food, pleasing to the eyes, and *desirable for gaining wisdom.* So she took some of its fruit and ate it, and she gave some to her husband, who was with her, and he ate it. Then the eyes of both of them were opened, and they realized that they were naked (Gen 3:4-7).

4. The Lord God said: "See! *The man has become like one of us,* knowing what is good and what is bad! Therefore, he must not be allowed to put out his hand to take fruit from the tree of life also, and thus *eat of it and live forever"* (Gen 3:22).

5. He stationed the cherubim and the fiery revolving sword to guard the way to the tree of life (Gen 3:24).

Like a pot of gold, shining with a bright light over the centuries, this stunning narrative from the Holy Bible (the collection of Jewish and Christian texts) is the Lord God's expressive statement: "See! *The man has become like one of us,* knowing what is good and what is bad."

Both the Old and New Testaments are rich mines of many similar parables. They reveal how we, like the Prodigal Son, may return home (reach our highest potential) and partake in divine providence. The quantity of these revered books differs in various religious traditions. The Hebrew canon recognizes twenty-four books. The Bible of the Roman Catholic Church acknowledges a total of seventy-three books. The Protestant canon accepts thirty-nine books. In the Greek Orthodox Church the total number of books comes to seventy-nine. The Ethiopian Church has eighty-one books, while the Samaritans recognize only five books (Genesis, Exodus, Leviticus, Numbers, and Deuteronomy).

Love One Another: We Are Many Colors of One Rainbow

The cryptic code of Israel's flight out of Egypt, the symbolic land of slavery, is a priceless epic of the *liberation of the soul* in the world of mortals through righteousness (the Ten Commandments). Indeed, it is more than a mere historic recording; the whole biblical plot is part of "the story of our life."

The Exodus narrative has its corresponding counterpart in the Ramayana and the Mahabharata. Ramayana is the "Life Story of Rama." The work contains twenty-four thousand couplets and is the oldest epic in Sanskrit literature. Mahabharata, next to the Ramayana, is the second most monumental and voluminous epic of Hindu literature of India. The work includes 106,000 verses in eighteen books. In the Book of Wisdom, the ascension of Enoch and Elijah draws us into a life as sons and daughters, in its deathless splendor, of God, and, of course, the classic statement of our being sons of the Creator is presented in the Psalms:

You are "gods"; you are all sons of the Most High (Ps 82:6).

Thales of Miletus, statesman, cosmologist, and discoverer of five geometric theorems, gave us in the sixth century BC a prescientific grand unification cosmology when he pointed out, "All things are full of gods." In Hafiz's language, "All the talents of God are within you." In one stroke, the Christ revealed the fundamental Oneness of the human family, creation, and the "Unchanging Hidden Order," which physicists refer to as the *invariance* of the laws of physics. Jesus presented this as the Father to the Apostle Philip, and Steven Weinberg terms this the "final theory":

Anyone who has seen me has seen the Father (Jn 14:9).

Here one is informed that "He [the Christ] is the image [visible likeness] of the invisible God" (Col 1:15). In other passages of the New Testament we learn what dwells in us:

> *Whoever sees me, also sees him* who sent me (Jn 12:45). If you really knew me, you would know my Father also. From this point on you know him; *you have seen him* (Jn 14:7). All that the Father has belongs to me (Jn 16:15).

Observe the connection: anyone who has seen the Galilean has seen the living God, the Infinite Splendor. We can say that whoever has observed a wave in water has observed the water. Also, whoever has seen the creation (image, reflection of the Infinite Splendor) has seen the Creator. Anyone who has seen the material universe has seen the "Unchanging Compassion." How heartbreaking! So many Christians do not know what treasures there are within them:

> Believe me that I am in the Father and the *Father is in me* (Jn 14:11).

Just as a wave is a part of the water, so the water is a part of the wave. The Christ ("unity consciousness") links himself to the inner nature of Reality, the Father ('1'). From physics and mathematics, we know that time is connected to space, space is connected to gravity, and we are linked to them. We are all a part of the '1'. We are different aspects, expressions, or qualities of the Unchangeable One. We see this in the statement:

> When that day [return of the memory of wholeness] comes, you will know that *I am in my Father,* and that *you are in me,* just as *I am in you* (Jn 14:20).

Ponder the Christ's words. Reflect on their ramification. Can they change your life and the world around you? Is the Galilean right?

Consider John 14:20. Is Christ in the Father, and you in Christ, and Christ in you? Now connect John 14:20 with John 12:45—"Whoever sees me [the Christ], also sees him [the Father] who sent me [the Christ]." What do you see?

Whoever sees the Christ is seeing the Father ('1'). Yes. Then, go one more step: combining the evangelist John 14:20 "Christ is in the Father, and *you in Christ*, and *Christ in you*," with John 12:45, "Whoever sees me, also sees him who sent me."

Please stop here. Do not go any further. Integrate John 14:20 and 12:45 in your mind. Listen to your heart. What do you feel? What do you glimpse? Of course, whoever sees the wave sees the water. Whoever sees *you* sees the Father! Yes, yes, WHOEVER SEES YOU SEES THE FATHER. Whoever sees you sees the Creator! Let Christ's words of John 14:20 and 12:45 take root in you.

"I Will Save Lives as Long as I Can: I Am Fulfilling My Duty"

Enjoy this intense moment. "Now the Son of Man's glory is revealed; now God's glory is revealed through him [in you]" (Jn 13:31). "Now that you have known me (the Christ), you will know my Father [in you] also; and from now on you do know him, and you have seen him" (Jn 14:7). "I (Christ) have told you this so that my (Christ's) joy may be in you, and that your joy may be complete" (Jn 15:11). Why? Simply put:

> For *you have been with me* ['1'] from the very beginning [of creation] (Jn 15:27). Before the world was created, the Word [Logos] already existed; he was with God, and he was *the same* as God. From the very beginning, the Word was with God. Through him God made all things [and continues to make all things]; not one thing in all creation was made without him. The Word had life in *himself*, and this life brought light to men. The light shines in the darkness, and the darkness has never put it out." (Jn 1:1-5).

Who is this evangelist John who presented the deepest, the finest, and the most sacred of Jesus' communication, and who wrote perhaps the most important gospel, the fourth Gospel—the Word made flesh, in which God is one with Christ and with humanity?

Can we trust him with this profound, the holiest of the holies meaning? Did Saint John, the son of Salome and Zebedee, understand what Jesus was saying and his account of the events that changed the course of human history? Was Saint John on intimate terms with the holy family? Why does he challenge us with his magical words before his passing away (Jerome places it sixty-eight years after the death of Christ): "Little children, love one another" (1 Jn 3:23)?

The Gospel of John is a great classic of world spirituality and the most important sacred text in Christianity. It demystifies some of the stranger aspects of life. It is written on many levels of spiritual sensitivity and from a still higher mind than ours. Saint Clement of Alexandria wrote in about 200:

> Last of all [after the other evangelists] John, perceiving that the external [historic, *ta somatika*] facts had been made plain in the [synoptic] Gospels, being urged by his friends, and inspired by the Spirit, composed a [deeper and more advanced] spiritual [*pneumatikon*] Gospel.[2]

Composed with relentless courage and utter compassion, in the Gospel of John, Saint John is less focused on the historical Jesus (no mention of his father Joseph, birth or early days) and more on his spiritual message, the sacred knowledge, and Jesus himself. In the synoptic gospels Jesus speaks in parables for the common Christianity, while in the Gospel of John the center is *God in Jesus and in humanity*. The synoptic gospels Clement suggested, instruct you "from the outside"; the beloved disciple John reveals the foundational heart of Jesus from the inside.

Saint Peter pointed out that John ("One of the disciples, whom Jesus loved, was sitting next to Jesus" [Jn 13:23]) had reclined on Jesus' chest at the supper. Also, Saint Irenaeus (190) informs us that John, son of Zebedee, lived at Ephesus until the reign of Emperor Trajan (98-117). We also know the apostles were key links between Jesus and the public. They knew the Christ as no one else did. Saint Irenaeus wrote, "Later John, the Lord's pupil, who reclined on the Lord's chest, himself published the gospel while staying at Ephesus in Asia."[3]

The disciple Jesus loved was also the eyewitness standing with his mother (the Lady of Light), his mother's sister, Mary, the wife of Clopa, and Mary Magdalene, beneath the cross:

> And there stood by Jesus' cross his mother [in the Gospel of John, she is never recognized as Mary] and his mother's sister . . . So Jesus, seeing his mother and the disciple whom he loved standing

by, said, "Woman, look: here is your son." Then he said to the disciple: "Look, here is your mother." And from that hour the disciple took her into his own home (Jn 19:25-27).

Notice, "the disciple whom Jesus loved . . . who reclined on the Lord's chest," was the one to whom the "Prince of Light" committed His mother, before passing away to the Other Side, and the only disciple near the cross. The other eleven disciples have deserted Jesus. Perhaps they were afraid of being killed; perhaps they did not internalize Jesus' message of our Oneness, or possibly both. We do not know. It is significant that the well-known disciples of Jesus do not even bury him, thus satisfying the token debt of goodwill in such horrifying circumstances. We learn that Joseph of Arimathea and Nicodemus took Jesus' body, and in accordance with Jewish burial custom buried him.

During the Soviet-Nazi era, when the persecutions and killings were rampant, populace in general, like in the days of the Christ, did not risk their lives to safe others from death. We all remember Simon Peter, who denied being one of Jesus' disciples (Jn 18:17). Yet there were incalculable others, like the apostle John, the Lady of Light, Mary Magdalene, Lazarus, and Jesus, who understood our Oneness, and who were not afraid of dying for others.

For example, our next-door neighbor Omelan Kowcz (1884-1944), a Ukrainian, Greek Catholic priest, who christened me, when I was seven years old, during the Russian occupation, was saving Jews from certain death by christening and providing to them Christian birth certificates. Kowcz had a great heart and an intense love for all people. He was warned by Hitler's Gestapo to stop Christianizing Jewish families. Glowing with kindliness and compassion Kowcz told my parents, "I will save lives as long as I can: I am fulfilling my duty." Similar to Carmelite nun, and a martyr for the Jewish-Catholic faith Saint Teresa Benedicta of the Cross, Kowcz perished in gas chambers of Majdanek (Poland) death camp.

"Greater love no one has but to lay down one's life for one's friends" (Jn 15:13), said Jesus. This applies to countless millions, including those who laid down their lives to liberate Western Europe from Hitler, Eastern Europe from the Communist System, Iraq from Hussein, and the like. Thank you from the bottom of my heart. I love you.

Saint Paul in the Galatian letter (2:9) refers to Saint John as one of the pillars of the church with Saint James and Saint Peter. We also know from the early Christian writings (Irenaeus, Polycarp, Justin) that John was the ultimate authority behind the Gospel, that he possessed remarkable spiritual understanding of the Christ's message, and had been on intimate terms with the holy family.

It is a noteworthy fact that Saint John was with Jesus, Peter and James at the death chamber of the synagogue ruler's twelve-year-old daughter (Mk 5:37) and witnessed the commotion, the wailing, and her restoration to life. He was present with Jesus, Peter and James at the Transfiguration (Lk 9:28) and during His deeply distressed "sorrow to the point of death," in Gethsemane (Mk 14:33). Saint John went together with Jesus, after His arrest by the Jewish officials, into the palace of the high priest Annas (who was the father-in-law of Caiaphas, the high priest that year) and then to Caiaphas (Jn 18:15). He was the first apostle to reach the tomb on the morning of the Resurrection (Jn 20:2), after Mary Magdalene told Simon Peter and him about the removal of the stone. Saint John was also the first to recognize the risen Christ standing upon the shore: "Then the disciple whom Jesus loved said to Peter, 'It is the Lord!'" (Jn 21:7).

"Every man," said Ebrard, "can see the sunset-glow on the Alps, but not everyone can paint it." Saint John discerned and painted the central idea of Jesus' message as no other evangelist did.

Michelangelo's work in the Sistine Chapel, one of the greatest artistic wonders of the world, marked a wholly new direction; the art of fresco would never be the same again. Likewise, Saint John's revelation of the Infinite Splendor, *Creator himself in us*, also gives a whole new direction and meaning to our lives, to religion, to science, and to our spirituality.

For those that have eyes to see, the brightness of Saint John's light is the Living Waters and the Bread of Heaven. Yes, whoever sees a wave sees the water; whoever sees you sees the Infinite Splendor, the '1'. You have unraveled one of the greatest mysteries of the ages: *who we are—* who is the knower.

Just as a wave cannot be without the water, so we cannot be without the '1'. "Remain in [*conscious*] union with me," said the Christ, "and I will remain in union with you. Unless you remain [every second conscious] in me you cannot bear fruit, just as a branch cannot bear fruit unless it remains in the vine . . . Whoever remains in me, and I in him, will bear much fruit (Jn 15:4-5).

In part 2 you will meet the same observation through physics. John 14:20 and 12:45 illustrate a profound insight into the deepest nature of our Being. The Father (the Mother of Infinity) is in the Christ, and the Christ is in the Father, "I am in you and you in me." You are in the Father, and the Father is in you. You are in Christ, and Christ is in you. Earlier, the Christ deployed parables to articulate the truth about the Father in us. Now through these profound statements Jesus speaks to us in plain words about the Father in us (Jn 16:25).

Therefore, "Love one another," said he, "just as I love you." *We are part of each other. We are part of one life—like rainbow colors of one light.* We each contribute toward our common progress into a single living organism, growth in freedom, prosperity, culture, social justice, wisdom, and peace. We are making our world a healthier habitat for free people.

Eileen Conn, writer and corporate transformation authority, in *Visions of Creation,* writes, "We are all part of creating the world in which we live. Each one of us is responsible for our own actions. Our images of our lives and ourselves can fundamentally change our individual and collective experience."

Can We Recognize Ourselves in Each Other?

The Christ revealed the principles and spiritual technology for a more significant and a more profound approach to life. He advocated making the world a better place, learning to care for another human life, and celebrating our mutual divinity. The procedure entailed understanding and modifying reality (science of miracles) through LSI (large-scale integration, which I've noted previously) of kindness, compassion, service-excellence, inner balance, goodwill, visualizing end results, and knowing in our heart with confidence that it is so. He applied the law of equilibrium ("turn the other cheek") through unconditional love and humility. Yet one of the most insightful and daring texts on conveying the reality of our Oneness, and one of his greatest contributions, is highlighted with grace and precision in John 14:9, 14:11, 14:20, 12:45, and 17:21:

I pray *that they may all be* [consciously] *one.* [We are now unconsciously one.] O Father! May they be in us, just as you are in me and I am in you. May they be one, so that the world will believe that you sent me. *I gave them the same glory you gave me* [yes, I GAVE THEM THE SAME GLORY YOU GAVE ME—I have made them realize who they are, as you made me realize who I am] so that they may be one, just as you and I are one: I in them and you in me, so they may be completely one [that they become a single life], in order that the world may know that you sent me and that you love them as you love me (Jn 17:21-23).

Enriching each other, serving each other, doing good, and loving one another have a rationale that becomes *self-evident*. When you are awake/ alert, aware/conscious, like breathing fresh air, realize that the stranger you are giving the helping hand to is God.

Individuals who understood the Christ's words questioned the authority of the old controlling institutions, causing them to fundamentally transform or crumble; we see the results in the incredible growth of Christianity. "The same power" of the people to challenge the legitimacy of the old order, stated Willis Harman, "was responsible for the changes in Eastern Europe in 1989 and brought down world Communism within a week in August 1991. Thus we need to look for signs that the legitimacy of the present social order is increasingly questioned."

"O righteous Father!" prayed Jesus, "I made you known to them and I will continue to do so, in order that the love you have for me may be in them, and I may be in them . . . So that they might have my joy in their hearts, in all its fullness" (Jn 17:26, 13). Mother Teresa of Calcutta asks us these sacred words of love, "Is my heart so clean that I can see the face [image] of God in my brother, my sister, who is that black one, that white one, that naked one, that one suffering from leprosy, that dying one?"[4]

Is there a need for Love to be rediscovered in us? Are we family of One Father ('1')? Will the "Little children love one another," as Saint John challenged us? "The good news is that," declared Harman, "perhaps through the unconscious wisdom of ordinary people, the transformation has already started. The depth of the transformation will startle us all."

Austrian theoretical physicist, Erwin Schrödinger (1887-1961), a towering genius, was a contributor to the wave theory of matter that helped elucidate the fundamentals of quantum mechanics. He shared the 1933 Nobel Prize in Physics with British physicist Paul Adrien Maurice Dirac (1902-1984) for developing the subtle and elegant wave equation, a widely used mathematical tool that became the heart of modern quantum mechanics. Schrödinger is highly prized for his purity of thinking and clarity of expression. He states:

> In Christian terminology to say, "Hence I am God Almighty," sounds both blasphemous and lunatic. But please disregard these connotations for the moment and consider whether the above inference is not the closest a biologist can get to proving God and immortality at one stroke.
>
> In itself, the insight is not new. The earliest records, to my knowledge, date back some 2,500 years or more. From the early great Upanishads the recognition ATMAN = BRAHMAN (the personal self equals the omnipresent, all comprehending eternal self) was in Indian thought considered, far from being blasphemous, to represent the quintessence of deepest insight into the happenings of the world. The striving of all the scholars of Vedanta was, after having learned to pronounce with their lips, really to assimilate in their minds this grandest of all thoughts . . .
>
> To Western ideology, the thought has remained a stranger, in spite of Schopenhauer and others who stood for it and in spite of those true lovers who, as they look into each other's eyes, become aware that their thought and their joy are numerically one, not merely similar or identical—but they, as a rule, are emotionally too busy to indulge in clear thinking, in which respect they very much resemble the mystic.[5]

As for the position of the personal self: "Everything is situated within Him ['1'],"[6] states the awe-inspiring "Song of the Exalted One" ("Gospel" of Hinduism) of the Bhagavad Gita. Similarly, "Lord, you have been our dwelling place" (Ps 90:1), sings the psalmist.

Aratus of Tarsus (310-245 BC) was the court poet of Antiochus Soter in Syria. In the vein of Lao-tzu in China and Vyasa in India, Aratus declared that the Most High, concealed as the Spirit, permeates all, and is always and everywhere present, and we shall return to Him, "Let us begin with the Most High (Dios), whose help we invoke incessantly. The Most High is present in every place where people live and are; he permeates the sea and the coasts, and everybody will return to him, for we are all his offspring."[7]

Similar to the Bhagavad Gita ("Everything is situated within Him" [8: 22], or "All beings rest in Me [9: 6]), Saint Luke made a profound observation concerning the '1' (the Christian God Almighty, the Maker of the Universe), when he referred to Aratus of Tarsus:

> The God who made the world and everything in it is the Lord of heaven and earth and does not live in temples build by hands . . . "For in him we live and move and have our being," as indeed some of your own writers [Aratus] have said: "We are all his offspring" [*Thoû gàr kaí génos semen*] (Acts 17:24, 28).

In summary: "In him [in the '1'—in the same invisible constant reality that is present everywhere] we live and move [exist, walk, and dance] and have our being [essence]."

Gustav Teres, a licentiate in philosophy, biblical exegesis, astronomy, and an adjunct astronomer of the Vatican Observatory, shares:

> The fifth century BC is the age of great Messianic revelations, prophets, and sages. We find Lao-tzu and K'ung Fu-tsu [Confucius] in China, the Buddha in India, Zarathustra in Persia, Ezekiel, Daniel, and Isaiah the Second in Babylon, Jeremiah in Judaea, Thales, Pythagoras, Heraclitus, and the anonymous Sibyls in Greece. What strange contemporaries! They seem to be able to perceive the inspiration of the same invisible spiritual Power ['1'], who is present everywhere. Although they do not speak each other's language, they preach the same ideas . . . [8]

Our worldview has changed more rapidly in the last few decades than in any previous era in human history. The Unchanging State has reached, through billions of years of advancement, a point of wakefulness and alertness wherein *it is beginning to know itself* and its relation to the origin: "I am in my Father, and *you* are in *me*, just as I am in *you*" (Jn 14:20).

Mother Teresa's insights are a light of hope in an age when at times people are unclear about their identity. She reminded us:

If sometimes people have had to die of starvation, it is not because God didn't care for them, but because you and I were not instruments of love in the hands of God, to give them bread, because WE DID NOT RECOGNIZE HIM when *once more the hungry* CHRIST CAME in distressing DISGUISE [God's marvelous masquerade—as us, emphasis added].[9]

Waking up to the incredible recognition of our Oneness ("Everything is situated within Him." "The whole universe is in God," that we are each other's brothers and sisters, "that the Universe is your own splendid glory"[10]) is not limited to major thinkers, philosophical and religious classics, or those men and women who lived and died suffering a godly life while in the midst of great poverty and deprivation. Scientists, educators, civil servants, businessmen, families, and many others have transformed a state of indifference or what they normally feel and do into a loving life of compassion, group altruism, and caring through kindness and vigilance.

Executive Edge: Widening Our Circle of Compassion, Becoming One Community

A young Swiss patent officer, Albert Einstein, was told by his teacher that physics is a dead-end street, and a young Israeli carpenter, Jesus the Christ, was told by his religious leaders that God is not his Father. Both Einstein and Jesus were two remarkably different men sharing a devotion to Oneness and peace, personal liberty, and progress. They were very conscious of the bondage of human "egocentric cravings, desires, and fears." Their expositions on the implications of higher values for their generations proved to be remarkably timely—even for the twenty-first century. Einstein, in the vein of the Christ (Jn 14:9, 14:11, 14:20), championed a crucial design for human Oneness and liberty:

A human being is a part of the whole, called by us the "Universe," a part limited in time and space. He experiences himself, his thoughts and feelings as something separated from the rest—a kind of optical delusion of his consciousness. This delusion is a kind of prison for us, restricting us to our personal desires and to affection for a few persons nearest to us. Our task must be to free ourselves from this prison by widening our circle of compassion to embrace all living creatures and the whole of nature in its beauty. Nobody is able to achieve this completely, but the striving for such achievement is in itself a part of the liberation and a foundation for inner security.[11]

Will Einstein's public statement remain "hidden under a bushel," or will more people experience infinite Oneness and freedom? What do you think?

How many scholars, policymakers and journalists, scientists, educators, and religious establishments, in the twenty-first millennium, realize what Einstein's proclamation means? It is not any different than what the Christ, the Buddha, and a host of others have publicly stated.

Arnold Toynbee (1889-1975) was the Koraes professor of Byzantine and modern Greek language, literature, and history in the University of London (1919-24), the director of studies in the Royal Institute of International Affairs and research professor of international history in the University of London until his retirement (1955). His major published work, *A Study of History*, is comprised of twelve volumes. In addressing "the relation between an individual living being and ultimate reality," Toynbee stated, "each single living being is coextensive with, and is therefore identical with, the entire universe."[12]

Albert Schweitzer (1875-1965) was a philosopher, German mission doctor in equatorial Africa, interpreter of Johann Sebastian Bach's works, theologian, and "reverence for life" servant of humanity. He received the 1952 Nobel Peace Prize for his work in support of "the Brotherhood of Nations." Similar to Einstein, Toynbee, and others, Schweitzer stated:

> The deeper we look into nature, the more we recognize that it is full of life, and the more profoundly we know that all life is a secret and the we are united with all life that is in nature. Man can no longer live his life for himself alone. We realize that all life is valuable and that we are united to all this life. From this knowledge comes our spiritual relationship to the universe.[12a]

Compassion is the actual name for the Lord Almighty and the presence of final physical principles within us. In the attitude of compassion, cosmic awareness and justice, breakthroughs and solutions to daily life challenges and miracles come into being. Through compassion a human becomes the Compassionate Light once again. Jesus advised, "Be compassionate as your Father in heaven is" (Lk 6:36-42).

John Archibald Wheeler provides us with a cosmological physicist's intimate glimpse within the perception and observation issue, "The universe does not exist "out there" independent of us. We are inescapably involved in bringing about that which appears to be happening. We are not only observers. We are participators. In some strange sense this is a participatory universe."[13]

Bernard d'Espagnat of France, another of the most celebrated physicists of our day, confirms this participatory interplay between nature and ourselves, cited analogously in John 14:9, 14:11, 14:20; Acts 17:28; the Bhagavad Gita; and by Albert Einstein and John Wheeler: "This notion of reality existing independently of man has no meaning whatsoever."[14]

We Are the Unsolved Mystery

Max Karl Ernst Planck (1858-1947), brilliant German physicist, was also counseled by his teacher (like Albert Einstein) to be a concert pianist because "physics is finished, young man. It's a dead-end street." Planck entered the University of Munich at age 16 and received his doctorate at age 21, with a thesis on the second law of thermodynamics. In spite of the great respect in which he was held all through his lifetime, Planck remained a man of extreme humility. For Planck, physics was more than a profession or problem solving; it was a holy path of life and a sacred way to the Mystery that he was trying to solve.

Planck formulated the mathematical relation of thermal radiation from a perfect absorber (blackbody, October 7, 1900). He was awarded the Nobel Prize in Physics (1918) "for the discovery of energy quanta," which illuminated the path to modern quantum mechanics. Planck predated both John Wheeler and Bernard d'Espagnat in suggesting that subject and object are inextricably connected—they are One: "In the last analysis, we ourselves are part of nature, and, therefore, part of the mystery that we are trying to solve."[15]

The German quantum physicist, philosopher, and the Nazis head of the nuclear effort Werner Karl Heisenberg (1901-1976) discovered a method to express quantum mechanics in terms of matrices (1925). For that insight, Heisenberg was awarded the 1932 Nobel Prize in Physics.

Erwin Schrödinger independently developed wave mechanics, and their works were shown later as two equivalent solutions. Through the assistance of Max Born, Paul Dirac, Pascual Jordan, and Wolfgang Pauli, matrix quantum mechanics was formalized. Heisenberg served as a director of the Kaiser Wilhelm Institute for Physics in Berlin and, after World War II, became director of the Max Planck Institute for Physics and Astrophysics in Göttingen. Heisenberg is best known for his brilliant indeterminacy principle. In studying the participatory interaction between nature and us, Heisenberg wrote, "Natural science does not simply describe and explain nature; it is part of the interplay between nature and ourselves; it describes nature as exposed to our method of questioning."[16]

His Heart Was Full of Joy: The Human Spirit Is a Universal Spirit

Abraham Isaac Kook (1865-1935), considered to be one of the foremost Jewish spiritual leaders of the twentieth century, had a loving heart by nature. He was a fervent Zionist and a prolific and eloquent author. Kook developed his philosophy in a number of essays, many of which are under the title *Orot ha-quodesh*, in three volumes (1963-1964; "Lights of Holiness"). He served as the first chief rabbi of Palestine Jewry, under the League of Nations mandate to Great Britain to administer Palestine, until his passing away just prior to the Second World War.

Kook never lost sight of our fundamental divinity, that we are sparks of light trapped in a delicate body, and Einstein, Toynbee, Wheeler, d'Espagnat, Planck, and Heisenberg's unity principle. Kook claimed that our mental separation from the Infinite One is not a physical actuality, but only an effect of human egocentric "forgetfulness" (amnesia) of a higher existence. Reinstatement of memory and man's unity with the divine can be achieved through the Torah. Addressing our unity, Kook wrote:

> Special individuals, the sages of great understanding, always knew the secret of spiritual unity. They knew that the human spirit is a universal spirit, that although many divergences, spiritual and material, tend to separate person from person and society from society, greater than all the differences is the essential unity among

them; that the processes of thought are constantly interacting, and ways of life tend to be harmonized. The objective of the harmonization is surely to embrace the best, the healthiest, and most sensitive in every society and to plant it on the soil of the larger human family.[17]

Robert Muller was chancellor of the United Nations University for Peace and former assistant secretary-general of the UN. With his office on the twenty-ninth floor of the United Nations Secretariat building and with an easy smile, serene blue eyes, an athletic build, and much compassion in his heart, Muller, for over thirty years, has coordinated the work of its thirty-two specialized agencies and world programs. He has seen disasters, battles, and natural and man-made catastrophes around the world. He is fondly called "the philosopher of the UN and its prophet of hope." Like Dag Hammarskjöld, to whom he was both a friend and advisor, Muller turned his gridiron enthusiasm to the clouds while keeping both feet planted firmly on the ground. He shares:

> I often feel as if my life were a lamp: a temporary container filled with light, a flow of energy, condensed and held together for a little while in a mysterious, marvelous living cosmos linked with the rest of the Earth and the heavens through material, touchable elements and immaterial, invisible elements. Someday the lamp will extinguish. The material elements will be reabsorbed by the Earth in its chains of life and energy. The immaterial elements will return to a universal soul to be reborn in other forms on this planet or elsewhere in the universe. We are cosmic matter come alive, partaking of the divine character of our Creator.[18]

Life Is Sacred: Feed the Poor with Bread of Love

Muller, akin to his caring brothers, Hammarskjöld and U Thant, is a great light of holiness and spontaneity shining in our midst. He is "an international sage" filled with an awareness of Oneness, the voice of the sacred, and is a "do good everywhere" compassionate friend. He has been with the UN since its inception. His father was a hatmaker who wanted Robert to track him into a hat-making career, while his mother wished that he would be an intellectual. He did better.

During World War II, Robert was a member of the French Resistance. He is a practical visionary who played a central role in having China admitted to the UN. His thesis on the Sarre region was a bible for Robert Schuman as he worked on the creation of the European Iron and Steel Community that evolved into today's EU. Prior to his UN retirement, Muller took pleasure in jogging early every morning in New York City. While running "his mile," he would pick up papers, cans, bottles, and other refuse. "This must be done," Robert would say with a rush of joy. He wanted "his mile" of New York City to be the cleanest. Robert Muller is a special individual and a superlative caring standard for all of us. He is a social reformer, poet, and a genius of integrity embarked to bring higher consciousness through peace and education in the world. With his very caring heart he is "partaking of the divine character of the Creator." He knows that the life of man is the life of God. Furthermore, he writes:

> One's family is his foremost church on Earth.
> The most sacred acts are conducted in it:
> love,
> the gift of life,
> care, protection, and education.[19]

"Why reinvent the wheel?" says Muller. "There are already time-tested maps to our realization and peace . . . allow the best to flower in each individual." Resembling Abraham Kook, Albert Einstein, Arnold Toynbee, Bernard d'Espagnat, Max Planck, Werner Heisenberg, and Dag Hammarskjöld, Muller often repeated, "Humanity is one living body made of human beings," and "Life is divine. *Das Leben ist göttlich.* I wish this exclamation of mine as a child were translated in all languages and displayed in every school on earth."[20]

Human love wears more than one face in God's brilliant disguise. Behind it, time and again, the same fundamental truth is shown. Not only is the truth of who is the knower elucidated by what we hold in common, it is refracted, colored, and repeated according to the genius of the presenter throughout history and within the many processes of scientific inquiry.

The love is marching on. "Come dance with Me ['1']. Come dance," in "God's magnificent masquerade—as us," declared Hafiz. Hurry. Let love, freedom, and peace come.

8

RISE, O MIGHTY ONE: WE HAVE ENTERED A UNIVERSE OF LOVE AND LIGHT!

> Give light to those that live in darkness
> and in the shadow of death . . .
>
> —Luke 1:79

Live as Children of Light

Let us visit another deep truth from the Adam and Eve parable: "The man has become like one of us, knowing what is good and what is bad!" This disclosure presents a condition existing prior to *becoming*, and prior to *knowing*. It construes that before eating of the tree of knowledge man and woman could not understand the truth. They were not conscious of their divinity: that "I am in my Father, and you in me and I in you," or as the Christlike saint Mother Teresa verbalized, "We did not recognize Him when once more the hungry Christ came in distressing disguise."[1]

A hint of humility: we did not cherish the fact that "A human being is a part of the whole," as Albert Einstein understood. That "he experiences himself, his thoughts and feelings as something separated from the rest—a kind of optical delusion of his consciousness. This delusion is a kind of prison for us, restricting us to our personal desires and to affection for a few persons nearest to us . . ."

We did not know what was "good" or "bad," as the Adam and Eve parable maintains. We were not enjoying the love and grace, the blazing Light and beauty of the Eternal Wisdom. We did not know that responsibility, gentleness, deep peace, human rights, freedom, and social and economic advancement are all interrelated. Some of us were living in fear, as millions do daily. We fought and persecuted our own being, as was the case with Genghis Khan, Hitler, Stalin, Mao Ze-dong, Hiroshima, Nagasaki, international terrorism in the name of Allah, drug traffic, unhappiness in many homes. The analogy is to our left hand beating up our right hand, the right side of our heart not working as one with the left side of our heart. Think. Where is our society today? Once humanity achieves the ability to make judgments that are in agreement with Reality, it is free.

Do you receive the same insight from Genesis, the Christ, Mother Teresa, Einstein, Toynbee, Heschel, and Hammarskjöld as I have? Do you perceive the same striking truth lit by a different lamp? Furthermore, a statement of *becoming* also acknowledges a vast potential in all of us: an upcoming realization of our essential value. A tomato seed cannot grow into an oak tree, but an acorn can become an oak.

Similarly, "the man has become like one of us" shows man and woman as the acorn, with the capability to transform—to metamorphose. This entails a complete change in nature, form, and structure from one stage to the next, as from the caterpillar to the pupa and from the pupa to the adult butterfly. As humans we open our eyes and see the truth—we make a quantum jump in awareness to where we can know ourselves as the Compassionate One, the Kindhearted One, the Infinite Splendor. This level of awareness discloses one essence, but in different splendors and forms, where we realize that all colors of a rainbow are a part of the same spectrum of white light.

The religious scholar and Sufi saint Jalal al-Din Rumi illustrated this experience in terms of the alchemical process. The base metal of the human soul transforms into the gold of Perfect Divinity, at which point Rumi realized: "Why should I seek? I am the same as he. His essence speaks through me. I have been looking for myself." Yes, as a spark of the one flame Rumi recognized: "I am the same as he . . . I have been looking for myself." In Meher Baba's words it means, "To find God is to come to one's own self."

Sathya Sai Baba (1926-present) is a world teacher and contemporary avatar with millions of followers in Puttaparthi, India, and around the world. Baba heals the sick, materializes various objects, awakens the superconscious state, inspires self-reliance and advocates to "offer and surrender everything [your deeds, words, and thoughts; the Christ's "Your ['I'] will be done"] to the Lord, without any desire for personal gain." Surrender, to six feet and four inches, Abraham Lincoln, meant "I believe I am a humble instrument in the hand of our Heavenly Father."

In the vein of the Christ, the Buddha, and others who revere the Everlasting Father in the human family, Baba recommends the development of truth, justice, freedom, and love. In order "to acquire the awareness of the Divine Splendor [within oneself] one must join the company of the holy and strive on the spiritual path." In the spirit of Rumi, Sai Baba corroborates:

> You need not search for God. You yourself are divine. How can you go in search of yourself? This is the mistake you commit. When everything is permeated by the Divine, who is the searcher of the Divine? It is because the world has lacked men who could proclaim this Vedantic truth with authentic experience that it has sunk to such degrading levels.[2]

Baba is correct. "How can you go in search of yourself?" *How can an ocean wave search for water?* Earlier I asked, given that the full light of truth about our essential nature has been known for over two thousand years, why this truth has not permeated in a more significant way throughout our planet. Sai Baba gives us a clue that it is very hard to see when one is blind; it is hard to hear when one is deaf. In his epistle to the Ephesians, Saint Paul magnificently related, "There was a time when you were darkness, but now *you are light* in the Lord. Well, then, live as children of Light. Light produces every kind of goodness and justice and truth," (Eph 5:8-9).

Today, light and knowledge and redemption are qualities available for everyone to cherish. Comparable to water in frozen ice, the Unchanging State is in each one of us. Scientific advances are part of the continuous revelation and celebration of the '1'. They help us to see more clearly the meaning and the purpose of life and discover what we should be and how to live the right way.

Our eyes are meant to see, to prove to oneself, that heaven, salvation, and emancipation are not some places out there in space to which we have to raise our hands, or something that begins after life on earth, but are here within each one of us. In this very moment, we can "offer our bodies as a living sacrifice, holy and acceptable to God, [which is] our spiritual worship."[3]

Every second that passes, every choice we make, every act we create, becomes our commitment and adoration of the '1'—the First Democracy or Democratic Spirit—to live in accordance with the laws that preside over the universe. In the Old and New Testaments we read of the same aids in our search for truth and individual liberty, "You shall love the Lord your God [the law of laws] with all your heart, soul, and might."[4]

Does this passage suggest any steps we might consider? It is counter to the hero worship of "the golden calf," symbolizing the continuing human tendency to turn from the divine and worship the creature[5] and to disregard the Highest Good *in us*. The Spirit of Love is already within and without us and among us, as the Prince of Peace in the Gospel of Thomas vividly stated. Otherwise, as the wise Rabbi Melech HaMoshiach declared, "In these days—the Days of Moshiach (the Messianic era)—which we are now in, all we need to do is open our eyes and then we see that the true and complete Geulah (Redemption) is already here, literally."

Arise, O Compassionate One from the Depths of Hades

Father Bede Griffith, a leading spiritual teacher in the world, is a writer and author of numerous books. In his exquisite book *River of Compassion*, commenting on the first chapter of the Bhagavad Gita he states, "Many people do not awaken to the reality of God, and to the experience of transformation in their lives until they reach the point of despair."

Alfred D'Souza characterized his despair this way: "For a long time it had seemed to me that life was about to begin—real life. But there was always some obstacle in the way, something to be got through first, some unfinished business to be served, a debt to be paid. Then life would begin. At last it dawned on me that these obstacles were my life."

The thoughts of Albert Schweitzer contain some of the most beautiful and most inspiring observation of nature. Here he speaks about a sleeping sickness of the soul:

> You know of the disease in Central Africa called sleeping sickness. There also exists a sleeping sickness of the soul. Its most dangerous aspect is that one is unaware of its coming. That is why you have to be careful. As soon as you notice the slightest sign of indifference, the moment you become aware of the loss of a certain seriousness, of

longing, of enthusiasm and zest, take it as a warning. You should realize your soul suffers if you live superficially.[6]

The "Source of Life" ('1'), or the universal divine consciousness in which the universe exists, pervades everything. Yet most of us are not conscious of this. Like atoms in the Void, we are in Love, and Love is in each one of us. Each saint and each creed is a new wake-up call. The "buglers" (Moses, Jesus, the Buddha, Hammarskjöld, etc.) broadcast the sacredness of our essence. It is time to wake up from our sleep, from our dreams and illusions, from our prejudices and fantasies. The present must become consciously grounded in eternity amid the vastness of space and its billion/trillion suns. We hear of Paul's towering achievement in his letter to the Ephesians, "Wake up, O sleeper, rise from the dead, and Christ will give you light," (Eph 5:14).

This is not a call to raise lifeless remains from a tomb, but to emerge from the deathlike unrealities of the world to a Christlike life of purity, responsibility, and splendor.

The great saint, poet, and humble weaver, Kabir (1440-1518), strived to bridge Hindu and Muslim elements, imagery, and viewpoints. He lectured on the fundamental *unity* (Aramaic: *Alaha*) of all religions and the basic *equality* of all males as well as females. Kabir spoke of the need for "awakening" from the unconsciousness of our existence and a new way of living:

> Friend, wake up! Why do you go on sleeping? The night is over—
> do you want to lose the day the same way? . . . So much was lost
> already while you slept . . . and that was unnecessary!
> My inside, listen to me, the greatest spirit, the Teacher [of
> Light: '1'], is near, wake up, wake up!
> Run to his feet—he is standing close to your head right now.
> YOU HAVE SLEPT FOR MILLIONS AND MILLIONS OF
> YEARS. WHY NOT WAKE UP THIS MORNING (author's
> emphasis)?
> Oh friend, I love you, think this over carefully! If you are in
> love, then why are you asleep?[7]

The mighty Kabir (Arabic: "Great") was a grandparent of Sikhism, instituted by his disciple, Guru Nanak (1469-1539). Kabir, instead of selecting the Hindu or Islam religions, took what appeared to him to be the best tenets of both and advocated a simple *union* ("sahaja" or the "natural," pre-quantum state of consciousness). Saint Paul's union, Christ's "worship in Spirit and truth," and the Buddhists' nirvana (or absolute union) with Love (the blazing Light) are examples.

The London-born poet, painter, engraver, and philosopher William Blake (1757-1827) depicted and wrote of life in its totality. He saw anew this unified image of the human being and its interconnectedness with the whole:

> Awake! Awake O sleeper of the land of shadows. Wake! Expand! I am in you and you in me, mutual in love . . . Lo! We are one.[8] [Also:] Arise, you little glancing wings, and sing your infant joy! Arise, and drink your bliss, for everything that lives is holy!

Blake possessed a mind of spectacular originality and vision. Similar to the incredible genius Nobelist Nikola Tesla, whatever Blake imagined, he also observed. Mozart, the miracle prodigy, perceived his symphonies within, in one unchanging flash, in one note.

Note: Nikola Tesla, the father of today's alternating-current (AC) electrical system, had the gift of eidetic imagery. Tesla could *see* and *test* his inventions in his mind. His ability to focus on fundamental principles enabled him to access the pre-quantum state, by liberating his unconscious for breakthrough insights. Tesla introduced us to the fundamentals of AC electric power generation and transmission, high-frequency currents, early fluorescent lamps, radio-controlled robotics, and assisted in paving the way for such space-age technologies as microwaves, satellites, and "star wars" beamed weapons.

The Encyclopaedia Britannica lists the following review of Blake's gift:

> Whatever he imagined, he also saw. The accounts of those who watched him, in his middle age, draw imaginary personages, make it plain that he had what is now called eidetic imagery—i.e., the rare ability to see mental images as if they are suspended outside the head, so that they can be inspected like solid figures by shifting one's gaze from one side to the other.[9]

Here is Blake's "awakening" to the fullness of love from the book of Psalms (44:23): "Awake, O Lord! Why do you sleep?" Yes. Awake, arise, O Lord to your divinity, or, "Rise up, O God, judge the earth, for all the nations are your inheritance," (Ps 82:8). The Indian poet Rabindranath phrased our sleepwalking thusly:

> Oh my heart, arise!
> Arise in this land of purity,
> On the shores of the sea of great humanity.[10]

"Arise, wake" is also Sai Baba's call to live in the divine state of righteousness, love, and reconciliation—to manifest our Holiness in all of our actions:

> Arise, awake, establish once again the royal era, resplendent with causes and projects which uphold Truth, Peace, and Righteousness. Love your brothers and sisters. Practice the Eternal Religion, quench the burning flames of ignorance, turmoil, injustice, and envy with the waters of Love, Forbearance, and Truth. Develop a feeling of mutual respect towards others . . . Live now in the divine state and manifest yourself as the God-force which is the core of your being. That is the real you, the spark of Divinity, for you yourself are part of that force, part of God, Divine. Realize your Divinity now and recognize that same Divinity in others, regardless of caste, color, or creed. Pay no attention to the way they may behave as many are still living at the lower levels of consciousness, confused and in a state of illusion. One day their time of awakening will also come.[11]

Darkness Can Be Lit, Thus Freeing Yourself

Call to mind what psalms "Rise, O God" meant to the benevolent Einstein, "Our task must be to free ourselves from this prison by widening our circle of compassion to embrace all living creatures and the whole of nature in its beauty."[12]

For John Wheeler, similar to Johann Wolfgang von Goethe before him ("Man must always in some sense cling to the belief that the unknown is knowable; otherwise, speculation would cease.") the awakening sound of a bugle signifies "The unknown is knowable . . . Every darkness can be lighted."[13]

For the Galilean, this waking up from darkness into the Light of lights, from the unknown into the knowable, is acting aligned with the One ('1') that governs the universe. "He who acts in truth ['1'] comes into the light" (Jn 3:21).

By doing His will, as stated earlier, one is doing what is right. One is on autopilot. One is employing the best solution in one's arsenal, acting in harmony with the internal software of '1'. Paramahamsa Yogananda turned into words: "God sent you here for a purpose. Are you acting in harmony with that purpose? You came on earth to accomplish a divine mission. Realize how tremendously important that is! Do not allow the narrow ego to obstruct your attainment of an infinite goal."

Therefore, he who acts in truth, he who does what is right, regains the consciousness of Light. Interestingly, the serpent from the Adam and Eve parable weaves this heart of hearts message: "The moment you eat of it you will be like gods who know what is good and what is bad" (Gen 3:4).

In Daily Life, Timing Is Everything: You Are Timeless

"There is a profound paradox in the spiritual journey," states John White. He explains:

> It is this: the goal of our journey, the answer we seek is none other than what we already are in essence—Being, the ultimate wholeness that is the source and ground of all Becoming. Enlightenment is realization of the truth of Being. Our native condition, our true self is Being, traditionally called God, the Cosmic Person, the Supreme Being, the One-in-all. (Incidentally, some enlightened teachers—the Buddha was one—prefer to avoid theistic terms in order to communicate better. Their intent is to bypass the deep cultural conditioning that occurs through such language and blocks understanding.) We are manifestations of Being, but like the cosmos itself, we are also in the process of Becoming—always growing, changing, developing, and evolving to higher and higher states that ever more beautifully express the perfection of the source of existence. Thus, we are not only human beings; we are also human

becomings. Enlightenment is understanding the perfect poise of being-amid-becoming.

When we finally understand that Great Mystery, we discover our true nature, the Supreme Identity, the Self of all. That direct perception of our Oneness with the Infinite Light, that Noetic realization of our identity with the divine is the source of all happiness, all goodness, all beauty, all truth. The experience is beyond time, space, and causality; it is beyond ego and all socially conditioned sense of "I." Knowing ourselves to be timeless, boundless, and therefore cosmically free ends the illusion of separateness and all the painful, destructive defenses we erect, individually and societally, to preserve the ego-illusion at the expense of others.[14]

As did the Bible, the Upanishads, starting about the sixth century BC in India, created the concluding segment of the revealed part of the Vedas or "sacred knowledge." In general, the Upanishads embody the attempt of woman and man's undertaking to understand the fundamental truths John White describes—selfless service, the meaning and value of "knowing," the foundation of the universe, and our destiny.

The singular interest of the Upanishads is with the study of ultimacy—the nature of the unified "theory of everything," summarized in the Chandogya Upanishad by the expression "That art thou" (the inner nature of Reality—Atman)—the Supreme One, the Self of all.

We Are the Temple of Love

In the Upanishads we become aware of the insufficiency of pagan idols and temple worship, the hollowness of pointless ceremonies and performance of rites. Ritualistic observances are useless unless one makes an inward journey and experiences in oneself God's peace, goodness of heart and compassion. We are back to what the Christ and the apostles taught[15]:

> Do not try to work together as equals with unbelievers [pagans], for it cannot be done. How can light and darkness live together? . . . How can *God's temple* come to terms with pagan idols? For WE ARE THE TEMPLE [the sanctuary] of *the living God* (2 Cor 6:14-16).

Yes, we are the place of worship (with our thoughts and actions) of the living God; our hearts are the heaven in which that light is enshrined. In the first chapter of Isaiah we read:

> "The multitude of your sacrifices—what are they to me?" says the Lord. I have more than enough of burnt offerings, of rams and the fat of fattened animals; I have no pleasure in the blood of bulls and lambs and goats. When you come to meet with me, who has asked this of you, this tramping of my courts? Stop bringing meaningless offerings! Your incense is detestable to me. New Moons, Sabbaths and convocations—I cannot bear your evil assemblies . . . They have become a burden to me. I am weary of bearing them . . . Stop doing wrong, learn to do right! Seek justice, encourage the oppressed. Defend the cause of the fatherless, plead the case of the widow (1:11-17).

The Upanishads were formulated prior to the rise of Buddhism and Taoism. The Upanishads stress, similar to the Bible that all expressions of nature are but manifestations of the "Infinite Presence": "The Alpha and the Omega, the One who is, and who was, and who is to come, the Almighty!" (Rev 1:8). They maintain that consciousness creates transitory phenomena, and that nothing exists unless it is either a mind itself or arises from the mind. We are the interpretation as well as the interpreter of the '1'. As the Maitrayana Upanishad, in basic language easily understood by all, expressed, "Having realized his own self as the Self, a person becomes selfless."[16]

The Mundaka Upanishad (or Mantra Upanishad), one of the most exquisite of the major Upanishads, greatly valued for its precision, lucidity, and purity of expression, sums up our self-realization ("seeing one's own true nature," self-recognition) through becoming this Absolute Splendor:

> It can neither be seen nor understood,
> It cannot be given boundaries.
> It is ineffable and beyond thought.
> It is indefinable.
> It is known only through becoming it.[17]

Secretary-General Hammarskjöld, in a radio program hosted by Edward Murrow, explained that selflessness not only leads to an appreciation of the meaning and purpose of life, the right way to live, and self-realization, but can also serve as an "overflowing of the strength" to meet the demands of life:

> On my father's side I inherited a belief that no life was more satisfactory than one of selfless service to your country—or humanity. This service required a sacrifice of all personal interests, but likewise the courage to stand up unflinchingly for your convictions.
>
> From scholars and clergymen on my mother's side I inherited a belief that, in the very radical sense of the Gospels, all men were equals as children of God, and should be met and treated by us as our masters . . . The explanation of how man should live a life of active social service in full harmony with himself as a member of the community of the spirit, I found in the writings of those great medieval mystics for whom "self-surrender" had been the way to self-realization, and who in "singleness of mind" and "inwardness" had found strength to say Yes to every demand which the needs of their neighbors made them face, and to say Yes also to every fate life had in store for them . . . Love—that much misused and misinterpreted word—for them meant simply an overflowing of the strength with which they felt themselves filled when living in true self-oblivion. And this love found natural expression in an unhesitant fulfillment of duty and an unreserved acceptance of life, whatever it brought them personally of toil, suffering—or happiness.[18]

Historian Arnold Toynbee, as Albert Einstein, Albert Schweitzer, and Bertrand Russell before him, was called "an international sage." Toynbee's discussions with Daisaku Ikeda (1928-present), president of Soka Gakkai, a scientific society for the creation of value in Japan, and a person dedicated to general welfare and world peace, concerning the ideal daily way of life and the goal of education, offers cherubic encouragement:

> Every entrant into any profession ought to pledge himself to use his special knowledge and skill for serving his fellow human beings and not for exploiting them. He should give his obligation of service priority over his incidental need to make a living for himself and for his family. Maximum service, not maximum profit, is the objective to which he should dedicate himself.[19]

9

GOD BECAME WHAT WE ARE

Nothing in life is to be feared,
It is only to be understood.

—Marie Curie

Passing the Torch: Keep That Spirit of Harmony

Saint Irenaeus (b. 120 to140, d. 200 to 203) was one of the principal theologians of the period of patristic studies, when the New Testament canon and the initial challenges to articulate a creed were settled. As a youngster, Irenaeus went to see and listen to Saint Polycarp, prior to the wise man being burned alive in 155. Polycarp was martyred for refusing to renounce Christianity. His life was based on the imitation of the Christ in his patience, tolerance, wisdom, and gentleness. Polycarp was embracing wholeness and sanctity of life: the state of being fully alive and human.

The apostle John the Evangelist walked and talked with Jesus of Nazareth; he also lived at Ephesus in the days when Polycarp was young. Irenaeus stated he learned from Polycarp himself that he had been a confidant of Saint John and had shared in mystical experiences of union ("worship in Spirit"—nirvana) with Love. This relationship, in Irenaeus' version of apostolic teaching and the vast importance of studying patristic literature, is a very valuable link between the apostle John's doctrinal understanding of *what* Jesus of Nazareth was revealing and its *initial* theological articulation by Christianity's second-generation spokesmen.

In 177 Irenaeus succeeded the martyred Bishop Pothinus as Bishop of Lugdunum (modern Lyon, southern France). Irenaeus was a very wise, prudent, hardworking, and effective teacher for the entire infant church, both in the East and in the West, and was able to bring out the best in people. In numerous instances he acted as mediator between various contending parties.

Illustration: the Roman Church celebrated Easter on a Sunday (the day of the Resurrection of Christ), whereas the churches of Asia Minor, where Polycarp observed, continued celebrating Easter (or the Christian Passover), on the fourteenth of Nisan, as did the Jews, regardless of the day of the week. Taking into consideration the meaning of the fundamental fact of who we really are, "the knowledge of the ineffable Greatness," the wise prudence of Irenaeus shows no anxiety to denounce either side. He maintained that differences in external issues such as dates of festivals and so forth need not be considered so vital as to destroy the "unity of the Spirit." Irenaeus quoted Saint Paul in his letter to the Ephesians,

> Do your best to preserve the unity which the Spirit gives, by the peace that binds you together. There is one body [manifestation] and one Spirit ['1'] . . . There is one God and Father of all men, who is Lord of all, *works through all*, and IS IN ALL (Eph 4:36).

The Return of the Eternal Return: Cosmic Grandeur of the Teaching

Irenaeus became the leading Christian theologian of the second century. He advanced the development of an authoritative canon of Scriptures, the creed (with the focal point being on God the Father, the Son, and the Holy Spirit), and the authority of the episcopal office. In his classic work of five books entitled *Adversus Haereses* (*Against Heresies*), Irenaeus communicates the Christ's message of our ancestry and our *around the loop* adventure: from Godhead to Godhead—from the Light of lights to the Light of lights—from nothingness (a single point or cosmic singularity) to nothingness (a single point or cosmic singularity). I will go into more detail in physics part 2: from nonbeing ("nothingness," a cornerstone in scientific theory today) to appearance (physical existence, manifestation) then back to nonbeing.

Jesus delineated the path of leaving the One (the Logos), narrated in the parable of the Prodigal Son, by means of entering the world of physical existence (including that of space-time), and finally, returning to the '1'. Irenaeus stated in AD 190:

GOD THE LOGOS BECAME WHAT WE ARE, IN ORDER
THAT WE MAY BECOME WHAT HE HIMSELF IS[1]
[emphasis added]

Irenaeus' statement is extremely significant. He reminds us that the
Old One himself took on a physical body and bears witness to our
sacred unity, i.e., "A human being is a part of the whole, called by us the
'Universe,'" as Einstein, Heisenberg, Schrödinger, and Hammarskjöld
recognized.

Irenaeus presents evolution contained *within* the '1', the clear Light
(consciousness)—not evolution *of* consciousness. How "you may
understand who you are, in what way you exist, and how you will come to
be," as Jesus declared (Lk 17:20), or, as noted before, "God the Logos
became what we are . . ."). This outlook radically improves the
"landscape" of the standard grasp, of the link between the "Unchanging
Infinity" and the manifest universe.

The insight traces a recurring blueprint in other traditions that
the present life is not the highest expression of reality, such as presented
by Shakyamuni Buddha and Lao-tzu, and predates by eighteen
centuries Pierre Teilhard de Chardin (1881-1955), the French Jesuit
paleontologist and seminal thinker of the Omega Point cosmology.[2]
The idea of our progression in awareness had to await later rediscovery
by contemporary science (Darwin, the big bang). Where we have come
from and to where are we heading as Irenaeus acknowledged earlier,
"God became what we are, in order that we may become what he
Himself is."

Notice: cosmic advancement (Ibn Arabi's "perpetual transformation":
the manifestations of Altruistic Love are in constant flux) from one state
to another (infant, teenager, adult) is an invariable process; our awareness
rises to higher and higher levels. The process continues from birth to
encampment on the other shore (infant, teenager, adult) every day,
although its results are not always perceptible.

Paraphrasing Irenaeus, it can be stated the Logos, or Uncreated Light
(*lux prima*), changed Her/Himself into us, disguised Her/Himself in
fancy masquerade costumes of a captivating woman or a charismatic
man, descended into a variety of grades of being, partaking in their
natures, so that we can grow forward to the totality of the unmanifest
and Constant Light.

A Profound Sense of Wonder:
We Originated from the Light

The Gospel of Thomas provides us with yet another view:

> Jesus said: "Blessed are the solitary and elect [those who have connected with purity of heart, love, and inner peace], for you shall find the kingdom; because you come from it [you have started off from the clear Light ('1'), Irenaeus' "God became what we are"] (and) you shall go there again" [Irenaeus' "that we may become what he Himself is"].
>
> Jesus said, "If they say to you: 'From where have you originated?' say to them: '*We have come from the Light, where the Light has originated through itself.*' [*Note:* in the creation saga of Manu, *Svayambhy* in Sanskrit is the First Cause, which is "existing out of itself," where all things in the universe exist through itself or the idea hidden within each of them.] It (stood) and It revealed itself in their image. If they say to you: '(Who) are you?' say: 'We are His sons and we are the elect of the Living Father.' If they ask you: 'What is the sign of your Father *in you*?' say to them: 'It is a movement [Becoming, manifestation] and a rest [Being, stillness, empty-space]'" (emphasis added, 49-50).[3]

Here we see two views of God: Being (Absolute Perfection = unmanifest reality = at rest consciousness = outside of space and time) = '1', and Becoming (relative perfection = manifest reality = thinking consciousness = in flux or motion of time and space) = physical quantities. The *rest* and *motion* idea has been expressed in the Old Testament by, "I Am What I Am" and "I will be what I will be" (Ex 3:14).

The explosive creation of the universe was postulated by the big bang theory (1950-55), as illustrated by Roger Penrose[4] and Steven Hawking,[5] at a single point ("where the Light has originated *through itself*") as (naked) singularity. Also, we know from physics: to every action (appearance) there is an equal and opposite reaction (disappearance). This means that creation at a *point* (singularity in empty-space) must be stabilized by annihilation at a point (singularity in empty-space).

212

What is my point? Jesus "knew that he had come from God and was going to God" (Jn 13:3). We start at the '1' and we end at the '1', from the so-called big bang to the so-called big crunch.

Does the book of Genesis in reality speak about the fall of Adam and Eve or is it the preface against a broader background? "We have come from the Light, where the Light has originated through itself." Also, the preamble to the *genesis of perfection and fulfillment* through "the tree of knowledge of good and bad."

What happens when we superimpose upon the Genesis equation Irenaeus' "God became what we are, in order that we may become what he Himself is?" When we add to the New Testament Paul's new Adam Christology in Romans 5 and 1 Corinthians 15, the book of Genesis: "See! The man has become like one of us . . ." To what does this traditional reading of the Bible point?

Irenaeus put it well. He does not assert God the Logos became the Christ, so that the Christ may become God the Logos. He declared God the Logos became *what we are.*

The Lord's Prayer is one of the most important Christian records. It is without a doubt the most recognized and the most regularly recited. The great prayer is a simple but concise blueprint for our growth. Jesus astutely formulated it with our development in view. The more I study the Lord's Prayer, the more profound I find its formula for the expansion of the spirit.

In the first two words "Our Farther" passage, Jesus presents the relationship between the nature of God and the nature of humanity, that of parent and the offspring of God. Notice, the Nazarene does not say *my* Father, but *our* Father. With one stroke Jesus confirms the Fatherhood of God *and* the Oneness (the sisterhood and the brotherhood) of the human family.

Do you appreciate Jesus' deep thinking? Do you understand why we should know who we are? Why "Our Father" thinking can free us from obscured theologies and belief systems? Why people who realized the highest, transcendent consciousness within themselves (through purity of heart, inner peace, union with the one great Life) keep urging others to "know Thy Self" (Socrates); "know the truth" (Jesus), "know the true nature of the visible world . . . who you really are" (Gnostic)? "All we need to do is open our eyes and then we [will] see that the true and complete Geulah [Redemption] is already here," as Melech HaMoshiach declared.

God Lives in You as You

Saint Athanasius (AD 293-373) was a recognized ecclesiastical statesman, theologian, Egyptian national leader, and ascetic and the great defender of the Council of Nicaea. In his *The Incarnation of the Word of God* (completed about 335), the first great classic of developed Greek Orthodox theology, he restated our great adventure:

> The Divine Word became human in order that every human being may become God.[6]

About 150 years earlier, Saint Clement of Alexandria phrased this point as follows:

> The Word of God became man that you also may learn from a man how a man becomes a God.

In his skillfully crafted diary like passage, Thomas Merton lays bare an analogous revelation by Irenaeus:

> God became man in Christ. In becoming what I am, He united me to Himself and made me His epiphany [appearance or manifestation], so that now I am meant to reveal Him.[7]

Meister Eckhart (1260-1327) of Cologne, Germany, was one of the spiritual giants of the Dominican order whose insights contributed to the development of Protestantism, Idealism, and Existentialism. He was exceptionally well-read, ecumenical in his thought, selfless, kind, and supportive of freedom and peace.

Eckhart practiced patience, righteousness, humility, and gratitude. Like Saint Paul and Shakyamuni Buddha, Eckhart understood the state of union with the Love of loves and Light of lights, described in both his Latin and German works. The "Nameless One" was his light and refuge. In Eckhart's outlook, most people are only partially awake and conscious. He was able to *let go* and laugh at himself while men in power, reminiscent of what they did to Jesus, his cousin Saint John the Baptist, Socrates, and others, did their best to bring him down. Eckhart was a man of immense talent, and a richly cultured mind, light-years ahead of his time in his part of the world in probing the nature of the ultimate ground of life. His life and practical wisdom offer a means of self-transformation. Addressing what we will become, he said:

> If it is true that God became man, it is also true that man became God.[8]

Forty years ago, the Indian holy man Muktananda, during one of his discourses in New York City, pointed out:

> Remember that God himself assumes human forms and lives in the world.[9]

Ibn Arabi (1165-1240), one of the greatest Islamic mystical teachers, symbolized the heart of early Christianity's "unity of the Spirit" in terms of the "unity of being" (the Real: *al-haqq*). Like Irenaeus' "unity of the Spirit" and the Sufis' "Unity of Existence," Ibn Arabi considered that "Everything is He" which is beyond all names and polarities.

Ibn Arabi's mind penetrated deep, enabling him to systematize his experiences and thoughts. "Everything is in perfect order," said he. Similar to Skovoroda, Yogananda, and Dag Hammarskjöld, Ibn Arabi declared the Real—his Beloved—existing as a reciprocal relationship, with various attributes refracted through the *prism of human consciousness* into the universe observed. He understood that like the spectrum of light:

> We ourselves are the attributes by which we describe God; our existence is merely an objectification of His existence. God is necessary to us in order that we may exist, while we are necessary to Him in order that he may be manifested to Himself.[10]

Ibn Arabi saw God, the Infinite Splendor, as disclosing it(self) to it(self) through it(self): "I give Him also life, by knowing Him in my heart." When Ibn Arabi asks who is the source of our perceptions, he then answers:

> When my Beloved appears,
> With what eye do I see Him?
> With his eye, not with mine,
> For none sees Him except Himself.[11]

"Seeing God means realization of the fact that God abides in our hearts," said Mahatma Gandhi, one of the most outstanding men of the twentieth century. "The yearning must persist until one has attained this realization, and will vanish upon realization. Realization is the final fruit of constant effort. God is there in the tabernacle of the heart." Meister Eckhart phrased Ibn Arabi's insight this way, "to see God means to see as God sees," and, "The eye with which I see God is the very eye with which God sees in me." Yes, God sees Himself through our eyes and hearts.

Saint Symeon the New Thoelogian, in *Hymns of Divine Love*, proclaims: "If you do not see Him, know that you are blind, though you are in the midst of the light." At another time he stated:

> Poor creature though I be, I am the hand and foot of Christ, I move my hand and my hand is wholly Christ's hand, for deity is become inseparable one with me. I move my foot, and it is aglow with God.

Ernest Renan (1823-1892), French philosopher, historian, and scholar of the history of religious origins, wrote:

> Were the men who have best comprehended God—Shakyamuni [Buddha], Plato, Saint Paul, Saint Francis d'Assisi, and Saint Augustine (at some periods of his fluctuating life)—Deists or Pantheists? Such a question has no meaning. The physical and metaphysical proofs of the existence of God were indifferent to them. They felt the Divine within themselves. We must place Jesus in the first rank of this great family of the true sons of God. Jesus had no visions; God did not speak to him as to one outside of himself; God was in him; he felt himself with God, and he drew from his heart all he said of his Father.[11a]

Seeing Our Own Footprint

Werner Heisenberg, one of the high priests of the orthodox quantum creed, wrote in his beautiful book *The Physicist's Conception of Nature*:

> Here already we get a foretaste of the essential insight of modern physics stated with such impressive brevity by Eddington: "We

have found that where science has progressed the farthest, the mind has but regained from nature that which the mind has put into nature. We have found a strange footprint on the shores of the unknown. We have devised profound theories, one after another, to account for its origin. At last, we have succeeded in reconstructing the creature that made the footprint. And lo! It is our own."[12]

Heisenberg concluded that this courageous insight by Eddington is impressive. The statement remains memorable as we consider recent developments and contributions by the grand theorists of contemporary physics: Bohr, de Broglie, Eddington, Einstein, Jeans, Pauli, Planck, and Schrödinger.

Those who have perceived their own nature, attained Irenaeus' "knowledge of the ineffable Greatness," have taken a journey of the self through the self to the self, and are aware of their root being (out of amnesia) can validate: the "strange footprint on the shores of the unknown . . . it is our own." Indeed, "We are a part of the mystery that we are trying to solve," declared Max Planck.

The Christ verbalized this perception to the paradox of identity, "I am in my Father, and you are in me, and I am in you." Shouldn't the poor, the handicapped, and the rejected find a new hope as Jesus stated? Shouldn't those who have not yet perceived their own nature, who have not yet taken a journey of the self to the self, be given the opportunity to realize that our cosmos is a friendly purposeful totality, and that we are an essential element of the continuing process of universal unfolding? Edgar Mitchel had this opportunity through the U.S. Navy and NASA:

Ever since I was a young child I've thought that there was more to life than meets the eye. As a scientist, it's been my passion to search for answers to the unknown—which is why I happened to be the sixth man to walk on the moon.

I was a 27-year-old test pilot for the U.S. Navy when the Sputnik satellite was launched into space in 1957. I knew that humans would soon follow and set my goal to be one of them. I volunteered for NASA, and thirteen years later I was a member of the Apollo 14 crew.

On the way back home from the moon, as I was gazing out the window at Mother Earth, the awe-inspiring beauty of the cosmos suddenly overcame me. While still aware of the separateness of my existence, my mind was flooded with an intuitive knowing that everything is interconnected—that this magnificent universe is a harmonious, directed, purposeful whole. And that we humans, both as individuals and as a species, are an integral part of the ongoing process of creation.

When I got back to Earth, I immediately shifted my exploration from the outer regions of space to the inner realms of the mind. It was to become my Holy Grail. Six months later, I resigned from NASA and founded the Institute of Noetic Sciences with the mission to scientifically study the nature and potential of consciousness.

Swami Rama was a knowledgeable teacher who spoke through his experience. In a journey of the individual self through the self to the self, he elaborated:

The Vedic Scriptures declare that the Brahman [nondual consciousness] became "Many" [individual selves] to realize its own glory and greatness. This manyness or plurality is but a transformation assumed by the Absolute, which in its totality remains the One without a second. Ignorant men make themselves mere toys in the hands of diversity. They go through this world of contingencies and delusions without gaining anything worth having. They create for themselves an eternal cycle of births and deaths from which they are unable to escape. The teachings of the Upanishadas show the path of liberation from this cycle of births and rebirths.[13]

10

BEFORE THE BEGINNING,
BEFORE THE HOT BIG BANG

We can see galaxies that cannot have seen each other.
How did they and their environments know to look so similar?

—P.J.E. Peebles

'1': A Simple Way of Saying Complicated Things

The Upanishads deal with the origin and general structure of the universe existing prior to the "creation" of space, time, and the self-evolution of nature towards greater consciousness. In today's terms, they address the state of the universe *before* the standard big bang event—a point outside contemporary big bang cosmology, yet not devoid of the laws of physics. The Upanishads describe preexisting archetypal patterns. A primordial pattern of this kind serves as a prototype of original models or blueprints from which a thing is made or copied prior to its excursion out of nonbeing (modern physics the world of possibilities) into the natural frontiers of physical existence. The Upanishads state:

> In the beginning this world was merely nonbeing [the pre-quantum fact], [1]

The *nonbeing* is Katha Upanishad's *consciousness,* Lao-tzu's *cosmic void,* the Christ's *Spirit,* Newton's *empty vacuum* or *absolute space,* Einstein's *ether.* [2] Physicists refer to this state as the not-modulated primordial empty-space, or a wave of possibilities. Also, the state of "nonbeing" can be viewed as the ordering principle of the universe, the universal source code, or the '1', which has passed rigorous tests of approval by the scientific community, without realizing it, in the laws of physics.[3]

In the beginning, it was not from a complete void in our familiar world of experience that an object suddenly appeared out of nowhere. Imagine leaving your living room for a second, going to the kitchen, and upon returning finding the living room filled to the ceiling with people, birds, and animals. In daily life we expect everything to come from something or from somewhere. So it does!

What sparked the bang of the big bang? What conditions existed just prior to this blossoming event to trigger the birth of the modern universe, as we know it? Does the phenomenon arise at all in the absence of an observer?

Potentiality: Uncarved Marble

Michelangelo Buonarroti (1475-1564), one of the greatest and most versatile artists (sculptor, painter, architect, and poet) of the Renaissance, who sculpted the *Pieta* (now in Saint Peter's Basilica), *David* (in Florence), *Madonna* (two sculptures), among others, maintained that his works were inside the blocks of marble awaiting his liberation with hammer and chisel. Jan Skacel, a Czech poet, relays it through another metaphor: "Poets don't invent poems. The poem is somewhere behind. It's been there a long long time. The poet merely discovers it."

Now visualize that you are a sculptor and that your life, like Michelangelo's works, exists inside an enormous block of marble ('1'), where you are freeing a particular experience into a space-time reality. Keep in mind all that exists, has existed, or will ever exist has been in existence as a potentiality, the undivided field of '1'. All that comes to pass, like carving a statue out of a slab of the "uncarved" marble, expresses how "dormant" elements of the undivided '1' are made manifest.

John von Neumann declared, "When I close my eyes, the whole world is a wave of [unmanifest] possibilities; when I open my eyes, consciousness collapses these waves of possibilities into [manifested] reality." The Katha Upanishad describes consciousness:

> That ['1'] which cannot be seen by the eyes, but because of which the eyes are able to see; that which cannot be heard by the ears, but because of which the ears are able to hear; that which cannot be

thought by the mind, but because of which the mind is able to think."

In the Gospel of John we read, "Before the world was created, the Word already existed; he was with God, and he was the same as God . . . The light shines in the darkness, and the darkness has never put it out" (Jn 1:1-5).

It is the same with your calculator. The calculator, as we all are aware, has the capability (preexisting internal program) to count/display numbers zero through nine in a particular changeless order. Likewise, the '1' ("cosmic DNA") has the potential to count, self-organize and to reveal an infinite variety of preexisting pure ideas (Plato) or archetypal images (C. G. Jung) in the cosmic calculator, according to an *invariant mathematical order*. Nick Herbert wrote:

> As a way of thinking about quantum reality, Heisenberg proposed that a quantum entity's unobserved attributes are not fully real but exist in an attenuated state of being called potentia ['1'] until the act of observation promotes some lucky attribute to full reality status.[4]

It should be noted that without the preexistence of an archetypal program in the '1', the scientific method, the procedure scientists use to acquire knowledge, such as transformation between two systems of coordinates (measuring the initial phenomena, then the phenomena after an experiment) would be impossible. Currently, physicists are learning through a Bose-Einstein condensate (BEC, where hundreds of thousands of atoms gather in the same quantum-mechanical state) and the renowned but strange Schrödinger's cat (which exists in a quantum state that is at the same time alive and dead) the subtle ways in the macroscopic world.

As light produces a precise spectrum of light, an electron leaps from "one orbit" around the nucleus of an atom to "another orbit," *without passing through the space in between or time delay*, or DNA generates a genetic alphabet, the preexistence of archetypes or primordial images makes such transformations in invariance possible. The experiment of two photons or light particles with the same spin or polarization shows that if the polarization of one photon changed, the second photon knows before a signal has reached it.

Jeremiah declared, "The word of the Lord came to me, saying, 'Before I formed you in the womb I knew you, before you were born I set you apart; I appointed you as a prophet to the nations'" (1:4). In the Gospel of Thomas, Jesus stated, "I am he who exists from the undivided ['1']" (Logion 62).

We Choose—We Create

Spinning the world's web, getting the real and unadorned facts on high-definition TV, human life, the texture of the universe, and their organization, are all *derivatives* of the preexistent "potentia" ('1'), accounting for the reality and meaning of all. However, the actual process of manifestation does not become visible until *we* start making choices ("creating," counting).

"How didst Thou make the heaven and the earth?" asked Saint Augustine. *We* (the observer) *must begin projecting patterns of excitation by our mind.* The state of nonbeing is the zero condition in the calculator's window, or the "uncarved" block of marble before carving is commenced.

In the quantum world of the Copenhagen interpretation (developed at Niels Bohr's Copenhagen Institute), it is maintained that the potentiality (the unmeasured atom) is not yet actual: its attributes are formed in the act of observation (creation, measurement).

Before manifesting begins, every preexistent image of time, space, high-definition home theater, or the baking of an edible delicacy in '1' is invisible. Each is only a potential possibility—the ordering principle within the infinity of potentialities ('1'). The baking of the cake occurs in the sequence of cake making—after everything has been mixed and not before. This is a condition *prior* to relativity and to the so-called hot big bang, wherein the "cosmic" calculator begins to "count and display." It is at this point that the unfolding universe manifests. The Upanishads suggest:

> In the beginning this world was merely nonbeing ['1']. It was existent. [The Word already existed (Jn 1:1)] It developed. It turned into an egg. It lay for the period of a year. [Then the projecting patterns and the space-time excitation began.] It was split asunder. One of the two eggshell-parts became silver, one gold. That which was of silver is this earth. That which was of gold is the sky. What

was the outer membrane is the mountains. What was the inner membrane is cloud and mist. What were the veins are the rivers. What was the fluid within is the ocean.[5]

Plato, Aristotle, and others deliberated on the question of preexistent pure ideas or archetypal patterns. In modern times, Werner Heisenberg (*Across the Frontiers*), Johannes Kepler (*Harmony of the World*), Wolfgang Pauli (*Philosophical Outlook*), and C. G. Jung, amongst others, also pondered this problem. Following is Heisenberg's summary of Pauli's position:

> The process of understanding in nature, together with the joy that man feels in understanding, i.e., in becoming acquainted with new knowledge, seems therefore to rest upon a correspondence, a coming into congruence of preexistent internal images of the human psyche with external objects and their behavior. This view of natural knowledge goes back, of course, to Plato and was . . . also very plainly adopted by Kepler. The latter speaks, in fact, of Ideas, preexistent in the mind of God and imprinted accordingly upon the soul, as the images of God. These primal images, which the soul can perceive by means of an innate instinct, Kepler calls archetypes. There is very wide-ranging agreement here with the primordial images or archetypes introduced into modern psychology by C.G. Jung, which function as instinctive patterns of ideation . . . As ordering operators and formatives in this world of symbolic images, the archetypes function, indeed, as the desired bridge between sense perceptions and Ideas, and are, therefore, also a necessary precondition for the emergence of a scientific theory. Yet, one must beware of displacing this a priori of knowledge into consciousness, and relating it to specific, rationally formulable Ideas.[6]

The '1' pervades everything. It is the preexistent God consciousness or Superconsciousness that the individual consciousness is able to perceive. It is the Ground of our human experience, and, thus, is everything we see and know. It is formless, timeless, and motionless. It is unchangeable, invisible, and appearing as *stillness* or *nothingness*.

As might be expected, *it* (the '1') itself is everything that exists or will ever exist. The '1' pervades present and future, like numbers within a calculator, or marble limestone before it is carved and polished. All that happens is a manifestation of the originally latent elements in the '1'.

Recall when Luke, the beloved physician (Col 4:14), declared: "He (the '1') is not far from each one of us. For "in Him we live and move and have our being" (Acts 17:27-28). Luke in essence said that the entire universe is the Absolute Presence. Marble limestone remains marble limestone, no matter what design you carve on it. Or as the Heart Sutra, one of the most profound sutras of Mahayana Buddhism, states, "Form is no other than emptiness, emptiness is no other than form."

Meaning: Distance between Points

Although each point of '1' is identical/dimensionless, and the empty-space of points is a transfinite ocean of potentiality, our perception of the '1' changes as we alter our point of view. Specifically, as we observe or measure the interval between points, or the boundaries between the initial ('1') and the final ('=') conditions of measurement. This interval between points, like interval between notes, determines the meaning of manifestation. The variation before/after enlightenment is not in the ultimate reality or God, but in our point of view. We awaken from a physical and spiritual death into a new life and the realization that the "All," which scientists characterize in the laws of physics with the '1', is everywhere, at every point in the universe.

As Jesus in the Gospel of Thomas affirms, we create our own personal reality:

> I am the light which is over everything. I am the All; (from me) the All has gone forth, and to me the All has returned. Split wood: I am there. Lift up the stone, and you will find me there (77).

Why are physical laws invariable, infinite? They describe "that which is" invariable, infinite. The laws of physics represent measurements between the unchanging points of '1' in equilibrium. They characterize the difference in their relation, between the Alpha (the initial conditions—zero) and the Omega (the final conditions—infinity) within the '1' (Absolute Infinity). In other words, physical laws describe the variation or distinction between "the First and the Last, the Beginning and the End" of the great book of God (Rev 22:13), which is explained in more detail, in part 2, chapters 5-8. What is seen and experienced is the empty-space, gap, or separation between the Alpha and the Omega boundaries in the '1', similar to measuring distance between the wingtips of a bird, or between steps.

Hierarchical Structure: The Pecking Order of Grace

The ocean of '1' or the great emptiness, reminiscent of the electromagnetic spectrum, has unique properties. In the electromagnetic spectrum, various frequency ranges assume different outward appearances. When interacting with matter, some wavelengths or frequencies, resembling various lengths of a jump rope, appear to our senses as sound, others as visible light or color, still others as heat, the fragrance of the forest, or a cool west wind under the stars.

Similarly, in pure nothingness (the unobstructed universe), different excitation lengths of the '1' (natural currencies), like various currency coins, bear different faces. Some natural units of measurement or archetypes of the '1' appear to us as time, others as people or matter, still others, like gems against the black velvet of space. The time/space/matter of physics, termed physical quantities, have been referred to by the Upanishads as membranes and eggshells.

We can also equate "membranes" and "shells" of the '1' plenum to a calculator's display window. Calculator windows have glass membranes on which numbers are etched. The numbers are arranged in a fixed sequence and can be energized according to a fixed formula. Although at a given moment one can display a particular number, each window has a capacity to display other numbers within the same space.

Just as the egg has a predetermined number of layers of shells and yolks, and the calculator has a fixed sequence on which numbers are etched, so does the smallest bit of the '1' have a fixed *hierarchical structure* of the natural units of measurement (physical quantities, elements [the Periodic Table of Elements], DNA, and so forth).

Creative Process: Working with Perfection

Gennady Shipov of the International Institute for Theoretical and Applied Physics, Russian Academy of Natural Sciences, wrote, "The idea that the great emptiness, or vacuum, is a source of the world that surrounds us dates back to centuries ago. According to the thinking of ancient philosophers of the Orient, all the material objects emerge from the great emptiness, are its integral part, and, in that sense, are illusionary. In the great emptiness itself, acts of creation of real objects continually occur."[7]

Theoretical physicist and 1933 Nobel laureate, Paul Dirac was the originator of many major breakthroughs. He devised a new form of quantum mechanics and developed a theory that predicted electron spin, introduced the quantum theory of radiation and was coinventor of Fermi-Dirac statistics. Today, his work underscores the ancient vision of creation in the Upanishads, that matter is created out of nonbeing (total emptiness, all-pervading nothingness), the zero-state in your calculator's window. Dirac stated:

> All matter is created out of some imperceptible substratum and . . .
> The creation of matter leaves behind it a "hole" in this substratum
> which appears as antimatter [matter composed of particles with opposite
> quantum number to standard particles]. Now, this substratum itself is
> not accurately described as material, since it uniformly fills all space and
> is undetectable by any observation. In a sense, it appears as
> nothingness—immaterial, undetectable and omnipresent. But it is a
> peculiarly material form of nothingness out of which all matter is
> created.[8]

The Bhagavad Gita, composed by the renowned sage Vyasa, most likely in the first or second century AD, forms part of Book VI of the Indian epic Mahabharata, and is the essence of the Vedas and the Upanishads. It has been called the most significant and most beautiful of the Hindu Scriptures. Henry David Thoreau wrote, "In the morning I bathe my intellect in the stupendous and cosmogonal philosophy of the Bhagavad Gita, in comparison with which our modern world and its literature seem puny and trivial."

Ralph Waldo Emerson declared, "I owed a magnificent day to the Bhagavad Gita. It was the first of books; it was as if an empire spoke to us, nothing small or unworthy, but large, serene, consistent, the voice of an old intelligence which in another age and climate had pondered and thus disposed of the same questions which exercise us." Mohandas K. Gandhi stated, "When doubts haunt me, when disappointments stare me in the face, and I see not one ray of hope on the horizon, I turn to Bhagavad Gita and find a verse to comfort me; and I immediately begin to smile in the midst of overwhelming sorrow. Those who meditate on Gita will derive fresh joy and new meanings from it every day." "The message of the Bhagavad Gita," confirmed Philip Novak,

> Is that each human life has but one ultimate end and purpose: to realize the Eternal Self within and thus to know, finally and fully, the joy of union with God, the Divine Ground of Being (Brahman). Whereas such knowledge was traditionally sought in retreat from the world, the Gita, without omitting that option, teaches that it may be attained in the midst of the world through nonattached action in the context of devotion (bhakti) to God.[9]

The religious genius and Hindu sage, Vyasa, went far beyond religious thought and ethical questions. He broadly considered, similar to our twentieth century physicists Paul Dirac, Albert Einstein, David Bohm, Erwin Schrödinger, and Wolfgang Pauli (as summarized earlier by Werner Heisenberg), *The Nature of God*—the nature of Paul Dirac's imperceptible substratum ('**1**')—and the means by which men and women can know themselves. Vyasa in simple yet masterly style composed:

> All created beings [all states of the universe, the Great Spectrum of Being] are unmanifest in their beginning [invisible like a film before its projection, suspended or frozen in time], manifest in their interim state [reactivated or projected on a movie screen], and unmanifest again [back on the shelf] when they are annihilated [2.28]. Never was there a time when I did not exist [as an archetype or a fundamental region of pre-physical potentiality ['**1**'] in the foundations of physics], nor you, nor all these kings; nor in the future shall any of us cease to be. As the embodied soul continually passes, in this body, from boyhood to youth to old age, the soul similarly passes into another body at death. The self-realized soul is not bewildered by such a change [2.12-13].[10]

The Psalmist, David, inscribed, "I knew you before you were in your mother's womb." The prophet Moses recalled his encounter with the Eternal '**1**', quoting "I am that I am." The great Rabbuni pointed out, "Before you existed I am."

Similar to Jesus, with his profound Sermon on the Mount (Mt 5), Lao-tzu suggested that the most effective "Way" to conquer hardships or challenges (part 2, chapter 10, '1': The Principle above the Laws of Nature) is by yielding (such as noncontention, "turn the other cheek," universal love) or taking the "Way" of least resistance, simplicity, and responsibility. He considered life softness and flexibility, death, rigidity, and inflexibility. Lao-tzu suggested that all opposites (day/night, man/woman) mutually support one another and are inseparable and complementary.

Tao Te Ching is a "Teacher of teachers" and a diamond mine of wisdom and insight on the nature of '1'. Of the many elucidations available, three are especially laudable: Wang Pi (Wang Bi), Ho-shang Kung (Heshang gong), and Han-shan Te-ch'ing (Hanshan Dwqing). Following are nine lines quoting Lao-tzu's characterization of the '1':

> There is a thing inherent and natural
> Which existed before heaven and earth.
> It is motionless and fathomless.
> It stands alone and never changes [is invariant];
> It pervades everywhere and never becomes exhausted.
> It may be regarded as the Mother of the Universe [foundation of
>   nature].
> I do not know its name [It's "nameless"];
> If I am forced to give it a name,
> I will call it Tao, and I name it as supreme.[11]

About the same time as Lao-tzu's philosophical school and the religious brotherhood of Taoism was being established in China, Pythagoras of Samos was founding a movement in southern Italy (Croton). Pythagoras proposed the divine origin and nature of the soul, Irenaeus' "God became what we are," and the possibility of its rising to union with the divine, that "we may become what he Himself is"—the cosmos blossoming consciously into divine being.

Akin to Paul Dirac, David Bohm, professor of theoretical physics at the University of London, gives us additional insight on how "God the Logos becomes visible" out of the "implicate order" or the *nothingness* plenum. In Bohm's model of "implicate order" the universal etching occurs by sustained patterns of excitation (constant unearthing of '1':

"continuous creation"), like projecting successive movie frames onto a screen. It is a deeply felt, powerfully conceived and beautifully explained work: the Logos projects onto a multidimensional screen of Reality. Bohm described the emergence in contemporary physical terms:

> It is being suggested here, then, that what we perceive through the senses as empty space is actually the plenum, which is the ground for the existence of everything, including ourselves. The things that appear to our senses are derivative forms [primordial images], and their true meaning can be seen only when we consider the plenum, in which they are generated and sustained, and into which they must ultimately vanish. This plenum is, however, no longer to be conceived through the idea of a simple material medium, such as ether, which would be regarded as existing and moving only in a three-dimensional space.
>
> Rather, one is to begin with the holomovement, in which there is the immense "sea" of energy described earlier. This sea is to be understood in terms of a multidimensional implicate order [the Absolue Infinity, '1', in equations of physics, to be discussed later], while the entire universe of matter as we generally observe it is to be treated as a comparatively small pattern of excitation [of infinities]. This excitation pattern is relatively autonomous and gives rise to approximately recurrent stable and separable projections into a three-dimensional explicate order of manifestation, which is more or less equivalent to that of space as we commonly experience it.[12]

Empty-Space = The Spirit of God

The Unchanging State has been characterized as the "colorless light of emptiness," from which all forms of existence can be abstracted. The '1' has also been described as the "self-activating" (in Wheeler's "self-excited circuit"), numerically based universal harmony found in the observations of Pythagoras[13, 14] and Euclid,[15] having the faculty to be observant of things in a mathematically discriminating manner.

Religious thinkers have characterized the ultimate reference point or the '1' as "Spirit" (Jn 4:24), such as, "It is the Spirit that gives life" (Jn 6:63); and, "From the Void comes a thousand things."[16] Modern ascriptions term the First Cause of the universe as an empty-space and cosmic vacuum, the Ground of our own Being, pure consciousness, nonexistence, and the Void.[17, 18]

Parmenides argued the "emptiness is nothingness."[19] Basil Hiley writes, "To him vacuum was a compact plenum which is regarded as being constituted as one continuous unchanging whole."[20] Plotinus (205-270), whose ideas bear some remarkable parallels to those of Ishvarakrishna's (350-425) Verses on the Sankhya, explained it in the following manner: "[Emptiness] is Everything and Nothing; it can be none of the existing things, and yet it is all."[21]

To Eckhart, "the Godhead is as void as though it were not." He states, "The Godhead gave all things up to God. The Godhead is poor, naked and empty as though it were not; it has not, wills not, wants not, works not, gets not. It is God who has the treasure and the bride in him, the Godhead is as void as though it were not."[22]

Jen Eddy wrote in *Rain on the Roof*, "Deep in the center of my being a boundless void with limitless space is drawing me to a place where I connect with my God." "I have made the journey into Nothing," affirmed Hafiz. "I have become that flame that needs no fuel."[23]

The void, "ultimate space," or empty vacuum, furnished an explanation for the development of Newtonian physics, with "corpuscles" moving through the vacuum. At the very beginning of Newton's *Principia*, we find the famous Scholium dealing with the concept of absolute space: "Absolute space, in its own nature, without relation to anything external, remains always similar and immovable. Relative space is some measure of the absolute space; which our senses determine by its position to bodies."[24]

Indeed, we shall see that the unity, truth, goodness and consistency of the universe points to a single cause. This deep insight is an unvarying theme within the framework of the sacred writers, prophets, evangelists and scientists who have revealed, exhaustively annotated and supported by credible evidence the '1' (see the One and the Many, part 2, chapter 5).

11

THE CREATOR PLAYS HIDE-AND-SEEK—AS US

The Spirit shall look out through matter's gaze
And matter shall reveal the Spirit's face.

—Sri Aurobindo

You Are Not a Butterfly:
You Are Older Than the Universe

If you could, would you change your present human form to that of an ant, Heschel's rooster, or Chuang-tzu's butterfly? What would it be like to live, eat, and school these life forms that there are no enemies, only brothers and sisters to be educated, as Jesus, Gandhi, and Martin Luther King Jr. did?

Would you accept the challenge to teach them advanced methods of unity and healing: forgiveness, reconciliation, selfless compassion, kindheartedness, or making a better livelihood, experiencing being human? Would you do so if you knew this would enable the lower forms of consciousness to recoup their memory loss of unity and transform themselves into members of the human race, brothers and sisters in Spirit—or as Willis Harman put it, "Look at all the evidence . . . we are all relatives."

The change to lower forms of living is no bed of roses. Who among us is equal to such a task? How much compassion would this changeover demand within our heart? How much love would be necessary if you knew you were going to think like a human in the ant/rooster/butterfly world? How much concern and love would be needed if you knew in advance that life was going to be dangerous, hand-to-mouth existence, with no sanitation or garbage-disposal systems other than the nearest door or window. And that they would harass you, rather than embrace you, spit on your eyes, smote your cheeks, and murder you for motivating them to become human beings who are consciously alive with God's own life breath? "Greater love no one has but to lay down one's life for one's friends" (Jn 15:13), we learn from the apostle Saint John.

The Son of Man validated his compassion, daring, mercy, and group altruism throughout his life. He lived and displayed the majesty of his spirituality in the splendor of his dealings, in the profundity and lucidity of his wisdom. He left the Godhead state and entered into dimensional multiplicity, becoming man that we might become God again.[1]

The Christ's bold and daring leap of loving-kindness and selfless compassion ushers us to embrace the transcendent immanence of the celestial light-consciousness—to ride on the ray of "unity" into a new frontier beyond that of special relativity and general relativity—beyond what Heisenberg referred to as the "uncertainty principle." Jesus' life calls for us to wake up out of our amnesia of identity and to come to a higher awareness and live the life of divine altruism on earth. His life shows us that we have been living in finite laws of form and relativity. He invites us to enter the ultimate source of all aliveness and connected life:

> *You are not of the world* anymore than I belong to the world (Jn 17:16). You have been with me from the very beginning (Jn 15:27). I have told you this so that my joy may be in you, and that your joy may be complete (Jn 15:11), your sadness will turn into gladness (Jn 16:20).

His life, in the words of "Abe" Lincoln, speaks the truth, "Stand by your principles, stand by your guns, and victory complete and permanent is sure at last . . . Leave nothing for tomorrow which can be done today." Yes, you are not of the world anymore than Jesus belongs to the world. That we have come out of that "imperceptible substratum [the undifferentiated '1'] . . . . out of which all matter is created," as Paul Dirac magnificently stated.

Now, how can the "Unchanging Presence" bring to light Itself in us? The psalmist characterizes our amnesia as a hiding process:

> How long, O Lord? Will you hide yourself forever? (Ps 89:47).

Chou Chuang-tzu (369-286 BC) was one of the greatest Taoist philosophers. He and Lao-tzu are considered the creators of "philosophical Taoism." Chuang-tzu is often credited with advancing "relativism": what is good for one person may not be good for another. Chuang-tzu advanced the illusory nature of the universe. He realized that he existed, without form or substance, in a previous state before birth.

Chuang-tzu's themes are similar to Lao-tzu's on such matters as the nature of the Tao ('1'), the importance of spontaneity and effortless action, the relativity of opposites, the capacity to perceive fine distinctions without judging experience in terms of an ideal alternative, and the experience of unity. He realized that on the fundamental level, we are projections of our mind, dreamers dreaming within a dream. In his book, *Chuang-tzu*, what can be termed philosophical Taoism, at the end of chapter 2, Chuang-tzu equates himself (Tao) to a butterfly that does not know who he is:

> Once Chuang Chou dreamt he was a butterfly, a butterfly flitting and fluttering around, happy with himself and doing as he pleased. He didn't know he was Chuang Chou. Suddenly he woke up and there he was, solid and unmistakable Chuang Chou. But he didn't know if he was Chuang Chou who had dreamt he was a butterfly, or a butterfly dreaming he was Chuang Chou.[2]

You Are the Light of the World

How long can we camouflage ourselves in this self-generated concealment? We have within us what we need to know, that the kingdom of Light, the connecting zero-state, is within us. Remember:

> All those who are led by the Spirit of God are sons [and daughters] of God (Rom 8:14).

"The best moments of life," Emerson wrote in chapter six of *Nature*, "are these delicious awakenings of the higher powers, and the reverential withdrawing of nature before its God." The Son of the Living One tried to shake us out of our memory loss through resurrecting the dead, feeding multitudes, acts of divine kindness, and reminding us (the butterflies):

233

YOU ARE GODS (Jn 10:34).
YOU ARE THE LIGHT OF THE WORLD (Mt 5:14).

This is the extraordinary subtle fidelity Jesus strove so hard to convey. It is the bottom line of the grand mystery, the magnanimity that sets us free. It is the truth by which we are one and the same essence (Jn 14:20). It is that by which we are the same thing, formed within different containers of consciousness. Saint Augustine, called Doctor of Grace, characterized life's unity in this manner:

> We are all members of one Body, whether we are here or anywhere else on earth, now or at any other time from Abel the just to the end of the world.[3]

You Are Holiness in the Costume of Your Cosmos

Emerson aimed to empower people. He read Sanskrit, the Bhagavad Gita, Persian poets, Goethe, Kant, Hegel, and Dante. In *Nature*, Emerson wrote, "As a plant rests upon the earth, so a man rests upon the bosom of God." He understood that we are each an expression or a display of the Universal Mind. Emerson reprimanded America for its inability to expand its spiritual strength and asked scholars to live what they know. In *Heroism*, Emerson stated:

> Every man is a divinity in disguise, a god playing the fool.

I have noticed, *the more we become conscious that God lives in us, as us, and that God is expressing Himself through us, the more the universe will manifest its perfection in us, the more serendipities and miracles we experience in our daily lives.* When we relate this statement to the writing on this page, instead of thinking that we are *a*, *b*, or *c* descriptions, we become conscious that we are the "white" area (the well-known boundary, the Common Ground, or the connecting zero-state) between the *a*, *b*, or *c* metaphors.

Jesus lived from that perspective: "Whoever has seen me has seen the Father" (Jn 14:9), "Whoever sees me also sees Him" (Jn 12:45). He used the connecting zero-state phrases like "I am the door," "Be perfect," "Thy will be done," "By myself I do nothing," and so forth, to convey

234

his walking on water and restoring to life authority. Sathya Sai Baba states:

> Concentrate on developing the firm conviction that you are Divine. With this conviction you can achieve anything.

To Merton, it is more prudent to come into God through our own living experience in the purity of selfless love (speak good, do good, and the like) than through theology. Says he:

> One of the paradoxes of the mystical life is this: that a man cannot enter into the deepest center of himself and pass through that center into God, unless he is able to pass entirely out of himself and empty himself and give himself to other people in the purity of a selfless love.[4]

We come to Infinite Splendor ('1': compassion, freedom, peace, and Oneness) not merely as a concept, but as a living experience; not merely by talking about God, but by living and manifesting His heart, presence, and splendor in us. For two thousand years the Christ's endless miracles and heroics have been discussed and admired. They were meant to be frames for our Fraternal Master Painting, an ideal for living together—caring for one another and ensuring the well-being of one another. It is time for the marital celebration of humanity to begin, to realize the unbroken wholeness of life's totality:

> I assure you, as often as you did [give a cup of water] for one of my least brothers, you did for me (Mt 25:40).

"It may sometimes happen," shared Hasidic (Jewish mystic or follower of the Kabbalah) rabbi Shmelke of Nikolsburg:

> that thine own hand inadvertently strikes thee. Wouldst thou take a stick and chastise thy hand for its heedlessness, and thus add to thy pain? It is the same when thy neighbor, whose soul is one with thine, because of insufficient understanding, does thee harm: shouldst thou retaliate, it would be thou who wouldst suffer.[5]

Yes, "Consider others as yourself," declared the Buddha in Dhammapada (10.1). Robert Muller of Alsace Lorraine, France, reminded members of the United Nations, "If you want to be in communion with God, you cannot be intoxicated. Period." Furthermore, he wrote:

> To be fully human, we must tap into the primal energy of the universe. Plato held that the soul of the universe, incarnated in a human being, lost much of its qualities and became imperfect. The effort of human beings should be to strive back to the perfection of the soul and to feel part of the mysterious flow and throbbing life of the universe.[6]

Moments of Landmark Experience: Discovering Yourself

"Reality and perfection are synonymous," said Benedict de Spinoza (1632-1677). Life is existence and existence is life. For this reason, articulated Ralph Waldo Emerson:

> The purpose of life seems to be acquainting a man with himself. [And,] It is the effect of science to explain man to himself . . . [Emerson hoped that] the knowledge of all the facts of all the laws of nature will give man his true place in the system of beings.[7]

Jewish theologian Abraham Heschel suggests, "Living is not a private affair of the individual. Living is what man does with God's time, what man does with God's world."[8]

The search for human identity has been central to every religious tradition, every eminent philosophy, classic literature, grand music, and great art throughout the ages. The celebrated fourteenth century intellect, Meister Eckhart, gave joyful form to Muller's striving for "the perfection of the soul," and David Bohm's "multidimensional implicate order." Eckhart, similar to Dame Julian of Norwich, Madame Guyon, Mother Cabrini, Hannah Rachel (Maiden of Ludomir), Henrietta Szold, or Alice Bailey, can be appreciated through this insight:

> When I came out of the Godhead into multiplicity, then all things proclaimed, "There is a God" (the personal Creator). Now this cannot make me blessed, for hereby I realize myself as creature. But

in the breaking through [becoming consciously one Spirit] I am more than all creatures; I am neither God nor creature; I am that which I was and shall remain, now and forever more. There I receive a thrust which carries me above all angels. By this thrust I become so rich that God is not sufficient for me, in so far as He is only God in his divine works. For in thus breaking through, I perceive that God and I are in common [a wave and the ocean are consciously one]. There I am what I was. There I neither increase or decrease. For there I am the immovable which moves all things. Here man has won again what he is eternally and ever shall be. Here God is received into the soul.[9]

Ninety years ago, John Dewey, head of the Department of Philosophy at Columbia University, in New York, described the place of the transcendent in immanent existence:

Intelligence has descended from its lonely isolation at the remote edge of things, whence it operated as Unmoved Mover, and ultimate good, to take its seat in the moving affairs of men.[10]

Cycle of Life in a Wireless World

Let us now look at the movement that Eckhart and Dewey have described. Figure 1 represents the Comparative Nomenclature and the Cycle of Life, from Absolute to Man and Man to Absolute, as the world's leading thinkers, scholars, and scientists have articulated.

In Appendix 1 you will find a Summary of Insights with references to the four states: 1. Absolute; 2. From Absolute to Man; 3. Absolute in the World; 4. From Man to Absolute.

Comparative Nomenclature and the Cycle of Life

(1) **Absolute** = '1' = The Unchanging State = The Foundational Condition of Nature = The Infinite Splendor = Godhead = The Kingdom of God = The Ordering Principle = The Theory of Everything = The Pre-Quantum Fact = The Common Ground = Pre-Physical Potentiality = Zero-State = The Great Silence = At Rest Consciousness = Nothingness = Oneness = Ultimate Reality =

The Empty-Space = The Most High = The Eternally Living One = He-Who-Is = Absolute Infinity
(2) **From Absolute to Man**
(3) **Absolute in the World** = Visible Reality = God Manifest = Dimensions = Infinities = Manifestations
(4) **From Man to Absolute**

Figure 1.

This Summary of Insights can be a useful tool to everyone desiring to study each of the areas individually. The listing is designed to present an integrative insight into the basic sense of who we are and where we are heading.

Why the Disguise?

In the context of our infinite adventure and amnesia, here are some unanswered questions. Why would one wish to forget the awesome life of our Origin, Life, and Finality? Why the shocking memory loss, of ultimacy, in our hearts and minds? Why would one set sail on the seas of cosmology into the enchanting places in our universe? Why are we summoned to live in a world of fast-moving particles, quarks and strings; of World Cup Soccer, global banks, theater and dance; of the Academy Awards, the Pulitzer Prizes, political powwows, and sushi shops; of the virtue of tolerance, intriguing games of lawmaking, parliamentary management, and billions of galaxies?

Why are we prevailed upon to depart from Paul Dirac's imperceptible "nothingness substratum" in order to live in the midst of the big bang fireworks, with large-scale cosmological structure, planets, genes, and microorganism; art, music, poetry, letters and books; the search for antigravity, interlocking shareholders, and so on ad infinitum? Why are we stirring the depths of our fraternal feelings to color our memories with love and desire? Why are we asked to place such a desperate wager on our limited lives of cellular ecology?

Here you are, in your "ground state" of quantum field theory, alone across the many dimensions and universes for zillions of years. You dwell all by yourself in "empty-space," withdrawn from sight, separated from seduction, strife, and strain; removed from everyday tasks of cooking, cleaning, shopping, and supporting others emotionally. You exist without mate or sweetheart, without someone to talk to, to share with. There is an absence of the challenge(s) of personal finance, product management, or a sales quota. There is nothing to do. You are the "primordial ground," the Source of all and All. You are in touch with everything in space/time. With perfect precision you are aware of yourself. You know all that was, is, or ever will be. You know all of cosmic history and can predict everything to $10\pm\infty$ following whichever big bang blast after one hundred billion years anywhere in the cosmic field of creation.

You made absolutely fail-safe, as will be noted later, that the tuning of the initial universal expansion Ω is exactly one ('1'), and after a zillion years of contractions and expansions, still with a value of Ω that has not gone away from unity ('1'). For every contingency, you know everything from beginning to end. *You have turned on and extinguished infinity of universes.* You are unchanging, ageless, and timeless. There is nothing to discover, nothing to learn. Everything that needed to be done has been done. You are speaking of yourself to yourself. Even never-ending bliss seems boring.

Would you make a change, perhaps do something as humiliating as forgetting everything you know (total amnesia): whence came I, whither go I? Hiding yourself from yourself, becoming the Andromeda Nebula, a tall mountain, a strikingly beautiful piece of music, a creative artiste, or a bluebird with pretty red eyes?

Let us leave this view of the never-changing Divinity. Let us contemplate our entrance into the Wild Playground and our appearance as one hundred trillion subatomic particles or suns in our universe. Imagine playing hide-and-seek with ourselves through mathematical cosmology, science/limits, colored quarks, curvature-tensors, AAASs, AMAs, royal societies, synagogues, traditions, churches, mosques, temples, multinational corporations, warring nations, cooperative governments, nanoscience, basic physical principles, and entire clusters of galaxies of intelligent civilizations engaged in equally intelligent conversations. In the Upanishads, we read:

> Lonely He felt, and all unsatisfied;
> So into Two He did divide Him-Self,
> To have a Playmate; Man and Wife He was;
> All wishes of each other they fulfill.[11]

With this, additional questions must be asked: how can we *recognize the obvious*—live from the point of view of God; celebrate our divinity all the time? Can we barter health for disease? Can we prevent nuclear war, cost overruns, inefficient management, and unlivable poverty? How can we promote creative excellence, increased intuitive capacities, greater productivity, and clarity of understanding? How do we assure optimal health, attain peak experiences, mastery of life, and—in the end— fulfillment? "Have fun, my dear;" acknowledged Hafiz,

> My dear, have fun,
> In the Beloved's divine game,
> O, in the Beloved's
> Wonderful
> Game.[12]

Home at Last: At the Heart of Things

Once immersed in this world, how long will it take us from the fog of "Temporary Disneyland" amnesia to discover our roots: *who we are* once again? It takes us quite a while, as stated by English astrophysicist, director of Cambridge Observatory and Nobel laureate Sir Arthur Eddington (1881-1944); "to regain from nature that which the mind has put into nature."[13]

With this notion are my personal, firsthand experiences that can lead us to a better future of the undivided totality:

> When I was a galactic cluster,
> I did not understand;
> When I was a neutron star,
> I did not recognize;
> When I was a salty ocean,
> I did not appreciate;
> When I was a mighty sequoia,
> I did not grasp;
> And when on my way I became an elderly woman,
> I still did not know;
> But, when I let the splendor of sacred teachings
> (Compassion, service-excellence, purity of life, boundless
> altruism, deep peace, joy, and the Light Triumphant)

Be my life,
I realized that I am, was,
And shall always be
The Absolute Reality.

We can rediscover pure consciousness, beauty, and the simplicity that we see in the world—this larger unity, which is the One—and learn with Meister Eckhart, and from religious texts,

I am that which I was and shall remain, now and forever more . . .
'One God and Father of all, who is blessed above all and *through all* and *in us all*' (Eph 4:6).[14]

It is a known fact that the Great Emancipator Abraham Lincoln "was never in a college or an academy as a student, and was never, in fact, inside of a college or academy building until after he had commenced the practice of the law. He studied English grammar after he was twenty-three years of age . . . he studied the six books of Euclid after he had served a term in Congress, when he was forty years of age, and was amid the pressure of an extensive legal practice."[15] Yet, it is also known that "Honest Old Abe" was a Christ icon, forgiving his enemies and dying for freeing the slaves and saving the Union.

"Old Abe" was "one of those peculiar [righteous] men who perform with admirable skill everything they undertake."[16] How? I suggest Honest Abe was a man of impeccable integrity and moral clarity. His reputation for personal character, responsibility and ethical fortitude was of the highest order. He gave more heed to his inner voice ("Right makes might") and less consideration to the outer voice of the world.

"Lincoln's knowledge of the Bible far exceeded the content-grasp of most present-day clergymen," wrote William Wolf in his book, *Lincoln's Religion*. Lincoln called it "the great book of God" and "the best gift God has given man . . . But for it we could not know right from wrong." Honest Abe drew on his inner strength, his *friend down inside* of him, and through living a righteous life, "He prepared himself [1849-1854] for his great lifework." Because of his incorruptible integrity of character and purity, firmness of will, and saintliness, Lincoln's perception improved ("Happy are the pure of heart; they will see God! [Mt 5:8]). His towering mind outshined his peers.

"In most areas," writes Michael Burlingame in *The Inner World of Abraham Lincoln*:

> He was a model of psychological maturity, a fully individuated man who attained a level of consciousness unrivaled in the history of American public life. Most politicians, indeed most people, are dominated by their own petty egos. They take things personally, try to dominate one another, waste time and energy on feuds and vendettas, project their unacceptable qualities onto others, displace anger and rage, and put the needs of their own clamorous egos above all other considerations. A dramatic exception to this pattern, Lincoln achieved a kind of balance and wholeness that led one psychologist to remark that he had more "psychological honesty" than anyone since Christ. If one considers Christ as a psychological paradigm, the analogy is apt. In short, what stands out about Lincoln's inner life is not his psychological weakness but his remarkable strength.[17]

"Lincoln is the only real giant in depth of feeling and in certain moral power," wrote (Count) Lev Nikolaevich Tolstoy (1828-1910), one of the world's greatest novelists, social thinkers, and reformers. Charles Dickens called Tolstoy "a genius such as is met but once in a century." Furthermore, stated Tolstoy:

> Lincoln is . . . a Christ in miniature, a saint of humanity whose name will live thousands of years in the legends of future generations. We are still too near his greatness, and so can hardly appreciate his divine power, but after a few centuries more our posterity will find him considerably bigger than we do . . . He was what Beethoven was in music, Dante in poetry, Raphael in painting, and Christ in the philosophy of life.[18]

"Oh human blindness!" lamented the pure at heart Carmelite, Saint Teresa of Avila, one of the greatest mystics of all times, whose wisdom and accomplishments, like Father Abraham, came to her without formal or academic schooling. Acclaim came to her although she never aspired to public fame. Saint Teresa continues:

> How long, how long shall it be before the dust is removed from our eyes?[19]

How long can members of our family and we camouflage ourselves in this self-generated hiding? How can our minds and hearts assimilate this grandest of all thoughts: "You are in me and I am in you" (Jn 14:20). Who does not remember the famous statements of the Bible?

> We, many though we are, are one body (1 Cor 10:17); the Spirit
> ['1'] of the Lord fills the whole universe and holds all things
> together (Wisdom 1:7);
> Whoever has seen me has seen the Father (Jn 14:9);
> The kingdom of God is within you (Lk 17:20-21).

The Bhagavad Gita phrased it this way: "The Supreme Lord is situated in everyone's heart" (18:61).

Your Personal Universe: Wash it White in Spirit

How can we be fully conscious of the most confidential of all knowledge? How can we remind ourselves that every moment is an opportunity to give birth to the greatest good within ourselves and to be a blessing to others, an opportunity for continuous re-creation of the world—for Love's life? How are we to experience the feelings and understandings that come to us from being at one with our Creator; being with, in and through our Creator; being cocreators of our personal universe, partakers in our personal resurrection of mind, body, and world?

Note: when night turns into day, or a negative pulse of an electromagnetic wave turns into a positive pulse, we go through a connecting zero-state, a no man's land. In this procreative state, the old creation (night) passes on and a new creation (day) comes back to life. In physics, for an electron particle, this cycle is very brief (t = 1.1812 x 10^{-22} seconds, that is, twenty-two zeros before 1, see the Nature of Time, in part 2, chapter 6).[20] To describe very small or very large numbers, I use power notation. Thus, 2 x 10^{-5} means 0.00002, and 2 x 10^5 means 200,000.

Why do I call attention to this? In the traditional Hebrew Old Testament and the current big bang model, it is understood there was one creation. In the Hebrew Genesis scenario this is 5760 years ago (in 2000) and in the big bang model approximately 13.7 billion years ago.

To be exact, "a universe of your own" is being created and re-created *continuously* by YOU! Yes, the old universe (like night) passes away and a new universe (day) comes into being in less than a second. Each one of us is fashioning our own personal world every 1.1812×10^{-22} (0.00000000000000000000011812) seconds. And according to Hawking, there is "nothing for a Creator to do."[21] Surprise! "Oh yes, absolutely," said Fritjof Capra, physicist and the founder and president of the Elmwood Institute, an ecological think tank in Berkeley, California. He writes:

> That is an old notion of God, a God who is separate from the creation, who sits out there somewhere in the void playing the dice and then reaches in according to what the dice show and meddles with the world . . .
> That, by the way, is exactly the position of Stephen Hawking. God sits out there and has various options, and Stephen Hawking wonders which option he will take. Hawking is one of the most brilliant scientists today, and his book, *A Brief History of Time* [sold more than 10 million copies in 40 languages], is brilliant in terms of physics and cosmology, but it is at the level of elementary-school catechism in terms of theology. And it's full of theology! God is in every chapter. Hawking says explicitly, "I want to understand the mind of God."[22]

Recently, many of us have been exposed to different varieties of virtual reality games. Along with our thoughts and actions, each one of us creates and re-creates our own virtual reality—our own personal universe—incessantly. "An individual has not started living," declared Martin Luther King Jr., "until he can rise above the narrow confines of his individualistic concerns to the broader concerns of all humanity." Great is she/he who controls her/his state of heart and mind. Therefore, let our impeccable life of integrity, unlimited love, service-excellence, freedom, and responsible free spirit be our universe.

Paramahamsa Yogananda (1893-1952) initiated over one hundred thousand students in Kriya Yoga, a scientific method for developing the divine consciousness. His mission in life was "to reveal the complete harmony and basic Oneness of original Christianity as taught by Jesus Christ [the conceptual foundations of quantum mechanics in physics] and original Yoga as taught by Bhagavan Krishna." He established the Self Realization Fellowship to make the perennial wisdom available in all parts of the world. In his profound book *Man's Eternal Quest,* Yogananda writes:

Everything is God ['1']. This very room and the universe are floating like a motion picture on the screen of my consciousness. When you look back at the booth, you see only the beam of light that is projecting the pictures on the screen. That this creation is naught but a motion picture, created out of God's light, seems incredible, but it is true. I look at this room and I see nothing but pure Spirit, pure Light, pure Joy. "He dwells in the world, enveloping all—everywhere." The pictures of my body and your bodies and all things in this world are only rays of light streaming out of that one sacred Light. As I see that Light I behold nothing anywhere but pure Spirit.[23]

Chogyam Trungpa (1939-1987), social visionary, author, and poet, founder of the Naropa University in Boulder, Colorado, the first Buddhist university in North America, the Shambhala Training program and Vajradhatu, an international association of Buddhist meditation centers (known under the name Shambhala International), is an esteemed scholar and one of the most influential exponents of Tibetan Buddhism in the West. In discussing our excursion into manifested duality, Trungpa stated:

At the beginning, duality is just a way of killing boredom [the never-ending bliss seemed boring]; then there is the realization that taking this kind of chance is very dangerous. As we continue on, things become more threatening [Hitler-Stalin-Mao Ze-dong death factories, nuclear and biological arsenals]. We begin to develop various perspectives, various tones of emphasis on various types of styles . . . [How to bring peace, how to create the improvement of human life and hope]. Then, after you have experienced the painful reality and feel that you have done a good job in relating to it [you and all the people on the planet enter the Land of Oneness, freedom and peace], then somehow you realize the whole thing doesn't exist [it's a play of consciousness]. This is also very painful, because you thought that at least you had achieved something. You thought you had broken the ice, and then suddenly no ice exists to be broken. That is the kind of thing that makes up the nature of the path.[24]

We end where we started, with the journey in between being a spine-chilling ride.

12

THE FLOURISHING OF REASON: RECOGNIZE THE OBVIOUS

Let the face of God shine through.

—Edna Saint Vincent Millay

See Yourself in Still Water: Speak to Me of Love

Similar to a chessboard, with its warring pieces, our mind can be an expression of the Divine Wisdom or a theater of war. The opponent's chess pieces can uplift, bringing unlimited happiness, altruism, and wisdom to us, or be our fears, worries, and so forth. To enhance the capacity to reason, or to grasp truth "together, all at the same time," as René Descartes recommended, it is crucial that the mind be at peace and that the heart be loving and pure.

If you desire to know how a rose smells, who can smell a rose for you? If you wish to spend more time with people you care about, you must do it yourself. Consider that what we want to experience or empirically verify, is a state of Godhead—a world governed by very precise mathematical laws or unchangeable stillness within us.

In the sciences, it is a condition in which all force, energy, and matter fields are in pre-physical potentiality ('1') or have zero intensity. Therefore, if you wish to see yourself as you are at your foundation, you have to discover with your own mind, heart and soul that you are the Infinite Splendor—where the Unchanging State is consciously within yourself.

The legendary Tibetan saint Jetsun Milarepa (1040-1123), for whom worldly concerns were the leash of the demons, in the *One Hundred Thousand Songs of Milarepa*, recommended:

It is through resting one's mind at ease [inner peace] that Buddhahood [the ubiquitous Buddha nature, Christian "unity of the Spirit" and an experience of inner enlightenment] is realized.[1]

In radio or TV reception, we tune in to the desired frequency of the program we wish to receive. Similarly, to experience the "inner light" of the Nameless One, it is essential we are receptive—we synchronize our intellect to inner peace or stillness. It is vital that, in daily living, we continually strive for harmony and selfless pursuit of one's occupation, and that we practice compassion and loving-kindness.

When we concentrate on the inner peace, our life energy nourishes our "inner light." The quality of our "inner light" produces the universe we experience. The more we are Godlike (Christlike), the more peace, freedom and happiness we come into contact with. Similar to John Wheeler's self-excited circuit, the more we "tune into" complete peace of mind, healthy living, and the Highest Good (not my program, not my strategy, not my way but "Thy ['1'] will be done"), the more beautiful a universe we *select* from the pre-physical potentiality in '1'.

"Do not imagine, do not think, do not analyze,"[2] suggested the great forefather of Tibetan Buddhism, the Kagyu lineage, Cakrasamvara Tilopa (988-1069). He passed on these teachings of mental ecology, the luminosity of mind, and devotion to high ideals to the spiritual family tree of Naropa (1016-1100), Lord Marpa (1012-1097), Milarepa, and others. One by one, they uplifted the human family through wisdom, good works, and perception of the "clear light" (Tibetan *ösel*). One by one, they transmitted the words of the Lord of Great Compassion and Purity (Siddhartha Gautama), that:

> All phenomena and their developments are simply manifestations of mind. All causes and effects, from great universes to the fine dust only seen in the sunlight, come into apparent existence only by means of the discriminating mind.[3]

"For him who has conquered the mind," states the Bhagavad Gita, "the mind is the best of friends, but for one who has failed to do so, his very mind will be the greatest enemy" (6.6).[4] In order to achieve self-understanding and appreciate the sacredness of Infinite Intelligence, as Saint Paul and Tibetan Vajrayana Buddhism suggested, the mind ought to be at peace. We have to hush our busy thoughts—we have to journey to light.

Knowledgeable world travelers concur that our journey is easier without excess baggage. We have to free our mind and learn to love others as both Jesus and the expressions of Mahayana Buddhism have counseled. Our brain neurons will tune into the pure consciousness if we are to observe the Problem Solver—the uncreated order where phenomena and objects of the universe come into being.

The great Guru Padmasambhava (b. 755), one of the historically identifiable founders of Tibetan Buddhism, venerated by his followers as the "second Buddha," recommended that we have to experience inner silence, compassion, equanimity, and a sense of inner balance within ourselves to grasp the totality of things, the unity of all in all: our own inner Buddha Mind and the Buddha qualities. "No one is more distracted and confused," counseled Milarepa, "than he who ceases to meditate in solitude! [Furthermore,] Nothing is more shameful than a learned Buddhist who neglects his meditation! Therefore, go to practice! To meditate."[5] Chuang-tzu, citing Confucius in his Taoist classic, *Chuang-tzu,* suggested,

A man does not see himself in running water but in still water.[6]

The Sound of Silence: Be Still, Be Still, and *Know*

The great Syriac writer, poet, and theological commentator of the fourth century, Ephraem the Syrian stated, "Good speech is silver, but silence is pure gold." What we cannot grasp by study and examination we become aware of in stillness—in "a still small voice" or "a sound of sheer silence" of the Bible. We are encouraged to pay attention to "the soundless voice" in Sanskrit, *the voice of the silence* within ourselves, to open our capacity to reason, to find ourselves.

The "still small voice" of the obvious has its own sound: the soundless sound, which, according to the great twelfth century mystics, Hildegard of Bingen, Elizabeth of Schoenau, Marie of Oigniens, Hadewijch, and Mechthild of Magdeburg, enables us to "see and taste the flowing godhead through your being." The issue of stillness is not stillness—the issue of stillness is God in us, who whispers: "This is I." As we read in the Psalms:

Be still, and know that I am God (Ps 46:10).

Dag Hammarskjöld wrote:

> The more faithfully you listen to the voice within you, the better
> you will hear what is sounding outside. And only he who listens
> can speak. Is this the starting point of the road towards the union
> of your two dreams—to be allowed in clarity of mind to mirror life
> and in purity of heart to mold it?[7]

On one occasion the Buddha was asked, "Is there God? I will not tell
you," he answered. "But, if you wish, I can show you how to find out for
yourself." Then the Compassionate One taught the art of inner silence,
compassion, and love. Paul von Ringelheim stated, "The essence of spirit
is the moment of silence within us all." Thomas à Kempis (1379-1471),
German ecclesiastic, said: "The more a man is united within himself,
and becometh inwardly simple, so much the more and higher things
doth he understand without labor . . ." For this reason, declared
Hammarskjöld, it is important:

> to preserve the silence within—amid all the noise. To remain open
> and quiet, a moist humus in the fertile darkness where the rain falls
> and the grain ripens—no matter how many tramp across the parade
> ground in whirling dust under an arid sky.[8]

"When the mind is disturbed, the multiplicity of things arises. When
the mind is quieted, the multiplicity of things disappears," stated
Ashvagosha in The Awakening of Faith, an early Buddhist passage. Sister
Theresina of the Missionaries of Charity, like her teacher Mother Teresa,
improved the lives of countless souls and gave dignity to the dying. She
offers her insights on silence:

> From what I have found, there is just too much noise in modern
> life—and because of this many people are afraid of silence. As God
> speaks only in silence, this is a big problem for those searching for
> God. Many young people, for instance, don't know how to reflect
> and just act instinctively.
>
> In cities these days there is so much chaos and physical
> violence, a lot of anger, frustration, and shouting, just the opposite
> of the peaceful countryside or the sound of a waterfall. People try
> to fill the emptiness they feel with food, radio, television, and

keeping busy with outside activities. But this emptiness can only be filled by the spiritual, by God.[9]

Similar to Sister Theresina, Sai Baba connects mental stillness with the search for God (Divine Splendor) and the experience of joy:

> When discrimination is keen and mental waves are stilled—and attention is one-pointed as a result of the contemplation of Pure Consciousness, then Divine Splendor is manifested, which can burn away evil and reveal joy.[10]

The Upanishad states, "When all the senses are stilled, when the mind is at rest, when the intellect wavers not—that, say the wise, is the highest state. This calm of the senses and the mind has been defined as yoga. He who attains it is freed from delusion."

The Heart's Responsibility Is to Love—to Understand

Reginald Ray, professor of Buddhist studies at the Naropa University in Boulder, Colorado, and member of the Religious Studies Department at the University of Colorado, shared:

> Resting in the nature of the empty, open, luminous awareness that is our essential nature, through abiding in this state of "peace beyond peace," one is able to respond to the suffering of others in a most natural way and to live a life that is uncontrived and endlessly creative.

The nineteenth century social scientist and poet Edward Carpenter presented methods and processes whereby the inhibition of thought tunes us into the '1' plenum and helps to verify *who the knower is?* Carpenter wrote:

> Of all the hard facts of science, I know of none more solid and fundamental than the fact that if you inhibit thought (and persevere), you come at length to a region of consciousness [utter silence] below or behind thought . . . and a realization of an altogether vaster self than that to which we are accustomed. And since the ordinary consciousness, with which we are concerned

in ordinary life, is before all things founded on the little local self, and is in fact self-consciousness in the ordinary self and the ordinary world. It is to die in the ordinary sense, but in another sense, it is to wake up and find that the I, one's real, most intimate self, pervades the Universe and all other beings—that the mountains and the sea and the stars are a part of one's body and that one's soul is in touch with the souls of all creatures. So great, so splendid is this experience, that it may be said that all minor questions and doubts fall away in face of it; and certain it is that in thousands and thousands of cases the fact of this having come even once to a man has completely revolutionized his subsequent life and outlook on the world.[11]

What does having purity of heart have to do with actualizing our "infinite possibilities"—training the heart and mind for happiness and improvement of our brain architecture? What does practicing goodness, integrity, and impeccable honesty have to do with realizing our divine (Christ) consciousness, Buddha nature, or God as the Lord within us (Antaryamin in Sanskrit)? What did Saint Paul mean in Ephesians (3:18, 19) when he said that the saints of God are able to be filled and understand all the fullness of God?

When our willingness to reach out and help others, our attitudes and actions toward others and our environment are carried out with unselfish love, we act with purity of heart. When our conscience—our "friend" deep down inside of us—is at peace, then we are at peace. Our perception and awareness, which naturally emerges from a clear mind, increase. This realization happens, as it happened to others: *God's face is reflected in all our experiences.* Thus, I am obliged to write:

I am the very people I help, and I am the very people I hurt.

How we think and what we do depends on the level of our consciousness. Serving unselfishly is akin to *cleaning the windows* of our homes. It allows us, by passing through the windows of our consciousness or soul, to see and understand Reality by being one with it. In a pure and peaceful heart, the subject and object are one in Love. You surrender to Love's voice—to Love's own self. Purity of heart expands our cognition and our commitment to continually work for the welfare of others.

Saint Paul wrote to the Ephesians: "I pray that you, being rooted and established in love, may have power, together with all the saints, to grasp how wide and long and high and deep is the love of Christ ['1'], and to know this love that surpasses knowledge—that you may *be filled to the measure of all the fullness of God*" (3:18, 19).

History bears out that when a certain level of need, knowledge, and consciousness appear *together* in different parts of the world, people will reach similar conclusions: creating fire to stay warm, determining the optimum planting and harvesting time in the fields, preventing infant mortality, discovering medicinal herbs/drugs, inventions, laws of physics, and so forth. It can also be seen from the great treasures of ancient texts that purity of heart and unity of mind and spirit occupied the central role of the Buddhist, Christian, Hindu, Judaic, and Taoist wisdom.

When we study the different religious traditions and their beliefs, practices, myths, symbols, rituals, deities, and institutions, we find that there is a captivating resonance with the great treasures of ancient literature. This resonance includes not only the great religions, but also the African tribal religions, the Australian aborigines, the American Indians, and the South American Indians such as Inca, Quechua, and Aymara of the Andes to the Carib, Tupi, and other groups of the Amazon jungle basin.[12]

The Nahuas of Mesoamerica were not in physical communication with the European or Asian continents, yet comparable insights and knowledge surfaced. Wrote James Maffie:

> Wisdom was actively embodied in Nahua sages or *tlamatinime* ("knowers of things"), among whose responsibilities were cultivating in people a "face and heart" (*in ixtli, in yollotl*) and reflecting upon and giving renewed expression to the ancient teachings through "flower and song" (*in xochitl, in cuicatl*) . . . Wisdom was not something one acquired or possessed but rather represented a characteristic of how one conducted oneself and one's affairs upon what the Nahuas saw as the dangerous, slippery surface of the earth. In short, the Nahuas understood wisdom in adverbial terms. Wisdom enabled humans to keep their balance as they walked upon the twisting, jagged path of life and thus afforded them some measure of equilibrium, rootedness, stability, and well-being in an otherwise evanescent life filled with pain, sorrow, struggle, and suffering, here on an impermanent, doomed earth . . . The Nahuas characterized

education as "the art of strengthening or bringing up men" (tlacahuapahualiztli) and "the act of giving wisdom to the face" (neixtlamachiliztli). Humans are born incomplete and "faceless" (i.e. without character) yet are perfectible through proper education. [Toward this end] Nahua education aimed at cultivating habits and dispositions that enabled individuals to live properly. Such enabling dispositions included self-control, self-sufficiency, moderation, modesty, and personal and domestic hygiene. Disabling dispositions included pride, intemperance, carelessness, sloth, duplicity, uncleanliness, gluttony, and drunkenness.[13]

The Greater the Purity, the Better the Judgment

Similar to the fundamental identity of the veritable teachings of Shakyamuni Buddha, the Christ, Krishna, Moses, Lao-tzu, and Zoroaster, Maffie maintains:

Nahuas wisdom involved an understanding of the nature, source, and limits of knowledge (*tlamatiliztli*). Nahuas conceived cognition dynamically and behaviorally as a way of acting or moving in the world and accordingly conceived knowledge as a characteristic of how one acts or moves. [Further,] the Nahuas also conceived knowledge as giving one the practical power and "know-how" needed to conduct one's life in such a way as to attain some measure of equilibrium, purity and hence well-being. [Therefore] The degree to which humans are able to understand *teotl* ['1': Spirit] reflects the degree to which they perfect equilibrium-and-purity.[14]

Muktananda put it best, "The purer you are, the greater your progress."[15] Meister Eckhart wrote, "A pure heart is one that is unencumbered, unworried, uncommitted, which does not want its own way about anything but which rather is submerged in the loving of God, having denied self."[16] We recognize the greatest good through purity of heart:

Purity of Heart = Clear Thinking (wisdom,),
            = Capacity to Reason (intelligence),
            = Ability to Make Decisions (judgment),
            = Perception of Truth (understanding); and
            = The Harvest of Good.

Just as energy (*E*) is directly related to mass (*m*) in $E = mc^2$, *so* purity of heart is directly related to clear thinking, high-quality decision-making, and creative actions. *The greater the purity of heart the better our awareness and capacity to harvest happiness,* and conversely, the less purity of heart the poorer the reasoning. In addition, the greater the perception of truth, the greater the compassion, the greater the compassion, the greater the illumination, and the deeper the wisdom. Wisdom translates to common sense, harmony-oriented functional structure, strong commitment and loyalty to the organization on the part of its members, low crime, and increased life expectancy.

Purity of heart advances personal responsibility, trust, cooperation, peace, liberty, cosmic consciousness, and beauty. It also refines perception and lets everything come into view as wisdom and exuberance. That is, "He who acts in truth ['1'] comes into the light" (Jn 3:21), or, as stated by Lincoln, "Right makes might." Recall Jesus' statement in his Sermon on the Mount:

> Happy are the pure of heart; they will see God (Mt 5:8)! [And] If you obey my teachings you are really my disciples; you will know the truth, and the truth will set you free (Jn 8:31).

God, '1', is Truth (source and standard of knowledge and highest freedom), and truth is God. Therefore, the statement that happy are the pure in heart for they will see the truth, and the truth will set them free, is not only real, it is also the breakthrough formula for profound growth, the cosmic awareness of who the knower is and how we relate to each other.

The eye's lens is a nature's awesome wonder. It consists of roughly one thousand layers of transparent tissue, facilitating light to pass across cell boundaries without scattering. The lens of the eye is the only perfectly clear living tissue in our body; all other cells scatter light rays. Clear layers of lens cells align in parallel, so that light passes perpendicularly through them. If the lens had any hint of color or speck, it would absorb light or disrupt the otherwise uniform index of refraction, creating lens-clouding cataracts in a person's field of vision. Molecules that make up our cells usually have half-lives of a few minutes to several weeks. Within six months or so, new ones replace 90 percent of the molecules that construct our bodies; lens cells have to operate for a lifetime without replacement. Age-related macular degeneration, retinitis pigmentosa, and years of elevated blood sugar from diabetes, ultraviolet radiation, chronic infections such as AIDS, Parkinson's disease, Alzheimer's disease, and severe dehydration causes the lens to activate a self-destruct (cellular suicide) program leading to blurred vision, cataracts, and blindness.

In 1899, Claude Monet painted the spectacular Japanese bridge in his beautiful Giverny garden near Paris. In 1912 Monet's doctor diagnosed a cataract in each eye and recommended surgery. Monet was afraid to do it. In his time surgically removing a cataract often wrecked an artist's productive life. From 1912 Monet's paintings exhibit fewer hues, tints, and shades; reds and browns prevail. Between 1912 and 1922, when advancing years seriously shaped his eyesight, Monet painted the same bridge when cataracts clouded his perception of gold, blues, and greens, leaving him in a state with foggy reds and browns. You have to see to believe it. In 1922 Monet stated that he was no longer able to paint anything of clarity. We are fortunate that we can study Monet's work over the final two decades of his life and how these common impairments skew human sight.

Analogous to the eye's one thousand—layers transparent lens is our lotus of a thousand-petals crown chakra. Similar to the lens of the eye that facilitates transmission of light, the crown chakra, called the sahasrara in India, acts as an information exchange of manifested universe to one's divine self. While lens cells are transparent in one's early years, the crown chakra, like infant's sex organs or the unawakened state of animal wakefulness (a la Hitler-Stalin-Mao Ze-dong-mujahedin blurry to black images) need development and peeling back the obscuring layers for self-realization, high-quality decision-making, and extraordinary creativity. The path of growth and self-purification recovers from the fog of amnesia and connects one with experience of higher planes, cosmic consciousness, knowledge of God, and the blazing Light of '1' within oneself. If we want to swim, we have to get into the water.

In 1923, Monet had cataract surgery to his right eye, which could only detect light. In 1925, at the age of 85, Monet stated that he can see well again and will create again. Today, doctors perform more than one million cataract operations annually in the U.S. alone. The procedure normally takes less than one hour with a success rate of nearly 100 percent. Similarly, when there is a caring, loving, and compassionate environment at home the journey from darkness into light unfolds quickly into a pure, radiant blossom. The success rate is also nearly 100 percent.

Do a Good Deed; Say a Caring Word

Ralph Waldo Emerson held, "If we live truly, we shall see truly."[17] Our actions shape our consciousness. They either strengthen or weaken it. The great peacemaker of our time, Dag Hammarskjöld, wrote:

> Give me a pure heart—that I may see Thee,
> A humble heart—that I may hear Thee,
> A heart of love—that I may serve Thee,
> A heart of faith—that I may abide in Thee.[18]

"The power to make distinction is a primary operation of intelligence," suggested Rabbi Heschel:

> We distinguish between white and black, beautiful and ugly, pleasant and unpleasant, gain and loss, good and evil, right and wrong.
>
> The fate of mankind depends upon the realization that the distinction between good and evil, right and wrong, is superior to all other distinctions . . . To teach humanity the primacy of that distinction is of essence to the Biblical message.[19]

We rise or sink by how we think and what we do. Every insightful teacher worth her/his salt started with purity of heart and ended with purity of heart. Purity of heart not only allows for a more orderly functioning of society; it is also the gateway to our own and other people's hearts and minds.

In a trustworthy, dependable, collaborative, pure, and compassionate heart, wisdom rises like butter from churning milk—Allah/Buddha/ Christ/Krishna ('1') is discovered in one's being. Strive, therefore, for direct, personal, unmediated experience of purity of heart: the Lord and Sustainer of the Worlds will be consciously reborn in you!

13

WHEN HEART SPEAKS TO HEART, WHAT MORE IS THERE TO SAY?

When you set on fire compassion,
You are the kingdom of Light.

—Orest Bedrij

Fill Your Heart with Love:
Experience the Light within Your Being

Most of us have been exposed to the essentials of personal responsibility, above-reproach integrity, commitment of each to the whole, and the maintenance of a social and moral order in our daily lives. We respect these principles by stopping at a red light, driving on the correct side of the road, and doing high-quality work in school, on the assembly line, and within our office(s). Without pulling together, gratitude, accountability, trustworthiness, conscientiousness, and learning our social and economic system would break down. Our standard of living would plummet. On this we all agree. Now bring to mind Jesus' relationship between *truth*, *knowledge*, and *freedom*: "know the truth, and *the truth will set you free*" (Jn 8:32).

Truth, like heart-to heart love and life, is the fundamental principle of the universe. Thus, to realize higher levels of freedom, higher levels of truth (i.e., responsibility, social harmony, universal love, altruism, and learning) have to be attained. Any freedom that is hostile to responsibility and education is bad freedom.

Case in point, to increase our chances of not having an accident and help eliminate traffic tie-ups and backups, we must drive on the appropriate side of the road, technically know how to drive with precision and sense, maintain a safe distance from another car or truck, have the vehicle in good working order, and not fall asleep at the wheel, or be intoxicated. We must convert our road knowledge and learning into action.

In the *Way of a Pilgrim* we find this insight: "Love usually grows with knowledge, and the greater the depth and extent of the knowledge, the more love there will be, the more easily the heart will soften and lay itself open to the love of God, as it diligently gazes upon the very fullness and beauty of the divine nature and His unbounded love for men."

Confucius (551-479 BC), known to the Chinese people as K'ung Fu-tsu, is a very significant personality in Chinese history. He maintained that the education of an individual is preparation for a peaceful, ordered society. Self-strengthening and self-realization are steps toward world peace. According to Confucius, the right method of governing is not by legislation, force, and law enforcement, but by character education and learning of what is right and what is wrong. He said, "When the personal life is cultivated, the family will be regulated; when the family is regulated, the state will be in order; and when the state is in order, there will be peace throughout the world."[1]

Mo-tzu (Master Mo, 468-376 BC), a contemporary of Socrates, tried to teach the Chinese people of his day how to create a united, productive, and strong populace built on values of universal love, appreciation, and social harmony. His ideas are included in a work known as *Mo-tzu*, compiled by his pupils. He realized that the cause of common discord is bias and the immersion into only personal needs, or those of one's own family.

Mo-tzu, similar to Lao-tzu and Jesus, suggested expressing absolute magnanimity and doing good directed to all peoples: to love everyone results in the greatest gain to oneself and to others. Mo-tzu's insights, "value in use" and "value in exchange," come into view in many truth seeking, social, and religious systems. Mother Teresa, 2,400 years later, wrote:

> The greatest disease in the West today is not TB or leprosy; it is being unwanted, unloved, and uncared for. We can cure physical diseases with medicine, but the only cure for loneliness, despair, and

hopelessness is love. There are many in the world who are dying for a piece of bread but there are many more dying for a little love. The poverty in the West is a different kind of poverty—it is not only a poverty of loneliness but also of spirituality. There's a hunger for love, as there is a hunger for God.[2]

Habits of the Heart: Greet Today with Love in Your Heart

Here I share with you the deeper meaning of personal responsibility, gratitude, working together, education, and the perfection of individuals. Listen to this excerpt from Og Mandino's scrolls, *The Greatest Salesman in the World:*

I will greet this day with love in my heart.

For this is the greatest secret of success in all ventures. Muscle can split a shield and even destroy life, but only the unseen power of love can open the hearts of men, and until I master this art, I will remain no more than a peddler in the market place . . . .

And how will I speak? I will applaud my enemies and they will become friends; I will encourage my friends and they will become brothers. Always will I dig for reasons to applaud; never will I scratch for excuses to gossip. When I am tempted to criticize, I will bite my tongue; when I am moved to praise, I will shout from the roofs . . . .

And how will I confront each whom I meet? In only one way. In silence and to myself I will address him and say, "I love you." Though spoken in silence, these words will shine in my eyes, unwrinkle my brow, bring a smile to my lips, and echo in my voice; and his heart will be opened. And who is there who will say nay to my goods when my heart feels my love?

I will greet this day with love in my heart.

And most of all I will love myself. For when I do I will zealously inspect all things which enter my body, my mind, my soul, and my heart. Never will I overindulge the requests of my flesh, rather I will cherish my body with cleanliness and moderation. Never will I allow my mind to be attracted to evil and despair, rather I will lift it with the knowledge and wisdom of the ages. Never will I allow my soul to become complacent and satisfied, rather I will feed it with meditation and prayer . . .

Henceforth will I love all mankind. From this moment all hate is let from my veins, for I have not time to hate, only time to love. From this moment I take the first step required to become a man among men. With love I will increase my sales a hundredfold and become a great salesman. If I have no other qualities, I can succeed with love alone. Without it I will fail though I possess all the knowledge and skills of the world.

I will greet this day with love, and I will succeed.[3]

Love Is Sacred: Love Ceaselessly

"A bit of fragrance always clings to the hand that gives you roses," is a Chinese proverb. There is nothing more beautiful than love. There is nothing greater than love. There is nothing more sacred than love. "I pray that your love will keep on growing more and more, together with true knowledge and perfect judgment, so that you will be able to choose what is best," said Saint Paul in his letter to the Philippians (1:9).

Love stands for the effort to be our best and to do things right, not just now and then but always—consistently. Love represents immaculate integrity and sincerity. Love begins with oneself: at home, in school, at work . . . Love begets more love. Love creates a rarified state we call liberty, harmony—your birthright. Each conceived baby is an expression of our love.

Lovemaking is an opportunity to raise and advance the human spirit. It is a way to infuse goodness and compassion into all aspects of our lives. It fills us to the brim with the spirit of freedom, deep inner peace, and joy. In loving others, we ourselves find love, and are filled with energy. Conversely, hating others or detesting what we do can cause pain to us and will drain us of energy. The pain we inflict on someone is inflicted above all on ourselves.

William Tiller, a world-leading scientist on the structure of matter, is an accomplished scholar and researcher (350 scientific papers, plus five books) with a distinguished career. He spent thirty-four years in academia (Stanford University, Oxford University) after nine years as an advisory physicist with the Westinghouse Research Laboratories in Pittsburgh. Tiller has been pursuing experimental and theoretical study in the field of crystallogenics, semiconductor processing, thin film formation, computer simulation, subtle energies, intentionality, and consciousness. In his groundbreaking work *Science and Human Transformation,* Tiller considers love through the window of physics:

> Love seems strange in that the more one gives of it the more one
> has of it.

It is because "Love generates love," said Rumi in *The Vakil of the Prince of Bokhara* story. Similar to John Wheeler, Bernard d'Espagnat, and Max Planck (with his participatory interplay between man and nature), Tiller maintains that human consciousness contributes to the creation and direction of the universe. He provides a solution to a very important challenge in the prevailing paradigm of science: how does one measure human intention upon matter, or consciousness? Tiller, with Walter Dibble Jr. and Michael Kohane, furnishes a comprehensive new theoretical and experimental framework.

In *Conscious Acts of Creation: The Emergence of a New Physics,* Tiller and his colleagues, utilizing new experimental techniques in measurement of materials, organic and inorganic, have been able to change the outcome of an experiment in the specific direction of the imbedded intention. They present experimental data on purified water, in vitro organic chemicals and in vivo living cells. They show that a human quality of conscious purpose can be imbedded and measured in a simple electronic device via a meditation process and then have the device influence the experimental space for that particular target experiment.

A New Spirit of Teamwork:
Try to Do Things Right All the Time

In 1958 the Green Bay Packers, the only small-town team to survive the Great Depression of the 1930s, was the National Football League's (NFL) butt of all jokes and the most distressing team in the league. College seniors prayed they wouldn't be drafted by Green Bay. The NFL troupe referred to the Packers, as "Siberia," and players were terrified of being traded to them. The beloved Green Bay Packers constantly humiliated their homeland supporters.

In 1958, the Packers finished with a 1-10-1 record (last in the league) and a 56-0 home loss to the Baltimore Colts, which was televised all over the Midwest. The 1958 was the eleventh straight losing season for the Packers. In the Green Bay club, there existed a crushing air of negativity, defeatism, and despair. The majority of Green Bay players did not care and showed up late for practice. A number of the Packers "had little respect for authority and actually took themselves out of games and put themselves back in whenever they felt like it," stated Donald Phillips in his scenic *Run to Win: Vince Lombardi on Coaching and Leadership.* Fundamentally, the Packers were members in the NFL but had no NFL-caliber leadership that understood the finer points of both the game of football and how to tame and direct the "big game."

In January of 1959 the Packers' selection committee singled out an "old man," a forty-five-year-old virtual unknown named Vince Lombardi (1913-1970), to be Green Bay's new head coach. Nearly every football aficionado in Wisconsin would repeat, "Who are they [Packers management] kidding?" "Who the hell is Vincent Lombardi?" In spite of everything, the fans had hope.

Lombardi made good on the opportunity. He understood that our calling is perfection: "You must be perfect" (Mt 5:48). "He was able to bring out the most in people," said Tom Landry, the tough Dallas Cowboys head coach.

Lombardi did not know about Stanford's Bill Tiller nor his experiments concerning a winning state of mind or intention, just as a bumblebee does not know that according to the laws of aerodynamics, it does not have the wingspan to fly. That is, winning is a state of mind, doing things right all the time, or having a quality of winning consciousness.

Striving for excellence and a spirit of teamwork was everything to Lombardi. He had three tenets for himself and his players: God, family and football, in that order. Vince knew, like Bill Tiller, that "battles are won primarily in the hearts of men."

Lombardi was a rough diamond, polishing the "big game." His impact on most of his players, teambuilding, enthusiasm, and his profession was profound. He had exceptional leadership ability, a well-hidden compassionate nature, deep spiritual strength, and was a perfectionist by nature. He wanted his players to *do the right thing*, and he wanted his players to *do things right all the time.* "Whatever you do, work at with all your heart" (Col 3:23), he would say. When the final gun sounded, after nine years with Green Bay, Lombardi always had a winning season and an overall .758 winning percentage. He was named

Coach of the Year four times and accumulated two Super Bowl victories, five NFL championships, and six Western Conference championships. Here are some of Lombardi's Principles:

- Success calls for singleness of purpose; success advances confidence.
- Teach people to be responsible—to think for themselves.
- Develop people's talents, abilities, and self-worth.
- Love is the answer for all; heart power is the might of your team.

"He never did anything without prayer," said his daughter, Susan. Of Green Bay pregame prayers, Lombardi stated that "we don't pray to win, we pray to play the best we can and to keep us free from injury. And the prayer we say after the game is one of thanksgiving." Lombardi was father, love, and kindness to many of his players. He made people grow up in mutual bonding, teamwork excellence, and life itself. "We are our brother's keeper," Lombardi stated to one audience. "If people can't find work, whether it's their fault or not, you've got to help them, clothe them, and house them properly and try to get rid of the conditions that have held them back." Donald Phillips stated, "Ultimate success can only be achieved in a person's heart. And Vince Lombardi's was the heart of a very good and decent man." He quoted Lombardi:

> Listen, I know you can't be perfect. No one is perfect. But boys, making the effort to be perfect, trying as hard as you can, is what life is all about. If you'll not settle for anything less than the best, you will be amazed at what you can do with your lives. You'll be amazed at how much you can rise in the world . . . The quality of a man's life [Bill Tiller's power of human intention to robustly influence physical reality] has got to be a full measure of that man's personal commitment to excellence and victory, regardless of what field he may be in . . . The ultimate victory can never be won, yet it must be pursued with all one's might . . .
>
> After the cheers have died down and the stadium is empty, after the headlines have been written, after you are back in the quiet of your own room and the championship ring has been placed on the dresser and all the pomp and fanfare have faded, the enduring thing that is left is the dedication to doing with our lives the very best we can to make the world a better place in which to live.[4]

While the Green Bay Packers dedicated themselves to teamwork excellence and being perfect in football in the 1960s, the Pittsburgh Steelers in the 70s, the San Francisco 49ers in the 80s, the Dallas Cowboys in the 90s, and the New England Patriots in the 2000s we should also understand what the game does to its players. According to the Center for the Study of Retired Athletes (a joint project of the University of North Carolina, at Chapel Hill, and the National Football League Players Association), of more than 2,500 former players survey respondents, writes *Scientific American* in April 2005 issue,

> 62.5 percent had gotten at least one concussion. The average was two concussions. A quarter suffered three or more concussions. This last group has three times the normal risk of depression. They also have an elevated risk of the kind of cognitive impairment that often precedes full-blown Alzheimer's disease. Moving from neurology to orthopedics, 38 percent of ex-players have osteodegenerative arthritis . . . Twenty percent of players damaged their knees' anterior cruciate ligament, which can lead to permanent mobility problems.

The Cuisine of the Heart:
Mother's Love Is Indispensable for Babies

Incredibly as it sounds, when a sense of responsibility, the commitment of each to the whole, goodness of heart and boundless compassion awaken within us, we achieve an exalted greatness; it woks like magic. The Righteous One engraved "on the tablets of every heart" these grains of truth:

> A new commandment I give you: Love one another. As I have loved you, so you must love one another. All men will know that you are my disciples if you love one another (Jn 13:33-5).

Five hundred years earlier the Buddha in Sutta Nipata stated:

> Just as a mother would protect her only child at the risk of her own life, even so, cultivate a boundless heart towards all beings. Let your thoughts of boundless love pervade the whole world. (149-150)

In Proverbs we find this insight, "Above all else, keep watch over your heart, for herein lie the wellsprings of life" (4:23). Count Tolstoy would like to know where in your life there is space for your heart:

> Compassion is one of the most precious faculties in the human heart. In taking pity on the suffering of a living being, the person forgets himself and understands the situation of misfortune. By his sentiment, he withdraws from his isolation and acquires the possibilities of uniting his existence to that of other living beings.

Dr. Clancy McKenzie is a brilliant, tenacious, and prevention-oriented physician. His face beams with compassion, happiness, and altruism. Loving-kindness, words of appreciation and encouragement are his trademark. He believes prevention is much better than cure; that is "It is more important to teach people to be responsible—to drive safely than to repair smashed cars." For over four decades McKenzie has been treating trauma victims, especially victims of the first twenty-four months of life. These include persons who have schizophrenia, depression, bipolar disorder, alcohol and drug dependence, ADHD (attention deficit/hyperactivity disorder), school violence, crime, and more.[5] According to McKenzie:

> Mother's love and care is indispensable for babies. To grow, flowers need sunshine; to blossom, babies need mother's love and care. Period. Experiencing mother's love and care not only helps in the nourishment of a healthy baby, but it teaches the baby how to love and care for others.
>
> What happens when the love and care is not there, or suddenly disappears? This produces "trauma" for babies and contemporary world-order problems for society later. The trauma of not having mother's love and care actually can cause babies to die in a failure-to-thrive syndrome. Babies who are traumatized by early separations from love and care of mothers often become alcoholic or criminals after experiencing similar stress or separation later in life. Research demonstrates that other primates traumatized by early separations are more susceptible to alcoholism.
>
> The same principle operates with other emotional disorders, including schizophrenia and depression. The mechanism is simple.

Everyone understands delayed post-traumatic stress related to the trauma of combat. Decades after war trauma, a loud noise can precipitate the heat of battle.

Nearly all infant traumas have one common denominator: a physical or emotional separation from a mother's love and care. This is not a result of being cast away, as literally was done in ancient Rome or in the days of the prophet Moses. The traumas usually are subtler, such as the birth of a sibling, moving to a new house, the mother being terribly upset for a period of time, or divorce.

Why should the baby be overwhelmed if a mother is upset or away for a few days? The answer becomes clear when we realize that, for 150 million years, mammalian babies die when separated from their mother. A separation of a mother from a baby is as terrifying as war trauma to a soldier.

The correlation between separation in the first two years of life and later development of schizophrenia has been confirmed with the 6,000 cases in the Finnish database on schizophrenia and the 2,669 cases in the Danish cohort on schizophrenia. The same separation in the next year of life correlates with the later development of nonpsychotic major depression. Decades after the trauma of infant separation in mother's love and care, a separation from some other "most important person" can precipitate the initial step back in time.

The Unibomber was nine months old when he was hospitalized and suffered the trauma of separation from his mother. This produced rage. When a lady friend left him forty years later, he returned to the rage of the earlier time and sent bombs indiscriminately to people. I profiled the Washington, D.C. sniper on Fox National TV as a person with early traumatic separation from mother, and subsequent separation from a lady friend or other important persons, which awakened the infant rage. This proved correct.

Pitirim A. Sorokin (1889-1968), Russian-American sociologist who founded the department of Sociology at Harvard University in 1930, is well known for his praiseworthy skill to weave complex social scientific methods of the day with extraordinary intellectual breadth and depth. In *The Mysterious Energy of Love*, Sorokin waves the white flag.

A rapid deterioration of the health of babies deprived of warm, motherly love is typically demonstrated by a careful, filmed study of what happened to [fifty-five] such babies in a well-managed New York foundling home. After three months of separation from their mothers the foundlings began to lose their appetite, failed to sleep, and became shrunken, whimpering, and trembling. During the additional two months their deterioration increased. Twenty-seven babies died during the first year; seven more died during the second year. Twenty-one survived longer, but were so altered that thereafter they could be classified only as idiots. Except for motherly love, these babies had all the care and attention necessary for their well-being. And yet, lack of genuine love made these conditions insufficient to secure the foundlings' survival and healthy growth.[6]

Parenthood Requires Skills in Human Technology

It is a known fact, most of our individual and social ills (which are discussed in more detail in part 2, chapter 10) start at home with many mothers and fathers not giving enough care, affection, and the holy compassion of love to their children; they don't give their children the tools to build a flourishing and successful life.

To drive a car, fly a commercial plane, transport people by train, or haul gasoline by ship, one needs basic training and a license to carry out these tasks. Without training or meeting basic proficiency requirements one would be endangering lives and property of others.

To market medicinal preparations for individual consumption, drug-makers must meet tough FDA (Food and Drug Administration) toxicity stamp of approval. To sell cows, pigs, or chickens to the general public, farmers, meat packers, and distributors also have to face demanding USDA (United States Agriculture Department), FSIS (Food Safety and Inspection Service), and the federal CDC (Center for Disease Control) modus operandi.

We all remember what happened in Britain: more than 130 people died, and millions of cattle had to be destroyed, because of the mad cow disease (otherwise known as bovine spongiform encephalopathy [BSE]) and the toxic BSE nourishments. In 2002, 61 million pounds of meat products were recalled in the U.S., because of food contamination. On the other hand, to produce humans for society there is no toxicology training or basic skill prerequisite, let alone living with compassion for the whole of human family and doing whatever one can for humanity's welfare.

Should children be traumatized; should general public not be protected from spiritual food contamination and mental toxicity? If you loved them, you would not do that to them! "Millions of fathers abandon their kids," states, a two-time Emmy Award winner for excellence in reporting, Bill O'Reilly in *Who's Looking Out for You*, "and it is rare that any of them sees a day in jail."[7] Columnist Kathleen Parker put into words: "Today having a baby is like swinging through McDonald's for a burger. One baby all the way, hold the dad." If what is produced is toxic to people or kills them, let the society worry about it.

Would you fly with a pilot of an airline or go to a doctor that was merely trained by his or her parents? If the father or mother was a pilot or a doctor you could be OK. But if not, you could be a statistic. Not all parents had parents that loved them, cared for them, and gave them emotional, educational, and spiritual tools for life and getting along with people in everyday business and social contacts. Many parents are disadvantaged—they need more training in the fine art of human technology: interrelation with people, arousing enthusiasm to their humanity and divinity, and in bringing up children. They should be helped to become problem solvers, not problem creators—before they embark on producing trauma for children and social chaos.

It is tragic, nerve-racking, and heavy going to most one-parent families. It is even more heartbreaking to the children and the public. Do the math. There are nearly twelve million one-parent families in the United States of America. Now fast forward. If the trend continues, over the next forty years, more than 50 percent of American babies will be born out of wedlock; now approximately 40 percent are born out of wedlock. According to the U.S. census, about 69 percent are African-American and 27 percent are whites. "For black women ages fifteen to twenty-four, that figure is astounding [at] 89 percent!" writes Bill O'Reilly:

> That is simply a cultural collapse on an unprecedented scale for a developed country. Just the fact that nearly [nine out of ten] all black girls and young women having babies today are unmarried is enough to ensure social chaos within the African-American

community for generations to come. A child without a secure support system will most likely be unable to compete with a child who has one. Thus, the cycle of hopelessness and deprivation will continue.

So let me ask you this question. When was the last time you heard Jesse Jackson or Al Sharpton or even Colin Powell address this issue? When was the last time there was a rally in Washington demanding that this colossal problem be addressed by all Americans?[8]

The U.S. census numbers become more chilling, more heartrending, when we realize that the 69 percent of the one-parent African-American and the 27 percent of the one-parent white population precipitates the bulk of social ills. Do your own research. You will take pity on the misfortune of the one-parent families *and* the public.

Oh, and one more thing. Parents that give love and care to their children in addition to their own personal challenges (health, finances, monogamy) have to deal with tons of un-neighborly assaults, cruelty, hype, buzz, and tease: toxic showbiz and media, deceit and corruption in high places (corporations, religious institutions, and out-of-touch governments as to our unity), child molestation, degenerate rap music, adultery and oral sex education from the World Wide Web, Oval Office, and the entertainment industry, the bottle, mind-numbing drugs, theft, and the like. What about children whose parents don't have the time or the tools to deal with these crippling influences? Will the Supreme Court, the ACLU (American Civil Liberties Union), and professionals, such as religious institutions and accountants protect them?

Something Is Not Kosher Here: You Cannot Legislate '1'

The empty-space is the fundamental nature of every atom. No atom of matter, or its spectral lines, comes marked in theistic or atheistic terms and the language of science and mathematics is standard. If the Supreme Court, ACLU, and the religious institutions understood the basic fact of the fundamental interconnectedness of every entity in the universe, and that the Common Ground ('1') is a "higher law" than the Constitution, and is a necessity for all the laws of nature and being, they would not be equating the "ultimate" or God with the legal concepts of religion. The irony here is that '1' is impartial and unyielding. '1' represents the ultimate law itself. Its job is to enforce principles and precedents regardless of the popularity of the outcome. Without the unchanging of the universe, there would be no existence.

Question: how do you legislate the unchanging or the empty-space out of our lives? That is what the Spirit of God is!

Do you remember the "Silly Billy" story, where people build houses with no windows? To have light in dwellings they caught sunlight into baskets and carried it into their homes. Did it work? No. They did not understand the physics of light. You cannot transport light in a basket; you have to make windows in a house. Equally, just as we cannot legislate laws of nature out of nature, we cannot legislate God out of the empty-space.

The unity of all existence does not depend on show of hands, nor is it a democratic choice or participation. It does not progress by majority rule or First Amendment, nor does it accept notions of belief. The unchanging is the Central Operating Principle of the universe and the fundamental structure of life. Additionally, states Sorokin,

> The grace of love—in both forms of loving and being loved—is necessary not only for survival and physical health sound citizens. Now we know well that the bulk of juvenile delinquents and psychoneurotics are recruited mainly from the ranks of persons who in their early life were deprived of a minimum of love in their families and in their "un-neighborly neighborhood." On the other hand, the Mennonite, the Hutterites, the Mormon and the Friends' communities in the United States yield either none or the lowest quota of criminals, mentally sick, drug addicts, sex perverts, and libertines. The main reason for this is that these brotherly communities not only preach love, but also steadily practice it, not only in regard to the members of their family, but to all members of their community, and even to all members of the human race.[9]

Yes, to participate is to make the right choice that helps your mind, body, and soul rise to the occasion and win its battle against all kinds of imbalances and wear and tear. To make the right choice means to be responsible. The responsibility is in the heart and mind. For this reason, we all need to accept the responsibility for our own development and advance. Robert Muller spoke with the voice of an unquenchable tenacity of purpose and Love Everlasting:

> To be able to say on the last day of one's life:
> I loved to live
> I lived to love
> I laughed a lot
> I gave much love
> I left the world a little better than I found it
> I loved the world's great beauty
> I sang life and the universe
> I looked for the best in others
> I gave the best I had.
> Thank you, O God, for this miracle of life.[10]

To Master Love Is to Practice Love

Similar to Muller's well-hidden poetic streak, Lincoln's mind was serenely consistent, so that "the common people will understand you." He stated to Joshua Speed that when he dies, "I want it said of me by those who know me best . . . that I always plucked a thistle and planted a flower where I thought a flower would grow."

Jeremiah suggested, "Circumcise [purify spiritually] yourselves to the Lord, remove the foreskin of your hearts" (4:4). In the Gospel of Thomas, Jesus' "disciples said to him, 'Is circumcision beneficial or not?' He said to them, 'If it were beneficial, their father would beget them already circumcised from their mother. Rather, the true circumcision in spirit has become completely profitable.'" (54)

Hafiz put it this way, "Old lovers say, 'We can do it one more time, how about from this longitude and latitude—swinging from a rope tied to the ceiling, maybe a part of God is still hiding in a corner of your heart our devotion has yet to reveal'"[11]

In a chat between the young Bishop of Belley and his friend Saint Francis of Sales (1567-1622), French ecclesiastic and writer on theology, bishop of Geneva (1602-1622), we learn the secret ways of becoming perfect:

There are many besides you who want me to tell them of methods and systems and secret ways of becoming perfect, and I can only tell them that the sole secret is a hearty love of God, and the only way of attaining that love is by loving. You learn to speak by speaking, to study by studying, to run by running, to work by working; and just so you learn to love God and man by loving. All those who think to learn in any other way deceive themselves. If you want to love God, go on loving Him more and more. Begin as a mere apprentice, and the very power of love will lead you on to become a master in the art. Those who have made most progress will continually press on, never believing themselves to have reached their end; for charity should go on increasing until we draw our last breath.[12]

Mother Teresa said, "It's not how much we give but how much love we put into giving." "Pure love can emanate only from a heart immersed in peace," says Sai Baba. For that reason, he exhorts:

Love all beings—that is enough. Love with no expectation of return; love for the sake of love; love because your very nature is love; love because that is the form of worship you know and like. When others are happy, be happy likewise. When others are in misery, try to alleviate their lot to the best of your ability. Practice love through service. By this means, you will realize Unity and dissolve the ego that harms . . . Live in love, live with love, move with love, speak with love, think with love, and act with love.[13]

Freedom Is Directly Related to the Right Choice: Live Consciously in His Heart

Love knows no bounds. Where love is, there you will find His heart; where God is, there you will find love. Love clears our mind and brings to light our Oneness with God and all of life. We become what we love. Love expands our life span and the advancement of knowledge. We realize love lives in us and we in love. Best of all, when love speaks to Love, what more is there to say? Saint John, saturated with love of God, enunciates the cosmic formula:

He that loveth not knoweth not God,
For God is love
And ANYONE WHO LIVES IN LOVE LIVES IN GOD,
And *God lives in him*.
Love will come to its perfection in us
When we can face the day of Judgment without fear;
Because *even in this world*
WE HAVE BECOME AS HE IS (1 Jn 4:13-17).

The Persian poet Yahya (ibn Mu´adh ar-Razi) and the author of many perceptive books, maintained: "One mustard seed of love is better than seventy years of worship without love."[14] Wolfgang Amadeus Mozart (1756-1791), who began composing music when he was five years of age and is regarded to be one of the greatest musical geniuses of all time, maintained, "A genius without heart is nonsense."[15] Or we can follow the path of sanctification through Saint Irenaeus' words that "God the Logos became what we are, in order that we may become what he himself is [through love]."

Jalal al-Din Rumi (the Sage of Rum) was a spiritual drunkard (as Sufis refer to him and others who place love at the center of their very lives) who hung out in God's tavern of love. He said: "The sect of lovers is distinct from all others; lovers have a religion and a faith all their own."[16] Additionally, said Rumi, "I pulled my own existence out of emptiness . . . love is the religion, the universe its book . . . Putting aside duality, I have seen that this world and the next are one. I seek the One, I know the One, I see the One, I invoke the One. Allah is the First and the Last, the Outward and the Inward."

"Being able to cure physical, mental, and moral sickness," confirms Sorokin,

> love-energy also contributes to the prolongation of human life. This fact is typically illustrated by the longevity of some 4,500 Christian saints studied. These saints lived in the first to the eighteenth centuries, when the average life span was much shorter than it is in the United States today. Most of the saints lived in the conditions, which, according to present standards of public health, were far from hygienic. Many of the saints were ascetic and deprived their bodies of the satisfaction of vital needs. In spite of these

adverse conditions, their average longevity was as high, at least, as that of contemporary Americans. An abundant and pure love of saints for God and for neighbors appears to be largely responsible for their outstanding longevity.

This conclusion is confirmed by the opposite, life-shortening effects of hate and enmity also ascertained by many recent studies.[17]

"Great is this challenge and power in our custody, to guide the generation of God into the Promised Land," rhapsodized Abraham Heschel. "Great is the challenge we face at every moment, sublime the occasion, every occasion. Here we are, contemporaries of God, some of His power at our disposal."[18]

The Jesuit monk Teilhard de Chardin, whose depth of insight strived to create a harmony and synthesis between religious and scientific thinking, very eloquently described that we are evolving, mentally and socially, toward a final spiritual unity (Christ [single] Consciousness—Rumi's, "I know the One, I see the One . . ."), and promised that one day, when we realize this awareness of Oneness within ourselves, humanity shall put a harness on the energy of love. "And then, for the second time in the history of the world, man will have discovered fire."[19]

14

WE CAN BE LIGHTS TO EACH OTHER: EXPERIENCE IT!

Every day is my best day, this is my life;
I'm not going to have this moment again.

—Bernie Siegel, MD

Divining Peace: I Have Never Felt So Happy in My Life

Just as in the equilibrium at the center of a wave, purity of heart, compassion, and deep inner peace in our mind creates a zero ('1', the clear Light) state. Energies in our body, similar to electric power, or a waterfall coursing down a mountainside, rush toward the lowest energy level (the electrical zero potential; Christ's "My power is strongest when you are weak" [2 Cor 12:9]), thus producing a regenerative and uplifting effect.

In this loving splendor and timeless bliss of "peace beyond peace," you will be slowly filling up your mind and body with the bioplasma or Kundalini energy (further explored in subsequent chapters). Your awareness will quicken and you will begin to break out of the chains of your present consciousness. The distinction between you and your surroundings—between knower and the known—will slowly disappear, and melt into the colorless light of emptiness, Japanese Zen satori or Buddhists nirvana. You will perceive, as did Bohm, Schrödinger, Skovoroda, Vernadsky, Gurvich, Shakyamuni, Gandhi, Plotinus, Emerson, Ramakrishna, Thoreau, Wilber, the Dalai Lama, and many others, the unity of the universe. Time and space, from here to there, and everywhere in between will become One, as a single light merges within the ocean of light.

You will then see that you yourself and the rest of Reality, large and small, are part of one and the same splendor and stillness, one and the same joy of conscious glory and light. You will transcend bliss, anticipation, and desire. You will, as René Descartes stated, "grasp together distinctly a number of these propositions so far as possible at the same time."[1]

Insight and Awakening: Eureka! I've Got It

Recall the towering Greek mathematician and engineer Archimedes (287-212 BC), noted for his insights into physical and geometrical principles and his mechanical inventions; his work on statics and hydrostatics of fluids is the foundation of both. Archimedes, discoverer of the lever and the principle of buoyancy, and forerunner of calculus, in one account was asked by King Hieron II of Syracuse, Sicily, to find out whether a goldsmith had substituted less valuable material, silver for gold, in creating his crown.

Archimedes knew that he needed to find the volume of the crown to unlock the mystery of its density. While getting into a bathtub, he "integrated" the untied parts—like we do when we cook a soup, bake a cake, or assemble a car. Archimedes realized that different materials not only weigh different amounts but when put into a tub of water would displace their own volume of water. He knew he had the answer. Archimedes instantly leaped out of his bath so overjoyed that he ran stark naked through the streets to King Hieron's palace shouting "Eureka! Eureka!" ("I have found [it], I have found [it]").

Nirvana: The Clear Light of Bliss

Ni in old Sanskrit stands for "no" and *rvana* signifies "broken." The state of nirvana is David Bohm's integrated wholeness—Oneness, complete cake, soup, and car. In this state of illumination, characterized by the fusion of the individual I in transcendent consciousness, Chuang-tzu disclosed, "The ten thousand things are all one."[2]

Why will it not be so, questioned the young disciple of Eckhart, German Dominican Henry Suso: "All creatures . . . are the same life, the same essence, the same power, the same one, and nothing less."

Those describing the Archimedes "eureka" moment or the Buddhist state of blissful nirvana explain the inner experience as "blowing out"—

exploding over the universe in the Hindu liberation or samadhi terms. Nirvana also suggests the state of perfect enlightenment (when one achieves the Oneness state, nothing/everything) attainable not merely after passing away, but here on earth while within our physical bodies. When the fires of desire are extinguished to "nothing" (complete stillness, joy beyond joy, and freedom beyond freedom), when our "mind" stops reflecting/projecting what we see and experience, we simultaneously come into contact with the opposite of nothing: everything ([Everything = 1/Nothing], where [Everything] x [Nothing] = 1).[3]

Nirvana has also been described as the "going out" of the flame of a candle, and an unimpeded or a still mind. Gautama Buddha associated nirvana with the "Emptiness of the Womb" and the subtle state of the unborn, uncreated, unformed (cosmic singularity: '1'). In Udana the Buddha stated:

> Verily, there is an unborn, unoriginated, uncreated, unformed. If there were not this unborn, unoriginated, uncreated, unformed, then an escape from the world of the born, the originated, the created, and the formed would not be possible. [viii, 3].

Einstein said that this state "is precisely not to be influenced, since it is changeless and unmovable, either by configuration of matter or by anything else."[4]

How Do We Know What We Know?

Scientists, in quantum physics, depict Einstein's "changeless" and "unmovable" state as the realm of possibilities, the world of potentialities, or, the not-modulated primordial vacuum. Buddhists represent the "changeless" nirvana state as the "ground state" of consciousness (consciousness devoid of mental states, where you eliminate the noise, fear, anxiety, and the static of everyday thought), the Great Perfection, or primordial awareness, out of which everything in the universe appears. Zen masters consider sitting in absorption of the "unmovable" (*zazen*) as the alpha and the omega of Zen. In its purest form, zazen is being in a state of "thought free," alertly wakeful attention. It is the most direct way to satori (the experience of awakening or enlightenment) and the "gateway to liberation."

For a visual illustration, we can compare the world of potentialities, or the clear Light of inner knowing, to the "zero" (reset) on a computer and our experiences and knowledge to the internal software of a computer. All problems and challenges just disappear to naught, zilch, or zip when you push that little reset button. Because all unmanifest knowledge preexist in the "realm of potentialities" (the Copenhagenists pre-quantum fact, Carpenter's I) '1', our Infinite Splendor, is accessible for understanding concepts, liberating the unconscious for breakthrough insights, and functioning at peak performance.

What is the best way to survive any crisis? Avoid it altogether. Imagine if you could see the ripple effects right through your organization and know the effects of a policy or operational decision—before you make that decision. Specifically, we can gain knowledge not only through reading, hearing, education, and computer simulation but also directly from the sacred-space (i.e., the "miracle zone," or simply "the zone"). That is, '1' can be deployed for remote viewing (fast-forward to today: visiting the future or the past, recovering memory loss of our identity), as well as, for decision-making, problem solving, how to design the right policies, create novel nanometer scale devices, deal with diminishing job security, and look forward to where a particular knowledge or a ripple effect is taking us.

Remote viewing is known as "inner viewing" (*nei-kuan* or *nei-shih*) in the Taoist tradition of China, or intuition in the West. Remote viewing has been employed to nurture new ideas, develop intellectual properties, solve crimes, in overhauls to bureaucracy, town planning, and for risk-minimizing, financial forecasting, pruning duplicated efforts, and locating missing objects or people, and spontaneous healing. Throughout the 1970s and 1980s the United States government, at the Stanford Research Institute, funded remote viewing research yielding "hit" rates of more than a million to one against chance. It was learned the human mind could go to distant locations, transcend space and time, and give the details of what is to be found there.

One of the joys of living, working, playing, and creating in a state of the "zone" is that it becomes apparent you can do no wrong. What appeared impossible earlier is now possible. The observer can discover superstrong nano materials, micro fuel-cells, software that's smart enough to write itself, processors that power all kinds of mobile gadgets, antivirus technology to track down virus writers, and female and male viruses that mate and have offspring. Furthermore, one can find out how to replace the light bulb with a minute scale nanocrystals that emit steady light, look at biomechatronics (which brings together robotics and biology), or the inner recesses of her/his body until the smallest features come into view with excellent lucidity before the inner eye. From heart disease to hepatitis, cancer to AIDS and real-time power grid control, it can help us in the development of new technologies, state-of-the-art drugs, investments, generate fresh advertising ideas, the structuring of corporate financial transactions, and the advancement of knowledge to new domains. It allows us to look into the very heart of the atom, see the universe making headway, uncover new gizmos and realize the practice of personalized medicine, where the right patients get the right drugs.

Example: let me indulge in a few personal reminiscences about the Infinite Ground and remote viewing utilization that illustrate themes from the experience of my own. In 1956 IBM started developing the Stretch (7030) Supercomputer for the Atomic Energy Commission (AEC) at the Los Alamos Scientific Laboratory (LASL) in New Mexico and the National Security Agency (NSA) in Langley, Virginia. Hungarian-born German American mathematician John von Neumann (1903-1957), who made extremely significant contributions in computer theory, urged Big Blue to build "the most advanced machine . . . possible in the present state-of-the-art."

Prior to Stretch, IBM computers glowed in the dark, all of which relied on vacuum tubes. Stretch was to be one of the first transistors-based computers, with all sorts of exotic innovations that became part of System/360 (a gutsy, bet-the-company move) and IBM's flagship product line for the next twenty years. It was to be Big Blue's scientific supercomputing masterpiece with the power of 75 to 100 IBM 704s to solve tremendously complex data-processing problems with the speed and capacity far beyond that of any system ever built. The LASL price (then $13.5 million) was comparable to more than $80 million in the year 2000. Supercomputers are used in a wide swath of applications, including molecular dynamics in biology, computational cosmology, human vision simulation, aerodynamic design, automotive development, and predicting climate change. Procter & Gamble, for example, engineers the superabsorbent materials in its baby diapers with a supercomputer.

In 1936, a paper by Cambridge University mathematician Alan Turing set the groundwork for the construction of electronic computers, and in 1950 he proposed a daring measure for machine intelligence. To be fair, various other people contributed, from mathematician Charles Babbage and Ada Lovelace in the 1830s to Herman Hollerith—whose tabulating company became IBM—at the turn of the century. But it was Turing who made the decisive fundamental advance of a "universal machine" that could be given *instructions* to perform a variety of tasks.

In 1956 I was part of the IBM Stretch research/development team. One of our major challenges was this: how can we add, subtract, multiply, and divide a googolplex sequence of numbers in a flash? The answer is to not perform these calculations consecutively in a serial fashion (as when we routinely add numbers), but rather to do this concurrently, in parallel. A googol is a number that a child wrote on the board in kindergarten. It is the mathematical term for a 1 followed by 100 zeros. A googolplex is 10 to the googol power (10^{googol}).

Normally, when numbers are added, the sum for each position is generated sequentially, incorporating the carry consecutively from one level to the next. The question was, is it mathematically feasible to bypass waiting for the carry propagation and add all numbers simultaneously, at the same time? Do you recollect the mechanical clink-clink adding machines? Sometimes answers appeared fast; other times the clink clinking went on forever.

On-Demand Solutions

In order to get a better perspective of what this "consecutive" serial fashion problem involves, let us consider an illustration from the early days of the formation of the American Republic. Having won independence from England, America faced a new challenge: mass-producing muskets. Prior to the discovery of mass (simultaneous or parallel) assembly, every handgun part was custom-built consecutively, one part after another, by a highly skilled craftsman. No two muskets were alike. However, there were not enough capable craftsmen to produce the thousands of muskets needed.

LeBlanc in France (who produced fifty musket locks) and subsequently two Connecticut Yankees, Eli Whitney, a manufacturer of muskets (who obtained a contract for ten thousand muskets in January 1798), and Simeon North, a maker of pistols (who acquired a contract for five hundred pistols in March 1799) came up with a solution—

"parts interchangeability through parts standardization." This eminent invention of the Industrial Revolution had a profound influence on the mechanization of industry. Now, interchangeable manufacturing (sometimes referred to as the "American System") allows automobiles and airplanes to be built concurrently, in parallel, by anyone. Unskilled craftsmen do mass assembly without fitting or further machining.

How does one simultaneously mass-assemble a googolplex of binary numbers (zeroes and ones) within a computer? How does one whiz through an incredible gazillions of calculations in a twinkle? "In the fields of observation, chance favors the mind that is prepared," wrote Louis Pasteur.[5]

To let you fix your high-tech car equipment, different cars have different "secret handshakes" to access the diagnostic codes. The first step in cracking the code or to an insight into depths of knowledge is a careful marshaling of the facts. Facts serve as "secret handshakes," triggers, couplings, and tuners to solutions, in the "world of potentialities" or the absolute ground of consciousness. Archimedes' law was triggered by rising water in a bathtub. A falling apple triggered Newton's gravity explanation (or so the story goes).

Because in most instances we can't get directly at the interior Software of '1' (quantum physicists world of potentialities), we have to examine its output. The trial-and-error method of experimentation, testing and verification are normally used. However, the trial-and-error method is costly, time-consuming, and does not always work. It is like breaking a watch and then observing where the wheels fall in order to determine how the internals are constructed. This is what is done for experimental research in elementary particle physics and with the most powerful accelerators in the world.

In addition, the equations of the theory—the properties of the particles and the forces themselves—are not present in the solutions. The symmetry breakdown of elementary particles (like when the watch falls apart) is not a straightforward product of the equations. Remote viewing can be a very effective tool to make new discoveries, especially compared to the now-standard trial-and-error approach. In the Bhagavad Gita this insight can be found:

> Whatever you wish to see can be seen all at once in this [human] body. This universal form can show you all that you now desire, as

well as *whatever you may desire in the future*. EVERYTHING IS HERE COMPLETELY [something Kurt Friedrich Gödel did not consider]. But you cannot see Me ['1', the clear Light] with your present eyes. Therefore I give to you divine eyes [the deepest state of consciousness—where all your might is] by which you can behold My mystic opulence (11:7-8).

Saint Symeon the New Theologian put it this way, "Search inside yourself with your intellect so as to find the place of the heart, where all the powers of the soul reside. To start with, you will find darkness and an impenetrable density. Later, when you persist and practice this task day and night, you will find, as though miraculously, an unceasing joy. For, as soon as the intellect attains the place of the heart, at once it seems things of which it previously knew nothing."

Living in the "Mivecle Zone"

Collecting all the basics possible, I prepared myself for a full-scale intuitive insight of the "realm of possibilities" ('1'). Centered in peace, stillness, and *certainty in my heart*, I had the notion that there should be (similar to interchangeable manufacture) a mathematical algorithm for *parallel processing* in the multidimensional Formless Infinity. I knew if there is a solution, I should be able to decipher this secret data-encryption algorithm with my mind's search engine.

To connect to '1' or "tune in" on the answer in the "miracle zone" of infinities, the mind must be clear, alert, free of thought processes, and prepared to infinite code breaking. The heart must be open and at peace. Albert Einstein once stated, "No problem can be solved from the same consciousness that created it."

For several weeks, while working in the laboratory and at home, I tried as much as possible to be in the silence of the heart and concentrated attention on the stillness of the mind (the silence between two thoughts) and detachment from the problem. Similar to tuning your radio to a particular station, I was tuning (while working and living my daily life) into the Absolute Infinity, '1': inner peace, compassion, and Oneness of all. In that sacred-space we experience pure consciousness itself, the ultimate level of infinity, the Infinite Splendor (discussed in part 2, chapter 5).

The Equations Were in the Air

Hosanna! Here it was. Unexpectedly, like cream rising to the top of milk, the answer surfaced in my mind. An "inner light" of insightful quality illuminated me. I was able to "visually observe" outside of my head a binary tree of Boolean equations of thousands exotic parallel microprocessors. I looked at the internal makeup of parallel supercomputers able to add new ten thousand problems to the old ten thousand problems, simultaneously in parallel. I picked up my pencil and began transcribing the vast string of *Boolean relationships that I vividly saw in front of me in the air* above my head.[6]

While I was transcribing the equations, which I had never seen before, an associate, Harry Reinheimer, who worked with me in the same office, started chatting. I told him with my hand I had to be silent. I was concerned that by conversing the equations would disappear from my view. Upon completion, I turned over the plans for the machine to be assembled and patented. It was built, patented,[7] and delivered to a number of customers. Now laptops, mainframes, and supercomputers employ these high-speed parallel processing, Carry Select, and Carry Look-Ahead principles in their computations.

The fascinating part of this experience is that even though I was the one who saw the Boolean equations suspended in the air, on the right side above my head, I did not fully understand how the parallel principle worked for several weeks—but my manager, Olin MacSorley, did right away.

Ludwig von Beethoven (1770-1827) used walking out of doors to trigger his remote viewing (compositions). In 1804 Beethoven went on a stroll with his student, who subsequently wrote:

> We went so far astray that we did not get back . . . until nearly 8
> o'clock . . . He had been all the time humming and sometimes
> howling, always up and down, without singing any definite notes.
> In answer to my question what it was he said, "A theme for the last
> movement of the sonata has occurred to me." When we entered
> the room he ran to the pianoforte without taking off his hat. I took
> a seat in the corner and he soon forgot all about me. Now he
> stormed for at least an hour with the beautiful finale of the sonata.
> Finally he got up, was surprised to see me and said: "I cannot give
> you a lesson today, I must do some more work."

The Search for Tomorrow:
Consciousness Generates Reality

This personal "eureka" experience took place when I was twenty-four years old. At that time I did not know entirely how to trigger on demand the state of lucid exaltation, the clear Light of inner knowing. Today, four decades later, I see a bit more clearly: *the quality of our consciousness determines the quality of our understanding and the nature of our universe.* We are the light for our own personal universe; we are dreamers dreaming our own personal dreams. When we smile, the mirror smiles; when we cry the mirror cries. Everything is produced by way of our consciousness!

Think of an atom. The empty-space between electrons, protons, and neutrons is one's real most intimate self, or the Infinite Splendor of inner knowing. Our consciousness tunes into imagery (the Forms of Plato) out of the collective cosmic foundation, the "ground state of potentialities" ('1'), that manifests to us as the universe or existence. Images that we see in our external "viewing screen" (daily happenings: the space-time universe around us) are essentially a projection of our own personal "light in us" that is constant to every observer, regardless of how she/he is moving about.

The '1' underpinning, the observer, and the observed are fundamentally one. The more we can "merge" our being and actions into the blueprint of '1', the more we can place ourselves into the current or stream of '1' (i.e., add like a calculator would, Christ's "Thy will be done") the more peace, happiness, and miracles we experience daily.

Jesus said, "If anyone loves me, he will obey my teachings. My Father will love him, and we will come to him and make our home with him" (Jn 14:23). Moreover, "If a man walks in broad daylight he does not stumble, because he sees the light of *this* world. But if he walks during the night he stumbles, because there is no light IN HIM" (Jn 11:9).

How so? Because, "you are like light for the whole world" (Mt 5:14); your consciousness brings light to your universe.

John Archibald Wheeler illustrates this personal "light in us" concept with one eye looking on another eye across a large "U." According to Wheeler, "The "U" in the universe stands for you. You are the Universe, looking in the mirror. When you observe the universe, you are observing Urself." So when you cry, the mirror cries; when you smile, the mirror smiles.

Elena Petrovna Blavatskaya (Helena Blavatsky, 1831-1891), born in Dnipropetrovsk, Ukraine, was a prolific remote viewing author. She wrote a letter to her sister, Vera, when transcribing her first book, *Isis Unveiled*:

> Well, Vera, believe it or not, some enchantment is upon me. You can hardly imagine in what a charmed world of pictures I live! . . . I am writing *Isis;* not writing, rather copying out and drawing that which she personally is showing me. Really, it seems to me as if the ancient Goddess of Beauty in person leads me through all the lands of bygone centuries which I have to describe. I am sitting with my eyes open and, to all appearances, see and hear everything real and actual around me; and yet at the same time I see and hear that which I write. I feel short of breath; I am afraid to make the slightest movement, for fear the spell might be broken . . . Slowly, century after century, image after image, float out of nowhere and pass before me as if in a magic panorama; and meanwhile I put them together in my mind, fitting in epochs and dates, and know positively there can be no mistake . . . It stands to reason, it is not I who do it all, but my Ego, the highest principles that live in me.

The Persian poet and major contributor to Sufism (*The Mystic Rose*), Mahmud Shabestari (1250-1320), put it this way:

> The world has become a man, and man a world. There is no clearer explanation than this. When you look well into the root of the matter, He is at once sees, seeing eye, and things seen.

William Makepeace Thackeray (1811-1863), English novelist, born in India, expressed similar insight, "The world is a looking-glass and gives back to every man the reflection of his own face. Frown at it and it in turn will look sourly upon you; laugh at it and with it, and it is a jolly, kind companion."

Anandamayi Ma ("the mother filled with bliss," 1896-1982) was born in East Bengal, now Bangladesh. "Mother" achieved enlightenment (realization), like Ramana Maharshi, without a guru or studying the Holy Scriptures. Ma, who journeyed through India to spiritually assist all classes, characterized Wheeler's "U" as follows: "This body is like a musical instrument; what you hear depends on how you play it." Try to be a flower, a bird, or a sequoia, and think what your universe would be like.

Immanuel Kant, roughly 150 years earlier, also "discovered" that the mind shapes reality in relation to is own makeup. This was such a breakthrough to Kant that he referred to it "the second Copernican Revolution." In London, just about the same time, William Blake stated, "As man is, so he sees." "Apart from thoughts, there is no independent entity called the world," declared Ramana Maharshi. "Just as the spider emits the thread (of the web) out of itself and again withdraws it into itself, likewise the mind projects the world out of itself and again resolves it into itself."

Not long ago it was thought that there was an exclusive absolute time for everyone. Currently, we know that according to the theory of relativity each observer has her/his own personal time that is relative to the observer. Now we think that there is an exclusive absolute space-time universe for everyone. In part 2, chapter 5, we shall see that because of the unity of the laws of physics and the Principle of the One and the Many, *each observer experiences her/his own personal universe.*

"Compared to what we ought to be," stated William James (1842-1910), "we are only half awake. We are making use of only a small part of our physical and mental resources. Stating the thing broadly, the human individual thus lives far within his limits. He possesses powers of various sorts which he habitually fails to use." Additionally, "The greatest revolution of our generation is the discovery that human beings, by changing the inner attitudes of their minds, can change the outer aspects of their lives." It is up to each of us to choose what we need to do, and to in fact see it through.

Linus Pauling worked on the molecular theory problem involving general anesthesia for ten years prior to finding the solution. Here is Pauling's story:

> Often my original ideas have come as a result of training my unconscious mind to think about a problem . . . I was in Boston as a member of the scientific advisory board of Massachusetts General Hospital in 1952, and this board was lectured to by the professor of anesthesiology at Harvard, Henry K. Beecher. Beecher said something that I hadn't known—that the noble gas xenon can act as a general anesthetic agent. So I said to my son (who was studying

medicine): "How do you think xenon can serve as a general anesthetic agent, since xenon doesn't form any compounds in the human body? It must be some sort of a physical action. I don't understand it." I thought about it day after day for several days; in the evening when I would go to bed, I would lie there and think about the problem . . . After a while I stopped that. Then, seven years later, I was reading a scientific paper on crystal structure, and I said to myself: "I understand anesthesia." I worked for about a year gathering data, and then I published my paper on "A molecular theory of general anesthesia." So I had trained my unconscious mind to keep this problem in view, and whenever any new thought entered my head, any new piece of information, I would connect it up with that problem to see if there was any connection.

Lincoln's old Illinois friend Ward Hill Lamon recalled that, "When Mr. Lincoln had a speech to write . . . he would put down each thought, as it occurred to him, on a small strip of paper, and, having accumulated a number of these, generally carried them in his hat or his pockets until he had the whole speech composed in this odd way. [After that would Honest Abe] sit down at his table, connect the fragments, and then write out the whole speech on consecutive sheets in a plain, legible handwriting."

In the Gospel of Thomas, Jesus makes a very interesting observation:

The images [preexistent answers or the "Unchanging Software" that] are manifest to man and the Light ['1'] which is within them is hidden in the Image of the Light of the Father. He will manifest himself and His Image is concealed by His Light. (84). Jesus said: When you see your likeness ['1'], you rejoice. [All well and good.] But when you see your images which came into existence before you, (which) neither die nor are manifested, how much will you bear! (85)

Here is the heart of the human predicament. As we think, as we desire, so we are. The fundamental seed born of the mind produces reality. With our actions, convictions, and expectations *we tune into* the "realm of possibilities" (patterns of potentialities, infinities, which exist prior to manifestation) within the '1'. "And then a miracle occurs." Like in a calculator, a potentiality of the '1', Absolute Infinity, becomes an actuality ('='), an experience in our consciousness. When "we see our likeness" of Light—our Infinite Splendor—we are happy, we rejoice; all well and good. But sometimes the images we tune into, project, scare the wits out of us ("how much will you bear!"). We are learning a new skill: with unconditional love, complete peace of mind, responsibility, and compassion, there is, in principle, no limit to what is possible. Like a sculptor, we are carving a new "face" out of the '1'. In the process we are entertaining ourselves with our own program. We are networking the concealed potentialities of our own being and cultivating new power to display more "miracles." Jesus said, "Everything is possible to the man who trusts" (Mk 9:23).

John von Neumann is a founder of modern set theory (whose use for basic physics language is only recently being explored), and he is a developer of quantum logic (the theory of "and," "or," "not," and "implies"). He made important contributions in quantum physics, meteorology, the theory of games, logic, and economic behavior. During World War II, John von Neumann (and Seth Neddermeyer) received a patent on the trigger of the implosion principle for inducing nuclear fuel to explode and then took part in the development of the hydrogen bomb.

Von Neumann made significant contributions in computer theory: the function of computer "memory," logical design for getting reliable solutions from a computer system with unreliable components, machine imitation of "randomness," and the concept of building machines that can reproduce their own kind. Von Neumann studied in great detail the act of choice, quantum measurement in physics, and the natural location of the "quantum jump" or the "wave function collapse."

How does the unobserved universe, the world of countless potential possibilities, become actuality? Similar to a calculator, within the universal '1' are untold potential possibilities to be unlocked by the mysterious act of choice. When we pick a set of numbers in an addition (analogous to the act of measurement in reality), one computation in a calculator (one quantum possibility in physics) is singled out. Taking one route suggests forsaking another route. Von Neumann concluded (as it had been known long ago to the Arhats [Sanskrit], Lohans [China], Rakans [Japan], Bodhisattvas [Mahayana Buddhism]) that the *observer's consciousness* is where the choice is ultimately made.

In an endeavor that rises above the confined outlook of theoretical physicists, Nick Herbert searched for a picture of "the way the world really is." In his scenic *Quantum Reality: Beyond the New Physics,* Herbert wrote,

> In von Neumann's consciousness-created world, things (or at least their dynamic attributes) do not exist until some mind actually perceives them, a rather drastic conclusion but one to which this great mathematician was forced by sheer logic once he decided to take the quantum measurement problem seriously.[8]

Robert Muller characterizes the problem thusly: "Each human being is a prism in which the whole universe is reflected."[9]

Nothing That Meets the Eye: A Point Cannot Be Divided

As will be seen in part 2, zero is unlike other mathematical numbers, just as a pure vacuum is unlike other physical quantities.[10, 11] A number divided by zero equals infinity. Zero divided by a number, including infinity, is always zero. To make any sort of measurement, we need a common starting point: zero in mathematics, the '1' in physics. Therefore, just as zero gives a glimpse of infinity, so the zero-dimension point provides a glimpse of the Absolute One (the Absolute Infinity in Georg Cantor's sets, discussed in part 2, chapter 4). Zero and the Absolute Infinity are the inverse of each other (discussed in part 2, chapter 5).

Consequently, there are no limits to zero in mathematics, or to initial conditions in physics. Also, there are no limits to an *inverse* of the zero-dimension point: the '1' in physics. There are no limits to our own divinity: *the infinitely small within us is the infinitely large without us,* letting everyone have her/his own personal universe, or as Muller earlier stated, "Each human being is a prism in which the whole [personal] universe is reflected."

What you believe, in time you see and experience. The microscopic order is also the macroscopic order. There are no limits to the development that we, as each point of consciousness, can experience. Projecting with our own consciousness makes our dreams come true. Jesus said,

> Believe me, if you *trust and do not falter,* not only will you do what I did . . . but if you say to this mountain, "Be lifted up and thrown

into the sea," even that will happen. You will receive all that you pray for, provided you have faith (Mt 21:21-2).

Julius Robert Oppenheimer (1904-1967), United States theoretical physicist, director of the Los Alamos laboratory during development of the atomic bomb (1943-1945) and director of the Institute for Advanced Study, Princeton (1947-1966), along with other physical theorists during the 1930s and early 1940s was faced with the catastrophic problem of infinities. When quantum mechanics were applied to electric and magnetic fields, it was found that the atom had an infinite energy (the same way the inverse-square law produces an infinite force when two point electrons are at the same location, or a point '1'). Physical theories were not capable of dealing with infinities, which are the inverse of a point, or the '1' (discussed in part 2, chapters 5 and 6). When infinities have come into view in theories, scientists let the infinities cancel each other out in a process known as "renormalization," which we term as the '1'. Addressing the challenge of infinities Weinberg wrote, "The problem of infinities is still with us, but it is a problem for the final theory."[12]

There's Lots of Muscle under the Hood
Enjoy the Presence of God

George Spencer Brown said:

> To arrive at the simplest truth, as Newton knew and practiced, requires years of contemplation. Not activity. Not reasoning. Not calculating. Not busy behavior of any kind. Not reading. Not talking. Not making an effort. Not thinking. Simply bearing in mind what it is one needs to know.[13]

Isaac Newton (1642-1727) characterized his way of discovery and advancement of the state of knowledge ("finding a smoother pebble or a prettier shell") accordingly:

> I know not what I may appear to the world, but to myself I seem to have been only like a boy playing on the seashore, and diverting myself in now and then finding a smoother pebble or a prettier

shell than ordinary, whilst the great ocean of truth ['1'ness of knowledge] lay all undiscovered before me.[14]

We all admire the Nobel Prize-winning physicist Luis Alvarez, who had a matchless capacity to integrate his creativity with the facts. Among Alvarez's many contributions, which enabled him to be elected to the National Inventors Hall of Fame, are a photographic lens that became stock in Polaroid cameras and an aircraft blind-landing system which saved countless lives by providing pilots a radar-guided path in poor-visibility environment. Who spurred Alvarez to creative thought? His father, the elder Alvarez, a physician and medical researcher, nurtured his son to dedicate a half hour *on a daily basis* to creative thought about his work, its implications, and its progress.

Saint Ignatius of Loyola stated that "a single hour of meditation . . . had taught him more truth about heavenly [cosmic] things than all the teachings of all the [spiritual] doctors put together." "This technique is looked down on today as being too 'low-tech,'" writes Mashelkar, director general of the Council of Scientific and Industrial Research, Government of India:

> Darwin used to take an hour's walk every day around a course he had laid out. He would become engrossed in his thoughts; therefore, he put some small stones at the start, kicking one off at each round so that he did not have to keep track of how many circuits he had made, or worry about time. It was during these walks that he wrestled with the deepest questions.
>
> The practice of taking long walks as an active part of intellectual activity used to be a common part of academic life. Professors would take their graduate students on walks to debate, discuss, and question. These days graduate students are lucky to even see their professor in the halls.[15]

Saint Thomas Aquinas' (1225-1274) goal in life was the philosophical exposition of theology (the unfinished *Summa Theologica*) and the reconciliation of faith with reason—man with God. He fashioned a commanding and thoughtful synthesis integrating Aristotelian and Neoplatonic fundamentals within a Christian framework. Aquinas was rejected by Catholic officialdom until the late nineteenth century. Toward the last part of his life, regularly spent in deep meditation ("infused contemplation"), Aquinas had a deep mystical experience, following which he alleged that what he had claimed, characterized, and composed throughout his life "was no better than straw or chaff"! Subsequently, he declined to work on his *Summa Theologica.*

In his masterpiece of psychological interpretation, *The Varieties of Religious Experience,* William James, Harvard professor of anatomy, physiology, psychology, and philosophy, wrote about overcoming the spider web of illusion:

> This overcoming of all the usual barriers between the individual and the Absolute is the great mystic achievement. In mystic states we become one with the Absolute and we become aware of our Oneness. This is the everlasting and triumphant mystical tradition, hardly altered by differences of clime or creed. In Hinduism, in Neoplatonism, in Sufism, in Christian mysticism, in Whitmanism, we find the same recurring note, so that there is about mystical utterances an eternal unanimity which ought to make a critic stop and think, and which brings about what the mystical classics have, as has been said, neither birthday nor native land, perpetually telling of the unity of man with God ['1'], their speech antedates language, and they do not grow old.[16]

In the Oneness of the Hidden Order, similar to *shifting grooves* on a record (shifting among points within '1'), we observe different realities. We manifest "the hidden benefits"—miracles. "Thus, the classical idea of the separability of the world into distinct but interacting parts is no longer valid or relevant," said David Bohm. He adds:

> Rather, we have to regard the universe [the groves on a record] as an undivided and unbroken whole. Division into particles, or into particles and fields, is only a crude abstraction and approximation. Thus, we come to an order that is radically different from that of Galileo and Newton—the order of undivided wholeness.[17]

In William Blake's writings, book lovers catch a glimpse of their own "infinite possibilities": "If the doors of perception were cleansed, everything would be seen as it is, infinite."[18] When a sense of purity of heart, selfless compassion, humility, cooperation, and responsibility are allowed entry into one's life, insight, understanding, and knowledge is achieved. The bond of deep peace, grasp, and awareness emerge, as a natural clarity of wakefulness and the voice of the sacred (the expression "sacred" to represent the highest state of consciousness).

The Spanish-born writer, thinker, and harmonizer of literature and philosophy George Santayana, who was a researcher under William James and in 1889 joined the faculty of philosophy at Harvard, sounds the calling truth as follows:

> I do not ask anyone to think in my terms if he prefers others. Let him clean better, if he can, the windows of his soul that the variety and beauty of the prospect may spread more brightly before him.

From Glory to Glory: God Addressing Himself

Yearning to banish the bedlam of human misery and to civilize the lives of people, the Nazarene prayed (paraphrased): Father, let them find the road to the unity of the universe that "I am in you, Father, and you are in me, Father, and that *we are in them*, Father." Let the sweet perfume of eternity move them closer toward the One without a second: "*That they may be one* [consciously], *as we are one—I living in them*, you living in me—that their unity may be complete" (Jn 17:22).

Dear reader, take a break here for a day or two and reflect on John 17:22. Allow Christ's profound wisdom to surface in your consciousness. Saint John's 17:22 conclusion is well worth considering. After your reflection, you might join Saint Paul in your thinking that:

> All of us . . . are being transformed from glory to glory into his very image by the Lord who is the Spirit (2 Cor 3:18).

The more we are at inner peace, the stronger our *life force* (the cosmic power that is in most people undeveloped; it can be awakened by spiritual growth), the sharper the image of God is in us. Erwin Schrödinger characterizes the Oneness of consciousness and world thusly:

> The reason why our sentient, percipient, and thinking ego is met nowhere within our scientific world picture can easily be indicated in seven words: because it is itself that world picture. It is identical with the whole, and therefore cannot be contained in it as a part of it.[19]

He is absolutely right! Just as we cannot have a reflection in a mirror without an image, so we also cannot have manifestation without the preexisting '1'. The reflection "is identical with the whole," as Schrödinger wrote, for "it itself is the projection of the world picture," the projection of the '1'.

"Reality is only one and that is the Self" (the "I AM" of Moses; the Father of Christ), confirms saint Ramana Maharshi (1879-1950), one of the most profound sages and liberated souls of current India. Ramana was adored and loved by Buddhists, Christians, Hindus, and Taoists equally for his spiritual power and teachings. Says he:

> All the rest are mere phenomena in it, of it and by it. The seer, the objects, and the sight, all are the Self only. Can anyone see or hear, leaving the self aside? . . . If you surrender yourself [to '1'] . . . all is well . . . Only so long as you think that you are the worker are you obliged to reap the fruits of your actions. If, on the other hand, you surrender yourself [to the Highest Good] and recognize your individual self as only a tool of the Higher Power, that power will take over your affairs along with the fruits of actions.
>
> They no longer affect you and the work goes on unhampered. Whether you recognize the power or not, the scheme of things does not alter. Only there is a change of outlook. Why should you bear your load on the head when you are traveling in a train? It carries you and your load whether the load is on your head or on the floor of the train. You are not lessening the burden of the train by keeping it on your head but only straining yourself unnecessarily. Similar is the sense of doership in the world by individuals.[20]

On another occasion, Maharshi pointed out:

> The whole of wisdom is contained in two biblical statements: "I am that I am" and "Be still and know that I am God." The sense of I pertains to the person, the body and the brain. When a man knows his true Self for the first time, something else arises from the depths of his being ['1'] and takes possession of him. That

something is behind the mind; it is infinite, divine, eternal. Some people call it the kingdom of heaven, others call it the soul, and others again Nirvana, and Hindus call it Liberation; you may give it what name you wish. When this happens, a man has not really lost himself; rather he has found himself. Unless and until a man embarks on this quest of the true Self, doubt and uncertainty will follow his footsteps through life. The greatest kings and statesmen try to rule others when in their heart of hearts they know that they cannot rule themselves. Yet the greatest power is at the command of the man who has penetrated to his Inmost depth . . . What is the use of knowing about everything else when you do not know yet who you are? Men avoid this inquiry into the true Self, but what else is there so worthy to be undertaken?[21]

Helena Blavatsky wrote:

> In his hours of silent meditation the student will find that there is one space of silence within him where he can find refuge from thoughts and desires, from the turmoil of the senses and the delusions of the mind. By sinking his consciousness deep into his heart he can reach this place—at first only when he is alone in silence and darkness. But when the need for the silence has grown great enough, he will turn to seek it even in the midst of the struggle with self, and he will find it.[22]

Saint Teresa of Avila explained the direct encounter with God in her meditations as "so subtle and delicate" that her awareness could not comprehend it: "It was granted me to perceive in one instant how all things are seen and contained in God. I did not perceive them in their proper form, and nevertheless the view I had of them was of a sovereign clearness, and has remained vividly impressed upon my soul . . . The view was so subtle and delicate that the understanding cannot grasp it."

"To live with the true consciousness of life centered in another is to lose one's self-important seriousness and thus to live life as "play" in union with a Cosmic Player," repeats Thomas Merton. He explains:

It is He alone that one takes seriously. But to take Him seriously is to find joy and spontaneity in everything, for everything is gift and grace. In other words, to live selfishly is to bear life as an intolerable burden. To live life selflessly is to live in joy, realizing by experience that life itself is love and a gift. To be a lover and a giver is to be a channel through which the Supreme Giver manifests His love in the world.[23]

15

LIGHT, LOVE, AND LIFE: THE CORE OF WISDOM

All things have meaning and beauty
In that space beyond time where you are.

—Dag Hammarskjöld

Your Thoughts and Actions Produce Your Personal Universe

The *garden*, or field, in the symbolic language of the various parables in the Bible, stands for our physical body, while the gardener represents the keeper of the garden. On another level, this can also be the one who weeds out one's vices and addictions. In Genesis we read that God took the man and settled him in the Garden of Eden (the Temple of Gladness, Paradise and delight) to cultivate and care for it (Gen 2:15).

In the *Vaisnav Baul Song* we have another type of parable, not too dissimilar from the "garden" story. Both of these parables can be interpreted on several levels. Outside of the sexual imagery which can come up in the beautiful *Vaisnav Baul Song*, we can, for instance, also picture a higher perspective of husband and wife circulating the energy of Christ Consciousness. Part of this higher consciousness level is the gaining of at least a temporary complete surrender of our ego selves to our Higher Self. Here is the *Vaisnav Baul Song*:

> When my beloved returns to the house, I shall make my body into a Temple of Gladness. Offering this body as an altar of joy, my letdown hair will sweep it clean. Then my beloved will consecrate this temple.[1]

297

The *fruit*, in the symbolic expression of that age, denotes the actual outgrowth of our actions. Jesus stated, "By your fruits [not by your roots] you shall be known," by your deeds you shall recognize the core of fire, the universe you observe. "God is hiding in the world," affirms Heschel, "Our task is to let the divine emerge from our deeds."[2]

Ken Carey, author of *Starseed: The Third Millennium*, sees the dimension of our deeds in terms of the cooperation of nations in the coming millennium. In this way:

> The coming millennium is to be a time of access to the infinite informational systems of Eternal Being ['1']. Fueled by divine motivation, technology will make leaps that will make the twentieth century appear to be the dark age that, in fact, it has been. Science will no longer deny the spirit within but will assist in the material implementation of the spirit's implicit designs and patterns. In these times the great floating cities of light will be constructed through the cooperation of the nations of the world, working together as [a] component organ of a single living whole.[3]

The Fruit of Knowledge Makes You Whole

Eating fruit from the tree of life and knowledge (Rumi calls it "that fruit-laden Tree of Life; the Katha Upanishad, an early Hindu classic, terms it "the tree of eternity") signifies our internal consumption of the fruit, the harvest of our thoughts and deeds. How can we consume something from the tree of life and knowledge, that imparts existence/wisdom/understanding?

Love begets love. That is the way of creation. We know the seed of life in lovemaking between husband and wife supplies the means of reproduction, which creates succeeding generations. It also appears from Genesis that there is something more to look forward to; there is an additional benefit. The heavenly fruit of blissful pleasure from the tree of life and knowledge is used for more than procreation. Based on our service and good deeds, somehow we can personally consume this nirvana fruit of the vital force and our level of awareness, concept of value, and degree of wisdom and understanding will flourish and expand.

On the surface, this suggestion may sound strange. Yet, upon further deliberation, it becomes clear that there ought to be some internal means within each species that enable its members to remember what each has learned during its existence, thus transmitting self-cultivation through a genetic code to future generations.

Scores of rich and diverse books have been written on this subject of using our basic sexual energy for more than merely procreation. You may desire to further explore the biological basis for improving your vitality, health, natural immunity, consciousness, and repairing the engines of life. I recommend that the topic of Kundalini (Sanskrit: "snake"), "serpent power," bioplasma, or the Taoist "secret elixir" of the life and heart of God be looked into.[4] This sleeping majestic life force is in every human being and, according to Eastern tradition, lies coiled at the base of the spinal column and finds expression in the form of creativity, vigor, spiritual knowledge, and mystical visions. In the Bible that vital lubricant of the soul is called "living water" (Jn 4:10; 7:38), "the River of Light," and "the water of life" (Rev 22:1).

Drink Living Water—Bring Peace and Joy to the Holy Dwelling of God

The Songs of Solomon (or Odes of Solomon) are compellingly profound wisdom teachings of Jewish-Christian origin about the sweet water of life and a return to the light. In Song 30 we hear, "Drink deeply from the living fountain of the lord. It is yours. Come, all who are thirsty, and drink, and rest by the fountain of the lord. How beautiful and pure. It eases the soul. That water is sweeter than honey. The combs of bees are nothing beside it." The Psalms state, "There is a stream whose runlets gladden the city of God, the holy dwelling of the Most High" (Ps 46:4). Notice the connection: "the holy dwelling of the *Most High*." And, in John we read:

> Jesus answered, "Everyone who drinks this [external] water will be thirsty again, but whoever drinks the [living] water I give him will never thirst. Indeed, the water I give him will become in him a spring of water welling up to eternal life" (Jn 4:14).

In another instance Jesus declared, "I tell you the truth, unless a man is born of [living] water and the Spirit, he cannot enter the kingdom of God" (Jn 2:5). Also, in the New and Old Testament we observe, "From within him rivers of living water shall flow" (Jn 7:38). For Islam, it is a fountain in the realms of peace, light, beauty, and joy: "the Mystic Fountain of Kafur."

Oksana and I, along with many other people we know, have come into contact with, experienced, and verified the existence of these inner "rivers of living water." Saint Gregory of Nyssa, in "*The Life of Moses*," referred to this biological living water (bioplasma) as "the bread of heaven." Saint Ignatius of Antioch called this living water the "drink of God."

"The bread of God" or "the true bread from heaven" (Jn 6:31-33) ensures our advancement to higher and more abundant frontiers of life, personal development, protection from disease (immunity, in the current parlance), and the unearthing of mysteries beyond the visible universe. The Holy One of God acknowledged, "I am the bread of life. He who comes to me will never go hungry, and he who believes in me will never be thirsty" (Jn 6:35). The potential is within us to realize our exceptional abilities and gain greater happiness, and to achieve reunion with the Absolute.

Through self-cultivation ("you have loved righteousness and hated wickedness," Heb 1:9), one can undergo the *redirection* of the subtle essence of bioplasma energy, "the oil of joy" (Heb 1:9), to the crown of the head. This step-up enables one to live her/his daily life more effectively—more productively in the heights of cosmic Oneness and omniscience, beyond the limits of ordinary consciousness. Saint John assures us that the person who is victorious in Christlike self management skills also will consume the orgasmic fruit that flourishes in the garden of God: "I will see to it that the victor [the one who transmutes vices into virtues] eats from the tree of life, which grows in the garden of God" (Rev 2:7).

Notice in the Old Testament, the "tree of knowledge of good and bad" (Gen 2:9) was off-limits to male as well as female. In the New Testament, John 8:32, Jesus said that by all means, "Know the truth, and the truth will set you free." What gives? More knowledge or no knowledge; should we eat from the "tree of knowledge" or not? Should we know what is good and what is bad or not? How can we know the truth if we don't know what is good and what is bad? Should we improve our life or not? Should we have more equality of opportunity, reconciliation, freedom, and happiness, or not?

Now a new twist enters, which is a contradiction to the Adam and Eve directive to be found in Revelations—"I will see to it that the victor eats from the tree of life, which grows in the garden of God" (Rev 2:7). Do you recall what Jesus, Saint Jerome, Origen, Maimonides, Skovoroda, and the Kabbalah have said about the deep wisdom in code language? Let us replay Origen again:

> What man is found such an idiot as to suppose that God planted trees in Paradise, in Eden, like a husbandman, and planted therein the tree of life, perceptible to the eyes and senses, which gave life to the eater thereof; and another tree which gave to the eater thereof knowledge of good and evil? I believe that every man must hold these things for images, under which the hidden sense lays concealed.

Remember the Christ's statement? "The kingdom of God is within you." So the tree of life and knowledge is within you. The Bhagavad Gita, one of the greatest and most scenic of the Hindu Scriptures, asserts, "A person who knows the Sacred Tree, with its roots in the Primal Being [Brahman], its trunk the body of Brahma [the attributes of creation] and its leaves the Holy Teachings, is a true knower of reality."[5] And, in the book of Revelation, written by Saint John, there are copious additional references to the tree of life:

> Happy are they who wash their robes [purify their hearts and minds] . . . to have access to the tree of life and enter the city [of light, which is within your Being] through its gates (Rev 22:14)!

Also, concerning the perfection of the virtuous life, "To him who overcomes, I will give some of the *hidden manna*" (Rev 2:17). Your comprehension and health will be lifted up to what is magnificent and heavenly. Therefore, "'Come!' Whoever is thirsty [for love, righteousness, peace], let him come; and whoever wishes, let him take free gift of *the water of life*" (Rev 22:17).

Wrote Huston Smith in *The Essential Kabbalah*:

> To regain access to the Tree of Life, people must cultivate their souls by discriminating between good and evil and practicing

the divine law. They must seek with great zeal the truth hidden behind the words of the scriptures.[6]

The whole of the Holy Qur'an is jam-packed with symbolism, "under which the hidden sense lies concealed," and this should always be considered in their interpretation: "The Devotees of Right: they attain the Mystic Fountain of Kafur: for purely out of love for Allah, they do good *to* Allah, they do good to Allah's *Creatures*, and *serve them* [not through jihad]. The Light of beauty and joy will be on them. In felicity and honor will they live in the garden of Delight, and share in the Banquet—the Presence and Glory Divine!"[7]

Secrets to Exceptional Living

Ralph Waldo Emerson, in his beautiful essay *Self-Reliance*, stated, "To believe your own thought, to believe that what is true for you in your private heart is true for all men—that is genius."[8] This is true, declared Schrödinger, because "you are a part, a piece, of an eternal, infinite being." Emerson maintained:

> Familiar as the voice of the mind is to each, the highest merit we ascribe to Moses, Plato, and Milton is that they set at naught books and traditions, and spoke not what men did but what they thought. A man should learn to detect and watch that gleam of light which flashes across his mind from within, more than the luster of the firmament of bards and sages. Yet he dismisses without notice his thought, because it is his. In every work of genius we recognize our own rejected thoughts: they come back to us with a certain alienated majesty.[9]

If one is to consider recent great theorists of modern relativity and quantum physics, such as Bohr, de Broglie, Eddington, Einstein, Heisenberg, Jeans, Pauli, Planck, Schrödinger, and Wheeler, all enjoyed a keen grasp of the unity of knowledge, the Invariance Principle, and the great unity of the universe. Namely, physical principles and the laws of physics are independent of any movement of the observer. Erwin Schrödinger, in *What is Life?*, condensed these elements into one sentence: "I am in the east and in the west, I am below and above, I am this whole world." The full passage shows much wisdom:

> What is it that has called you so suddenly out of nothingness to enjoy for a brief while a spectacle which remains quite indifferent to you? . . .
>
> For we should then have the same baffling question: which part, which aspect are you? What, objectively, differentiates it from the others? No, but, inconceivable as it seems to ordinary reason, you—and all other conscious beings as such—are all in all. Hence this life of yours which you are living is not merely a piece of the entire existence, but is, in a certain sense, the whole; only this whole is not so constituted that it can be surveyed in one single glance. This, as we know, is what the Brahmins express in that sacred, mystic formula which is yet really so simple and so clear: *Tat tvam asi*, this is you. Or, again, in such words as "I am in the east and in the west, I am below and above, I am this whole world."
>
> Thus you can throw yourself flat on the ground, stretched out upon Mother Earth, with the certain conviction that you are one with her as she with you. You are as firmly established, as invulnerable, as she—indeed, a thousand times firmer and more invulnerable. As surely as she will engulf you tomorrow, so surely will she bring you forth anew to new striving and suffering. And not merely, "some day": now, today, every day she is bringing you forth, not once, but thousands upon thousands of times, just as every day she engulfs you a thousand times over. For eternally and always there is only now, one and the same now; the present is the only thing that has no end.[10]

16

YOUR SEED OF PURE PLEASURE:
IT ADDS BRIGHTNESS TO THE SUN

Reveal your light.

—Saint Symeon

High-Quality Actions Purify and Amplify Awareness

So I ask you this question: how can we purify our bioplasma fabric of life for greater creativity, productivity, health, excellence and longevity? How does Saul of the fundamentalist God become Paul of Christ? How can larger quantities (twenty or more times the norm) of our inner flowing energy be more effectively directed to the crown of the head? How do we celebrate our divinity? How do we "sanctify the dwelling of the Most High" (Ps 46:4)?

The Adam and Eve parable does not elaborate upon the actions that precipitate the primordial essence or the internal "nectar fruit" being released and purified (separating the poisonous seed essence from the pure seed essence) to "refresh the city of God." Nevertheless, prudent thinkers and physicians of the human soul the world over— Buddhist, Christian, Hindu, Islamic, Persian, and Taoist authorities— suggest this is achieved via a transfiguration of the interior universe through service-excellence (righteous deeds) and fasting of the heart. Each one speaks of this transformation being realized by a life of personal responsibility, compassion, and purity of motive; doing your best each day, and abstention from undesirable habits.

Robert Muller, who insisted on cleaning litter from the streets of New York City while jogging on his route, reminds us of our responsibilities:

Decide to live joyfully, exultantly, gratefully, openly, and then miracles will begin to happen. [Furthermore,] what is the greatest work of art on Earth? A healthy, beautiful, well-educated, loving child. Fathers and mothers are the greatest artists there can be on Earth. A happy, loving family is more precious than any Rembrandt or Leonardo da Vinci painting.[1]

"This kind of personality" declared Joseph Wu, professor of philosophy at California State University, "will not be corrupted by wealth or fame, will not be bent by power or force, and will not be moved by poverty or mean conditions." Addressing the cultivation of our bioplasma seed essence, Chinese *qi* [*chi*], Wu stated:

The phrase "cultivation of *qi*" means almost the same as "development of moral or spiritual power." Such a spiritual power is developed through constant accumulation of righteous deeds and is not to be obtained by occasional moral acts. This is comparative to the Eightfold Path of the Buddha, which integrates right mindfulness and right conduct.

Thus, by "washing their robes, that they may have the right to the tree of life" (Rev 22:14)—by transmuting vices into virtues—one eats from the tree of life and knowledge: releasing Kundalini energy, bringing about enlightenment, health, and a higher majesty of living.

Right Makes Might

Alexander Kelly McClure, who as friend and advisor saw President Abraham Lincoln practically daily during our American Civil War, has written:

Of all the Presidents of the United States, and indeed of all the great statesmen who have made their indelible impression upon the policy of the Republic, Abraham Lincoln stands out single and alone in his individual qualities . . . He was patient, tireless, and usually silent . . . When he reached his conclusion, he was inexorable . . . His judgment of men was next to unerring, and when results were to be attained, he knew the men who should be assigned to the task, and he rarely made a mistake.[2]

Judge David Davis noted in his eulogy of Father Abe, "His presence on the circuit was watched for with interest, and never failed to produce joy and hilarity. When casually absent, the spirits of both bar and people were depressed." One may perhaps marvel how an extremely poor, would-be village blacksmith advanced into a successful lawyer of austere honesty, then up to our country's presidency?

Honest Abe walked four miles to repay 6 1/2 cents to a woman who overpaid him for dry goods. He was admired in the Illinois capital as a "man of uncorrupted if not incorruptible integrity." Newspaperman Horace Greeley, upon Lincoln's election, composed, "Never till now has a President been chosen who was known to regard Human Bondage as . . . evil and . . . wrong."

John Milton Hay, Lincoln's assistant personal secretary, wrote in his diary on July 31, 1863, "While the rest are grinding their little private organs for their own glorification, the old man is working with the strength of a giant and the purity of an angel to do this great work." On another occasion Hay told John George Nicolay, Lincoln's White House private secretary, that "There is no man in the country, so wise, so gentle and so firm. I believe the hand of God placed him where he is." His lack of selfishness facilitated Lincoln to connect to the people of the North with ease, so that, in James Russell Lowell's words, "When he speaks, it seems as if the people were listening to their own thinking aloud." James Humes, in *The Wit and Wisdom of Abraham Lincoln*, wrote, "If democracy is a secular religion, Lincoln is a Muhammad or a Moses . . . a Statue of Liberty in the flesh."

Lincoln put into practice individual responsibility, self-reliance, extraordinary industriousness, idealistic enthusiasm, love, and service. He lived them. He struggled, suffered, and endured agonizing years as a son of a Kentucky frontiersman, and as a president during one of the worst crises our country faced. He showed exceptional compassion, wisdom, and patience in the way he listened to what others had to say. Lincoln was also unafraid of his own ideas and held firm to his beliefs.

Honest Abe was known for care, a superb memory, accuracy in his dealings, a winning smile, and a rare skill in the management of people. He was courteous, polite, and helpful and would not be a slave, nor be a master. He stood strong by for freedom, unity, education, books, morality, and "Good God Almighty." Lincoln was an intrepid man. He bridged the ideal with the everyday experiential world. Like the Christ, the Buddha, Mahatma Gandhi, and Martin Luther King Jr., Lincoln was convinced of the ultimate triumph of righteousness, liberty, justice, and self-determination. His speeches (the Gettysburg Address, at Cooper Union) held a mystic songlike quality: "Let us have faith that right makes might, and in that faith, let us, to the end, dare to do our duty as we understand it."[3] William Herndon told of his law partner:

> Mr. Lincoln had a strong, if not terrible, passion for women. He could hardly keep his hands off a woman, and yet, much to his credit, he lived a pure and virtuous life. His idea was that a woman had as much right to violate the marriage vow as the man—no more and no less. His sense of right—his sense of justice—his honor forbade his violating his marriage vow. Judge [David] Davis said to me, "Mr. Lincoln's honor saved many a woman." This I know. I have seen Lincoln tempted and I have seen him reject the approach of woman![4]

The Chief Magistrate of the Nation was above all a nation builder. He sought to build a country in which high moral and ethical values at home, business and government were esteemed, practiced and lived. Lincoln's life and drive for meaning is best presented in his own words:

> I have never had a policy. I have simply tried to do what seemed best each day, as each day came . . . I desire so to conduct the affairs of this administration that if at the end, when I come to lay down the reins of power, I have lost every other friend on earth, I shall at last have one friend left, and that friend shall be down inside of me.[5]

Francis Grierson, who listened to Lincoln debate Stephen A. Douglas at Alton in 1858, stated:

> From every feature of Lincoln's face there radiated the calm, inherent strength that always accompanies power . . . Here, then, was one man out of all the millions who believed in himself, who did not consult with others about what to say, who never for a moment respected the opinion of men who preached a lie . . . What thrilled the people who stood before Abraham Lincoln on that day was a

sight of a being who, in all his actions and habits, resembled themselves, gentle as he was strong, fearless as he was honest, who towered above them all in that psychic radiance that penetrates in some mysterious way every fiber of the hearer's consciousness . . . Lincoln's presence infused into the mixed and uncertain throng something spiritual and supernormal. His looks, his words, his voice, his attitude, were like a magical essence dropped into the seething cauldron of politics, reacting against the foam, calming the surface and letting the people see to the bottom.[6]

Aldous Huxley wrote:

The nature of a man's being determines the nature of his actions; and the nature of his being comes to manifestation first of all in the mind. What he craves and thinks, what he believes and feels—this is, so to speak, the Logos, by whose agency an individual's fundamental character performs its creative acts. These acts will be beautiful and morally good if the being is God-centered, bad and ugly if it is centered in the personal self. "The stone," says Eckhart, "performs its work without ceasing, day and night." For even when it is not actually falling the stone has weight. A man's being is his potential energy directed towards or away from God; and it is by this potential energy that he will be judged as good or evil—for it is possible, in the language of the Gospel, to commit adultery and murder in the heart, even while remaining blameless in action.[7]

Be the Best to Benefit the Most

For nearly sixty years previous to his passing away in 1952, George Santayana, endowed with many brilliant gifts, poetical and philosophical, advised students, "Live as much as may be in the eternal."[8] The Tibetan prince of light Milarepa, an original genius in his discipline, addressing the liberation of Kundalini, said, "Your inability to drink the nectar [seed of pure pleasure] was because your central channel [*sushumna* in Sanskrit] was not yet opened. You should practice certain vigorous bodily exercises."[9]

The two practices, cultivation of inner energy and commitment to outer ethical behavior, go hand in hand. The groundbreaking sage

Ashtavakra, like Albert Einstein, envisioned the path of uninterrupted success and progress as being in the service of humanity.[10] In his famous book *Ashtavakra Samhita* (not recommended for beginners) he warns his royal disciple (King Janaka)

> not to rest content with mysticism, ordinary yoga, or religion alone, but to take the further step necessary to acquire a knowledge of the philosophy of truth—not to flee to caves or sit idly in ashrams but be constantly engaged in work for the welfare of others.[11]

Yes, nothing happens until someone makes it happen. We are asked to see, judge, and act. The power exists in our conscience, minds and hearts to choose the best. We hold in our hands the power to do our very best. We are called to see clearly and to choose the good that we see.

Shankara, the greatest of all Hindu philosophers, made this declaration in his immortal work *Viveka-Chudamani*:

> Disease is never cured by [pronouncing] the name of medicine, but by taking the medicine. Liberation is not achieved by repeating the word Brahman, but by directly experiencing Brahman . . . The nature of the one Reality must be known by one's own clear spiritual perception [living Christlike . . . the Buddhalike life]; it cannot be known through a pundit [learned man]. Similarly, the form of the moon can be known only through one's eyes. How can it be known through others?[12]

The Gospel of Thomas, in its own distinctive manner, declared: "Love your brother as your own soul, guard him as the pupil of your eye."[13]

Why such a severe requirement? Why, as the spiritual peacemaker the Dalai Lama, in *A Simple Monk*, stated:

> Each of us must learn to work not just for oneself, one's own family, or one's nation, but for the benefit of all mankind. Universal responsibility is the best foundation for world peace . . . The more we become interdependent, the more it is in our own interest to ensure the well-being of others.[14]

Why must the fundamentalist Saul or the jihadist Muslim transform himself from persecuting and taking life to become the great Paul or Muslim of altruistic love and compassionate deeds? Why must we appreciate that *sexual intercourse creates a spiritual bond—a union* having nothing to do with the sociopolitical context of officially authorized marriage? Why must our actions be in tune with Lincoln's relentless honesty, humility, integrity, inner peace, and Christ's way, before we can experience a profound change of perspective and realize the unbroken wholeness of totality? See God face-to-face; experience the living godhead through our being.

Comparable to hydrogen and oxygen united to become water, through the sacrament of sexual union, two individuals through the interchange of energy fields are merged to become one new being. We can see this through chemistry—we can observe this through physics. Also, the Jewish Zohar, the Christian Gospels, the Islamic Koran, and the sacred books of the East underscore this fact. Saint Paul, in his first letter to the Corinthians, explains:

> Someone will say, "I am allowed to do anything." Yes; but not everything is good for you. I could say, "I am allowed to do anything"; but I am not going to let anything make a slave of me. Someone else will say, "Food is for the stomach, and the stomach is for food . . ."
>
> You know that *your bodies are parts of* THE BODY OF CHRIST ['1']. Shall I take a part of Christ's body and make it part of the body of a prostitute? Impossible! Or perhaps you don't know that the man who joins his body to a prostitute *becomes physically one with her?* The scripture says quite plainly, "*The two will become one body.*" But he who joins himself to the Lord becomes spiritually one with him (1 Cor 6:12-17).

Furthermore, each time a new "union" is consummated, one partner not only links oneself up to the other's electromagnetic network, but, similar to mixing paints or chemicals, she/he acquires the idiosyncrasies and energy fields of the other's personality and karma! The two people become emotionally and spiritually coupled, and the network of people they are united to. Each time we "connect" ourselves with someone new in a sexual relationship, we place another energy hookup to our being.

Having different sexual linkups is equivalent to having an oil pipeline with many people siphoning off the flow along its length.

Intimacy then, is a special form of caring that uplifts both concerned at the same time. "Your body is the temple of the Holy Spirit, who lives in you," said Saint Paul. "So use your bodies for God's glory" (1 Cor 6:19-20).

Safety Locks on Our Inner Energy

Why do we have to purify our bioplasma seed essence before we can enter through the door of the Light of lights and tap the "pure experience" orgasm of the tree of life and knowledge?

Life is full of opportunities. To raise us to a higher energy level, life has to be cultivated; energy loss has to be prevented. The various growth components are health, inner peace, compassion, wisdom, excellence, and service. We cannot increase the quantity and quality of our garden until we prepare the soil, eliminate the weeds, and take care of the plant. We cannot increase the quantity and quality of our precious life energy if we decide to live carelessly and be half asleep, spiritually; we have to sidestep real and potential energy leakage.

At one time, humans produced fire by rubbing sticks together, and made use of caves for shelter. Now we create fire with matches, and for housing we build beautiful thermostat-controlled homes. By internal consumption of our "seed of pure pleasure," we are unlocking the centuries-old secrets of inner power, productivity, growth, happiness, creativity, and insight gleaned by our greatest human achievers.[15]

Moreover, this tremendously powerful cosmic energy can be used constructively: for productive endeavors, improvement of our consciousness, health, joy, prosperity, and advancement of the human family. In a "toxic waste" environment (anger, fear, tension, compulsion, worry), or a misdirection of our life force, the negative energy is very stressful on our mind, body, and soul. This may lead to stress-related illnesses, including ulcers, heart attacks, and insanity. It can also cause us to fall short of our goals in life.

Recall when the Galilean, in frustration, projected negative energy toward the fig tree? It died the next day. Imagine the same force projected inward. World literature has many similar examples. Luckily, when we become angry, worried, or upset, in most cases in our present stage of development we do not channel much life force to ourselves, the throttle to our "central channel has not opened yet," as Milarepa said. Therefore, not much damage is done to our surroundings or ourselves, except for such minor maladies as a headache, upset stomach, lower back pain, or nervous tension.

The fact is, life is protecting itself. A margin of safety exists. Through pain, hunger, and affliction, you, a newborn creator, are "gently" being guided, like the Prodigal Son, homeward to enlightenment and a higher quality of life. For this reason, as in an atom bomb or in a central bank, there are various safety measures and "locks" (chakras[16]). They are a part of our body that guards the doorway to the inner sanctum: "He stationed the cherubim and the fiery revolving sword, to guard the way to the tree of life" (Gen 3:24). These "locks" will not open the "central channel," the large electrical conductor feeding our inner tree of knowledge, until we have achieved a high degree of goodness and purity of living. The Perfect One said, "I am the door"—the Light itself—the resurrection that is individual, collective, and cosmic. It is a door for all in all aspects of our lives, both in the present and in the ultimate future.

The Serpent: Raises Consciousness, Accelerates Evolution

The "serpent"[17] is taken as an allegorical symbol of the Divine Logos, existence, wisdom, and life—the power that puts physical, mental, and emotional existence in motion. The bioplasma energy is coiled like a serpent at the base of the spine. The sperm, whose head, like a snake's, is pushed forward by a highly efficient system of propulsion—the undulating movement of a long, slender tailpiece—resembles a snake. The people who saw this in stillness gave it a very good name.

A similar symbol was used by the early people of Mesoamerica (Coatl, the serpent; Quetzalcoatl, the Feathered Serpent); the Gnostics (in association with life, advancement and the transformation of the woman/man imprisoned in the world into light); Egyptians (the snake on Cleopatra's head in a bas-relief within the Temple of Hathor, Dandarah, Egypt); by the wise Nagas of Hindu literature (the Rig-Veda: Vak); by the Chinese; by Moses; and the Nazarene.

In the Eastern world, the serpent represents the awesome energy of Kundalini, the seed of pure pleasure, or "the serpent fire." It is referred to in the Bible as the "bread of angels" (Ps 78:25), the fruit of "the tree of the knowledge of good and evil" (Gen 2:9), the "bread from heaven" (Ex 16:4), "the free gift of the water of life" (Rev 21:17), the "bread of the mighty ones," the Heavenly Manna, the philosophers stone, and the rivers of honey and delight.

"A character which plays a great role in the history of Adam and Eve is the Serpent," wrote Edouard Schure in his study of the secret history of religious symbols. He explains:

> Genesis calls it *Nahash*. Now what did the serpent mean in the ancient temples? The mysteries of India, Egypt, and Greece reply with a single voice: the serpent arranged in a circle means universal life, whose magic agent is starlight. In a still deeper sense, *Nahash* means the power which puts life in motion, the attraction of the self for self. In the latter meaning Geoffrey Saint-Hilaire saw the basis for universal gravity. The Greeks called it Eros, Love, or Desire. Now apply these two meanings to the story of Adam and Eve and the Serpent, and you will see that the Fall of the first couple, the celebrated original sin, suddenly becomes the vast revealing of divine and universal nature with its kingdom, its classes and its species, in the tremendous, ineluctable cycle of life.[18]

For centuries the ancients have carefully guarded the secrets of the serpent and its accelerating evolutionary power that adds brightness to the "sun behind the sun." Gene Kiefer, director of the Kundalini Research Foundation in New York, in his introduction to *Kundalini for the New Age* states:

> Gopi Krishna [modern world-renowned verifier of Kundalini] said more than once that Kundalini was the most jealously guarded secret in history. Though millions of ordinary people may know about the great breakthroughs in physics, astronomy, medicine, chemistry, and other branches of science, hardly anybody is familiar with a far more important development: the almost unbelievable potential lying dormant in their own brain. It is this power center in the human body that the sages of India knew as Kundalini and that adepts in other parts of the world called by names as varied as the "sun behind the sun" and the "philosopher's stone."[19]

17

I AM THE ONE—I AM ALSO THE MANY

When one door of happiness closes, another opens;
But often we look so long at the closed door that
we do not see the one that has opened for us.

—Helen Keller

The Splendor of Life

As the transfiguration of our interior universe begins to take place through a life of purity of heart, peace of mind, and excellence, minute amounts of bioplasma are released. They ascend like sap from the root system to the leaves, carrying dissolved nutrients from the base of our spine (the Hindus call it the Muladhar Chakra, where Kundalini lies dormant) to the rest of our body, culminating at the top of our heads. As this happens, we have more energy; our consciousness becomes illuminated and amplified.

Initially, the state of this rapturous experience is momentary, with exhilarating happiness and exaltation. Later, as we spiritually mature, and we become more Christlike (reveal perfection) in our actions, decisions, attitude, and sensitivity toward our family, neighbors, coworkers, and environment, the "central channel," like a river, begins to widen, allowing greater amounts of our life force to pass through it. The invigorating elations become more frequent and of longer duration, lasting for hours and extending even into sleep. Eventually, as the interior development under the Spirit's direction progresses over the years, we achieve a very powerful connection with our Infinite Splendor. We realize that He-Who-Is—the Almighty One—lives in us and we in Him. "We begin to realize," wrote Wingate in his remarkable *Tilling the Soul:*

That we are joined in the most deeply intimate communion with every other Soul in the Cosmos. That we are joined with the One Soul. That It is in us. That we and the One Soul are One. And we begin to realize who and what the One Soul really is: no longer are we bogged down by the teachings and dogmas of an age when it was believed that the Universe was only 3,000 years old and 3,000 miles in diameter. Now we are free to experience the One Soul in whatever way It needs to manifest Itself to us, in whatever way It needs to reveal Itself to us, for us to be able to understand It and accept It.[1]

Nineteen centuries earlier, Saint Paul expressed our connection thusly: "We, many though we are, are one body (1 Cor 10:17), [and]; We are members of one another" (Eph 4:25). Ken Carey restates in *Vision:*

The Creator and Creation are joined in physical flesh; for it is One Life that pulses within every body. We have only to be joined in consciousness, in awareness, and all will be fulfilled according to the prophecy.[2]

Circulating internally in normal daily dealings, during meditation, or in moments of deep compassion for other people or nature, large amounts of Kundalini can produce "pure experience"—a continuous whole-body orgasmic bliss many times greater than normal sexual orgasm. Initially we might not be consciously aware that Kundalini is active or that we can direct its flow to any part of the body, natural environment, or activity. But once we learn how to manage Kundalini, the Kundalini enables us to heal, be more productive, overcome obstacles and remove blinders to what is possible. We unite our will, our brain's neural antenna, and our heart to internal guidance from our own inner nature.

There's a difference between *knowing* God and *knowing about* God, eating food and talking about food. As Saint Paul testified in the First Epistle to the Corinthians, "The kingdom of God does not consist in talk but in power" (1 Cor 4:20).

The Magic Never Ends

The Highest Good means not living in pain, hunger, or worry, but in peace, working for the good of others. It means the power to heal, to produce new wonders, and to be the light to each other. Deng Ming-Dao in *Chronicles of Tao* describes the secret life of a Taoist master:

> The more you learn, the more you must use your knowledge for others. The wiser you become, the more unselfish you must also become. As your experience deepens, and with it your humility, you will realize unfathomable depths of knowledge. You can never become arrogant and narrow-minded if you perceive how small your abilities are when contrasted to those of the greatest.
>
> Remember to use your knowledge in the service of others, but expect nothing in return.[3]

"We are all either ministers of the sacred or slaves of evil," articulated Rabbi Heschel. Also:

> The only safeguard against constant danger is constant vigilance . . . . We carry the gold of God in our souls to forge the gate of the kingdom. The time for the kingdom may be far off, but the task is plain: to retain our share in God in spite of peril and contempt. There is a war to wage against the vulgar, against the glorification of the absurd, a war that is incessant, universal. Loyal to the presence of the ultimate in the common, we may be able to make it clear that man is more than man, that in doing the finite he may perceive the infinite.[4]

Furthermore, pointed out Heschel, unless we wake up (self-remember) out of our egocentric dementia, we will either forfeit or enrich the legacy of ages. He states:

> A world has vanished. All that remains is a sanctuary hidden in the realm of spirit. We of this generation are still holding the key. Unless we remember, unless we unlock it, the holiness of ages will remain a secret of God. We of this generation are still holding the key—the key to the sanctuary which is also the shelter of our own deserted souls. If we mislay the key, we shall elude ourselves.[5, 6]

The more you use your knowledge for others, the more you become human, stated Hafiz:

Once a man came to me and spoke for hours about "His great visions of God" he felt he was having. He asked me for confirmations, saying, "Are these wondrous dreams true?" I replied, "How many goats do you have?" He looked surprised and said, "I am speaking of sublime visions and you ask about goats!"

And I spoke again saying, "Yes, brother—how many do you have?" "Well, Hafiz, I have sixty-two." "And how many wives?" Again he looked surprised, then said, "Four." "How many rose bushes in your garden, how many children, are your parents still alive, do you feed the birds in winter?" And to all he answered. Then I said, "You asked me if I thought your visions were true, I would say that they were if they make you become more human, more kind to every creature and plant that you know."[7]

All Is Yours

The Christ reminded us of our Infinite Splendor and the necessity to expand our exuberance, a sense of duty to the deeper human nature in each other, the universality of human rights, and to the universe we share. It breathes life-giving air for the advancement of human liberty, promoting one civilization that ensures the well-being of others: *All that the Father has is yours.* "All the talents of God are within you. How could this be otherwise when your soul derived from His genes!"[8]

Observe that at every point of the universe there is the '1'. At every point of the universe all the laws of physics can be tested. At every point of the universe "All that the Father has is yours."

In surveying historical scholarship and personally experiencing the '1', Wingate navigates theological topologies in an expansive mode:

Call Me Omega
Or God, or Jehovah, or Brahman, or Allah,
Or anything else you would like to call Me.
I AM all of these. Yet I AM also none of them.
I AM the Cosmos, the Universe. Everything That Is . . .
I AM the First Cause.
I AM the Last Effect.
I AM Every Cause and Every Effect.
I AM Spirit.

I AM Soul.

I AM Matter.

As Spirit, I AM the inexpressible,
    indefinable Source of All Being, infinite and eternal.

As Soul, as Spirit manifest for an evolution,
    I AM Mind. I Am Consciousness. I AM Beingness.

And as Matter, as Soul manifest for a lifetime,
    I AM Everyone and Everything.

I AM Perfect; and Every Cause and Every Effect and
Everyone and Everything are Part of My Perfection.

I AM THE ONE.

I AM ALSO THE MANY.

AND WHATEVER IT IS THAT SAYS I AM,

I AM THAT I AM.[9]

Intoxicated with love, Sufi Sachal Sarmast (1739-1826) reveals
Wingate and Einstein's grasp of the unity of being:

He is Abu Hanifa and He is Hanuman,
He is the Koran and He is the Vedas,
He is this and He is that,
He is Moses, and He is Pharaoh.[10]

We Live in His Heart; His Heart Lives in Us

Joseph Benner in his wonderful *The Impersonal Life* follows Carey's and
Wingate's "I Am Consciousness" map through cells, forming group
intelligence. He writes:

You have been told that each cell of your body has a consciousness
and an intelligence of its own: that were it not for this consciousness
it could not do the work it so intelligently does.

Each cell is surrounded by millions of other cells, each
intelligently doing its own work and each evidently controlled
by the united consciousness of all these cells, forming a group
intelligence, which directs and controls this work; this group
intelligence apparently being the intelligence of organ which the

cells comprising it form. Likewise, there are other group intelligences in other organs, each containing other millions of cells, and all these organs make up your physical body.

Now, you know You are the Intelligence that directs the work of the organs of your body, whether this directing is done consciously or unconsciously; and that each cell of each organ is really a focal center of this directing Intelligence; and that when this Intelligence is withdrawn the cells fall apart, your physical body dies and exists no more as a living organism.

Who is this You who directs and controls the activities of your organs, and consequently of each cell composing them? You cannot say it is your human or personal self who does this, for you of yourself consciously can control the action of scarcely a single organ of your body.

It must then be this Impersonal I AM of you, who is You, and yet is not you. Listen!

You, the I AM of you, are to Me what the cell consciousness of your body is to your I AM Consciousness.

You are a cell, as it were, of My Body, and your consciousness (as one of My Cells) is to Me what the consciousness of one of the cells of your body is to you.[11]

"The only way to get rid of misconceptions" to what is real, to have the awareness and realization of "I AM" Consciousness of Christ living in us and we in Him, articulates Thomas Merton,

is to experience it. One who does not actually know, in his own life, the nature of this breakthrough and this awakening to a new level of reality cannot help being misled by most of the things that are said about it . . . And all is summed up in one awareness— not a proposition, but an experience: "I AM" . . . that Creating Spirit (Creator Spiritus) [the central principle of the universe, '1' in physics] dwells in us, and we in Him. That we are "in Christ" and that Christ lives in us. That the natural life in us has been completed, elevated, transformed and fulfilled in Christ by the Holy Spirit . . . in some sense experience, of what each Christian obscurely believes: "It is now no longer I that live but Christ lives in me."[12]

We all remember René Descartes' *cogito ergo sum* ("I think therefore I am"). Yet in experiencing I AM we have to be still. We have to put all thoughts aside. "There is no *cogito* ("I think") and no *ergo* ("therefore") but only *SUM*, 'I AM,'" discloses Merton.[13]

Gopi Krishna, who studied the impact of Kundalini (Parashakti, Mahamaya) on the peoples in India, Tibet, China, Japan, and the Middle East, and who experienced the "I AM" Consciousness personally, attests:

> Probably no other spectacle, not even the most incredible supernormal performances of the mystics and mediums, so clearly demonstrates the existence of an All-pervading, omniscient intelligence behind the infinitely varied phenomena of life as the operations of a freshly awakened Kundalini.
>
> It is here that man for the first time becomes acutely aware of the staggering fact that this unimaginable Cosmic Intelligence is present at every spot in the universe and that our whole personality—ego, mind, intellect, and all—is but an infinitely small bubble blown on this boundless ocean. But to suppose that even a particle of this ocean of consciousness can ever become extinct or cease to be is more absurd than to imagine that there can be night on the sun.[14]

In the words of Ibn Arabi:

> When the mystery—of realizing that the mystic is one with the Divine—is revealed to you, you will understand that you are no other than God and that you have continued and will continue . . . without when and without times. Then you will see all your actions to be His actions and all your attributes to be His attributes and your essence to be His essence, though you do not thereby become He or He you, in either the greatest or the least degree. "Everything is perishing save His Face," that is, there is nothing except His Face, "then, whithersoever you turn, there is the Face of God."[15]

18

THE WINE OF HEAVEN:
AN OCEAN OF UTMOST PEACE

If you just set out to be liked, you would be prepared
to compromise on anything at any time,
and you would achieve nothing.

—Margaret Thatcher

The Living Waters from Your Private Spring

The Christian mystics and saints, perhaps not always being aware of a
"great underground river" in the human anatomy, experienced the
effects of Kundalini in their daily activities and through meditation.
They employed phrases similar to those used by Kundalini
practitioners—beatific peace, raptures, brilliant light, wine of pure
pleasure, the heavenly Wine of Life, or, as Saint Teresa of Avila stated,
"The raptures . . . carry the soul out of its senses.[1] [It] penetrates the
very marrow of your bones."[2]

Your senses can be fused into one ineffable act of perception. The
distinction between bounded time/space/motion will cease to exist. Each
one of us can find ourselves in the center of stillness, immersed in a
living glow of nirvanic light and bliss so brilliant that the dissimilarity
between our surroundings and us vanishes. We discover that we are one
with the rest of our environment in light and love, in conscious joy,
happiness, and freedom. It can take place when we settle down or are on
the go, are in meditation or working. This experience of life in its most
fundamental and heavenly splendor is available when the seeker is ready.
It is beatific peace, beyond thought and emotion, where we come to an

end as a disconnected being and become part of one infinite and loving Spirit.

Additionally, we can dive into the ocean of knowledge, where the fundamental concepts of science, technological inventions, works of literature, poetry, music, and art become illuminated and clear to us, as in the case of parallel computer processing (chapter 14). This is a method par excellence by which problems can be solved quickly and the hidden truth can be known with the speed of light. The shining knowledge of existing things, above and beyond all empirical reason and beyond all discursive thought, is nearer to us than we are to ourselves. We can experience this when we fine-tune our neural antennae from the manifestation ('=') to the "Unchanging Pure Consciousness" ('1').

Saint Catherine of Siena (1347-1380), a deeply spiritual Italian girl of great commitment and virtue, was the youngest of twenty-four children of a local wool dyer and his wife. At the age of six she saw the Christ in a vision. At twenty-five years she stopped eating and slept little, until her passing away eight years later. Saint Catherine performed many miracles. While being in an elevated state of cosmic grace, her inner voice said to her:

> If you will arrive at a perfect knowledge and enjoyment of Me, the Eternal Truth, you should never go outside the knowledge of yourself, and by humbling yourself in the valley of humility you will know Me and yourself, from which knowledge you will draw all that is necessary.[3]

Saint Teresa of Avila was striking, playful, and gifted. While the Inquisition was watching her carefully (the Inquisition was paying close attention to the Jews who had converted to Christianity), Teresa filled her life with the passion of the Absolute Infinity, and drank "the wine of pure pleasure" from her "spring," whereby she could see the mystery a bit more deeply. Teresa relates in her meditations:

> There will suddenly come to it [the soul] a suspension in which the Lord communicates most secret things, which IT SEEMS TO SEE WITHIN GOD HIMSELF . . . The brilliance of this vision is like that of infused light or of a sun covered with some material of the *transparency of a diamond* [the clear Light] . . . For as long as

such a soul is in this state, it can neither see nor hear nor understand [shunyata or nirbita-samadhi state, in which all thought waves have turned off and all manifestation shut down]; the period is always short and seems to the soul even shorter than it really is. *God implants Himself in the interior* of that soul in such a way that, when it returns to itself, *it cannot possibly doubt* that GOD HAS BEEN IN IT AND IT HAS BEEN IN GOD [emphasis by the author].[4]

Yes, "When that day [of joining together] comes, you will know I am in my Father, and that you are in me, just as I am in you," said the Christ (Jn 14:20).

Cosmic Religious Feeling: To See within His Heart

Saint Catherine of Genoa's discourses parallel those of Saint Basil the Great, Archbishop of Caesarea in Cappadocia. She was one of the most penetrating gazers into the ocean of utmost peace and the utter transformation of the self in God, stating: "My Being is God, not by simple participation, but by a true transformation of my being,"[5] akin to Saul becoming Paul or a grain of wheat transforming into many grains of wheat. Active, with mind undisturbed, with heart full of tranquility, Saint Catherine put pen to paper:

> When the loving kindness of God calls a soul from the world [of fear and worry, and pain], He finds it full of vices and sins; and first He gives it an instinct for virtue, and then urges it to perfection, and then by infused grace leads to true self-naughting, and at last to true transformation. And this noteworthy order serves God to lead the soul along the Way; but when the soul is naughted and transformed, then of herself she neither works nor speaks nor wills, nor feels nor hears nor understands, neither has she of herself the feeling of outward or inward, where she may move. And in all things it is God who rules and guides her without the mediation of any creature. [We consciously live in a state of the Highest Good, or the Buddhist "it thinking": complete equanimity, purity, love, nonconcern, and detachment from results.] And the state of this soul is then a feeling of such utter peace and tranquility that it

seems to her that her heart, and her bodily being, and all both within and without is immersed in an ocean of utmost peace; from whence she shall never come forth for anything that can befall her in this life. And she stays immovable, imperturbable, impassible. So much so that it seems to her in her human and spiritual nature, both within and without, she can feel no other thing than sweetest peace. And she is so full of peace that though she press her flesh, her nerves, her bones, no other thing comes from them than peace.[6]

Recall the Adam and Eve narrative: "The moment you eat from it [the "tree of life and knowledge"] you are surely doomed to die." Did they die? Did Saul pack it in to be reborn as Paul? Yes, but only metaphorically. They left behind fear, worry, and moral discrepancy to be resurrected into purity, great lucidity, and spiritual consciousness as offspring of the Creator: as the Christ.

"I tell you the truth," said the Righteous One, "a grain of wheat is no more than a single grain unless it is dropped into the ground and dies. If it does die, then it produces many grains . . . Whoever wants to serve me must follow me, so that my servant will be with me where I am. My Father will honor him who serves me" (Jn 12:24). What this means, said Saint Paul to Ephesians, is this:

Your hearts and minds must be made completely new. You must put on the new self, which is *created in God's likeness*, and reveals itself in the true life that is upright and holy.

No more lying, then! Everyone must tell the truth to his brother, for *we are all members together in the body of Christ* . . . The man who used to rob must stop robbing and start working to earn an honest living for himself, and to be able to help the poor. Do not use harmful words in talking. Use only helpful words, the kind that build up and provide what is needed, so that what you say will do good to those who hear you (Eph 4:23-29).

When you plant a grain of wheat, it does not sprout to life unless it dies. Einstein referred to this new rebirth, of Oneness, as "cosmic religious feeling."[7] Canadian psychiatrist Maurice Bucke (1837-1902) called it "cosmic consciousness,"[8] while the Japanese Nishida Kitaro (1870-1945) described it as "pure experience." That is, the experience of knowing the

Greatest Secret, the state of being consciously unified with ultimate reality in which subject and object are one.[9]

Recall the moment (Numbers 13 and 14) when the scouts ventured out to explore the Promised Land. They returned with accounts of the riches, but also of the people who resided there. The scouts struck terror in the hearts of the people of Israel, who elected not to go into the Promised Land. We learn that the entire generation must wander in the wilderness, die off, and then it is the offspring who enter the Promised Land. In due course, each person has to work out his or her deliverance and come to the point of partaking personally in the divine life.

When "coal" transforms into a "diamond" or Saul becomes Paul, we transfigure from the religion of fear, vindictive morality, and paganism of idols and the many gods to the consciousness of Christ or One Being. Through the death of the self—the realization of true Selfhood, says Kitaro—we encounter the bliss of knowledge of the Absolute Perfection (*basho* or Absolute Nothingness) in personal life. We know ourselves as a "reflection" of the foundation of the totality. We enter into a higher life; we come into the Promised Land. Then God becomes an actuality, an active power in our being.

The eyes of Adam and Eve were opened. The naked truth was seen: the subject and object are identical. We are a part of "the whole family," the nation, and the global community (Amos 3:1). Or, as Thomas Merton in his *New Seeds of Contemplation* stated: "An awakening to the Real within all that is real. A vivid awareness of infinite Being at the roots of our own limited being."[10]

We realize that we are a part of the deepest sacred roots of '1': "The Lord God said, 'See! The man has become like one of us . . . [Gen 3:22]!'" When a planted seed dies, something more majestic, a new lovely plant, is born—the heir of Absolute grace, beauty, and power.

Do Not Stop These Beautiful Feelings

Albert Einstein, reflecting on spiritual development from the religion of fear to moral religion and the New Testament, to a third state of religious experience, to the superconscious state, recorded his remarkable observation written expressly for *The New York Times Magazine* in 1930:

The Jewish scriptures admirably illustrate the development from the religion of fear to moral religion, a development continued in the New Testament. The religions of all civilized peoples, especially the peoples of the Orient, are primarily moral religions. The development from a religion of fear to moral religion is a great step in people's lives. And yet, that primitive religions are based entirely on fear and the religions of civilized peoples purely on morality is a prejudice against which we must be on our guard . . .

Common to all these types is the anthropomorphic character of their conception of God. In general, only individuals of exceptional endowments, and exceptionally high-minded communities, rise to any considerable extent above this level. But there is a third state of religious experience which belongs to all of them, even though it is rarely found in a pure form: I shall call it cosmic religious feeling. It is very difficult to elucidate this feeling to anyone who is entirely without it, especially as there is no anthropomorphic conception of God corresponding to it.

The individual feels the futility of human desires and aims the sublimity and marvelous order which reveal themselves both in nature and in the world of thought. Individual existence impresses him as a sort of prison [Plato's chained prisoners in a cave, Tagore's "weeping in this dungeon"] and he wants to experience the universe as a single significant whole ["I am in my Father, and you in me, and I in you" (Jn 14:20)]. The beginnings of cosmic religious feeling already appear at an early stage of development, e.g., in many of the Psalms of David and some of the Prophets. Buddhism, as we have learned especially from the wonderful writings of Schopenhauer, contains a much stronger element of this.

The religious geniuses of all ages have been distinguished by this kind of religious feeling, which knows no dogma, no God conceived in man's image; so that there can be no church whose central teachings are based on it. Hence it is precisely among the heretics [of the established religious order: Saint John the Baptist, Jesus, early followers of Christ, al-Hallaj, Suhrawardi, etc.] of every age that we find men who were filled with this highest kind of religious feeling and were, in many cases, regarded by their contemporaries as atheists, sometimes also as saints. Looked at in this light, men like Democritus, Francis of Assisi, and Spinoza are closely akin to one another.

How can cosmic religious feelings be communicated from one person to another if it can give rise to no definite notion of a God and no theology? In my view, *it is the most important function of art and science to awaken this feeling and keep it alive* in those who are receptive to it [emphasis added].[11]

Considering the long history of persecution and clashing antagonism between science and religion, Einstein offered these insights:

We thus arrive at a conception of the relation of science and religion very different from the usual one. When one views the matter historically, one is inclined to look upon science and religion as irreconcilable antagonists, and for a very obvious reason. The man who is thoroughly convinced of the universal operation of the law of causation cannot for a moment entertain the idea of a being who interferes in the course of events—provided, of course, that he takes the hypothesis of causality really seriously . . .

It is, therefore, easy to see why the churches have always fought science and persecuted its devotees. On the other hand, I maintain that the cosmic religious feeling is the strongest and noblest motive for scientific research. Only those who realize the immense effort and, above all, the devotion without which pioneer work in theoretical science cannot be achieved are able to grasp the strength of the emotion out of which alone such work, remote as it is from the immediate realities of life, can issue . . .

Only one who has devoted his life to similar ends can have a vivid realization of what has inspired these men [Newton, Kepler, etc.] and given them the strength to remain true to their purpose in spite of countless failures. It is cosmic religious feeling that gives a man such strength. A contemporary has said, not unjustly, that in this materialistic age of ours the serious workers are the only profoundly religious people.[12]

The development of a third state of religious experience, of deep interconnectedness and cosmic meaning, has appeared in all walks of life throughout the history of humanity. Maurice Bucke,[13] Aldous

Huxley,[14] and Evelyn Underhill[15] gave excellent general presentations on the nature and development of spiritual consciousness. They covered the psychology of awakening, purification, and training of the self in its ascent up the path of the Christlike, the Buddhalike, and Godlike life. Ken Wilber[16] brought together seminal thoughts from virtually every major physicist: de Broglie, Eddington, Einstein, Heisenberg, Jeans, Pauli, Planck, and Schrödinger. To those who know the literature of these prominent scholars of ultimate reality, no praise will be necessary. To others, it may be commended as works of authoritative significance which show the perennial meaning behind the great religious writings of our own and other civilizations: link it to the best thinking of all times and all ages.

Since Bucke, Huxley, Underhill, and Wilber primarily focus on Judeo-Christian classics of the Western World, in chapter 21 I have listed sixty-three illuminated thinkers and their works from the Eastern world: China, India, Japan, Korea, and Islam. My purpose is to indicate that the West and the East corroborate each other in reference to the '1'.

Executive Focus: Sacred Unity in the Corporate Setting

In business setting many corporate leaders and business luminaries of the world are cognizant of a "line below the bottom line": the fundamental unity of all existence and the unfoldment of the inherent Light within every human being. They are fostering new and liberating horizons that go beyond fear and hope and clever management. They value perennial wisdom, bonding with children, families, and customers. They emphasize teambuilding, learning, communication, and improving human performance in such areas as work effectiveness, and total-quality through investment in developing our precious human capital.

In our country America, for example, to attract the best and the brightest, nurture the entrepreneurial spirit, new technologies, growth, and profit, when the computer giant had less than $100 million in sales (now over $90 billion, or 900 times more), Thomas J. Watson Sr. based IBM's corporate policy, or mission statement, on the development of people and the need for Big Blue to serve others first. IBM's motto to outsiders: "Customers Come First."

Tom Sr., and later Watson Jr., made IBM into the leading authority in what became the world's vital industry. With the guidance of Walter

Russell and a religious fervor for basic research, business, and policymaking Tom Sr. and Jr. built IBM into a key player in the world of computers, by converging human potential, innovation, technologies, and top-to-bottom quality management. IBM's computers turned out to be the "gold standard" worldwide. IBM's great success, and its priceless contribution toward raising the standard of employee decision-making, the breadth of ingenuity, product and service quality, and company growth and profitability, can be attributed to Tom Sr.'s corporate policy to Big Blue insiders:

> This is a man age. To make a business grow, begin growing men.
> We are all one brotherhood. We have but one thought, one creed—
> mutual helpfulness to each other.

Tom Sr. recognized that to facilitate a change in people's behavior, a change that would endure and serve as an example to others, one must create a community around corporate values, where they can be nurtured, practiced, and expressed. Simple. When you want to have quality timber, you need to grow quality trees; when you want to have quality decision makers, you need to grow quality people. Period.

19

BOUNDLESS LOVE AND JOY IN YOUR BEING

Happiness does not reside in money or material things.
Its seat is in the heart.

—Munishri Chitrabhanu

Discovering Infinity within Oneself

The apostle Paul was born in Tarsus, capital of the Roman province of Cilicia. He was a prophet, theologian and writer, Hebrew and Hellenist, Roman and Christian. Initially, as a pureblooded Pharisee, he had little room for the nature of Compassionate God, its contemporary implications for Jews, or refinements of his decision-making ("Be ye perfect") as suggested by the Christ.

Paul of Tarsus was a staunch defender of a particular strand of religious betterment within the framework of the "sacred history" of salvation and the old fundamentalist God of fear, terror, and persecution without mercy (Gal 1:13). His parents were strict Orthodox Jews. Paul was proud of his heritage: "I am Paul, a Jew of Tarsus." He arrested, imprisoned, and persecuted men and women to the point of loss of life. Here is what Paul had to say, in Hebrew, about himself in Jerusalem:

> I received strict instruction in the Law of our ancestors, and was just as dedicated to God as all of you [Jews] here today are. I *persecuted to the death* the people who followed this [Christ] Way. I arrested men and women and threw them into prison. The High Priest and the whole Council can prove that I am telling the truth. I received from them letters written to the Jewish brothers in Damascus, so I went there to arrest these people and bring them back *in chains* to Jerusalem to be punished [stoned to death].

> And as I was traveling and coming near Damascus, about midday a bright light suddenly flashed from the sky around me. I fell to the ground and heard a voice saying to me, "Saul! Saul! Why do you persecute me?" "Who are you, Lord?" I asked. "I am Jesus of Nazareth, whom you persecute," he said to me. The men with me saw the light but did not hear the voice of the one who was speaking to me. I asked, "What shall I do, Lord?" and the Lord said to me, "Get up and go into Damascus, and there you will be told everything that God has determined for you to do." I was blind because of the bright light, and so my companions took me by the hand and led me into Damascus (Acts 22:3-11).

Paul had his being enlightened to divine radiance, presaging the large-scale Christianization of society:

> Are you not aware that you are the temple [the central sanctuary, the Holy of Holies) of God and that the Spirit of God ['1'] lives in you . . . For the temple of God is holy, and *you are that temple* (1 Cor 3:16-17).

Therefore, we need to honor our true nature. We need to make our sanctuary (body/mind/soul) a habitable place in which the Spirit of the Compassionate One can live consciously. Paul instructed the Corinthians, "Imitate me, then, just as I imitate Christ" (1 Cor 11:1).

Also, the '1' is not limited to a heaven of riches and knowledge, name and fame, nor restricted to any particular place, point in time, creed, ideology, synagogue, church, or science. The '1' is present everywhere: at every point in nature, and within us. Physicists characterize it as invariance in the laws of physics, though in its totality it is extra physical, like peace, democracy, or freedom. The great book of God centers this ubiquitous nature:

> Your body is a temple of the Holy Spirit, who is in you (1 Cor 6:19).

Each one of us is a Seventh Heaven wherein final physical principles dwell. The First Epistle of John shares that God is love—love is his very being. To love God is to know Him ('1') and to share His life:

331

God is love. Whoever lives in love lives in God, and God in him (1 Jn 4:16).

Thus, to experience the abundance of life and to serve others with excellence, we need to do our best, be responsible, and be truthful to our divine heritage, as exemplified by Saint Paul:

Glorify God in your body (1 Cor 6:20).

Celebrate your divinity. Yes. Strangely, we are called to become consciously that which *we already are* unconsciously. Jesus declared:

The kingdom of God [the Highest Good] is within you (Lk 17:20-21).

Or, as a parallel passage in the Gospel of Thomas[1] bears out:

The kingdom of the Father is spread upon the earth and people do not see it (111).

God Is Walking in Human Form

In our noble outing into manifested existence, *we* (as images of the '1', Love in the world) *have assumed many forms of physical reality*: forms of time/space, gravity/matter, exotic particles, and elements. We have clothed ourselves in clusters of galaxies, large-scale structure and history. We walk the streets of New York, London, Moscow, Peking, Delhi, Tokyo, and so forth. *On the whole, we do not recognize ourselves in other beings.* By and large, we do not appreciate nor understand our common bond. And within this makeup we are called to return home to one Glory—to the Infinite Life.

This return to Home, to the personification of Love, has been addressed and reflected upon by Judeo-Christian, Buddhist, Hindu, and Muslim scholars and scribes. In Ephesians, the fullness or completion of Christ is to occur in the future:

This plan, which God will complete when the time is right, is to bring all creation together, everything in heaven and on earth, with Christ ['1'] as head (Eph 1:10).

All roads lead to the same goal. I was waiting for my wife and children on a bench in Disney World, Florida. People were rushing from one fantasy ride to another. A man sat next to me and we exchanged a few thoughts. He was also waiting for his family. He told me that in the perennial worldview, he was the prodigal son sidetracked by the husks of desires and the limitations of our universe. But now, following his bliss, he had found his way home.

I was very moved by his serenity, sagaciousness, and keen-eyed observation. He understood the greatest secret of the universe: the fundamental Oneness of the human family with the Spirit of God. My Disney friend realized that "Anywhere you turn, there is the face of God!" In scientific phraseology: the physics of the very big and of the very small are different aspects of the Common Ground: '1'. What was once the province of a few saintly folks is now our common heritage of quantum physics.

In the ultimate sense, to decipher the fine structure of time and space it means this: the Spirit of God—the Unchanging Principle that set off the creation of the universe and moves the sun and galaxies—is present in all places; every day is the Shabbas day and Christmas; the location whereon you stand is holy ground; and your neighbor's face is but your own. My friend also knew that unlimited freedom, wisdom, growth, and prosperity are available to each of us by trusting God. He quoted Jesus:

> I have come that they may have life, and have it to the full (Jn 10:10). So do not worry, saying, "What shall we eat?" or "What shall we drink?" or "What shall we wear?" For the pagans run after all these things, and your heavenly Father knows that you need them. But seek first his kingdom [within you] and his righteousness [genuine striving to be your best], and all these things will be given to you as well (Mt 6:31-33).

Then, we just sat in silence. My family came; we hugged and parted. I saw an indescribable light on his face. In the midst of Snow White and the Seven Dwarfs, Donald Duck, Mickey Mouse, Minnie, Pooh, and Goofy, there was enormous peace, happiness, and gratitude in my heart. I came across a soul who knew his roots of sanctity. After many years of wandering through the woods of time and encounters with many kinds of birds, wolves, and bears of the world, at that moment I felt that I had found a "human being." I couldn't keep tears of joy from coming to my eyes.

Teilhard de Chardin's agenda of luminous, direct vision and promise of fulfillment brings the future into the present:

> Someday after mastering the winds and the waves, the tides and gravity, we shall harness the energy of love. And then, for the second time in the history of the world, man will have discovered fire.[2]

Why someday, why not now?

The Highest Revelation: His Heart Is in Every Person

The bond of love is behind the flaming sword of Israel. It is also the love of the fullness of knowledge given witness to by the Hebrew cherubim. The fiery revolving sword, which looks like the compressor of a spinning jet engine, is a high-energy transformer, or the "lotus guard" that protects our "fruit of pure pleasure" from prematurely being released into our body. It is also the chakra of the Hindus and the Buddhists,[3] and the "Gateway reserved for Gods" of the Egyptians. The heavenly fruit of pure pleasure is the dancing creative energy unleashed for those who have achieved a high degree of inner peace, single-mindedness, and stillness of the mind.

In the symbols of the Adam and Eve parable, we notice an expression of the eternal truths related to the unlocking of the highest energies of self-illumination and spiritual evolution. The potential exists for Saul to be changed into Paul, and for Einstein's cosmic religious feeling to materialize on earth through science and education. Certain biblical passages guide us to this cosmic sense in a roundabout way through mythological fables, symbols, and cryptic code language:

> The reign of God is like a buried treasure [within your consciousness], which a man found in the field. He hid it again, and rejoicing at his find went and sold all he had and bought that field (Mt 13:44).

In another instance the Holy Scripture articulates it directly: "Is it not written in your own Law that God said, "You are gods'? If he called them 'gods,' to whom the word of God came—and the Scripture cannot be broken—" (Jn 10:34-5). The Book of Psalms, known in Hebrew as "the Book of Praises," conveys the same inspiration:

> They know nothing, they understand nothing. They walk about in darkness; all the foundations of the earth are shaken. I said: "You are 'gods'; you are all sons of the Most High" (Ps 82:5-6).

In Galatians, one more insight can be found: "You are my children, and you put me back in labor pains until Christ [Compassion] is formed [consciously realized] in you" (Gal 4:19).

Our own life and work, like those of Emerson, Einstein, and Hammarskjöld, continue to shape our self-reliance and self-perception. Emerson's extended crusade against slavery is similar to Moses', the Christ's, and Lincoln's. Emerson could read before he was three. On self-reliance he said, "All that can be done for you is nothing to what you can do for yourself."[4] On self-perception, like Descartes, Emerson maintained, "I know that I exist, and that a part of me, as essential as memory or reason, is a desire that another being exist."[5]

Emerson was enthusiastically active in all venues (reading, writing, talking and walking in every direction), spoke his mind convincingly, and understood "the Unity of All," and "The immediate presence of God" in humanity. He wrote, blazing with God within:

> The highest revelation is that God is in everyman . . . [as Socrates, Skovoroda and others observed] know thyself a man and be [consciously] a God. [6]

Precious One, can you feel the immanence of divine reality, the immediate presence of the God within? Is the Highest Good '1' within all of us and without all of us? Is this our destiny? Quietly think, ponder, and apply it in your sacred life.

To Know Yourself Is to Know God

The Upanishads, in a style of great breadth and poetic beauty, inform us, "What is within us is also without. What is without us is also within." In the Gospel of Thomas, Jesus presents us with a similar statement of how complete the kingdom of the *Infinite* and intimate is: "The kingdom is inside of you, and it is outside of you" (2). Furthermore, said Jesus of Nazareth,

> When you come to know yourselves,
> Then you will become known,
> And you will realize that it is you
> Who are the sons of the living Father ['1'].
> But if you will not know yourselves,
> You dwell in poverty
> And it is you who are that poverty (2).[7]

In addition,

> Let him who seeks continue seeking until he finds.
> [Which sounds a lot like "Seek and you shall find"]
> And when he finds,
> He will become troubled,
> And when he becomes troubled,
> He will be astonished,
> And he will rule over the all (1).[8]

On the surface, the Gospel of Thomas appears a bit cryptic. Together, in light of what we know, let us attempt to decode it as follows:

1. The most significant aspect of the first part of the Gospel of Thomas is that the unchanging ("kingdom" of the Father, the Book of Life [Dan 12:1; Lk 10:20; Rev 21:27], all that has happened and will happen) is within every point in the universe—it is within you and it is without ("outside of") you. This is also seen in passages (111 and 83) of the Gospel of Thomas: "the kingdom of the father is spread out upon the earth, and men do not see it" (111). The reason we do not see the '1' says the Christ is because: "the images are manifest to man, but the [unchanging] light in them remains concealed in the image of the light of the father [the empty-space]. He will become manifest, but his image will remain concealed by his light [the pre-quantum fact]." (83)

    We do not observe the '1' until we tune in mentally and emotionally to the "undivided" '1'. We do not dwell in the light until we synchronize our consciousness (unite, become one) with the light. Stated another way, we don't know what sex is until we have sex; we don't know what God is until we have union with God. Also, the '1', the changeless self-essence, is everywhere. However, "if you do not know yourselves" (who you are at your foundation), not only "you are in poverty" (unable to help yourself and others) but "you are the poverty."

2. Furthermore, let the one who seeks the truth (who looks for the common denominator in different forms) not stop searching until she/he finds it—until she/he discovers the Highest Good within her/himself.

3. In the beginning, when one realizes this truth, one can be amazed or even disturbed. You may have been taught that God is someplace far away in outer space (heaven). Suddenly, you discover that the "kingdom of the Eternal Light is within you," wherever and whoever you are. I know. Coming into contact with the clear Light of absolute peace stirred me. The first time I experienced the transparent Light I was so moved that for a long time I did not venture there again. It was shattering to see the Unutterable, whom I had always regarded in terms of infinity, actually shining as the clear Light in me.

At first I could not comprehend how the Absolute, the Prime Mover and the Highest Good could be a pure Light in me. It is only after I understood that the middle rest-line of the electromagnetic wave, the no-movement empty-space, is where manifestation is generated, and after I realized that *zero contains within itself the very essence of all possible mathematical relationships*, that I could once again gaze at the limitless all-pervading Light.

The view is beautiful. You see not only the breathless grandeur of creation aglow in blazing light; you are also flooded by the splendor of transcendent beauty, force, and love. Numerous times, in my daily spiritual exercises, I found that the distinction between my surroundings and myself had disappeared. I saw that all is One and the same splendor of conscious love, light, joy, peace, and wonder.

The manifestation may be likened to a glowing spark. As the spark, at first full of brilliance and speed, is ejected, as if exploded from the fire ('1'), it begins to expand—to inflate in '1'. As it expands, it cools, loses its brilliance, and slows down—decelerates. But as it starts traveling homeward again, as some of the galaxies in our universe do now, it accelerates, and increases in brilliance, until finally it ends its history and unites with the '1'.

The process or cycle is repeated endlessly. Every electromagnetic wave, every particle, and every universe come to manifestation in this manner. Further, every time the electromagnetic wave or the universe exhausts itself, it returns to the Absolute to be regenerated. And all manifestations, at different electromagnetic vibrations, appear as networks of beautifully interconnected flashing lights, which on the surface glitter as if real, but when one penetrates this moving foreground of atoms, through higher levels of inner peace, one finds she/he is involved in an illusion of the grossest kind. If you could stop the electromagnetic movements with a high-speed camera, the solid matter would disappear, and only immense distances between the tiny clouds—doughnut like electromagnetic groups of waves, particles, would be left. Then, if you could increase your camera speed again and examine the tiny electromagnetic waves, they also would disappear and only the Absolute Light would be left.

There will be no movement, no deception, and no illusion. All, finally, like the physical law, will be immovable and at rest. One will see that the manifest reality, which seconds ago appeared so very real, is only a simulated play of reflection within the '1'. In this joyous and subtle ecstasy one will understand that all is a momentous Disneyland playground created by you for your own enjoyment, that all-that-is is you, and that you are the one who takes yourself on the ride of self-inflicted horrors and joys.

My observations are imperfect and limited. Additionally, it is difficult to relate what one sees with the knowledge and the symbolic language we have. It's like using the words "black" and "white" to describe color, or water to describe orange juice.[9]

All This Time You Were Me

When I shared my experiences with Oksana, she advised me to be prudent in disclosing this knowledge to others. One wonders why it took so long to discover the precious truth, to find out who one is—to realize that she/he is I.

"All this time you were me and I was you, and we did not know it," a friend informed me in a dream. Yes, all this time we were Christ—all this time we were a Buddha—but we were not "awakened" to this reality. Hans Denk lamented in this fashion:

> O my God, how does it happen in this poor old world that Thou art so great and yet nobody finds Thee, that Thou callest so loudly and nobody hears Thee, that Thou art so near and nobody feels Thee, that Thou givest Thyself to everybody and nobody knows Thy name? Men flee from Thee and say they cannot find Thee; they turn their backs and say they cannot see Thee; they stop their ears and say they cannot hear Thee.

"I have come to the stage of realization in which I see that God is walking in every human form and manifesting himself alike in the sage and in the sinner," stated Sri Ramakrishna. Consequently, when one realizes her/his Christ-Buddha nature for the first time, one begins to experience the brilliant Light within oneself and thanksgiving, filled with great joy, that life is wonderful and each of us is everywhere within each other. Finally, after all of the amazement, marveling and gratitude, each of us will, in the words of Einstein, "place [our] powers freely and gladly in the service of mankind."[10]

And science without borders shall reign over all, consciously influencing the events in our lives, the laws of nature, our environment, and the cosmic field of creation. Jesus phrased it like this, "If you do not doubt in your heart, but believe that what you say will happen, it will be done for you" (Mk 11:23).

World literature is jam-packed with humans attaining "clarity of thought" and deep inner peace—creating "miraculous" phenomena. Think of the discovery of language, fire, the invention of agriculture and paper, the birth of cities, knitting, dancing, music, the wheel, communication through the written word, poetry, judicial systems, governments, piped water, indoor bathrooms, pianos, elevators, petrochemicals, microchips, merchant banking, the printing press, free enterprise, telescopes, mass production, teamwork, electricity, submarines, computers, telephones, fiber-optic networks, bomb-sniffing detectors, refrigerators, temperature control at home, automobiles, airplanes, radios, television, electron microscopes, solar energy, freeways, underwater tunnels, skyscrapers, plastics products, electric appliances, footwear, the United Nations, rockets, genetics as a human endeavor, walking on the moon, the broadband Internet and World Wide Web, space stations, the nanoscale science and devices, Nanobiotechnology, and more. These are some of the marvels and miracles to those who do not recognize the fundamental laws powering them. For others, it requires the knowledge and understanding of the basic principles to create a "miraculous" experience: "Know the truth, and the truth shall set you free" (Jn 8:32).

As might be expected, if one understands the simple rules at the initial conditions of all that is, and knows how to implement them, then seeming miracles become self-evident truths to higher levels of freedom and a more abundant life. They enable us to live a richer and more meaningful existence. You will search no more for the knowledge and freedom, because you will be knowledge and freedom itself.

All Is for the Good: Let's Focus on That First Goal

We all have goals and desires. The challenge is being able to fulfill them. For that, we need a bedrock mate with a proven record of success. The bedrock on which everything rests is the '1'. As you will find in part 2, chapters 10 and 11, the '1' is the foundation for "all states of being." The Hindu sage Vyasa speaks of the different disguises and masks of the '1' in the Bhagavad Gita:

> There is no Truth superior to Me. Everything rests upon Me [the ultimate '1'], as pearls are strung on a thread . . . I am the taste of water, the light of the sun and the moon, the syllable om in the Vedic mantras; I am the sound in ether [empty-space] and the ability in man. I am the original fragrance of the earth, and I am the heat in fire. I am the life of all that lives, and I am the penance of all ascetics . . . I am the original seed of all existence, the intelligence of the intelligent, and the prowess of all powerful men. All states of being—be they of goodness, passion, or ignorance—are manifested by My energy. I am, in one sense, everything [manifestation]— but I am independent [empty-space]. I am not under the modes of this material nature (7.7-12).[11]

Rejoice. Celebrate your divinity every second in every act. You are looking at yourself through your brother's eyes!

The Hindu scripture Chandogya Upanishad, aiming to describe the origin, nature, and destiny of man and his universe, assures us that we don't have to go far to find the ultimate totality (God, Brahman, Atman), for the entire world is a reflection of God:

> Verily, this whole world is Brahma [the attributes of creation]. Tranquil, let one worship It as that from which he came forth, as that into which he will be dissolved, as that in which he breathes,[12] [and] Atman alone is the whole world.[13]

Chandogya Upanishad continues the theme "That art thou"—You are He:

> As the bees, my dear, prepare honey by collecting the essences of different trees and reducing the essence to a unity, as they are not able to discriminate "I am the essence of this tree," "I am the essence of that tree"—even so, indeed, my dear, all creatures here, though they reach Being, know not "We have reached Being" . . . . These rivers, my dear, flow, the eastern toward the east, the western toward the west. They become the ocean itself. As there they know not "I am this one," "I am that one"—even so, indeed, my dear, all creatures here, though they have come forth from Being, know not "We have come forth from Being."[14] I Myself am He![15]

In point of fact, affirms the Brihadaranyaka Upanishad:

> The world is His ['1']; indeed, He is the world itself.[16] Verily, this Soul is the overlord of all things, the king of all things. As all the spokes are held together in the hub and felly of a wheel, just so in this Soul all things, all gods, all worlds, all breathing things, all these selves are held together.[17]

Jesus is quoted as saying: "I am the vine ['1'] and you are the branches [manifestations]." In his dispatch to the Galatians, Saint Paul corroborates this most fundamental actuality:

Each one of you is a son [reflection—image] of God ['1']
(Gal 3:26).

Ken Wilber, in his striking book *Quantum Physics*, dealing with the
writings of the world's greatest physicists, brings this two-thousand-
year-old message of the Epistle to the Galatians to the present-day:

> All things, including subatomic particles, are ultimately made of
> God [the inner nature of reality].[18]

The Universe:
A Very Tiny Ripple on a Background of Infinity
David Bohm, a leading-edge researcher, spent forty years exploring the
"hidden variables in the quantum theory . . . the enfolding-unfolding
universe and consciousness" and their "common ground" at the Lawrence
Radiation Laboratory in Berkeley, California and during his appointments
at Princeton, the University of Sao Paolo, and the University of Haifa.
Comparable to Einstein, Bohm wrote:

> The entire universe [with all its "particles," including those
> constituting human beings, their laboratories, observing
> instruments] has to be understood as a single undivided whole, in
> which analysis into separately and independently existent parts
> has no fundamental status . . . That is, the entire Universe is a very
> tiny ripple on a background of emptiness, which is also fullness! . . .
> and there might be other levels of reality beyond anything we are
> able to know so far. This would suggest that we are only scratching
> the surface of reality.[19]

The Svetasvatara Upanishad, akin to the great Hindu sage Vyasa, in the
Bhagavad Gita, presents another breathtaking treasure:

> You are woman. You are man.
> You are the youth and the maiden too.
> You as an old man totterest with a staff
> Being born, you becomest facing in every direction.
> You are the dark blue bird and the green (parrot) with red eyes.

You hast the lightning as thy child.
You are the seasons and the seas.
Having no beginning.
You do abide with all-pervadingness.
Wherefrom all beings are born.[20]

The apocryphal Acts of Peter reiterates:

Thou art perceived of the spirit only ['1'], thou art unto me father,
thou my mother, thou my brother, thou my friend, thou my
bondsman, thou my steward: thou art All and All is in thee: and
thou art, and there is naught else that is save thee only.

Yes, let us look for a profounder understanding; yes, let us realize our
relationship with God, '1'. '1' is All: all inclusive, all pervading, and all
encompassing. '1' is in all of us: nothing apart from '1', nothing outside
of '1', nothing other to '1'.

Isaiah articulated: "I am the Lord, and there is none else." Some
twenty-five centuries later, Ken Carey offers his own thought:

I am always with you . . . You and I are one in your consciousness
as we have ever been one in Reality. I beat with every throb of your
heart, feel with every touch of your hand, cry your every tear,
breathe your every breath. I am never far away.[21]

Saint Bernard shares with us a similar treasure:

Who is God? I can think of no better answer than He who is.
Nothing is more appropriate to the eternity which God is. If you
call God good, or great, or blessed, or wise, or anything else of this
sort, it is included in these words, namely, He is.[22]

Mohandas Karamchand Gandhi, well known to us as Mahatma Gandhi,
was a spiritual giant, and a social and political leader of the twentieth
century. He deployed armory of love, truthfulness, purity, self-
discipline, and nonviolence (also recognized as civil disobedience) in
his spiritual advancement and against destructive political, social, and
military forces.

Mahatma ("Great Soul," as he was called) studied Christ's Sermon on the Mount and Tolstoy's teachings, and saw the presence of God (the "Omnipresent, Omniscient, and Omnipotent God of gods"; '1') in all beings. His ambition: wiping every tear from every eye, universal self-realization, and seeing that no one in the world is hungry or homeless. Albert Einstein said of Gandhi, "Generations to come will scarcely believe that such a one as this walked the earth in flesh and blood."

When Gandhi was thirty-seven, he became aware of the power of "the inner voice," self-surrender in complete love to the Highest Good (*bhakti*; Christ's "Thy will be done"), selfless action, and service-excellence with no attachment to the results (karma; Christ's washing the feet of the apostles example [Jn 13:14]).

God was Truth and Love for Gandhi. Where Truth was equated to ultimate reality, Love was the ultimate value of life. All principal religions were true and equal; all men and women were brothers and sisters as they have the same absolute consciousness—'1'. He stood for the very highest principles: "the truly noble know all men are one"; the relation between economic development and political freedom cannot be separated from spiritual values; humanity's fundamental goal is self-liberation.

For Gandhi, "Noncooperation with evil is as much a duty as is cooperation with good," yet the path of liberation was that of the love of all creatures and adherence to moral values and action. His concept of God displays this philosophy:

> To me God is truth and love. God is ethics and morality; God is fearlessness. God is the source of light and life, and yet he is above and beyond all these. God is conscience. He is even the atheism of the atheist. For in his boundless love, God permits the atheist to live. He is the searcher of the hearts. He knows us and our hearts better than we do ourselves . . . He transcends speech and reason. He is a personal god to those who need his personal presence. He is embodied to those who need his touch. He is the purest essence. He simply is to those who have faith. He is long-suffering. He is patient but He is also terrible. He is the greatest democrat the world knows, for he leaves us unfettered to make our own choice between evil and good. He is the greatest tyrant ever known for he often dashes the cup from our lips and under

cover of free will leaves us a margin so wholly inadequate as to provide only mirth for himself at our expense. Therefore, it is what Hinduism calls all this sport—Lila, or calls it an illusion Maya.[23]

Gandhi's life is a remembrance of human destiny. His expressions are just as true for Muslim Sufis:

> The "world" is but forgetfulness [amnesia] of God; it is not spouse and child, silver and gold. Who from this world did turn his face away, he was not lost; indeed, instead, he found his long forgotten and lost Self again. No bar guards His palace-gateway, no veil screens His Face of Light—you are my heart! By your own selfness, are enwrapped in darkest night.[24]

The Irani avatar, great sage, and spiritual genius Merwan Sheriarji, known as Meher Baba, is an invaluable gift to humanity. In his discourses Meher Baba explains:

> There is only one question. And once you know the answer to that question, there are no more to ask . . . Out of the depths of unbroken Infinity arouse the Question, Who am I? And to that Question there is only one Answer—I am God![25] The problem is that people do not know who they really are: you are Infinite. You are really everywhere; but you think you are the body, and therefore consider yourself limited. If you look within and experience your own soul in its true nature, you will realize that you are infinite and beyond all creation.[26]

Yes, "you are the infinite come in the finite," restates Sai Baba:

> The formless Infinite appearing as the form-full infinitesimal, the Absolute pretending to be the relative, the Atman behaving as the body, the metaphysical masquerading as the merely physical . . . The self in man and the divinity that dwells within him are one and the same. Add infinity onto yourself and you become the divinity itself. Unfortunately, having become embodied you have forgotten your divinity, your unlimited infinity; you are aware

only of your limited individuality. If you want to attain the infinity, you must make an inquiry into the divinity which is inherent in you.[27]

I Went to Look for God: You Remind Me of Me

If you enter into your Being through the point of peace you will feel unity with the world. You will experience the joy of God of the Catholic mystics, the Sufis of Islam, Baha'is, and the wisest of the Protestant tradition, the Charismatics, Quakerism, the Methodists, the Waldensians and Hussites, the Baptists, the Hutterites, the Mennonites, the Bruderhof community, and the Latter-day Saints. For:

> *I am in your own souls!*
> *Why see you not?*
> *In every breath of yours am I,*
> *But you are blind.*
> *Without true eye,*
> *And see Me not.*[28]

The whole of life is one continuous act of conscious living, of advancing toward the humanly perfect as the ultimate is perfect: Universal Christ, Universal Buddha, and Universal Vishnu. Yes:

> He who is absent, far away from God—
> His heart can only say: "God is" somewhere;
> He who has found the Loved One in Him-Self
> For him God is not he, nor you, but I.
> Whom may I take for guide upon the Way
> One who himself away from it does stray?
> He is content to say "God is," while I
> Am desolate till I "God am" can say![29]

The pearls of the eternal wisdom are ad infinitum. Eventually, when we find God within ourselves, we will compose similar insights:

> If you find God, then you have found all things! Just think! If the Creator you do find, can His creation still remain behind? Is the

One ever separate from the Other? "Indeed I am this All, All This is Mine"—this word resoundeth ever from within! You are Your-Self the Thinker, and this world but your own thought, and God but Your-Self.[30]

In our search through the wilderness of meaningful investments, where can we locate the finest and greatest return on our capital? Is "it" to be found in euro capital markets, derivatives (the Oracle of Omaha and investment legend Warren E. Buffett has called them "financial weapons of mass destruction"), structured finance, real estate holdings, synthetic CDOs (collateralized debt obligations), CDOs cubed—or derivatives that invest in derivatives of derivatives, foreign currencies, bonds, stocks, corporate takeovers, or restructurings? Is "it" in high technology, monetary policy, liquidity in economy, global financial markets, Eurobonds, or mortgage-backed securities, and so forth?

The finest, most enduring and most rewarding return on investment (to get your portfolio sparkling) is in the cutting-edge asset: *people*. The best gain on that asset is in unleashing the infinite human energy that rests undeveloped within each of us. A good decision maker is a national asset; a bad decision maker a national liability. The Hindu Vedanta magnificently restates our search:

Why will you wander in the wilderness!
You who are seeking God!
Yourselves are He!
You need not search!
He is you, verily![31]

Tukaram Maharaj (1598-1650) was of oceanic heart, magnanimity, and the most keen-eyed mind, translates:

I went to look for God, but didn't find God. I myself became God.
In this very body, God revealed Himself to me.[32]

The Biblical book of Psalms (a psalm of Asaph) affirms:

They know nothing, they understand nothing;
They walk about in darkness;

all the foundations of the earth are shaken.
I said: "You are 'gods';
you are all sons of the Most High."
But you will die like mere men;
you will fall like every other ruler.
Rise up, O God, judge the earth,
for all the nations are your inheritance (Ps 82:5-8).

Truth Is One: Greet the Future with a Warm Embrace

Similar to Gandhi, Tolstoy, and Thoreau, the *Tasawwuf* restates:

> *The wise see in their heart the face of God,*
> *And not in images of stone and clod!*
> *Who in themselves, alas! can see Him not,*
> *They seek to find Him in some other spot.*[33]

Hui-neng (638-713), the sixth patriarch of Zen in China, had scarcely any formal education and had to take care of his widowed mother by collecting and selling firewood. He wrote some of the most profound passages in Zen literature and displayed a streak of genius when he declared:

> When not enlightened, Buddhas are no other than ordinary beings;
> when there is enlightenment, ordinary beings at once turn into
> Buddhas.[34]

When nonenlightened Saul is Saul—when there is enlightenment, Saul turns into Paul. Let us pray that Wahhabi strain of Islam turns into Ibn 'Arabi, Ibn al-Farid, al-Hallaj, Suhrawardi, Rumi, and Hafiz's strain of Islam.

Insight into one's pure nature is possible by allowing the Voice of Truth to come to the surface. That is, to achieve insight into one's foundation (enshrined in many different symbols: the Christ consciousness, liberation, etc.), one's mind must be pure, loving, and at peace, free from attachment and error. This type of life leads through the samadhi of Oneness, a state of deep stillness and inner peace ("absence of thought" or "no-thought") to sudden enlightenment.

Hui-neng maintained that the absolute consciousness—pure Buddha-nature ("I am that I am," Christ's "kingdom")—is in everyone and in all things. Through the New Rebirth we tune into the '1'. We experience what the Gospel of Thomas described: "I am the light which is over everything . . . Split wood: I am there. Lift up the stone, and you will find me there." (77).

Penetrating genius Erwin Schrödinger possessed great breadth and acuteness of intellect. He developed new models for cross-discipline and cross-sector fertilization. Schrödinger was a student of self-realization amongst sages and mystics. He said:

> Again, the mystics of many centuries, independently, yet in perfect harmony with each other (somewhat like the particles in an ideal gas) have described, each of them, the unique experience of his or her life in terms that can be condensed in the phrase: DEUS FACTUS SUM (I have become [one with] God).[35]

Their descriptions differ, but they share in a fundamental truth what the Upanishads state simply:

> *Cows are of many different colors,*
> *But the milk of all is one color, white;*
> *So the proclaimers who proclaim the Truth*
> *Use many varying forms to put it in,*
> *But yet the Truth enclosed in all is One.*[36]

Once a high degree of purity of heart is achieved, one's limited thoughts concerning one's self are removed. There is a consciousness shift from the part (paradigm thinking of Cartesian, Newtonian, and Baconian type) to the whole (paradigm thinking of Einstein, Schrödinger, Bohm, Mother Teresa, Pope John Paul II, and Copenhagen), from the many (leadership, media, education, religion, and government that separates people from people) to the One (leadership, media, education, religion, and government that brings together people with people). We begin to understand, at first hazily and later quite lucidly, that true joy is not to be found someplace "out there" or somewhere "deep under one's skin," but rather, it is blazing forth from all of us. As Vedas proclaim:

> Truly, you are Godhead yourself . . . He is you.[37]

Actions Are Speaking Louder Than Words:
Let Us Do Our Duty

It is most moving and chilling that these thoughts include the Stalins, Hitlers, Mao Ze-dongs, Husseins, and terrorists of the world, as well as the millions of people they destroyed. It embraces the saints and the saviors, the sages, wise ones, and the "awake ones" (Buddha[s], Baba[s]). "God is in all and all is in God." Our brothers and sisters are one and the same Being, existing in enduring, beautiful, eternal Oneness. As the New Testament proclaims:

> We are members of one another (Eph 4:25); all are one in Christ
> Jesus (Gal 3:28).

Saint Francis of Assisi describes the fire and water, the sun and the moon, his brothers and his sisters. In our many roles we take on the form and character of the joyous self and occasionally the shadow self, always moving toward what we perceive to be the light. The nearer we come to the light ('1') the more light, order, and goodness we experience; the farther we move away from the light, the more darkness, disorder, and evil we live through. Every atom, every human, every planet, and every starburst galaxy, near and far, goes through this cycle. We share in the same celebration and the Oneness of Infinity.

Understanding the stunningly beautiful Oneness—the Cause of Existence—is subtle. Our mind's circuitry is subject to physical laws. It is difficult to drive a fifty-ton truck through a two-inch hole. The same applies to our mind's neural antenna. The full light of truth is that the Highest Good, '1', is within each and every one of us: *we are all one.*

The personal experience of unity is so vast, the awareness is so immense, and our mind's opening so small, that although this truth has been presented, verified, and corroborated by direct experience and experimentation by thousands of individuals, today, most people still cannot grasp it. In part 2 this truth will be shown to be verified by science.

If we can only understand the Oneness of all, we will close the freeways to destructive behavior. We will not be brooding in the darkness of some desperate isolation or alienation. We will not be holding onto inflexible boundaries among Buddhists, Christians, Hindus, Jews, and Muslims, amid blacks, whites, and other races, between nations, corporations, and families. There would not be the need for a *Mein Kampf*, a *Book of Mao*, and anthrax to be used against people, or human rights abuses. The Dachaus, Gulag Archipelagos, jihad training camps, suicide bombing teams, and thirty thousand nuclear warheads (Russia 18,000, U.S. 11,000, China 400, France 350, Britain 200, Israel 100, India 70, Pakistan 44) would not exist. The leaders would not state, "We have to kill for Allah . . . We have to war for God . . ." There would be no murders, rapes, robberies, nor the corrosive devastation of families.

Sir James Hopwood Jeans (1877-1946), physicist and mathematician who made fundamental contributions to the continuous-creation theory, binary and multiple star systems, the dynamic theory of gases, the mathematical theory of electromagnetism, the evolution of gaseous stars, the investigation of spiral nebulae, and the theory of giant and dwarf stars, goes on to write:

> Things are not what they seem; it is the general recognition that we are not yet in contact with ultimate reality. We are still imprisoned in our cave, with our backs to the light, and can only watch the shadows on the wall.[39]

Change must develop from within our hearts and minds. Then we shall free ourselves and enter the Promised Land. Dennis Gabor (1900-1979) gives additional insight:

> Till now man has been up against Nature; from now on he will be up against his own nature.[40]

20

MANY THOUGH WE ARE, WE ARE ONE BODY

Rise up, O God . . .
for all the nations are your inheritance.

—Psalm 82:8

Where There Is Goodness, There Is God

The insight that "His ('1') heart resides in everything" has been observed and experienced throughout the centuries, in the East and West. In the Gospel according to John we hear, "In him was life, and that life was *the light of men*. The light shines [on in the darkness], but the darkness has not understood [overcome] it," (Jn 1:4-5). Aldous Huxley, in *The Perennial Philosophy*, writes:

> It is because we don't know who we are, because we are unaware that the kingdom of heaven is within us . . . that we behave in the generally silly, the often insane, the sometimes criminal ways that are so characteristically human. We are saved, we are liberated and enlightened, by perceiving the hitherto unperceived good that is already within us, by returning to our eternal ground and remaining where, without knowing it, we have always been.[1]

Meister Eckhart, the penetrating genius, verbalized, similar to Jetsun Milarepa, the burning with love man, when he said:

> A man has many skins in himself,
> Covering the depths of his heart.

352

Man knows so many things;
He does not know himself.
Why, thirty or forty skins or hides,
Just like an ox's or bears,
So thick and hard, cover the soul.
Go into your own ground
And learn to know yourself there.[2]

On one occasion Eckhart shared the following story:

God give you good morning, brother!
  "The same to you, sir, but I have never yet had a bad one."
  How is that, brother?
  "Because whatever God has sent me, I have borne gladly for his sake, considering myself unworthy of him. That is why I have never been sad or troubled."
  When did you first find God?
  "When I left all creatures, then I found God."
  Where, then, did you leave him, brother?
  "In any clear, pure heart."
  Who are you, brother?
  "I am a king."
  Of what?
  "Of my flesh: whatever my spirit wants from God, my flesh is more eager and ready to take than my spirit is."
  A king must have a kingdom. Where is yours, brother?
  "In my soul."
  How so?
  "When I have shut the door of my five senses, earnestly desiring God, I find him in my soul as clearly and as joyful as he is in eternity."
  You could be holy! What made you so, brother?
  "Meditation, high thinking, and union with God have drawn me to heaven, for I never could be content with anything less than God. Now I have found him and I am eternally content and happy in him and that is worth more than any kingdom, as long as we continue in time. No pious practice is so perfect that it may not be an obstacle to spirituality."[3]

The *Theologia Germanica*, a work by the fourteenth century German mystic Johan Tauler, edited and published in 1516-1518 by Martin Luther (1483-1546), maintains that, "Goodness needeth not enter into the soul, for it is there already, only it is unperceived."[4] Dag Hammarskjöld wrote, "Goodness is something so simple: always to live for others, never to seek one's advantage."[5]

By God! Everything Is He

Earlier, we examined the Gospel of Thomas regarding "the one who knows himself . . . [that person] has at the same time already achieved knowledge about the Depth of the All." Here, Rumi speaks in a similar frame of mind: "He who knows himself knows his Lord."[6] Also, said Rumi, in *Masnavi*, "The Beloved is all in all, . . . The Beloved is all that live."[7] As Jesus was to exclaim,

All are one (Gal 3:28), one body and one spirit (Eph 4:4).

Thomas Merton, a brilliant young mind working in great haste and prompted by a sense of utmost urgency, declared, "Our very life loses its separate voice and resounds with the majesty and the mercy of the Hidden and Living One."[8]

In the late fifteenth century Maulana 'Abdurrahman Jami called out:

Neighbor and associate and companion—everything is He.
In the beggar's coarse frock and in the king's silk—everything is He.
In the crowd of separation and in the loneliness of collectedness
By God! Everything is He and by God! Everything is He.[9]

All is He, the very same essence and Being, but in different forms, wonders and perfumes that can be directly experienced by us. According to the first epistle of Paul to the Corinthians, as stated earlier, we are all part of the body of God ('1'), "The body is one and has many members, but all the members, many though they are, are one body."

Additionally, each of the members of the body works not for itself alone but as a team, for the whole body, as for example the ear hears for each member of the body, the eye sees for each member of the body, and the head thinks for each member of the body. Teamwork excellence of each member is what the '1' consists of. The scriptural bedrock of the Hindu tradition, the Vedas, gives a related perspective: "The countless heads, eyes, ears, and hands and feet of living beings are all parts of One Man."[10]

A car, ship, rocket, computer, or washing machine, and so forth, similar to our body, consists of many parts. Each part works in a "team" with all of the other parts. Each part operates, not for itself, but as a member of the whole!

The Parts Are Not Separate from the Whole

Personal experience that the Infinite is everywhere and everything was skillfully expressed by Jami:

> Sometimes we call Thee wine, sometimes goblet,
> Sometimes we call Thee corn, and sometimes snare,
> There is no letter save Thy name on the tablet of the word—
> Now: by which name shall we call Thee?[11]

Two centuries later, regarding the insight that God is everywhere, Dara Shikoh would proclaim, "In the name of Him Who has no name, who appears by whatever name you will call Him . . ."[12]

Furthermore, "Everything that lives, lives not alone, nor for itself," said William Blake. Willis W. Harman, president of the Institute of Noetic Sciences, and professor emeritus of engineering-economic systems at Stanford University, was a seminal thinker in the area of consciousness and human transformation. In his search for knowledge and for a higher synergy society at Stanford, he did not limit himself to one school of thought or one partisan explanation, but instead journeyed far and wide throughout the entire spectrum of scholarship, science, and reason. Willis expressed Blake's suggestion to me this way:

> When reality is wholeness, there is no greater error than separateness thinking. Imagine if the stomach were to get the idea that it could pursue its self-interest independent of the well being of the whole body/mind/spirit. Justifying its appetites with the maxims "What's good for the stomach is good for the whole,"

and "The business of the stomach is growth of the stomach," it seeks to maximize its absorption of nutrients and minimize the fraction going to other parts of the body. It worries about such indicators as getting its "market share" of food value, and "gross abdominal product." It sounds absurd, of course, because the stomach doesn't do anything of the sort. It concentrates on performing its function with regard to the whole system, and trusts that if it does that, the system will see to it that its nutrient, protection, and other needs are met.[13]

And one more observation of the essential unity of God and us, that "we" and "Thou" are not independent from each other:

> The progeny of Adam,
> All are parts and limbs of one
> And the same organism,
> Risen from the same essence, everyone;
> And can it be, while one limb is in pain,
> That other limbs should feel at restful ease?[14]

"This that I am now uttering unto you," revealed the Blessed One of Islam, Muhammad:

> The Holy Qur'an—it is to be found within the ancient Seers' writings too; for Teachers have been sent to every race. Of human beings no community is left without a warner and a guide. And aught of difference we do not make—for disagreement there is none between these Prophets. All that have been sent, have been so sent but One Truth to proclaim—"I, verily the I All-One, am God, there is no other God than I [the '1': the universal all-pervading Self], and I alone should be adored by all.[15]

Show Me Yourself and I Will Show You My God

It is evident that no community has been left without a bugler to awaken us from our lingering sleep, or a leader to proclaim the Good News of our roots and heritage. However, "Mind is patient," said quantum physicist Freeman Dyson:

Mind has waited for three billion years on this planet before composing its first string quartet. It may have to wait for another three billion years before it spreads all over the galaxy. I do not expect that it will have to wait so long.

But if necessary, it will wait. The universe is like a fertile soil spread out all around us, ready for the seeds of mind to sprout and grow. Ultimately, late or soon, mind will come into its heritage. What will mind choose to do when it informs and controls the universe? That is a question which we cannot hope to answer.

When mind has expanded its physical reach and its biological organization by many powers of ten beyond the human scale, we can no more expect to understand its thoughts and dreams than a monarch butterfly can understand ours . . . In contemplating the future of mind in the universe, we have exhausted the resources of our puny human science.[16]

Yes, "Like a reflection in a mirror, all is a projection of mind," relates the child of joy, and profound thinker saint Milarepa. He expounds:

External phenomenal objects: forms, sounds, smells, tastes, and objects of touch, all these phenomena are no other than the magical tricks of mind. Like a child who builds sand castles, it is mind that fixates on names. Realizing that this is unreal is also mind . . . Know that all manifestations are like reflections of the moon in water.[17]

Jesus inspires us: "I come not to destroy the law or the prophets, but to fulfill them. That you might be filled with all the fullness of God." That you might experience pure happiness and holiness within yourself through heightened awareness, expansion of human consciousness, and highly productive work. When this takes place, as it surely will, your heart will feel as if it is going to explode with happiness and holiness. Every cell in your body will sing with joy. Everything you see, everyone you meet, everything you do at home, work, on the street, will be touching your heart with joy. You will go to bed with joy. You will wake up with the pure joy of holiness in your being.

Professor Martin Buber (1878-1965) was a contemporary German-Jewish religious philosopher, theologian, biblical translator, and political leader. He became editor of the Zionist weekly *Die Welt* (1901), and founded *Der Jude* (1916), the central resource for German-reading Jewish intellectuals. Because of his hostility to Nazi principles, in Frankfurt (on Main), he was forbidden (in 1938) to make public lectures. Through his *Paths in Utopia,* Buber advanced to the Israeli kibbutz, a courageous step in collective living. Buber describes one's experiences of holiness in these celebrating words:

> One should, and one must, truly live with all, but one should live with all in holiness, one should hallow all that one does in one's natural life. No renunciation is commanded. One eats in holiness, tastes the food in holiness, and the table becomes an altar. One works in holiness, and he raises up the sparks which hide themselves in all tools. One walks in holiness across the fields, and the soft songs of all herbs, which they voice to God, enter into the song of our soul. One drinks in holiness to each other with one's companions, and it is as if they read together in the Torah. One dances the roundelay in holiness, and a brightness shines over the gathering. A husband is united with his wife in holiness, and the Shekhina rests over them.[18]

Krishna, the most revered Indian avatar, declared: "To but One Goal are marching everywhere, all human beings, though they may seem to walk on paths divergent; that goal is I."[19] Our goal is to regain the inner nature of Reality (Christ, Buddha, Tao, the Creator, the Way, Joy, and Holiness) within us. That's the test.

Saint Theophilus of Antioch (115-181) was the sixth bishop of Antioch, Syria (modern Antakya, Turkey). In all probability, he was the first to articulate a trinity, or triad, in the divine existence: God, his Word (Logos), and his Wisdom. Theophilus was one of the earliest commentators upon the Gospels, if not the first, and he appears to have been the earliest Christian historian of the Church of the Old Testament. Theophilus maintained that the consciousness of God's reality manifests as widespread occurrence of the sensitive spirit and affects all of human activity. In *Theophilus to Autolycus* he stated:

> But if you say, "Show me thy God," I would reply, "Show me yourself, and I will show you my God."[20]

I Was Deeply Moved by These Insights

Yes, says Theophilus, God will manifest to you, all around you, when you cleanse yourself from all impurity:

> For God is seen by those who are enabled to see Him when they have the eyes of their soul opened: for all have eyes; but in some they are overspread [like cataracts], and do not see the light of the sun. Yet it does not follow, because the blind do not see, that the light of the sun does not shine; but let the blind blame themselves and their own eyes. So also thou, O man, hast the eyes of thy soul overspread by thy sins and evil deeds. As a burnished mirror, so ought man to have his soul pure. When there is rust on the mirror, it is not possible that a man's face be seen in the mirror; so also when there is sin in a man, such a man cannot behold God.[21]

When the eyes of the soul are purged, God can be seen all the time, everywhere, in everyone and everything, attested Saint Paul in his letters to the Colossians, "Christ is everything ['**1**'] in all of you" (Col 3:11), and the Ephesians,

> And so we shall all come together to that Oneness . . . ; we shall become mature men, reaching to the very height of Christ's full stature. Then we shall no longer be children, carried by the waves and blown about by every shifting wind . . . Instead, by speaking the truth in a spirit of love, we must grow up in every way to Christ ['**1**'], who is the head. Under his ['**1**'] control all the different parts of the body fit together, and the whole body is held together by every joint with which it is provided. So when each separate part works as it should, the whole body grows and builds itself up through love" (Eph 4:13-16).

Drenched in the love of Christ, Sathya Sai Baba found that:

> The highest level on the spiritual path is achieved when the devotee and God become One. His consciousness expands to the level of God consciousness or superconsciousness and for him all distinctions between Sai [the Mother of the Universe], God, and

himself disappear and he becomes "THAT." Having annihilated his ego completely and achieved total desirelessness, he transcends body consciousness to achieve total equanimity and remain eternally immersed in God-consciousness—Sath-Chith-Ananda [a supreme state of being, translated as Being-Awareness-Bliss]; I am Existence, I am Knowledge, I am Bliss.[22]

In the *Cidade Caleixnese* manuscript (the so-called *Dialogue of Jesus and John*) another insight appears:

The kingdom of heaven is within you,
and whosoever shall know himself shall find it . . .
strive therefore to know yourself
and you shall know that you are in the City of God,
and you are the City.[23]

21

GREAT MINDS OF THE EASTERN WORLD

Let the past serve the future.

—Munishri Chitrabhanu

Giants on Whose Shoulders Others Have Stood

The Western reader, in all probability, is familiar with the key ideas of the Judeo-Christian thinkers in Western intellectual tradition. Moses to the Christ, Isaac Newton to Albert Einstein, all have profoundly influenced and advanced the development of our civilization.

Similarly, just as the Western culture has been blessed with the giants of human thought and spirit, revealing insights and revolutionary ideas that have advanced Western humanity, the Eastern world has also been blessed, in a comparable way, with outstanding intellects, groundbreaking works, and fundamental concepts that have advanced our planetary civilization.

For expanded research into '1', the Path of Knowledge, attaining unlimited life and the realization of one's true nature, please refer to the references in the Notes section of this book. The listing of sixty-three thinkers emanates from China (11), India (25), the Muslim world (7), Japan (15), and Korea (5). They are arranged chronologically, from 600 BC through the twenty first century, with a cross reference to their key thoughts and major works (180): China (36), India (67), the Muslim world (22), Japan (42), and Korea (13). The authors of these gems are as follows:

China (11)
Lao-tzu (Laozi) (sixth century BC)[1]
Tseng Tzu (Zengzi) (505-? BC)[2]
Tzu Ssu (Zi Si) (492-431)[3]
Mo-tzu (Mozi) (470-391 BC)[4]

Lieh Tzu (Liezi) (fifth to fourth century BC)[5]
Kuo Hsiang (Guo Xiang) (third century to 312 BC)[6]
Chuang-tzu (Zhuangzi) (370-301 BC)[7]
Mencius (Meng Tzu/Mengzi) (371-289 BC)[8]

Hui-neng (638-713)[9]
Fa-Tsang (Fazang) (643-712)[10]
Chou Tun-i (Zhou Dunyi) (1017-1073)[11]

India (25)
Upanishads. Authors Unknown (600-400 BC): the work of many Indian thinkers[12]
Mahavira (599-527 BC)[13]
The Buddha (Siddharta Gautama) (563-483 BC)[14]
Badarayana (fifth century BC)[15]

Vyasa (exact dates unknown: between fifth and first centuries BC)[16]
Patanjali (exact dates unknown: 400-150 BC)[17]
Nagarjuna (exact dates unknown: between second and third centuries AD)[18]
Vasubandhu (fourth or fifth century)[19]

Ishvarakrishna (350-425)[20]
Gaudapada (exact dates unknown: eighth century)[21]
Haribhadra (459/700-529/770)[22]
Shankara (788-822)[23]

Vacaspati Mishra (842-?)[24]
Sureshvara (ninth century)[25]
Ramanuja (1017-1137)[26]
Nanak (1469-1539)[27]

Jiva Gosvamin (1511-1596)[28]
Vijnanabhikshu (exact dates unknown: sixteenth to seventeenth century)[29]
Madhusudana Sarasvati (exact dates unknown: seventeenth century)[30]
Dharmaraja Adhvarin (exact dates unknown: seventeenth century)[31]

Rabindranath Tagore (1861-1941)[32]
Mohandas Karamchand Gandhi (1869-1948)[33]
K.C. Bhattacharyya (1875-1949)[34]
Aurobindo (1872-1950)[35]

Sarvepalli Radhakrishnan (1888-1975)[36]

The Muslim World (7)
Rabi'a al-Adawiyya (717-801)[37]
Ibn Sina (Avicenna) (980-1037)[38]
Qushayri (986-1074)[39]
Suhrawardi (1153-1191)[40]

Ibn 'Arabi (1165-1240)[41]
Sirhindi (1564-1624)[42]
Sadr al-Din Shirazi (Mulla Sadra) (1571-1641)[43]

Japan (15)
Kukai (774-835)[44]
Eshin Sozu (Genshin) (942-1017)[45]
Jichin (Jien) (1155-1225)[46]
Myoe (1173-1232)[47]

Shinran (1173-1263)[48]
Dogen (1200-1253)[49]
Nichiren (1222-1282)[50]
Ippen (1139-1289)[51]

Fujiwara Seika (1561-1619)[52]
Suzuki Shosan (1579-1655)[53]
Hayashi Razan (1583-1657)[54]
Nakae Toju (1608-1648)[55]

Kaibara Ekken (1630-1713)[56]
Nishida Kitaro (1870-1945)[57]
Nishitani Keiji (1900-1990)[58]

Korea (5)
Wonhyo (617-686)[59]
Chinul (1158-1210)[60]
Hyujong (1520-1604)[61]
Yi Yulgok (1536-1584)[62]

Han Yongun (1879-1944)[63]

22

LIFE FROM HOLY LIFE: MAKE TODAY COUNT

I cannot and will not cut my conscience
to fit this year's fashions.

—Lillian Hellman

The Spiritual Renaissance: I See the Light in All

Can we look toward the day when Christ, Buddha, and Absolute Infinity become a single life in our consciousness as Tagore suggested? Are we part of one Spirit, which scientists term invariance and the ancients called the City of God? Can we delve deep into our being and find the voice of the sacred in us?

Mahatma Gandhi, Dag Hammarskjöld, Martin Luther King Jr., Mother Teresa of Calcutta, Aurobindo, and a universe of other trailblazers are witnesses to this possibility. Their lives are a challenge to us, encouraging us to know the truth, and in so doing, to expand our state of happiness. They disclose that to know the Infinite in us, we have to reach for the infinite powers of God within us.

Reveal compassion from compassion, altruism from altruism, responsibility from responsibility, and freedom from freedom, counsel great thinkers of the Eastern and Western worlds; let your Higher Self be your guide to fuller ways of living! They hearten us to seek out the extraordinary in our everyday world. They encourage us to be the best one is capable of being. They tell us to use our capabilities to the fullest, to let the splendor of God be our splendor, behold ourselves as Christ. Mother Teresa of Calcutta personified this kind of splendor, this type of understanding,

The poor are our Lord![1] In serving the poorest we directly serve God.[2]

Mother Teresa's exemplary life mirrors the words of Jesus.

"Come, you who are blessed by my Father; *take your inheritance,* the kingdom prepared for you since the creation of the world. For [when] I was hungry [for food, love, and compassion] and you gave me something to eat, I was thirsty [for water, peace, and freedom] and you gave me something to drink, I was a stranger and you invited me [into your hearts and homes], I needed clothes and you clothed me, I was sick and you looked after me, I was in prison and you came to visit me." Then the righteous will answer him, "Lord, when did we see you hungry and feed you, or thirsty and give you something to drink? When did we see you a stranger and invite you in, or needing clothes and clothe you? When did we see you sick or in prison and go to visit you?" The King will reply, "I tell you the truth, whatever you did for one of the least [important] of these brothers of mine, you did for me" (Mt 25:34-40).

Life is full of choices. Jesus provided us with an unconditional standard for living:

"I tell you the truth, whatever you did not do for one of the least of these, you did not to do it for me" (Mt 25:45).

Srimad-Bhagavatam, known as "the ripened fruit of the tree of Vedic literature," is the most complete and authoritative exposition of timeless Vedic wisdom. Srimad-Bhagavatam is widely acclaimed as the Bible of Indian devotionalism par excellence. After compiling the Vedas, Srila Vyasadera (Vyasa) integrated their profound essence in Srimad-Bhagavatam. Vyasa wrote:

Learn to look with an equal eye upon all beings, seeing the one Self in all.[3]

Hafiz put it this way,

There I bow my head—at the feet of every creature.
This constant submission and homage, of kissing God all over,
Someday, every lover will do.

Only there I prostrate myself—against the beauty of each form—
For when I bring my heart close to any object
I always hear the Friend ('1') say,
Hafiz, I am here.[4]

For we are one and the same being says the Christ, like the cellular tissue
of our heart. Yes, "I am in my Father, and you [are] in me, and I [am] in
you" (Jn 14:20). At one time we lived in an unconscious state. Now it is
our "daily manna." Compassion is our highest form of thought, deed, and
holiness. When pure and mindful, it is more precious than diamonds:
"In our era, the road to holiness necessarily passes through the world
of action," stated Hammarskjöld. Specifically,

The road to self-knowledge [gnosis] does not pass through faith.

But only through the self-knowledge [that in yourself lie all the
powers of God] we gain by pursuing the fleeting light in the
depth of our being do we reach the point where we can grasp what
faith is. How many have been driven into outer darkness by empty
talk about faith as something to be rationally comprehended,
something "true."[5]

Furthermore says Hammarskjöld, that road consists of:

love and patience,
Righteousness and humility,
Faith and courage,
Stillness.[6]

Experiencing the Infinite: Letting Go and Letting Be

The means to self-knowledge or to liberation are the self-disciplined
practices reviewed earlier. Self-knowledge or liberation is achieved when
the Spirit discriminates its own existence as imperishable and
indestructible, or pure consciousness. The Bhagavad Gita states:

Know that which pervades the entire body is indestructible ['1'].
No one is able to destroy the imperishable soul (2.17) . . . For the
soul there is never birth or death. Nor, having once been, does he

366

ever cease to be. He is unborn, eternal, ever existing, undying and primeval. He is not slain when the body is slain (2.20).

The emptying of the lower mind precedes its being filled with the fullness of unity, truth, goodness and agape love in its higher state. Sai Baba, the twentieth century Bangalore saint, sang:

> Wash your hearts with your tears of joy so that God might install himself therein . . . Engage always in good deeds and beneficial activities. Speak the truth, do not inflict pain by word or deed—or even by thought. That is the way to gain true peace, and that is the highest gain you can earn in this life. God is the inner Splendor in every being. He is in you as much as in everyone else . . . Know yourself as the indestructible Supreme Being.[7]

The Ancient One, as some called Meher Baba, elaborates:

> The God-realized knows himself to be God as surely as a man knows himself to be a man. It is for him not a matter of doubt, belief, self-delusion, or guesswork; it is a supreme and unshakeable certainty, which needs no external corroboration and remains unaffected by contradiction, because it is based upon self-knowledge. Such spiritual certainty is incapable of being challenged. A man thinks himself to be what in reality he is not; a God-realized knows what in reality he is.[8]

In his letter to the Colossians, Saint Paul recommended to move from ignorance to knowledge, that knowledge by which we are known in this way:

> Put aside your old self with its past deeds and put on a new man, one who grows in knowledge as he is *formed anew in the image of his Creator.* There is no Greek or Jew here, circumcised or uncircumcised, foreigner, Scythian, slave or freeman. Rather, Christ is everything in all of you (Col 3:9-11).

And what you are surely to become, by letting go and letting be is the universal harmony of all things (*universitas*). You already are part of the Common Ground.

"The seed of God is in us," reveals the remarkable Eckhart. Further,

> If the seed had a good, wise, and industrious farmer, it would
> thrive all the more and grow up to God whose seed it is, and the
> fruit would be equal to the nature of God. Now the seed of a pear
> tree grows into a pear tree, a hazel seed into a hazel tree, the seed
> of God into God.[9]

The seven systems of Indian philosophy (Buddhism, Mimamsa, Nyaya,
Sankhya, Vaisheshika, Vedanta, and Yoga) arrive at similar time-tested
conclusions. To be relaxed, we have to relax. To experience an embrace,
we embrace. One cannot swim in the ocean while standing on the shore.
Aldous Huxley writes:

> That is why we can attain to the unitive knowledge of God, only
> when we become in some measure Godlike, only when we permit
> God's kingdom to come by making our own kingdom go.[10]

An article on *"Shakespeare and Religion,"* written during Huxley's last
weeks in this dimension, contains perhaps his simplest and yet most
profound statement about life and happiness:

> The world is an illusion, but it is an illusion which we must take
> seriously, because it is real as far as it goes, and in those aspects of the
> reality which we are capable of apprehending. Our business is to
> wake up. We have to find ways in which to detect the whole of
> reality in the one illusory part which our self-centered consciousness
> permits us to see. We must not live thoughtlessly, taking our illusion
> for the complete reality, but at the same time we must not live too
> thoughtfully in the sense of trying to escape from the dream state.
> We must continually be on our watch for ways in which we may
> enlarge our consciousness. We must not attempt to live outside the
> world, which is given to us, but we must somehow learn to transform
> it and transfigure it. Too much "wisdom" is as bad as too little
> wisdom, and there must be no magic tricks. We must learn to come
> to reality without the enchanter's wand and his book of words.
> One must find a way of being in the world while not being of it. A
> way of living in time without being completely swallowed in time.[11]

"It is through discrimination and renunciation that man understands who he really is,"[12] says Sai Baba. The Second Vatican Council goes to the core of the issue:

All men are called to one and the same goal, namely God himself.[13]

"After the attainment of God-realization," articulates Meher Baba,

> the soul discovers that it has always been the Infinite Reality, and that its looking upon itself as finite during the period of evolution and spiritual advancement was an illusion. The soul also finds that the infinite knowledge and bliss that it enjoys have been latent in the Infinite Reality from the beginning of time and that they became manifest at the moment of realization . . .
>
> The process of attaining God-realization is a game in which the beginning and the end are identical [God became what we are, in order that we may become what he Himself is]. The attainment of realization is nevertheless a distinct gain. There are two kinds of advantages. One consists in getting what we did not previously possess; the other consists in realizing what we really are. God-realization is of the second kind. However, there is an infinite difference in the soul that has God-realization and one that does not have it. Though the soul that has God-realization has nothing it did not already possess, its explicit knowledge makes God-realization of the highest significance. The soul that is not God-realized experiences itself as finite and is constantly troubled by the opposites of joy and sorrow. But the soul that has realization is lifted out of them and experiences the Infinite.[14]

Science Can Assist Religion; Religion Can Assist Science

Once we realize that we are the life force of all, we will be walking consciously in the majesty and the celebration of life and our divinity. Every moment will be our moment. We will drink One life. We will drink love's joy. We will lose ourselves in our inner Splendor. We will understand, as I did, that truly we are the visible parts of the Creator, sons of the Trinity—the triumphant Light Manifest:

When the blazing avalanche of light, and
  finest perfume of flowers are emanating out of your body;
When the head spinning love and happiness are
  exploding out of your heart;
And when gentle shining peace and joy
  permeate every cell of your being;
You'll understand that there is only God—
  the I am who I am;
That it is the splendor of Absolute Infinity
  that pervades the entire universe;
That you are looking at yourself through your brother's and sister's eyes.
And that the Creator of everything that is and
  everything that you experience,
Is really you, yourself.
There will be the clear Light!
There will be great Joy.

Your spirit will know no bounds. You will but to think and it is done, it is so. Albert Einstein maintained,

> The more a man is imbued with the ordered regularity of all events, the firmer becomes his conviction that there is no room left by the side of this ordered regularity for causes of a different nature. For him, neither the rule of human nor the rule of divine will exist as an independent cause of natural events.[15]

Therefore, scientific reasoning can advance religious spiritualization of life, suggested Einstein.

> If it is one of the goals of religion to liberate mankind as far as possible from the bondage of egocentric cravings, desires, and fears, scientific reasoning can aid religion in yet another sense. Although it is true that it is the goal of science to discover rules which permit the association and foretelling of facts, this is not its only aim. It also seeks to reduce the connections discovered to the smallest possible number of mutually independent conceptual elements. It is in this striving after the rational unification of the manifold that it encounters its greatest successes, even though it is precisely this attempt which causes it to run the greatest risk of falling a prey to illusion.

But whoever has undergone the intense experience of successful advances made in this domain is moved by profound reverence for the rationality made manifest in existence. By way of the understanding he achieves a far-reaching emancipation from the shackles of personal hopes and desires, and thereby attains that humble attitude of mind toward the grandeur of reason incarnate in existence, and which, in its profoundest depths, is inaccessible to man. This attitude, however, appears to me to be religious in the highest sense of the word. And so it seems to me that science not only purifies the religious impulse of the dross of its anthropomorphism, but also contributes to a religious spiritualization of our understanding of life.[16]

23

BEYOND THE EVOLUTIONARY ADVENTURE—BEYOND CREATION

Practice abstinence,
See how it invigorates your soul!

—Rumi

The Dawn of Evolutionary Theory

British naturalists Charles Robert Darwin (1809-1882) and Alfred Russell Wallace (1823-1913) independently brought forth similar evidence concerning the theory of evolution by natural selection. Darwin had come to his conclusion, comparable to the historian Jacob Burckhardt, after years of careful research and thought. Wallace's solution, similar to the Greek mathematician and inventor Archimedes, surfaced in his mind unexpectedly, like a sudden lightning bolt of intuition.

Both authors' papers on the theory of evolution by natural selection were presented at the meeting of the Linnaean Society on the evening of July 1, 1858. Almost a year and a half later, in 1859, John Murray published Darwin's "Abstract" of his massive work titled *On the Origin of Species by Means of Natural Selection, or the Preservation of Favoured Races in the Struggle for Life*, now known simply as the *Origin of Species*. By a remarkable parallel, Darwin's *Origin of Species*, Marx's *Das Kapital*, and Adam Smith's *Wealth of Nations* were each seventeen years in the writing. Subsequently, Darwin wrote *The Descent of Man*, suggesting that species are the modified descendants of other classes of species, and that by this line of thought, according to Darwin, "light would be thrown on the origin of man and his history."

"The [modified descendants of other classes of species] idea is older than Aristotle and Lucretius," wrote Robert Downs. He adds:

> Such brilliant minds as Buffon, Goethe, Erasmus Darwin [Charles' grandfather], Lamarck, and Herbert Spencer had supported the doctrine. Charles Darwin's contribution was notable in two directions. First, he accumulated more indisputable evidence to show the fact of evolution than had ever been offered before. Secondly, he advanced his famous theory of natural selection as a reasonable explanation for the method of evolution.[1]

The general principle of evolution—the modification and transformation of organisms between generations that reach back over 500 million years, as revealed in all its richness by Darwin and Wallace, is profound. It has been strengthened with fossils, their radiocarbon dating and their tens of thousands of peer-reviewed journal articles. A comparable unification on the microscopic level had been achieved by the cell theory made known by Theodor Schwann and Matthias Schleiden in 1838, whereby cells were held to be the fundamental building blocks of all tissues.

In addition we see the beauty of orderly stepwise mofification, transformation, and progression in "the periodic law" of the elements, in the order of increasing atomic weights and structure, discovered in 1869 by the Russian chemist Dmitry Mendeleyev, and in the periodic recurrence of the fundamental physical quantities[2, 3] to be discussed in part 2. Also we see it in the structure of DNA, the carrier of the genetic code and thus the key molecule of heredity, developmental biology and evolution, pieced together by Francis Crick and James Watson in 1953.

There are three basic aspects pertaining to the endless march of growth, transformation of states, and advancement of species (natural selection of Darwin) that I wish to note:

a) Growth, transformation of states, and advancement of species (where species are the modified descendants of other classes of species), is much broader than what Darwin, the periodic law of elements, or the fundamental physical quantities suggest. As equations of physics suggest, the direction of evolutionary changes in development and advancement is encoded and progressing according to *the cosmic blueprint* or *the infinite source code* ('**1**'), discussed in part 2. It moves onward on infinite levels, producing new diversity and manifested environments, is a case in point.

That is, every form of existence is a modified successor of a previous form. Each manifested structure (the form in which the Absolute Infinity manifests itself)—each physical quantity, element or life form in the universe—starts its own *self-evolution* (the Alpha cycle: beginning of manifestation, the initial conditions) and ends its own self-evolution (the Omega cycle: end of manifestation, final conditions, big crunch).

b) Similar to the elements, or the physical quantities (in the modification and transformation, stretching upward through the vast universe and beyond) there is an *invariant* hierarchy of life forms (Saint John Climacus' revered rungs of life: *The Ladder of Divine Ascent*), intelligences and a hierarchical order in the infinite source code.

c) Modification, growth and transformation of species (relation between observer and milieu) are governed by each form's consciousness (such as atom, plant, animal, human, galaxy) *and free will*, which grows and strengthens, within the principle of '**1**'.

Previously, we learned from Saint Irenaeus, regarding our own transition from the Divine to humanity and to the Divine: "God the Logos became what we are, in order that we may become what he himself is."[4] Saint Athanasius repeated the point: "The Divine Word became human in order that every human being may become God."[5] And Jesus advised his good brother:

> Brother Thomas . . . examine yourself that you may understand who you are, in what way you exist, and how you will come to be. Since you are called my brother, it is not fitting [for a brother] that you be ignorant of yourself.[6]

Every Pilgrim Is Advancing: Spiffing Up the Look

From Emerson we discover "the worm stirring to be a man, mount through all the spires of form." Mirza Khan Ansari (eighteenth century), a descendent of Bayezid Ansari, who could have inspired the lines of

Sachal, cited earlier, echoes Rumi's life in his own words, "How shall I define in evolutionary progression what thing I am?" Ansari states:

> Wholly existent [as a form], and nonexistent [as sacred-space,
>   Absolute Infinity],
> I am, . . . Sometimes a mote in the disc of the sun,
> At others, a ripple of the water's surface.
> Now I fly about on the wind of association,
> Now I am a bird of the incorporeal world . . .
> I have enveloped myself in the four elements.
> I am the cloud on the face of the sky . . .
> In the lot of the devoted, I am the honey,
> In the soul of the impious, the sting.
> I am with every one, and in all things;
> Without imperfection—immaculate I am.[7]

Guru Arjan characterized the process of passing from one form to another in this way:

> Many lives have you had as insects and worms.
> And many lives as elephants, fish and deer;
> In many lives were you born a snake or a bird,
> And countless times, you lived as a tree.
> After aeons you've obtained the glory of human birth:
> Now it's your chance—meet the Lord![8]

Goethe, Ralph Waldo Emerson, Pushkin, Turgenev, Carlyle, and Garcia Lorca admired Hafiz's poems. Even Sherlock Holmes quotes Hafiz in one of the narratives by Arthur Conan Doyle. In "I Know I Was the Water," Hafiz writes:

> I know I was the water that quenched the Christ's thirst.
> I know I am the food and water that goes into every mouth . . .
> I know I was a tree that stood near,
> Leaned down and took notes.
> I know I was the earth that measured the infinite arch in His feet . . .
> Pilgrim, if it is your wish, you will someday see you sat inside of
>   Hafiz.[9]

Six centuries prior to Charles Darwin's theory of evolution by natural selection, which generated hot debate and controversy when it was introduced, Rumi, in his Mathnawi (M 3:3901-6), deemed by some to rank in importance with the Koran, observed in deep stillness the chronology of the Alpha to the Omega unfoldment and metamorphosis. He considered it the underpinning for the existence of everything, and into which they [everything] must ultimately vanish. In Rumi's words, "To Him ['1', nonexistence of form] we shall return." Here are Rumi's changes of life forms:

> I died as mineral and became a plant,
> I died as plant and rose to animal.
> I died as animal and I was Man.
> Why should I fear? When was I less by dying?
> Yet once more I shall die as Man,
> To soar with angels blest;
> But even from angelhood I must pass on:
> All except God ['1'] perishes.
> When I have sacrificed my angel soul,
> I shall become what no mind e'er conceived.
> O let me non-exist,
> For Nonexistence [the absence of manifested objects] proclaims in
> organ tones,
> "To Him we shall return."[10]

We Are No Longer Alone

Darwin's insights are not particularly cutting-edge interdisciplinary research. Darwin's evolution took Rumi through: "I died as mineral and became a plant, I died as plant and rose to animal. I died as animal and I was Man"; then it stops. Rumi, similar to other Great Ones (Mahavira, Lao-tzu, Krishna, Yeshua, Muhammad Iqbal), goes beyond Francis Crick and James Watson, and the double-helix DNA, with the evolutionary advancement to Nonexistence. That is, the emptiness state previous to manifestation, and prior to the modern day's big bang, the *neti neti* of the Upanishads, Abhava in Sanskrit, or the kingdom of the Father of Christ.

Those thinkers reflecting on the deepest Self seem to have arrived at a common destination. Placed side by side, "To Him shall we return" becomes Irenaeus' statement "God became what we are, in order that we may become what he Himself is." Also, compare Rumi's "I shall become what no mind e'er conceived," with Jesus' "I shall give you what no eye has seen and what no ear has heard and what no hand has touched and what has never occurred to the human mind . . ." They are the same meaning and significance.

The lord Mahavira (599-527 BC) was a great saint who founded Jainism as a religious community. He was a contemporary of Gautama the Buddha. Mahavira was the twenty-fourth or last of the great teachers of Jainism bearing the title Tirthankara, or master. Like other profound thinkers, Mahavira searched for the Unchanging Absolute. Through a gradual process of *purification* (avoidance of injury to any life form, nonviolence, truthfulness, great kindness, not stealing, fasting, meditating, and renouncing all possessions— Jesus' Mt 5:1-12; Lk 6:20-42) Mahavira achieved elevated awareness and remote viewing of hundreds of previous lifetimes. In Christian terms, Mahavira entered "the kingdom of heaven" (Mt 5:20) or "beatific vision" (the "lasting union with God"). Namely, he penetrated into the Janists "kevala," Hindus "moksha," or the Buddhists nirvana.

Subsequent to an experience of enlightenment, Mahavira and his eleven disciples were the first to be anti-Brahmans and to oppose their sacrificial rites. There is a correlation to the Christ and his apostles challenging the teachers of the Law and Pharisees (Mt 23; Mk 12:38; Lk 11:39). The Brahmans considered themselves the spiritual guardians of ancient hymns and sacrificial ceremonies. They maintained that only through such hymns, and the sacrificial observances related with them, would an appropriate relationship with the gods be achievable, such relationship in turn being held to facilitate one's wealth, triumph over enemies, contentment, and the like.

According to the Acaranga Sutra, the oldest of Jaina texts, dating from the fifth or fourth century BC, Mahavira describes a metamorphosed "hierarchy" and "evolution" of life forms. Life forms are modified progeny of other classes of life forms. This hierarchy of life forms we can see now through the double-helix DNA that carries the instructions for making living things from one life form to another and one generation to the next. In deep stillness of the mind or high quality remote viewing, Mahavira observed emanation of phenomenal reality and its metamorphosing hierarchical process within manifestation, and identified manifested existence with the cosmic process. His description

377

started with most simple forms of *nigoda* (modern microorganisms) and progressed through plants, animals, human beings, and at long last to the world of the *siddha loka* (liberated beings).

Erwin Schrödinger, in his book *What Is Life?* suggested that one of life's fundamental features is the storage and communication of information—that is, a genetic code that passes from parent to offspring. Because the storage and transmission of information had to be both complex and compressed to fit inside a cell, this code had to be composed at the molecular level. Crick and Watson were impressed with Schrödinger's genetic code notion. With a series of brilliant experiments they solved the double-helix structure of DNA, which has advanced with many breakthroughs including officially launching (1990) the Human Genome Project, an international effort to map and sequence human DNA.

Sathya Sai Baba describes the evolutionary process this way:

> Man has evolved from the stone through plant and tree, worm and insect, bird and mammal; but some are still groveling in the early stages though they have achieved the human form . . . So you should cast off all the impediments, all the encumbrances that drag you down and make you a boulder instead of a Devotee of God and a realized person, or even a Paramatma [Eternal Consciousness, '1'].[11]

'1': The True Entertainer

Who is transforming through different forms in our cosmos? Who has disguised her/himself in masquerade costumes of physical quantities, whirling particles and DNA's in the universe? Who pretends to be a bottomless ocean, gigantic sequoia, a captivating woman, or a charismatic man? Who has, in temporary amnesia, forgotten who one is?

Recall when Mahatma Gandhi said, "I am a man of God disguised as a politician," or what Moses heard nine hundred years prior to Mahavira,

> I am that I am ['1': Spirit]; I will be what I will be [existence: manifested form].

Yes, "I am the Alpha [A, beginning of manifestation] and the Omega" [Ω, ending of manifestation] of Revelation (1:8; 21:6). "I am the first [the initial conditions] and I am the last" [the final conditions] of Isaiah (44:6). "In Him we live [have our existence: form] and move [through an invariant cosmic process on a hierarchical ladder of manifestation] and have our being [existence]" (Acts 17:28).

Who is expanding through a process of progressive change, metamorphosis, and advancement via personal, social and economic structures? "This is the God to Whom the Christian refers when he says 'in Him we live, and move, and have our being,'" says Alice Bailey in *The Consciousness of the Atom*:

> This is the force, or energy, which the scientist recognizes; and this is the universal mind, or the Oversoul of the philosopher. This, again, is the intelligent Will which controls, formulates, binds, constructs, develops, and brings all to an ultimate perfection. This is that Perfection which is inherent in matter itself, and the tendency which is latent in the atom, in man, and in all that is. This interpretation of the evolutionary process does not look upon it as the result of an outside Deity pouring His energy and wisdom upon a waiting world, but rather as something which is latent within that world itself [John Wheeler's, Bernard d'Espagnat's, and Max Planck's participating universe and not Stephen Hawking's "nothing for a Creator to do," mentioned earlier], that lies hidden at the heart of the atom of chemistry, within the heart of man himself, within the planet, and within the solar system. It is that something which drives all on toward the goal, and is the force [the Existence, the Logos, the enfolding consciousness whom we call God] which is gradually bringing order out of chaos [empty, formless reality]; ultimate perfection out of temporary imperfection; good out of seeming evil; and out of darkness and disaster that which we shall some day recognize as beautiful, right, and true. It is all that we have visioned and conceived of in our highest and best moments.[12]

No matter what one's state of life, from the consciousness of the '1', the fundamental atom, a lump of earth, to a multiplicity of forms, or a liberated being, one has the discriminating power to expand and contract one's evolutionary process. The '1' emanates form, expresses itself, gains experience, expands its consciousness (the Parable of the Yeast, Mt 13:33; Lk 13:20), and through the deployment of that particular form attains higher knowledge and deeper contact with Life. It is a part of the great life cycle—a cycle where a dimensionless point (singularity) originates phenomenal form (connects to more points within itself; as in an atom, creating larger and larger light units), which then, in the course of billions of years, metamorphoses into Saul and then into Paul.

You Are Your Friend, You Are Your Enemy

To illustrate the emergence of materialization, we can consider the Common Ground, 1', as water in an ocean and the manifestations as the "waves" (dimensions) of the ocean. The rate at which "waves" are transferred determines the specific characteristics of each dimensional form. In addition, each point, form or pattern in Reality (physical quantity—natural units of measurement), can exert influence through its own free will and intentionality, or can be affected by other patterns. These are added to, and subtracted from, the original state (measurement).

The '1', like a calculator or your PC, keeps track of events and displays the status. There is a Hidden Order to every infinitesimal point of the One in the universe. This can be verified with the Grotthus-Draper law: For light to produce an effect upon matter, it must be absorbed.[13] Atoms, molecules, and cells absorb energy and become excited only when they can accept photons whose energy equals the energy difference in question— the photon energy must equal exactly the energy needed to raise the configuration from one level to another: "everything is a modified successor of another class." Thus, only energy of a specific frequency will be absorbed. Absorption will continue as long as there is less energy in the lower energy level than in the higher. In effect, the gas tank in your automobile can only be filled to the brim. Similarly, if our actions have not created the proper absorption condition, we cannot participate in the effect.

Observe: everything that we do every second of our lives creates spacetime patterns [see the Nature of Time and the Nature of Space in part 2, chapter 6] that are added to, or subtracted from, the original count in direct relationship to our actions. This makes us into a sort of tuning fork that attracts the same field that it generates. "The mind yields fruits corresponding to its thoughts," says Muktananda, adding:

"One is one's own friend or one's own enemy." Whether you are in hell or in heaven depends entirely on you.[14]

Shakyamuni Buddha put it this way, "There are causes for all human suffering, and there is a way by which they may be ended, because everything in the world is the result of a vast concurrence of causes and conditions, and everything disappears as these causes and conditions change and pass away." We are subject to '1': we live and move and have our being in '1'. To put that in gambling terms: the house ('1', the stabilizing equilibrium) has set the odds so that every action produces an equal and opposite reaction. When you're betting with the house, guess who wins?

All pleasant and unpleasant experiences are therefore the consequences of our own actions. They would not exist had we not created them. If the necessary electromagnetic field did not exist within us, there would be no way for us to "tune into" the experience. Although there are thousands of radio stations and TV channels being broadcast, we only see and hear those we "tune into." The Buddha in Majjhima Nikaya suggested, "If anyone should give you a blow with his hand, with a stick, or with a knife, you should abandon any desires [repaying] and utter no evil words" (21:6).

Suppose we create abundance and happiness for someone. Consider these facts: what we did involved quantities of time, space, energy, and the like. The force intensity of our actions set appropriate physical laws in motion. We cannot escape our personal history or the '1'. *The action produced must be repaid back to us with abundance and happiness,* or as John Wheeler stated, "You are the Universe, looking in the mirror."

The Books of the Cosmos Must Balance

The Buddhist-Hindu theory of karma (every action has a reaction; good acts earn a recompense, and bad deeds beget punishment), the Dharma sastra (do not do unto others what you do not wish done unto yourself, and wish for others too what you desire and long for yourself), the Judeo-Christian notion of "whatsoever you sow you shall reap," and Newton's principle that "every action produces an equal and opposite reaction" are well known. Notice that the concept of karma maintains that current events are the result of earlier proceedings and current actions will, in turn, affect yet-to-come events. This effect is exerted from moment to moment, as well as from life to life, including black holes and the cosmos. That means, since virtual particles are appearing and disappearing everywhere all the time, every black hole and the cosmos will eventually disappear.

What is not always considered is the fact that energy of actions is added/subtracted and transformed to other forms. We eat, we get heavier; we fast, and we get lighter. Christopher Chapple wrote:

> The theory of karma in Jainism is quite unique, being significantly more developed than karma theory in Buddhism or Hinduism. According to Jainism, karma is a material, sticky, colorful substance, composed of atoms, that adheres to the life force and prevents ascent to the siddha loka, the world of the liberated. This karma is attracted to the *jiva* [life form: existence that creates duality and causality] by acts of violence, and the most violent of beings are said to be shrouded with clouds of blackish matter. Beings with increasingly less violent natures are said to be successively cloaked in blue, gray, orangish-red, and yellow karma, while the person of nonviolence is said to have only white karma.[15]

In the future, we will not only have to understand the nature of '1', but will have to know the truth and act accordingly, thereby achieving a higher degree of serenity, poise and freedom. We will have to consciously build our life, as if it were a work of magnificent art. A new being will be born. A new glory and Great Light will be manifest upon the earth. "And then," as Teilhard de Chardin stated, "for the second time in the history of the world, man will have discovered fire."[16]

This rebirth, not a return to the mother's womb and rebirth therewith, but a metaphorical rebirth, through perfectibility and illumination to higher consciousness, is alluded to by the Christ in his dialogue with Nicodemus:

> I tell you the truth, unless a man is born again, he cannot see the kingdom of God . . . You must be born again (Jn 3:5-7).

We find a correlate in Ch'an (Zen). The "great death" (*daishu*) expression in Zen does not refer to physical demise, but rather to the downfall of ego, which leads through the practice of abstinence (like cleaning the window) to the experience of awakening ("unity of the Spirit" in Christian tradition) and "glimpses of self-nature" (enlightenment—satori) to "great rebirth" (profound enlightenment—*daigo-tettei*). Profound enlightenment arrives at the Absolute Infinity and differs in degree from less-deep experiences of glimpses of self-nature or satori.

Hindus have a similar term, "twice-born;" which refers to interior rebirth, illumination, and enlightenment—giving birth to God within oneself. This emergence is associated with the widening of our "central channel" for greater production, release, and conscious control of large amounts of our life force (Kundalini). The total, life-dilating process provides the fuel for explosive intellectual growth, productivity, altruism within a group, happiness, and fulfillment.

This is the goal of our liberation—to bring about an informed world made up of free individuals whose creative energies have been put to fuller usage. Included in this awareness is that *the life of humanity is an integral part of the life of God.* Our birthright is to live in a world of light, splendor, peace, and goodness, more breathtaking and more beautiful than anything we can imagine now.

24

FOLLOW YOUR BLISS:
YOUR FUTURE IS VERY BRIGHT

> Doing the best at this moment puts you
> in the best place for the next moment.

> —Oprah Winfrey

Making Our Way Home: Freedom! Freedom!

William Law (1686-1761) carefully researched the union between God and humanity, as articulated in works *The Spirit of Prayer* (1749), *The Way to Divine Knowledge* (1752), and *The Spirit of Love* (1752). He characterized the Christian ethical ideal and its actualization through the disciplined life, expressed in his *Practical Treatise Upon Christian Perfection* (1726) and his *Serious Call to a Devout and Holy Life* (1728). Here is how Law untied the knots of salvation:

> In what does salvation consist? Not in any historic faith or knowledge of anything absent or distant, not in any variety of restraints, rules and methods of practicing virtue, not in any formality of opinion about faith and sanctification, not in any truth or righteousness that you can have from yourself, from the best of men and books, but solely and wholly from the life of God, or Christ of God, quickened and born again in you, in other words in the restoration and perfect union of the first twofold life in humanity.[1]

Twenty-eight centuries earlier, Lao-tzu stated: "If you want to awaken all of humanity, then awaken all of yourself . . . Truly the greatest gift you have to give is that of your own self-transformation."

In his letter to the Romans, Saint Paul uncovered a very important element in our excursion through "creative nothingness": we were not created to be in bondage. In fact, the entire universe impatiently waits for personal revelation—bringing to light our union with God (the story of the Prodigal Son is the saga of the universe): that we are one family, being unified with ultimate reality. The universe waits for us to at last make our exodus out of "slavery." Consider this passage:

> I consider that what we suffer at this present time cannot be compared at all with the glory that is going to be revealed to us. All of creation waits with eager longing for God to reveal his sons [and daughters] . . . Yet there was this hope: that creation itself would one day be set free from its slavery to decay, and share the glorious freedom of the children of God. For we know that up to the present time all of creation groans with pain like the pain of childbirth (Rom 8:19-21).

On the other side of our planet the Third Patriarch of Zen counseled:

> One in all,
> All in One—
> If only this is realized,
> No more worry about not being perfect![2]

Swami Muktananda considers this notion as follows:

> Just as a river after flowing for a long time merges in the ocean and becomes the ocean, when Kundalini [serpent power] has finished Her work and stabilized in the sahasrara [seventh chakra, located above the crown of the head], you become completely immersed in God. All your impurities and coverings are destroyed, and you take complete rest in the Self. The veil, which made you see duality drops away, and you experience the world as a blissful play of Kundalini, a sport of God's energy. You see the universe as supremely blissful light, undifferentiated from yourself, and you remain unshakeable in this awareness. This is the state of liberation, the state of perfection.
>
> A being who has attained this state does not have to close his eyes and retire to a solitary place to get into samadhi.

Note: Samadhi is a state of consciousness of deep inner peace and calming of mental activity. The ability to attain the state of samadhi is a precondition for dhyana where our mind is stilled so that absolute consciousness is liberated from any overlay. Christian mystics (Origen, Gregory of Nyssa, Gregory Nazianzen in the East, Ambrose, Augustine and Pope Gregory the Great in the West) refer to it as union (unitive life) with God, and Buddhists as nirvana. In this spiritual union,[3] the Kundalini continually, day and night, flows in large quantities through you. You taste, as if you had an uninterrupted "whole body orgasm," a "wine of pure pleasure." Muktananda continues:

> Whether he is meditating, eating, bathing, sleeping, whether he is alone or with others, he experiences the peace and joy of the Self. Whatever he sees is God, whatever he hears is God, whatever he tastes is God, whatever words he speaks are God's. In the midst of the world, he experiences the solitude of a cave, and in the midst of people, he experiences the bliss of samadhi . . . the bliss of the world is the ecstasy of samadhi.
>
> It is to attain this that we should meditate, that we should have our Kundalini awakened. We do not meditate to attain God, because we have already attained Him. We meditate so that we can become aware of God manifest within us.[4]

"I am sure," stated Eckhart, "that if a soul knew the very least of all that Being means, it would never turn away from it." "Father," the man of Galilee petitioned:

> I pray . . . that all of them may be one, Father, just as you are in me and I am in you. May they also be in us so that the world may believe that you have sent me. I have given them the glory that you gave me, that they may be one as we are one: I [living] in them and you in me. May they be brought to complete unity . . . (Jn 17:20-23).

Experiencing Cosmic Consciousness

Richard Maurice Bucke, MD, after experiencing illumination at age thirty-five (1872), began a study in the evolution of the human mind.

His work covered the relationship between the sympathetic nervous system and the moral nature of man, ultimately arriving at a description of cosmic consciousness and "the most pure, the most noble, the most honorable, and the most tender-hearted." The *Proceedings and Transactions of the Royal Society of Canada* has this account of his experience:

> He [Bucke] and two friends had spent the evening reading Wordsworth, Shelley, Keats, Browning, and especially [Walt] Whitman. They parted at midnight, and he had a long drive in a hansom. His mind deeply under the influence of the ideas, images, and emotions called up by the reading and talk of the evening, was calm and peaceful. He was in a state of quiet, almost passive, enjoyment.
>
> All at once, without warning of any kind, he found himself wrapped around, as it were, by a flame-colored cloud. For an instant he thought of fire—some sudden conflagration in the great city. The next (instant) he knew that the light was within himself.
>
> Directly after there came upon him a sense of exultation, of immense joyousness, accompanied or immediately followed by an intellectual illumination quite impossible to describe. Into his brain streamed one momentary lightning-flash of the Brahmic Splendor which ever since lightened his life. Upon his heart fell one drop of the Brahmic Bliss, leaving thenceforward for always an aftertaste of Heaven.[5]

Describing Bucke's experience, George Acklom writes:

> To Bucke, it [this experience] had nothing whatever to do with mysticism or formal religion, or with conscious preparation and intention. He was a student of the human mind, a psychologist, and he treated illumination from the standpoint of psychology, as a very rare but definite and recognizable mental condition, of which many well-authenticated instances are on record and available for examination . . . [the illumination] enables man to realize the Oneness of the Universe, to sense the presence in it and throughout it of the Creator, to be free of all fears of evil, of disaster or death, to comprehend that Love is the rule and basis of the Cosmos—this is

cosmic consciousness, which Bucke prophesied will appear more and more often until it becomes a regular attribute of adult humanity.[6]

Bucke tabulated and described fifty examples and ages of individuals at illumination—transformation of individual consciousness (self-consciousness, possessed by ordinary people) into the superconscious state or cosmic consciousness. They include fourteen instances of cosmic consciousness and thirty-six of lesser vintages. In the first grouping Bucke lists: Gautama the Buddha, Jesus the Christ, Saint Paul, Plotinus, Muhammad, Dante, Bartolomé Las Casas, Saint John of the Cross, Francis Bacon, Jakob Böhme, William Blake, Honoré de Balzac, Walt Whitman, and Edward Carpenter.

In the second category we find Moses, Isaiah, Socrates, Roger Bacon, Blaise Pascal, Benedict de Spinoza, Alexander Pushkin, Ralph Waldo Emerson, Alfred Lord Tennyson, and Henry David Thoreau. William James wrote this to Bucke regarding his *Cosmic Consciousness* book:

> I believe that you have brought this kind of consciousness "home" to the attention of students of human nature in a way so definite and unescapable that it will be impossible henceforward to overlook it or ignore it . . . But my total reaction on your book, my dear Sir, is that it is an addition to psychology of first-rate importance, and that you are a benefactor of us all.[7]

Bucke made two very important observations. Firstly, "the new sense [of awareness] will become more and more common and show itself earlier in life, until, after many generations, it will appear in each normal individual at age of puberty or even earlier,[8] and secondly, having experienced this cosmic sense, a person becomes more creative, more productive, and more effective.

Rabindranath Tagore (1861-1941) has been applauded as possibly being the greatest literary personage in history. He composed twelve novels, thirty-eight plays, more than two hundred short stories, one thousand poems, two thousand songs, and numerous essays dealing with the social, educational, religious, cultural, and political issues of his time. He acted on the stage, directed, and produced plays and dance-dramas. Tagore also ventured into painting and drawing, producing over

2,500 compositions. Throughout India, Tagore is a household name. His writing is a sacred influence above class, doctrine or creed. At age fifty-two, Tagore was honored with the Nobel Prize in Literature. Thirty-four years earlier, Tagore first experienced a form of Bucke's cosmic sense. In *My Reminiscences* Tagore shares:

> When I was eighteen, a sudden spring breeze of religious experience came to my life for the first time and passed away leaving in my memory a direct message of spiritual reality.[9]

As Tagore matured, he had deeper spiritual experiences and yielding more literary works. His experiences validated his insight on the unity of the individual self and the Absolute Self. He became skilled at harvesting the "tree of life and knowledge." Tagore maintained that human beings must rise from self-centeredness to altruistic love for all, and *nations must grow to love other countries and their cultures.* Among his principal compositions is *Gitanjali* (Song Offerings), presenting discussions between the human being and Vishnu (the third aspect in the Hindu trinity of Brahman, Vishnu [preservation], and Shiva [dissolution]). His novel *Gora* is a sort of modern-day Mahabharata. In *Gitanjali* (1912) Tagore wrote:

> Where the mind is without fear and the head is held high;
> Where knowledge is free;
> Where the world has not been broken up into fragments by narrow
>   domestic Walls . . .
> Where the clear stream of reason has not lost its way into the dreary
>   desert sand of dead habit . . .
> Where the mind is led forward by thee into ever-widening thought
>   and action—
> Into that heaven of freedom, my Father, let my country awake.[10]

I'm on Your Side:
Shape the Universe of Love, Joy and Wonder

Eckhart described it this way:

> In the kingdom of heaven all is in all, as is one, and all is ours.[11]

When this takes place, we will (as did Erwin Schrödinger, David Bohm, John Wheeler, and others) validate that the observer and the observed are fundamentally One. You and everyone else are luminous cells of that one living body of God (Eph 4:44; Cor 10:17; Gal 3:28). One living heart. One splendor. One eternal You.

"As soon as the man is at one with God, he will not beg," states Emerson:

> he will then see prayer in all action. The prayer of the farmer kneeling in his field to weed it, the prayer of the rower kneeling with the stroke of his oar, are true prayers heard throughout nature . . . [12]

The leading Jesuit philosopher and paleontologist, Teilhard de Chardin, brilliantly presented a fascinating and wonderful story, one of exuberance, awe, beauty, and inspiration, in his *Future of Man*:

> The Incarnation is a making new, a restoration, of all the universe's forces and power; Christ is the instrument, the Center, the End, of the whole of animate and material creation: through Him, everything is created, sanctified, and vivified. This is the constant and general teaching of Saint John and Saint Paul [that most "cosmic" of sacred writers], and it has passed into the most solemn formulas of the Liturgy; and yet we repeat it, and generations to come will go on repeating it, without ever being able to grasp or appreciate the profound and mysterious significance, bound up as it is with understanding of the universe.[13]

Additionally:

> The men of the future will form, in some way, but one single consciousness; and since, once their initiation is complete, they will have gauged the strength of their associated minds, the immensity of the universe, and the straightness of their prison, this consciousness will be truly adult and of age . . . It is then, we may be sure, that the Parousia [the arrival or presence of Oneness] will be realized in creation that has been taken to the climax of its capacity for union. The single act of assimilation and synthesis that

has been going on since the beginning of time will then at last be made plain, and the universal Christ will blaze out like a flash of lightning in the storm clouds of a world whose slow consecration is complete.[14]

The astrophysicist John A. Wheeler furnishes this additional insight:

> The universe not only must give rise to life, but . . . once life is created, it will endure forever, become infinitely knowledgeable, and ultimately mold the universe to its will . . . thus, man—or Life—will be not only the measure of all things, but their creator as well.[15]

25

FAR-REACHING IMPLICATIONS:
LOOSENING THE KNOTS OF BONDAGE

When man and woman become one,
Thou are that One!

—Rumi

In the Valley of Silence:
The Knower and the Known Are but the Same

It will be noted in part 2, chapter 8, that all creation manifests different aspects (dimensions) of the same Reality ('1')—the same Ocean of Light. Also, the human mind is the universe itself, and is one and the same as the '1'.

Actually, all human beings, and all manifestations are aspects (images) of the '1'. In addition, like numbers, there is a *hierarchical relationship* (the Principle of Position[1]) between matter, energy, time/motion, electric/magnetic flux density, electric/magnetic fields, and so forth. Thus we encounter the '1' in all things! Similarly, in spiritual terms, these truths are observed: God within and God without; "That art thou"; "Behold but One in all things."

Gautama the Buddha in the Lotus Sutra (one of the most important sutras of Mahayana Buddhism, especially popular in China and Japan) stated:

I am the Father. All living beings are my children.

Notice, in John 14:9, Jesus also affirmed, "Whoever has seen me has seen the Father." And Muhammad reaffirmed in Hadis (the Sayings of the Holy Prophet),

He who hath seen Me surely hath seen God.
He who hath known Him-Self hath known his God.
He who forgetteth God forgets Him-Self.[2]

The laws of physics demonstrate that every physical relationship has the '1'. Therefore, *when the '1' (That-Which-Is) is united to all points, then each point is united through the '1' to every other point.* Consider the Christ's message: "I am in my Father, and you in me, and I in you" (Jn 14:20). This applies to Chinese, Indian, Arab, American, Japanese, German, white, black, yellow, and all other peoples; the man one helps/hurts is really oneself in a different form. Jesus understood this, as did Schrödinger, Fo-Hi, Ruysbroeck, Suso, Huang Po, Kabir, William Law, Buddhamitra, Asvaghosha, and Nagarjuna.[3]

They all perceived that the same foundational essence is not only without, but also within. The observer/observed are fundamentally one: dimensionally inverted through the Principle of the One and the Many, discussed in part 2, chapter 5[4] Therefore, you yourself are a part of the same living essence: the '1'.

The understanding that we are the Light of life is one that is corroborated by other cultures and has been referred to by Christians as "Christ formed within you." Pan-Asians know it as becoming a Buddha (Awakened or Enlightened One).[5] Sri Aurobindo described it as evolving to the Mind of Light.[6] Patanjali in the Yoga Sutras referred to absolute consciousness as Samadhi-Bhavana.[7] Swami Rama understood it as reaching the state of Absolute Samadhi or superconsciousness.[8] Shankara called the superconscious state *adhyatma-prasada.* Canadian psychiatrist Maurice Bucke called it cosmic consciousness.[9]

Let us look at other men and women who have made the exuberant ascent to spiritual heights and achieved this holy illuminated state of sensitivity, profound humility, gentleness, sanctity, and earnest care to avoid giving offense. Moses did not just break into the heart of "I Am." It took a great deal of "mountain climbing" the ladder that leads to perfection (Saint John Climacus' *The Ladder of Divine Ascent*), such as renouncing undesirable habits (purification), before he reached the top (illumination) of Mount Sinai.[10] But once he did, he must have trembled in joy and wonder when he grasped the Truth. Oh, what happiness— what glory . . . "I am who I am" (Jn 13:19)—I am the very same essence in different states and forms—was understood.

Saint Gregory of Nyssa wrote in his beautiful *Life of Moses,* "In the same way that Moses on that occasion attained to this knowledge, so now does everyone who, like him, divests himself of the earthly covering and looks to the light shining from the bramble bush, that is (as the Gospel says) the true light and the truth itself." "Now the Son of Man's glory is revealed; now God's glory [in us] is revealed through him" (Jn 13:31).

Jesus, the Greatest Living Light, also had to undergo inner growth and overcome obstacles (Jn 16:33) on the spiritual path leading toward knowledge of the '1'. He learned to obey through suffering (Heb 5:8) and endless testing (Mk 1:13). He was, "tempted in every way that we are" (Heb 4:15). And He prayed, "Abba [Oh Father] . . . take this cup away from me. But let it be as you would have it, not as I" (Mk 14:36).

"Jesus," wrote Maurice Nicol, in his interpretation of parables and miracles of the Christ, *The New Man,*

> had to pass through all the stages of this evolution in himself by trial and error, until it was perfected, through endless inner temptations, of which we are only given a few glimpses.[11]

Had he not, we could have questioned the whole development process of a young Creator for not having to face the same hardships we do. Yet, in the earliest reference to the Son of God's growth, it is said, "Jesus, for his part, progressed steadily in wisdom and age and grace before God and men." (Lk 2:52). John Haughey analogized in his *The Conspiracy of God*:

> Like a seed in the beginning [he] progressed from there to seedling, to plant, to tree, to glorious fulfillment . . . And at some point in his life, he knew something that only the Spirit could eventually teach men when time had provided a sufficient cushion for them to accept what must have made Jesus gasp when he saw the truth.[12]

When Jesus understood that he is the Creator himself—when he had enough courage to say, "Whoever has seen me has seen the Father" (Jn 14:9), he became the Light, the Path, and the Happiness for others. Yes, yes, whoever has seen the wave has seen the water.

"I am the way, and the truth, and the life," to freedom, radiance, profundity, and more abundant living, he said. "No one goes to the Father ['1'] except by me" (Jn 14:6), through the letting go of all detrimental baggage, revealing Perfection in the Christlike life of love, forgiveness, fearlessness, deep inner harmony, and the way to unlimited health, happiness, and success. The kingdom is not a place you travel to, Jesus enumerated on various occasions. It is a mode of living and rejoicing with what is perfect. Love ('1'), mercy ('1'), courage ('1'), and deep inner harmony ('1'), are good for our physical and emotional health, peace of mind, and our souls. It is a state of love and exuberance. It is the source from which higher understanding is attained, experiencing the "unity of the Spirit" through the bond of peace in your own being.

The "steady progression in wisdom and grace before God" Lord Buddha equates to the loosening of knots in order to enter here/now the true Stream of Life:

> The unloosening of knots is a gradual process one must begin with the knots of the five sense-organs, after which the knots of the sixth sense—the perceiving and discriminating mind—will loosen of themselves. Therefore, it is wise to begin with the sense organ that is most yielding and accommodating, and by means of it, it will be easier to enter the true Stream of Life that flows into highest perfect Wisdom.[13]

To understand what Jesus is saying, he suggests we apply his words ("I am the way . . ."); that we become Christlike. "Reform your lives," advises he (Mt 4:17). "You must be perfect—just as your Father in heaven is perfect" (Mt 5:48).

Milarepa, similar to the poets of Persia, particularly Rumi, Jami, and Sa'di, recommended, "Remove the rust of wrong ideas . . . root up all errors from within!"[14]

Our Chains Will Fall Away

Throughout the centuries the Holy Ones suggested: wherever you go, whatever you do, help people to overcome their adversities. Spread loving-kindness, happiness, and wisdom of responsibility and well-being. Live a life of love in action. *The more you love, the more you will understand—*

the more your effectiveness will increase. There will be Light Triumphant manifested in your being. There will be life divine. There will be Happiness without boundaries.

The Son of Man and the Judeo-Christian tradition advises us to love our God with all of our heart and with all of our soul and with all of our mind, and our neighbor as ourselves. Mother Teresa stated: God is everywhere, including in your neighbor. We should, therefore, love everything, including our neighbor, for she/he is us. Then we shall experience peace and love. Then we will experience joy that surpasses all understanding. We will be abiding in the Translucent Light of the '1'.

Our mission on earth will be accomplished. The unloosening of knots will have taken place. Our chains will fall away. There will be a jailbreak. We shall be set *free*. Freed from what? From our self-imposed restraints: the Disneyland space-time movie that we have entertained ourselves with. Ken Carey shares:

> For I am the first and the last, the beginning and the end, the Creator of all that is and of all that is to be. My potential is infinite, my being eternal. All creation is an ever-unfolding picture of what I conceive. The star fields are my canvas, humans are my brushes, biology is my paint.[15]

And Aldous Huxley writes:

> It is only by becoming Godlike that we can know God. And to become Godlike is to identify ourselves with the divine element which in fact constitutes our essential nature, but of which, in our mainly voluntary ignorance, we choose to remain unaware.[16]

Albert Schweitzer, Martin Buber, Jayata, Manura, Vasasita, Thomas Merton, Rabindranath Tagore, Mahakasyapa, and a universe of saintly forbearers in all climes and cultures give us a similar story. The great Fathers of the Church and major theologians, Athanasius, Irenaeus, Chrysostom, Clement of Alexandria, Ignatius of Antioch, Gregory of Nyssa, Cyril of Alexandria, Augustine, and particularly Basil the Great,[17] all understood that each person slowly progresses through stages of awakening and gradually becomes perfected in the image and likeness of her/his Creator.

Saint Basil the Great (328-379), archbishop of Caesarea in Cappadocia of Asia Minor, was a spiritual giant with a great generosity of heart and an incisive mind. He understood the Oneness of life that the human being is a divine being, and that life is about character development and human growth in the broadest sense. The development of character is the education par excellence and of fulfilling and creative living. His influence of "making yourself manifest—that you are alive" (considered through immense masterpieces of thousands of pages of St Basil's works), converges upon countless concerns of our era, including in the spheres of the liturgy and the monastic life. Here I would like to share with you his insights describing the stages of awakening and transformation into God:

> Through His aid, hearts are lifted up, the weak are led by the hand, and they who are advancing are brought to perfection. By His illumination of those who are purified from all defilement, He makes them spiritual by fellowship with Him. Just as bright and transparent bodies, in contact with a ray of light, themselves become translucent, and emit a fresh radiance from themselves, so souls wherein the Divine Spirit dwells, being illuminated thereby, themselves become spiritual and give forth their grace to others. Hence comes their foreknowledge of the future, the understanding of mysteries, the comprehension of what is hidden, the distribution of good gifts, the heavenly citizenship, a place in the choir of angels.
>
> Hence comes to them unending joy, abiding in God, being made like unto God, and which is the highest of all, being made God.[18]

Your Heart Is Happy and Leaps

The great Paul rejoices in the art of living: "The life I live now is not my own; Christ [the Author of all things] is living in me" (Gal 2:20). "Or perhaps it might be more accurate to use the verb transitively and say," recommended Aldous Huxley:

> I live, yet not; for it is the Logos [Eternal God] who lives in me— lives in me as an actor lives his part.[19]

Saint Catherine of Genoa trusted her "inner voice." She exclaimed in happy wonder:

> My Me is God, nor do I recognize any other Me except my God himself.[20]

Isaiah described it this way: "I am the Lord and there is none else, there is no God beside me," (45:5). Also, "I am the first ['1'] and the last ['='], and beside me there is no God," (44:6), and, "Is there any God beside me? Yes, there is no God. I know not any," (44:8). Jalal al-Din Rumi represents the pinnacle in the achievement of Persian mystical poetry. In the same words as Jesus ("You are in me and I am in you" [Jn 14:20]) and the blessed Angela of Foligno, Rumi enters the limitless Valley of Love:

> I am you and you are me.[21]

And in his poem Be Melting Snow Rumi repeats:

> Lo, I am with you always means when you look for God, God is in the look of your eyes, in the thought of looking, nearer to you than your self, or things that have happened to you. There's no need to go outside. Be melting snow. Wash yourself of yourself. A white flower grows in the quietness. Let your tongue become that flower.[22]

The Upanishads joyfully sang:

> *I am the Infinite;*
> *What you are, that same am I;*
> *You are all This;*
> *I am all This.*[23]

Mechthild of Magdeburg (1210-1297) developed the same kind of singular eloquence:

> I am in you and you are in me. We cannot be closer. We are two united, poured into a single form by an eternal fusion.[24]

The daily preoccupation with survival can easily cause us to lose sight of our personal needs. This overpowering closeness—this blissful splendor that is concealed beneath the mask of each and every particle—blinds the day-by-day mind to the '1', and blinds it to the fact that the whole world is filled with the "Infinite Presence," just as a strong light blinds our sight of objects and makes them appear to be temporarily invisible.

Among many quotations from the mystics of the Muhammadan faith, this Sufi verse sets the divine harmony to rhyme:

> There's naught within your robe but God Himself
> The knower and the known are but the same.
> He who knows God is God;
> God knows Himself.[25]

The Hakuin's *Song of Meditation* further elaborates:

> All sentient beings are from the very beginning the Buddhas:
> It is like ice and water;
> Apart from water no ice can exist.
> Outside sentient beings, where do we seek the Buddha
> Not knowing how near the Truth is,
> People seek it far away, what a pity!
> They are like him who, in the midst of water,
> Cries in thirst so imploringly;
> They are like the son of a rich man
> Who wandered away among the poor.
> The reason why we transmigrate through the six worlds
> Is because we are lost in the darkness of ignorance;
> Going astray further and further in the darkness,
> When we are able to get away from birth-and-death?
> As the Truth eternally calm reveals itself to them,
> This very earth is the Lotus Land of Purity,
> And this body is the body of the Buddha.[26]

Yes, you are me and I am you: this can only be sought within our own hearts and minds. For I am in your heart and mind, and you are in mine. "Thoughts of the ecstatic saints release rapture in the heart," discloses Muktananda. "I had once heard it sung":

When I realized the Pure, I became pure;
My ego was obliterated, I myself became God.[27]

Annie Besant was an educator with high aims and ideals, a political leader of unflagging youthfulness of spirit, with the balance of beauty of character and maturity of age. She was a brilliant teacher, regarded by Bernard Shaw as a woman of swift decision and the most exceptional orator of the century. Besant has to her credit thirty-two books on religion and two hundred and eighteen books on theosophy. She stated:

> Men have sought for God in many ways, but have not found him, because they sought amiss. They sought him in the forest and jungle, in desert and cave; they sought him through austerity and torture, through knowledge and argument, but He ever escaped them. In one place can He surely be found, never to be lost again, and that is a place beyond emotion and intellect, in the depth of your own Spirit, who verily is He. There He abides ever in the Cave of the Heart, the hidden God, the Light beyond the darkness, the Eternal, who is Strength and Love and Beauty. Find him there, and you will thereafter see him everywhere, in every human being, in every animal, in every plant, in encircling space, in joy and sorrow, in delight and in agony, even in the darkness of evil and of shame. Worship him in all beings; serve him in all needs; feed him in the hungry; teach him in the ignorant; love him in the unloving; make your life a temple, and your acts his sacrifice. Then shall your eyes one day behold the King in his beauty, the highest manifestation of God on earth, and you shall grow into Man made perfect, Man divine.[28]

Saint Augustine was one of the greatest of the Fathers and Doctors of the Church. He composed almost four hundred sermons and two hundred treatises. His legendary works are *Confessions*, a landmark masterpiece; *City of God*, a superb elucidation of a Christian philosophy of history; *De Trinitate*; *De doctrina christiana*, etc. Similar to Annie Besant, Saint Augustine shares with us this insight:

> Lord, I have sought you in all the temples of the world and lo, found you within myself . . . If a man does not find the Lord within himself, he will surely not find Him in the world.[29]

Sathya Sai Baba expresses Saint Augustine thusly:

> The distance between you and God is the same as the distance between you and yourself. If a person is far removed from himself, then only God is removed from him. Therefore, you (should) become close to yourself. Then only you will understand and experience divinity in the true sense.[30]

26

IS ANYBODY HERE APART FROM GOD?

Let everything that has breath:
Praise the Lord. Praise the Lord.

—Psalms 150

Exult in God's Glory

Long before Saint Catherine of Genoa cried out, "My Me is God, nor do I recognize any other Me except my God himself," Bayazid of Bistun declared:

How wonderful am I! Salutations unto Me! How great is my glory!

On another occasion, someone knocked at this Sufi saint's door and called out, "Is Bayazid here?" Bayazid responded:

Is anybody here except God?[1]

In a similar fashion Walt Whitman declared, "I am vast. I contain multitudes." Gustav Teres wrote: "The development of human awareness and culture, the evolution of the individual and society, progresses together with the rhythm of historical and cosmic time. The ultimate aim of all this is 'the full maturity with the fullness of Christ.'"[2]

Annie Besant stated,

We are part of one great Life, which knows no failure, no loss of effort or strength, which "mightily and sweetly ordering all things" bears the worlds onward to their goal. The notion that our little life is a separate independent unit, fighting for its own hand against countless separate independent units, is a delusion of the most tormenting kind. So long as we thus see the world and life, peace broods far off on an inaccessible pinnacle. When we feel and know that all selves are one, then peace of mind is ours without any fear of loss.

All our troubles arise from thinking of ourselves as separated units, and then revolving on our own mental axes, thinking only of our separate interests, our separate aims, our separate joys and sorrows . . . Peace is not to be found in the continual seeking for the gratification of the separate self, even though the gratification be of the higher kind. It is found in renouncing the separated self, in resting on the Self that is One, the Self is manifesting at every stage of evolution, and in our stage as much as in every other, and is content in all.[3]

How amazing it must have been for Einstein's contemporaries to appreciate his perspective that "A human being is part of the whole . . . [that] Our task must be to free ourselves from this prison by widening our circle of compassion to embrace all living creatures and the whole of nature in its beauty." How much more challenging it must have been for the generation of Saint John of the Cross (John Yepes, 1542-1591) to listen to one of the greatest Christian mystics and poets (*Spiritual Canticle* and *Dark Night of the Soul*), and cofounder of the Contemplative Order of Discalced (or "shoeless," because of the extreme poverty to which they subjected themselves) Carmelites, when he wrote that:

> The heavens are mine, the earth is mine, and the nations are mine
> Mine are the just, and the sinners are mine;
> Mine are the angels and the Mother of God; all things are mine.
> God himself is mine and for me, because Christ is mine and all for me.
> What do you ask for, what do you seek for, O my soul?
> All is yours—all is for you.
> Do not take less nor rest with the crumbs which fall from the table
>   of your Father.
> Go forth and exult in your glory, hide yourself in it, and rejoice,
> And you shall obtain all desires of your heart.[4]

Almost one hundred years later, Oxford-educated Thomas Traherne (1637-1674), the mystical poet of the Anglican clergy, which included in particularly George Herbert and Henry Vaughan, in *Centuries of Meditation*, acknowledged:

> All tears and quarrels were hidden from mine eyes. Everything was at rest, free and immortal. I knew nothing of sickness or death or exaction . . . . The streets were mine, the temple was mine, the people were mine, their clothes and gold and silver were mine, as much as their sparkling eyes, fair skins, and ruddy faces. The skies were mine, and so were the sun and moon and stars, and all the world was mine: and I the only spectator and enjoyer of it. I knew no churlish proprieties, nor bounds nor divisions; but all proprieties and divisions were mine, all treasures and the possessors of them. So that with much ado I was corrupted, and made to learn the dirty devices of this world, which now I unlearn, and become, as it were, a little child again that I, may enter into the kingdom of God.[5]

Yes, all things belong to '1'; all things are thus united to us. Our separateness is an illusion, for '1' knows only unity. Sixteen centuries earlier Saint Paul sent a similar communication to the Corinthians, "All things are yours, whether Paul or Apollos or Cephas [Peter] or the world or life or death or the present or the future—all are yours, and you are of Christ, and Christ is of God (1 Cor 3:21-23).

You Are the Yearning of Each Heart

Walt Whitman (1819-1892), poet, journalist, and essayist, widely read Homer, the Bible, Shakespeare, Coleridge, Sir Walter Scott, and Dickens. According to Bucke, who knew Whitman personally,[6] at age thirty-four, Whitman experienced the cosmic sense. Two years later Whitman published, with no author's or publisher's name, a thin pamphlet of twelve poems called *Leaves of Grass*. In this 1855 publication, Whitman deserted the conventional Victorian structure and writing style. The book upset many people who read it, stated the publishers of the *Leaves of Grass* special edition, which was prepared in observance of the one hundredth anniversary of Whitman's loss.

Thirty-seven years after the twelve-poem pamphlet was published, the 1892 version of *Leaves of Grass* included more than three hundred poems, producing an indisputably American classic. The poems encouraged the American populace to be mighty and generous in spirit, a race of races nurtured in liberty, and possessed of united souls and bodies. Similar to the proclamation of Saint John of the Cross three hundred years earlier, "The heavens are mine, the earth is mine, and the nations are mine," *Leaves of Grass* by Whitman broadcasts:

> The east and the west are mine,
> And the north and the south are mine.
> I am larger, better than I thought,
> I did not know I held so much goodness . . .
>
> And I know that the hand of God is the elder hand of my own,
> And I know that the spirit of God is the eldest brother of my own,
> And that all the men ever born are also my brothers . . .
> And the women my sisters and lovers,
> And that a kelson of the creation is love . . . [7]

Barbara Benjamin, whose insight parallels the Svetasvatara Upanishad, shares these wonderful gems:

> *You are The Source of warmth and light;*
> *You are the Risen Sun;*
> *You are The God made manifest;*
> *You are The Joyous One.*
> *You are The Way we learn to walk;*
> *You are The Word sublime;*
> *You are The Energy of life;*
> *You are The Quantum Time.*
> *You are The Yearning of each heart;*
> *You are The Growing Soul;*
> *You are The Parent of the world;*
> *You are Our Only goal.*

You Have Taken a Giant Step:
All Desire Is Now Fulfilled

When Pope Paul VI expressed the following rapturous love song, his heart must have embraced happiness, grace, and light, not only for all of humanity, but also for blessed eternity:

> Let us rejoice and give thanks that we have become not only Christians but Christ. My brothers, do you understand the grace of God, our Head? Stand in admiration, rejoice; we have become Christ.[8]

Firsthand knowledge is best. This Sufi saint, in perfect harmony with a thousand others,[9] exclaimed gratefully in joy and happiness:

> I saw you not before—I see you now,
> Belov'd! You peep forth from every face!
> I saw you not before—behind the clouds
> Beloved! You did not hide. I see you now![10]

And in the Brihadaranyaka Upanishad we find:

> As loving man and wife, when they embrace,
> Are both dissolved in but one feel of Love,
> One feel of Unity, and know naught else
> Outside their body or inside their mind;
> Even more, the Soul when it embraces God,
> And feels its Unity with the All-Self,
> Passes beyond all sorrow, all desire;
> For all desire is now fulfilled.[11]

End of Part 1

PART 2

Breakthrough

to

The Theory of Everything

In the beginning this world was merely nonbeing. It was existent.

—The Upanishads

There is a thing inherent and natural, which existed before heaven and earth.
It is motionless and fathomless. It stands alone and never changes;
it pervades everywhere and never becomes exhausted.
It may be regarded as the Mother of the Universe. I do not know its name;
if I am forced to give it a name, I will call it Tao, and I name it as supreme.

—Lao-tzu

Absolute space, in its own nature, without relation to anything external,
remains always similar and immovable.
Relative space is some measure of the absolute spaces;
which our senses determine by its position to bodies.

—Isaac Newton

This unimaginable Cosmic Intelligence is present at every spot in the universe,
and our whole personality, ego, mind, intellect and all—
is but an infinitely small bubble blown on this boundless ocean

—Gopi Krishna

He whom I enclose with my name
Is weeping in this dungeon.
I am ever busy building this wall all around;
And as this wall goes up into the sky day by day
I lose sight of my true being in its dark shadow.

I take pride in this great wall,
And I plaster it with dust and sand
Lest at least hole should be left in this name;
And for all the care I take I lose sight of my true being.

—Rabindranath Tagore (*Gitanjali*)

1

TOWARD THE FOUNDATION OF NATURE: THE STAKES HAVE NEVER BEEN HIGHER

Beautiful are the things we see
More beautiful those we understand
Much the most beautiful those we do not comprehend.

—Niels Steensen (Steno)

Climbing to Solutions: A Basis for Predicting the Results

Our search for the nature and destiny of the human family and the universe, the ultimate source from which all things emanate, and for the key to how our universe actually operates, can be traced throughout the pages of history. Humankind has been striving to interpret these questions through a common thread, a simple universal basis of the unchangeable law of cosmic order. "One of the curious features of modern physics," noted Nick Herbert in his *Quantum Reality*, "is that in spite of its overwhelming practical success in explaining a vast range of physical phenomena from quark to quasar, it fails to give us a single metaphor for how the universe actually works."[1]

"Can we guess the shape of theories yet to come," wrote David Wick in *The Infamous Boundary: Seven Decades of Controversy in Quantum Physics?* "History dampens our expectations, with quantum mechanics itself throwing the coldest water." Recall how the world's most keen-eyed individuals in various parts of the world and during different timeframes have had parallel insights into our unity with all life and "the unchanging nature of His purpose" (Heb 6:17). A known fact is that some of the great achievers in their search for the underlying fundamental principles were elevated to gods, acclaimed as supernatural beings, and worshiped as deities. Others were persecuted, purposely suppressed, and even put to death.

Case in point. In 1543, Polish astronomer and a canon of the cathedral chapter of Warmia, Mikolaj Kopernik (Nicolaus Copernicus, 1473-1543) published his groundbreaking work *De Revolutionibus orbium coelestium* ("On the Revolutions of the Celestial Spheres"). His theory, which was more than thirty years in the making, challenged the idea that the planets revolved around the Earth, taking Earth out of the center of the Ptolemaic universe. Copernicus proposed that Earth and other planets in our solar system revolved around a fixed sun. The heliocentric model appears to incorporate elements drawn from: (1) the writings of Aristarchus of Samos and Heraclides of Pontus (388-315 BC); (2) the work of the Arab astronomers al-Tusi and Ibn al-Shatir (1304-1376); and (3) the work Giovanni della Mirandola (1463-1494).

In Copernicus' day the geocentric (Earth-centered) cosmology placed the Earth solidly fixed in a privileged position: the center of the universe. Just recently (the twentieth century) have cosmologists realized that the Earth is but a tiny planet of a faint star in the outer edge of the Milky Way galaxy, made of one hundred billion or more stars with about one hundred fifty billion of other galaxies in the universe.

Copernicus initially described his heliocentric theory (1514) in a manuscript summary of his *Commentarius* ("Little Commentary"), which he disseminated to a small number of colleagues. In 1541, his student Rhaeticus, in *Narratio Prima,* explained in more detail the heliocentric theory. Copernicus did not want to broadcast his findings. He was afraid of the vested interests of the Holy Office and ridicule of conservative scholars, who adhered to Aristotle and Ptolemy. Twenty-six years after his *Commentaries,* Copernicus was finally persuaded to publish his complete work. Unfortunately, it was not possible to make definitive observations and to substantiate his findings.

Most astronomers continued to follow the Ptolemaic physics, until Galileo Galilei telescopic observations (1609/10) and Johannes Kepler (1571-1630) published his *Astronomia Nova* ("New Astronomy," 1609) and *Tabulae Rudolphine* (the "Rudolphine Tables," 1626). Kepler was a brilliant genius and the originator of the three laws of planetary motion now known as Kepler's Laws.

Had Copernicus not died at the time his book came out, he would most likely have had to face the Holy Office. In 1616, the Roman Catholic Church placed Copernicus' *De Revolutionibus* on the *Index Librōrum Prohibitorum* ("Index of Forbidden Books"), a list of books that were barred by church authority as harmful to the faith or morals of Roman Catholics. The last (twentieth) edition of the *Index* was published in 1948; a supplement listing titles and authors came out in 1959. The *Index* was banned in June 1966.

Giordano Bruno (1548-1600), Italian philosopher and member of the Dominican order from 1565-76, until he was suspected of heresy, was reduced to ashes in Rome. Bruno published *De l'infinito universe e mondi* ("On the Infinite Universe and the World's," 1584). Similar to the Italian astronomer, natural philosopher, mathematician, and physicist Galileo Galilei, Bruno supported the Copernicus' heliocentric theory of the solar system. For contradicting the fundamental views of the cosmology of Aristotle and backing Copernicus, Bruno was arrested by the Venetian Inquisition (1592) and passed on to the Roman Inquisition[2] (1593), which burned him alive at the stake for theological heresy. A challenge on the universally accepted physics of Aristotle (who lived approximately four centuries before the New Testament was written) and the established Ptolemaic system of an Earth-centered model suggested an unequivocal assault on the Keys of the Kingdom, the Holy Office, church canon and Scripture.

Galileo Galilei, a towering intellect and seismic achiever, was a major instigator of the Scientific Revolution of the seventeenth century. His mind was exceptional for its sharpness and clarity of thought. Galileo is often considered the father of mathematical physics. He created physics as a branch of learning based on mathematical theory and experimentation.

The fire of his genius, mathematical elegance, and wisdom cut deep. Galileo invented a device for raising water (air thermoscope), a computer for calculating quantities in geometry and ballistics, the isochronism of the pendulum, and hydrostatic balance. His *Discourse Concerning Two New Sciences* (1638) facilitated the modern science of mechanics. He was one of the first to deploy the telescope for astronomical work. His telescopic observations have enabled him to discover the moon's mountains, the sunspots, the phases of Venus (which illustrated that Venus orbited the sun), four of Jupiter's satellites (the Galilean satellites), and the expanse of the Milky Way.

In 1611, Galileo demonstrated the operation of his telescope to the renowned dignitaries at the Holy Office. Galileo supported the Copernican heliocentric model in planetary dynamics, stating that Ptolemy was wrong and Copernicus was right. The Aristotelian forces, seeing their vested interests threatened, united against him. The Copernican theory appeared to his enemies more dangerous "than Luther and Calvin put together."

On February 26, 1616, the Holy Office forbade Galileo from "teaching or discussing Copernicanism in any way." On February 13, 1633, the Inquisition faced Galileo with a trial. Galileo was forced to go down onto his knees and renounce the Copernican theory of the solar system under intimidation of torture. The Inquisition condemned Galileo to incarceration for life; his term was soon converted to house detention. Galileo spent the last years of his life under house arrest in Florence.

Were Galileo's intellectual breadth and scientific and technological accomplishments not so vast, Galileo would in all probability have been burned alive at the stake like Bruno or Servetus before him. At the 350 anniversary of Galileo's passing in 1992, Pope John Paul II made a formal apology to Galileo's estate for the actions of the Inquisition.

Michael Servetus (1511-1553), a perceptive Spanish physician and theologian, matriculated in medicine at Paris in 1538. Servetus described the pulmonary circulation of blood in animals eighty-five years before William Harvey did in *On the Motion of the Heart and Blood in Animals*. He published, anonymously, a treatise entitled *Christianismi Restitutio*, for which he was convicted with these words: "We condemn you, Michael Servetus, to be bound and taken to Champel and there attached to a stake and burned with your books to ashes."

Servetus was burned alive for heresy, mostly on his ideas of the Trinity, stating that the Word ['1'] is eternal, a form of *God's self-expression*, while the Spirit is the faculty within the hearts of people. Akin to the Greeks on Socrates and the Muslims on al-Hallaj, both Catholics and Protestants did not understand Servetus' deep insights on the Trinity.

As we have seen, procedures by which our creative intelligence is put to work illuminate not only the broad patterns of accumulated knowledge to reach the highest summits in both theory and experiments, but also newly established fundamental physical principles. New pathways generalizing and extending older principles have been carefully scrutinized, tested, validated, confirmed, and recorded, providing the framework into which new discoveries must be fit and the means for interpreting them. Likewise, religious beliefs and doctrine have been consecrated or enshrined into "holy books" and "divine texts" to preserve their grasp of insight into the central principle of the universe and our nature. Religions came about to animate and transmit the collective knowledge of the Unchanging State.

To extend the "Unchanging Values" or religion itself, numerous heated disputes, holy wars and crusades have been waged. Populations having different points of view or value were persecuted and victimized. Nations were systematically eradicated, ironically, over differing views of that which is transcendent and unchanging.

Today, differences flourish between and within the various kingdoms of religion, in Buddhism, Christianity, Hinduism, Islam, Judaism, Shinto, Taoism, Zen, Zoroastrianism, and others. Religions do not work together for a common understanding of the foundational cornerstone (underlying '1'ness), the foundational essence (compositional '1'ness), and the foundational purpose of existence (unifying '1'ness). Yet, the idea of the Unchanging Values is necessary to gain higher consciousness and to create sustainable living environments.

Is the Highest Good beyond Human Understanding?

Opinions differ on how far we are from a central principle of the universe. Saint Thomas Aquinas, one of the most significant Roman Catholic scholars of the medieval period, made great contributions as a moral and theological voice. Concerning the question of whether the human mind is capable of ever knowing what ultimate principles and fundamental explanations must be like, and having no reductive explanation of more fundamental and deeper principles, Aquinas stated, "The divine essence, the divine law, and the divine intention lie in this life beyond human sight."[3]

Is Aquinas correct concerning our helplessness to grasp the central principle of the universe? Consider the following insight from the Gospel of Saint John, "If you live according to my teaching, you are truly my disciples; then you will know the truth, and the truth will set you free" (Jn-8:31). Moreover, said the Perfect One:

He who lives [consciously] in me and I in him [in the unity of the Unchanging State] will produce abundantly, for apart from me

413

[being Christlike, Mt 5:48] you can do nothing. A man who does not live in me [in my values] is like a withered, rejected branch, picked up to be thrown in the fire and burnt. If you live in me, and my words stay part of you, you may ask what you will, it will be done for you . . . that my joy may be yours and your joy may be complete (Jn 15:5-11).

Professionals, operating in different disciplines, have erected territorial roadblocks toward the realization of the Highest Good, the Unchanging State. Consider the most inspiring intellectual adventure of our times— "the greatest quest in all of science" toward the epochal search for the foundations of physical science. Just as religions in most cases choose not to scrutinize and embrace the Unchanging Principle which other faiths and sciences have unlocked, so scientists in most cases, working at the foundations of groundbreaking research, choose not to probe and appreciate what evidentiary matter religions can contribute. The movement in the knowledge traffic in the search for nature's unchanging laws and the primordial quest to understand the cosmic field of creation and our place in it has reached a gridlock status. The situation can be compared to studying '1' with the sense of touch, but not listening to '1' with the sense of hearing, or observing '1' with the sense of seeing.

To establish broad patterns of information, in an increasingly competitive marketplace, means to be critically aware of ourselves as we are of the other. No business can prosper for long without reliable intelligence and understanding its competitors. In corporations, it makes business sense to have competitive analysis departments that examine products, services, and technology of their competitors in the marketplace. Military intelligence professionals and strategists study their allies, rivals, security issues, and potential threats (foreign weapons development and proliferation, information warfare and emerging technologies) in great detail. Going shopping: before buying a car, refrigerator, or a washing machine, most consumers compare different brands.

Comparable to our body needing all of our senses, our "manifested body," with which we perceive as the universe, needs all of us in each of our diverse capacities. Akin to our heart requiring large arteries, and these arteries in turn requiring smaller arterioles and capillaries, we need each other. We learn from each other. We add to each other. Personal knowledge is freedom and power; collective knowledge is universal freedom and universal power.

The central prerequisite in mankind's search for the Holy Grail of science, the Unchanging Software that explains the universe and everything that happens in it, is a willingness to undertake the process of knowing through a purely unitary consciousness, that is, through the clear Light state of awareness; without mental constructs, or images, or, as Isaiah stated, "Strip and make yourselves bare" (32:11).

Those who would agree with Steven Weinberg's characterization, of course, can contradict this point of view, along with the similar conclusions of Saint Thomas Aquinas we heard earlier:

> Perhaps there is a final theory [a central principle of the universe], a simple set of principles from which flow all arrows of explanation, but we shall never learn what it is. For instance, it may be that humans are simply not intelligent enough to discover or to understand the final theory . . . The best reason for hope that our species is intellectually capable of continued future progress is our wonderful ability to link our brains through [collective knowledge and] language, but this may not be enough.[4]

Nobel laureate Eugene P. Wigner, one of the leading physicists in the community of learning, was caught up in the initial development of nuclear technology, and had in mind, in the same way to Einstein, nuclear energy's social and political implications. In the 1960s, he embarked on developing the idea of civil defense against nuclear attacks. Wigner made contributions to physical chemistry, statistical mechanics, and symmetries in quantum mechanics of the relativistic wave equations, relativistic particle theory, and field theory. He introduced what is now known as the Wigner function, and found splendor in "The Unreasonable Effectiveness of Mathematics." In the *Proceedings of the American Philosophical Society*, Wigner gave notice of "The Limits of Science": "We have no right to expect that our intellect can formulate perfect concepts for the full understanding of inanimate nature's phenomena."[5]

Stephen Hawking is a distinguished scientist with pristine scholarship. Hawking was born 300 years to the day after Galileo died. He holds Newton's chair as Lucasian Professor of Mathematics at Cambridge University, a position once occupied by Isaac Newton and afterwards by P.A.M. Dirac. Queen Elizabeth named Hawking "Commander of the British Empire." Hawking is one of the standard-bearers of the quest for a theory to explain the universe. His research has covered such fundamental areas as black holes, so coined by John Wheeler in 1969, the arrow of time, the unification of physics, and the origin and fate of the expanding universe. Hawking wrote:

But can there really be such a unified theory? Or are we perhaps just chasing a mirage? There seems to be three possibilities:

1) There really is a complete unified theory, which we will someday discover if we are smart enough.
2) There is no ultimate theory of the universe, just an infinite sequence of theories that describe the universe more and more accurately.
3) There is no theory of the universe; events cannot be predicted beyond a certain extent but occur in a random and arbitrary manner.[6]

British philosopher and Nobel laureate Bertrand Russell, in his *Mysticism and Logic,* sided with the notion of an ultimately unpredictable universe, using Hawking's option three, while some elements of option two also entered his philosophy.

The idea of an ultimate explanation, put forth by Karl Popper, must be viewed in terms of an infinite chain of more and more fundamental or deeper and deeper principles (Hawking's second option). That is, "Every explanation may be further explained, by a theory or conjecture of a higher degree of universality. There can be no explanation [complete final formula], which is not in need of a further explanation . . ."[7]

Murray Gell-Mann, CalTech (one of the most prestigious scientific-technological institutions in the U.S.), holds a Nobel laureate in physics (1969). This was awarded to him for his work on quarks, and he is a celebrated theoretician. He served on the President's Science Advisory Council (PSAC) and is one of our most highly respected thinkers. Gell-Mann stated:

> It is the most persistent and greatest adventure in human history, this search to understand the universe, how it works and where it came from. It is difficult to imagine that a handful of residents of a small planet circling an insignificant star in a small galaxy have as their aim a complete understanding of the entire universe, a small

speck of creation truly believing it is capable of comprehending the whole.[8]

Robert Muller resonates with Gell-Mann, "Our planet is so small and part of such a tiny solar system among trillions of solar systems of a small galaxy among trillions of galaxies that our efforts to understand Creation resemble those of a flea trying to comprehend planet Earth."[9]

Thomas Merton, a courageous thinker, prolific writer and one of the most celebrated monks of the twentieth century, had a fertile and lively lucidity of mind. Reflecting on our challenge, Merton observed:

> Either you look at the universe as a very poor creation out of which no one can make anything, or you look at your own life and your own part in the universe as infinitely rich, full of inexhaustible interest, opening out into the infinite further possibilities for study and contemplation and interest and praise. Beyond all and in all is God ['1'].[10]

Live in the Present Because it Is Eternity

The Great Ones, whose "direct knowledge" of the Unchanging State is deeply steeped in the philosophy and practice of relentless honesty, kindness, selfless compassion, and collective wisdom, independently, at different times and in different parts of the world, have stated:

> The kingdom of God ['1', the foundation of everything] is within you and it is without you.[11] I ['1'], indeed, am below. I am above. I am to the west. I am to the east. I am to the south. I am to the north. I, indeed, am this whole world.[12] I ['1'] am the Light, which is above them all. It is I who am the all. From me did the all come forth, and unto me did the all extend. Split a piece of wood, and I am there. Lift up the stone, and you will find me there.[13] By God! Everything is He ['1'] and by God! Everything is He.[14] God is nearer to me than I am to myself . . . the knower [observer] and the known [observed] are one.[15] Everything [the universe with all its laboratories] is situated within Him ['1'].[16] In him ['1'] we live and move and have our being.[17] The countless heads, eyes, ears, and hands and feet of living beings are all parts of One Man.[18] Where

can I go from your spirit ['1']? From your presence where can I flee? If I go up to the heavens, you are there; if I sink to the nether world, you are present there.[19]

It should be noted that the "direct knowledge" is realized through observation or personal experience. The "indirect knowledge" is secondhand knowledge, as when one knows a subject from others, books, maps, or scriptures without actually being there or experiencing it. The foundation of everything we learn "is like treasure hidden [out of sight] in the field [epiphany, appearance, manifestation]" (Mt 13:44). The certainty of "direct knowledge," enlightenment, or immediate perception of the underlying nature of each thing is accessible to all of us: "Happy are the pure in heart; they will see God (Mt 5:8). The awakening of man begins when he discovers his own identity," states Sai Baba,

> and at the same time, he begins to recognize the identity of all around him, for all are one, all are Divine, all are part of the whole and I am that whole. I am there now residing in the heart of each one of you, but few of you realize it and even fewer experience the Divinity that is within . . .[20]

Additionally, articulates the Child of Light, "Anyone who withdraws into meditation on compassion can see Brahman [the clear Light of Peace] with his own eyes, talk to him face to face and consult with him."[21]

The link to the First Cause, as avowed by the great sages, is within everything. Also, as noted earlier (part 1, chapter 2), we have the potential to see the Light of the world, or the central principle of the universe, because we ourselves are "the light of the world" (Mt 5:14) in the disguise of manifestation. "Fortunately," maintains Sai Baba,

> Today there is a growing number of more evolved souls who are beginning to see the light ['1'] and there are signs of a new awakening. That awakening is in its early stages but it will gradually spread to every corner of the globe. It is the light that shines from within and it springs from the heart as the heart opens and the love of God begins to flow and shine like a great beacon. That light is there now, with each one of you, just waiting for you to switch it on through your own awakening.[22]

To See the Highest Good ('1'),
Look at the Highest Good ('1')

In immediate experience, you and I are at least partially open/united (consciously) to the '1'. As subtle and profound as the Silent One is, we are capable of penetrating the camouflaged Life, reducing observations to precise mathematical structures and extracting the Highest Good state through exact empirical equations.

Galileo Galilei, possibly more than any other truth seeker of the Western scientific revolution of the sixteenth and seventeenth centuries, including Copernicus, Descartes, Kepler, Leibniz, and Newton, attained a critical mass of general verifiable insights and a synthesis of theory and observation. As mentioned earlier, he challenged established Aristotelian notions of astronomy and physics. Galileo was responsible for reducing empirical observations to mathematical language, which facilitated the dawn of *mathematical physics* and current science. Unlike Saint Thomas Aquinas, Wigner, and Popper, Galileo was one of the first contemporary scientists to make a case that we can grasp the Highest Good. Namely, we can grasp ultimate reality by understanding the analytical language of mathematics, consisting of numerical and geometrical relationships hidden behind the sensory surface of the universe. He explained:

> Philosophy is written in that great book whichever lies before our gaze—I mean the universe—but we cannot understand if we do not first learn the language and grasp the symbols in which it [the Unchanging State] is written. The book is written in the mathematical language, and the symbols are triangles, circles and geometrical figures, without the help of which it is impossible to conceive a single word of it, and without which one wanders in vain through a dark labyrinth.[23]

Galileo espoused the notion of the mathematical unity of all nature, which he deeply appreciated—or a unified theory through the symbols of the disciplines, i.e., physics, philosophy, cosmology, sociology, art, music and medicine. The breadth of mathematical-linguistic symbolism implies that the *awareness refining process is a function of each observer*. The residence where we live is the reflection of our awareness. An observer will become aware of what she/he is conditioned to see. Dependent on individual consciousness, there exists, and can be, many forthcoming meanings of the First Cause ('1'): as the eye, so the sight; as the purity, so the clarity; as the light, so the visibility.

Each observer (physical quantity, atom, plant, animal, person, or galaxy) perceives the '1' based on the observer's position (simplicity, sensitivity, assumptions, environment, categories of thinking, cultural atmosphere, experiences and training) to '1'. The closer one is to the light the brighter the light; conversely, the further one is from light, the dimmer the light. Our awareness (the sacredness and serenity of personal space) and our universe constitute our most personal art. *We see what we see because we are where we are. We understand what is understood because we are who we are.* Aristotle put it this way, "as we *are*, so we shall *see.*" Therefore, the world, which is transformed by each observer (prism), is not the same as '1', but has a reality that is observer dependent.

To hear the "Unchanging One," to see the Unchanging One, to know the Unchanging One," we have to get in tune, or synchronize our mind and measurements, with the unchanging. What Galileo suggested for astronomic observations is true for life in general. Direct experience of the unchanging in our own being is the foretaste in our lives of what the sense of wonder and sacredness within a heart immersed in loving service will be like when we spread ourselves consciously over the universe.

To construct a unified reasoning for the Unchanging Software, it is possible, comparable to stilling the mind as previously discussed in part 1, to examine and characterize the foundation of physical science with precision measurements and the mathematical equations of physics. Repeated steps involving experiments, testing, and empirical methods in physics and mathematics realize this goal. Broadly, the different disciplinary viewpoints, added together, empower a researcher to find the "zero-point" of view from which the central unified idea appears in its absolute simplicity, beauty, structure, order, and relations, hidden in the Unchanging One. Or as William Blake captured in his beautiful poem "Auguries of Innocence":

To see a World in a grain of sand,
And Heaven in a wild flower,
Hold Infinity in the palm of your hand,
And Eternity in an hour.

2

PRECISION SCIENCE: AGREEMENT AT EVERY POINT OF THE UNIVERSE

Every problem contains within itself
the seeds of its own solution.

—Norman Vincent Peale

Oh, How Could It Have Been Otherwise!

I have noted what Steven Weinberg, Eugene Wigner, Karl Popper, and Stephen Hawking put forth regarding the central principle of the universe. Weinberg, being as unenthusiastic as he was with his "this may not be enough" statement, offered on further reflection:

> My own guess is that there is a final theory, and we are capable of discovering it. [However,] we are not likely to discover it soon . . . Physicists do sometimes underestimate the distance that still must be traveled before a final theory is reached . . . But from time to time we catch hints that it is not so very far off. Sometimes in discussions among physicists, when it turns out that mathematically beautiful ideas are actually relevant to the real world, we get the feeling that there is something behind the blackboard, some deeper truth foreshadowing a final theory that makes our ideas turn out so well.[1]

Hawking, taking into account his three possibilities of "the long sought-after unified theory of physics," and considering Popper's "boxes within boxes" of concealed principles, concluded similarly to Weinberg:

421

It does seem that the sequence of more and more refined theories should have some limit as we go to higher and higher energies, so that there should be some ultimate theory of the universe. [Therefore] I think there is a good chance that the study of the early universe and the requirements of mathematical consistency will lead us to a complete unified theory within the lifetime of some of us who are around today, always presuming we don't blow ourselves up first.[2]

What do you think; can the great quest in science be realized? Will we ever recognize the obvious? Will we ever understand the obvious? The answer is simple.

John Archibald Wheeler, one of the most notable nuclear and relativity theorists, an active proponent of observer-created reality, and a student of truth-seeking writings of our own and other civilizations, sounds a more positive note:

Can we ever expect to understand existence? Clues we have, and work to do, to make headway on that issue. Surely someday, we can believe, we will grasp the central idea of it all as so simple, so beautiful, so compelling that we will all say to each other, "Oh how could it have been otherwise! How could we all have been so blind so long!"[3]

The Common Ground Is Constant: Constancy Implies Unity and Infinity

What are some of the characteristics of a central unifying idea that could be so simple, so beautiful, so compelling? What crucial formalism in the philosophy of understanding empowers a researcher to reveal the common features of plainness and universal order hidden in the Unchanging State? What innermost knowledge of the physical world gives us the power to restructure our environment and improve our living conditions? What compelling grasp of the Finality will enable us to reshape ourselves and create an emancipating quality of life?

Let us look deeper into the inner sanctum of the foundations of physics. Let us consider why the stunning labor of love to dig deep for the facts in the scientific method is important: why the measurement of phenomena is essential for understanding the most sacred frontier of science, why verifying the Unchanging Principle that is behind manifested phenomena, at every point of the universe, means recognizing the obvious.

Patricia Barnes-Svarney, with a strong background in the physical sciences as well the halls of learning, wrote in *The New York Public Library Science Desk Reference*, "One of the most important developments in the history of science was the scientific method; the procedure scientists use to acquire knowledge in any field of science. Measurement of phenomena is essential to the scientific method—including measuring the initial phenomena and/or measuring the phenomena after an experiment—because it helps to quantify the experiment's results. The general format of the scientific method is as follows:

1. *The observation of the phenomena and the recording of facts.* The phenomena are what occurs in the environment; the facts are descriptions of what is observed.

2. *The formulation of physical laws from the generalization of the phenomena.* Physical laws are the way nature usually behaves based on what has been observed.

3. *The development of a theory that is used to predict new phenomena.* The theory is a general statement that explains the facts. A theory can lead to a new conclusion or the discovery of a phenomenon. Development of a theory often results in a change in paradigm—that is, looking at or thinking about a scientific problem in a totally different way.[4]

or scientific method would'nt work

Science is one of the central authorities of our time. While science, at its very heart, must remain flexible to accomplish new goals, *that* ('1', the ordering principle of the universe) *which science measures, defines, analyzes, and verifies never changes,* '1' is constant; '1' is infinite. '1' makes physics possible!

What's more, just as parts standardization enables mass production of automobiles, computers, and planes, so the constancy of '1' provides foundational consistency to conduct scientific inquiry into all branches of knowledge and learning. That which never changes permits to characterize the nature of mathematics, language, science, and much more. Lacking the constancy of '1', lacking infinities in physical quantities, none of the above, or existence, as we understand it, would be possible.

Think of a universe where there is no atomic constancy or order (i.e., the Periodic Table of Elements), no DNA, no fugue of Bach with its consistency or organization, and no invariability in the laws of physics. Everything hinges on everything else, in an unchanging way, in the universe. Infinities and simultaneous equations of the laws of physics provide evidence to this. What kind of world would you have if you established inconsistency or no infinities at the foundation of nature? Think of a computer infected with an epidemic of viruses, worms, Trojan horses, and other plagues.

Experiments and Theory Validate the '1'

In the domain of exact concepts and formulations, a world filled with elegant experiments along with high-caliber theory, high-energy particle accelerators, thermonuclear fusion, thermodynamics, radioactivity, relativity, quantum physics, cosmology, and beyond, the "Unchanging Operating Software" ('1'), which is at every point of the universe, is actually carefully studied, measured, verified, characterized, and classified. Through the scientific method, we are able to uncover and simplify lengthy expositions, differentiate and integrate the various laws of nature, and show their mathematical relationship and unity.

This is all history now. Scientific explorers bring to light the beauty and majesty of the central idea: the invariable foundation of physical science. In truth, scientists, comparable to the founders of the great religions (Moses, Lao-tzu, the Buddha, Krishna, Jesus) deal with the unchanging, infinite, character of the foundation of nature. The great news is that in the formulation of physical laws, scientists characterize the unchanging, the Imperishable, personality of '1'. In every equation of physics, scientists express the unified "theory of everything." It is a closed system.

Equipped with the scientific method, science has been observing, measuring, validating, analyzing, and predicting the organization of the unchanging mathematical structure of '1', and our observers' relationship to it. In most cases, the acquisition of knowledge has been taking place through micro-science: the bottom-up approach embedded in the scientific method of characterizing '1', the zero-point to be explained in chapter 5. In contrast, the Great Ones, their followers, and modern cosmologists in most cases have been employing macro-science: the top-down approach of knowing the Unchanging State via observation or spiritual experiences with '1'.

At the accessible horizon of '1' both the micro and the macroscientists seek to know the Unchanging Software—the "Book of the Old One," where human limitation often forces the seeker to peer through Plato's "shadows on the cave wall." Weinberg, in accepting the Nobel Prize (1979), shared from Plato's seventh book of the *Republic*:

> Plato describes prisoners who are chained in a cave and can see only shadows that things outside cast on the cave wall . . . We are in such a cave, imprisoned by [our consciousness and] the limitations on the sorts of experiments we can do . . . We have not been able to get out of this cave, but by looking long and hard at the shadows on the cave wall, we can at least make out the shapes of symmetries, which though broken are exact [invariant] principles governing all phenomena, expressions of the beauty of the world outside.[5]

The Unchanging:
Shared Property of Science and Religion

"The frank realization that physical science is concerned with a world of shadows, [which the Bible refers to as the images of God and the Rigveda as Maya, where creation and dissolution takes place] is one of the most significant of recent advances,"[6] explained Eddington. He adds:

> Briefly the position is this. We have learnt that the exploration of the external world by the methods of physical science leads not to a concrete reality but to a shadow world of symbols, beneath which those methods are unadapted for penetrating. Feeling that there must be more behind, we return to our starting point in human consciousness—the one centre where more might become known . . . Physics most strongly insists that its methods do not penetrate behind the symbolism [of quantities and physical laws]. Surely then that mental and spiritual nature of ourselves, known in our minds by an intimate contact transcending the methods of physics, supplies just that . . . which science is admittedly unable to give.[7]

Religious tradition portrays a comparable emergence from imprisonment: the tyranny of slavery and the principle of liberty. "God in exile" language describing captivity, prison and slavery experiences, and the end of the exile, where we are transformed "into His very likeness" (2 Cor 3:18), dominates much of the Hebrew and the New Testament Bibles. For example, the life of Jesus is commonly understood in the Gospels as a reenactment of ancient Israel's flight for freedom. Baptism is identified as a personal exodus from slavery (Plato's cave) to a new life of Light in the knowledge of the unchanging—"in an ever greater degree of glory" (2 Cor 3:18).

In Islam, the Holy Qur'an and subsequent traditions echo the biblical account of the Exodus in their description of the Hejira, the flight of Holy Prophet Muhammad from Mecca to Medina. From the Dead Sea scrolls, the biblical text that are conceivably the most important archeological discovery in the Holy Land, we read of the Essene community (an ascetic group of Jews) at Qumran continuing the interpretive tradition of relating the experience of the Exodus to itself. In Buddhism and Hinduism, the Buddha and Krishna discuss these basic notions. In the same vein, Einstein, as noted earlier, stated:

> A human being is a part of the whole. He experiences himself, his thoughts and feelings as something separated from the rest—a kind of optical delusion of his consciousness. This delusion is a kind of prison for us [Saint Peter's "prison" (1 Pet 3:19), Shantiveda's "the great ocean of suffering," Isaiah's: "dungeon in darkness . . . the land of the shadow of death" (42:7, 9:2), Plato's: "chained prisoners in a cave," Saint Paul's: "slavery" (Rom 8:19), Rumi's "prisoners," Sir Jeans' "cave," Rabindranath Tagore's: "dungeon"], restricting us to our personal desires and to affection for a few persons nearest to us. Our task must be to free ourselves from this prison by widening our circle of compassion to embrace all living creatures and the whole of nature in its beauty.[8]

Scores and Highlights:
The Great Advancement in Science

It is difficult to believe that the proverbial thread of constancy, measurement, and advancement to ever-higher levels of knowledge of the unchanging, as related to the scientific method, was born less than four hundred years ago. There were important scientists and mathematicians prior to 1600, some of whom are listed in Table 1,[9] who pondered and debated the micro/macro issues of the unchanging '1'. However, more than 90 percent of all scientists and mathematicians who have ever lived are alive today; Fifty percent of the world's inventions have been created in the last decade alone. Advancement was accomplished through unifying and simplifying the Unchanging State in every branch of human endeavor, i.e., the physical quantities, constants, and the usual laws of physics. The chapter on the unchanging mathematical logic has been written on the crowded canvas of human history by great scientists and mathematicians, some of whom are listed in Table 2.[10]

The Unchanging State of nanophysics, astrophysics, quantum computing and gravity, nanotechnology, bioengineering, economics, measurement, medicine, and comparative studies of symbolic reasoning goes far back to ancient Sumeria, Mesopotamia, and Egypt. People kept records of their possessions; government officials measured land and its known goods for tax purposes, while priests and philosophers reflected on the general nature of the mysterious, unfathomable forces. Initially, progress was slow. As time went on, the overall knowledge base expanded at a more rapid pace. Just think about what we have learned in the last fifty years. Now imagine the learning possibilities in the next one hundred thousand or one hundred million years awaiting humanity.

Contemporary scientists and mathematicians have elegantly summarized the numerous laws behind the forms into mathematical relations through the rigors of the scientific method, deploying "boundary" relationships behind every law of physics. Collectively, they have proven the connecting zero-state or the "Unchanging Boundary" relations behind every law of physics. Specifically, they have characterized the '1' through the universal constants and the initial conditions of the universe. They have summarized the invariant ratios of physical quantities and fundamental constants between the '1' (the Alpha Point: fixed zero-point or node) and the equality boundaries ('=': the Omega Point: empty interval or zero-state) which we term laws of physics. In cosmology, these two zero-state boundaries represent either of the two points at which the orbit of a cosmic body intersects a given plane, especially the plane of the ecliptic or of the celestial equator. In mathematical interpolation, this "boundary" is termed a joint knot, one of the points at which the values of a function are assigned.

In walking, the difference (delta, discrete or "quantal" property observed) between one's first step (the '1', starting point of measurement—the initial conditions) and one's second step (the '=', ending point of measurement—the final conditions) could distinguish the dimension, or quantum, of each person's step. When penetrating deeper into the domain of quantum theory, which Niels Bohr and others sought to characterize, the quantification is the result.

However, a comprehensive description of the physical world contains not only one type of packet or quanta, but different packets (the difference in their relation, steps) in the guise of physical quantities, elements, DNA, and so forth. Through measurement and symbolic representation, an illustrator may compare one person's walk with another person's walk in terms of individual physical steps, such as expression of the form, or quanta. Therefore, to travel from one place to another on a planet, one could characterize people through different step sizes, an incremental change in a variable, as delta or quanta.

Equally, to the way material processes can be used to express physical quantities, intervals in '1' (meaning), can be used to characterize quantities. The laws of nature, which characterize relationships bounded by '1' and '='points, do not change, when one goes from one system of coordinates to another. They are scale invariant. Thus, in physics, because of the "Unchanging Nature" of '1', we can express the same meaning in different ways. *- Ratios exist b/c of 1*

Example: mass and energy are interchangeable. The rate of exchange was laid out by Einstein in his well-known special relativity mass-energy equation, $E = mc^2$. Mass (m) and energy (E) can be viewed as two different ways (expressions of the form) to convey an equivalent idea underlying the constant structure of '1'.

What is interesting in this setting is that while we are concentrating on measuring the size of steps (quantal properties, packets or quanta) and their relationships to other steps, such as the relations between quantities in the laws of physics, we have disregarded the central principle of the universe. The entire picture should also contain the Unchanging State or global operating software: the planet we are walking on and the rules it abides by. The reason mass and energy are interchangeable in $E = mc^2$ is because mass and energy are locked into an invariant relationship in the Unchanging State ('1')—a universal foundation or connectivity for equivalent integrity of nature. *- closed system?. Same as?.*

428

The Overlooked First Principle: Make Physics Real

Erwin Schrödinger, the pick and flower of Austrian culture, asserted that it takes roughly fifty years before a major scientific advance enters public awareness—before the general population understands what science knows. In 1543, Nicolaus Copernicus made it known that Earth and the other planets in our solar system move around the sun. Yet 460 years later, "at least half of Americans polled in a recent (2002) survey by the National Science Foundation did not know that Earth orbits the sun, and that it takes a year to do so . . ." writes Lawrence Krauss in the *APS* (American Physical Society) *News*.

In the towers of science, '1' is an integral underpinning of every law of physics. Yet, in "the observation of the phenomena [and] the development of a theory that is used to predict new phenomena," the central principle of the universe has not yet knowingly been considered. This is to say the most important underpinning, the Imperishable '1', in which the laws of physics are carefully researched, verified, and painstakingly documented has been overlooked.

Is it possible to drive and not be conscious that we are driving? Is it possible to eat and not know that we are eating? Yes. The same is true with '1'. '1' is a central foundation of every equation of physics, but not part of our consciousness. The most important factor behind the invariance is not the nature of measurement but the ground on which science lives, moves, and has its being. Consider: "In him we live and move and have our being" (Acts 17:28). Also, "Where can I go from your Spirit[11] ['1']? From your presence where can I flee? If I go up to the heavens, you are there; if I sink to the nether world, you are present there."[12]

The fusing essence of all reality and the underpinning of each of the sciences, with laws that each have fixed zero boundaries of '1' (absolute beginning), and an equality '=' (absolute ending) is unchanging under all transformations. Freeman Dyson, taking a worm's eye view of our universe, stated in his beautiful book, *Infinite in All Directions*:

> Now it is generally true that the very greatest scientists in each discipline are unifiers. This is especially true in physics. Newton and Einstein were supreme as unifiers. The great triumphs of physics have been triumphs of unification. We almost take it for

The more experiments + unification, just getting the same information over + over again..... Have to look at it differently.

granted that the road of progress in physics will be a wider and wider unification, bringing more and more phenomena within the scope of a few fundamental principles. Einstein was so confident of the correctness of this road of unification that at the end of his life he took almost no interest in the experimental discoveries, which were then beginning to make the world of physics more complicated. It is difficult to find among physicists any serious voices in opposition to unification.[13]

Through advanced theory, mathematics, instrumentation, experimentation, and confirmatory verification, we are on the verge of realizing mankind's age-old dream of a unified understanding of our universe—who we are, what we are, why we are, and what kind of world this is. "Everybody likes adventure stories," wrote Paul Davies, professor of natural philosophy, at the University of Adelaide, Australia, and Templeton Prize laureate, in his *Superforce*. He explains:

> One of the greatest adventures of all time is happening now, in the shadowy world of fundamental physics. The characters in the story are scientists and their quest is for a prize of unimaginable value—nothing less than the key to the universe.
>
> The most important scientific discovery of our age is that the physical universe did not always exist. Science faces no greater challenge than to explain how the universe came to exist and why it is structured in the way it is.[14]

Hidden Connections in Symbolic Logic

In 1665, twenty-three-year-old (Sir) Isaac Newton (1642-1727), apparently while lying in the orchard of Woolsthorpe, Lincolnshire, England, saw an apple fall to ground. This unremarkable event set him to work on the problem of what caused both the apple to fall and the moon to orbit. He discovered that bodies attract each other with a force inversely proportional to the square of the distance between them. You can repeat this experiment any place at whatever time, because of the Unchanging Nature of '1', and the results will always be the same. Apples will fall to the ground. With the law of universal gravitation, Newton integrated the quantities of mass, force, and distance. In addition to discovering the first and second laws of motion, which were perhaps one of the greatest generalizations and most useful theorems of natural sciences, Newton unified the quantities of acceleration with mass and force.

Newton's laws of gravity and motion are relatively simple mathematically, even by high school standards. The scientific revolution that accompanied the work of Newton's law of universal gravitation provided a classic example of what is a very involved, random behavior of physical relationships utilizing the elegant mathematical descriptions that can be integrated through simple physical quantities that will support a vast range of complex activities in nature. These physical quantities are encoded through the universal, compact, mathematical relationships of physical laws in a cryptic and often subtle way, not always apparent to someone observationally studying nature.

Alfred North Whitehead (1861-1947) was a world-renowned mathematician (*Treatise on Universal Algebra*, 1903; *An Introduction to Mathematics*, 1911), possessing a philosophical bent (*Enquiry Concerning the Principles of Natural Knowledge*, 1919; *The Concept of Nature*, 1920) with a metaphysical outlook (*Process and Reality*, 1929). Whitehead attempted to grasp existence and to devise a general representation that would rise above classic dualism. Instead of just senior lectureship (Trinity College, Cambridge) or discovering new mathematical theorems, Whitehead was moved toward obtaining an understanding of fragmented ideas, such as connecting interrelated concepts and elucidating a bigger view of nature—the philosophical fundamentals for physics and the foundations of mathematical logic in its general expression.

Whitehead worked with Bertrand Russell on *Principia Mathematica* and developed a comprehensive metaphysical theory while teaching at Harvard University starting in the mid-1920s. He became a Fellow of the Royal Society (in 1903), was elected to the British Academy (1931), and received the Order of Merit (1945). Whitehead wrote:

> Consider how all events are interconnected, when we see the lightning, we listen for the thunder; when we hear the wind, we look for the waves on the sea; in the chill autumn, the leaves fall. Everywhere order reigns, so that when some circumstances have been noted, we can foresee that others will also be present. The progress of science consists in observing these interconnections [in

'1'] and in showing, with a patient ingenuity, that the events of this ever-shifting world are but examples of a few general connections or relations called laws. To see what is general in what is particular and what is permanent in what is transitory is the aim of scientific thought. In the eye of science, the fall of an apple, the motion of a planet around a sun, and the clinging of the atmosphere to the earth are all seen as examples of the law of gravity. This possibility of disentangling the most complex evanescent circumstances into various examples of permanent laws is the controlling idea of modern thought.[15]

By utilizing symbolic logic to integrate simultaneous equations between the "Unchanging Points" of physical quantities in '1', we can decipher a broad range of hidden connections, symmetries, and superhuman insights about '1' never suspected on physical grounds.

Journey to Mars

The value of symbolic manipulation in everyday reality can be illustrated from the following example. In the not-too-distant future, NASA will undertake sending voyagers to Mars. The round-trip mission could take as long as three years. Medical researchers at Ames Research Center, at Moffett Field, California, in the heart of Silicon Valley, are developing science and technology for potential flight missions germane to exobiology, that is, the study of the effects of outer space environment on living organisms from the planet Earth. They are concerned about the damage incurred by the human body from such a prolonged absence of gravity.

Soviet cosmonaut Oleg Atkov, landing after eight months in space station Salyut 7, had become so weak that he had to be carried off by stretcher. His muscles withered in the punishing world of zero-g despite intensive daily exercise. Atkov's bones, no longer needed for supporting his body, gave up calcium and lost density. The question arises: how can we create an artificial gravitational field for a mission to Mars and other deep-space probes? Can we leave Earth to visit distant galaxies in some type of vehicle and remain healthy?

I have noticed that when one evaluates the mathematical notation of astronomical gravitation with symbolic reasoning, Newton's law of universal gravitation can be extended via the principle of substitution from the simple relationship of force, F, divided by mass, m ($g = F/m$) to an expression whereby the gravitational field strength, g, equals linear velocity, v, times angular velocity, w ($g = v$w). Because the space vehicle will have forward or linear velocity, NASA will need to rotate it, like nature does with Earth. If we choose not to rotate the spacecraft, but utilize other means to produce gravitational field strength, we can create additional relationships, thus modifying each electron, proton, and neutron on the spacecraft to produce gravity. Hence, in every field of thought, careful scrutiny of the mathematical symbolism can yield a range of hidden connections, solutions, and possibilities.

Translating Science into Life

Between 1780 and 1789, the French physicist and inventor Charles Augustin de Coulomb (1736-1806) discovered that magnetic poles attract or repel each other in proportion to the inverse square of their distances. He also found that the same law holds for electric charges. Coulomb's law, which appears very similar to Newton's law of universal gravitation, unified the quantities of force, charge, and distance.

Following Coulomb, the Danish physicist and natural philosopher Hans Christian Oersted's (1777-1851) discovery in 1820 of electric currents exerting a force on magnets paved the way for the French physicist André Marie Ampère (1775-1836) to formulate the mathematical law of force and to show that the quantities of electric currents exert force upon each other.

British physicist Michael Faraday (1791-1867) made immeasurable contributions to physics, chemistry, materials science, and electrical engineering. In 1831-32, through the laws of induction between currents and between currents and magnets, Faraday showed that magnetism and electricity are also closely related, each feeding off of the other. He revealed the phenomenon of electromagnetic induction—the production of electric current through a change in magnetic intensity.

In 1873, the talented Scottish mathematical physicist James Clerk Maxwell (1831-79) achieved a tremendous breakthrough with his electromagnetic theory. Building upon Faraday's work, he developed equations to show that electricity and magnetism are intimately related forces that can be described through a unified electromagnetic field. Maxwell united the quantities of electrical and magnetic fields, force, velocity, distance, and charge. He proved, with mathematical elegance, that what at first sight could appear as two distinct forces of nature are, in fact, just two different facets of the same force. The stunning success of Maxwell and Faraday's unification can best be measured by the tremendous impact that electrical power and electronics, which emerged from the electromagnetic field concept, have had on our lives. In 1888 Heinrich Rudolph Hertz (1857-94), a German physicist, building on Maxwell's work, produced electric vibrations by the direct electrical method. His experiments laid the groundwork for our present wireless communications.

Albert Einstein, whose life, in his own words, was "divided between politics and equations," proved that the quantities of energy and mass are interchangeable. They are of the same essence, the same cosmic core, but in different forms. Furthermore, Einstein demonstrated, with French mathematician Jules Henri Poincaré (1854-1912) and Dutch theoretical physicist Hendrik Antoon Lorentz (1853-1928) and one of the greatest scientists of his time, that the quantities of space and time are not independent entities, but are interwoven. His final ambition, to link "all natural phenomena" into a single descriptive scheme, proved a little bit more elusive. Einstein's lifelong quest, at the turn of the twentieth century, to construct a "unified theory" of everything in the universe, all at one go, would probably have been realized had he been given a little more time on Earth.

The Unchanging Light through the Equations of Physics

Paul Davies, reflecting on the magnitude of significant developments realized in fundamental physics over the last decades, rhapsodized in his *Superforce*:

> For the first time in history we have within our grasp a complete scientific theory of the whole universe in which no physical object or system lies outside a small set of basic scientific principles . . . These dramatic developments stem directly from a number of major advances made in fundamental physics over the last decade, especially in the area known as high-energy in theoretical understanding are, if anything, even more spectacular. Two new conceptual schemes are currently forcing the pace. One goes under

the name of "grand unified theories," or GUTS, the other is called "supersymmetry." Together these investigations point towards a compelling idea, that all nature is ultimately controlled by the activities of a single superforce. The superforce would have the power to bring the universe into being and to furnish it with light, energy, matter, and structure. It would represent an amalgamation of matter, spacetime, and force into an integrated and harmonious framework that bestows upon the universe a hitherto unsuspected unity.[16]

In previous times, the rishis, prophets, messiahs, saints, avataras, arhats, Buddhas, nabis, and spiritual leaders kept alive the concept of the Unchanging Light through the "unity of the Spirit." Now the Unchanging Light shines through high-precision science in the equations of physics.

3

PHYSICAL QUANTITIES:
A MEANS TO ULTIMACY

I have always thought it curious that,
while most scientists claim to eschew religion,
it actually dominates their thoughts more than it does the clergy.

—Fred Hoyle

Wider and Wider Unification of Knowledge

Let us consider the notion of "unity" and "unified theory." What is unity? Unity is a state of being one, the condition or reality of being unified or fused into one, as of parts of a totality regarded as one quantity. What is unified theory? Basically, unified theory is one that unifies all phenomena by means of identical laws, physical concepts, or mathematical structures. As we know from the works of Newton, Maxwell, Lorentz, Poincaré, Planck, Einstein, and others, contemporary science recognizes the unity of the universe. The central issue in our search for the greatest prize in all of science is the shape of nature's final law.

There are many ideas and a variety of conceptual approaches that attempt to bring together the seemingly different phenomena of nature and to present a complete picture of modern physics. These proposals range from the integration of (1) fundamental theories, such as Newton's theory of gravitation, Maxwell-Lorentz's electrodynamics, and Einstein's theory of gravitation, (2) phenomenological or constructive theories, such as the theory of nuclear forces, the theory of electromagnetic form-factors, and (3) semi-phenomenological theories, such as the theory of

436

electroweak Weinberg-Salam-Glashow interactions, to the c̶c̶
the universal principle of relativity and the theory of a physical vacu̶
to string theories. Some of the world's most distinguished thinkers
scholars suggest, as previously noted, that there is no common starting
point, or a complete final formula, to which all explanations may be
traced. That is, "Every explanation may be further explained, by a theory
or conjecture of a higher degree of universality."[1]

The search continues for a "wide and wider unification" of knowledge,
and the effects its discovery may have on the foundations of science and
beyond.[2] I have taken the liberty of bringing this challenge to unite
phenomena into sharper focus, by connecting the fundamental physical
quantities and the fundamental constants, which are the most elementary
entities in nature. Through unity, absolute simplicity, and universal
applicability of constancy, or invariance, in the laws of physics, we may
find answers to our deepest questions such as: what is ahead of us after
we go beyond our current understanding of today's theories of physics,
the big bang theory, and the psalmist's view of the "glory of God."

To permit this greater depth of exploration and the inclusion of the
general thrust of modern physics into the vital issue of who we are and
where we have come from, let us start again at the basics. What exactly
is a physical quantity?

David Halliday, professor of physics at University of Pittsburgh,
and Robert Resnick, professor of physics at Renesselaer Polytechnic
Institute, record:

> The building blocks of physics are the physical quantities in terms
> of which the laws of physics are expressed. Among these are force,
> time, velocity, density, temperature, charge, magnetic susceptibility,
> and numerous others. [Furthermore,] All physical laws are the
> same [unchanging] in all reference frames. Observers in different
> frames [of reference] may obtain different numerical values for
> measured physical quantities, but the relationship between the
> measured quantities, that is, the laws of physics, will be the same
> for all observers.[3]

The invariance of relationships assures that physical laws will pertain to
more than just our particular sector of the universe. A final unifying
theory would apply to the universe as a totality.

cy: The Key to the Unfolding Universe

ustrated parallel evidence of some of the world's , thinkers, and scholars in Eastern and Western e concept of the universe, our unity with all life, question. Let us now evaluate further, through the specifics of the Halliday and Resnick definition.

The building blocks of physics are the physical quantities. This is true. Therefore, time, space, energy, matter, and other quantities are the fundamental units of nature that physics can measure. Time can be measured. You do this with your watch. Velocity and length can also be measured. You do this with your speedometer, your yardstick, nanometer, and many other measurement devices.

We customarily state that physical laws are expressed through relationships of physical quantities. In mathematics, this is analogous to saying that mathematical relationships can be expressed through numbers, $10 = 2 \times 5$, or that a dime equates to two nickels. Moreover, because in physics we have not yet come to grips with what the common essence of time and gravity is, or what the fundamental core of matter and energy is, we utilize relationships among physical quantities to express (or barter) concepts in terms of each other.

The situation is comparable to that of trading or bartering before money, the common currency to which our goods and services convert, existed. We exchanged chickens for goats, pigs for skins, and so forth. Recently I viewed a touching TV documentary on PBS wherein one tribe, in a bidding auction, negotiated barter with another tribe using black pigs, grass skirts, and arrows. The bride and goods were swapped. There was a lot of joy and dancing at the wedding. Wonderful story.

Global Classification of Information:
The Ordering Principle of Numbers

Suppose in your attempt to improve and extend the state of the principles of the universe and the now-standard world picture, the hot big bang model of the expanding universe, you went on a voyage to a planet in the Andromeda Nebula, a northern constellation between the Square of Pegasus and the "W" of Cassiopeia. The Andromeda Galaxy, which is essentially moving toward us, is the nearest giant spiral galaxy outside the Milky Way, some 2.4 light-years away, wherein 10^{11} (100,000,000,000) stars and our own sun are located. While visiting the great nebula in Andromeda, scientists present you with hard evidence of the central elements in their cosmology. You are given their theoretical explanation of the physics of the very early universe and the cornerstone of their mathematical relationships: 6 = 2 x 3; 10 = 5 x 2; 2 = 8/4; and 7 = 14/2.

In addition, you have learned, based on their observations of the Andromeda constellation, which is surrounded by about nine galaxies, the Milky Way, encircled by about thirteen other galaxies, and the nearby Alpha Centauri triple system, which is about 270,000 astronomical units or 4.4 light-years away, that the above mathematical relationships are always true and unchanging.

Note: one astronomical unit (AU) is the mean Sun-Earth distance, or half the semimajor axis of the Earth's orbit—equal to just over one billion trips around Earth.

The Local Group, containing the Milky Way, the Andromeda Galaxy, the Triangulum Galaxy, the two Magellanic Clouds, etc., covers an area about five million light-years in diameter and includes about forty galactic systems. One of the great Andromeda scientists, John One-Stone, has made a career of observing the behavior of the Local Group. He informs you of his observational evidence that the *empty-space* in which its galactic members are moving smoothly is *not* a part of the big bang expansion. That is, the empty-space (vacuum) in which this region of the universe lives and moves and has its being, is constant: invariable, continuous, and unbounded, making local mathematics the same, at all times. Additionally, all the galaxies of the Local Group are gravitationally connected and are not receding from one another. Each star, including the sun, is moving relative to the local standard of zero-point rest.

Furthermore, you are informed, the relationship between the mathematical numbers in your possession (the laws of numbers) will be the same no matter how fast you travel or the stars expand in the empty-space. Namely, the mathematical relationships are an integral part of the empty-space—they are infinite, and not the moving objects.

Although inhabitants of the Andromeda Galaxy understand relationships between numbers, which they call "mathematical laws," they have not yet solved the *global order*, or sequence, as first, second, third, and so on, *of numbers*. Your mission on this trip to the Andromeda

Nebula, should you decide to accept it, is to unravel for them the *ordering principle,* the hierarchy of successive patterns, wherein numbers are organized or classified from small to large, for the numerical sequence 6, 2, 3, 10, 5, 8, 4, 7, and 14. Of course, you smile—you know the decimal system of numeration from planet Earth. Elatedly, you name them *consecutively* as: 2, 3, 4, 5, 6, 7, 8, 10, and 14.

Zero Cannot Be Divided: Common Starting Point of Numbers

Now, what does this have to do with the *ordering principle* of physical quantities, infinities, and the common zero-point reference frame giving them structure and value? I was hoping you would ask. Thank you so much for reminding me.

It should be noted that the scientists on the distant planet of the Andromeda Galaxy together with our scientists concluded that the relationship between numbers and the interactions between physical quantities will always be the same: invariable, unchanging. The mathematical correlations of 7, 14, and 2 (7 = 14/2), and the physical relationships between energy, E, mass, m, and the velocity of light, c ($E = mc^2$) will be the same no matter how fast we travel through empty-space. Eureka! We are getting very close to the fundamental starting frame of reference. How?

As part of your approach to the global ordering problem posed by the Andromedans you unified every number in *affiliation to the starting point of numbers*: the *zero*. Surprised? You shouldn't be. This initial point of counting is a concept the Andromeda mathematicians have not yet fathomed, and it is also one that the Western civilization on planet Earth could not grasp for nearly two millennia.

Observe: when you place a sequence of numbers on a ruler, such as 1, 2, 3, 4, 5, each number must be positioned in relation to the common ("initial") reference frame—the universal starting point of counting: the zero, nada, zilch. One *from* zero, two *from* zero . . . five *from* zero. A stopwatch or a car's odometer starts at zero (0:00.00). NASA, prior to blasting rockets into outer space, counts backwards to zero: . . . seven, six, five, four, three, two, one, *liftoff.* In Hiroshima or Nagasaki, when you go in the direction of the spot where the Fat Man or the Little Boy were deployed against civilian city dwellers you are going to ground zero. The bombs were not detonated against their number one targets. By the time Fat Man and Little Boy were ready, the Germans had capitulated. The same applies to New York City's WTC site, where the terrorist attack took place. For you, zero is ordinary: a "nothing special" reference frame. Nonetheless, there was a time when there was no zero, zip, or zilch in our system of counting, and without it, what we now consider the normal sequence of numbers was not so easy to explain.

Zero's Place in Human Civilization

Zero may rightly be deemed one of the most unprecedented achievements of the human mind. The Babylonian system of numeration, developed around 350 BC, began using an empty column (our zero) on the abacus. Maya's mathematics included the zero, which was their common reference frame to positional numeration. While in India zero was conferred with many powers, in Europe the concept of the zero was rejected and not grasped. The man who brought zero from the Muslims to the West was the son of an Italian trader, Leonardo of Pisa, known to us as Leonardo Fibonacci.

In unfolding the life story of zero, which was considered a treacherous concept for the West, Charles Seife wrote in his scenic *Zero: The Biography of a Dangerous* Idea:

> Zero clashed with one of the central tenets of Western philosophy, a dictum whose roots were in the number-philosophy of Pythagoras and whose importance came from paradoxes of Zeno [of Elea 490-430 BC]. The whole Greek universe rested upon this pillar: there is no void [empty-space].
>
> The Greek universe, created by Pythagoras, Aristotle, and Ptolemy, survived long after the collapse of Greek civilization. In that universe there is no such thing as nothing. There is no zero. Because of this, the West could not accept zero for nearly two millennia. The consequences were dire. Zero's absence would stunt the growth of mathematics, stifle innovation in science, and, incidentally, make a mess of the calendar. Before they could accept zero, philosophers in the West would have to destroy their [prevailing concept of the] universe.[4]

A historical fact is that "the Laughing Philosopher" Democritus (460-370 BC) and Leucippus (fifth century BC) Greeks from Abdera on the seacoast of Thrace, maintained that the physical phenomena were composed of tiny eternal and uncaused "atoms" (*atoma*), differing from one another in shape, arrangement, position, and magnitude, and which move through "infinite space," or the "void" (*kemon*, or *vacuum*). The suggestion was detestable to the common notion of that day. Plato voiced the deep-seated desire that all of the literature pertaining to "atoms and the void" be destroyed by fire! It did not agree with his thinking.

While the West could not grasp the zero (they also felt endangered by the idea of the void, or nothingness), years earlier, both the Mesoamerica Maya and the East had already embraced the zero concept. In the classic Maya long count catalog the cycles have elapsed since a zero date in 3113 BC.

In India,[5] the ultimate void, the supreme nothing—the Shiva "without parts"—has an ancestry preceding Democritus and Leucippus. Their zero (the *sunya*) embraced the notion that emptiness and nonbeing were absolute goodness, and prospered. The Rig-Veda states: "Existence was born from nonexistence [empty-space]."[6] Rabindranath, similar to Irenaeus, opening his heart in admiration and delight, said: "God [the First Cause] has taken the form of man here, man is to become God here."[7]

For nearly two thousand years, beginning with Pythagoras, the West had an unreasonable apprehension of the zero. The Aristotelian cosmos dominated the knowledge base of Western philosophers and scientists. As the West awakened from the Dark Ages, it was inclined to see the zero that is at the heart of all mathematics. This also meant that it would have to do away, per Nicolaus Copernicus, Galileo Galilei and Kepler, with the Ptolemaic view of the universe.

4

THE GOLDEN ALPHABET: FROM ZERO TO INFINITY

Everything should be made as
simple as possible, but not simpler.

—Albert Einstein

'1': A New Language for Understanding Solutions

As with the Copernican theory of the solar system for the Roman Inquisition, or "atoms and the void" for Plato, a similar state of affairs exists to some extent in science today. Contemporary science has an unreasonable uneasiness of *the abstract realm of all possible states*: '1', the Absolute Infinity. Yet '1' is the foundational information and mathematical structure of the physical laws that govern them (the Principle *above* the laws of physics), and the Common Ground in which the universe expands, interacts with, and atoms revolve in.[1]

Sigmund Freud, unfailing in his steadfast atheism and agnosticism, declared to his friend Oscar Pfister, a Lutheran minister, that he was a "godless Jew." Freud "prided himself on being an intrepid man of science, a conquistador of the mind, who cherished his 'enlightenment' attitude toward religion and clung to his avowed agnosticism until the end of his life . . . He even quipped at one point that the writings of Karl Marx seemed to have replaced the Bible and the Qur'an as sources of revelation,"[2] wrote William Meissner, university professor of psychoanalysis at Boston College.

Steven Weinberg, a towering scientific intellect, in his book, *The First Three Minutes,* dealing with the idea of the original cosmic bang,

443

stated that "the more the universe seems comprehensible, the more it seems pointless." In *Dreams of a Final Theory*, Weinberg wrote:

> It would be wonderful to find in the laws of nature a plan prepared by a concerned creator in which human beings played some special role. I find sadness in doubting that we will . . . . The more we refine our understanding of God to make the concept plausible, the more it seems pointless . . . On the rare occasions when conversations over lunch or tea touch on matters of religion, the strongest reaction expressed by most of my fellow physicists is a mild surprise and amusement that anyone still takes all that seriously. Many physicists maintain a nominal affiliation with the faith of their parents, as a form of ethnic identification and for use at weddings and funerals, but few of these physicists seem to pay any attention to their nominal religion's theology.[3]

A question can be raised: is God irrelevant relic of the past? Why have conventional scientific quarters of inquiry neglected advances into the nature of ultimate reality, infinities, consciousness, and biblical scholarship? Are we back to only hearing the individual instruments of the orchestra playing our beloved Symphony, in part 1, chapter 1, or the story of the "Six Blindfolded Men and the Elephant?" These efforts call for joint collaboration among scholars and the steady building of a body of knowledge.

Srinivasa Ramanujan (1887-1920) was India's phenomenal mathematician and the icon of Indian mathematical thought on the Light of God. When fifteen years old, Ramanujan acquired a copy of George Carr's two volumes (1880 and 1886) of approximately 4,400 theorems—classical results, no proofs. Having validated the results in Carr's work (*Synopsis of Elementary Results in Pure and Applied Mathematics*), Ramanujan was developing his own theorems. With a profound insight, untrained and unfamiliar with the accumulated state of knowledge and methods of rigorous proof, he developed his own mathematics and results that went past Carr's work. Ramanujan made contributions to the theory of numbers, the functional equations of the zeta function and the theory of divergent series, and he constructed a theory of nature around *zero* and *infinity*. Zero, to Ramanujan, symbolized *the starting point of everything*, or ultimate reality ('**1**'). Infinity, to him, represented the countless expressions ('=') of ultimacy. The mathematical result of infinity into zero was not one number, but all numbers, each of which relates to discrete acts of nature. He said, "An equation means nothing to me unless it expresses a thought of God." Ramanujan is right! An equation without the Unchanging has no meaning. The reason something is unchangings it is because it is infinite. *We can repeat an experiment an infinite number of times and an equation should remain unchanging.* To Ramanujan, every relationship was an expression of Absolute Reality. To associates, his statements were like what our computer chips would be to Babylonians.

There is a zero in mathematics, but no zero in the fundamental equations of physics! There is infinity in mathematics, but no infinity in the equations of physics. Or is there? More precisely, how are physical quantities generated? How do the concepts of the universal starting boundaries, such as the zero in calculus, and ending boundaries, or the infinity in calculus, enter into the physics of quantities in empty-space?

Akin to zero and infinity in calculus, there is no commonly recognized physical state in the equations of physics expressing the initial conditions (the common starting point boundary) and the final conditions (the common ending point boundary) in empty-space. To compare to the writing on this page, we have not reflected sufficiently enough on format spacing (margins, left and right alignment, left and right indentation, line and page breaks, line spacing) between the letters, nor the medium of this writing. In physical language, we have not reflected sufficiently enough on mathematical terms (the *infinities*) of the void (the Absolute Infinity in which the universe lives and moves and has its being). Why are these boundaries, infinities, always rigid? Why are the laws of physics unchanging? What creates mathematical order, coupling, the Lamb shift, and interaction between the laws of physics?

Emptiness: A Common Starting Point for Science

"Will we ever discover that point? How close are we now?" Steven Weinberg wanted to know. He wrote:

> Speaking of a final theory, a thousand questions and qualifications crowd into the mind. What do we mean by one scientific principle "explaining" another? How do we know that there is a common

starting point for all such explanations? Will we ever discover that point? How close are we now? What will the final theory be like? What parts of our present physics will survive in a final theory? What will it say about life and consciousness? And, when we have our final theory, what will happen to science and to the human spirit?[4]

In walking or measuring steps, we start at the beginning, the zero "boundary" of both activities. That zero starting point forms a common "boundary," or reference frame, to which all explanations may be traced. As a matter of fact, when we measure an object, such as the size of our shoe, there exists a unifying theme of an empty space, receptacle, a *boundary* (in empty-space) and a *limit* (considered empty) to the object and measurement. No matter how close we bring our shoes together, we will have empty-space (zero) between the shoes.

Likewise, when you take steps, no matter how long or short your steps are, you have limit points between steps. In physics the limit points are invariant. The fundamental physical constants attest to the invariance. The Bolzano-Weierstrass theorem states that infinite sequences in a bounded space have limit points. What is the boundary of a boundary? "The boundary of a boundary is zero," declared John Wheeler. But where is zero coupling in the equations of physics? Are there no boundaries between physical quantities, shoes, or letters on this page? Following is what Wheeler wrote of the *zero* boundaries:

> This central principle of algebraic topology, identity, triviality, tautology, though it is, is also the unifying theme of Maxwell electrodynamics, Einstein geometrodynamics, and almost every version of modern field theory. That one can get so much from so little, almost everything from almost nothing, inspires hope that we will someday complete the mathematization of physics and derive everything from nothing, all law from no law.[5]

When a child's balloon keeps shrinking, there is a point at which gas takes up no space at all. Charles' law states that a balloon of gas has to reduce in size to zero space. Zero is at the center of the coordinate system, and zero is embedded in each geometric "boundary."

The big bang model suggests a *point* of cosmic singularity (zero), a frame of reference (boundary) and a one-time cataclysmic explosion (in empty-space) creating all the gas, dust, stars, galaxies, radiation, and spacetime in the universe some 13.7 billion years ago. In the atomic domain, singularities can be observed in parity-violating effects (the symmetry between physical phenomena occurring in right-handed and left-handed coordinate systems, developed by Yang Chen Ning and Tsung-Dao Lee) when elementary particles decay. And when two particles unite, they converge at a point of singularity.

Furthermore, the virtual particles that are constantly appearing and disappearing out of existence and the "cosmic microwave background" radiation, commonly known as the CMB (uniformly and isotropically distributed), exist in empty-space. Light travels in empty-space. Additionally, every type of particle and atom that the laws of physics describe can subsist in zero-dimension empty-space, which endows empty-space with the selfsame "Ultimate Software." The capability for a particular type of particle to exist is a property of every point in the universe.

There are other types of singularities as well. Illustration: the curve $1/x$ has a singularity at the $x = 0$ that mathematicians call a pole. Yet, in the standard laws of physics, neither the zero-dimensional singularity nor the empty-space (Wheeler's "boundary" of a "boundary") is officially recognized. Or is it? Steven Weinberg maintains: "String theory has provided our first plausible candidate for a final theory."[6] Charles Seife makes this point in his own way:

> In string theory, zero has been banished from the universe; there is no such thing as zero distance or zero time. This solves all the infinity problems of quantum mechanics.
>
> Banishing zero also solves the infinity problems in general relativity [the fundamental basis for reasoning of general relativity are: (a) spacetime is a four-dimensional continuum; and (b) the principle of equivalence of gravitational and inertial mass] . . . This singularity makes no sense in quantum mechanics or in general relativity. Zero is the wrench in the works of both great theories. So physicists simply got rid of it.
>
> It is not obvious how to get rid of zero, as zero appears and reappears throughout time and space.[7]

To the particle physicist, strings represent the limit of what they consider to be the smallest entity still having some degree of substantiality, not quite physical zero in essence.

Orders of Infinity: Brilliant and Fascinating

Similar to the challenge of grasping the zero concept, mankind had problems comprehending infinity. As cited in part 1, a number of people in history have been given a glimpse of infinity. Infinity, in its profession, has been recognized as boundless, immeasurable, and limitless. Amir Aczel, describing the mystery latent in the search for infinity, wrote in his *Mystery of the Aleph*:

> Sometime between the fifth and sixth centuries BC, the Greeks discovered infinity. The concept was so overwhelming, so bizarre, so contrary to every human intuition, that it confounded the ancient philosophers and mathematicians who discovered it, causing pain, insanity, and at least one murder. The consequences of the discovery would have a profound affect on the worlds of science, mathematics, philosophy, and religion two and a half millennia later.[8]

The Greek expression for infinity is *apeiron,* denoting unbounded, undefined, or unlimited (Aristotle, 384-322 BC). Infinities made their way into physics (1930) via the young American theorist, Julius Robert Oppenheimer. Oppenheimer found in his calculations that the atom had infinite energy. For four decades infinities seemed a horrendous impediment to the advancement of physics. Physicists get around infinities in their equations by the cancellation of infinities, or through an esoteric new theory of strings. The problem of infinities has not been solved in physics. Or as Weinberg put it, "The problem of infinities is still with us, but it is a problem for the final theory, not for a low-energy approximation like the Standard Model."[9]

Ferdinand Ludwig Philipp, known to us as Georg Cantor (1845-1918), was a brilliant mathematician and the founder of the modern mathematical theory of the infinite. He attempted to solve with mathematics the problem of "orders of infinity" (the well-ordering principle) in an unbroken continuum by deploying sets. In the language of physics, we could characterize his work as follows: Cantor was attempting to decipher orders of infinity by deploying the *ordering principle of physical quantities*, comparable to you explaining the ordering principle of numbers (1, 2, 3, 4, . . .) to the Andromeda scientists.

Bertrand Russell (1872-1970), English mathematician and philosopher, described Cantor in his *Autobiography* as one of the greatest intellects of the nineteenth century. By his own deep research, and penetrating analysis of the central concepts in mathematics, Cantor gained considerable mathematical understanding, the result of a series of leaps of insight into the nature of infinity.

There were others before Cantor (the ancients noted in part 1), as well as his contemporaries, such as Newton, Leibniz, Gauss and Euler, who in their derivations *approached* infinity (the potential infinity of limits). It took the mathematical foresight of Galileo Galilei, and later Cantor, to discover and develop a key property of *actual* infinity. On the basis of his *set* theory, Cantor demonstrated that there are different "orders (the hierarchy) of infinities." In the words of physics we could describe there being different "orders (the hierarchy) of physical quantities."

In embarking upon infinity, Cantor was dealing with the classical problem of "the One and the Many" (One/Many) of the great books of antiquity. Can the world be considered as a unity, as a single fixed object (One), or not? Can the Many independent parts of reality, like dollars, be rolled up into the One currency, or not? In Cantor's terms, "A set is a Many that allows itself to be thought of as a One."[10]

Example: one can have a set (galaxy) of gold, another set (galaxy) of beryllium, and a third set (galaxy) of helium. Thus, we can treat multiplicity (gold, beryllium, and helium) as a mathematical unity in the universe. Further, the amounts of gold, beryllium, and helium, individually could extend to infinity. Here we see a potentiality for a hierarchy of infinities, the hierarchy of successive patterns, like numbers, wherein infinities are organized or classified from small to large.

Cantor symbolized infinity by the letter aleph (א), the first letter in the Hebrew alphabet. For Cantor, the aleph stood for the infinity and Oneness of the Absolute. The logic of set theory was introduced by the British mathematician George Boole (1854) in his *An Investigation of the Laws of Thought*.[11] Boole introduced modern symbolic logic, now called Boolean algebra, the foundation for the logical design of digital computers.

Of specific significance in Cantor's development of set theory is the *empty set*, or the one location that has nothing in it: zero. Similar to numbers 0, 1, 2, 3, Cantor arranged his sets consecutively: "$\aleph_0$, $\aleph_1$, $\aleph_2$, $\aleph_3$, . . ." and so on. Cantor described the smallest (zero) order of infinity (the *empty set* or *null set*) as his aleph-zero ($\aleph_0$). He also determined that for any set there is a larger set, ad infinitum. Thus, he assumed the reality of a hierarchical sequence (connected series, following one another in unbroken order) of alephs. Cantor labeled his hierarchical sequence of alephs ($\aleph_0$, $\aleph_1$, $\aleph_2$, $\aleph_3$, . . .) with the name taf, ת, the last letter in the Hebrew alphabet. Taf, ת, represented the ultimate level of infinity, the Absolute, in which all infinities exist.

The Absolute to Cantor was the ultimate reality, otherwise known as the Most High God. It was an inaccessible and unreachable state of infinity. Consequently, each and every set had to be a part of taf, ת, possessing all alephs. Taf, ת, was the connection between sets. In a sense, it was what the white *empty-space between the letters on this page* signifies for us. Taf, ת, is also what the empty-space between the particles, planets, stars, and galaxies in our universe stands for in physics, astronomy, and astrophysics.

Cantor wanted to demonstrate mathematical *continuity* and the hierarchical structure of "the well-ordering principle" of infinities within the taf, ת. Using our previous example, Cantor sought to do with infinities what the Andromeda scientists wanted to do with numbers. Here is another illustration: Cantor's task was akin to proving mathematically the connection between the empty-spaces of this writing and establishing the ordering principle between the letters (such as a, b, c, d, e, f). Can we help Cantor? Can we unravel the infinite sequence, the global ordering principle, where infinities are ordered from small to large, as we did for the Andromedans with numbers?

The Lessons of Experience: An Ordering of Quantities?

For continuity to work, connectedness of everything to everything and order must exist between sets. One addresses the question: what is the order of infinity of different things (gold, beryllium, and helium) of various dimensions? The well-ordering principle required Cantor to establish a continuity of sequence between the different orders (a consecutive hierarchy of dimensions) of infinity. The challenge concerning the different orders of infinity became known as the Continuum Hypothesis.

It is one challenge to characterize a sequence of alephs ($\aleph_0$, $\aleph_1$, $\aleph_2$, $\aleph_3$, . . .) in taf, ת, on paper, another to place levels upon levels of uncountable infinite numbers in mathematical order, as is done with numbers, or with a, b, c's. We have to be able to compare every possible set with all other sets. Are they equal, or is one greater than the other? What is the ordering principle? This is the crux and the core test of the foundations of physical science, and the shape of nature's final law. Applying the Continuum Hypothesis to the familiar laws of physics, what is the common denominator (global operating software—Cantor's taf, ת) between the physical quantities? What is the "smallest quantity" (Cantor's aleph-zero, $\aleph_0$)? Finally, what is the ordering between time, energy, matter, gravity, electric and magnetic fields, and so forth? Can we express it simply with mathematics in every law of physics?

Associated questions also arise. Are physical quantities, like energy and matter, the same essence (currency) in different containers (amounts, receptacles, sets)? What is that essence? Which fundamental physical quantity is greater, and which is smaller? How do physical quantities connect to zero, infinities, and the empty-space containing all the laws of nature, in which the universe, like a heart, is pulsating (expanding and contracting)? Can we arrange fundamental physical quantities (infinities) consecutively, as we organize the numbers or letters in the alphabet?

To put it another way, which sequence in the International Atomic Weights is right? Gold (G), beryllium (B), helium (H): GBH, GHB, BHG, BGH, HBG, HGB? In our case, I have specified only three chemical elements: gold, beryllium, and helium. Now, find a hierarchical periodic classification of the 118 elements, as Mendeleyev did in chemistry.

For a unified theory of physics, the researcher would need to determine what the common "currency" and the ordering principle of Cantors infinities, the hierarchical periodic classification of the 120 or so fundamental physical quantities, is. No more bartering with grass skirts, black pigs, and arrows. Try to imagine this challenge.

Cantor realized that alephs, like numbers in mathematics (0, 1, 2, 3), letters in an alphabet (a, b, c, d), and elements in the Periodic Table of Elements (hydrogen [atomic number 1]; helium [atomic number 2]; lithium [atomic number 3]; beryllium [atomic number 4]; gold [atomic number 79]), had ordering principles and sequences. However, Cantor could not name another aleph higher than the empty set ($\aleph_0$). Aczel stated:

> Over the next few years, Cantor continued his touch-and-go relationship with the Continuum Hypothesis. After weeks of intensive work he would suddenly be convinced that he found a proof of the theorem. Then he would find a fatal flaw in his derivations, and a few weeks later he would suddenly be sure that he did find a proof of the opposite result. Through this ordeal, and aggravated by Kronecker's continuing attacks, Cantor slowly went mad.[12]

Indeed, Kabbalistic sages warned that the ever-receding environment of infinities and the Absolute Infinity (the knowledge of Ein Sof) and shifting solutions conjured by seekers of ultimacy would be enough to drive the less than virtuous mad. A certain dedication, inner peace, purity of heart, and mental stability is required in reaching for ultimate patterns, be they material or cosmic.

Reexamine Your Beliefs

Leopold Kronecker (1823-1891) was one of Cantor's professors. He had ordinary mathematical insight and usual scholarly competence. Cantor and Kronecker, analogous to Semmelweis, the "Savior of Mothers" from puerperal fever, and his Viennese superior, had different perceptions of the inner nature of reality. Comparable to the Athenians accusing Socrates of corruption of the young with his "Know thyself," Kronecker accused Cantor of being a "corruptor of youth" for teaching the concept of infinities. To Kronecker, infinity was without meaning—nonsense, an act against nature, similar to the chlorine hand wash that a number of Viennese medical men felt to be nonsensical, or to the "atoms and the void" in Plato's view. To Cantor, infinity was the realm of ultimate reality. Kronecker openly mocked and persecuted Cantor on many levels, blocking publication of Cantor's works, referring to his toil as "humbug," and calling him names.

Max Planck made a very interesting observation concerning the conversion of its opponents:

An important scientific innovation rarely makes its way by gradually winning over and converting its opponents; it rarely happens that Saul becomes Paul. What does happen is that its opponents gradually die out, and that the growing generation is familiarized with the ideas from the beginning.[13]

The heart that pursues truth is the heart that loves truth. In ancient times, oppressive beliefs were perpetrated largely through superstition, ignorance, and religion, or dictated by the state. Today, mankind is more developed in its mutual tolerance, charity, and the "holy feeling" of love (an immense love for the whole of humanity), yet the outcome is every now and then related. Even the prodigies of the world can, from time to time, be surprisingly off course.

Case in point: we all recall the flat-Earth philosophy, the Earth-centered universe and the rejection of the Copernican theory. Yet how many of us remember English physicist and mathematician Lord William Thomson Kelvin (1824-1907), who in 1900 declared that science had discovered all the laws of nature? Or Thomas Jefferson's (1743-1826) response to a reported by Silliman and Kingsley on a rain of rock from the sky (meteorite shower), which fell in Weston, Connecticut, in 1807? "I [Jefferson, who revered Newton, studied the *Principia*, mastered calculus, and ranked science as his "supreme delight"] could more easily believe that two Yankee professors would lie than that stones would fall from heaven."[14]

Or Albert Einstein's reasoning on attaining the energy of the atom: "There is not the slightest indication that energy will ever be obtained from the atom."[15] Einstein was not unaccompanied. The British physicist Ernest Rutherford's (1871-1937) influence in science may be equated with that of Faraday and Newton. He was awarded the Nobel Prize in Chemistry (1908) and made president of the Royal Society (1925). In 1909-1911, together with his collaborators in a Manchester, England, laboratory, Rutherford examined an atom by bombarding it with heavier particles. Lord Rutherford, who suggested that the atomic nucleus has internal structure and is composed of protons around which electrons orbit, was still heard to say twenty-two years later, "The energy produced by the breaking down of the atom is a poor kind of thing. Anyone who expects a source of power from transformation of these atoms is talking moonshine."[16]

Likewise, another American experimentalist, Robert Millikan, who was honored with the 1923 Nobel Prize in Physics for his study of the photoelectric effect and elementary charge, and who represented the U.S. (1922-32) on the League of Nations committee for international cooperation, stated in 1928, "There is no likelihood that man can ever tap the power of the atom. The glib supposition of utilizing atomic energy when our coal has run out is a completely unscientific Utopian dream."[17]

Today we know better. Science has not discovered all the laws of nature. Meteorites fall to Earth quite frequently, but because of our atmosphere and our Earth being 70 percent ocean, most of these extraterrestrial missiles are neither known nor ever found. As to Einstein, Rutherford, and Millikan's logic, the heavy, unstable atoms (U-235) can be split by fission. Nuclear fission generates steam, which rotates turbogenerators, thus producing electricity and nuclear waste.

The error of ways into which outwardly flawless humans have fallen, such as the Hubble telescope blunder, the Challenger space shuttle, the Chernobyl and World Trade Center disasters, the burning alive of heretics, the Katyn Massacre, the Hitler-Stalin-Mao Ze-dong devastations, the murdering of Jesus Christ and his apostles, give us a useful perspective on being careful about our preconceived notions and unassailable dogmas.

Prince Louis de Broglie (1892-1987), discoverer of the wave nature of electrons and other particles, for which he was awarded the Nobel Prize (1929), stated:

> History shows that the advances of science have always been frustrated by the tyrannical influences of certain preconceived notions that were turned into unassailable dogmas. For that reason alone, every scientist should periodically make a profound reexamination of his basic principles.[18]

For advancement in any undertaking, an open-minded attitude is a must; rigorously honest *interdisciplinary* peer review and corroboration is a good way to valid science.

Impossible Problem in Mathematics

Georg Cantor was working relentlessly on a tough mathematical challenge; some mathematicians would term it an impossible mathematical problem.

The disappointment Cantor experienced at not being able to crack the well-ordering riddle, along with the Kronecker pressure placed a great deal of stress on Cantor's life. Aczel elaborated:

> Today we understand that Cantor's predicament was not at all due to faulty reasoning. What Cantor didn't know—couldn't possibly know—was that he was working on an impossible problem. We know that the Continuum Hypothesis has no solution within our system of mathematics. Cantor felt alternately sure that the Continuum Hypothesis was true and that its converse was true because there really is no correct answer here . . . The Continuum Hypothesis is undecidable within the realm of our mathematics.[19]

German mathematician Ernst Zermelo also tried his hand at Cantor's unsolved problem in mathematics, through his "axiom of choice." Although Zermelo's proof of the well-ordering principle, through his axiom of choice, was well designed, Zermelo, and later the Israeli mathematician Abraham Fraenkel, could not recommend a method for selecting a choice infinitely many times. Namely, Zermelo could not give an exact solution as to how an infinite sequence of selections could be made.

Kurt Gödel, another brilliant logician-mathematician, known for his two Incompletess Theorems, devoting himself to his project with intensity—and a passion to finding answers to the "problem without a solution" of Cantor's mystery of the alephs and the Continuum Hypothesis of actual infinity. Gödel worked at the University of Vienna and later at the Institute for Advanced Study in Princeton, where he had many inspiring discussions with Einstein. Building on the ideas of Charles Hartshorne, Gödel provided a proof of the existence of a logical God. Aczel, characterizing Gödel's work in set theory, stated:

> Upon his return to Vienna [1935], Gödel is said to have made the statement: *Jetzt, Mengenlehre!* ("Now, set theory!") indicating his desire to devote all his energies to working on the impossible problems of Cantor's actual infinity. He must have been aware that his concentration on these topics was slowly driving him mad, but, like Cantor, he was drawn to infinite light like a moth to fire . . . Gödel's proof, completed during the night of June 14-15, 1937,

implied that the Continuum Hypothesis might work within the set of axioms forming the foundations of mathematics. If the back-implication was proved, the axiom of choice and the Continuum Hypothesis would be shown to be completely independent of mathematics, meaning that within the present system we can't know whether or not Cantor was right about the orders of infinity.[20]

Analogy: How Far Can a One-Winged Bird Fly?

Cantor was attempting to solve without a solution mathematical problem. The vastness of the infinity field (the Continuum Hypothesis) has no answer within our system of mathematics. That is, complex levels of infinity in the Continuum Hypothesis, according to Kurt Gödel, have undecidable ordering. Certain descriptions of the mathematical universe have no solution within the realm of our mathematics, and are completely independent of the axioms of set theory.

Does that mean there is no solution to Steven Weinberg's dreams of a "final theory" and infinities within the foundations of mathematics? The answer is an unquestionable "yes" when viewed through the window of mathematics that Cantor, Zermelo, Gödel, Stephan Banach, Srinivasa Ramanujan, and others, such as Nikolai N. Luzin, L. Bukovky, Paul Cohen, Jack Silver, and Saharon Shelah pursued. Specifically, the Continuum Hypothesis has no solution within our system of mathematics!

In essence, one-winged birds do not fly; flight is possible only with two wings. Namely, we do not hear with our eyes, see with our tongue, or smell with our ears. The limits of the mathematical system cannot differentiate what is bigger and what is smaller without measurement.

A Happy Marriage of Two Methods: A Match Made in Heaven

Can we recall the orchestra example wherein each musician was isolated in a soundproof booth, or the fable of the six blindfolded men characterizing an elephant? One revealed the tail, a different man the ear, one the trunk, another the tusk, still another the leg, and another the eye. Each was "right" about the elephant, but only about one portion. To get an global version of your most beloved symphony or the elephant we have to relate each individual part to the whole.

These examples are similar to the different religions describing the Infinite One, or the various mathematicians characterizing the Continuum Hypothesis. The well-ordering principle is reasonably different by each of their interpretations, and yet they all know that they are characterizing the same creature. The challenge, therefore, is whether we can enter the labyrinth of understanding by the *collective efforts* of many disciplines, as combining seeing, hearing, tasting, smelling, touching and marshaling a more comprehensive picture of the "elephant."

Werner Heisenberg is the "Christopher Columbus" or discoverer of the uncertainty principle, which places limits on our knowledge of the simultaneous values of concurrent atomic level attributes. Heisenberg, when studying the road to knowledge in the days of Democritus, Pythagoras, Plato, Aristotle, and other great thinkers, made a very incisive observation:

> If we look back on the history of the exact sciences, it can perhaps be asserted that correct representation of natural phenomena has evolved from this very tension between the two opposite views. Pure mathematical speculation becomes unfruitful because from playing with the wealth of possible forms it no longer finds its way back to the small number of forms according to which nature is actually constructed. And pure empiricism becomes unfruitful because it eventually bogs down in endless tabulation without inner connection. Only from the tension, the interplay between the wealth of facts and the mathematical forms [the convergence of natural and human science into the unity of knowledge such as integration of what we see, hear, smell, taste, and touch into one] that may possibly be appropriate to them, can decisive advances spring.[21]

When Cantor's foundations of mathematics are unified with the measurements of physics, comparable to hearing with seeing, the complex infinities can be seen in a new light. What is a "problem without a solution" in mathematics has a solution with the measurements of physics!

Example: deep relationships between properties of elements can be ascertained by their atomic weights through the periodic classification of elements, which, as is known, was developed by Mendeleyev. In the same vein, deploying mathematics with the high-precision measurements of physics, I suggest, the well-ordering riddle of an all-encompassing theory—a "theory of everything"—can be deciphered.

5

'1' VIA THE ONE AND THE MANY PRINCIPLE

The notes I handle no better than many pianists.
But the pauses between the notes—ah,
that is where the art resides!

—Arthur Schnabel

One House, Many Windows

Earlier, we saw how Georg Cantor attempted to state the standard challenge of the One and the Many in terms of set theory. Cantor was unifying widely divergent phenomena through different orders (windows) of infinity. He was searching for a way to fit particularized infinite sequences of alephs ($\aleph_0$, $\aleph_1$, $\aleph_2$, $\aleph_3$, . . .) into the ultimate level of infinity, the Absolute, symbolized by the letter taf, ת. Cantor's all-encompassing central core (the Absolute) ultimately integrated and included all orders of infinity, just as this page integrates the different letters of the alphabet.

How do we reconcile, on a common ground, the modern idea of a final Absolute Principle of nature as One ('1') with the classical notion of the Absolute as Many (laws of physics and physical quantities of time and space *in* the '1')? Is there an end to this interpolating process, or as Karl Popper and others have suggested, an infinite chain of more and more fundamental (deeper and deeper) principles churning out an endless sequence of approximations, with no single guiding principle visible at the end? How can we clear away these obscurities for the foundations of physical science?

In the tradition of the Great Books of the Western (and Eastern) thought, the problem of the One and the Many has been addressed largely through the windows of religion, philosophy, mathematics and metaphysics.[1] In the Great Books, the One is expressed as the Being and Oneness, or the Oneness of a Being, togetherness in nature, unity at the heart of Trinity, and so forth. The Many, on the other hand, is presented as emanation of the many *in* the One, duality of God in the world, and types of wholes or complex unities. Clearly, the Bible, the Tao Te Ching, the Bhagavad Gita, the Koran, Plato, Aristotle, Aurelius, Plotinus, Augustine, Aquinas, René Descartes, Benedict de Spinoza, William James, and, to a degree, scientists such as Galileo, Newton, Einstein and Francis Bacon, have served as references.[2]

Aristotle (384-322 BC), recognized as one of the most influential thinkers of ancient times, held that *unity* (a "unity of the Spirit" in Christianity) is the first property of being. For him, as for the many others I have noted, there is no separation between God and the world. They are one:

> Being and unity are the same, and are one thing in the sense that they are implied in one another as are principle and cause. [Furthermore,] "Being" and "Unity" [the House] are among the number of attributes [windows] that follow everything . . . For the same soul ['1'] is usually thought to be a principle alike of rest [stationary house] and of motion [movable windows], so that, if rest is the better of the two, this is the genus into which the soul should have been put.[3]

Benedict de Spinoza, in addressing the One and the Many subject, held like Aristotle that:

> Besides God ['1', the central principle of the universe], no substance can be nor can be conceived. Since God is Being absolutely infinite, of whom no attribute can be denied which expresses the essence of substance, and since He necessarily exists, it follows that if there were any substance besides God, it would have to be explained by some attribute of God, and thus, two substances would exist possessing the same attribute, which is absurd; and therefore there cannot be any substance excepting God, and consequently none other can be conceived.[4]

Spinoza was "God intoxicated," a deep thinker and philosopher who fashioned one of the finest metaphysical structures in Western philosophy. Similar to Henry David Thoreau, Ralph Waldo Emerson, and Alexander Pushkin, Spinoza experienced illumination, spiritual intoxication, and insight, which reveal[5] cosmic (pure) consciousness[6] in the midst of his philosophical writings.

Cutting-Edge Predictability:
The One and the Many through Science

The One/Many concept seems to recur in every period of Eastern and Western thought. Previously we saw that "for hundreds of years there had been speculation concerning the basic structure of both plants and animals. Not until optical instruments were sufficiently developed to reveal cells, however, was it possible to formulate a general hypothesis, the cell theory that satisfactorily explained how plants and animals are organized."[7]

A curious thought arises. How do we characterize the One/Many as it relates to the scientific method? Can we determine a correspondence among infinitely many things through physics, the way Georg Cantor did with the elements of set theory in mathematics? Can the theory of evolution be quantitative and predictive? Can the One/Many relationship be established, connecting corresponding physical quantities with one another? Is it possible, deploying observation, testing, and measurements of the One/Many principle, to predict the laws of physics for new phenomena?

With this in mind, while using the general format of mathematics *and* the high-precision measurements of physics, we will aim to discover those few fundamental principles from which the more detailed rules of law can be derived. Furthermore, together we will attempt to unravel Cantor's continuum problem. Also, we will demonstrate how, by utilizing this method, prediction of new phenomena is possible. In so doing, we will combine practical reason with the cultural-religious traditions of the Great Books and the procedures scientists use to acquire knowledge. Practical reason at this point refers to principles of action, values in business, moral values, and political principles.

When studying physical quantities and fundamental physical constants with high-precision measurements in the usual laws of physics, it is possible to make a *reciprocal* (inverse) relationship between the One and the Many for each physical quantity and constant.[8, 9] Physical quantities and fundamental physical constants of *individual quantities*—the One (such as wavelength, period of harmonic motion)—are the inverse of *group quantities*—the Many (number of waves, frequency)—as shown in Table 3 of the Notes.[10]

Table 3

'1' and the One/Many through the Laws of Physics

(Partial Table 3: see the Notes[10] for a more complete Table 3)

Individual Quantity (q_k)	Group Quantity (Q_k)
Wavelength λ_c	Number of waves n (= $1/\lambda_c$), where $\lambda_c n = 1$.
Period of harmonic motion T	Frequency f (= $1/T$), where $Tf = 1$.
Conductance G	Resistance R (= $1/G$), where $GR = 1$.

Summarizing Table 3:

$$\text{(Individual Quantities)} \times \text{(Group Quantities)} = 1.$$

Or,

$$\text{One} = 1/\text{Many}; \text{Many} = 1/\text{One}.$$

What is significant about the One/Many relationships of physical quantities and fundamental constants, in Table 3, is the *point of inversion*. The central principle in these relations is '1'.[11] The coupling point of inversion is John Wheeler's "boundary of a boundary,"[12] the initial condition of the universe, or the "miracle zone" where the One, individual quantity (i.e., harmonic motion) becomes the Many, group quantity (i.e., frequency) and the Many turn into the One.

The '1', in Table 3, and in all the customary laws of physics, is the *ultimate reference frame*, the principle of maximum transformation, and is *above* the standard laws of physics. '1' materializes in every law of physics and interacts with every law of physics. It obstructs nothing, pervades everything without impediment, and is free from changeability. '1' forms a common *inverting* reference frame (zero starting point, the initial conditions or absolute beginning) to which all respective explanations may be traced. *Each point generates its own reference frame.* In NASA's work of rocket launching, '1' is at the point of liftoff. On the seesaw, '1' is the pivot or the fulcrum point. With numbers, it is the common reference frame of zero. In mathematics the common inverting reference can be demonstrated via the elliptic functions and elliptic integrals, as well as the hyperelliptic functions and hyperelliptic integrals.

The inverse relationship is established by studying the formulations of elliptic functions devised by Karl Gustav Jacob Jacobi (1804-51), German mathematician, and by Niels Henrik Abel (1802-29) of Norway, who, unaware of each other's endeavors, separately founded the theory of elliptic functions. Jacobi was originally recognized for his work on number theory, which gained the respect of Carl Friedrich Gauss (1777-1855), one of the greatest mathematician and physicists of his era, who made major contributions to celestial mechanics. In his 1829 work, *New Foundations of the Theory of Elliptic Functions*, Jacobi demonstrated that elliptic functions can be achieved by inverting elliptic integrals, and, in 1832, that hyperelliptic functions can be achieved by inverting hyperelliptic integrals. The Hamilton-Jacobi equation, which performs an important part in the staging of quantum mechanics, is yet another example of the point of inversion.

Pythagoras explored music experimentally and mathematically. He discovered musical intervals whilst experimenting with the monochord, a one-stringed musical instrument with a movable bridge (fulcrum), to study the principles of tuning theory. Pythagoras found that the most pleasant musical intervals are produced by the simple numerical ratios of the first four integers that derive, respectively, from the relations of string length: the eight, the fifth, the fourth. Upon closer scrutiny of the mathematics of harmonic mediation, the Principle of the One and the Many can be observed. Similar to quantities (Table 3), there is a reciprocal relation between string-length and vibration-frequency (Table 4).[13] By stopping the string at the geometric nodal points, the harmonic overtones may be individually accentuated.

Table 4

'1' and the One/Many through the Harmonic Nodal Points and Overtone Series on the Monochord

q_k (String Length)	Q_k (Vibration Frequency)	Tonal Value
1/8	8, where $(1/8)(8) = 1$	c^2
1/3	3, where $(1/3)(3) = 1$	g
1/2	2, where $(1/2)(2) = 1$	c
1/1	1, where $(1/1)(1) = 1$	C

Deploying Table 3 examples suggests that very weak fields (One) can produce very large effects (Many), not only by interacting in immediate proximity, but throughout systems (galaxies) separated by large distances, and instantaneously, without an upper limit to the speed of transmission. Does this not contradict the accepted rule that information cannot be transmitted faster than the speed of light? Yes. Nevertheless, because '1' is everywhere, '1' does it instantaneously. Notice that comparable to planets and galaxies in the void ('1'), letters and words are placed on this page. Just as changing one word or sentence will directly have an effect on the meaning of the page, so will modifying planets and galaxies at once affect the universe.

Singularity in Physics: The Big Bang Born Anew

Let us call to mind that in the tradition of Eastern and Western wisdom, the problem of the One (the Absolute) and the Many (emanation from the One, duality of God and the world, kinds of complex unities) has been addressed largely through the windows of religion, philosophy, mathematics, and metaphysics. While these approaches are revealing, additional insight can be obtained through physics, as shown in Table 3. Explicitly, every relationship in Table 3 utilizes the same zero dimension point of inversion ('1'), Georg Cantor's empty or null set, thereby providing a framework in which unity and knowledge of the world can be realized. I characterize the zero dimension point in the laws of physics as the "laws of physics singularity." In the logarithmic, or natural log scale, the law of laws singularity ('1') is *zero* $(1 = 10^0 = e^0 = x^0)$.[14]

Smaller than the smallest, a single *point* ('1') is so basic that in modern formulations of Euclidean geometry it is regarded as a fundamental geometrical object, requiring no definition. The law of laws singularity, around which Table 3 relationships and every law of physics revolve (observation, measurement, and the experience of meaning and value), is the *zero-point boundary* for all cosmic (stars, galaxies and clusters of galaxies) and atomic (electrons, protons, and neutrons) structures. '1' is everywhere. By its most profound elegance, unassuming simplicity, and economy, the zero-dimension point is too simple for illustration, too sacred for decoration, and too unpretentious for consideration. The vastness of a point exceeds anything anyone has ever stated of a point.

The "New Testament" of Hinduism is the Upanishads. Upanishads deal with the meaning of ultimacy, life and the universe. The Katha Upanishad characterizing the Unmanifest stated:

It ['1'] is soundless, touchless, formless, imperishable,
Likewise tasteless, constant, odorless,
Without beginning, without end . . . (3.15)

The point has no length, no string or quanta, zero volume, and zero everything. It transcends our normal experience in classical physics. The '1', as a system of infinitely many degrees of freedom, is prior to the definition of any metrical structure, matter, force, or geometry. It has no spatial or temporal relationships, but it is still a topological manifold. Each laws of physics singularity, like a computer chip, in its entire splendor, *contains an imprint of the whole universe*, ad infinitum, so that there is no point-to-point correspondence and recorded image. Everything that has happened, is happening, or is going to happen, is programmed (enfolded) into the '1', the same way that from a block of marble you can carve infinite expressions. The universe exists in the unobserved point (marble) and in a state with a zero total cosmological constant before it is visible in the sphere of observation.

"There are various different 'alternative realities' which are potentially there in quantum state," stated Sir Roger Penrose, Rouse Ball professor of mathematics at the University of Oxford. "Upon measurement, only one of these alternatives becomes realized, and that realization of a particular alternative constitutes the second quantum procedure: the measurement process." For example, electrons appear in two slits at the same time, but, when measured, become visible in a single location. Deploying David Bohm's language, a work artfully written and based on first-rate scholarship and insight, with clarity and wit:

> That is to say, the form and structure of the entire object may be said to be enfolded . . . In terms of the implicate order one may say that everything [like in a hologram, see the Nature of Time and the Nature of Space in chapter 6 below] is enfolded into everything. This contrasts with the explicate order now dominant in physics in which things are unfolded in the sense that each thing lies only in its own particular region of space (and time) and outside the regions belonging to other things.[15]

The curvature of space and time at a point is an unbounded *zero* and *infinity*. The point is irreducible and invariant under all transformations. The '1' makes it possible for the laws of nature to be the same in all reference frames and for all observers, because it brings uniformity to, and connects, them all. The law of physics singularity ("Singularity") enforces mathematical consistency and naked simplicity on the equations of physics. It provides the ground of "renormalization" from which experimental measurements of space, time, and gravity can be derived,[16] facilitating a distinctive nature to our Standard Model of elementary particles throughout all empty-space.

Understanding Complexity in Terms of an Underlying Simplicity

The big bang model at the explosive creation of the universe, from a single point, about 13.7 billion years ago, predicted that distance between next-door galaxies was zero and at the same time the temperature at time zero was on the order of 10^9 K. When one studies cosmic singularity with equations of physics, one realizes that at zero distance and zero time ('1'), the unchanging laws of nature are "no law," like the empty-space between letters on this page. At the Singularity, space and time come to a sudden end and the known laws of science, and our capability to predict the future breaks down. Also, at the Singularity, time and space come into being with the universe, and the known laws of physics are transformed into other laws of physics, quantities, and fundamental constants.[17]

The '1' is the Law without law, free zone, or "no man's land" of physics. It is the Principle *above* the laws of physics, wherein "the hidden benefits" of great cosmic shift, or the transformation (miracles) from one state to another state, take place. We can go from A to Z in empty-space. Positioned as a "boundary of a boundary" midway between microcosm and macrocosm, order and disorder, a point can have infinity of points within itself. It is a crossroad of any number of planes or dimensions and the pivot zone of miscellaneous physical events in the universe.

According to Einstein, the force of gravity determines the arrangements of everything in space. Consistent with conventional physics, in Table 3, how things behave in the universe come from the '1'. To be exact, the Unchanging State, '1', determines the blueprint of the laws of physics, not gravity.

Paul Dirac and others thought it was unreasonable to assume that the laws of physics have never changed. In line with the '1' mathematics, the laws of physics can never change. However, *what is constantly changing, are the relationships between points (fundamental physical constants)*. For example, the same laws of physics apply to the electron, proton and neutron, yet, their fundamental constant are different.[18]

The '1' (Table 3) is so rigid, so severe, that it cannot be distorted into some altered mathematical principle without interjecting nonsense. '1' can be considered the overlooked a priori principle, and the meeting ground for various levels of reality. It is the synchronization point to absolute balance, freedom, and measurement. It is the foundation of all objects, events and processes, boundless and independent of nature but interacting with it. '1' extends the range of human experience leading to mathematical secrets that are at the heart of the universe, like a cosmic "Rosetta stone," making that which is verified by measurement physics and the sacred One.

Kingdom of God: The Smallest of All Seeds

Jesus likens the smallest of all seeds (mustard seed: Mt 13:31; Mk 4:31; Lk 13:19) to the kingdom of God. Tukaram Maharaj, a great poet-saint of India, wrote, "The Lord of the universe builds a tiny house the size of a sesame seed and lives inside it." Sanskrit characterizes the point as *bindu*, *sunya-bindu* (an empty dot, spot), or *Mahabindu* (the Great Point). Bindu denotes a starting point from which all lines and forms may emerge, the emanation of something from nothing. It contains all possibilities of becoming and is a representation for the universe in its unmanifest state.

John D. Barrow is the professor and director of the Astronomy Centre at the University of Sussex, United Kingdom. He has written more than 240 research papers and 10 books in astrophysics and cosmology. In his magisterial *The Book of Nothing*, packed with insight and written with clarity and enthusiasm, Barrow examines different aspects of "nothingness" ('1'), from the void of philosophers to the zero of mathematicians, from the ether to the quantum vacuum, and from Shakespeare to the null set of Cantor. Addressing the Indian use of the word *bindu*, Barrow wrote:

> *Bindu* is used to describe the most insignificant geometrical object, a single point or a circle shrunk down to its centre where it has no finite extent. Literally, it signifies just a "point," but it symbolizes the essence of the Universe before it materialized into the solid world of appearances that we experience. It represents the uncreated Universe from which all things can be created. This creative potential was revealed by means of a simple analogy. For, by its motion, a single dot can generate lines, by whose motion can be generated planes, by whose motion can be generated all of three-dimensional space around us. The *bindu* was the Nothing from which everything could flow. [19]

Brihad-Aranyaka Upanishad represents the ruler of everything with a grain of rice or barley and states that this person is made of *mind*:

> This person (*purusa*) here in the heart is made of mind, is of the same nature of light, is like a little grain of rice, is a grain of barley.

> This very one is ruler of everything, is lord of everything, governs this whole universe, whatsoever there is.

When we consider the zero-dimension point in the One and the Many relationship, depicted in Table 3, we find that '1'—*One* (where log of '1' is zero) and the inverse of '1', *Many* (where inverse of log '1' is undeterminable, Absolute Infinity) are also equal to '1'. Thus, the central principle of the universe, the Law of laws, is in zero (the point)—and the Absolute Infinity (empty-space, Spirit).

Note: time and space (like the basic monetary currency of United Kingdom, the pound, or of the United States, the dollar), are distinctive physical quantities (monetary measures), and have therefore different quantization (currency exchange), i.e., discrete values to calculate or express the behavior of a physical system. A four-dimensional spacetime continuum is made up of three spatial dimensions (three dollars) and one time (one pound) dimension. The problem with general relativity is that spacetime as a four-dimensional continuum, which without converting space into time and vice versa, will defy quantization in elementary particle physics. That is, without converting pounds into dollars or vice versa, you cannot add up pounds to dollars in a vertical column of numbers, at the same time. Empty-space is based on the assumption of the pre-quantum state of no time or space: '1'.

Divide any number by infinity, and zero is the result; divide any number by zero, and we have infinity. Square zero, and the resultant is zero. Square infinity, and cause infinity. In effect, '1', the Brunelleschi's (1425) vanishing point in the axis of a drawing of a prominent Florentine structure, the Baptistery, characterizes the smallest of the smallest and the largest of the largest.

The smallest of the smallest is the zero-dimensional point or Cantor's null set. The largest of the largest is radiation-free empty-space, equivalently the "continuum in its ground state," equivalently Cantor's ultimate level of infinity, or the lowest energy state. Zero and infinity are united in the vanishing point ('1')! Here, "at home," when stilling the mind, one can simultaneously experience the zero and infinity condition of the crystal-clear Light or pre-physical potentiality. Maharaj Tukaram characterized his zero and infinity experience thusly,

> I am even smaller than the atom, but I have expanded to the outer limits of space . . . I have transcended space and time.

Through the One and the Many means of high-precision measurements of science, Cantor's smallest order of infinity (the empty or null set), aleph-zero ($\aleph_0$), and the ultimate level of infinity, the Absolute, symbolized by letter taf, ת, are collectively shared by '1' in physics. The '1' enables the zero order of infinity and the ultimate level of infinity to be present at every point of the universe, thus making physics at its foundation, extraordinarily beautiful, stunningly simple, continuous, based on a straightforward underlying principle, and embodied in a rigid mathematical structure. As the vacuum has structure in classical general relativity, '1' (Table 3) has structure in the general formalism of physics.

Just as the point and its inverse can be represented with the '1', so the equality and its inverse can be represented with equality '=', in the standard laws of physics, making '1' with equality '=' Absolute and infinite at every point of the universe.[20]

The Empty-Space in Science:
New Vision through Old Eyes

The underpinning of the electromagnetic field is the empty-space. Hendrik Antoon Lorentz, one of the greatest minds in fundamental physics, demonstrated, with empirical science, that in order to have the electromagnetic field empty-space is required. Michael Faraday, James Clerk Maxwell, André Marie Ampere, Carl Friedrich Gauss, Georg Friedrich Bernhard Riemann, and other brilliant thinkers formulated diverse laws and experiments involving atoms and particles moving through the "empty-space" ('1'), "medium," or "ether," as it was then expressed.

Recently, the empty-space or "vacuum" is considered by a stellar list of contributors as the fundamental edifice of modern physics. The list includes, David Finkelstein (Georgia Institute of Technology), Roger Penrose (Oxford University), Simon Saunders (Harvard University), Harvey Brown (Oxford University), Gordon Fleming (Pennsylvania State University), D. Sciama (International School for Advanced Studies, Trieste), I. Aitchison (Oxford University), Robert Weingard (Rutgers University), Basil Hiley (University of London), Michael Atiyah (Trinity College, Cambridge), and Peter Braam (University of Utah).

Einstein, one of the world's greatest minds, played a significant part in the intellectual life around the world spanning from relativity, atomic energy, and religion, to economics, government, and human rights. Einstein characterized the '1' as "ether," which "is precisely not to be influenced, since it is changeless and unmovable, either by configuration of matter, or by anything else. For this reason, one may call it "absolute." Einstein wrote:

> That this ether is not to be supposed a phantasy of the Newtonian theory, but that there corresponds to the concept of a certain reality in nature . . . We therefore have to consider the mechanical ether which Newton calls "absolute space" as some kind of physical reality . . . we will not be able to do without the ether in theoretical physics, i.e., a continuum [is employed to signify a continuous region of mathematical space, such as a line, area, or volume] which is equipped with physical properties; for the general theory of relativity, whose basic points of view physicists surely will always maintain, excludes direct distant action. But every contiguous action theory presumes continuous fields, and therefore also the existence of an "ether."[21]

In a message conveyed at Leyden, Holland, in 1953, for the commemoration of the one-hundredth anniversary of the birth of Hendrik Antoon Lorentz, Einstein equated "ether" to empty-space:

> At the turn of the century, the theoretical physicists of all nations considered H. A. Lorentz as the leading mind among them, and rightly so. The physicists of our time are mostly not fully aware of the decisive part which H. A. Lorentz played in shaping the fundamental ideas in theoretical physics . . . He meant more to me personally [Einstein] than anybody else I have met in my lifetime . . . He [Lorentz] based his investigation [of all electromagnetic phenomena known at the time] with unfaltering consistency upon the following hypotheses:
> The seat [foundation] of the electromagnetic field is the empty-space . . . It is a work of such consistency, lucidity, and beauty as has only rarely been attained in an empirical science . . . Indeed, the essential step was just the reduction of electromagnetism to Maxwell's equations in empty-space or—as it was expressed at that time—in ether.[22]

Stark Truths:
Nudity in Richness and Freshness of Detail

Leonardo da Vinci described the nothing as the greatest among us, stating, "Among the great things, which are found among us the existence of nothing is the greatest."[23] The Emperor of Emperors ('1'), when at home, not in exile as manifestation, has no clothes—not a stitch.

Currently, scientists depict the "ultimate space" as a fathomless structure—an uncountable "infinite manifold of coordinate systems,"[24] abandoning the traditional starting point of space-time. Basil Hiley, in "Vacuum or Holomovement," a chapter in the book *Philosophy of Vacuum*, calls this fundamental point prior to the introduction of matter or geometry "pre-space."[25] Other theorists characterize that which is clear of relative space/time, along with all other physical manifestations, as an un-modulated primordial vacuum.

It has also been described as the "Absolute Nothingness" or a vacuum state lacking field quanta, by Aitchison,[26] Ambjorn and Wolfram,[27] Atiyah,[28] Coleman,[29] Fleming,[30] Weingart,[31] and many others. In the language of quantum theorist David Finkelstein (head of the School of Physics at Georgia Institute of Technology), based on his work supported by the National Science Foundation, the not-modulated vacuum prior to space is denoted by preexistent "causal networks":

> A general theory of the vacuum is thus a theory of everything, a universal theory. It would be appropriate to call the vacuum "ether" once again, as long as we remember its local Lorentz invariance. The most workable theories of the vacuum today are quantum field theories. In these the vacuum serves as the law of nature, as reviewed below. The structure of the vacuum is the central problem of physics today; the fusion of the theories of gravity and the quantum is a subproblem.[32]

John Davidson in his epic, *The Secret of the Creative Vacuum*, reveals the significance of the vacuum as a real energy field, outlining some of the profound and fascinating technological changes it will bring, including unconstrained energy supplies:

While a number of physicists, including Harold Aspden, Paul Dirac, Shiuji Inomata, Thomas Bearden and many others, have postulated the existence of the vacuum as a real energy field, the conventional view remains that it really is nothing—but with special dimensions. To contemplate that it could indeed be something carries too many implications, not the least of which is a return to the concept of an ether—a subject considered medieval, if not downright heretical . . .

Probably the nearest that quantum theorists have come to considering the vacuum as a real entity is in *quantum field* and *S-matrix* theories. There is no doubt that physicists do consider the vacuum to be of considerable importance, a seething mass of *virtual* particles, particles which arise and disappear at ultra-high speeds, and this fascinating topic will not be neglected.[33]

Thus, from Lorentz to Einstein to modern theorists, the zero-point boundary ('1') refuses to disappear. It remains a tangible placeholder in the universe of science.

One More Time:
The Fabric of Consciousness Is Emptiness

Mahamudra,[34] Milarepa,[35] Taimni,[36] and Rinpoche[37] considered the "empty-space" as the "still mind" (the deepest state of consciousness) or the ground state of phenomena out of which the universe materializes. Gautama set forth his most profound teachings on "emptiness" in the Prajna Paramita Sutra (Perfection of Wisdom Sutras), wherein he pointed out, "Mind is emptiness." In addition, "All phenomena are preceded by the mind. When the mind is comprehended, all phenomena are comprehended." Period.

This means, from the Imperishable or consciousness the universe comes out (God or Brahman created the world out of Himself) and into the Imperishable the universe will dissolve or vanish. Therefore, *the essence of our mind causes the type of world we manifest and experience.*

The makeup of our mind or consciousness assists in the construction of interactions, establishing what is recognized and blossoms in '1': "All appearances perceived and/or experienced by the mind are, in fact, mental projections [modulations]. They are the mind's play.[38] Emerson put it this way: "The whole of nature is a metaphor [image] of the human mind."[39]

Previously, we took into consideration John von Neumann's "consciousness-created world," and Max Planck's statement, "In the last analysis, we ourselves are part of nature, and, therefore, part of the mystery that we are trying to solve." Planck, whom I place in a league of Isaac Newton, Hendrik Antoon Lorentz, Albert Einstein, Srinivasa Ramanujan, John von Neumann, and Kurt Gödel, similar to Jesus and Gautama understood that "This Mind" is the foundation of all visible and invisible Reality,

> As a man who has devoted his whole life to the most clearheaded science, to the study of matter, I can tell you as the result of my research about the atoms, this much: there is no matter as such!
>
> All matter originates and exists only by virtue of a force which brings the particles of an atom to vibration and holds this most minute solar system of the atom together . . . We must assume behind this force the existence of conscious and intelligent Mind. This Mind is the matrix of all matter.[40]

I should like to emphasize that invariance in the laws of physics and the physical notion of a transformation between two systems of coordinates suggest the existence of the Absolute, whether named the Great Unseen Power of the universe or a cosmic principle, as the source of all things that is *above* the laws of nature. Furthermore, the One and the Many examples, in Table 3, suggest that the fundamental ideas of the Judeo-Christian thinkers in the Western world correlate with the insights of the Eastern world.

Everything resides within the ordering principle of the universe that is prior to time and space and the definition of any metrical structure. Or as we read earlier: "Where can I go from your spirit ['1']? From your presence where can I flee? If I go up to the heavens, you are there; if I sink to the nether world, you are present there."

6

THE THEORY OF EVERYTHING: '1'

Unless there is a void with a separate being of its own,
"what is" cannot be moved—nor again can it be "many," since there
is nothing to keep things apart.

—Leucippus

Singularity = 1/(Empty-Space)

Steven Weinberg, in his remarkable *Dreams of a Final Theory*, discusses
Einstein's struggle in the search for a unified theory of physics:

> In our century it was Albert Einstein who most explicitly pursued
> the goal of a final theory. As his biographer Abraham Pais puts it,
> "Einstein is a typical Old Testament figure, with the Jehovah-type
> attitude that there is a law and one must find it." The last thirty
> years of Einstein's life were largely devoted to a search for a so-called
> unified field theory that would unify James Clerk Maxwell's theory
> of electromagnetism with the general theory of relativity, Einstein's
> theory of gravitation. Einstein's attempt was not successful, and
> with hindsight we can now see that it was misconceived. Not only
> did Einstein reject quantum mechanics; the scope of his effort was
> too narrow. Electromagnetism and gravitation happen to be the
> only fundamental forces that are evident in everyday life (and the
> only forces that were known when Einstein was a young man),
> but there are other kinds of force in nature, including the weak
> and strong nuclear forces. [The weak force and the strong force are
> relatively very strong forces, compared with the gravitational force,
> but have limited range.] Indeed, the progress that has been made

toward unification has been in unifying Maxwell's theory of the electromagnetic force with the theory of the weak nuclear force, not with the theory of gravitation, where the problem of infinities has been much harder to resolve. Nevertheless, Einstein's struggle is our struggle today. It is the search for a final theory.[1]

As I suggested in part 2, chapter 5, through the means of the Principle of the One and the Many, compelling evidence has surfaced of two crucial fundamentals leading to the central principle of the universe: (1) the dimensionless point (the dimensionless One or the Singularity); and (2) the inverse of the dimensionless point (the dimensionless Many, the empty-space or Absolute space). Namely, the "dimensionless smallest of the smallest" or zero, and the dimensionless "largest of the largest" or Absolute space have been formulated and verified, without conscious realization, in our laws of physics.

Additionally, there is experimental evidence that the "smallest of the smallest," the point, and the inverse, the "largest of the largest," the empty-space continuum, including the infinities, present at every point of nature, are represented with a '1' in the laws of physics. Therefore, the vacuum equation for the ordering principle of the universe or the theory of physical vacuum takes the form of '1'.

The Empty-Space: Explore! Understand! Learn!

The empty-space serves as the absolute receptacle or a container behind the relative manifestation. That is, '1' or empty-space (analogous to zero '0'—pre-number) has underlying constancy, priority with profound relevance to our own existence. '1' is the timeless ground of being or participatory consciousness, often equated with God of the universe, and where all of its activities come to pass. The early Christian church referred to this principle as "creation ex nihilo"—creation out of or from nothing.

Max Planck in "From the Relative to the Absolute," a lecture presented at the University of Munich in 1924, speaks of the absolute behind the relative,[2]

If space and time have been denied the character of the absolute, that does not mean that the absolute has been removed as such—

it has been moved further out, into the metrics of the four dimensional manifold . . . this metric represents something independent of all arbitrariness and therefore something absolute. Thus also in the often-misunderstood "theory of relativity," *the absolute is not abolished*. On the contrary, it has been more precisely articulated [through fundamental constants], that, and how, *physics is founded everywhere on an absolute in external reality* [emphasis added].[3]

Martin Buber depicts God in his famous book *I and Thou* (1923) as the ultimate Thou (Absolute Infinity), the Thou who can never become an It. While writing the book, Buber was reflecting on his conception of two primary relationships: I-Thou and I-It. When in that deep state of thought on edgelessness or infinity without a beginning or end, similar to Georg Cantor, Kurt Gödel, and others (i.e., the Greeks, Kabbalists) who tried to contemplate infinity, Buber noticed that the more he thought of the Infinite, the more he was at risk of the menace of madness:

> A necessity I could not imagine swept over me: I had to try again and again to imagine the edge of space, or its edgelessness, or time without a beginning or end, and both were equally impossible, equally hopeless . . . Under an irresistible compulsion I reeled from one to the other, at times so closely threatened with the danger of madness that I seriously thought of avoiding it by suicide.[4]

Recall that American nuclear physicist Robert Oppenheimer observed in his calculations that the atom had an infinite energy, which means infinities exists at every point in the universe. Also known is that Hindu, Buddhist and Taoist contemplatives entered the secret orchard of the Infinite Splendor with much preparation and purification. The Kabbalists require mental and emotional strength, the stability of a marriage, high moral values, and prior rabbinic knowledge before entering the closeness of the Ein Sof, the knowledge of Absolute Infinity.

Greeks and others, not approaching the Infinite Splendor with prior grounding, experienced mental pressure and sometimes pain. Gopi Krishna, in his writings, goes into a great depth about the dangers of pursuing Absolute Infinity without adequate grounding and purification. In the early days of my spiritual growth, I discovered that when I synchronized my mind to the clear Light, or tried to merge myself in it, it was challenging to remain in that state for a long extent of time. Initially, the duration would be five to ten minutes. Then it would be four or six months between individual occurrences. It was not easy to recreate the state of awareness of one's identity with the Absolute. I did not come to understand the fine points of the process.

However, as time passed, by doing my best every time, and making love with every moment, as discussed in part 1, chapter 3, I was able to "get the bugs out of the process." Now, most of the time, I can arrive at the clear Light of Oneness within a minute or two, and dwell in that state for hours. You realize that the Blessed Holy Love, similar to ocean for waves, is not out there in outer space but within us and around us. Also, when my daily life is peaceful, I am very creative and productive. Conversely, whenever there is stress, my productivity drastically diminishes.

Motion: Tick-tock, Tick-tock, the Nature of Time

"What is time?" wrote Saint Augustine. "If no-one asks me, I know. If I want to explain it to someone who asks me, I do not know." "Space and time form the very fabric of the cosmos," writes Freeman Dyson in *The New York Review of Books*. "Yet they remain among the most mysterious of concepts. Is space an entity? Why does time have a direction? Could the universe exist without space and time? Can we travel to the past?"

In examining interactions between particles through the inversion process, physicists have observed "duality" (the Principle of the One and the Many) between different segments of mathematical concepts in string and superstring theories. John Barrow, in his superb book *The Universe That Discovered Itself* is an inspiration to those who want to explore innovative approaches to time and timelessness:

> Duality may yet be the route to the deepest secrets of Nature. The form possessed by string theories corresponds to being able to change any distance, D, into its inverse, 1/D, yet leave the theory unchanged. This is remarkable because physicists are used to being able to solve their equations in the situation where the distance between interacting particles is large, so that the interactions are weak. But when the distances are small,

interactions get stronger, and everything becomes intractably complicated [the closer one is to the light the more light, and conversely the farther one is from the light the less light]. String theory offers a tantalizing hint that a solution found in the "easy" regime of large distances and low energies might allow itself to be straightforwardly manipulated into the solution for the small-distance high-energy regime . . . Physically, these duality transformations linking the high—and low-energy behaviors of the strings are analogous to the way in which some substances can manifest themselves in superficially different ways, for example as steam, water, or ice, despite the fact that all of these phases possess the same chemical makeup.[5]

John Barrow has a point, "Duality may yet be the route to the deepest secrets of Nature." What has been disguised in the ever-moving world of D and its inverse, 1/D, in the equations of physics, is the ultimate furniture of timelessness, the '1'; John Wheeler's "boundary of a boundary" facilitating D to become its inverse, 1/D.

Table 3 illustrates that inversion affects not only distances, or an abstract infinite-dimensional space called Hilbert space, as the theorists have discovered, but Augustine's awareness of time, Einstein's theory of relativity, and the ever-moving universe of daily events.[6] Next, inversion incorporates limits enabling us to predict inverse quantities, inverse fundamental constants, laws of physics, and their hierarchical structure,[7] which I will discuss in the next chapter, and which Georg Cantor was trying to solve through his well-ordering principle.

"Predictions are hard to make, especially about the future," said Nobel physicist Niels Bohr. For instance, is it feasible to find eternity in the midst of time? Speculations on the fabric or the "nature of time," the quantum universe splits over time into multiple universes, the slowing of time, the relativity of simultaneity, the origin of time, ultramicroscopic makeup of time, time travel, time without a beginning or end, departing to the future, the age of the universe, or visiting the past have long fascinated philosophers, physicists, and lay people alike. "Time is at the heart of all that is important to human beings," said Bernard d'Espagnat. "Despite all this," writes Igor Novikov, in *The River of Time*, "in spite of all the progress, the nature of time remains to a large extent a mystery for us."

Brian Greene, one of the world's leading string theorists, in his elegant *The Fabric of the Cosmos: Space, Time, and the Texture of Reality*, writes, "After centuries of thought, we still can only portray space and time as the most familiar of strangers. They unabashedly wend their way through our lives, but adroitly conceal their fundamental makeup from the very perceptions they so fully inform and influence." Time, by its very nature, like a young stallion, rigorously resists being put in straps and buckles.

"We are still a long way from solving the riddle of time," states Paul Davies, in his magnificent book *About Time*. Furthermore, Davies portrays with richness and freshness of detail, "If we identify Einstein's theory of relativity with the modern era of physics, then I contend that modern physics will not solve the riddle of time."

Earlier I pointed out that Einstein's general relativity spacetime is a four-dimensional continuum and that without conversion of time into space and vice versa (by means of simultaneous equations and fundamental physical constants in the laws of physics), spacetime will defy quantization; without a currency exchange, you cannot compute with pounds and dollars at the same time and be right. Another example. You probably recall the Readers Digest airliner-refueling story. Instead of the British imperial gallon (4.546 liters per gallon), which the pilot called for, a mechanic used the liter measure to refuel the jumbo jet. You appreciate the end result of 10,000 British imperial gallons and the 10,000 liters on the mileage of an airliner? Less than halfway to destination, at 33,000 feet, one engine after another died out. There was no fuel in the tanks. You know the rest of the story: the pilot glided the airliner and then crash-landed it on a deserted airstrip. The aircraft was destroyed; no one died.

Paul Davies is right; the nature of time will not be solved from physics that does not relate to some standard or measure; the obstacles to doing so are far from insignificant. However, deploying identical measure (scale invariance) with information of the formalism of physics, through the Principle of the One and the Many, we can dig up rare gems of time.

Let me illustrate this point. *Motion between two points in* '1' can be described in terms of *linear velocity*, *v*, in meters per second, *angular velocity*, *w*, in radians per second, and *frequency of motion*, *f*, in cycles per second. It should be noted that the meter, second, radian, and cycle are each a unit of measurement between two agreed points in '1'. To measure meters per second, we need four points, two for meter and two for second, and so on. Utilizing the One and the Many principle, we learn that *the inverse of motion is time*. Specifically, *time is the quantum* (packet, slice, or step) *of motion*; time is the smallest excitation of a quantized motion. When velocity is 299,790,000 meters per second then time is 1/ (299,790,000) seconds per meter.

In 1900 Max Planck showed that thermal radiation, such as light, is emitted, transmitted, and absorbed in discrete energy packets, or quanta. The significance of Plank's mathematical formulations in this context is that *motion, is made up of many quanta or portions of time*, just as a mile is a unit of distance on land that is made up of many (5,280) feet or (1609) meters. Utilizing the equilibrium point of inversion, '1', we derive three quantities of time.

Linear time, t (1/linear velocity), is symbolized in units of *seconds* per meter. Linear time is a measure of time delay in electric wires of computers per meter of wire or the astronomical distance that light travels in a year. The elementary quantum of linear time, or the elementary quantum of the speed of light in vacuum is t = 3.3356×10^{-9} ($1/2.9979 \times 10^8$) seconds/ meter, where the speed of light in vacuum is 2.9979×10^8 meters per second. And so a light-year is equivalent to 9.4607×10^{15} meters/second, or 2.8362×10^{24} (2.8 with 24 zeros) elementary quanta of linear time.

Angular time, t (1/angular velocity) is characterized in *seconds* per radian. Angular time is a rotational measure of time used in our everyday clocks. The elementary quantum of angular time is t = 1.1812×10^{-22} seconds/radian. Indeed, very, very small.

Periodic time, T (period of harmonic motion = 1/frequency) is described in *seconds* per cycle. A pendulum demonstrates a characteristic frequency or periodicity. The elementary quantum of periodic time is T = 8.0933×10^{-21} seconds/cycle.

Thus, because the inverse of motion is time, we can observe six states (descriptions, expressions) of motion. Three in quantum form, as "one" physical quantity (linear time, angular time, and periodic time), and three in non-quantum form, "many" physical quantities (linear velocity, angular velocity, and period of harmonic motion).

In the past we have used cycles of astronomical phenomena, mechanical vibrations (such as those of a pendulum or a quartz crystal), and radiation frequency to measure time. Because we made no distinction between the different quantities of time (linear, angular, and periodic), we found it difficult to understand *time dilation* in relativity theory, the slowing of clocks (the so-called clock paradox), atomic reactions, and biological processes (twin paradox), such as aging.

What is within time and what is beyond time? What does "now" mean? Is the present (the universe's endeavor to entertain itself and to become aware of itself) constantly changing vis-à-vis the future in '1'? Recall that Einstein found in the principle now known as the "relativity of simultaneity" that the present ("now") is not identical for everyone; "time is relative." Namely, because time is the inverse of motion, time is essentially personal and subjective: you determine your tune of life, the quality of your understanding of yourself, and the nature of your personal universe.

Einstein is right, from the perspective of '1', the present is not the same for everybody. Are not the future and the past relative to the in-motion point of the turning present? Put simply, the "arrow of time," wherein each observer has her or his own measure in relationship to '1', can fascinate us with its unexpected implications, depending on how we are moving through timeless reality ('1'). In effect, *each part of '1' has its own methods for "music"* (inner peace, purity of heart, service) *and "performance."* Two hundred seventy years before Einstein, Angelus Silesius made this statement: "Time is of your own making, its clock ticks in your head [consciousness]. The moment you stop thought [the relativity of motion], time too stops dead."[8]

'1' and Motion: The Nature of Space

Similar to the nature of time, it has been a challenge for both physicists and mathematicians (Poincaré, Lorentz, Maxwell, Einstein, Riemann, Leibniz, Minkowski, Reichenbach, Hilbert, Connes, etc.) and philosophers (Kant, Locke, Berkeley, Descartes, Hume, Whitehead, et al.) to arrive at the fundamental nature of space. Can it be solved? Can we turn these words into a precise mathematical statement? Let us explore.

As stated earlier, the ultimate concept of the zero-state space ("In him we live and move and have our being" [Acts 17:28]) has been perceived by the ancients: Moses,[9] David,[10] Solomon,[11] Jeremiah,[12] John,[13] Virgil,[14], Philo,[15] Bhagavad Gita,[16] Pythagoras, Thales, Anaxagoras, et al.

Newton had inspired insights into the nature of the absolute space. Gauss, who used to joke that he could calculate before he could talk, considered the three dimensions of space as a specific peculiarity of the human soul. Poincaré attempted to show the three dimensions of space through the concept of dimension and topological consideration. His thoughts are particularly welcome:

> The most important of all theorems of analysis is the statement that space has three dimensions . . . What do we mean when we say that space has three dimensions? . . . To separate space into parts, cuts are necessary which we call surfaces; to disconnect surfaces, cuts are necessary which we call lines; to divide lines, cuts are necessary which we call points. But we cannot go further, since a point, not being a continuum, cannot be divided. Therefore, lines that can be disconnected by cuts, which themselves are not continua, are continua of one dimension; surfaces that can be separated into parts by parts by one dimensional continua are continua of two dimension; and finally space, which can be separated by two-dimensional continua, is a continuum of three dimensions.[17]

Yes, space has the three dimensions. But how do we cut up the symbolic bread? In balls, or rings, or do we reduce it to tidbit crumbs? How do we unify these mathematical space dimensions with physics and the foundation of our understanding of ourselves as Infinite Splendor? Heraclitus argued that our limited senses, "Eyes and ears are bad witnesses to men with souls who do not understand their [unlimited] language."

As with time, through '1', motion, and the Principle of the One and the Many, we can shed additional light on the nature of space and our Infinite Splendor. Specifically, I notice six states (metaphors, expressions) of space. Two are dimensionless and four are dimensional.

The *dimensionless states of space* are the *point* (Singularity), which, as Poincaré pointed out, cannot be divided, and its *inverse*, the *Absolute* or *empty-space*. Both the point (as "one") and the empty-space (as "many"), between the stars or the particles in an atom, are characterized in the laws of physics with a symbol '1'. Similar to our consciousness, or white page for letters, '1', our Infinite Splendor, has neither limits nor dimensions. Empty-space, or the connecting zero-state, can be expressed in *meters* per meter and I equate to unmanifest reality or the pre-quantum fact. From the mathematical physics point of view it means the '1' state is the state in which all modes are unexcited, and the field is in its ground (zero) state, where '1' underlies, penetrates, transforms, unifies, and is prior to all manifestation, curved space, black holes, quantum superpositions, or knowledge.

Both the point and the empty-space is the Common Ground that continues beyond the confines of our observable universe and in which an infinite number of other universes (a multiverse), like our heart, pulsate. Quantum mechanics predicts a vast number of such parallel universes by broadening the concept of "elsewhere." These universes are located elsewhere, not in dimensional space but in an abstract realm of the pre-quantum space. Empty-space is the Unchanging State where the points and the primes in the world of mathematics line up and from where the CMB radiation starts. Because the empty-space is unchanging, all laws of physics are unchanging, enabling us, like tuning in to TV programs to interact in a multiverse.

The four *dimensional states of space* are *periodic space* (as "one" physical state and its inverse as "many" physical states) and *angular space* (as "one" physical state and its inverse as "many" physical states). Periodic space and angular space are *compound motions* in '1'. That is, pair of motions when integrated tends to neutralize each other thus producing a compound "secondary motion," which manifests as periodic or angular space. We can draw a parallel to complementary color where one of a pair of colors opposed to the other element of the pair on a schematic chart or scale, as green opposed to red, that when integrated tend to neutralize each other. In a complementary angle either of two angles that added together produce and angle of 90^0

Periodic space, as "one" physical state (quantum) quantity, is characterized in the laws of physics as wavelength, λ (2.4263×10^{-12}), in meters per cycle, while periodic space as "many" is characterized as number of wavelengths ($n = 1/\lambda$, see Table 3) and is expressed in cycles per meter. Periodic space is a compound motion quantity. It consist of linear velocity (v) and periodic time (T) in '1', where $\lambda = vT$ and v is velocity of light in vacuum (2.9979×10^8), in meters per second, and T is the elementary quantum of periodic time (8.0933×10^{-21}), in seconds per cycle, discussed previously.

Angular space, as "one" physical state (quantum) quantity is characterized in physical relationships as radius of gyration, a line, or distance, S (3.5411 x 10^{-14}),[18] in meters per radian. Angular space or a line, being "many" quanta, is characterized in physical relationships as 1/S. Like periodic space, angular space is a compound motion quantity. It consists of linear velocity (v) and angular time (t) in '1', where $S = vt$ and v is velocity of light in vacuum and t is angular time (1.1812 x 10^{-22}) in seconds per radian, discussed earlier.

A quantum of angular space as surface *area*, A ($S^2 = v^2t^2$), is a compound motion in four dimensions (vv and tt) in '1', and a quantum of angular space as *volume*, V ($S^3 = v^3t^3$), is a compound motion in six dimensions (vvv and ttt) in '1'. Observe, when Poincaré addresses three-dimensional space, in which material objects are located and events occur, in physics to characterize volume in '1' we require six dimensions of motion ($S^3 = v^3t^3$); when Poincaré refers to a surface area in two dimensions, in physics we need four dimensions of motion $S^2 = v^2t^2$; and when Poincaré speaks of linear distance, as between objects, in physics we call for two dimensions of motion $S = vt$.

At an earlier time, we talked about a journey to Mars and the *gravitational field strength*, g, relationship, where g = vw. We can also express gravity, like time and space, in terms of motion, where g = v/t. The gravitational field strength, g, as a quantum quantity equals 1/g. According to Einstein's theory of general relativity, gravity warps and bends space, deforming a beam of starlight. And so it does. However, gravity distorts only angular and periodic space, not the Absolute Space, '1'.

Dimensional space consists of a plane curve generated by a point moving around a fixed point ('1') while constantly receding from or approaching it, or when a screw is driven into wood. In video recorders, to get maximum packing of information, we make use of the angular and periodic space; we spin the recording head while moving the tape, also, when atoms or planets spin in their orbits, they revolve around the nucleus of an atom or an elliptical path around a celestial body. It takes twenty-four hours for Earth to do one spin; it requires roughly 364 Earth spins to complete one year.

Albert Einstein, Jules Henri Poincaré, and Hendrik Antoon Lorentz demonstrated that the quantities of time and space are not independent entities, but are interwoven. From the relationships above we see that time and space are intimately related quantities (they are different facets of '1') that can be described through motion in empty-space. In the Gospel of Thomas, as was acknowledged before (part 1, chapter 9), Jesus said, "If they ask you: 'What is the sign of your Father [Infinite Splendor, '1'] in you?' say to them: 'It is a movement and a rest.'" When we consider that to become visible manifestation requires movement (time, space, gravity, etc.) and rest (empty-space, '1'), we see how literal the Gospel of Thomas statement is.

Nick Herbert (part 1, chapter 10) stated that "As a way of thinking about quantum reality, Heisenberg proposed that a quantum entity's unobserved attributes are not fully real but exist in an attenuated state of being called potentia ['1'] until the act of observation promotes some lucky attribute to full-reality status." Saint John (part 1, chapter 6) declared, "Before the world was created, the Word [Logos, '1'] already existed; he was with God, and he was the same as God" (Jn 1:1-5). In the Gospel of Thomas we read, "I am he who exists from the undivided" (Logion 61).

All that exists or will ever exist, the different orders of infinity (physical quantities, elements, DNA, and so forth), has been in existence as a potentiality in the empty-space, similar to a statue in a slab of "uncarved" marble, or the preexisting internal program in a computer. Through periodic and angular space, potential elements of the empty-space (potentia of '1') are made manifest. A more comprehensive discussion on the nature of space and time can be found in the Principle of Trinity and Self-Organization.[19]

Keep it Simple, Keep it Clean: '1' in Infinite Series

There are other surprises of mathematical simplicity, beauty, and profound order at every point behind the universe. The constant e (2.71828) is central to the formula for compounding financial interest and mathematical modeling of such basic life processes as growth and decay. The e base of the so-called natural, hyperbolic or Naperian, logarithms reduces "multiplication" and "division" to *addition* and *subtraction* of the physical quantities. The 2.71828 number is generated by an infinite series using the '1' as a reference for every position of the e base, physical quantity or fundamental physical constant:

$$e = 1 + 1/(1) + 1/(1 \times 2) + 1/(1 \times 2 \times 3) + 1/(1 \times 2 \times 3 \times 4) + 1/(1 \times 2 \times 3 \times 4 \times 5) \ldots$$

The constant *e* facilitates manipulation of quantities, or the different orders of infinity, depending on which side of '1' the quantity or the infinity is. Thus, the inverse of a quantity, John Barrow's distance, D, and its inverse, 1/D, (the Principle of the One and the Many, discussed in part 2, chapter 5) is the "same number" only with an *opposite sign*. Again, determination of square root (evolution) becomes division, while raising to a power (involution) is transformed into a simple product.

The Fine Structure Constant

The well-known expression for pi (p = 3.14159) has captivated many generations of mathematicians. Pi appears in the calculations of probabilities, physics, and is the ratio of the circumference of every circle to its diameter. Similar to *e*, pi is a never-ending expression:

$$\pi = (1 - 1/3 + 1/5 - 1/7 + 1/9 - \ldots) \times 4$$

The classical electron radius, *r* (2.817×10^{-15}), is obtained through the radius of gyration in angular space, *S*, and pi, where $r = S/4\pi$. In nuclear dimensions of quantum electrodynamics, because of scale invariance, pi becomes the fine structure constant.[20] The fine structure constant, α (7.29735×10^{-3}), is a fundamental physical constant related to the strength of the interactions among photons, muons, and electrons. It can be expressed in cycles per radian. The fine strucure constant can be derived through angular space, *S*, and periodic space, λ, where $\alpha = S/2\lambda$, or through angular time, *t*, and periodic time, *T*, where $\alpha = t/2T$.

The Rydberg Constant

The Rydberg constant, $\mathfrak{R}$ (1.0974×10^7 per metre), is another fundamental constant of atomic physics that emerges (1890) in the equations of the Swedish physicist Johannes Rydberg. It characterizes the wavelengths or frequencies of light in an assortment of spectral lines, such as those emitted by hydrogen atoms. The Rydberg constant can be generated through the fine structure constant and angular space, where $\mathfrak{R} = \alpha^3/S$, or the fine structure constant and periodic space, where $\mathfrak{R} = \alpha^2/2\lambda$. The reason I am mentioning these relationships is to show the infinite wit, precision, and common sense at the '1' level, as well as the profound logic, symmetry, and splendor of interconnections between different physical quantities, constants, and frames of reference.

What do the seed arrangements in an apple, the positions of the petals in a red rose, the breeding of rabbits, the growth of spiral shells, the Frank Lloyd Wright's spiral ramp in the Guggenheim Museum in New York City, the Salvador Dali's "Sacrament of the Last Supper" all have in common? The answer, they have sagaciously harmonious relationships or geometrical proportions that are arranged according to a mathematical rule that relies on the Golden Ratio. The Golden Ratio phi (ϕ = 1.61803) involves square roots that go on, like e and pi, forever without displaying any repetition:

$$\phi = (1 + (1 + (1 + (1 + (1 + \ldots)^{1/2})^{1/2})^{1/2})^{1/2})^{1/2}$$

Sometimes, it is necessary to transform the electron base to the proton base,[21] or the surface of the Earth π base to the nuclear π base, as was mentioned earlier. Again, the transformations (John Barrow's duality) are made simple by e and in accord with John Napier's *Constructio*. The expression log 1 = 0 holds for any base B of reality, or constant, because B^0 = 1 for all (nonzero: $\neq$ 0) values of B. Similarly, for any B ($\neq$ 0), $\log_B B = 1$, because $B^1 = B$.

Strings, Superstrings, and M-Theory: Colossal Achievement to the Summit of Everest

Werner Heisenberg and Austrian physicist Wolfgang Pauli (1929) characterized forces and particles as bundles of energy in various quantum fields, known in the more general formalism as quantum field theory. Forty-five years later (1974) John Schwarz (CalTech) and Joël Scherk (Paris, France) in collaboration described the gravitational force in terms of lines or strings. The approach had limited predictive power.

However, in 1984, John Schwarz and Michael Green (Queen Mary College, London) and Edward Witten (Princeton University, 1985), as well as others, described *lines* (strings and superstrings) with ten- and twenty-six dimensional superstring theories (entailing nine and twenty-five dimensions of space), including the M-theory. Stephen Hawking, in characterizing string theories wrote:

In these theories, the basic objects are not particles, which occupy a single point of space, but things that have a length, but no other dimension, like an infinitely thin piece of string. These strings may have ends (the so-called open strings) or they may be joined up with themselves in closed loops (closed strings). A particle occupies one point of space at each instant of time. Thus its history can be represented by a line in space-time (the "world-line"). A string, on the other hand, occupies a line in space at each moment of time. So its history in space-time is a two-dimensional surface called the world-sheet. (Any point on such a world-sheet can be described by two numbers: one specifying the time and the other the position of the point on the string).[22]

The string, like a rubber band, defines the centerline of action within space measured with a complex dimensional set of axes, the line about which a rotating mass, such as the Earth rotates. String theorists found that they require worlds with many dimensions; the more, the better. To express the dimension of a line, strings need "two numbers: one specifying the time and the other the position of the point on the string."

The challenge with strings is that they need space and time to exist, which we have seen is motion in '1'. What string theory requires is a fully spaceless and timeless framework, what physicists call a "background-independent" formulation. Also, strings have not been connected to verifiable physics. While the string theory community, with monumental originality, has mapped out quantum mechanics; special and general relativity; extra dimensions of Kaluza and Klein; supersymmetry; gauge theories of the strong, weak, and electromagnetic forces; it has not provided a spaceless and timeless framework (with exact equations and adequate precision) to enable evaluation with experiment. To reach the highest bedrock in the world (the modern quest for the deepest laws of nature), where infinities (like a rubber band in a golf ball) are tightly curled up into the enfolded Unchanging rest (Everest), string theorists need to formulate the concept of "duality"[23] and the coupling physics[24] around the rather subtle "scale invariance"[25] and the "wormhole" of '1'. Then, we will put quantitative rigor behind the "theory of everything" and be at the summit of Mount Everest.

7

THE SAME ESSENCE IN DIFFERENT CONTAINERS

Your beauty is extraordinary,
Your appearance is without comparison.
Your magnificence is inexpressible,
Your glory is beyond human language.

—Saint Symeon the New Theologian

Natural Units of Measurement

Now let us take a trip, similar to the explorers going to a distant galaxy, to unravel the numerical sequence within the decimal system of numeration, at the physical quantities. Let us see how the fundamental building blocks of nature are globally arranged in the grand hierarchical superstructure. Let us unravel, as with numbers, the *global quantity sequence* from the '1'.

When we attended grade school, we were instructed in our arithmetic classes that we must always multiply apples with apples and oranges with oranges. For the multiplication to work, we were taught not to mix apples with oranges. By the time we were in high school, we learned to bundle apples or oranges into boxes, truckloads, and shiploads, but still no mixing was allowed. These larger units of measurement did not change the apple-with-apple multiplication or division game. They enabled us, however, with higher-level systems to bundle together identical essence, to establish a one-one relationship within the same essence, to more subtly speed up our counting processes.

Eureka! There is our grand unification of apples with apples, but only in different-sized containers—in different natural units of measurement. "In seeking a definition of a number," Bertrand Russell in his *Introduction to Mathematical Philosophy* wrote:

> Number is a way of bringing together certain collections, namely, those that have a given number of terms. We can suppose all couples in one bundle, all trios in another, and so on. In this way, we obtain various bundles of collections, each bundle consisting of all the collections that have a certain number of terms. Each bundle is a class whose members are collections, i.e., classes, thus each is a class of classes . . . It is obvious to common sense that two finite classes have the same number of terms if they are similar, but not otherwise. The act of counting consists in establishing a one-one relationship between the set of objects counted and the natural numbers [excluding 0] that are used up in the process.[1]

Likewise, Maxwell proved, as noted earlier, that the physical quantities of magnetism and electricity are different aspects of the same thing, the very same essence packaged in different containers. *The reason physical quantities are able to interact at all is because they are all made of the same essence.* Energy is made of the same essence as light, and light is made out of the same essence as gravity or electromagnetism. It would be impossible to do any kind of quantity transformation if the core content—the essence we were dealing with ('1')—was of unrelated substance. In addition, as formerly stated, the laws of physics measure constant difference between the Unchanging Points, *infinities*, such as '1' and the '=' within a vacuum in physics, or the First and the Last in the Bible (Rev 22:13).

Similar to taking various-sized steps in walking, what is observed in physics is the "boundary" separation between the initial and final condition of measurement in '1'. That is, observational measurements based on physical quantities take place within a spatiotemporal milieu. Time, space, gravity, and so on are not only fundamental building blocks of nature that physics can measure, but also *the very same fundamental essence in different natural units of measurement.* They are "the very same reality in different sized containers." Basically, similar to numbers, because we can multiply and divide physical quantities by each other, the quantity difference is in the unit of measure.

Notice: we cannot multiply nor divide oranges by apples (or time by energy, gravity by mass, etc.) and vice versa unless they are of identical essence, or they are normalized, as energy and mass are normalized in Einstein's famous formula through the *gravitational potential* expressed as c^2. However, you can bring together truckloads and shiploads of apples, just as you can bundle collections of oranges.

Consciousness at Physical Boundaries

The manifestation or measurement of a solitary point or infinity is unattainable. However, separation between points, or infinities, can be measured and described. Each physical quantity is a precise "natural unit of measurement" with specified boundaries, defined by fundamental physical constants in '1'. The algorithmic compressibility for the *initial* condition (zero "0") of each natural unit of measurement in the laws of physics is the '1'.

For example, $1 = E/mc^2 = mc^2/E$, where the natural logarithm of $1 = 0$, and E, m, c are energy, mass, and speed of light. By the same token, the "empty interval" of each natural unit of measurement in the laws of physics is the point of equality '=' ($E = mc^2$). The final conditions ('=') occur after the initial "0" and a number of event points. Equality signifies the fact that two expressions (for example, 48 and 6 x 8 or E and mc^2) represent the same quantity upon substitution of some of the variables involved by suitable numbers.

That is, it is possible to transform one expression into the other (6 x 8 into 48) using any permissible operation. Also, E serves as the "surrogate equilibrium" between m and c^2. '1' and the '=' perform inversion, equalization and transformation. These two terms, '1' and '=', are precise, mathematical, and internationally communicable in the language of science. They transcend cultural differences, hold predictive power, and can be reexamined, tested, and compared.

The natural units of measurement are accessible to the observer in the interval between the '1' and '=' points in the empty-space. The interval also serves as a quantization ("size of step") constant. In Einstein's world of relativity, one finds the invariant space-time interval giving rise to the notion that the universe is four-dimensional, consisting of three spatial dimensions and one-time dimension. The space-time interval is a kind of "size of step" in that four-dimensional space. If the measurement of a quantity involved energy E as a variable, the "boundary" of the initial conditions ('1', empty-space on this page) would start before E, while the "boundary" after the final condition of measurement ('=') would be after E ($1E=$).

Previously I noted, "The knower [observer] and the known [observed] are *one*." Question: where does the interaction or observational process between the observer (or the observation equipment) and the observed (the object under study) take place? I suggest that the linkage occurs at the '1' and the equality '=' boundaries. Matter, information and forces are unified at '1' and the equality '=' points. Specifically, at '1' and the '=' points, in vacuo, observer-dependent *consciousness* and *free will* enter. At the point, we can adopt a unified view and from that vantage point identify what is required and fill that need. Here, at the common boundary of '1', the observer, through his free will, constructs the world (manifestation) on his own behalf. Here, space can tell matter how to move, and matter can tell space how to curve. Here is where the observer, in the state of deep meditation, can equate her—or himself to '1', or see her—or himself as the observed.

A few physical quantities of time, space, energy, and velocity make an atom. Enough atoms of hydrogen, oxygen, aluminum, silicon, and iron make a brick. A collection of bricks makes up a wall. A set of walls and a roof make a house. Hence, the physical quantity, the atom, the brick, and the wall, like numbers, "bring together certain collections, namely, those that have a given number of terms," as Bertrand Russell stated. They bring together "different container-sizes"—different systems (dimensions) of the selfsame fundamental essence ('1').

Quantum or wave mechanics summarizes how radiant energy is itself quantized to discrete values rather than to a continuous set of values. Radiation and absorption processes, instead of being continuous, as had been supposed prior to Max Planck, are discontinuous. Radiant energy is absorbed and emitted in definite units called *quanta*, with the container-size being called the Planck constant. Electricity is quantized in the container-size form of electrons. Ordinary matter exists in its own quanta, named atoms.

The zero of the placeholder notation has no value itself but gives value to other numerals. Similarly, the '1' in physical equations has no value itself but gives value (through '1' and '=') to physical quantities. Based on the Logarithmic Slide Rule for Physical Relationships, I am suggesting that similar to zero's role as a shifter, or modifier, in mathematical value, the role of '1' is also as shifter (transformer) in the physical value. Considered in this context, nature not only quantizes things according to the rules of quantum physics, but everything is quantized in a hierarchy of different-sized *containers* known as physical quantities (mass, energy, time). Each individual physical quantity is further quantized in what quantum physics calls units of quanta.

Additionally, transformation (i.e., conversion, shifting) between quantities (relative infinities) is instantaneous. That is, without any space-time signals—without traversing time or space in between, "nonlocality" in '1'. For example, electrons instantly leap from one orbit to another orbit, around the nucleus of an atom, without navigating the time or space between them. They exist as probability waves in more than one point of '1', showing up in diffraction pictures as fuzzy orbits or clouds of uncertainty. The choice of experiment or consciousness brings them from unmanifest ('1': the pre-quantum fact, the Ground of the First Cause) into manifest space-time reality ('='). Deploying this (without traversing time or space in between) know-how, in supercomputer development, will facilitate instantaneous quantum-computing data-processing machinery.

8

THE GRAND HIERARCHICAL STAIRWAY

A million galaxies are a little speck
on that shoreless ocean of non-being.

—Rumi

Any Place I Hang My Hat:
A Staircase in the Universal Ranking

When looking beneath the surface of each element, a very orderly periodic system of classification is seen. Atoms differ from one another in the number of protons and neutrons in the nucleus, and in the number of electrons spinning around the nucleus. The atomic number, which indicates each element's position in the table, is of fundamental significance in that it gives the number of protons possessed by the atom of the element. Also, the number of electrons, protons, and neutrons and their arrangement determine almost "all the properties of the element" is the agent for "governing its position in the Periodic Table of Elements."

Observe: as we go up the Periodic Table of Elements, developed by Dmitry Ivanovich Mendeleyev, Russian chemist, between 1869 and 1871, and add a few more protons, neutrons, and electrons, the face of each element changes. Similar to boxes and truckloads of apples, electrons, protons, and neutrons are bundled in a hierarchy of different-sized "containers." When there is "a package" of one proton and one electron in the atom, you can be certain that the element will be hydrogen. With two protons, two neutrons, and two electrons spinning in an atom, the atom will be helium. In a package of ninety-five protons, the element will be americium.

Periodical Classification of the Elements

Number of Protons (Atomic Number)	Element Name (Container)	Number of Protons (Atomic Number)	Element Name (Container)
1	Hydrogen	11	Sodium
2	Helium	12	Magnesium
3	Lithium	13	Aluminum
4	Beryllium	14	Silicon
5	Boron	15	Phosphorus
6	Carbon	27	Cobalt
7	Nitrogen	47	Silver
8	Oxygen	79	Gold
9	Fluorine	92	Uranium
10	Neon	95	Americium

Nature keeps score of the same essence—natural currencies—*natural units of measurement,* by assigning unique container-sizes to discrete units of '**1**'. Just as it is possible to interpret the atomic structure of elements through atomic numbers, so with the coded language of DNA (deoxyribonucleic acid) can we decipher every single component of every gene—every letter, so to speak—in that unfolded six-foot-long "code" or "blueprint" of life. Fold the code of life back, and it reduces in size to trillionths of an inch, petite enough to put into any one of our one hundred trillion cells. DNA is written in words of *four* chemical letters: A, T, G, and C. It is the central part of a cell that has the biochemical recipe for how to make everything needed for the functioning of a living organism. The ingredients are the same for everything that lives. We are one life, one creation, brothers and sisters to flowers, animals, and all humans.

Of course, mapping the "genome sequence" is not a simple matter of stretching our genes and reading of the base-pair combinations, but just as with the numerical sequence of numbers and atomic-number sequence, every single component of every gene, like physical quantities, has a very specific description and location (the Principle of Position)[1] in the lengthy chain of Being—the long chain of '1'. We have a similar idea of iteration in the sequence of natural numbers, such as the counting of money. The green stuff can be counted in one-hundred-dollar bills, twenty-dollar bills, quarters, nickels, pennies, or as five twenty-dollar bills, or four hundred quarters of the same one-hundred-dollar currency.

Each law of physics expresses a quantity relationship. Because all of the laws are interrelated, each, therefore, is an expression of one grand relationship among the physical laws in empty-space ('1'),[2] where everything is *encrypted into organized sequential steps* at every point of '1'. Hence, just as currency has a sequence of different denominations (nickels, dimes, quarters), and a spectrum of light has a sequence of colors (red, green, blue), so then collective building blocks of the very same essence ('1') represent a higher level system of different physical quantities (natural units of reality, hierarchical ladder of quantization), such as time, space, matter, elements, animals, people, planets, and galaxies.

The *decryption* process or algorithm requires the performance of a number of exact sequential steps. Similar to code breaking, there are certain problems that have to be solved. Every single step in the decryption must be carried out exactly in the correct sequence. The encryption solution can be right, statistical, chaotic complexity, or garbage. It all depends wherever one has the cipher text, or the exact decryption algorithm, alongside a piece of equipment to run it. Just as hydrogen must go through a sequence of steps to become gold, so must time, space, or energy must go through a sequence of steps to become gravity.

There are over seventy known physical quantities and over 100,000 four-term ($A = BCD$) mathematical relationships that these seventy quantities can enter into. Just as the Rosetta stone was used to decode the writing on a roll of ancient Egyptian papyrus, it is possible—with the tools of physics, disarmingly simple mathematical analysis, and high-speed computers—to unify the fundamental physical quantities of time, space, matter, electromagnetism, and gravity into one cohesive global network, similar to creating a planetary map of oceans, mountains, and cities. The values of the physical quantities represent hierarchical levels (quantum values) of the same essence.[3]

Physical Quantities Spectrum:
Progression of Larger and Larger Infinities

As the basic building blocks organize to form different parts, the physical quantities change. The fundamental building block of nature is a point

(Singularity). Every point is adjoining another point, '1'. Also, between any two points there is always one more point, and so on. Through an impulse of mental projection, which we commonly term creation, points are energized by the mind. A number of vibrating points bring into being *resonant frequencies* and *reflections* (images) within the '1'. A few resonant patterns of vibration generate moment of inertia. A number of moments of inertia create volume. Volume forms mass; mass causes time; time becomes energy; energy gives birth to gravity; and so forth. This process of creation takes place simultaneously, at the same time, in parallel. Starting with the moment of inertia, a partial list of the Physical Quantities Spectrum[4] follows in order of size:

Table 5

Physical Quantities Spectrum

Natural Units of Reality (Physical Quantities)	Dimensional Units
Moment of Inertia (Individual Quantity)	10^{-57} kg-m^2
Volume (Individual Quantity)	10^{-41} m^3
Angular Momentum (Individual Quantity)	10^{-36} kg-m^2/sec
Mass (Individual Quantity)	10^{-31} kilograms
Time (Individual Quantity)	10^{-22} seconds
Electric Flux (Individual Quantity)	10^{-19} coulombs
Energy (Individual Quantity)	10^{-14} joules
'1'	10^{0} dimensionless
Magnetic Potential (Group Quantity)	10^{3} amperes
Velocity (Group Quantity)	10^{8} meters/second
Electric Field (Group Quantity)	10^{19} volts/meter
Pressure (Group Quantity)	10^{27} new/m^2
Gravity (Group Quantity)	10^{30} m/sec^2
Angular Acceleration (Group Quantity)	10^{43} rad/sec^2

As noted in part 1, chapter 10, though each electromagnetic wave is of the same essence, different frequencies, different groups of the same essence, appear to our senses, our windows of perception, differently. We decode some wavelengths as sound, others as heat, still others as visible light within a spectrum of colors. Similarly, while '1' is the same essence (empty-space), some excitation ranges of '1' are decoded by our consciousness as velocity, others as space, still others as matter. What is seen and experienced depends on where we, the observer (decryption), consciously are in awareness, in relation to that which is being observed. When we are looking through a yellow pane of glass, colors will appear to us in a different way than when looking through a purple pane of glass. When we are happy the world will look differently to us than when we are tired or homeless. "All appearances perceived and/or experienced by the mind, are, in fact, mental projections," said one of the greatest Tibetan yogis of the century, Kalu Rinpoche. Spending over thirty years meditating in hermitages and caves in the Himalayas, he achieved a profound level of realization and has often been compared to the great saint Milarepa. Further, "they are the mind's play; as mind itself is insubstantial, so are these projections."[5] My work discloses that the very same essence is everywhere, but is packaged (encrypted) in different building blocks—in different sized containers of physical quantities, particles, elements, chemical and organic compounds, molecules, micro-organisms, plants, animals, and humans.

John Napier (1550-1617), eminent Scottish mathematician and theological writer, presented science and mathematics with a very simple system of notation and computation through the concept of logarithms. Logarithms transform multiplication into addition, division into subtraction, the taking of powers into multiplication, and the taking of square roots into division. Solutions could be quickly determined from tables displaying exponents of a fixed base.

German mathematician Michael Stifel, in 1544, as well as Simon Stevin, in 1586, of the Netherlands, denoted exponents (repeated products) by indices, but their notation was awkward and most likely unfamiliar to Napier. The Swiss mathematician Joost Bürgi also developed a system of logarithms (1603-1611), published in 1620.

Napier likely commenced working on logarithms in 1594, publishing in 1614. He discovered that the foundation for calculation is a relationship involving an arithmetical progression—a sequence of numbers in which each number is generated, following a geometric progression, from the one directly preceding it, by multiplying numbers by a constant factor when larger than unity, 1 (such as 4, 8, 16, 32 . . .), or dividing when smaller than unity, 1 (1/2, 1/4, 1/8, 1/16 . . .). I have established a similar correlation between physical quantities and fundamental physical constants in the laws of physics.[6] Napier employed the *decimal point* (.) as the demarcation to segregate the fractional from the integral part of a number. I have noticed that the laws of physics, as set forth in the examples of Table 3, and the Physical Quantities Spectrum, utilize '1' (Georg Cantor's aleph-zero, $\aleph_0$) to separate the One (individual quantities) from the Many (group quantities).[7]

Predictive Power: A New Frame of Reference

English mathematician Edmund Gunter plotted logarithms (1620) on a two-foot straight line, making multiplication and division of numbers possible through the addition and subtraction of lengths via a pair of dividers, thus facilitating calculations through an analogue device known as the *slide rule*. William Oughtred (1621), Robert Bissaker (1654), Matthew Boulton and James Watt (1779), Peter Mark Roget (1815), Amédéé Mannheim (1859), plus others provided improved versions of the slide rule, making it an indispensable tool in the mathematics of science, engineering, and industry prior to the electronic computer era.

Recall that both Cantor and Gödel attempted to decipher the well-ordering principle deploying set theory in mathematics. I found that similar to a mathematical slide rule, when base *e* (see '1' in Infinite Series, part 2 chapter 6) is integrated with fundamental physical constants and plotted to a natural log scale, one can produce a *natural scale of measurement of infinities*. This natural scale of measurement serves as a foundational principle of logical consistency for physical quantities, fundamental physical constants, and the laws of physics.[8] Instead of the mathematical sequence of the natural numbers (1, 2, 3.) in reference to a zero, '0,' there is the physical sequence of the natural quantities, fundamental constants, and the laws of physics in reference to '1'.

To transform one set of quantities, fundamental constants, or physical laws into another, I utilized two natural scales of measurement to construct a Logarithmic Slide Rule for Physical Relationships (LSPR).[9] The LSPR operates on the same mathematical principle as a logarithmic slide rule for mathematical numbers. In place of zero and numbers in a logarithmic slide rule, in an LSPR we have '1' (0 and ∞) and physical quantities.

The LSPR is a practical instrument with the *mathematically predictive power of physics*. LSPR demonstrates a correspondence between the intellectual structure of comprehension and the structure of foundation, making one conscious of immediate-ultimate reality dependence by emancipating and articulating new potentialities of knowledge as a whole. The LSPR generates, in algorithmically compressed terms, experimentally verified equations of the laws of physics and fundamental physical constants.

Additionally, an LSPR can, in simple equations, give form to undiscovered and unexplored potential possibilities in '1', such as the ability to *predict new* fundamental physical constants and relationships within physics.[10] It demonstrates immediate-ultimate reality relations (classification, sequence, order, and position of physical quantities and laws of physics) in reference to '1'. The LSPR suggests, with fundamental physics and high-precision measurements, that the laws of physics and fundamental constants are mutable and emerge from the '1'. It demonstrates that immediate reality is relative and actualized in the unchanging empty-space. Conversely, '1' is invariant and equilibrating (transforming) in all frames of reference.

'1' may be viewed as an organizing principle of logical consistency, equilibrating the *one* to the *many*, and the *many* to the *one*. LSPR enables one to explore verification of ultimate principles and Unchanging Values through the use of scientific method and simple mathematization of physics. The ability to predict pure constants is the real touchstone of the LSPR. Its transforming power enables an equation, in the causal nexus of physics, to characterize '1'.

9

ALL PEOPLE ARE MEMBERS OF YOUR IMMEDIATE FAMILY

The universe begins to look more like a great thought
in the mind of God than like a great machine.

—Sir James Jeans

Advancement through Our United Efforts

Albert Einstein said:

> When we survey our lives and endeavors, we soon observe that almost the whole of our actions and desires is bound up with the existence of other human beings . . . We eat food that others have produced, wear clothes that others have made, live in homes that others have built. The greater part of our knowledge and beliefs has been communicated to us by other people through the medium of a language which others have created . . . the individual, if left alone from birth, would remain primitive and beastlike in his thoughts and feelings to a degree that we can hardly conceive. The individual is what he is and has the significance that he has not so much in virtue of his individuality, but rather as a member of a great human community, which directs his material and spiritual existence from the cradle to the grave.
>
> A man's value to the community depends primarily on how far his feelings, thoughts, and actions are directed toward promoting the good of his fellows.[1]

As I examine the evidence between the great branches of learning (the natural sciences, the social sciences, and the humanities), the affirmation of the sacred at the highest levels of scholarship and talent, the creation of values for society, the debate over first principles, and the insights of who we are,[2] I am deeply moved and delighted with the quality of knowledge humanity has amassed. I am keenly aware of how the partitioning of knowledge has promoted the fragmentation of learning and multiplication of disciplines, each with its own standards of validation, philosophy, and approaches. Yet interdisciplinary studies and the breaking down of scientific barriers have been rapidly increasing, attracting many dedicated scholars.

What all of these breakthroughs add up to is a very important finding of fundamental significance. The early giant trail blazers, Moses, the Buddha, Zoroaster, Krishna, Jesus, Erwin Schrödinger, the Dalai Lama, Pope John Paul II, and Mother Teresa, crossed the high mountains of cosmic consciousness and, through personal observation and verification, left their legacy of the golden coast of unity and Oneness amongst us. Utilizing forms of simplicity and beauty, we can now solidify their point of view. It is now provable with physics and mathematics that indeed everything is intimately linked through the '1' and into the One. The Bhagavad Gita put it best: "And when you have thus learned the truth, you will know that all living beings are but part of Me ['1']—and that they are in Me, and are Mine" [4.35]. Or as Hafiz declared, in *Where the Drum Lost Its Mind*: "Indeed, indeed, you are one of us."

Each Is in All and All Is in Each

It can be demonstrated that each of us exists in the selfsame, single, all-embracing multidimensional system of hidden symmetries, fundamental physical quantities and infinities, the relationships and properties of which are determined by their function in the whole. Beneath the plane of ordinary subjective perspective, all existence corresponds with and moves along an invariable hierarchical chain of being.

Just as in a hologram each particle contains a three-dimensional image of the whole object, or in nature each seed contains the whole tree, so each (individual point, '1') is in All ('1') and All is in each one of us. Our everyday world of human beings, animals, trees, plants, and galaxies is connected to everything else in such a way that careful study of any individual element could theoretically reveal detailed information about other elements in the universe. Metaphorically, the universe resembles an underlying order, a unity, in a *dictionary*—wherein every word's definition also contains definitions of every other word in the dictionary, "the One" of which forgotten saints laboriously wrote on tablets of stone, wood, or pages of palm leaves. In a Hindu sutra, we find this gem:

> In the heaven of Indra there is said to be a network of pearls [individual points] so arranged that if you look at one, you see all the others reflected in it. In the same way, each object in the world is not merely itself but involves every other object, and in fact is in every other object.

Johann Wolfgang von Goethe (1749-1832), commonly recognized to be one of the giants of world literature, was a natural philosopher, statesman, journalist, critic, painter, and possibly the last European to endeavor the multifaceted character of the Renaissance perfection. Goethe had keen lucidity and unending wisdom, as well as a realistic side with clarity and elegance. He characterized the All in each of us as follows: "Every natural form to the smallest, a leaf, a sunbeam, a moment of time, a drop, is related to the whole and partakes of the beauty of the whole . . . A leaf is a compend of Nature, and Nature a colossal leaf.[3] Similar to Goethe, Ralph Waldo Emerson subscribed to the "all-in-each" principle. He wrote:

> I believe in the omnipresence; that is; that the all is in each particle; that entire Nature reappears in every leaf and moss. I believe in Eternity—that is, that I can find Greece and Palestine and Italy and England and the Islands—the genius and creative principle of each and all eras in my own mind.[4]

Using religious nomenclature: The First Cause [I Am That I Am-'1'] is everywhere, but in different forms. Basically, at the heart of it all, we are, through the '1', invisibly united into a single framework underlying the physical reality. It is God. It is You! The world is our lifeblood, and all of its citizens are our immediate family. They are You. You are they. We are One Essence.

Footprints on the Shores: They Are Our Own

We are the Creator in Exile who, in a sense, has taken a nap for a few billion years, who slept through the formation of the stars, the development of the many forms of consciousness, and finally to where we are in the last ten thousand years or so. At this time, humanity and divinity are slowly waking up—unfolding to ever-increasing inner richness and glory. Previously, I quoted Eddington's essential insight of modern physics:

> We have found that where science has progressed the farthest, the *mind has but regained from nature that which the mind has put into nature.* We have found a strange footprint on the shores of the unknown. We have devised profound theories, one after another, to account for its origin. At last, we have succeeded in reconstructing the creature that made the footprint. And *Lo! It is our own* [my emphasis].[5]

For thousands of years, mystics, saviors, and saints, through personal insight and sustained encouragements, have been restating the same wonderful song of Oneness—of God within us and of living unity among us. This is one of the most precious moments in our conscious history. Like a twentieth century Moses, today through the "unity of knowledge" and the hard verification tools of physics and mathematics, we can finally part the modern-day Red Sea of blood, nuclear and biological bombs, widespread violence, pain, and bondage. This deployment will lead to more freedom, peace, free will, productivity, and service-excellence—to One Family. We can finally recognize our common humanity and live together as members of a single family.

Now, I would like to share with you a dream I saw. It was Holy Thursday, and there before me on a table lay the unleavened bread. From within the bread I heard a voice: "This is my body." It was the Perfect One, and he affirmed again, as did the Buddha, Schrödinger, Einstein, Robert Muller, Dalai Lama, Pope John Paul II, Mother Teresa, and others more recently, that we are all one body.

Yes, eat, experience, and consciously bond again: "Every time you eat this bread and drink this wine, remember me,"[6] remember the Christ; we are all connected; we are One at the Absolute Ground.

New vistas of increasing certainty, knowledge, harvests of good, and tremendous opportunity are opening up before us as never before. New wisdom—new ways of creation—will be forging new pathways for enormous energy releases, higher levels of attainment, human closeness, prosperity, and peace. A very exciting phase in our human adventure is emerging.

We Are All Part of It: I Am Rejoicing at Your Success

Together, let us sum up some of the key findings:

1. Know the truth, and the truth shall set you free.
2. The world is but a self-forgetfulness of God. You have assumed human form: now you are entertaining yourself in this limited space-time movie on Earth.
3. The very same essence, the Eternal Light from which all things emanate, is everywhere, but appears in different natural units of measure: different sized containers of physical quantities. You are a part of the physical quantities. You are a part of '1'.
4. Everything is part of everything else. The observer and the observed are fundamentally one, or as the Brihad-Aranyaka Upanishad stated, "I, indeed, am this creation, for I emitted it all from myself" (1:4.5).
5. You are part of the Creator Her/Himself. Your universe and all of its manifestations are creations of your own consciousness. It is with your mind that you see. It is with your mind that you hear.
6. You are me; I am you! You are looking at yourself through your brother's eyes!
7. The Most High God = the "theory of everything" = You, at your foundation = a priori dimensionless state = Consciousness beyond all contents or overlay = '1'.
8. Through the example of your own life, you can help to awaken other human beings to a realization of their essential value.
9. Great opportunities have opened up before us at this point of convergent knowledge and action.

10

WINNING OPTIONS:
COMPREHEND THE INCOMPREHENSIBLE

Opportunity is missed by most people because
it is dressed in overalls and looks like work.

—Thomas Edison

Where Do We Go from Here?:
Success Is Not an Accident

Now, let us peer into the future. Similar to the logarithmic slide rule for
mathematical numbers, which makes possible multiplication, division,
and prediction of numeric answers, so the Logarithmic Slide Rule for
Physical Relationship (LSPR) facilitates multiplication, division, and
the *prediction* of quantity relationships, laws of physics, and fundamental
physical constants. Just as a mathematical slide rule would not be feasible
without a zero, the LSPR is not possible without the '1'. '1' is way of
separating the positive and negative frequency parts of field amplitudes,
fundamental physical constants, physical quantities, and infinities. '1'
enables predictability in physics. And is the unchanging wholeness of
the world, the borderless knowledge, and the ordering principle of the
universe.

The more skills one has, the more tasks one can perform. The more
refined the pebble, the more holes it can go through. Like a zero that
serves every number, so a point (the smallest pebble) serves every process
and each manifestation. It is the central point that precedes form and is
inherent within each form. '1' transcends space and time, and is the Ground
Zero from which the entire cosmic field of creation is derived. '1' represents

the fundamental level of reality on which all of our lives and activities are based. It pervades the whole universe that forms the matrix of all appearance, like an ocean out of which all waves arise and into which, after its course is run, it once again vanish. Today, we realize that mathematical computations without "zero" would not be possible. The same is with '1'. Without '1', existence is not possible!

The Price of Freedom:
Systematic Pursuit of the Unchanging

Invariance ('1') in nature is not a democratic state or process. It does not advance by majority rule or First Amendment guidelines, nor does it accept notions of belief. Invariance is the Central Operating Principle of the universe and the inner structure of '1'. Although all human endeavors, like health, social, political, philosophical, and scientific activities, are rooted in a realm of the '1', the scope and applicability of '1' extends to each and every part of our universe.

While the pursuit of knowledge and social and economic development has led to a great deal of excellent accomplishments, much learning and dissemination of that knowledge remains to be done. We the people, should we want to navigate the upcoming challenges more effectively, must choose our future. We must dedicate our resources to the solution of problems before they actually become problems. We must search for and discover more meaning in our world and in all existence—to foster and strengthen the voices of responsibility, peace, human rights, physical safety, and freedom's holy cause.

I saw myself in a dream with one of my teachers. I asked him, "What is this place?" meaning Earth. He said, "A hospital." Then I asked, "What do they call it?" meaning from where he comes. He responded, "Hell." I asked, "Do they ever get out of here?" He said, "Yes, when they heal." When I asked, "What heals them the fastest?" He said, "Pain."

Currently, despite being fundamentally one single life and divine, or as the Christ said, "You are the light of the world" (Mt 5:14), *we are eagles with our wings tied!* We are in "slavery" (Rom 8:21; Isaiah's "the dungeon of darkness," 42:7; David's "the valley of the shadow of death," Ps 23:4; Plato's "cave"; Einstein's "prison"). From the ultimacy point of view we are the Infinite Splendor incarcerated by the limitations and the complexities of the totality of situations. One might examine the various metaphors that have been applied to our state of existence (i.e., dungeon, slavery, mental hospital for gods, etc.). In view, what has been happening and is happening in our society (see the Nuremberg [1945-46] indictments[1]), you make the call. Sri Aurobindo wrote:

> The present evolutionary crisis comes from a disparity between the limited faculties of man—mental, ethical, and spiritual—and the technical and economical means at his disposal. At present mankind is undergoing an evolutionary crisis in which is concealed a choice of its destiny; for a stage has been reached in which the human mind has achieved in certain directions an enormous development while in others it stands arrested and bewildered and can no longer find its way . . . Man has created a system of civilization which has become too big for his limited mental capacity and understanding and his still more limited spiritual and moral capacity to utilize and manage, a too dangerous servant of his blundering ego and its appetites.[2]

If Slavery Is Not Wrong Nothing Is Wrong

The monstrous injustice of the institution of slavery, which imprisons mankind in hopeless and needless conflicts, shedding blood, pain, and crime, must be addressed. "Slavery is wrong and ought to be dealt with as a wrong," said Lincoln.

The spectacle of the slaves shackled all together with irons was "a continual torment" to him, wrote Lincoln to Joshua Fry Speed in 1855. At numerous occasions, until an assassin's bullet felled him in Ford's Theater on Good Friday (10:13 p.m. on April 14, 1865, the year Leo Tolstoy published *War and Peace* and Lewis Carroll *Alice in Wonderland*), and until his last breath at 7:21 the next morning, Lincoln denounced slavery as:

- a "monstrous injustice" (October 4, 1854)
- a "cancer" (October 16, 1854)
- an "odious institution" (August 27, 1856)
- "the sum of all villainies" (December 1857)
- a "deadly poison" (May 18, 1858)
- "an unqualified evil" (September 11, 1858)

- a "tyrannical principle" (October 15, 1858)
- a "moral, social, and political wrong" (March 1, 1859)
- a "wrong [which] ought to be dealt with as a wrong" (March 1, 1859)
- atrocious "morally and politically" (September 17, 1859)
- "the greatest wrong inflicted on any people (August 14, 1864)

The patriotic song "Rule, Britannia!" (1740), with its proclamation, resonates, "Britons never will be slaves," and the American Declaration of Independence (1776) asserts, "We hold these truths to be self-evident, that all men are created equal, that they are endowed by their Creator with certain unalienable rights, that among these are life, liberty, and the pursuit of happiness."

Similar pronouncements for the protection of human rights and fundamental freedoms exist in every country on our planet and on the two tables of the United Nations' 1948 Universal Declaration of Human Rights. However, when we compare our common humanity's fears, pains, poverty, and collective sufferings in the last seven thousand years, vis-à-vis who we are at our foundation, we are in slavery! "The real slavery of Israel in Egypt was that they had learned to endure it," said Rabbi Hanokh of Alexander. Anthropologist Margaret Mead (1901-1978) expressed it this way, "If we are to achieve a richer culture, rich in contrasting values, we must recognize the whole gamut of human potentialities, and so weave a less arbitrary social fabric, one in which each diverse human gift will find a fiting place."

The Joy of God:
Advancement and Diffusion of the Knowledge of '1'

"Without an inner change," stated Aurobindo, "man can no longer cope with the gigantic development of the outer life." "What is required," declared Julius Stulman in *Evolving Mankind's Future*, "is a new social model through which to organize the search for solutions to man's problems and thereby to break down the walls of ignorance and hostility which divide men." Apostle Paul acknowledged this need in his letter to the Romans, so "that creation itself would one day be set free from its slavery to decay, and share the glorious freedom of children of God" (Rom 8:21).

Dealing with "our slavery" is a long-term effort and must me dealt with carefully, tolerantly, and responsibly—help the poor people to help themselves. In Lincoln's words,

> Slavery is somewhat like the vein that you see on the back of a man's neck. If it were cut off immediately without the necessary precautions, the man could easily bleed to death. However, if it were allowed to grow unattended, and without any kind of medical surgery, it could easily spread until it would completely disfigure or incapacitate the man. As the man submit to carefully planned surgery to save his life from being destroyed by the vein, so must the nation carefully and tolerantly treat the problem of slavery in a way so as not to destroy the Union.

To provide the basic facts on which more responsible choices—furthering the advancement and diffusion of the knowledge of '1' and its application to economic, political, social, scientific, technological, self-development, free market, and human welfare—can be made, I see an urgent need for the "systematic pursuit" of the Unchanging Software behind the universe. In religious terms it means entrusting us with treasures; God calls us to "invest" in his ('1') kingdom. In Psalms we find, "Teach me to do thy will, for thou art my God: thy spirit is good . . . (143:10).

What is known today of '1', the field of potential action, is minuscule compared to the infinite dimensions of '1'. We are to that infinite knowledge of '1', stretching across billions of light-years through to infinity, what an amoeba is to us. As our knowledge of '1' increases, so will the free play of reason and the power to engage and influence nature increase. Bruce Murray, director of the Jet Propulsion Laboratory at CalTech, where I directed an IBM team forty years ago in the development and integration of a computer complex and software that controlled the first interplanetary flight and soft landing on the moon, stated:

> We are all desperately in need of a new world-view, consistent with the facts of science but much broader and more encompassing. The new world-view must provide reasonable guides to how men should behave toward one another. We must know how to rise above animals and act like gods.

I assert the primary intellectual event of the next several hundred years will be the development of this new world-view. The suffering and seemingly purposeless disorder and destruction which are the hallmarks of the twentieth century (and perhaps much of the twenty-first as well) will sharpen men's views of themselves and their world. It will create part of the basis of what must truly be a new theology whose effects may be even more enduring than those of previous great religions.[3]

Albert Einstein was of the same opinion as Bruce Murray. Einstein said:

It is not enough to teach man a specialty. Through it he may become a kind of useful machine but not a harmoniously developed personality. It is essential that the student acquire an understanding of and a lively feeling for values. He must acquire a vivid sense of the beautiful and of the morally good. Otherwise he—with his specialized knowledge—more closely resembles a well-trained dog than a harmoniously developed person. He must learn to understand the motives of human beings, their illusions, and their sufferings in order to acquire a proper relationship to individual fellowmen and to the community.[4]

Edgar Mitchel, moonwalk astronaut, had intuitive insight into reality while in space, and stated upon his return: "When looking at this magnificent Earth and the cosmos that surrounded it, the view inspired me and caused me to realize we need to do some different thinking about who and what we are."[5] Robert A. F. Thurman declared, "We can continue suffering the periodic hells that our ignorance produces . . . Or we can start by allowing that it might be possible to make an enlightened society."[6] David Bohm, who was painstaking and thorough in the study of our challenge, stated:

What I am proposing here is that man's general way of thinking of the totality, his general world-view, is crucial for overall order of the human mind itself. If he thinks of the totality as constituted of independent fragments, then that is how his mind will tend to operate, but if he can include everything coherently and harmoniously in an overall whole that is undivided, unbroken, and without a border (for every border is a division or break) then his mind will tend to move in a similar way, and from this will flow an orderly action within the whole.[7]

A Crime against Humanity: I Feel Your Pain

An old saying asserts it is hard to appreciate someone until you walk a mile in her or his shoes. Most of us know by now the repulsive statistics of our "post-genocidal world." Two out of every three inhabitants on our planet go to sleep hungry each night. One out of every five people lives in poverty on $1.00 a day or less. Five million persons on average starve to death each year. Mahatma Gandhi addressed this issue, "Earth provides enough to satisfy every man's need, but not every man's greed."

Two million children expire each year of diseases for which vaccines are already available. Over two million humans are dying from diarrhea every year, one million from malaria and almost three million from AIDS (eighteen million have breathed their last breath thus far and thirty eight million are infected). It is estimated that some six hundred thousand to eight hundred thousand people are trafficked for sexual exploitation, to the Middle East, Central and Western Europe, the United States, etc. In this modern-day slavery and atrocity, 47 percent are women, 34 percent are girls, and 16 percent are boys under the age of eighteen— meaning more than 80 percent of victims are female and 50 percent are children. (For "modern-day slavery," torture, and incommunicado incarceration, see the U.S. State Department "Trafficking in Persons Report.")

There are over one hundred million homeless worldwide; three million Americans live on the street that believe they have nothing to benefit others. There are 2.2 million hard-core drug users in the United States; one thousand drug-addicted babies are born every day. We now have mountains of empirical evidence on the global social and public costs of pervasive turmoil and collapse in the family, and the moral and spiritual crisis in education. There is the combustible material, devastation and gang warfare in our inner cities, sclerotic (hard hearted and animosity-ridden) political system, unemployment, the spiraling federal deficits (Americans borrow about $2,000,000,000 from foreigners every working day) and debt (more than $7,500,000,000,000), and escalating welfare.

There is a tragedy of values in the Christian church (sexual atrocities by bishops and priests, etc.), a general breaking of the social contract between society and worker, and the enormity of the problem of human sexual violence. There is a catastrophe of values, alleged accounting improprieties in corporate America: the Arthur Andersen, Enron, Global Crossing, PwG (PricewaterhouseCooper), Tyco, WorldCom, and other companies that shook world confidence in American business. We have armed our society to the hilt. Our way of life has fostered reckless proliferation of weapons, environmental pollution, pollution by words, and terrorism in cyberspace, inflicting trillions of dollars of damage.

We are all aware of identity theft, toxic nuclear waste problem, declining clean water supplies, and water contamination. Lack of clean water in parts of our planet promotes disease and fuels civil conflicts. We see increased harshness of weather patterns, land turning to desert, destruction of vegetation, species extinction, soil depletion and erosion, the punctured ozone layer, environmental degradation, and disappearing forests. Global warming threatens our health, our children's future, our natural resources, and our economies. Researchers under the support of the National Academy of Sciences and the Intergovernmental Panel on Climate Change have concluded that we must act fast to resist global climate change and the hazard it poses to the world.

There is bloodshed between Israel and the Palestinians. Acts of genocide were perpetrated not only by Hitler, Stalin, and Mao Ze-dong, but also by leaders in Iraq, Sudan, Rwanda, and elsewhere. Islamic radicals have called for the destruction of other religions and have stated that the acquisition of weapons of mass destruction is a "religious duty."

Is a war on terror, jihadist bombers, and struggle against military Islam winnable? Can a democracy successfully wage a war on terrorism without sacrificing civil liberties?

In 2001, like a badly beaten boxer staggering round the ring, a bipartisan task force for the U.S. Department of Energy presented President Bush with this report: "The most urgent unmet national security threat to the United States today is the danger that weapons of mass destruction or weapons-useable material in Russia could be stolen, sold to terrorist or hostile nation states, and used against American troops abroad or citizens at home." The volatility of fiscal prudence, national security, and global relationships makes the edges of the sword seem to get sharper.

To carry the analogy further, crime and violence continue to spiral. To anticipate national and international troubles, the spy shops of Washington encompass fifteen separate agencies, spreading through six Cabinet departments, that gather and analyze intelligence and employ an estimated one hundred thousand people and spend $40 billion a year.

What is the cost of the U.S. criminal justice structure and the price tag to our people? The criminal justice endeavor, designed to deter and prosecute individuals and corporations throughout the United States, costs over $150 billion per year. It is composed of over 69 federal agencies with law enforcement authority, more than 16,000 federal, state and local courts, 16,600 state and local police agencies, almost 780,000 sworn law enforcement officers, nearly 5,000 detention facilities, and a total of 2.2 million employees within the homeland security and justice system. The national security system, designed for deterring targets operating outside the U.S., has a price tag of $275 billion, with 1.4 million active duty and 2.2 million aggregate personnel. The total tabs of the two structures is $421 billion and 4.4 million personnel, excluding individual and corporate expenditures related to protecting our developing society.

To relieve nervousness, worry, emotional depletion, physical exhaustion, and even addiction, in an average day Americans puff their way through 1.17 billion cigarettes and 3.5 million joints, pop 2.8 million antidepressants and 145, 000 tabs of Ecstasy, and drink 330 million alcoholic drinks. The list goes on and on. In all probability, you have an additional listing of your own.

Martin Luther King Jr. (1929-1968) studied Gandhi's nonviolence and civil disobedience methods and borrowed from the wisdom of Jesus ("I want you to love your enemies"). To "meet hate with love," harness people's anger, and direct it into action through core values of justice and fairness King stated, "What is so disturbing is not the appalling actions of the 'bad' people, but the appalling silence of the 'good' people."

There is a pressing need for a global strategy, a common vision, and exact principles to protect and enhance the planet and all its life—to persuade mankind to apply its genius to the fundamental challenges that keep in chains our human family. From Proverbs we learn: "Where there is no vision, the people perish." As Marilyn Wilhelm stated, "You can not maintain democracy with an illiteracy."

Schools of '1': Expand Science—
Take What We Know One Step Further

Life requires meeting very high standards: the acquirement of knowledge, blessing of liberty, cultural and scientific literacy, and the capacity to reason and make quality decisions of those who aspire to be the participators and priests of our private and public institutions. "As liberals," said Milton Friedman, "we take freedom of the individual, or perhaps the family, as our ultimate goal in judging social arrangements. Freedom as a value in this sense has to do with the interrelations among people."[8] This means that we must take responsible participation and understanding that *we are one life*, as Einstein and others have realized.

The power to do good is also the power to do bad. In order to advance life and balanced social and economic development, preserve law and order, enforce private contracts, and foster viable markets, we borrow from Lincoln, "We can succeed only by concert . . . With firmness in the right, begin with head, heart and guts."

Hate, crime, war, terrorism, and other principal challenges can be drastically reduced through prudent research, investment, and education on the shackling nature of hate, crime, and war. Dr. L. Sharma, president of Himachal Pradesh State Veterinary Council in India, states:

> "Fundamentalists," as Dr. Radhakrishnan said, "want us to go by the beaten track, like horses in blinkers, looking neither to the right nor to the left." They go by the scriptures, and that too not by any scripture or all the scriptures, but by only their scriptures, and anything and everything that the other scriptures, or any other branch of knowledge says, is heresy. These fundamentalists, when they acquire arms and get charges to kill the followers of other faiths, become terrorists . . . The events in Israel, Afghanistan, Pakistan, Bangladesh and other places prove that the situation today is not much better. Jihad continues to be the war cry. Christians continue to believe that only their flock will be saved. Mussulmans will see the Christians in hell while Christians clamp eternal damnation on the Muslims. And both of them claim that Hindus, Buddhists, Jains, and Sikhs have no chance of emancipation. Out of concern for the 'Kafirs' or the "nonbelievers," they are carrying

on conversions, and killing people if they refuse to be converted. The terrorists, it seems, kill us out of mercy, to save us from flames of hell!"[9]

Robert Muller, who, through the United Nations University for Peace, is forging one human family education, calls this new worldview "a peacemaking vision . . . an education for global citizenship." He writes:

> Loving peace is not enough. We also need a peacemaking vision, science, strategy, and action . . . THE REALLY UNDEVELOPED PEOPLE ON THIS PLANET ARE THOSE WHO HAVE NO WORLD CONSCIOUSNESS . . . Wrong education is the principal cause of the political disorder on this planet. *People with limited vision can only produce limited solutions.* We need on this planet a host of people with a world vision. If your child was taught that Westchester County is the most important place on Earth and that out there is the rest of the world, you would protest with anger, and yet this is how most children are still educated about their own nations [emphasis added].[10]

Prevent Challenges by Truth:
Avoid Problems via the Unchanging Knowledge

We are about to enter an accelerated linking of humanity and sustaining solutions, solutions that do not produce new problems in the future. The wheel, the written word, navigation, education, the democratic system of government, the rise of a global economy, the printing press, electric power, telephone, radio, automobile, airplane, computer, television, the technology of communication and information processing, and the Internet have been progressively linking humanity and advancing our civilization.

For example, in 1992 the World Wide Web (Arpanet) consisted of sixty-four sites; today a count revealed more than 350,000,000 sites. The inspiration for each advance has been mankind's deeper understanding of the Common Ground—the collective cosmic foundations of '1'. As stated by Richard Feynman, "Science is not about what we know, it's about what we don't know." Judah Folkman, a renowned physician, highlights that the medical encyclopedias depict some fifteen to twenty thousand known human ailments, but fewer than a thousand can be "cured" or fully reversed.

Can we do better? Can we integrate the best of the human spirit, scientific rigor, religious insight, education, and creative problem solving? Can we revive that heart-to-heart experience of community and communion within the broad context of our Oneness? Can we accelerate the discovery and the grasp of the subtleties, new forms of knowledge, and new principles of '1' more scientifically? Can we raise our sights about what kind of people we can be, the kind that would allow us to commit ourselves to a common idea of freedom, democracy, the development of social skills, kinship, systematic consideration of international affairs, happiness, and boundless compassion, without deserting personal liberty or social divergence? Can we unleash the inherent powers of human existence and advance to a more just and better life? The hour is urgent. Will you help?

At the moment, physics is the most fundamental science into the Unchanging Nature of '1'. To make the focus of inquiry into the "Unchanging Sciences" more systematic (orderly, logical, rigorous, and enduring), I suggest *expanding the scientific method* and physics into a broader branch of learning. This more encompassing branch of '1' would be based on experimentation, personal experience, and mathematical theory: *The schools for the increase and diffusion of the Unchanging Knowledge*—the Schools of '1'.

Advancements to the deepest secrets of the universe, habits of the heart, creating a close-knit community and progress in society inevitably require groundbreaking research and the cooperation of many minds. These interdisciplinary institutions would be involved in the "systematic pursuit" (promoting research, exploration, and teaching, graduate and undergraduate studies) of the fundamental ground rules of the Unchanging Nature of '1'. They would link up and bring together contributors from a number of disciplines (i.e., the arts, sciences, and professions, including archaeology, fine art, architecture, astronomy, biological sciences, business and management, chemistry, economics, education, engineering, finance, health, history, international relations, law, linguistics, literature, mathematics, philosophy, physical sciences, political science, psychology, religion, social sciences, theology, and other subjects). Knowledge of individual disciplines linked together would lead to a greater understanding of higher principles such as the laws of economics, family life, materiality, freedom, peace, justice, consciousness, and a transcendent universal vision.

Acting in the Interests of the Human Family: A Treasure beyond Price

Is it possible? Can it happen? The answer is yes! With '1', the issue is only when.

You probably remember the story of a small boy and a wise old man: "I have a bird in my hands," said the boy to the wise man. "Is it alive or is it dead?" asked the old man. "I will trap him," thought the boy. "If he says it is dead, I will let the bird fly away. But if he says it is alive, I will crush the life out of it."

What is your answer? "His life is in your hands," replied the man. So is the Schools of the Unchanging—Schools of '1', to heal the sufferings of poor humanity.

Muller, in his farsighted work, *New Genesis*, shares "A Parable," by Jon Rye Kinghorn, where the students expressed disapproval of their teacher, a program of the Commission on Schools, North Central Association and the Charles F. Kettering Foundation:

> "Why was I not warned? Why was I not better educated? Why did my teachers not tell me about the problems and help me understand I was a member of an interdependent human race?" With even greater anger the student shouted, "You helped me extend my hands with incredible machines, my eyes with telescopes and microscopes, my ears with telephones, radios, and sonar, my brain with computers, but you did not help me extend my heart, love, concern to the entire human family. You, teacher, gave me half a loaf."[11]

"As knowledge advances," said Oliver Wendell Holmes (1841-1935), one of the foremost jurists of his day as a justice of the United States Supreme Court:

> science ceases to scoff at religion, and religion ceases to frown on science. The hour of mockery by the one, and of reproof by the

other, is passing away. Henceforth, they will dwell together in unity and goodwill. They will mutually illustrate the wisdom, power, and grace of God. Science will adorn and enrich religion; and religion will ennoble and sanctify science.

Science—in other words, knowledge—is not the enemy of religion; for, if so, then religion would mean ignorance; but it is often the antagonist of school-divinity.[12]

Mahatma Gandhi put it in simplicity of feeling and wholeness of being, "How beautiful it would be if all of us, young and old, men and women, devoted ourselves wholly to truth ['1'] in all that we might do—in our waking hours, whether working, eating, drinking or playing, till pure dreamless sleep claimed us for her own. God as truth has been for me a treasure beyond price. May he be so to every one of us!"[13]

When we devote ourselves wholly to the unchanging ('1'), in all that we might do, then we shall have no other gods.

Cutting-Edge Science of the Future: The Principle *above* the Laws of Nature

The question before eternity: why is the basic research and systematic study of '1' (the "Unchanging Jigsaw Puzzle" of the universe) so fundamental and so practical an investment to us? Why the betterment of human relations and the unfoldment of the inherent genius and the Light within every human being so essential to us?

The '1' speaks to us in code, which must be understood. Simply, winning (making family, business, and society healthy and prosperous) takes more than teamwork—it takes team software and management that understands the software. Great software in the company of excellent teamwork produces teamwork excellence. For the Green Bay Packers, that software and management was Vincent Lombardi. For such companies as American Express, Bank of America, The Chase Manhattan Bank, Disney, Federal Express, Genentech, IBM, Marriott, Microsoft, Nordstrom, Omniscience, Service Master, Snap-On Tools, Stew Leonard, and others, who understand that customer responsiveness, top-quality products, service-excellence, accountability, and trust pays, it is their management.

'1' is the software and our "Guiding Light" to help us cocreate and manage the universe and infinity. Business leaders, educators, and scientists understand the value of freedom, integrity, tolerance, social justice, intellectual property, curriculum planning, design, and implementation, and the power of knowing the laws of shaping their own discipline. Through the interdisciplinary study of '1' that power will be expanded, amplified, and focused on the core problems that are haunting humanity, people building, and ultimately nation and planetary life building.

At the heart of everything is the '1'. We live and move and have our being in '1'. '1' is the essence of life, the goal of all growth, progress, and evolution. Also, '1' is the crucial part of science and the crux of all pathfinding. Furthermore, the state of '1' is *above all* and *beyond all* the laws of physics. It is a law unto itself. At a point of Singularity we make our choice. At a Singularity ('1'), the universe and the laws of physics come into being; at a Singularity, the universe and the laws of physics vanish. Saint Paul, in a letter to the Ephesians, wrote: "One God ['1'] and Father of all, who is above all, and through all, and in you all (Eph 4:6).

'1' is the Light of Life, a time-tested and world-honored map of reality. At present, most of us are of the opinion that because the laws of physics are invariant, we are their hostages. Not so. Just because a calculator's software is tightly set it does not mean we don't have a choice in our addition. "No elementary phenomenon is a phenomenon until it is a registered phenomenon."[14] If you decide to lift your hand, you lift your hand. It is your thought and *free will* that decide what comes into being in your environment.

One of the key elements of the LSPR is its ability to make predictions of physical relationships and fundamental physical constants. This comes through '1'. The use value and exchange value of '1' is *above* all the laws of physics. As a fulcrum of a seesaw creates a balance between two sides, so '1' creates a balance between the laws of physics! '1' *determines what the laws of physics will be!* '1' is the Book of Life and the software guiding us to our future!

The ramifications are momentous and awe inspiring. We, individual images of '1' are the center that structures and organizes "a universe of our own"—our own personal world and life. We bring into being our horizons and, therefore, our experiences. John Wheeler, in his observer-participatory universe, describes this "higgledy piggledy" process in electrical terms of "a self-excited circuit."[15]

That is, by applying the '1' principles to our decision-making and actions, we, as a self-excited circuit, have dominion over the laws of nature and the direction of events in our lives. Now is the opportunity of the scientific community to utilize their genius to the core problems that are challenging the human race. Here is the potential for the birth of a new science (the a priori science at the foundation of all sciences) and new reverence for the laws of nature and to help us to navigate our future more effectively. In the Epistle to the Galatians, Paul declared:

> If you are led by the Spirit ['1'], you are not under law [i.e., law of nature. You are above the laws of nature. You are in the miracle territory of John Wheeler's "law without law."] (5:18) . . . the fruit of the Spirit is love, joy, peace, patience, kindness, goodness, faithfulness, gentleness and self-control. Against such things there is no law . . . [When you move the fulcrum of the seesaw you change the balance]. Since we live by the Spirit, let us keep in step with the Spirit (5:22-5).

Katha Upanishad stated it thusly, "*When all desires that cling to the heart are surrendered, then a mortal becomes immortal.* This is the sacred teaching."[16] This is also the cornerstone to the elementary act of creation, achieving a higher quality of life (to what has been referred to as "miracles" in religion) and space-time transformations in physics. Christians hold miracles to be God's omnipotence working through us, and Buddhists see them as perfecting of the mind. No one can do wonders for us. Each individual, if she/he desires to change her/his world, has to do this on her/his own behalf.

No More Doubt about the End
We Will Emerge Victorious and Thankful

The central point in a seesaw is the fulcrum. If the fulcrum is heavyweight, it can support a big load. If it is fragile, you know the rest. In an electrical system, to transmit heavy-duty power across high-voltage lines one needs *heavy-duty grounding*. Similarly, in the elementary act of creation, in quantum phenomena (transformation from one state to another, expressed with equality '=' in physical relationships), one needs effective zero neutralizing force ('='). We have not yet quantized this force in science, as we did in mathematics by adding more zeros. The more zeros behind a number in your bank account, the larger your total. Similar to zero's role as a *shifter in mathematical value*, the role of '**1**' is as a *shifter in physical value*! We can see this visually on the LSPR.

The long-lasting grounding in our lives is the neutralizing zero force of the Law of Life in the Beatitudes (Mt 5:3) and the Law of Liberty for the lovers of Freedom "that gives freedom, and continues to do this" in James (1:25). This correspondence can be demonstrated with the laws of physics in the LSPR. How we distill simplicity out of complexity in our lives, how we ascend to the better view—and from that vantage point distinguish what is missing in the next step, and fill the gap—and how we wield the knowledge of '**1**' ("the will of God" of the Scriptures, the power of Freedom in our Constitution) will determine the quantum outcome of our personal choice, views of reality, and our experiences. A Tibetan abbot of a lamasery stated:

> Let the forces of light bring illumination to mankind.
> Let the spirit of peace be spread abroad.
> May men of goodwill everywhere meet in the spirit of cooperation.
> May forgiveness on the part of all be the keynote at this time.
> Let power attend the efforts of the great ones.
> So let it be, and help us do our part.[17]

"When the heart is filled with compassion," confirmed Sai Baba, "the hands are dedicated to the service of others, the body is engaged in constant help to others, the life of such a person is sacred, purposeful, and noble."[19] John Wheeler declared, "Philosophy passes the judgment; human idealism raises the flag. Science shows the possibilities. Education spreads the motivation. We, the human species, can and must take control of our own fate. How else can we survive over the long haul?"[19] On March 1, 1859, Lincoln would reveal:

> All you have to do is to keep the faith, to remain steadfast to the right, to stand by your banner. Nothing should lead you to leave your guns. Stand together, ready, with match in hand. Allow nothing to turn you to the right or to the left. Remember how long you have been in setting out on the true course; how long you have been in getting your neighbors to understand and believe as you now do. Stand by your principles; stand by your guns; and victory complete and permanent is sure at the last.[20]

And in his address at Cooper Union (in February of 1860) practical visionary Lincoln would proclaim: "Let us, to the end, dare to do our duty . . ." Daniel Webster (1782-1852) wrote:

> If we work marble, it will perish;
> If we work upon brass, time will efface it;
> If we rear temples, they will crumble into dust;
> But if we work upon immortal minds
> And instill into them just principles,
> We are engraving upon tablets
> Which no time will efface,
> But will brighten and brighten to all eternity.

Access to the Principle *above* the laws of nature, the Law of '1', opens a new range of choices from a higher, more endearing and very caring perspective. In the end, the highest degree of choice is to advance the interests of every person.

Let us rejoice, for the hours of the Highest Good are at hand.

11

I AM WHO I AM; I WILL BE WHAT I WILL BE

Indeed, indeed,
You are one of us.

—Hafiz

What Are We Searching For?

I am the sky, the smile, and the sorrow;
I am the little ant and the graceful sparrow.
I am the child you kick, and the man you hang;
The fragrance you love, the beat of your heart,
And the woman you hug.

I am everywhere equally:
The beginning, the middle and the end;
Everyone and everything is me;
And there is no one else but me.
I am gazing out of every face, including yours!
Indeed, I am who I am.
Indeed, I will be what I will be.

Remember my dearest;
Before this journey you were in Light and Bliss.
There was no time or space, no birth or death.
You decided to celebrate life—
To limit the spectrum of your perception.

You have assumed many forms:
As a flower, a waterfall, or the bright sky,
Your own brother, sister, mother and father.
Yet, you made certain that the pressure of self-discovery
Takes you back to your original knowledge.

Do not be uneasy, my love,
About this great excursion;
Do not be troubled, my joy,
With so many different faces and forms.
They are all carved out of the same One Light of '1'.
They are you!

Find Your Own Inner Light

Know thyself.
Trust your insights.
Rise to the larger view.
Press onward to the "unity of knowledge."
Achieve, through self-cultivation, purity of heart,
Love of your neighbor, detachment from results,
And stillness of the mind:
Pristine peace, harmony, and freedom.

Rejoice.
Be perfect.
Simplicity is the essence, unity the common binding thread.
Deploy more free will with responsibility.
Cherish each opportunity to serve and to love.
Live with unceasing consciousness in God.
Celebrate your divinity.

You will be enraptured in your blissful glory.
Yes my Happiness, yes my Light, and yes my Love;
Dressed in righteousness, kindness, caring and compassion,
You will perceive the Triumphant Light in your own being.

Through your personal example,
By your contacts at home, work,
While talking, walking, and serving,
Reading, writing and traveling,
Bring this message to others.

In a scientific context,
Each one teach '1'.

It is a luminous road of radiant beauty,
Happiness, splendor and life.
It is a captivating pilgrimage
You have prepared for yourself.

It is Joy,
It is Light,
It is Unconditional Love,
It is Wonder,
It is You!

May the Compassion of the Holy One,
Peace, Goodness, Abundance, Freedom,
Love and Happiness abide with you always.
Thank you so much. I love you. God bless you!

—Orest Bedrij

ACCLAMATIONS

Hosanna!

O, Father, my Sweetheart, and Lover,
Oh, Infinite Wisdom and Light,
Immeasurable love to you
For letting me experience you:
In freedom, peace and kindness;
Excellence, choice and humility;
Teamwork, gentleness and responsibility;
Simplicity, longer and more abundant life;
My precious parents;
My dearly beloved wife and children;
My treasured coworkers and neighbors.

O, Great Joy, Goodness, and Happiness
Oh, Holy Compassion and Care.
When I contemplate your nature,
Words are incapable to describe your
Vastness, beauty, perfection and abundance;
Only the music of purity, service-excellence and silence . . .

O, Bliss of bliss and Door of doors,
Oh, clear Light of light in my being,
Please allow me to love you and glorify you,
With all my heart, all my soul and all my being.

Glory to you, Grace, Glory to you, Father, and
On earth peace, goodwill toward all.

I Love You: Thank You for Changing My Life

This book would not have been possible without the assistance of many people, including authors and publishers. I am enormously grateful to all of you, authors and publishers, for your advice and for the usage of print materials listed in Notes and for illuminating and helping me in the preparation of this study. Thank you from the bottom of my heart for your wisdom, guidance, and the wealth of precious jewels you provided.

My deepest love and gratitude to you my dearly beloved spiritual father, brother, sweetheart, and Light of liberation, Jesus the Christ, for your loving guidance, support, selfless compassion, wisdom, and encouragements, to lead an immaculate holy life in the fullness of God. Glory to you, holy One. Glory to your glory.

Absolute love and gratitude to you blessed Lady of Light, Mary, our Universal Mother (Buddhists Kuan Yin), our lover and sweetheart, for your infinite love and compassion and for your perseverance to rescue all beings from suffering.

Divine love and compassion to you archangels Gabriel and Uriel for revealing to me, in the most basic sense, the Spirit and the fragrance of the knowledge of the Source of Life, which in the language of science, translates to the central principle of the universe, characterized in the laws of physics by the symbol '1'.

Unconditional love, indebtedness, and gratitude to you Lords of Light, Sanat Kumara, Maitrea, Avalokiteshvara, Shakyamuni Buddha, Melchizedek, Saint John the Baptist, Moses, Kashyapa, Dipamkara, Lord Krishna, Djwhal Khul, Babaji, Bodhidharma, Omelan Kowcz, my precious parents, and to the many who influenced my thinking long before this study was conceived.

Absolute love, gratitude, and sincere acclamation to you most pure, most caring, and most supportive compassion, my noble wife and sweetheart Oksana, for your unlimited love and wisdom, and for enjoining me in this task as intimate advisor and companion.

My deepest love, gratefulness, and blessings to you our wise children, Orest, Roksana, Chrystyna, Adrian, Christopher, and Christiaan, for your great compassion, wonderful hugs, and for being the most supportive family unit.

Abounding love, acclamation, and gratitude to Professor Stephen Modell, Bernice Neben, Marsante G. Alison, Helen Marie S. Tabaranza,

Kevin Desabelle, Nadia Joy Ador-Javier, Andrew I. Lenec, Bill Hungerford, Maya Martin, Jinni Richards, and Dr. E. Stanley Kardatzke, for your painstaking editing, indexing, and suggestions.

My gratitude, brotherly love, and special thanks to Richard Knouse for applying mathematical programming and computer modeling highlighting the relationships between the laws of physics, the fundamental physical constants, and '1'.

A heartfelt thanks, appreciation, and brotherly love to Richard Payne for your enlightening thoughts and feedback, which made this work more lucid.

Sincerest thanks, love, and appreciation to Cathy Amon, John Balme, Jen Eddy, Professor John Fizer, Professor Wilhelm I. Fushchych, Jim Giorgi, Professor Peter Kotzer, Mario William III Larrabure, Jim Lasko, Arthur Lockard, Professor Peter Roche de Coppens, and Professor Marilyn Wilhelm, for reading the manuscript and offering valuable comments and suggestions. Your generosity is gratefully acknowledged.

Countless individuals, publishers, corporations, and foundations have contributed to what I know. It is impossible to catalog you all. I shall list a few. Brotherly love, reverence, and profound indebtedness to Stefan Banach, Hendrik Antoon Lorentz, Hermann Minkowski, Wolfgang Pauli, Enrico Fermi, Subrahmanyan Chandrasekhar, Marie Curie, Victor Weisskopf, Linus Carl Pauling, (Jules-) Henri Poincaré, Walter and Lao Russell, Freeman Dyson, Nikola Tesla, Hideki Yukawa, Ian Barbour, John Polkinghorne, Vyasa, Sathya Sai Baba, Hryhoryj Skovoroda; Evelyn Underhill, Taras Shevchenko, Ibn Arabi, Paramahamsa Yogananda, Hui-neng, Patanjali, Kabir, Ralph Waldo Emerson, Robert Muller; archangels Michael and Raphael; His Holiness the Fourteenth Dalai Lama, Pope John Paul II, authors of the Bible, and many others who served as advisors on this project, and whose insights and literary works furnished more specific glimpses of '1'. To a great degree this work is yours too; the blessings of God upon you.

To all you reading this book, there is not enough space to acknowledge my profound thanks and appreciation for joining me in the Spirit of unity, peace and love. May the grace and wisdom of the All Highest be with you always. I am extremely grateful, and I love you all.

ABBREVIATIONS

A	The Alpha
ACLU	American Civil Liberties Union
AD	In the year of the Lord
ADHD	Attention deficit/hyperactivity disorder
AEC	Atomic Energy Commission
a.*m.*	Before noon
AU	Astronomical Unit
BBC	British Broadcasting Corporation
BC	Before Christ
BSE	Bovine Spongiform Encephalopathy (mad cow disease)
CDC	Center for Disease Control
CMB	"Cosmic microwave background" radiation
DNA	Deoxyribonucleic Acid
EST	Eastern Standard Time
EU	European Union
FDA	Food and Drug Administration
FSIS	Food Safety and Inspection Service
IBM	International Business Machines Corporation
LASL	Los Alamos Scientific Laboratory in New Mexico
LSI	Large-scale integration
LSPR	Logarithmic Slide Rule for Physical Relationship
NASA	National Aeronautics and Space Administration
NFL	National Football League
NSA	National Security Agency
NSF	National Science Foundation
PC	Personal Computer
p.*m.*	After noon
SSC	Superconducting Super Collider
TB	Tuberculosis
UN	United Nations

USDA   U.S. Department of Agriculture
WTC   World Trade Center
YHWH   Yahweh, the personal name of the God of Israelites, called
          the Tetragrammaton
Ω   The Omega

APPENDIX 1

A Summary of Insights

The appendix 1 contains a Summary of Insights with references to the four states: (1) Absolute, '1'; (2) From Absolute to Humanity; (3) Absolute in the World; (4) From Humanity to Absolute. The Summary of Insights can be a valuable tool to examine each of the areas individually. The list is intended to show an integrated meaning of *who we are* and where we are heading. Orientation code to references and chapters is shown as: part 1 or 2, chapter (ch.) yy, reference[xx]. Specifically, as in Saint Augustine, part 1, chapter 25, reference [29]: 1 ch. 25:29

Summary of Insights: (1) Absolute, '1'

Augustine, Saint
Lord, I have sought you in all the temples of the world and lo, I found you within myself. If a man does not find the Lord within himself, he will surely not find Him in the world. 1 ch. 25:29.

We are all members of one Body, whether we are here or anywhere else on earth, now or at any other time from Abel the just to the end of the world. 1 ch. 11:3.

Baba, Meher
Out of the depths of unbroken Infinity arouse the Question, Who am I? And to that Question there is only one Answer—I am God! 1 ch. 19:25.

If you look within and experience your own soul in its true nature, you will realize that you are infinite and beyond all creation. 1 ch. 19:26.

Bernard, Saint
Who is God? I can think of no better answer than He who is. Nothing is more appropriate to the eternity which God is. If you call God good, or great, or blessed, or wise, or anything else of this sort, it is included in these words, namely, He is. 1 ch. 19:22.

Bhagavad Gita
Everything is situated within Him ['1']. 1 ch. 7:6.

There is no Truth superior to Me. Everything rests upon Me ['1'], as pearls are strung on a thread. I am the taste of water, the light of the sun and the moon, the syllable om in the Vedic mantras; I am the sound in ether [empty-space] and the ability in man. I am the original fragrance of the earth, and I am the heat in fire. I am the life of all that lives, and I am the penance of all ascetics. I am the original seed of all existence, the intelligence of the intelligent, and the prowess of all powerful men. All states of being—be they of goodness, passion or ignorance—are manifested by My energy. I am, in one sense, everything—but I am independent. I am not under the modes of this material nature (7.7-12). 1 ch. 19:11.

Bible, The
The Spirit ['1'] of the Lord fills the whole universe and holds all things together (Wis 1:7). 1 ch. 11.

"I am who I am": "I will be what I will be" (Ex 3:14). 1 ch. 6.

Lord, You have been our dwelling place (Ps 90:1). 1 ch. 7.

The God who made the world and everything in it is the Lord of heaven and earth and does not live in temples build by hands (Acts 17:24). 1 ch. 7.

You are gods, all of you sons of the Most High (Ps 82:6). 1 ch. 7.

You are the light of the world (Mt 5:14). 1 ch. 11.

Is it not written in your own Law that God said, "You are gods" (Jn 10:34). 1 ch. 11.

Whoever has seen me has seen the Father (Jn 14:9). 1 ch. 7.

I am in my Father, and you in me, and I in you (Jn 14:20). 1 chs. 5, 7.

In him we live and move and have our being (Acts 17:28). 1 chs. 1, 8, 11.

We, many though we are, are one body (1 Cor 10:17). 1 ch. 11.

Each one of you is a son of God (Gal 3:26). 1 ch. 19.

All are one (Gal 3:28). 1 ch. 20.

One body and one Spirit (Eph 4:4). 1 ch. 20.

Whoever looks on me is seeing him who sent me (Jn 12:45). 1 ch. 7.

All that the Father has belongs to me (Jn 16:15). 1 ch. 7.

You are in me and I am in you (Jn 14:20). 1 ch. 11.

The body is one and has many members, but all the members, many though they are, are one body (1 Cor 12:12). 1 ch. 20.

If one member suffers, all the members suffer with it; if one member is honored, all the members share its joy (1 Cor 12:26). 1 ch. 20.

Now the body is not one member, it is many. If the foot should say, "Because I am not a hand I do not belong to the body," would it then no longer belong to the body? . . . There are, indeed, many different members, but one body. The eye cannot say to the hand, "I do not need you," any more than the head can say to the feet, "I do not need you." Even those members of the body which seem less important are in fact indispensable . . . If one member suffers, all the members suffer with it; if one member is honored, all members share its joy. You, then, are the body of Christ. Every one of you is a member of it (1 Cor 12:12-27). 1 ch. 20.

Blake, William
I am in you and you in me. 1 ch. 8:8.

Bohm, David

What we perceive through the senses as empty space is actually the plenum, which is the ground for the existence of everything, including ourselves. The things that appear to our senses are derivative forms, and their true meaning can be seen only when we consider the plenum, in which they are generated and sustained, and into which they must ultimately vanish. 1 ch. 10:12.

The entire universe has to be understood as a single undivided whole, in which analysis into separately and independently existent parts has no fundamental status. 1 ch. 19:19.

Buddha, Gautama the

Verily, there is an unborn, unoriginated, uncreated, unformed. If there were not this unborn, unoriginated, uncreated, unformed, then an escape from the world of the born, the originated, the created, and the formed would not be possible. 1 ch. 14.

Carey, Ken

I am always with you . . . You and I are one in your consciousness. As we have ever been one in Reality. I beat with every throb of your heart, feel with every touch of your hand, cry your every tear, breathe your every breath. I am never far away. 1 ch. 19:21.

Catherine of Genoa, Saint

Then of herself she neither works nor speaks nor wills nor feels nor hears nor understands, neither has she of herself the feeling of outward or inward where she may move. 1 ch. 18:6

The state of this soul is then a feeling of such utter peace and tranquility that it seems to her that her heart, and her bodily being, and all both within and without is immersed in an ocean of utmost peace; from whence she shall never come forth for anything that can befall her in this life. 1 ch. 18:6

And she stays immovable, imperturbable, impassible. So much so, that it seems to her in her human and spiritual nature, both within and without, she can feel no other thing than sweetest peace. And she is so full of peace that though she presses her flesh, her nerves, her bones, no other thing comes from them than peace. 1 ch. 18:6

My Me is God, nor do I recognize any other Me except my God himself. 1 ch. 26:20

Cidade Caleixnese
The kingdom of heaven is within you, and whosoever shall know himself shall find it. 1 ch. 20:23

Eckhart, Meister
In thus breaking through, I perceive what God and I are in common. There I am what I was. There I neither increase or decrease. For there I am the immovable which moves all things. Here man has won again what he is eternally and ever shall be. Here God is received into the soul. 1 ch. 11:9.

I am that which I was and shall remain, now and forevermore. 1 ch. 11:14.

The seed of God is in us, if the seed had a good, wise, and industrious farmer, it would thrive all the more and grow up to God whose seed it is, and the fruit would be equal to the nature of God. Now the seed of a pear tree grows into a pear tree, a hazel seed into a hazel tree, the seed of God into God. 1 ch. 22:9

The Godhead gave all things up to God. The Godhead is poor, naked and empty as though it were not; it has not, wills not, wants not, works not, gets not. It is God who has the treasure and the bride in him, the Godhead is as void as though it were not. 1 ch. 10:22.

Einstein, Albert
[Reality] is precisely not to be influenced, since it is changeless and unmovable, either by configuration of matter or by anything else. 1 ch. 14:2.

A human being is a part of the whole, called by us the "Universe," a part limited in time and space. He experiences himself, his thoughts and feelings as something separated from the rest—a kind of optical delusion of his consciousness. This delusion is a kind of prison for us, restricting us to our personal desires and to affection for a few persons nearest to us. 1 ch. 7:11; 1 ch. 8.

Emerson, Ralph Waldo
Every man is a divinity in disguise, a god playing the fool. 1 ch. 11.

al-Farid, Ibn
Everything you see is the action of the One ['1']. 1 ch. 4:20.

I knew for sure that we are really One, and the sobriety of union restored the notion of separation, and my whole being was tongue to speak, an eye to see, an ear to hear, and a hand to seize. 1 ch. 4:21.

Gandhi, Mahatma
To me God is truth and love. God is ethics and morality. God is fearless. God is the source of light and life and yet He is above and beyond all these. God is conscience. He is even the atheism of the atheist. He transcends speech and reason. He is a personal God to those who need His touch. He is the purest essence. He simply *is* to those who have faith. He is long suffering. He is patient but He is also terrible. He is the greatest democrat the world knows, for he leaves us unfettered to make our own choice between evil and good. He is the greatest tyrant ever known for he often dashes the cup from our lips and under cover of free will leaves us a margin so wholly inadequate as to provide only mirth for himself at our expense. Therefore, it is what Hinduism calls all this sport—Lila, or calls it an illusion—Maya. 1 ch. 19:23.

Hammarskjöld, Dag
Goodness is something so simple: always to live for others, never to seek one's advantage. 1 ch. 20:5.

John of the Cross, Saint
The heavens are mine, the earth is mine, and the nations are mine! Mine are the just, and the sinners are mine; mine are the angels and the Mother of God; all things are mine, God himself is mine and for me,

because Christ is mine and all for me. What do you ask for, what do you seek for, O my soul? All is yours—all is for you. 1 ch. 26:4.

Krishna, Gopi
This unimaginable Cosmic Intelligence is present at every spot in the universe, and our whole personality, ego, mind, intellect and all—is but an infinitely small bubble blown on this boundless ocean. 1 ch. 17:14.

Lao-tzu
There is a thing inherent and natural, which existed before heaven and earth. It is motionless and fathomless. It stands alone and never changes; it pervades everywhere and never becomes exhausted. It may be regarded as the Mother of the Universe. I do not know its name; if I am forced to give it a name, I will call it Tao, and I name it as supreme. 1 ch. 10:11.

Maharshi, Ramana
Reality is only one and that is the Self, all the rest are mere phenomena in it, of it, and by it. The seer, the objects, and the sight, all are the Self only. Can anyone see or hear, leaving the self aside? . . . If you surrender yourself . . . all is well . . . Only so long as you think that you are the worker, are you obliged to reap the fruits of your actions. If, on the other hand, you surrender yourself and recognize your individual self as only a tool of the Higher Power, that power will take over your affairs along with the fruits of actions. 1 ch. 14:20.

Jami, Maulana 'Abdurrahman
Neighbor and associate and companion—everything is He. In the beggar's coarse frock and in the king's silk—everything is He. In the crowd of separation and in the loneliness of collectedness by God! Everything is He and by God! Everything is He. 1 ch. 20:9.

Mechthild of Magdeburg:
I am in you and you are in me. We cannot be closer. We are two united, poured into a single form by an eternal fusion. 1 ch. 25:24.

Merton, Thomas
Our very life loses its separate voice and resounds with the majesty and the mercy of the Hidden and Living One. 1 ch. 20:8.

Muslim Sufis

What marvel! that a Being colorless displays a hundred thousand hues, tints, shades! What wonder! That being void of form enrobes in forms beyond all numbering!—May we behold Him in all hues and forms! Yet lifts to every name an answering head, the name of Him who is the changeless One amidst the changing many, and within whose oneness all this many is confined, may we begin our loving work of peace. 1 ch. 6:20.

There's naught within your robe but God Himself, the knower and the known are but the same. He who knows God is God; God knows Himself. 1 ch. 25:25

I saw you not before—I see you now, Belov'd! You peep forth from every face! I saw you not before—behind the clouds, Beloved! You did not hide. I see you now! 1 ch. 26:10.

Muhammad, Holy Prophet

I, verily the I All-One, am God, there is no other God than I [the '1': the universal all-pervading Self], and I alone should be adored by all. 1 ch. 20:15.

Muktananda, Swami

I see the soft conscious mass of light trembling delicately and shining in all conditions—whether I am eating, drinking, or bathing. It surrounds me even during sleep . . . Thou art That—is, in fact, my own Self— vibrating subtly within me . . . The universe belongs to you. You are its Soul. Different levels of manifestations arise from you. They are your own forms. You are perfect in your aspect as the in dwelling Universal Spirit. Remain continuously aware that the universe is your own splendid glory. 1 ch. 4:25.

All this, indeed, is the Absolute . . . God pervades everywhere . . . This universe is a true image of the Supreme Reality. 1 ch. 7:1.

Al-Rumi, Jalaluddin

The Beloved is all that lives. 1 ch. 20:7.

I am you and you are me. 1 ch. 25:21.

Schimmel, Annemarie
God is visible in every trace of His creation, and although the common folk, the blind and dumb, animal-like, do not recognize Him, the mystic drinks not a single drop of water without discovering His vision in the cup. 1 ch. 5:9.

Schrödinger, Erwin
I am God Almighty. 1 ch. 7:5.

ATMAN = BRAHMAN (the personal self equals the omnipresent, all-comprehending, eternal self). 1 ch. 7:5.

"I am in the east and in the west, I am below and above, I am this whole world." 1 ch. 15:10.

Spinoza, Benedict de
Reality and perfection are synonymous. 1 ch. 11.

Subramuniya
At first you feel light shining within you. 1 ch. 4:19.

Tasawwuf
The wise see in their heart the face of God, and not in images of stone and clod! Who in themselves, alas! can see Him not, they seek to find Him in some other spot. 1 ch. 19:33.

Teresa of Avila, Saint
God implants Himself in the interior of that soul in such a way that, when it returns to itself, it cannot possibly doubt that God has been in it and it has been in God. 1 ch. 18:4.

Thales of Miletus
All things are full of gods. 1 ch. 7.

Upanishads, The
The One God hidden in all living beings, the Living Witness biding in all hearts—the Wise who seek and find Him in them-Self, to them, the None Else, is Eternal Joy. The all-pervading Inner Self of all, who from

His Formlessness creates all Forms—the Wise who see that One within them-Self, to them alone belongs Eternal Joy . . . The Colorless, who from His secret store exhaustless, countless colors draws, to paint, efface, repaint the worlds upon the face of empty-space with Mystic Potency— may He endow us with the lucid mind! 1 ch. 6.19.

In the beginning this world was merely nonbeing. It was existent. 1 ch. 10:5.

Cows are of many different colors, but the milk of all is one color, white; so the proclaimers who proclaim the Truth use many varying forms to put it in, but yet the Truth enclosed in all is One. 1 ch. 19:36.

Verily, this whole world is Brahman. Tranquil [still and calm], let one worship It, as that from which he came forth, as that into which he will be dissolved, as that in which he breathes. 1 ch. 19:12.

Atman alone is the whole world. 1 ch. 19:13.

As the bees, my dear, prepare honey by collecting the essences of different trees and reducing the essence to a unity, as they are not able to discriminate "I am the essence of this tree," "I am the essence of that tree"—even so, indeed, my dear, all creatures here, though they reach Being, know not "We have reached Being" . . . . These rivers, my dear, flow, the eastern toward the east, the western toward the west. They become the ocean itself. As there they know not "I am this one," "I am that one"—even so, indeed, my dear, all creatures here, though they have come forth from Being, know not "We have come forth from Being." 1 ch. 19:14.

You are woman. You are man. You are the youth and the maiden too. You as an old man totterest with a staff being born, you becomest facing in every direction. You are the dark blue bird and the green (parrot) with red eyes. You hast the lightning as thy child. You are the seasons and the seas. Having no beginning. You do abide with all-pervadingness. Wherefrom all beings are born. 1 ch. 19:20.

I Myself am He! 1 ch. 19:15.

The world is His ['1']; indeed, He is the world itself. 1 ch. 19:16.

Verily, this Soul is the overlord of all things, the king of all things. As all the spokes are held together in the hub and felly of a wheel, just so in this Soul all things, all gods, all worlds, all breathing things, all these selves are held together. 1 ch. 19:17.

I am the Infinite; what you are, that same am I; you are all This; I am all This. 1 ch. 19:20.

Vedas, The
Truly, you are Godhead yourself . . . He is you. 1 ch. 19:37.

The countless heads, eyes, ears, and hands and feet of living beings are all parts of One Man. 1 ch. 20:10; 2 ch. 1:18.

The progeny of Adam, all are parts and limbs of one and the same organism, risen from the same essence, everyone; and can it be, while one limb is in pain, that other limbs should feel at restful ease? 1 ch. 20:14.

Wilber, Ken
All things, including subatomic particles, are ultimately made of God. 1 ch. 19:18.

Wingate
Call Me Omega or God, or Jehovah, or Brahman, or Allah, or anything else you would like to call Me. I AM all of these. Yet I AM also none of them. I AM the Cosmos, the Universe. Everything That Is . . . I AM the First Cause. I AM the Last Effect. I AM Every Cause and Every Effect. I AM Spirit. I AM Soul. I AM Matter. As Spirit, I AM the inexpressible, indefinable Source of All Being, infinite and eternal. As Soul, as Spirit manifest for an evolution, I AM Mind. I Am Consciousness. I AM Beingness. And as Matter, as Soul manifest for a lifetime, I AM Everyone and Everything. I AM Perfect; and Every Cause and Every Effect and Everyone and Everything are Part of My Perfection. I AM THE ONE. I AM ALSO THE MANY. AND WHATEVER IT IS THAT SAYS I AM, I AM THAT I AM. 1 ch. 17:9.

Summary of Insights: (2) From Absolute to Humanity

Athanasius, Saint
The Divine Word became human in order that every human being may become God. 1 ch. 9:5.

Bhagavad Gita
All created beings are unmanifest in their beginning, manifest in their interim state, and unmanifest. [2.28] There never was a time when I did not exist [as an archetype or a potential], nor you, nor any of these kings. Nor is there any future in which we shall cease to be. Just as the dweller in this body passes through childhood, youth and old age, so at death he merely passes into another kind of body. (2.12-13). 1 ch. 10:10.

Bohm, David
The entire universe of matter as we generally observe it is to be treated as a comparatively small pattern of excitation. 1 ch. 10:12.

The excitation pattern is relatively autonomous and gives rise to approximately recurrent stable and separable projections into a three-dimensional explicate order of manifestation. 1 ch. 10:12.

Dewey, John
Intelligence has descended from its lonely isolation at the remote edge of things, whence it operated as Unmoved Mover, and ultimate good, to take its seat in the moving affairs of men. 1 ch. 11:10.

Dirac, Paul
All matter is created out of some imperceptible substratum. 1 ch. 10:8.

The creation of matter leaves behind it a "hole" in this substratum which appears as antimatter. Now, this substratum itself is not accurately described as material, since it uniformly fills all space and is undetectable by any observation. In a sense, it appears as nothingness—immaterial, undetectable and omnipresent. But it is a peculiarly material form of nothingness out of which all matter is created. 1 ch. 10:8.

Eckhart, Meister
If it is true that God became man, it is also true that man became God.
1 ch. 9:8.

When I came out of the Godhead into multiplicity . . . 1 ch. 11:9.

Gospel of Thomas, The
I am the light which is over everything. I am the All; (from me) the All
has gone forth, and to me the All has returned. Split wood: I am there.
Lift up the stone, and you will find me there also. (77). 1 ch. 10.

Blessed are the solitary and elect, for you shall find the kingdom; because
you come from it (and) you shall go there again. 1 ch. 9.3.

Jesus said, "If they say to you: 'From where have you originated?' say
to them: *'We have come from the Light, where the Light has originated
through itself.'* It (stood) and It revealed itself in their image. If they say
to you: '(Who) are you?' say: 'We are His sons and we are the elect of the
Living Father.' If they ask you: 'What is the sign of your Father *in you?*'
say to them: 'It is a movement and a rest [emphasis added]'" (49-50). 1
ch. 9:3.

Irenaeus, Saint
God the Logos became what we are, in order that we may become what
He Himself is. 1 ch. 9:1; 1 ch. 23:4.

Merton, Thomas
God became man in Christ. In becoming what I am, He united me to
Himself and made me His epiphany [appearance or manifestation], so
that now I am meant to reveal Him. 1 ch. 9:7.

Muktananda, Swami
Remember that God himself assumes human forms and lives in the
world. 1 ch. 9:9.

Muller, Robert
The soul of the universe, incarnated in a human being, lost much of its
qualities and became imperfect. 1 ch. 11:6.

Rama, Swami
The Vedic scriptures declare that the Brahman [the Eternal] became "Many" [individual selves] to realize its own glory and greatness. This manyness or plurality is but a transformation assumed by the Absolute, which in its totality remains the One without a second. 1 ch. 9:13.

Schrödinger, Erwin
What is it that has called you so suddenly out of nothingness to enjoy for a brief while a spectacle which remains quite indifferent to you? . . . Looking and thinking in that manner you may suddenly come to see, in a flash, the profound rightness of the basic conviction in Vedanta: it is not possible that this unity of knowledge, feeling, and choice which you call your own should have sprung into being from nothingness at a given moment not so long ago; rather this knowledge, feeling, and choice are essentially eternal and unchangeable and numerically one in all men, nay in all sensitive beings. But not in this sense—that you are a part, a piece, of an eternal, infinite being, an aspect or modification of it . . . 1 ch. 15:10.

Shipov, Gennady
According to the thinking of ancient philosophers of the Orient, all the material objects emerge from the great emptiness, are its integral part, and, in that sense, are illusionary. In the great emptiness itself acts of creation of real objects continually occur. 1 ch. 10:7.

Trungpa, Chogyam
At the beginning, duality is just a way of killing boredom. 1 ch. 11:24.

Upanishads, The
In the beginning this world was merely nonbeing. It developed. It turned into an egg. 1 ch. 10:5.

Lonely He felt, and all unsatisfied; so into two He did divide Him-Self, to have a Playmate; Man and Wife He was; all wishes of each other they fulfill. 1 ch. 11:11.

Summary of Insights: (3) Absolute in the World

Arabi, Ibn
We ourselves are the attributes by which we describe God; our existence

is merely an objectification of His existence. God is necessary to us in order that we may exist, while we are necessary to Him in order that he may be manifested to Himself, 1 Ch. 9.10.

When my Beloved appears, with what eye do I see Him? With his eye, not with mine, for none sees Him except Himself, 1 Ch. 9.11.

I give Him also life, by knowing Him in my heart, 1 Ch. 9.10.

Baba, Meher

Who am I? And to that Question there is only one Answer—I am God! The problem is that people do not know who they really are: you are Infinite. You are really everywhere; but you think you are the body, and therefore consider yourself limited. If you look within and experience your own soul in its true nature, you will realize that you are infinite and beyond all creation. 1 ch. 19:26.

He who is absent, far away from God—his heart can only say: "God is" somewhere. 1 ch. 19:29.

Just think! If the Creator you do find, can His creation still remain behind? 1 ch. 19:30.

The God-realized knows himself to be God as surely as a man knows himself to be a man. It is for him not a matter of doubt, belief, self-delusion, or guesswork; it is a supreme and unshakeable uncertainty, which needs no external corroboration and remains unaffected by contradiction, because it is based upon self-knowledge. Such spiritual certainty is incapable of being challenged. A man thinks himself to be what in reality he is not; a God-realized knows what in reality he is. 1 ch. 22:8.

Sai Baba, Sri Sathya

Arise, awake, establish once again the royal era, resplendent with causes and projects, which uphold Truth, Peace and Righteousness. Love your brothers and sisters. Practice the Eternal Religion, quench the burning flames of ignorance, turmoil, injustice and envy with the waters of love, forbearance and Truth. Develop a feeling of mutual respect towards others. 1 ch. 8:11.

Bedrij, Orest

I am the very people I help, and I am the very people I hurt. 1 ch. 12.

All this time you were me and I was you, and we did not know it. 1 ch. 19.

Bible, The

I assure you, as often as you did for one of my least brothers, you did for me (Mt 25:40). 1 ch. 11.

He who acts in truth ['1'] comes into the light (Jn 3:21). 1 ch. 8.

How long, O Lord? Will you hide yourself forever? (Ps 89:47). 1 ch. 11.

Are you not aware that you are the temple of God and that the Spirit ['1'] of God lives in you? . . . For the temple of God is holy, and you are that temple (1 Cor 3:16-17). 1 ch. 19.

All of us . . . are being transformed from glory to glory into his very image by the Lord who is the Spirit (2 Cor 3:18). 1 ch. 14.

We, many though we are, are one body (1 Cor 10:17). 1 ch. 17.

We are members of one another (Eph 4:25). 1 chs. 17; 19.

All are one in Christ Jesus (Gal 3:28). 1 ch. 19.

They know not, neither do they understand; they go about in darkness; all the foundations of the earth are shaken. I said: You are gods; all of you are sons of the Most High; yet like men you shall die, and fall like any prince. Rise, O God, judge the earth, for yours are all the nations (Ps 82:5-8). 1 ch. 19.

For [when] I was hungry and you gave me something to eat, I was thirsty and you gave me something to drink, I was a stranger and you invited me [into your homes], I needed clothes and you clothed me, I was sick and you looked after me, I was in prison and you came to visit me . . . when did we see you hungry and feed you, or thirsty and give you something to drink? When did we see you a stranger and invite you in, or needing clothes and clothe you? When did we see you sick or in prison and go to visit you?" The King will reply, "I tell you the truth, whatever you did for one of the least [important] of these brothers of mine, you did for me" (Mt 25:34-40). 1 ch. 22.

We are the temple of the living God (2 Cor 6:14). 1 ch. 8.

Rise, O God; judge the earth, for yours are all the nations (Ps 82:8). 1 chs. 8; 19.

Know the truth, and the truth will set you free (Jn 8:32). 1 chs. 2; 7; 12; 13; 16; 19.

Your body is a temple of the Holy Spirit, who is within (1 Cor 6:19). 1 ch. 19.

Do not give what is holy to dogs or toss your pearls before swine. They will trample them underfoot, at best, and perhaps even tear you to shreds (Mt 7:6). 1 ch. 5.

The kingdom of God [God's Spirit] is within you (Lk 17:20-21). 1 ch. 19.

It is written in your own Law that God said, "You are gods" (Jn 10:34). 1 ch. 19.

You are my children, and you put me back in labor pains until Christ [Ultimate Perfection] is formed [realized] in you (Gal 4:19). 1 ch. 19.

God is love and he who abides in love abides in God, and God in him (1 Jn 4:16). 1 ch. 19.

Live as children of light. Light produces every kind of goodness and justice and truth (Eph 5:8-9). 1 ch. 8.

Glorify God in your body (1 Cor 6:20). 1 ch. 19.

Blake, William
Awake! Awake O sleeper of the land of shadows, wake! Expand! I am in you and you in me, mutual in love . . . Lo! We are one. 1 ch. 8:8.

Carey, Ken

The Creator and Creation are joined in physical flesh; for it is One Life that pulses within every body. We have not only to be joined in consciousness, in awareness, and all will be fulfilled according to the prophecy. 1 ch. 17:2.

Catherine of Siena, Saint

If you will arrive at a perfect knowledge and enjoyment of Me, the Eternal Truth, you should never go outside the knowledge of yourself; and by humbling yourself in the valley of humility you will know Me and yourself, from which knowledge you will draw all that is necessary. 1 ch. 18:3.

Eckhart, Meister

A man has many skins in himself, covering the depths of his heart. Man knows so many things; he does not know himself. Why, thirty or forty skins or hides, just like an ox's or bear's, so thick and hard, cover the soul. Go into your own ground and learn to know yourself there. 1 ch. 20:2.

In the kingdom of heaven all is in all, as is one, and all is ours. 1 ch. 24:11.

Einstein, Albert

Our age is characterized by perfecting the means, while confusing the goals. 1 ch. 1:4

Place [your] powers freely and gladly in the service of mankind. 1 chs. 2:2; 19:10.

Emerson, Ralph Waldo

All that can be done for you is nothing to what you can do for yourself. 1 ch. 19:4.

The purpose of life seems to be acquainting a man with himself. 1 ch. 11:7.

The highest revelation is that God is in everyman . . . know thyself a man and be a God. 1 ch. 19:6.

To believe your own thought, to believe that what is true for you in your private heart is true for all men—that is genius. 1 ch. 15:8.

D'Espagnat, Bernard
This notion of reality existing independently of man has no meaning whatsoever. 1 ch. 7:14.

D'Estaing, Valéry Giscard
The world is unhappy. It is unhappy because it doesn't know where it is going and because it senses that if it knew, it would discover that it was heading for disaster. 1 ch. 1:2.

Gabor, Dennis
Till now man has been up against Nature; from now on he will be up against his own nature. 1 ch. 19:40.

Gospel of Thomas, The
Brother Thomas, while you have time in the world, listen to me and I will reveal to you the things you have pondered in your mind. Now since it has been said that you are my twin and true companion, examine yourself that you may understand who you are, in what way you exist, and how you will come to be. Since you are called my brother, it is not fitting that you be ignorant of yourself. 1 ch. 5:13.

The kingdom is inside of you, and it is outside of you. When you come to know yourselves, then you will become known, and you will realize that it is you who are the sons of the living father ['1']. But if you will not know yourselves, you dwell in poverty and it is you who are that poverty (3). 1 ch. 19:7.

The kingdom of the Father is spread upon the earth and people do not see it (113). 1 ch. 19.

Whoever knows the All but fails (to know) himself lacks everything (65). 1 ch. 7.

Heschel, Rabbi Abraham Joshua
Living is not a private affair of the individual. Living is what man does with God's time, what man does with God's world. 1 ch. 11:8.

Great is the challenge we face at every moment sublime the occasion, every occasion. Here we are, contemporaries of God, some of His power at our disposal. 1 ch. 13:18.

We carry the gold of God in our souls to forge the gate of the kingdom. The time for the kingdom may be far off, but the task is plain: To retain our share in God in spite of peril and contempt. There is a war to wage against the vulgar, against the glorification of the absurd, a war that is incessant, universal. Loyal to the presence of the ultimate in the common, we may be able to make it clear that man is more than man, that in doing the finite he may perceive the infinite. 1 ch. 17:4.

Huxley, Aldous
[It is] because we are unaware that the kingdom of heaven is within us . . . that we behave in the generally silly, the often insane, the sometimes criminal ways that are so characteristically human. We are saved, we are liberated and enlightened, by perceiving the hitherto unperceived good that is already within us, by returning to our eternal ground and remaining where, without knowing it, we have always been. 1 ch. 20:1.

The world is an illusion. 1 ch. 22:11.

Our business is to wake up. We have to find ways in which to detect the whole of reality in the one illusory part which our self-centered consciousness permits us to see. 1 ch. 22:11.

We must not live thoughtlessly, taking our illusion for the complete reality, but at the same time we must not live too thoughtfully in the sense of trying to escape the dream state. 1 ch. 22:11.

Jeans, Sir James
Things are not what they seem; it is the general recognition that we are not yet in contact with ultimate reality. We are still imprisoned in our cave, with our backs to the light, and can only watch the shadows on the wall. 1 ch. 19:39.

Jerome, Saint
The most difficult and most obscure of the holy books, Genesis, contains as many secrets as words concealing many things even under each word. 1 ch. 5:20.

John Paul II
The more human beings know reality and the world, the more they know themselves in their uniqueness, with the question of the meaning of things and of their very existence becoming ever more pressing. 1 ch. 2:34.

Kabir
You have slept for millions and millions of years. Why not wake up this morning? 1 ch. 8:7.

Kook, Abraham Isaac
Special individuals, the sages of great understanding, always knew the secret of spiritual unity. They knew that the human spirit is a universal spirit, that although many divergences, spiritual and material, tend to separate person from person and society from society, greater than all the differences is the essential unity among them. 1 ch. 7:17.

Lincoln, Abraham
Let us have faith that right makes might, and in that faith, let us, to the end, dare to do our duty as we understand it. 1 ch. 16:3.

Maharshi, Ramana
Why should you bear your load on the head when you are traveling in a train? It carries you and your load whether the load is on your head or on the floor of the train. You are not lessening the burden of the train by keeping it on your head but only straining yourself unnecessarily. 1 ch. 14:20.

Mandino, Og
Muscle can split a shield and even destroy life, but only the unseen power of love can open the hearts of men, and until I master this art, I will remain no more than a peddler in the market place. 1 ch. 13:3.

Milarepa, Jetsun

Your inability to drink the nectar [seed of pure pleasure] was because your central channel was not yet opened. You should practice certain vigorous bodily exercises. 1 ch. 16:9.

External phenomenal objects: Forms, sounds, smells, tastes, and objects of touch, all these phenomena are no other than the magical tricks of mind. Like a child who builds sand castles, it is mind that fixates on names. Realizing that this is unreal is also mind . . . Know that all manifestations are like reflections of the moon in water. 1 ch. 20:17.

Ming-Dao, Deng

The more you learn, the more you must use your knowledge for others. The wiser you become, the more unselfish you must also become. As your experience deepens, and with it your humility, you will realize unfathomable depths of knowledge. You can never become arrogant and narrow-minded if you perceive how small your abilities are when contrasted to those of the greatest.

Remember to use your knowledge in the service of others, but expect nothing in return. 1 ch. 17:3.

Mozart, Wolfgang Amadeus

A genius without heart is nonsense. 1 ch. 13:15.

Muller, Robert

Decide to live joyfully, exultantly, gratefully, openly, and then miracles will begin to happen. [Furthermore,] What is the greatest work of art on Earth? A healthy, beautiful, well-educated, loving child. Fathers and mothers are the greatest artists there can be on Earth. A happy, loving family is more precious than any Rembrandt or Leonardo da Vinci painting. 1 ch. 16:1.

One's family is his foremost church on Earth. The most sacred acts are conducted in it: Love, the gift of life, care, protection, and education. 1 ch. 7:19.

Life is divine. *Das Leben ist göttlich.* I wish this exclamation of mine as a child were translated in all languages and displayed in every school on Earth. 1 ch. 7:20.

Each human being is a prism in which the whole universe is reflected. 1 ch. 14:9.

Neng, Hui

When not enlightened, Buddhas are no other than ordinary beings; when there is enlightenment, ordinary beings at once turn into Buddhas. 1 ch. 19:34.

Pasteur, Louis

In the fields of observation, chance favors the mind that is prepared. 1 ch. 14:5.

Plato

To find out the Maker and Father of this universe is difficult; and, when found, it is impossible to declare Him to all. 1 ch. 5:15.

Planck, Max Karl Ernst

In the last analysis, we ourselves are part of nature, and, therefore, part of the mystery that we are trying to solve. 1 ch. 7:15.

Rabindranath

Oh my heart, arise! Arise in this land of purity, on the shores of the sea of great humanity. 1 ch. 8:10.

Al-Rumi, Jalaluddin

He who knows himself knows his Lord. 1 ch. 20:6

Schrödinger, Erwin

The reason why our sentient, percipient, and thinking ego is met nowhere within our scientific world picture can easily be indicated in seven words: Because it is itself that world picture. It is identical with the whole, and therefore cannot be contained in it as a part of it. 1 ch. 14:19.

Tauler, Johan

Goodness needeth not enter into the soul, for it is there already, only it is unperceived. 1 ch. 20:4

Teresa of Avila, Saint

Oh human blindness! How long, how long shall it be before the dust is removed from our eyes? 1 ch. 11.19.

Teresa of Calcutta

The greatest disease in the West today is not TB or leprosy; it is being unwanted, unloved, and uncared for. We can cure physical diseases with medicine, but the only cure for loneliness, despair, and hopelessness is love. There are many in the world who are dying for a piece of bread but there are many more dying for a little love. The poverty in the West is a different kind of poverty—it is not only a poverty of loneliness but also of spirituality. There's a hunger for love, as there is a hunger for God. 1 ch. 13:2.

Is my heart so clean that I can see the face [image] of God in my brother, my sister, who is that black one, that white one, that naked one, that one suffering from leprosy, that dying one? 1 ch. 7:4.

If sometimes people have had to die of starvation, it is not because God didn't care for them, but because you and I were not instruments of love in the hands of God, to give them bread, because we did not recognize Him when once more the hungry Christ came in distressing disguise. 1 ch. 7:9.

In serving the poorest we directly serve God. 1 ch. 22:2.

Upanishads, The

When they say to a man who sees with his eyes, "Have you seen?" and he says, "I have seen," that is the truth (iv, 1, 4). 1 ch. 2.

Wheeler, John Archibald

The unknown is knowable . . . Every darkness can be lighted. 1 ch. 8:13.

The universe does not exist "out there" independent of us. We are inescapably involved in bringing about that which appears to be happening. We are not only observers. We are participators. 1 ch. 7:13.

Yahya (ibn Mu'adh ar-Razi)

One mustard seed of love is better than seventy years of worship without love. 1 ch. 13:14.

Summary of Insights: (4) From Humanity to Absolute

Ashtavakra
Be constantly engaged in work for the welfare of others. 1 ch. 16:11.

Athanasius, Saint
The Divine Word became human in order that every human being may become God. 1 chs. 9:6; 23:5.

Baba, Meher
He who has found the Loved One in Him-Self for him God is not he, nor You, but I. 1 ch. 19:29.

If you find God, then you have found all things! 1 ch. 19:30.

After the attainment of God-realization, the soul discovers that it has always been the Infinite Reality, and that its looking upon itself as finite during the period of evolution and spiritual advancement was an illusion. The soul also finds that the infinite knowledge and bliss that it enjoys have been latent in the Infinite Reality from the beginning of time and that they became manifest at the moment of realization. 1 ch. 22:14.

The process of attaining God-realization is a game in which the beginning and the end are identical. The attainment of realization is nevertheless a distinct gain. There are two kinds of advantages. One consists in getting what we did not previously possess; the other consists in realizing what we really are. God-realization is of the second kind. However, there is an infinite difference in the soul that has God-realization and one that does not have it. Though the soul that has God-realization has nothing it did not already possess, its explicit knowledge makes God-realization of the highest significance. The soul that is not God-realized experiences itself as finite and is constantly troubled by the opposites of joy and sorrow. But the soul that has realization is lifted out of them and experiences the Infinite. 1 ch. 22:14.

Basil the Great
Through His aid, hearts are lifted up, the weak are led by the hand, and they who are advancing are brought to perfection . . . Hence comes to

them unending joy, abiding in God, being made like unto God, and which is the highest of all, being made God. 1 ch. 25:18.

Bedrij, Orest
When our mind is still and our heart is pure we tune into the '1'. We grasp Oneness and the Creator within ourselves. 1 ch. 12.

Purity of Heart = Clear Thinking (wisdom,),
= Capacity to Reason (intelligence),
= Ability to Make Decisions (judgment),
= Perception of Truth (understanding); and
= The Harvest of Good. 1 ch. 12.

When I let the Christ's teachings be my life, I realized that I am, was, and shall always be the Absolute Reality. 1 ch. 11.

Bhagavad Gita
Make Me ['1'] the ultimate goal of life (6.13). 1 ch. 2:24.

Bible, The
Happy are the pure of heart; *they will see* God! (Mt 5:8). 1 ch. 12.

Know the truth, and the truth will set you free (Jn 8:32). 1 ch. 12.

If your eye be single, your whole body will be full of light (Mt 6:22). 1 ch. 4.

"See! The man has become like one of us, knowing what is good and what is bad!" (Gen 3:22). 1 chs. 7-9, 18.

Make every effort to keep the 'unity of the Spirit' through the bond of peace. There is one body and one Spirit ['1'] . . . one God and Father of all, who is over all and through all and in all (Eph 4:3-6). 1 ch. 9.

You shall love the Lord your God with all your heart, soul, and might (Deut 6:5; Mk 12:30 par.). 1 chs. 2, 8.

He that loveth not knoweth not God, for God is love and anyone who lives in love lives in God, and God lives in him. Love will come to its perfection in us when we can face the day of Judgment without fear; because even in this world we have become as He is (1 Jn 4:13-17). 1 ch. 13.

You must be made perfect as your heavenly Father is perfect (Mt 5:48). 1 ch. 25.

Be still, and know that I am God (Ps 46:10). 1 ch. 12.

If you live according to my teaching, you are truly my disciples; then you will know the truth, and the truth will set you free (Jn 8:31-2). 1 ch. 16.

Be compassionate as your Father in heaven is (Lk 6:36-42). 1 ch. 7.

[Father, I pray . . .] that all may be one as you, Father, are in me, and I in you; I pray that they may be [one] in us . . . I living in them, you living in me—that their unity may be complete (Jn 17:21-23). 1 ch. 7.

Indeed, the whole created world eagerly awaits the revelation of the sons of God . . . because the world itself will be freed from its slavery . . . and share in the glorious freedom of the children of God (Rom 8:19, 21). 1 ch. 24.

Now I will show you the way, which surpasses all the others. If I speak with human tongues and angelic as well, but do not have love, I am a noisy gong, a clanging cymbal. If I have the gift of prophecy and, with full knowledge, comprehend all mysteries, if I have faith great enough to move mountains, but have not love, I am nothing. If I give everything I have to feed the poor and hand over my body to be burned, but have not love, I gain nothing. Love is patient; love is kind. Love is not jealous, it does not put on airs, it is not snobbish. Love is never rude, it is not self-seeking, it is not prone to anger; neither does it brood over injuries. Love does not rejoice in what is wrong but rejoices with the truth. There is no limit to love's forbearance, to its trust, its hope, its power to endure (1 Cor 13:1-7). 1 ch. 13.

I give you a new commandment: Love one another. Such as my love has been for you, so must your love be for each other. This is how all will know you for my disciples; your love for one another (Jn 13:33-5). 1 ch. 13.

"Come!" Whoever is thirsty [for God: Love, truth, peace], let him come; and whoever wishes, let him take free gift of the water of life (Rev 22:17). 1 ch. 15.

Awake, O sleeper, arise from the dead, and Christ will give you light (Eph 5:14). 1 ch. 8.

To him who overcomes, I will give some of the hidden manna (Rev 2:17). 1 ch. 15.

Blake, William
If the doors of perception were cleansed, everything would be seen as it is, infinite. 1 ch. 14:18.

Buddha, Gautama the
All phenomena and their developments are simply manifestations of mind. All causes and effects, from great universes to the fine dust only seen in the sunlight come into apparent existence only by means of the discriminating mind. 1 ch. 12:3.

Carpenter, Edward
Of all the hard facts of science, I know of none more solid and fundamental than the fact that if you inhibit thought [and persevere], you come to a region of consciousness below or behind thought . . . and a realization of an altogether vaster self than that to which we are accustomed. And . . . the ordinary consciousness with which we are concerned in ordinary life is before all things founded on the little local self, and is in fact self-consciousness in the ordinary self and the ordinary world. It is to die in the ordinary sense, but in another sense, it is to wake up and find that one's real, most intimate self, pervades the universe and all other beings . . . So great, so splendid is this experience, that it may be said that all minor questions and doubts fall away in the face of it; and certain it is that in thousands and thousands of cases the fact of this having come even once to a man has completely revolutionized his subsequent life and outlook on the world. 1 ch. 12:11.

de Chardin, Teilhard

Someday after mastering the winds and the waves, the tides and gravity, we shall harness the energy of love. And then, for the second time in the history of the world, man will have discovered fire. 1 ch. 19:2.

Confucius

When the personal life is cultivated, the family will be regulated; when the family is regulated, the state will be in order; and when the state is in order, there will be peace throughout the world. 1 ch. 13:1.

Eckhart, Meister

A pure heart is one that is unencumbered, unworried, uncommitted, which does not want its own way about anything but which rather is submerged in the loving of God, having denied self. 1 ch. 12:16.

The seed of God is in us, if the seed had a good, wise, and industrious farmer, it would thrive all the more and grow up to God whose seed it is, and the fruit would be equal to the nature of God. Now the seed of a pear tree grows into a pear tree, a hazel seed into a hazel tree, the seed of God into God. 1 ch. 22:9.

Eddington, Arthur

The mind has but regained from nature that which the mind has put into nature. 1 ch. 9:12.

We have succeeded in reconstructing the creature that made the footprint. And Lo! it is our own. 1 chs. 9:12, 35:5.

Emerson, Ralph Waldo

If we live truly, we shall see truly. 1 ch. 12:17.

Einstein, Albert

Our task must be to free ourselves from this prison by widening our circle of compassion to embrace all living creatures and the whole of nature in its beauty. Nobody is able to achieve this completely, but the striving for such achievement is in itself a part of the liberation and a foundation for inner security. 1 ch. 7:11.

Gospel of Thomas, The

Jesus said, "I shall give you what no eye has seen and what no ear has heard and what no hand has touched and what has never occurred to the human mind . . . When you come to know yourselves, then you will become known, and you will realize that it is you who are the sons of the living Father" (17). 1 ch. 4:8.

Love your brother as your own soul, guard him as the pupil of your eye. 1 ch. 16:13.

Hammarskjöld, Dag

The more faithfully you listen to the voice within you, the better you will hear what is sounding outside. And only he who listens can speak. Is this the starting point of the road towards the union of your two dreams—to be allowed in clarity of mind to mirror life and in purity of heart to mold it? 1 ch. 12:7.

To preserve the silence within—amid all the noise. To remain open and quiet, a moist humus in the fertile darkness where the rain falls and the grain ripens—no matter how many tramp across the parade ground in whirling dust under an arid sky. 1 ch. 12:8.

Give me a pure heart—that I may see Thee, a humble heart—that I may hear Thee, a heart of love—that I may serve Thee, a heart of faith—that I may abide in Thee. 1 ch. 12:18.

Herbert, Nick

The world is not objectively real but depends on the mind of the observer. [And,] The observer may be said to partially create the attributes he observes . . . A rainbow appears in a different place for each observer—in fact, each of your eyes sees a slightly different rainbow. Yet the rainbow is an objective phenomenon; it can be photographed. 1 ch. 2:15

Heschel, Rabbi Abraham Joshua

God is not always silent, and man is not always blind. In every man's life there are moments when there is a lifting of the veil at the horizon of the known, opening a sight of the eternal. Each of us has at least once in his life experienced the momentous reality of God. Each of us has once caught a glimpse of the beauty, peace and power that flow through the souls of those who are devoted to Him. But such experiences are rare events. To some people they are like shooting stars, passing and unremembered. In others they kindle a light that is never quenched. The remembrance of that experience and the loyalty to the response of that moment are the forces that sustain our faith. 1 ch. 3:3

We distinguish between white and black, beautiful and ugly, pleasant and unpleasant, gain and loss, good and evil, right and wrong. The fate of mankind depends upon the realization that the distinction between good and evil, right and wrong, is superior to all other distinctions . . . To teach humanity the primacy of that distinction is of essence to the Biblical message. 1 ch. 12:19.

Huxley, Aldous
We must continually be on our watch for ways in which we may enlarge our consciousness. We must not attempt to live outside the world, which is given us, but we must somehow learn how to transform it and transfigure it. 1 ch. 22:11.

It is only by becoming Godlike that we can know God. And to become Godlike is to identify ourselves with the divine element which in fact constitutes our essential nature. 1 ch. 25:16.

Irenaeus, Saint
God the Logos became what we are, in order that we may become what he himself is. 1 chs. 9:1; 23:4.

James, William
This overcoming of all the usual barriers between the individual and the Absolute is the great mystic achievement. In mystic states we become one with the Absolute and we become aware of our Oneness. This is the everlasting and triumphant mystical tradition, hardly altered by differences of clime or creed. In Hinduism, in Neoplatonism, in Sufism, in Christian mysticism, in Whitmanism, we find the same recurring note, so that there is about mystical utterances an eternal unanimity which ought to make a critic stop and think, and which brings about what the mystical classics have, as has been said, neither birthday nor

native land, perpetually telling of the unity of man with God, their speech antedates language, and they do not grow old. 1 ch. 14:16.

John of the Cross, Saint
Go forth and exult in your glory, hide yourself in it, and rejoice, and you shall obtain all desires of your heart. 1 ch. 26:4.

Krishna, Gopi
Probably no other spectacle, not even the most incredible supernormal performance of mystics and mediums, so clearly demonstrates the existence of an All-Pervading, Omniscient intelligence behind the infinitely varied phenomena of life as the operations of a freshly awakened Kundalini. 1 ch. 17:14.

Lincoln, Abraham
I have never had a policy. I have simply tried to do what seemed best each day, as each day came . . . I desire so to conduct the affairs of this administration that if at the end, when I come to lay down the reins of power, I have lost every other friend on earth, I shall at last have one friend left, and that friend shall be down inside of me. 1 ch. 16:5.

Logan, Alastair
Salvation, then, is special knowledge of one's true self, of one's kinship with the unknown transcendent God and of the true nature of the visible world . . . the knowledge (gnōsis) of our origin, nature and destiny, a knowledge which tells Gnostics who they really are and frees them from their present state of ignorance and imprisonment in an alien body and a hostile world governed by Fate. 1 ch. 3:1.

Maharaj, Tukaram
I went to look for God, but didn't find God. I myself became God. In this very body, God revealed Himself to me. 1 ch. 19:32.

Mandino, Og
Henceforth will I look on all things with love and I will be born again. I will love the sun for it warms my bones; yet I will love the rain for it cleanses my spirit. I will love the light for it shows me the way; yet I will love the darkness for it shows me the stars. I will welcome happiness for

it enlarges my heart; yet I will endure sadness for it opens my soul. I will welcome obstacles for they are my challenge. 1 ch. 13:3.

I will applaud mine enemies and they will become friends; I will encourage my friends and they will become brothers. Always will I dig for reasons to applaud; never will I scratch for excuses to gossip. When I am tempted to criticize, I will bite my tongue; when I am moved to praise, I will shout from the roofs . . . 1 ch. 13:3.

Merton, Thomas

One of the paradoxes of the mystical life is this: that a man cannot enter into the deepest center of himself and pass through that center into God, unless he is able to pass entirely out of himself and empty himself and give himself to other people in the purity of a selfless love. 1 ch. 11:4.

Milarepa, Jetsun

It is through resting one's mind at ease [peace] that Buddhahood [the all-pervading Buddha-nature—Christian "unity of the Spirit"—an experience of inner enlightenment] is realized. 1 ch. 12:1.

Muktananda, Swami

The purer you are, the greater your progress. 1 ch. 12:15.

Muller, Robert

To be able to say on the last day of one's life:

> I loved to live
> I lived to love
> I laughed a lot
> I gave much love
> I left the world a little better than I found it
> I loved the world's great beauty
> I sang life and the universe
> I looked for the best in others
> I gave the best I had.

Thank you, O God, for this miracle of life. 1 ch. 13:10.

Paul VI, Pope
Stand in admiration, rejoice; we have become Christ. 1 ch. 26:8.

Rumi, Jalaluddin
The sect of lovers is distinct from all others; lovers have a religion and a faith all their own. 1 ch. 13:16.

I died as mineral and became a plant, I died as plant and rose to animal. I died as animal and I was Man. Why should I fear? When was I less by dying? Yet once more I shall die as Man, to soar with angels blest; but even from angelhood I must pass on all except God ['1'] perishes. When I have sacrificed my angel soul, I shall become what no mind e'er conceived. O let me non-exist, for Nonexistence proclaims in organ tones, "To Him we shall return." 1 ch. 23:10

Sai Baba, Sri Sathya
When discrimination is keen and mental waves are stilled—and attention is one-pointed as a result of the contemplation of Pure Consciousness, then Divine Splendor is manifested, which can burn away evil and reveal joy. 1 ch. 12:10

It is through discrimination and renunciation that man understands who he really is. 1 ch. 22:12.

Love all beings—that is enough. Love with no expectation of return; love for the sake of love; love because your very nature is Love; Love because that is the form of worship you know and like. When others are happy, be happy likewise. When others are in misery, try to alleviate their lot to the best of your ability. Practice Love through service. By this means, you will realize Unity and dissolve the ego that harms . . . Live in Love, live with love, move with love, speak with love, think with love, and act with love. 1 ch. 13:13.

Santayana, George
Let him clean better, if he can, the windows of his soul, that the variety and beauty of the prospect may spread more brightly before him. 1 ch. 14.

Live as much as may be in the eternal. 1 ch. 16:8.

Schroedinger, Erwin

Again, the mystics of many centuries, independently, yet in perfect harmony with each other (somewhat like the particles in an ideal gas) have described, each of them, the unique experience of his or her life in terms that can be condensed in the phrase: DEUS FACTUS SUM (I have become [one with] God). 1 ch. 19:35.

Shankara

Disease is never cured by [pronouncing] the name of medicine, but by taking the medicine. Deliverance is not achieved by repeating the word Brahmam, but by directly experiencing Brahmam . . . The nature of the one Reality must be known by one's own clear spiritual perception; it cannot be known through a pundit. Similarly, the form of the moon can be known only through one's eyes. How can it be known through others? 1 ch. 16:12.

Simonetti, Manlio

Indeed, neither the prophets nor Our Lord himself expressed the divine mysteries in a simple way which would be accessible to all, but they spoke in parables (i.e., allegories) as the apostles themselves declared (Mt 13:34).

There were various reasons for this: To encourage the more zealous to sustained and skillful research, and because those who are not sufficiently prepared would receive more injury than help from a knowledge of Scripture. The sacred mysteries are reserved for the elect; those predestined for this "gnosis." This explains the characteristic use of the parable-style in Scripture (*Strom.* VI 15:124). 1 ch. 5:3.

Subramuniya

As you release desires and cravings through daily meditation, the external mind releases its hold on your awareness and you dive deeper, fearlessly, into the center of this blazing avalanche of light beyond form and formlessness. 1 ch. 4:19.

As you come out of that samadhi, you realize you are the spirit, the life force of all. 1 ch. 4:19.

Sutra, Lankavatara

With the lamp of word and discrimination one must go beyond word and discrimination and enter upon the path of realization. 1 ch. 2:31.

Teresa, of Calcutta

I always begin my prayer in silence, for it is in the silence of the heart that God speaks. God is the friend of silence—we need to listen to God because it's not what we say but what He says to us and through us that matters. Prayer feeds the soul—as blood is to the body, prayer is to the soul—and it brings you closer to God. It also gives you a clean and pure heart. A clean heart can see God, can speak to God, and can see the love of God in others. When you have a clean heart it means you are open and honest with God, you are not hiding anything from Him, and this lets Him take what He wants from you. 1 ch. 4:15.

Tilopa, Cakrasamvara

Do not imagine, do not think, do not analyze . . . 1 ch. 12:2

Tzu, Chuang

A man does not see himself in running water but in still water. 1 ch. 12:6.

White, John

When we finally understand that Great Mystery, we discover our true nature, the Supreme Identity, the Self of all. That direct perception of our Oneness with the infinite, that noetic realization of our identity with the divine is the source of all happiness, all goodness, all beauty, all truth. The experience is beyond time, space, and causality; it is beyond ego and all socially conditioned sense of I. Knowing ourselves to be timeless, boundless, and therefore cosmically free ends the illusion of separateness and all the painful, destructive defenses we erect, individually and societally, to preserve the ego-illusion at the expense of others. 1 ch. 8:14.

Wu, Joseph

This kind of personality will not be corrupted by wealth or fame, will not be bent by power or force, and will not be moved by poverty or mean conditions. 1 ch. 16.

The phrase "cultivation of *qi*" means almost the same as "development of moral or spiritual power." Such a spiritual power is developed through constant accumulation of righteous deeds and is not to be obtained by occasional moral acts. This is comparative to the Eightfold Path of the Buddha, which integrates right mindfulness and right conduct. 1 ch. 16.

Upanishads, The
From the unreal lead me to the real, from darkness lead me to light. From death lead me to immortality, 1 ch. 4:10.

Vedanta
Why will you wander in the wilderness! You who are seeking God! Yourselves are He! You need not search! He is you, verily! 1 ch. 19:31.

Wheeler, John Archibald
The universe not only must give rise to life, but once life is created, it will endure forever, become infinitely knowledgeable, and ultimately mold the universe to its will . . . thus, man—or Life—will be not only the measure of things, but their creator as well. 1 ch. 24:15.

APPENDIX 2

Perfections

Be perfect as your Father within you is perfect,
Advised the Teacher of Righteousness.
How do we do it?
Let us reveal the light of the Eternal One within us.

Let the *will* of the Most High be my will;
Let the *peace* of the Most High be my peace;
Let the *purity* of the Most High be my purity;
Let the *freedom* of the Most High be my freedom;
Let the *generosity* of the Most High be my generosity;
Let the *order* of the Most High be my order;
Let the *service* of the Most High be my service.

Let the *integrity* of the Most High be my integrity;
Let the *perception* of the Most High be my perception;
Let the *grace* of the Most High be my grace;
Let the *harmony* of the Most High be my harmony;
Let the *kindness* of the Most High be my kindness;
Let the *abundance* of the Most High be my abundance;
Let the *dedication* of the Most High be my dedication.

Let the *humility* of the Most High be my humility;
Let the *compassion* of the Most High be my compassion;
Let the *commitment* of the Most High be my commitment;
Let the *perseverance* of the Most High be my perseverance;
Let the *understanding* of the Most High be my understanding;
Let the *indefatigability* of the Most High be my indefatigability;
Let the *noninterference* of the Most High be my noninterference.

Let the *consciousness* of the Most High be my consciousness;
Let the *fearlessness* of the Most High be my fearlessness;
Let the *forgiveness* of the Most High be my forgiveness;
Let the *excellence* of the Most High be my excellence;
Let the *confidence* of the Most High be my confidence;
Let the *altruism* of the Most High be my altruism;
Let the *goodness* of the Most High be my goodness.

Let the *justice* of the Most High be my justice;
Let the *health* of the Most High be my health;
Let the *prudence* of the Most High be my prudence;
Let the *forethought* of the Most High be my forethought;
Let the *simplicity* of the Most High be my simplicity;
Let the *gentleness* of the Most High be my gentleness;
Let the *patience* of the Most High be my patience.

Let the *courage* of the Most High be my courage;
Let the *healing* of the Most High be my healing;
Let the *equanimity* of the Most High be my equanimity;
Let the *perfection* of the Most High be my perfection;
Let the *innocence* of the Most High be my innocence;
Let the *holiness* of the Most High be my holiness;
Let the *wisdom* of the Most High be my wisdom.

Let the *caring* of the Most High be my caring;
Let the *unity* of the Most High be my unity;
Let the *truth* of the Most High be my truth;
Let the *love* of the Most High be my love;
Let the *fidelity* of the Most High be my fidelity;
Let the *beauty* of the Most High be my beauty;
Let the *joy* of the Most High be my joy.

Let it be.

And now,
Let me bow my head in peace and love and joy
To the Absolute Light in you
And to the Eternal One in all.

NOTES

The Old Testament and the New Testament quotations are from:

The Holy Bible: New International Version. Grand Rapids, MI: Zondervan Bible Publishers, 1978.

The Holy Bible: New Revised Standard Version. London: Collins Publishers, 1989.

The New American Bible. Confraternity of Christine Doctrine. Translated from the Original Languages with Critical Use of All the Ancient Sources. Washington, D.C.: The Catholic Press, 1970.

Holy Bible: From the Ancient Eastern Text. George M. Lamsa's Translation from the Aramaic of the Peshitta. Philadelphia: A.J. Holman Co., a division of J.B.Lippincott Co., 1933.

Part 1

THE ULTIMATE JOY OF PARADISE— SEEING GOD FACE-TO-FACE
Introduction

1. Robert Marc Friedman, *The Politics of Excellence* (New York: W.H. Freeman, 2001).
2. Dialogue with Trypho. Qu C.C. Martindale, *St. Justin Martyr*, London, 1921, p. 40.

1-1.2
Where Is God? Who Are We, My Friend?

1. Ralph Waldo Emerson, *The Works of Ralph Waldo Emerson* (Roslyn, NY: Black's Readers Service, 2000), p. 1.
2. Giscard d'Estaing, *U.S. News and World Report*, March 3, 1975, p. 34.
3. Kenneth Clark, *Civilization: A Personal View* (New York: Harper & Row, 1969), p. 344.

4. Alan L. Mackay, *A Dictionary of Scientific Quotations* (Bristol and Philadelphia: Institute of Physics Publishing, 1992), p. 82.

5. Dag Hammarskjöld, *Markings,* trans. from the Swedish by Leif Sjöberg & W.H. Auden (New York: Ballantine Books, 1993), p. xv.

6. *Ibid.,* p. 143.

7. *Ibid.,* p. 53.

8. Abraham Joshua Heschel, *I Asked for Wonder: A Spiritual Anthology,* Edited by Samuel H. Dresner (New York: Crossroad, 2000), p. 46.

9. *Ibid.,* p. 43.

10. Peter Russell, *The Global Brain: Speculations on the Evolutionary Leap to Planetary Consciousness* (Los Angeles: J.P. Tarcher, 1983), pp. 17-18.

11. *Ibid.,* p. 18.

12. Ralph Waldo Emerson, *The Works of Ralph Waldo Emerson* (Roslyn, NY: Black's Readers Service, 2000), p. 2.

13. "Democracy," according to Lenin, in *The Socialist Revolution and the Right of Nations to Self-Determination* (theses), "of course, is also a form of state which must disappear when the state disappears, but that, will only take place in the transition from conclusively victorious and consolidated socialism to full communism."

14. Professor of Statistics Kurganov lists that "from the beginning of the October Revolution up to 1959 the internal repression cost the USSR sixty-six million— 66,000,000 lives": Aleksandr Solzhenitsyn, *The Gulag Archipelago Two,* (New York: Harper and Row, 1975), p. 10.

    The Black Deeds of the Kremlin: A White Book (Toronto: Basilian Press, 1953).

    J. W. Brugel, "The Crime of Genocide," Central European Observer, XXIV (October 17, 1947).

    Zbigniew K. Brzezinski, *The Permanent Purge* (Cambridge: Harvard University Press, 1956).

    Robert Conquest, *The Great Terror: Stalin's Purge of the Thirties* (New York: The Macmillan Co, 1969).

    Nikita Khrushchev, *Secret Report to the Twentieth Party Congress K.P.S.S. v Rezolyutsiakh* (Moscow: Marx-Engels-Lenin Institute, 1953)

    Boris Nicolaevsky, ed., *The Crimes of the Stalin Era* (New York: The New Leader, 1962).

    Alexander Orlov, *The Secret History of Stalin's Crimes* (New York: Random House, 1953).

    U.S. Congress House Committee on Un-American Activities, *The Crimes of Khrushchev,* Hearings (Washington D.C.: Government Printing Office, 1959).

U.S. Congress Senate Committee on Foreign Relations, *The Genocide Convention: Hearings Before a Subcommittee*, January 23-February 9, 1950, on Executive Order (Washington D.C.: Government Printing Office, 1950).

U.S. Congress Senate Committee on Judiciary, *Soviet Empire: Prison House of Nations and Races* (Washington D.C.: Government Printing Office, 1958).

U.S. Congress Senate Committee on Judiciary, *Soviet Empire: A Study in Genocide, Discrimination and Abuse of Power* (Washington D.C.: Government Printing Office, 1958).

15. Dachau, northwest of Munich, held more than 200,000 "registered" prisoners with over 30,000 "certified" deaths between 1933 and 1945.

16. Oświęcim, German Auschwitz (city), Bielsko-Biala (province), southern Poland: Nazi concentration camp ("death factory"), established in 1940—where 4,000,000 to 5,000,000 people were gassed and burned.

17. Orest, [Bedrij] *One*. (San Francisco: Strawberry Hill Press, 1978), pp. 16-23. For the crimes of the Stalin Era see Ref. 14, above. For the crimes of the Hitler Era see *Nazi Conspiracy and Aggression, Official Records of the International Military Tribunal at Nüremberg* (8 Vols. 1946). For the crimes of the Mao Ze-dong (Mao-Tse-tung) Era see the *Walker Report*, published by the U.S. Senate Committee of the Judiciary, July 1971. It's accounting of the mass murder toll since 1949 was between 32 and 61 million. A similar report issued April 1971 by the Taiwan cabinet listed the mainland death toll between 1949 and 1969 as "at least 39.9 million." The USSR government also has a report covering the period 1945 to 1965 listing 26,300,000 killings.

18. Abraham J. Heschel, *The Prophets* (New York: HarperCollins, 1969), p. 185.

19. Jelaluddin Rumi, *The Essential Rumi*, trans. by Coleman Barks with John Moyne, A.J. Arberry, Reynold Nicholson (New York: Quality Paperback Book Club, 1998), pp. 4-5.

20. Hafiz, trans. by Daniel Ladinsky, *The Gift* (New York: Arkana, Penguin Group, 1999), p. 186.

21. Also, (Mt 4:23; Mk 1:15; Jn 3:3).

22. Also, (Mk 4:30; Lk 13:18; the Gospel of Thomas 20).

23. Albert Einstein, *Mein Weltbild* (Amsterdam: Querido Verlag, 1934).

24. Athenagoras the Athenian, "A Plea for the Christians," trans. by Rev. B.P. Pratten, *Fathers of the Second Century* (Peabody, MA: Hendrickson Publishers, 1999), Vol. II, p. 145.

25. Hafiz, trans. by Daniel Ladinsky, *The Gift* (New York: Arkana, Penguin Group, 1999), p. 318.

26. Mt 6:22; Lk 11:34.

2
Humanity Crucified and Risen:
Happiness Is Our Responsibility

1. David Bohm, *Wholeness and the Implicate Order* (London: Ark Paperbacks Ltd., 1983), pp. 138-9.

2. Albert Einstein, "Science and Religion." From an address at Princeton Theological Seminary, May 19, 1939; published in Out of My Later Years, New York: Philosophical Library, 1950).

3. *Ibid.,* Address at Princeton Theological Seminary.

4. David Hughes, *The Star of Bethlehem Mystery. An Astronomer's Confirmation.* (New York: Walter & Co., and London: Dent & Sons, 1979).

5. Gustav Teres, S. J. *The Bible and Astronomy. The Magi and the Star in the Gospel* (Budapest: Springer Orvosi Kiado Kft., 2000).

6. Neil Douglas-Klotz, *The Hidden Gospel* (Wheaton, Illinois: Quest Books, 1999), p.10.

7. Moses, 13th century BC (Jn 5:46); Isaiah, 742 BC (2:12); Ezekiel, 593 BC (30).

8. Mk 13:32; 1 Thess. 5:2-3.

9. Is 7:14, 8:8, 10.

10. Phil 2:4; 1 Cor 10:24; Luke's sermon on the plain, Matthew's sermon on the mount, and Jesus' sayings, now called Q (from *Quelle*, German for "source").

11. Mt 5:1-12; Lk 6:20-23.

12. Ex 21:23-25; Lev 24:20; Deut 19:21.

13. David Bohm, *Wholeness and the Implicate Order* (London: Ark Paperbacks Ltd., 1983), pp. 138-9.

14. Carl Friedrich von Weizacker, quoted in Victor Gollancz, *Man and God* (Boston: Houghton Mifflin Company, 1951), p. 406.

15. Nick Herbert, *Quantum Reality: Beyond the New Physics* (New York: Doubleday, 1985), pp. 135, 162, 189.

16. Deut 6:5; Mt 22:37; Mk 12:30.

17. Gal 3:28; Ep 4:25; 1 Cor 10:17; Jn 17:22.

18. Mt 26:42; Mk 14:36; Lk 22:42.

19. Hafiz, trans. by Daniel Ladinsky, *The Gift* (New York: Arkana, Penguin Group, 1999), p. 270.

20. *Ibid.* p. 48.

21. Jn 4:48; Mt 16:4.

22. Ex 20:1-6; Deut 5:6-10; Mt 4:10; Lk 4:8

23. Deut 6:5; Lk 10:27; Mk 12:30 par; 1 Cor 13. Further, "I appeal to you . . . to present your bodies as a living sacrifice, holy and acceptable to God, which is your

spiritual worship" (Rom 12:1; cf. 1 Cor 6:18-20; 2 Cor 6:6-7:1). The veneration of "the golden calf" symbolizes the recurrent human tendency to turn from the designer (the '1') and revere the design (manifestation) (Ps 96:5; Rom 1:21-25).

24. *The Bhagavad Gita* in Sanskrit. Many English translations are available, among them that of Swami Prabhavananda and Christopher Isherwood (New York: New American Library, 1954); that of Ann Stanford (New York: Herder & Herder, 1971); that of P. Lal (Calcutta: Writers Workshop, 1965); that of Swami Nikhilanada (New York: Ramakrishna-Vivekananda Center, 1952); and that of A.C. Bhaktivedanta Swami Prabhupada, *Bhagavad Gita As It Is*, (Los Angeles: Macmillan Publishing, 1973), p. 321.

25. Lao-tzu, *Tao Te Ching: The Classic Book of Integrity and the Way*. Translated, Annotated, and with an afterword by Victor H. Mair (New York: Quality Paperback Book Club, 1990), p. 15.

26. Revelation of the Buddha's teachings can be found in "Discourse on the Adornments of the Buddha" in Avatamsaka-sūtra.

27. Karl Raimund Popper, *The Logic of Scientific Discovery* (London: Hutchison, 1959).

28. S F Mason, *A History of the Sciences* (London: Routledge, 1953), p. 123

29. Marilyn Wilhelm, *Education: The Healing Art* (Houston, TX: Paideia Press, 1995), p. 2.

30. Stephen Mitchel, *The Enlightened Mind* (New York: Harper Perennial, 1993), p. 9.

31. Aldous Huxley, *The Perennial Philosophy* (New York: Meridian Books, 1968), p. 133

32. Steven Weinberg, *Dreams of a Final Theory* (New York: Pantheon Books, 1992), p. 6.

33. René Descartes, "Rules for the Direction of the Mind," trans. by Elizabeth S. Haldane and G.R.T. Ross, *The Great Books of the Western World* (Chicago: Encyclopaedia Britannica, Inc., 1971), Vol. 31, p. 17.

34. John Paul II, *Encyclical Letter of John Paul II to the Catholic Bishops of the World On the Relationship between Faith and Reason* (Rome: L'Osservatore Romano, 1998).

3
Setting Yourself Free: Worth Working For

1. Alastair H.B. Logan, *Gnostic Truth and Christian Heresy: A Study in the History of Gnosticism* (Edinburgh, Scotland: Hendrickson Publishers, 1996), p. 211.

2. Irenaeus of Lyons, *Libros quinque adversus haereses*, ed. by W. W. Harvey (2 vols. Cambridge, 1857), 1.21.4.

3. Abraham Joshua Heschel, *I Asked for Wonder: A Spiritual Anthology*, Edited by Samuel H. Dresner (New York: Crossroad, 2000), p. 17.

4. *Ibid.*, p. 53.

5. Eknath Easwaran, *A Man to Match His Mountains: Badshah Khan, Nonviolent Soldier of Islam* (Berkeley, California: Nilgiri Press, 1984), p. 55.

6. Bhagavan Das, *The Essential Unity of All Religions* (Wheaton, Ill: The Theosophical Publishing House, 1973).

7. *Ibid.*, p. 305.

8. William Law quoted in Aldous Huxley, *The Perennial Philosophy* (New York: Meridian Books, 1968), p. 81.

9. St. Francis of Assisi quoted in Victor Gollancz, *Man and God* (Boston: Houghton Mifflin Company, 1951), p. 335.

10. Abraham Joshua Heschel, *I Asked for Wonder: A Spiritual Anthology*, Edited by Samuel H. Dresner (New York: Crossroad, 2000), p. 17.

11. Mother Teresa, *A Simple Path*, Compiled by Lucinda Vardey (New York: Ballantine Books, 1995), pp. 204.

12. Jn 14:20; 1 Cor 11:29; 2 Cor 13:5.

13. William Beidler, *The Vision of Self in Early Vedanta* (Delhi: Motilal Banarsidass, 1975). This study presents a helpful discussion on the notion of "self" (such as Ātman, Brahman, and purusha).

14. Orest Bedrij, ed., *Yes, It's Love: Your Life Can Be A Miracle.* (New York: Pyramid Publications, 1974), pp. 45-50.

15. Albert Einstein, "Religion and Science," *The New York Times Magazine*, November 9, 1930, pp. 1-4. The German text was published in *The Berliner Tageblatt*, November 11, 1930.

16. Turgenev, quoted in Victor Gollancz, *Man and God* (Boston: Houghton Mifflin Company, 1951), p. 51-2.

17. *Gregory of Nyssa: The Life of Moses*, trans. by Abraham J. Malherbe and Everett Ferguson (New York: Paulist Press, 1978), pp. 61, 98.

18. Orest Bedrij, "Scale Invariance, Unifying Principle, Order and Sequence of Physical Quantities and Fundamental Constants," *Ukrainian Mathematical Journal*, A trans. of the Proc. of the Nat. Acad. of Sci. of Ukraine (New York: Allerton Press, 1994), N. 4, pp. 67-73).

19. John Archibald Wheeler, *At Home in the Universe* (Woodbury, NY: American Institute of Physics, 1994), p. 86.

20. Jaroslav Pelikan, *The Idea of the University: A Reexamination* (New Haven, CT: Yale University Press, 1992), p. 18.

4
Birth of a Notion: Exciting Possibilities Ahead

1. Ricky Alan Mayotte, *The Complete Jesus* (South Royalton, Vermont: Steerforth Press, 1997), p. 234.

2. John Dominic Crossan, *The Historical Jesus: the Life of a Mediterranean Jewish Peasant*, San Francisco: Harper Collins, 1992, p. 427.

3. *Ibid.*, pp. 428-432.

4. Ricky Alan Mayotte, *The Complete Jesus* (South Royalton, Vermont: Steerforth Press, 1997), pp. 221-238.

5. Neil Douglas-Klotz, *The Hidden Gospel* (Wheaton, Illinois: Quest Books, 1999), p.12.

6. Stephen J. Patterson and James M. Robinson, Hans-Gebhard Bethage et al. *The Fifth Gospel: The Gospel of Thomas Comes of Age* (Harrisburg, PA: Trinity Press International, 1998).

7. James M. Robinson, "The Gospel According to Thomas" in *The Nag Hammadi Library in English*, Gen. Ed., Coptic Text Established and Translated by A. Guillaumont et al. (San Francisco: Harper & Row, 1988), p. 125.

8. Willis Barnstone, ed., *The Other Bible*, "The Gospel of Thomas" (San Francisco: HarperCollins Publishers, 1984), pp. 301, 300.

9. Ricky Alan Mayotte, *The Complete Jesus* (South Royalton, Vermont: Steerforth Press, 1997), p. 174.

10. Robert Ernest Hume, trans. from the Sanskrit, *The Thirteen Principal Upanishads* (London: Oxford University Press, 1971), p. 71, (*Brihad-Aranyaka Upanishad* 1. 3.28).

11. Orest Bedrij, *La Preuve Scientifique de L'Existence de Dieu* (Montreal: Courteau Louise, 2000).

12. *The New Encyclopaedia Britannica* (Chicago: Helen Hemingway Benton, 1973-4), Vol. 2, p. 101.

13. Arthur Koestler, *The Act of Creation* (New York: Dell, 1964).

14. Mother Teresa, *A Simple Path*, Compiled by Lucinda Vardey (New York: Ballantine Books, 1995), p. 55.

15. *Ibid.*, pp. 7-8.

16. Thomas Merton, Edited by Patrick Hart and Jonathan Montaldo, *The Intimate Merton* (New York: Harper Collins Publishers, 1999), p. 103.

17. *Ibid.*, p. 354.

18. Orest Bedrij, ed., *Yes It's Love: Your Life Can Be A Miracle* (New York: Pyramid Publications, 1974), pp. 46-49.

19. Subramuniya, "Spiritual Unfolding" in *Spiritual Community Guide* (San Rafael: Spiritual Community Publications, 1974), p. 13.

20. Annemarie Schimmel, *Mystical Dimensions of Islam* (Chapel Hill: The University of North Carolina Press, 1975), p. 278.

21. Ibid., p. 277.

22. Hafiz, trans. by Daniel Ladinsky, *The Gift* (New York: Arkana, Penguin Group, 1999), p. 191.

23. St. Symeon the New Theologian, *Hymns of Divine Love* (Denville, NJ: Dimension Books, 1968), p. 5.

24. James Maffie, "Like a Painting, We Will Be Erased; Like a Flower, We Will Dry Here on Earth: Ultimate Reality and Meaning According to Nahua Philosophy in the Age of Conquest." *Ultimate Reality and Meaning* (Toronto: University of Toronto Press, 2000), Vol. 23:4, p. 300.

25. Swami Muktananda, *Guru* (New York: Harper & Row Publishers, 1971), pp. 168, 175.

5
Deep Secrets in Code Language

1. Heinz Pagels. *The Cosmic Code.* New York: Bantam, 1983), p.156

2. Fritz Buri, *Der Pantokrator, Ontologie und Eshatologie als Grundlange der Lehre von Gott* (Hamburg-Bergstedt: Herbert Reich, 1969), pp. 56-64.

Geoffrey Hodson, *The Hidden Wisdom in the Holy Bible* (an examination of the idea that the contents of the *Bible* are partly allegorical), 3 vols. (Wheaton, Ill.: The Theosophical Publishing House, 1978); idem, *The Christ Life from Nativity to Ascension* (London: The Theosophical Publishing House. 1975); idem, "Lecture Notes," *The School of Wisdom*, Vol. II (Adyar, Madras: The Theosophical Publishing House, 1955).

Manlio Simonetti, Translator John A. Hughes, *Biblical Interpretation in the Early Church: An Historical Introduction to the Patristic Exegesis* (Edinburgh: T&T Clark, 1994).

Gerald Tranter, *The Mystery Teachings and Christianity* (Wheaton, Ill.: The Theosophical Publishing House, 1969).

R. C. Zaehner, *Matter and Spirit: Their Convergence in Eastern Religions, Marx and Teilhard de Chardin* (New York: Harper & Row, 1963), pp. 44-67.

3. Manlio Simonetti, Translator John A. Hughes, *Biblical Interpretation in the Early Church: An Historical Introduction to the Patristic Exegesis* (Edinburgh: T&T Clark, 1994), p. 36.

4. Confraternity of Christian Doctrine, *The New American Bible* (New York: Catholic Book Publishing Co., 1986), p. 27.

5. Hryhoryj Savych Skovoroda, *Sad Pisen* (Orchard of Songs: Kyiv, 1972), p. 90.

6. *The Zohar* III, Soncino ed., 1528, Vol. V, p. 211), is the most important book of the Kabbalah. A good edition of the book of *The Zohar* (meaning the light of the infinity of God) is that by Christian Knorr von Rosenroth, with Jewish commentaries (Schulzbach, 1684). Reprints with additional index (Amsterdam, 1714, 1722, 1728, 1805, 3 vols.). Later editions of *The Zohar* were published at Breslau (1866, 3 vols.); Livorno (1877-8 in 7 parts), and Wilna (1882, 3 vols.; 1882-3 in 10 parts).

7. Al-Hallaj, in full Abu al-Mughith al-Husayn Ibn Mansur al-Hallaj.

8. "Exchanging of acts" was the doctrine of the *isqāt al-farā'id*. We can equate this to "transformation" in mathematics or physics.

9. Annemarie Schimmel, *Mystical Dimensions of Islam* (Chapel Hill: The University of North Carolina Press, 1975).

10. Suhrawardī, in full Shihāb al-Dīn Suhrawardī, known as Shaīkh al-Ishrāq.

11. Sri Aurobindo, *The Future Evolution of Man: The Divine Life upon Earth*. Compiled with a summary and notes by P. B. Saint-Hilaire (Wheaton, Ill.: The Theosophical Publishing House, 1974), p. 45.

12. Evelyn Underhill, *Mysticism: A Study in the Nature and Development of Man's Spiritual Consciousness* (New York: E.P. Dutton & Co., Inc., 1961).

13. Ricky Alan Mayotte, *The Complete Jesus* (South Royalton, Vermont: Steerforth Press, 1997), p. 174.

14. Orest, [Bedrij] One (San Francisco: Strawberry Hill Press, 1978), pp. 16-23.

15. Plato, "Timaeus." *Great Books of the Western World* (Chicago: Encyclopaedia Britannica, Inc., 1952), Vol. 7, p. 442.

16. Milton Friedman, *Capitalism & Freedom* (Chicago: The University of Chicago Press, 1975), p. 19.

17. Dean Abrahamson, "So You Want To Become A Critic," *Physics and Society*. (College Park, MD: American Physical Society, 2000).

18. Ralph Waldo Emerson, *The Works of Ralph Waldo Emerson* (Roslyn, NY: Black's Readers Service, 2000), p. 133.

19. Quoted in Geoffrey Hodson, *The Hidden Wisdom in the Holy Bible* (Wheaton, Ill.: The Theosophical Publishing House, 1978), p. 42.

20. *Ibid.*, p. 97.
21. Orest Bedrij, "Union Without Ceasing," *Yes It's Love: Your Life Can Be A Miracle* (New York: Pyramid Publications, 1974), pp. 32-53.
22. The *Kū* or Void state in the *Upanishads* is recognized as *turīva*, and in yoga as *nirbīja-samādhi*. In the *Bhagavad Gita* it is acknowledged as *brahman-nirvana*, and in *Vedanta* as *nirvikalpa-samādhi*.
23. Sri Aurobindo, *The Future Evolution of Man: The Divine Life upon Earth.* Compiled with a summary and notes by P. B. Saint-Hilaire (Wheaton, Ill.: The Theosophical Publishing House, 1974), p. 50.
24. *The New Encyclopaedia Britannica* (Chicago: Helen Hemingway Benton, 1973-4), Vol. 13, p. 736.
25. Origen, *Origenes Werke* (Leipzig, 1899-1925), 8 vols.
26. Origen, "Selectra Psalmos, Patrologia Graeca XII," *Origenes Werke.*
27. Manlio Simonetti, Translator John A. Hughes, *Biblical Interpretation in the Early Church: An Historical Introduction to the Patristic Exegesis* (Edinburgh: T&T Clark, 1994), p. 51: Here and elsewhere Origen supports this concept by quoting or alluding to Mt 7:6 (do not throw your pearls before swine), a text which we have also seen Clement use in an analogous context.
28. *Ibid.,* p. 42.
29. Clement of Alexandria, "The Stromata, or Miscellanies," *Ante-Nicene Fathers* (Peabody, Mass: Hendrickson Publishers, 1999), Vol. 2, p. 302.
30. *Ibid.,* p. 344.
31. William Law quoted in Victor Gollancz, *Man and God* (Boston: Houghton Mifflin Company, 1951), p. 395.

6
We Can't Improve on God:
We Are Meant to Reveal Him in Us

1. Ramakrishna, *Ramakrishna: Prophet of New India,* trans. by Swami Nikhilananda (New York: Harper & Brothers, n.d.).
2 Arnold Toynbee made this statement in an interview, Marcus Bach, *Major Religions of the World* (New York: Abingdon Press, 1959), p. 15.
3. Hafiz, trans. by Daniel Ladinsky, *The Gift* (New York: Arkana, Penguin Group, 1999), p. 250.
4. Philip Schaff, *History of the Christian Church* (Peabody, Massachusetts: Hendrickson Publishers, Inc., 2002), Vol. 2, p. 9.
5. June Hager, *Pilgrimage: A Chronicle of Christianity Through the Churches of Rome* (London: Weidenfeld & Nicolson, 1999), p. 17.

6. Philip Schaff, *History of the Christian Church* (Peabody, Massachusetts: Hendrickson Publishers, Inc., 2002), Vol. 2, p. 68.

7. Steven Weinberg, *The First Three Minutes: A Modern View of the Origin of the Universe* (New York: Basic Books, 1977).

8. Alexander Roberts, D.D. & James Donaldson, LL.D., ed., "Introductory Note to Clement of Alexandria," *Ante-Nicene Fathers* (Peabody, Mass: Hendrickson Publishers, 1999), Vol. 2, p. 168.

9. Alexander Roberts, D.D. & James Donaldson, LL.D., eds., *Ante-Nicene Fathers* (Peabody, Mass: Hendrickson Publishers, 1999), Volumes 1-10—the writings of the Fathers down to CE 325. Also, Philip Schaff, D.D. & LL.D., ed., *Nicene and Post-Nicene Fathers* (Peabody, Mass: Hendrickson Publishers, 1999), Volumes 1-28—a select library of the Christian Church.

10. Sri Aurobindo, *The Future Evolution of Man: The Divine Life upon Earth.* Compiled with a summary and notes by P. B. Saint-Hilaire (Wheaton, Ill.: The Theosophical Publishing House, 1974), p. 42-3.

11. Philip Schaff, *History of the Christian Church* (Peabody, Mass: Hendrickson Publishers, 2002), Vol. 2, p 36—(Ante-Nicene Christianity, from the death of John the Apostle to Constantine the Great, AD 100-325).

12. *Ibid.* p. 78.

13. Sri Aurobindo, *The Future Evolution of Man: The Divine Life upon Earth.* Compiled with a summary and notes by P. B. Saint-Hilaire (Wheaton, Ill.: The Theosophical Publishing House, 1974), p. 44.

14. Abraham J. Heschel, *The Prophets* (New York: HarperCollins, 1969), p. 176.

15. Evelyn Underhill, *Mysticism: A Study in the Nature and Development of Man's Spiritual Consciousness* (New York: E.P. Dutton & Co., Inc., 1961); also, *Gregory of Nyssa: The Life of Moses*, trans. by Abraham J. Malherbe and Everett Ferguson (New York: Paulist Press, 1978), p. xiii.

16. John White, ed., *What is Enlightenment?* (Los Angeles: Jeremy P. Tarcher, Inc. 1984), p. 63.

17. Steven Weinberg, *Dreams of a Final Theory* (New York: Pantheon Books, 1992), p. 5.

18. *The New Encyclopaedia Britannica* (Chicago: The University of Chicago, 1987), Vol. 16, p. 274.

19. Bhagavan Das, *The Essential Unity of All Religions* (Wheaton, Ill: The Theosophical Publishing House, 1973), pp. 1-2.

20. *Ibid.*, p. 2.

21. Francis Thompson, quoted by Sir George Trevelyan in "Gateway to the Infinite," *The Spirit of Science: From Experiment to Experience* by David Lorimer, ed. (New York: The Continuum Publishing Company, 1998), p. 305.

22. Orest, [Bedrij] One. (San Francisco: Strawberry Hill Press, 1978), pp. 83-89.

23. Orest Bedrij, "Revelation and Verification of Ultimate Reality and Meaning Through Direct Experience and the Laws of Physics." *Ultimate Reality and Meaning*, Toronto: University of Toronto Press, 2000), Vol. 23:1, pp. 49-50.

24. *Ibid.*, p. 51.

7
Seek God's Face: A Child's Story Decoded

1. Swami Muktananda, *Guru* (New York: Harper & Row Publishers, 1971), p. 5.

2. Clement of Alexandria in Eusebius, *Ecclesiastical History* 6.14.7.

3. Irenaeus, *Against All Heresies* (Refutation of So-called Gnosis or Knowledge) 3.11.

4. Mother Teresa, *The Joy in Loving* (New York: Viking, 1997), p. 115

5. Erwin Schrödinger, *What is Life?* (Cambridge: The MacMillan Company, 1946), p. 88.

6. A.C. Bhaktivedanta Swami Prabhupada, *Bhagavad Gita As It Is* (Los Angeles: Macmillan Publishing, 1973), p. 432.

7. G. Zannoni, *Arato di Soli, Fenomeni e pronostici* (Florence: Sansoni, 1948), *Phenomena*, I. 1-6. Greek text of Aratus with an Italian translation by G. Zannoni.

8. Gustav Teres, S. J. *The Bible and Astronomy. The Magi and the Star in the Gospel.* (Budapest: Springer Orvosi Kiado Kft., 2000), pp. 278-279.

9. Mother Teresa, *The Joy in Loving* (New York: Viking, 1997), p. 148

10. Swami Muktananda, *Guru* (New York: Harper & Row Publishers, 1971), p. 174.

11. Albert Einstein, in *The New York Post*, November 18, 1972.

12. Arnold Toynbee and Daisaku Ikeda, *Choose Life: A Dialogue* (London: Oxford University Press, 1976), p. 25.

13. Quoted in Henryk Skolimowski, "Global Philosophy as the Canvas for Human Unity," (*The American Theosophist*. May 1983,) p. 163.

14. *Ibid.*, p. 163.

15. Max Planck, *Where is Science Going?* (New York: Norton, 1932).

16. Werner Heisenberg, *Physics and Philosophy* (London: Allen & Unwin, 1959).

17. Rabbi Ben Zion Bokser, ed. and trans., *The Essential Writings of Abraham Isaac Kook* (Warwick, NY: Amity House, 1988), pp. 167, 170.

18. Robert Muller, *A Planet of Hope* (Warwick, NY: Amity House, 1985), p. 21.

19. Ibid, p. 4.

20. Ibid, p. 5.

8
Rise, O Mighty One:
We Have Entered a Universe of Love and Light!

1. Mother Teresa, *The Joy in Loving* (New York: Viking, 1997), p. 148

2. Charlene Leslie-Chaden, *A Compendium of the Teachings of Sathya Sai Baba* (Prasanthi Nilayam: Sai Towers Publishing, 1997), p. 215.

3. Rom 12:1; cf. 1 Cor 6:18-20; 2 Cor 6:6-7:1.

4. Deut 6:5; Mk 12:30 par.

5. Ps 96:5; Rom 1:21-25.

6. Albert Schweitzer, quoted by Richard Carlson and Benjamin Shield in *Handbook for the Soul* (Boston: Little, Brown and Company, 1995), p. 85.

7. Kabir, quoted in Meister Eckhart, Introduction and Commentaries by Matthew Fox, O.P. *Breakthrough: Meister Eckhart's Creation Spirituality in New Translation* (New York: Doubleday, 1980), p. 129.

8. Geoffrey Keynes, ed., *The Writings of William Blake* (London, 1925) 3 vols.

9. *The New Encyclopaedia Britannica* (Chicago: Helen Hemingway Benton, 1973-4), Vol. 2, p. 1100.

10. Acharya Debendranath, *Ultimate Reality of Hinduism* (Calcutta: Indranil Basu, Basu Mandir, 2000), p. 118.

11. Satya Sai Baba, *Teachings of Sri Satya Sai Baba*, first compiled by N. Kasturi, and published in India. This edited version is by Roy Eugene Davis (Lakemont, Georgia: CSA Press, 1974), p. 53. Also, Charlene Leslie-Chaden, *A Compendium of the Teachings of Sathya Sai Baba* (Prasanthi Nilayam: Sai Towers Publishing, 1997), p. 37.

12. Albert Einstein, in *The New York Post,* November 18, 1972.

13. John Archibald Wheeler, *At Home in the Universe* (Woodbury, NY: American Institute of Physics, 1994), p. 3.

14. John White, ed., *What is Enlightenment?* (Los Angeles: Jeremy P. Tarcher, Inc. 1984), p. xv.

15. ""Sir," answered the woman, "I can see you are a prophet. Our ancestors worshiped on this mountain, but you people claim that Jerusalem is the place where men ought to worship God." Jesus responded: "Believe me woman, an hour is coming [that is beyond pagan worship of today] when you will worship the Father neither on this mountain nor in Jerusalem. You [pagan] people worship what you do not understand, while we [who were reborn in Christ] understand what we worship . . .

Yet an hour is coming, and is already here, when *authentic worshipers will worship the Father in SPIRIT and truth. Indeed, it is just SUCH worshipers the Father seeks. God is Spirit, and those who worship him must worship in Spirit and truth.*"" (Jn 4:19-24).

Also, "I did not see a temple in the city [of Absolute Unity], because the Lord, God Almighty [in whom we live and move and have our being, Acts 17:28] and the Lamb (the risen Christ—the Spirit of truth) is its lamp. The nations will walk by its light, and the kings of the earth will bring their splendor into it" (Rev 21:22-24).

Therefore, "present your bodies as a living sacrifice, holy and acceptable to God, which is your spiritual worship" (Rom 12:1; cf. 1 Cor 6:18-20; 2 Cor 6:6-7:1).

16. Robert Ernest Hume, trans. from the Sanskrit, *The Thirteen Principal Upanishads* (London: Oxford University Press, 1971); also quoted in Aldous Huxley, *The Perennial Philosophy* (New York: Meridian Books, 1968), p. 206.
17. *Ibid.*, p. 366.
18. Dag Hammarskjöld, *Markings*, trans. from the Swedish by Leif Sjöberg & W.H.Auden (New York: Ballantine Books, 1993), pp. vi-vii.
19. Arnold Toynbee and Daisaku Ikeda, *Choose Life: A Dialogue* (London: Oxford University Press, 1976), p. 62.

9
God Became What We Are

1. St. Irenaeus, *Adversus Haereses,* Book V, ch. 28, 4, in *The Ante-Nicene Fathers*, Vol. 1, A. Roberts and J. Donaldson, Eds. (Grand Rapids: Eerdmans, 1958), p. 557.
2. Pierre Teilhard de Chardin, *The Phenomenon of Man,* translated by Bernard Wall (London: Collins, 1959; New York: Harper & Row, 1959); Science & Christ, translated by Rene' Hague (London: Collins; New York: Harper & Row, 1968).
3. *The Gospel According to Thomas*, Coptic Text Established and Translated by A. Guillaumont, et al. (San Francisco: Harper & Row, 1959), p. 29.
4. Roger Penrose, "Gravitational Collapse and Space-Time Singularities" (*Physical Review Letters*, 1965), pp. 14, 57-9; "Singularities in Cosmology." In M.S. Longair (Ed.), *Confrontation of Cosmological Theories with Observational Data.* (Boston: D. Reidel). Also, *Cosmology* (London: BBC Publications, 1974); "Singularities and Time-asymmetry." In *General Relativity: An Einstein Centenary Survey*, ed. by Stephen Hawking and W. Israel. (Cambridge: Cambridge University Press, 1979).
5. Steven Hawking, "Singularities in the Universe." (*Physical Review Letters* 17, 1966); "Theoretical Advances in General Relativity." In H. Woolf (Ed.), *Some Strangeness*

in the Proportion (Reading, MA: Addison-Wesley, 1980); A *Brief History of Time: From the Big Bang to Black Holes.* (New York: Bantam Books, 1988).

6. St. Athanasius, *De Incarnatione Verbi*, p. 5, 192B.

7. Thomas Merton, ed. by Patrick Hart and Jonathan Montaldo, *The Intimate Merton* (New York: Harper Collins Publishers, 1999), p. 254.

8. Meister Eckhart, *Meister Eckhart: A Modern Translation,* trans. by Raymond Bernard Blankney (New York: Harper Torchbook, 1941), p. 244.

9. Swami Muktananda, *Guru* (New York: Harper & Row Publishers, 1971), p. ix.

10. Henri Corbin, "Imagination créatrice et prière créatrice dans le soufisme d'Ibn Arabi," *Eranos-Jahrbuch* 25 (1956), p. 182.

11. Abū'l-'Alā Affifi, *The Mystical Philosophy of Muhyid'Dīn Ibnul-'Arabī* (Cambridge, 1936), pp. 172.

12. Werner Heisenberg, *The Physicist's Conception of Nature* (New York: Harcourt and Brace, 1955).

13. Swami Rama, *The Book of Wisdom* (Kanpur, India: Himalayan International Institute of Yoga, Science and Philosophy, 1972), pp. 4-5.

10
Before the Beginning, Before the Hot Big Bang

1. Robert Ernest Hume, trans. from the Sanskrit, *The Thirteen Principal Upanishads* (London: Oxford University Press, 1971), p. 11.

2. S. Saunders and H.R. Brown, Eds., *The Philosophy of Vacuum.* (Oxford: Oxford University Press, 1991).

3. Orest Bedrij, "Scale Invariance, Unifying Principle, Order and Sequence of Physical Quantities and Fundamental Constants," *Dopovidi* (Kyiv: National Academy of Sciences of Ukraine, April 1993), #4, p. 67.

4. Nick Herbert, *Quantum Reality: Beyond the New Physics* (New York: Doubleday, 1985), p. 126.

5. Robert Ernest Hume, trans. from the Sanskrit, *The Thirteen Principal Upanishads* (London: Oxford University Press, 1971), p. 11.

6. Werner Heisenberg, *Across the Frontiers* (New York: Harper & Row, 1974).

7. Gennady Shipov, *A Theory of Physical Vacuum: A New Parading* (Moscow: Russian Academy of Natural Sciences, 1998), p. 47.

8. Richard F. Plzak Jr., *Paradox East and West* (Senior Dissertation), MIT, 1973, p. 54.

9. Philip Novak, *The World's Wisdom: Sacred Texts of the World's Religions.* (New York: Harper Collins Publishers, 1994), p. 24.

10. A.C. Bhaktivedanta Swami Prabhupada, *Bhagavad Gita As It Is* (Los Angeles: Macmillan Publishing, 1973), pp. 86-9, 109.

11. Chu Ta-kao, trans., *Tao-te Ching* (Boston: Mandala Books, 198), ch. 25.

12. David Bohm, *Wholeness and the Implicate Order* (London: Ark Paperbacks Ltd., 1983), pp. 191-2.

13. Aristotle, "The Works of Aristotle." *Great Books of the Western World*. (Chicago: Encyclopaedia Britannica, Inc., 1952) Vol. 8, p. 612.

14. Kenneth Sylvan Guthrie, Comp. and trans., *The Pythagorean Sourcebook and Library* (Grand Rapids, Michigan: Phanes Press, 1987).

15. Sir Thomas L. Heath, trans., The "Thirteen Books of Euclid's Elements," *The Great Books of the Western World* (Chicago: Encyclopaedia Britannica, Inc., 1952), Vol. 11.

16. Takpo Tashi Namgyal, trans., and annotated by Lobsang P. Lhalungpa, *Mahamudra: The Quintessence of Mind and Meditation* (Boston: Shambhala Publications, Inc., 1986), p. 296.

17. Kalu Rinpoche, *Gently Whispered: Oral Teachings.* Compiled, edited. and annotated, by E. Selandia (Tarrytown, NY: Station Hill Press, 1994), p.13.

18. Lao Tzu, *The Tao Teh King: Sayings of Lao Tzu,* trans. with Commentary by C. Spurgeon Medhurst (Wheaton, Ill: The Theosophical Publishing House, 1972), p. 27.

19. Plato, "Dialogues of Plato: Parmenides." *Great Books of the Western World* (Chicago: Encyclopaedia Britannica, Inc., 1971), p. 486.

20. Basil Hiley, "Vacuum or Holomovement." *The Philosophy of Vacuum.* (Oxford: Oxford University Press, 1991), p. 216.

21. Plotinus, "*The Six Enneads.*" *Great Books of the Western World* (Chicago: Encyclopaedia Britannica, Inc., 1952), Vol. 17, 7.3.2.

22. Meister Eckhart, *Works*, trans. by C. B. Evans (London, 1924); also quoted in Aldous Huxley, *The Perennial Philosophy* (New York: Meridian Books, 1968), p. 25.

23. Hafiz, trans. by Daniel Ladinsky, *The Gift* (New York: Arkana, Penguin Group, 1999), p. 148.

24. *Principia*, condensed title of Isaac Newton's *Philosophiae naturalis principia mathematica* ("Mathematical Principles of Natural Philosophy"), brings together his observations and mathematical analysis into physics and astronomy, published in three volumes in 1686-1687; Isaac Newton, "Mathematical Principles of Natural Philosophy." *Great Books of the Western World* (Chicago: Encyclopaedia Britannica, Inc., 1971), Vol. 34, p. 8.

11
The Creator Plays Hide-and-Seek—as Us

1. Athanasius, *De Incarnatione Verbi, p. 25.*

2. Burton Watson, trans. *Chuang Tzu: Basic Writings* (New York: Columbia University Press, 1964), p. 45.

3. Augustine, *Sermones* 341.9.11

4. Thomas Merton, *New Seeds of Contemplation* (New York: New Directions Books, 1961), p. 64.

5. Rabbi Shmelke of Nikolsburg quoted in Victor Gollancz, *Man and God* (Boston: Houghton Mifflin Company, 1951), p. 183.

6. Robert Muller, *A Planet of Hope* (Warwick, NY: Amity House, 1985), p. 62.

7. Robert D. Richardson Jr., *Emerson: The Mind on Fire* (Berkeley: University of California Press, 1995), p. 154.

8. Abraham Joshua Heschel, ed. by Samuel H. Dresner, *I Asked for Wonder: A Spiritual Anthology* (New York: Crossroad, 2000), p. 55.

9. Meister Eckhart, *Works*, trans. by C. B. Evans (London, 1924); also quoted in Aldous Huxley, *The Perennial Philosophy* (New York: Meridian Books, 1968), p. 25.

10. John Dewey, *The Influence of Darin on Philosophy* (New York, 1910), p.55.

11. Bhagavan Das, *The Essential Unity of All Religions* (Wheaton, Ill: The Theosophical Publishing House, 1973), p. 39.

12. Hafiz, trans. by Daniel Ladinsky, *The Gift* (New York: Arkana, Penguin Group, 1999), p. 331.

13. Arthur Stanley Eddington, *Nature of the Physical World* (Cambridge: Cambridge University Press, 1928), p. 219.

14. Meister Eckhart, Introduction and Commentaries by Matthew Fox, O.P. *Breakthrough: Meister Eckhart's Creation Spirituality in New Translation* (New York: Doubleday, 1980), p. 188.

15. John Locke Scripps interview with Lincoln and Lincoln's 2,500-word autobiography distilled in a 32-page pamphlet titled "Life of Abraham Lincoln," which was published simultaneously by the Chicago *Tribune* and the *New York Tribune*: Carl Sandburg, *Abraham Lincoln* (Norwalk, Conn.: The Easton Press, 1954), p. 179.

16. *Ibid.,* p. 179: Stephen Douglas (1858) debate.

17. Michael Burlingame, The Inner World of Abraham Lincoln (Chicago: University of Illinois Press, 1994), pp. 361-2.

18. Carl Sandburg, *Abraham Lincoln* (Norwalk, Conn.: The Easton Press, 1954), p. 733.

19. Saint Teresa of Avila, trans. and ed. by E. Allison Peers, *The Interior Castle* (Garden City, NY: Image Books, 1944), p. 154.

20. Orest Bedrij, "Fundamental Physical Constants," *Dopovidi* (Kyiv: National Academy of Sciences of Ukraine, March 1993), #3.

21. Stephen W. Hawking, *A Brief History of Time: From the Big Bang to Black Holes* (New York: Bantam Books, 1988), p.174.

22. Fritjof Capra and David Steindl-Rast with Thomas Matus, *Belonging to the Universe: Explorations on the Frontiers of Science and Spirituality* (San Francisco: Harper Collins Publishers, 1991), p. 136.

23. Paramahamsa Yogananda, *Men's Eternal Quest* (Los Angeles: Self-Realization Fellowship, 1982), p. 453.

24. Chögyam Trungpa, *Orderly Chaos: The Mandala Principle* (Boston: Shambhala, 1991), pp. 105, 111.

12
The Flourishing of Reason: Recognize the Obvious

1. Jetsun Milarepa, *One Hundred Thousand Songs of Milarepa,* trans. and annotated by Garma C. C. Chang (Boulder: Shambala, 1977), Vol. 2, p. 437.

2. *Ibid.,* pp. 425, 481.

3. Dwight Goddard, ed., *A Buddhist Bible* (Boston: Beacon Press, 1994), p. 125.

4. A.C. Bhaktivedanta Swami Prabhupada, *Bhagavad Gita As It Is* (Los Angeles: Macmillan Publishing, 1973), p. 314.

5. Jetsun Milarepa, *One Hundred Thousand Songs of Milarepa,* trans. and annotated by Garma C. C. Chang (Boulder: Shambala, 1977), Vol. 2, p. 481.

6. Burton Watson, trans., *Chuang Tzu Basic Writings* (New York: Columbia University Press, 1964), p. 65.

7. Dag Hammarskjöld, *Markings*, trans. from the Swedish by Leif Sjöberg & W. H. Auden (New York: Ballantine Books, 1993), p. 8.

8. *Ibid*, p. 70.

9. Mother Teresa, *A Simple Path*, compiled by Lucinda Vardey (New York: Ballantine Books, 1995), pp. 25-6.

10. Satya Sai Baba, *Teachings of Sri Satya Sai Baba*, first compiled by N. Kasturi, and published in India. This edited version is by Roy Eugene Davis (Lakemont, Georgia: CSA Press, 1974), pp. 7, 11.

11. Edward Carpenter, *The Drama of Love and Death* (London: George Allen & Unwin Ltd.).

12. Lawrence E. Sullivan, *Icanchu's Drum: An Orientation to Meaning in South American Religions* (New York: Macmillan Publishing Company, 1988).

13. James Maffie, "'Like a Painting, We Will Be Erased; Like a Flower, We Will Dry Here on Earth': Ultimate Reality and Meaning According to Nahua Philosophy in the Age of Conquest." *Ultimate Reality and Meaning* (Toronto: University of Toronto Press, 2000), Vol. 23: 4, pp. 227, 311.

14. *Ibid.*, pp. 313, 316.

15. Swami Muktananda, *Guru* (New York: Harper & Row Publishers, 1971), p. 59.

16. Thomas Merton, Edited by Patrick Hart and Jonathan Montaldo, *The Intimate Merton* (New York: Harper Collins Publishers, 1999), p. 143.

17. Ralph Waldo Emerson, *The Works of Ralph Waldo Emerson* (Roslyn, NY: Black's Readers Service, 2000), p. 106.

18. Dag Hammarskjöld, *Markings*, trans. from the Swedish by Leif Sjöberg & W. H. Auden (New York: Ballantine Books, 1993), p. 83.

19. Abraham Joshua Heschel, *I Asked for Wonder: A Spiritual Anthology*, Edited by Samuel H. Dresner (New York: Crossroad, 2000), p. 58.

13
When Heart Speaks to Heart What More Is There to Say?

1. Ian P. McGreal, ed. *Great Thinkers of the Eastern World* (New York: Harper Collins Publishers, 1995), p. 7.

2. Mother Teresa, *A Simple Path*, Compiled by Lucinda Vardey (New York: Ballantine Books, 1995), p. 79.

3. Og Mandino, *The Greatest Salesman in the World* (New York: Frederick Fell Publishers, 1973), pp. 58-62.

4. Donald T. Phillips. *Run To Win: Vince Lombardi on Coaching and Leadership* (New York: St. Martin's Press, 2001), p. 171.

5. Clancy D. McKenzie, Md. & Lance S. Wright, Md. *Delayed Post Traumatic Stress Disorders from Infancy and the Two Trauma Mechanism: Clinical Examples* (Bala Cynwyd, PA: American Health Association, 1990).

6. Pitirim A. Sorokin, "The Mysterious Energy of Love," *Vedanta and the West* (Hollywood, CA: Vedanta Centre), No. 136, p. 4.

7. Bill O'Reilly, *Who's Looking Out for You* (New York: Broadway Books, 2003), p. 8.

8. *Ibid.* p. 178.

9. Pitirim A. Sorokin, "The Mysterious Energy of Love," *Vedanta and the West* (Hollywood, CA: Vedanta Centre), No. 136, p. 5.

10. Robert Muller, *A Planet of Hope* (Warwick, NY: Amity House, 1985), p. 20.97.

11. Hafiz, trans. by Daniel Ladinsky, *The Gift* (New York: Arkana, Penguin Group, 1999), p. 184.

12. Jean Pierre Camus, *The Spirit of St. Francis de Sales* (London, n.d.); also quoted in Aldous Huxley, *The Perennial Philosophy* (New York: Meridian Books, 1968), p. 90.

13. Satya Sai Baba, *Teachings of Sri Satya Sai Baba*, first compiled by N. Kasturi, and published in India. This edited version is by Roy Eugene Davis (Lakemont, Georgia: CSA Press, 1974), pp. 17.

14. Annemarie Schimmel, *Mystical Dimensions of Islam* (Chapel Hill: The University of North Carolina Press, 1975), p. 51.

15. Robert Muller, *A Planet of Hope* (Warwick, NY: Amity House, 1985), p. 38.

16. Jalāl al-Din Rūmi, *Teachings of Rumi the Masnavi*, trans. and abridged by E. H. Whinfield (New York: E.P. Dutton & Co., 1975); also quoted in Aldous Huxley, *The Perennial Philosophy* (New York: Meridian Books, 1968), p. 91.

17. Pitirim A. Sorokin, "The Mysterious Energy of Love," *Vedanta and the West* (Hollywood, CA: Vedanta Centre), No. 136, p. 5.

18. Abraham Joshua Heschel, *I Asked for Wonder: A Spiritual Anthology*, Edited by Samuel H. Dresner (New York: Crossroad, 2000), p. 60.

19. Piere Teilhard de Chardin, "The Evolution of Chastity" in *Toward the Future* (New York: Harcourt Brace Jovanovich, 1975), p. 87.

14
We Can Be Lights to Each Other: Experience It!

1. René Descartes, "Rules for the Direction of the Mind," trans. by Elizabeth S. Haldane and G.R.T. Ross, *The Great Books of the Western World* (Chicago: Encyclopaedia Britannica, Inc., 1971), Vol. 31, p. 17.

2. Burton Watson, trans. *Chuang Tzu: Basic Writings* (New York: Columbia University Press, 1964), p. 65.

3. Orest Bedrij. "Revelation and Verification of Ultimate Reality and Meaning Through Direct Experience and the Laws of Physics." *Ultimate Reality and Meaning* (Toronto: University of Toronto Press, 2000), Vol. 23:1, pp. 59-61.

4. Albert Einstein. "Über den Äther," *Schweizerische Naturforschende Gesellschaft* (Verhanflungen, 1924) 105:85-93.

5. John Barlett, *Familiar Quotations,* 16th ed. (Boston: Little, Brown, 1982), p. 502; originally quoted in Rene Valley-Radot, *The Life of Pasteur* (1927).

6. O. J. Bedrij, Carry-Select Adder, *IRE Transactions on Electronic Computers*, Vol. EC-11, Number 3, June, 1962, pp. 340-346.

7. Orest J. Bedrij, *Selecting Adder* (Filed Jan. 6, 1960; Patented Aug. 13, 1963, US Patent 3100,835), Also, *Electronic Binary Parallel Adder* (International Classification: G 06 f, London: The Patent Office, # 963,429).

8. Nick Herbert, *Quantum Reality: Beyond the New Physics* (New York: Doubleday, 1985), p. 148.

9. Robert Muller, *A Planet of Hope* (Warwick, NY: Amity House, 1985), p. 63.

10. Orest Bedrij, "Scale Invariance, Unifying Principle, Order and Sequence of Physical Quantities and Fundamental Constants," *Dopovidi* (Kyiv: National Academy of Sciences of Ukraine, April 1993), #4.

11. Orest Bedrij. "Revelation and Verification of Ultimate Reality and Meaning Through Direct Experience and the Laws of Physics." *Ultimate Reality and Meaning* (Toronto: University of Toronto Press, 2000), Vol. 23:1, pp. 59-61.

12. Steven Weinberg, *Dreams of a Final Theory* (New York: Pantheon Books, 1992), p. 207.

13. George Spencer Brown, *The Laws of Form* (London: Allen & Unwin, 1969).

14. [Sir] Isaac Newton, in D Brewster Memoirs of Newton (1855), Vol. 2 chapter 27.

15. R. A. Mashelkar, "Resurgence of Springs of Scientific Creativity: The Indian Challenge." *The Theosophist* (Adyar, India: The Theosophical Society, March 2002), p. 214.

16. William James, *The Varieties of Religious Experience* (London: Longmans Green, 1919).

17. David Bohm, *Wholeness and the Implicate Order* (London: Ark Paperbacks Ltd., 1983), pp. 124-5.

18. Quoted in Aldous Huxley, *The Perennial Philosophy* (New York: Meridian Books, 1968), p. 189.

19. Erwin Schrödinger, *What is Life?* (Cambridge: The MacMillan Company, 1946), p. 218.

20. Arthur Osbourne, *Ramana Maharshi and the Path of Self-Knowledge* (New York: Samuel Weiser, 1973).

21. *Ibid.*, pp. 20-21.

22. Helena H. Blavatsky, *The Secret Doctrine* (Wheaton, Ill.: The Theosophical Publishing House, 1993), Collected Writings, Vol. 8, pp.127-8.

23. Thomas Merton, *The Asian Journal of Thomas Merton,* ed. by Naomi Burton, Brother Patrick Hart, and James Laughlin (New York: New Directions Press, 1973).

15
Light, Love, and Life: the Core of Fire

1   Stephan Schuhmacher, *The Encyclopaedia of Eastern Philosophy and Religion* (Boston: Shambhala, 1994), p. 397.

2. Abraham Joshua Heschel, *I Asked for Wonder: A Spiritual Anthology*, edited by Samuel H. Dresner (New York: Crossroad, 2000), p. 46.

3. Ken Carey, *Starseed: The Third Millennium* (San Francisco: Harper Collins Publishers, 1991), p. 149.

4. Elizabeth Haich, *Sexual Energy and Yoga* (London: George Allen & Unwin Ltd.).

    Marilyn Ferguson, *The Brain Revolution* (New York: Taplinger Publishing Company, 1973).

    Gopi Krishna, *Kundalini: The Evolutionary Energy in Man* (Berkeley, CA, 1970); idem, *The Awakening of Kundalini* (New York: Dutton, 1975); idem, *The Biological Basis of Religion and Genius* (New York: Harper & Row, 1972); idem, *Higher Consciousness: The Evolutionary Thrust of Kundalini* (New York: The Julian Press, Inc., 1974).

    Jetsun Milarepa, *One Hundred Thousand Songs of Milarepa,* trans. and annotated by Garma C. C. Chang (Boulder: Shambala, 1977), 2 vols.

    Swami Muktananda, *Kundalini: The Secret of Life* (South Fallsburg, NY: SYDA Foundation, 1987).

    Vasant Rele, *The Mysterious Kundalini* (India: D. B. Taraporevala Sons & Co.).

    Lee Sannela, MD, *Kundalini-Psychosis or Transcendence?* (San Francisco: Sannela, 1976).

    Swami Mahjaraj Vishnu Tirtha, *Devatma Shakti,* India.

    John White, ed., *The Highest State of Consciousness* (New York: Doubleday, 1972); idem, *Kundalini, Evolution and Enlightenment* (New York: Anchor Books/ Doubleday, 1978).

5. A.C. Bhaktivedanta Swami Prabhupada, *Bhagavad Gita As It Is* (Los Angeles: Macmillan Publishing, 1973).

6. Daniel C. Matt, *The Essential Kabbalah* (New York: Quality Paperback Book Club, 1998), p. xiv.

7. 'Abdullah Yusuf 'Ali, *The Meaning of The Holy Qur'an* (Beltsville, MD: Amana Publications, 1994), p. 1570.

8. Ralph Waldo Emerson, *The Works of Ralph Waldo Emerson* (Roslyn, NY: Black's Readers Service, 2000), p. 97.

9. *Ibid.,* p. 97.

10. Erwin Schrödinger, *What is Life?* (Cambridge: The Macmillan Company, 1946).

16
Your Seed of Pure Pleasure: Adds Brightness to the Sun

1. Robert Muller, *A Planet of Hope* (Warwick, NY: Amity House, 1985), pp. 29, 2.
2. Donald J. Hawkins, ed., *Famous Statements, Speeches, and Stories of Abraham Lincoln* (Scarsdale, NY: Heathcote Publications, 1981), p. 2.
3. Carl Sandburg, *Abraham Lincoln* (Norwalk, Conn.: The Easton Press, 1954), p. 165
4. *Ibid.,* p. 151.
5. Donald J. Hawkins, ed., *Famous Statements, Speeches, and Stories of Abraham Lincoln* (Scarsdale, NY: Heathcote Publications, 1981), pp. 16, 38.
6. Michael Burlingame, The Inner World of Abraham Lincoln (Chicago: University of Illinois Press, 1994), p. 9.
7. Aldous Huxley, *The Perennial Philosophy* (New York: Meridian Books, 1968), p. 179.
8. George Santayana, *Reason in Common Sense* (New York: Charles Scribner and Sons, 1927), p. 28.
9. Jetsun Milarepa, *The Hundred Thousand Songs of Milarepa (Milagrubum)*, trans. and Annotated by Garmac C. Chang (Boulder Co.: Shambhala Publications, Inc., 1977), Vol. II.
10. Albert Einstein, Address at Albany, NY, on the occasion of the celebration of the tercentenary of higher education in America, October 15, 1936. Published in *Out of My Later Years* (New York: Philosophical Library, 1950)
11. Paul Brunton, *The Hidden Teaching Beyond Yoga* (New York: Samuel Weiser, 1972), p. 36.
12. Shankara, *Viveka-Chudamani* ("The Crest Jewel of Wisdom"); see the new, independent translation with commentary by Ernest Wood, *The Pinnacle of Indian Thought* (Wheaton, Ill.: The Theosophical Publishing House, 1970), Op. cit., verses 56, 57, 64.
13. Stephen J. Patterson, James M. Robinson, and Hans-Gebhard Bethage, et al., *The Fifth Gospel: The Gospel of Thomas Comes of Age* (Harrisburg, PA: Trinity Press International, 1998), p. 26.
14. Tom Morgan, ed. *A Simple Monk* (Novato, CA: New World Library, 2001), p. 137-8.
15. Maurice R. Bucke, *Cosmic Consciousness: A Study in the Evolution of the Human Mind* (New York: E.P. Dutton & Co., 1901 and 1975).

     Gopi Krishna, *Kundalini: The Evolutionary Energy in Man* (Berkeley, CA, 1970); idem, *The Awakening of Kundalini* (New York: Dutton, 1975); idem, *The Biological Basis of Religion and Genius* (New York: Harper & Row, 1972);

     John White, ed., *The Highest State of Consciousness* (New York: Doubleday,

1972); idem, *Kundalini, Evolution and Enlightenment* (New York: Anchor Books/ Doubleday, 1978).

16. C. Leadbetter, *The Chakras,* (Wheaton, Ill.: the Theosophical Publishing House, 1969).

17. Elizabeth Haich, *Sexual Energy and Yoga* (London: George Allen & Unwin Ltd.).

    Gopi Krishna, *Kundalini: The Evolutionary Energy in Man* (Berkeley, CA, 1970); idem, *The Awakening of Kundalini* (New York: Dutton, 1975); idem, *The Biological Basis of Religion and Genius* (New York: Harper & Row, 1972); idem, *Higher Consciousness: The Evolutionary Thrust of Kundalini* (New York: The Julian Press, Inc., 1974).

    Swami Muktananda, *Kundalini: The Secret of Life* (South Fallsburg, NY: SYDA Foundation, 1987).

    Vasant Rele, *The Mysterious Kundalini* (India: D. B. Taraporevala Sons & Co.).

    Swami Mahjaraj Vishnu Tirtha, *Devatma Shakti,* India.

    John White, ed., *The Highest State of Consciousness* (New York: Doubleday, 1972); idem, *Kundalini, Evolution and Enlightenment* (New York: Anchor Books/ Doubleday, 1978).

18. Edouard Schure, *The Great Initiates,* trans. from the French by Gloria Rasberry (San Francisco: Harper & Row, 1980), pp. 192-3.

19. Gene Kieffer, ed., *Kundalini for the New Age: Selected Writings by Gopi Krishna* (New York: Bantam Books, 1988), p. 1.

17
I Am the One I Am Also the Many

1. Wingate, *Tilling the Soul* (New York: Aurora Press, 1984), pp. 65-7.
2. Ken Carey, *Vision* (Kansas City, MO: Uni Sun, 1985), p. 11.
3. Deng Ming-Dao, *Chronicles of Tao* (New York: Harper Collins, 1993), p. 82
4. Abraham Joshua Heschel, *I Asked for Wonder: A Spiritual Anthology*, Edited by Samuel H. Dresner (New York: Crossroad, 2000), pp. 107, 110.
5. *Ibid.*, p. 109.
6. *Ibid.*, p. 103.
7. Hafiz, trans. by Daniel Ladinsky, *The Gift* (New York: Arkana, Penguin Group, 1999), p. 323-4.
8. *Ibid.*, p. 207.
9. Wingate, *Tilling the Soul,* pp.69-71.
10. Annemarie Schimmel, *Mystical Dimensions of Islam* (Chapel Hill: The University of North Carolina Press, 1975), p. 394

11. Joseph S. Benner, *The Impersonal Life* (Marina del Ray, CA: DeVorss & Co., Publishers, [1941] 1986), pp. 50-52.

12. Thomas Merton, *New Seeds of Contemplation* (New York: New Directions Books, 1961), pp. 6, 4, 5.

13. *Ibid.*, p. 9.

14. Gene Kieffer, ed., *Kundalini for the New Age: Selected Writings by Gopi Krishna* (New York: Bantam Books, 1988), p. 41.

15. R. S. Bhatnagar, *Dimensions of Classical Sufi Thought* (Delhi: Motilal Banarsidass, 1984), p. 92.

18
The Wine of Heaven: An Ocean of Utmost Peace

1. Saint Teresa of Avila, *The Interior Castle,* trans. and ed. by E. Allison Peers (Garden City, NY: Image Books, 1944), p. 149.

2. *Ibid.*, p. 179.

3. Saint Catherine of Siena, *The Divine Dialogue of Saint Catherine of Siena*, trans. by Alger Thorold, 2d ed., (London, 1926).

4. Saint Teresa of Avila, *The Interior Castle,* pp. 186, 194.

5. Evelyn Underhill, *Mysticism: A Study in the Nature and Development of Man's Spiritual Consciousness* (New York: E.P. Dutton & Co., Inc., 1961), p. 129.

6. Saint Catherine of Genoa, *Vita Mirabile e Dottrina Celeste di Santa Catherina de Genova,* Insieme Col Trattato del Purgatorio e col Dialogo della Santa, 1743, CAP.

7. Albert Einstein, "Religion and Science," *The New York Times Magazine,* November 9, 1930, (pp. 1-4). The German text was published in *The Berliner Tageblatt,* November 11, 1930.

8. Maurice R. Bucke, *Cosmic Consciousness: A Study in the Evolution of the Human Mind* (New York: E.P. Dutton & Co., [1901]; 1975).

9. Nishida Kitarō, *Intelligibility and the Philosophy of Nothingness,* trans. by R. Schinzinger (Tokyo: Muruzen, 1958), also reprint: (Westport, Conn.: Greenwood Press, 1973).

10. Thomas Merton, *New Seeds of Contemplation* (New York: New Directions Books, 1961), p. 3.

11. Albert Einstein, "Religion and Science," *The New York Times Magazine,* November 9, 1930, (pp. 1-2). The German text was published in *The Berliner Tageblatt,* November 11, 1930.

12. *Ibid.*, pp. 3-4.

13. Maurice R. Bucke, *Cosmic Consciousness: A Study into Evolution of the Human Mind.* (New York: E.P. Dutton & Co, [1901]; 1975).

14. Aldous Huxley, *The Perennial Philosophy* (New York: Meridian Books, 1968).

15. Evelyn Underhill, *Mysticism: A Study in the Nature and Development of Man's Spiritual Consciousness* (New York: E.P. Dutton & Co., Inc., 1961).

16. Ken Wilber, *Quantum Questions* (London: New Science Library, 1984).

19
Boundless Love and Joy in Your Being

1. James M. Robinson, "The Gospel According to Thomas" in *The Nag Hammadi Library in English*, Gen. Ed., Coptic Text Established and Translated by A. Guillaumont et al. (San Francisco: Harper & Row, 1988), p. 138.

2. Piere Teilhard de Chardin, "The Evolution of Chastity" in *Toward the Future* (New York: Harcourt Brace Jovanovich, 1975), p. 87.

3. C. Leadbetter, *The Chakras* (Wheaton, Ill.: the Theosophical Publishing House, 1969).

4. Robert D. Richardson Jr., *Emerson: The Mind on Fire* (Berkeley: University of California Press, 1995), p. 69.

5. *Ibid.*, p. 69.

6. *Ibid.*, pp. 152-3.

7. James M. Robinson, "The Gospel According to Thomas" in *The Nag Hammadi Library in English*, Gen. Ed., Coptic Text Established and Translated by A. Guillaumont et al. (San Francisco: Harper & Row, 1988), p. 126.

8. *Ibid.*, p. 126.

9. Orest [Bedrij], *One* (San Francisco: Strawberry Hill Press, 1978), pp. 85-87.

10. Albert Einstein, in *The New York Post,* November 18, 1972.

11. His Divine Grace A. C. Bhaktivedanta Swami Prabhupada, trans., *The Bhagavad Gita,* with original Sanskrit text and elaborate purports (New York: Collier Books, 1973), pp. 371-7.

12. Robert Ernest Hume, trans., *The Thirteen Principal Upanishads,* from the Sanskrit, with an outline of the philosophy of the *Upanishads* (London: Oxford University Press, 1971), p. 209, (Chandogya Upanishad 3. 14.1).

13. *Ibid.*, p. 31 (Chan. 7. 25.2).

14. *Ibid.*, p. 50-51 (Chan. 6. 9-10).

15. *Ibid.*, p. 157 (*Brihad-Aranyaka Upanishad,* Fifth Adhyaya, Fifteenth Brahmana).

16. *Ibid.*, p. 43 (Brih. 4. 4.13).

17. *Ibid.*, p. 104 (Brih. 2. 5.15).

18. Ken Wilber, *Quantum Questions* (London: New Science Library, 1984), p. 27.

19. David Bohm, *Wholeness and the Implicate Order* (London: Ark Paperbacks Ltd., 1983), pp. 174; second part of quote from a lecture delivered at the 1983 Mystics and Scientists conference in David Lorimer, ed. "Cosmos, Matter, Life and Consciousness" *The Spirit of Science: From Experiment to Experience* (New York: Continuum, 1999), p. 55.

20. *The Thirteen Principal Upanishads*, p. 32, Svet. 4. 2-4.

21. Ken Carey, *Vision*, (Kansas City, MO: Uni Sun, 1985), p. 87.

22. Saint Bernard of Clairvaux, *The Steps of Humility* (Cambridge, MA, 1940); his thoughts may also be located in *The Mystical Doctrine of Saint Bernard*, by Etienne Gilson (London and New York, 1940).

23. Dhirenda Mohan Datta, *The Philosophy of Mahatma Gandhi* (Madison, WI: The University of Wisconsin Press, 1972), p. 30.

24. Bhagavan Das, *The Essential Unity of All Religions* (Wheaton, Ill: The Theosophical Publishing House, 1973), p. 93.

25. Meher Baba, *The Everything and the Nothing* (Berkeley, CA, 1971), p. 78.

26. Meher Baba, *Sparks from Meher Baba* (Myrtle Beach, SC: Sheriar Press, 1962), pp. 9-10.

27. Charlene Leslie-Chaden, *A Compendium of the Teachings of Sathya Sai Baba* (Prasanthi Nilayam: Sai Towers Publishing, 1997), p. 268.

28. Bhagavan Das, *The Essential Unity of All Religions* (Wheaton, Ill.: The Theosophical Publishing House, Quest Book Edition, 1973), p. 98.

29. *Ibid.*, p. 103.

30. *Ibid.*, p. 94.

31. *Ibid.*, p. 110.

32. *Ibid.,* p. 158.

33. Quoted in Aldous Huxley, *The Perennial Philosophy* (New York: Meridian Books, 1968), p. 56.

34. Philip Yampolsky, ed. and trans. *The Platform Sūtra of the Sixth Patriarch: The Text of the Tunhuang Manuscript* (New York: Columbia University Press, 1967).

35. Erwin Schrödinger, *What is Life?* (Cambridge: The MacMillan Company, 1946), p. 88.

36. Bhagavan Das, *The Essential Unity of All Religions* (Wheaton, Ill.: The Theosophical Publishing House, Quest Book Edition, 1973), p. 60.

37. *Ibid.*, p. 61.

39. [Sir] James Jeans, *The Mysterious Universe* (Cambridge University Press, 1931), p. 111.

40. Dennis Gabor, *Inventing the Future* (Harmondsworth: Penguin, 1964), p. 89

20
Many Though We Are, We Are One Body

1. Aldous Huxley, *The Perennial Philosophy* (New York: Meridian Books, 1968), p. 14.
2. Meister Eckhart, *Meister Eckhart: A Modern Translation,* trans. by Raymond Bernard Blankney (New York: Harper Torchbook, 1941); also quoted in Aldous Huxley, *The Perennial Philosophy* (New York: Meridian Books, 1968), p. 162.
3. Meister Eckhart, *Meister Eckhart: A Modern Translation,* trans. by Raymond Bernard Blankney (New York: Harper Torchbook, 1941), pp. 251-2.
4. *Theologia Germanica,* Winkworth's translation (London: 1937).
5. Dag Hammarskjöld, *Markings,* trans. from the Swedish by Leif Sjöberg & W.H. Auden (New York: Ballantine Books, 1993), p. 74.
6. Jalal al-Din Rūmi, *The Discourses of Rumi,* transl A. J. Arberry (London: Murray, 1961).
7. Jalal al-Din Rūmi, *Teachings of Rumi the Masnavi,* trans. and abridged by E. H. Whinfield (New York: E.P. Dutton & Co., 1975), p. 3.
8. Thomas Merton, *New Seeds of Contemplation* (New York: New Directions Books, 1961), p. 3.
9. Maulānā 'Abdurrahmān Jāmī, *Lawā'ih* (Tehran, 1342 ah.1963), chap. 21; see the English translation by Edward Henry Whinfield and Mirza Muhammad Kazwini (London, 1914); also, Annemarie Schimmel, *Mystical Dimensions of Islam* (Chapel Hill: The University of North Carolina Press, 1975), p. 283.
10. Bhagavan Das, *The Essential Unity of All Religions* (Wheaton, Ill: The Theosophical Publishing House, 1973), p. 176.
11. Maulānā 'Abdurrahmān Jāmī, *Dīwān-I kāmil,* ed. by Hāshim Rizā (Tehran, 1341 sh./1962), p. 810; also, Annemarie Schimmel, *Mystical Dimensions of Islam* (Chapel Hill: The University of North Carolina Press, 1975), p. 283.
12. Annemarie Schimmel, *Mystical Dimensions of Islam* (Chapel Hill: The University of North Carolina Press, 1975), p. 284.
13. Willis W. Harman, "Business as a Component of the Global Economy," *Noetic Sciences Review,* Nov. 1971.
14. Bhagavan Das, *The Essential Unity of All Religions* (Wheaton, Ill: The Theosophical Publishing House, 1973), p. 62.
15. *Ibid.,* p.167.
16. Freeman J Dyson, *Infinite In All Directions* (New York: Harper & Row, 1988), pp. 118-9.
17. Jetsun Milarepa, *One Hundred Thousand Songs of Milarepa,* trans. and annotated by Garma C. C. Chang (Boulder: Shambala, 1977), Vol. 2, p. 102.

18. Martin Buber, *Hasidism* (New York: Philosophical Library).

19. A.C. Bhaktivedanta Swami Prabhupada, *Bhagavad Gita As It Is* (Los Angeles: Macmillan Publishing, 1973), pp. 371-7.

20. Theophilus of Antioch, "Thoeophilus to Autolycus," trans. by the Rev. Marcus Dods, A. M., *Fathers of the Second Century* (Peabody, MA: Hendrickson Publishers, 1999), Vol. II, p. 89.

21. *Ibid.*, p. 89.

22. Charlene Leslie-Chaden, *A Compendium of the Teachings of Sathya Sai Baba* (Prasanthi Nilayam: Sai Towers Publishing, 1997), p. 182.

23. *Cidade Calelixnese* manuscript, found in Oxyrynchus, Egypt, is located in the British Library, Department of Manuscripts, London.

21
Great Minds of the Eastern World

China

1a. Robert G. Henricks, trans. *Lao Tzu: Te-Tao Ching: A New Translation Based on the Recently Discovered Ma-wang-tui Texts* (New York: Ballantine, 1989).

—b. Gia-Fu Feng and Jane English, trans. *Lao Tsu: Tao Te Ching* (New York: Vintage, 1972).

—c. Arthur Waley, *The Way and Its Power: A Study of the Tao Te Ching and Its Place in Chinese Thought* (New York: Evergreen, 1958).

—d. Ariane Rump, *Commentary on the Lao Tzu by Wang Pi* (Honolulu, Hawaii: University of Hawaii Press, 1979).

—e. Eduard Erkes, *Ho-shang Kung's Commentary on Lao-tse* (Ascona, Switzerland: Artibus Asiae, 1958).

—f. Alan K.L. Chan, *Two Visions of the Way: A Study of the Wang Pi and the Ho-shang Kung Commentaries on Lao Tzu* (Albany, NY: SUNY Press, 1991).

2a. David Collie, ed. and trans. *The Chinese Classical Works Commonly Called "The Four Books"* (Gainesville, Fla.: Scholars' Facsimiles and Reprints, 1970), from the Mission Press 1828 edition.

3a. E. R. Hughes, *The Great Learning and the Doctrine of the Mean-in-Action: Confucius' Ta Hsüeh* (New York: AMS Press, 1943).

—b. David Collie, trans. *Chung Yung or the Golden Medium.* In: *The Chinese Classical Works Commonly Called "the Four Books"* (Gainesville, Fla.: Scholars' Facsimiles and Reprints, 1970), from the Mission Press 1828 edition.

4a. Yi-Pao Mei, *The Ethical and Political Works of Motse* (Westport, Conn.: Hyperion Press, 1973).

—b. Burton Watson, *Basic Writings of Mo Tzu, Hsun Tzu, and Han Fei Tzu* (New York: Columbia University Press, 1967).

—c. A.C. Graham, *Later Mohist Logic, Ethics and Science* (Hong Kong: The Chinese University Press, 1978).

—d. Alfred Forke, *Me Ti des Sozialethikers und seiner Schüler philosophische Werke* (Berlin: Mitteilungen des Seminars für Orientalische Sprachen (Vol. 23-25), 1922).

—e. Augustinus A. Tseu, *The Moral Philosophy of Mo-tzu* (Taiwan: Fu Jen Catholic University Press, 1965).

5a. A.C. Graham, trans. *The Book of Lieh-tzu: A Classic of Tao* (New York: Columbia University Press, 1990).

6a. Yu-lan Fung, trans. *Chuang Tzu, A New Selected Translation with an Exposition of the Philosophy of Kuo Hsing* (Shanghai: Commercial Press, 1933).

—b. Yu-lan Fung, *A History of Chinese Philosophy*, trans. by Derk Bodde. 2 Vol. (Princeton, NJ: Princeton University Press, 1953).

—c. Brook Ziporyn, "The Self-so and Its Traces in the Thought of Guo Xiang," *Philosophy East and West*, 43/3, July 1993, pp. 511-539.

7a. Burton Watson, *Complete Writings of Chuang Tzu* (New York: Columbia University Press, 1968).

—b. A.C. Graham, *Chuang-tzu: The Inner Chapters* (London: George Allen & Unwin, 1981).

—c. Yu-lan Fung, *A Taoist Classic: Chuang Tzu* (Beijing: Foreign Language Press, 1989).

—d. Burton Watson, trans. *Chuang Tzu: Basic Writings* (New York: Columbia University Press, 1964).

—e. Bruya Chung, *Zhuangzi Speaks!* (Princeton, NJ: Princeton University Press, 1992).

—f. English Feng, *Chuang Tsu: The Inner Chapters* (NY: Vintage Books, 1974)

8a. I. A. Richards, *Mencius on the Mind* (London: Kegan Paul, Trench, Trubner & Company, 1932).

—b. James Legge, ed. and trans., *The Life and Work of Mencius* (Oxford: Clarendon Press, 1895).

9a. Philip Yampolsky, ed. and trans. *The Platform Sūtra of the Sixth Patriarch: The Text of the Tunhuang Manuscript* (New York: Columbia University Press, 1967).

—b. Wing-tsit Chan, ed. and trans. *The Platform Scripture* (New York: St. John's University Press, 1963). An unabridged translation of the Tun-huang (Dunhuang) manuscript, found in a cave in Dunhuang, northwest China, in 1900.

—c. Edward Conze, ed. and trans. *Buddhist Wisdom Books: The Diamond Sūtra and Heart Sūtra* (London: Giorge Allen & Unwin, 1958).

10a. Garma C.C. Chang, *The Buddhist Teaching of Totality: The Philosophy of Hwa Yen Buddhism* (University Park, Pa.: Penn State Press, 1971).

—b. Ming-wood Liu, *The Teaching of Fa-Tsang: An Examination of Buddhist Metaphysics* (Ann Arbor, Mich.: University Microfilms International, 1979).

—c. Wing-Tsit Chan, trans. and comp. *A Source Book in Chinese Philosophy* (Princeton, NJ: Princeton University Press. 1963).

—d. Yu-lan Fung, *A History of Chinese Philosophy,* trans. by Derk Bodde. 2 vols. (Princeton, NJ: Princeton University Press, 1953).

11a. Wing-Tsit Chan, trans. and comp. *A Source Book in Chinese Philosophy* (Princeton, NJ Princeton University Press, 1963). Chapter 28 gives a variety of selections from his books.

—b. Yu-lan Fung, *A History of Chinese Philosophy,* trans. by Derk Bodde. 2 vols. (Princeton, NJ: Princeton University Press, 1953).

—c. Percy J. Bruce, *Chu His and His Masters* (London: Probsthain, 1923).

India

12a. Swami Nikilananda, *The Upanishads* (New York: Harper and Brothers, 1959), 4 vols.

—b. Robert Ernest Hume, *The Thirteen Principal Upanishads Translated from the Sanskrit* (London: Oxford University Press, 1934).

—c. Sarvepalli Radhakrishnan, *The Principal Upsanishads* (New York: Harper and Brothers, 1953).

—d. Paul Deussen, *The Philosophy of the Upanishads* (Edinburgh: T. and T. Clark, 1906).

13a. Nathmal Tatia, *Studies in Jaina Philosophy* (Banares, India: Jaina Cultural Research Society, 1951).

—b. Paul Dundas, *The Jainas* (London: Routledge, 1992).

—c. R. Williams, *Jaina Yoga: A Survey of the Mediaeval Sravkacaras* (London: Oxford University Press, 1963).

—d. Padmanabh S. Jaini, *The Jaina Path of Purification* (Berkeley, Calif.: University of California Press, 1979).

14a. A.K. Warder, *Indian Buddhism* (Delhi: Motilal Banarsidass, 1980)

—b. Edward Conze, *Buddhist Scriptures* (Harmondsworth: Penguin Books Ltd., 1959).

—c. Walpola Rahula, *What the Buddha Taught* (New York: Grove Press, 1974).

—d. Edward Conze, *Buddhist Thought in India* (London: George Allen and Unwin Ltd., 1963).

15a. B.N.K. Sharma, *The Brahmasūtras and their Principal Commentaries: A Critical Exposition* (Bombay: Bharatiya Vidya Bhavan, 3 vols: Vol. 1, 1971; Vol. 2, 1974; Vol. 3. 1978).

—b. George Adams, *The Structure and Meaning of Bādarāyana's Brahma Sūtras* (Delhi: Motilal Banarsidass, 1933).

16a.   R.C. Zaehner, *The Bhagavad Gita, with Commentary Based on Original Sources* (London: Oxford University Press, 1069).

—b.   S. Radhakrishnan, *The Bhagavad Gita* (London: Allen and Unwin, 1948).

17a.   Surendranath Dasgupta, *Yoga as Philosophy and Religion* (Delhi: Motilal Banarsidass, 1924)

—b.   Christopher Chapple and Yogi Ananda Viraj, trans. by Eugene P. Kelly, Jr, *The Yoga Sūtras of Patanjali: An Analysis of the Sanskrit with Accompanying English Translation* (Delhi: Sri Satguru Publications, 1990)

—c.   Georg Feuerstein, *Yoga-Sūtra of Patanjali: A New Translation and Commentary* (Folkenstone, Kent: Dawson, 1979).

18a.   Kenneth Inada, *Nāgārjuna: A Translation of his Mūla-madhyamaka-kārikā with an Introductory Essay* (Tokyo: Hokuseido Press, 1970).

—b.   David J. Kalupahana, *Nāgārjuna: The Philosophy of the Middle Way* (Albany, NY: SUNY Press, 1986).

19a.   Leo Pruden, trans. *Abhidharma Kośa Bhāsyam* (Berkeley, Calif.: Asian Humanities Press, 1988-90), 4 vols.

—b.   Thomas Kochumuttom, *A Buddhist Doctrine of Experience: A New Translation and Interpretation of the Works of Vasubandhu the Yogācārin* (Delhi: Motilal Banarsidass, 1982).

—c.   Stefan Anacker, *Seven Works of Vasubandhu* (Delhi: Motilal Banarsidass, 1984).

20a.   Ganganatha Jha, *Pūrva-Mīmāmsa in Its Sources* (Varanasi, India: Banares Hindu University, 1964).

—b.   Sarvepalli Radhakrishnan and Charles Moore, *A Sourcebook in Indian Philosophy* (Princeton, NJ: Princeton University Press, 1957).

—c.   Surendranath Dasgupta, *A History of Indian Philosophy* (Cambridge: Cambridge University Press, 1922).

21a.   Swami Nikhilananda, trans. *The Māndukyopanisad with Gaudapāda's Kārikā and Samkara's* Commentary (Mysore, India : Sri Ramakrishna Ashrama, 1974).

—b.   T.M.P. Mahadevan, *Gaudapāda: A Study in Early Advaita* (Madras, India: University of Madras, 1975).

22a.   K.K. Dixit, *The Yogabindu of Acārya Haribhadrasūri* (Ahmedabad, India: Lalbhai Dalpatbhai Bharatiya Sanskriti Vidyamandira, 1968).

—b.   *Yogadisamuccaya and Yogavimśikā of Acārya Haribhadrasūri* (Ahmedabad, India: Lalbhai Dalpatbhai Bharatiya Sanskriti Vidyamandira, 1970).

—c.   S.M. Desai, *Haribhadra's Yoga Works and Psychosynthesis* (Ahmedabad, India: L.D. Institute of Indology, 1983).

23a.   Eliot A. Deutsch, *Advaita Vedānta: A Philosophical Reconstruction* (Honolulu, Hawaii: University of Hawaii Press, 1968)

—b. Sarvepalli Radhakrishnan and C.A. Moore, *A Source Book of Indian Philosophy* (Princeton, NJ: University of Princeton, 1957).

24a. S.S. Sastri and C.K. Raja, trans. and eds. *The Bhāmāti of Vācaspati* (Madras, India: The Theosophical Publishing House, 1933).

—b. S.S. Hasurkar, *Vācaspati Miśra and Advaita Vedānta* (Darbhanga, India: Mithila Institute, 1958).

25a. A.J. Alston, trans. *The Naiskarmya Siddhi of Śrī Sureśvara* (London: Shanti Sadan, 1959).

—b. R. Balasubramanian, *The Taittirīyopanisadbhasya with Sureśvara's Vārtikā* (Madras, India: University of Madras, 1984).

—c. T.M.P. Mahadevan, *Superimposition in Advaita Vedānta* (New Delhi: Sterling Publishers Pvt. Ltd., 1985).

26a. K.C. Varadachari, *Srī Rāmānuja's Theory of Knowledge* (Madras, India: Devasthanama Press, 1943).

—b. George Thibaut, trans. "The *Vedānta Sūtras* with the Commentary of Rāmānuja" in *The Sacred Books of the East,* Vol. 48 (Oxford: The Clarendon Press, 1904).

—c. S.R. Bhatt, *Studies in Rāmānuja Vedānta* (New Delhi: Heritage Publishers, 1975).

27a. Gopal Singh, trans. and ed. *Sri Guru Granth Sahib: An Anthology* (Calcuta: M.P. Birla Foundations, 1989).

—b. Ernest Trump, *The Adi Granth, or the Holy Scriptures of the Sikhs* (New Delhi: Munshiram Manoharlal, 1970).

—c. Pritam Singh Gill, *The Doctrine of Guru Nānak* (Jullundher: New Book Company, 1969).

28a. Stuart Elkman, *Jīva Gosvāmin's Tattvasandarbha: A Study of the Philosophical and Sectarian Development of the Gaudiya Vaisnava Movement* (Delhi: Motilal Banarsidass, 1986).

—b. Sushil Kumar De, *Early History of the Vaisnava Faith and Movement in Bengal from Sanskrit and Bengali Sources* (Calcuta: Firma K.L. Mukhopadhyay, 1961).

29a. T.S. Rukmani, *Yogavārttika of Vijnānabhiksu,* Vol. I. *Samādhipada* (New Delhi: Munshiram Manoharlal, 1891).

—b. A. Berriedale Keith, *A History of the Sāmkhya Philosophy* (Delhi: Nag Publishers, 1975).

30a. Sanjukta Gupta, *Studies in the Philosophy of Madhusūdana Sarasvatī Madhusūdana Sarasvatī* (Calcutta: Sanskrit Pustak Bhandar, 1966).

31a. Swami Madhvananda, *Vedānta Paribhāsā* (Calcutta: The Ramakrishna Mission, 1972).

—b. Swami Satprakashanada, *Methods of Knowledge* (Calcutta: Advaita Ashrama, 1974).

—c. D.M. Datta, *Six Ways of Knowing* (Calcuta: University of Calcutta, 1972).

32a. Krishna Kripalani, *Rabindranath Tagore: A Biography* (New York: Grove Press, 1962).

—b. E.J. Thomson, *Rabindranath Tagore: Poet and Dramatist* (London: Oxford University Press, 1948).

—c. Amiya Chakravarty, ed. *A Tagore Reader* (New York: Macmillan, 1961).

33a. Margaret Chatterjee, *Gandhi's Religious Thought* (Notre Dame, Ind.: University of Notre Dame Press, 1983).

—b. Joan Bondurant, *Conquest of Violence* (Berkeley, Calif.: University of California Press, 1965).

—c. Raghavan N. Iyer, *The Moral and Political Thought of Mahatma Gandhi* (Oxford: Oxford University Press, 1973).

34a. K.C. Bhattacharyya, *The Subject as Freedom* (Amalner, Bombay: Indian Institute of Philosophy, 1930)

—b. —, *Studies in Vedantism* (Calcutta: Calcutta University Press, 1907).

35a. Aurobindo, *Birth Centenary Library*, thirty Volume set (Pondicherry, India: Sri Aurobindo Ashram Press, 1972).

—b. Beatrice Bruteau, *Worthy Is the World: The Hindu Philosophy of Sri Aurobindo* (Rutherford, NJ: Fairleigh Dickinson University Press, 1971).

—c. K.R. Srinivasa, *Sri Aurobindo: A Biography and A History, 2 Vols.* (Pondicherry, India: Sri Aurobindo Centre of Education, 1972).

36a. Sarvelli Gopal, *Radhakrishnan, A Biography* (London: Unwin Hyman Ltd. 1989).

—b. J.G. Arapura, *Radhakrishnan and Integral Experience* (New York: Asia Publishing House, 1966).

—c. Paul A. Schilpp, ed. *The Philosophy of Sarvepalli Radhakrishnan* (Library of Living Philosophers, New York: Tudor Publishing Company, 1952).

The Muslim World

37a. Margaret Smith, *Rabi'a the Mystic* (Cambridge: Cambridge University Press, 1928, 1984).

—b. Michael A. Sells. "Foundations of Islamic Mysticism." *Classics of Western Spirituality* (New York: Paulist Press, 1994).

—c. Fariduddin Attar, *Muslim Saints and Mystics,* trans. by A.J. Arberry (London:Routledge and Kegan Paul, 1966).

38a. H. Corrbin, *Avicenna and the Visionary Recita,* trans. from the French by W. Trask (Princeton, NJ: Princeton University Press, 1990).

—b.   V. Courtois, ed. *Avicenna Commemmoration Volume* (Calcutta: Indo-Iranian Society, 1956).

—c.   G. Wickens, ed. *Avicenna, Scientist and Philosopher: A Millenary Symposium* (London: Luzac Press, 1952).

—d.   H. Davidson, "Avicenna's Proof of the Existence of God as a Necessarily Existent Being." In: *Islamic Philosophical Theology*, edited by P. Morewedge (Albany, NY: SUNY Press, 1979), pp.167-187.

39a.   Abu l-Qasim 'Abn al-Karim b. Hawazin al-Qushayri, *Risālah al-Qushayriyya*, trans. from the Arabic by Richard Gramlich as *Das Sendschreiben al-Qushayris Über das Sufitum* (Stuttgart: F. Steiner Verlag, 1989).

—b.   Michael A. Sells, "Foundations of Islamic Mysticism," *Classics of Western Spirituality* (New York: Paulist Press, 1994)

—c.   al-Qushayri, *Principles of Sufism*, trans. from the Arabic by B.R. von Schlegel (Berkeley, Calif.: Mizan Press, 1990).

40a.   Seyyed Hossein Nasr, *Three Muslim Sages* (New York: Carvan Books, 1969).

—b.   W.M. Thackston, *Mystical and Visionary Treatise of Suhrawardi* (London: The Octagon Press, 1982).

—c.   Kazem Tehrani, *Mystical Symbolism in Four Treatises of Suhrawardi*. Ph.D. Dissertation, Columbia University, 1974 (Ann Arbor, Mich.: Xerox University Microfilms).

41a.   Ibn 'Arabī, "Bezels of Wisdom," *Classics of Western Spirituality*, trans. by Ralph Austin (New York: Paulist Press, 1980).

—b.   *Les Illumination de La Mecque* [*The Meccan Illuminations*], trans. by Michel Chodkiewicz, et al. (Paris: Sindbad, 1988).

—c.   S. Hirtenstein, ed. *Journal of the Muhyiddin Ibn 'Arabi Association* (Oxford, 1981).

42a.   Yohanan Friedmann, *Shaykh Ahmad Sirhindī* (Montreal: McGill University, 1971).

—b.   J.G.J. ter Haar, *Follower and Heir of the Prophet: Shaykh Ahmad Sirhindī (1534-1924) as Mystic* (Leiden, the Netherlands: Het Oosters Instituut, 1992).

—c.   Muhammad Abdul-Haq Ansari, *Sufism and Shari'ah: A Study of Shaykh Ahmad Sirhindi's Effort to Reform Sufism* (Leicester, England: The Islamic Foundation, 1986).

43a.   Fadl al-Rahman, *The Philosophy of Mullā Sadrā* (Albany, NY: SUNY Press, 1975).

—b.   James Morris, *Introduction to Wisdom of the Throne* (Princeton, NJ: Princeton University Press, 1981), a translation of Mullā Sadrā's *al-Hikmat al-'arshiyyah*.

—c.   Seyyed Hossein Nasr, *Sadr al-Dīn Shīrāzī and His Transcendental Theosophy* (Tehran: Iranian Academy of Philosophy, 1978).

Japan

44a. Yoshito Hakeda, trans. *Kūkai: Major Works* (New York: Columbia University Press, 1972).

—b. Minoru Kiyota, *Shingon Buddhism: Theory and Practice* (Los Angeles: Buddhist Books International, 1978).

45a. A.K. Reischauer, "Genshin's Ōjō Yōshu: Colected Essays on Birth into Paradise," *Transactions of the Asiatic Society of Japan.* 2nd ser., Vol. 7 (Tokyo, 1930), pp. 16-97.

—b. Allan A. Andrews, *The Teachings Essential for Rebirth: A Study of Genshin's Ōjōyōshu* (Tokyo: Sophia University Press, 1973).

46a. Fujiko Manaka, *Jichin Kashō oyobi shūgyokushū no kenkyū* [Master Jien and the Collection of Gleaned Jewels] (Kawasaki, Japan: Mitsuru Bunko, 1974).

—b. Robert E. Morrell, *Sand and Pebbles: The Tales of Mujū Ichien, A Voice for Pluralism in Kamakura Buddhism* (Albany, NY: SUNY Press, 1985).

47a. Hayao Kawai, *The Buddhist Priest Myōe: A Life of Dreams,* trans. by Mark Unno (Venice, Calif.: Lapis Press, 1992).

—b. George J. Tanabe Jr. *Myōe the Dreamkeeper* (Cambridge, Mass.: Harvard University Press, 1992).

48a. Daisetz Teitaro Suzuki, *Collected Writings on Shin Buddhism* (Kyoto: Shinshu Otaniha, 1973).

—b. Takamichi Takahatake, *Young Man Shinran: A Reappraisal of Shinran's Life* (Waterloo, Ontario: Wilfrid Laurier University Press, 1987).

—c. Yoshifumi Ueda and Dennis Hirota, *Shinran: An Introduction to His Thought* (Kyoto: Hongwanji International Center, 1989).

—d. Shinran. Translations of his works are available in the Shin Buddhism Translation Series (Kyoto: Hongwanji International Center): *The True Teaching, Practice and Realization of the Pure Land Way* [popularly known as *Kyōgyōshinshō,* in four volumes, 1983-1990], *Letters of Shinran* (1978).

49a. Tōru Terada and Mizuno Yaoko, eds. *Dōgen.* 2 Vols. (Tokyo: Iwanami, 1971).

—b. Kazuaki Tanahashi, *Moon on a Dewdrop: Writings of Zen Master Dōgen* (San Francisco: North Point Press, 1985).

—c. William R. La Fleur, ed. *Dōgen Studies* (Honolulu, Hawaii: University of Hawaii Press, 1985).

—d. Hee-Jin Kim, *Dōgen Kigen—Mystical Realist* (Tucson, Ariz.: University of Arizona Press, 1975).

—e. Masao Abe, *A Study of Dōgen: His Philosophy and Religion.* Edited by Steven Heine (Albany, NY: SUNY Press, 1992).

50a. Masaharu Anesaki, *Nichiren, the Buddhist Prophet* (Cambridge, Mass.: Harvard University Press, 1916).

—b. Philip B. Yampolsky, ed. *Selected Writings of Nichiren*, trans. by Burton Watson, et al. (New York: Columbia University Press, 1990).

—c. Laurel Rasplica Rodd, *Nichiren: Selected Writings* (Honolulu, Hawaii: University Press of Hawaii, 1980).

51a. Denis Hirota, *No Abode: The Record of Ippen* (Kyoto: Ryukoku University, 1986).

—b. James Harlan Foard, *Ippen and Popular Buddhism in Kamakura Japan*. Ph.D. Dissertation, Stanford University, 1977 (Ann Arbor, Mich.: Xerox University Microfilms).

52a. Herman Ooms, *Tokugawa Ideology: Early Constructs, 1570-1680* (Princeton, NJ: Princeton University Press, 1985).

—b. Ryusaku Tsunoda, Wm. Theodore de Bary, and Donald Keene, *Sources of Japanese Tradition*. Vol. 1 (New York: Columbia University Press, 1964), pp. 336-41.

53a. Royall Tyler, trans. *Selected Writings of Suzuki Shōsan*, Cornell University East Asia Papers, no. 13 (Ithaca, NY: China-Japan Program, Cornell University, 1977).

—b. Winston L. King, *Death Was His Kōan: The Samurai-Zen of Suzuki Shōsan*. Nanzan Studies in Religion and Culture, Vol. 5 (Berkeley, Calif.: Asian Humanities Press, 1986).

—c. Herman Ooms, *Tokugawa Ideology: Early Constructs, 1570-1680* (Princeton, NJ: Princeton University Press, 1985).

54a. Ryusaku Tsunoda, Wm. Theodore de Bary, and Donald Keene, *Sources of Japanese Tradition*. Vol. 1 (New York: Columbia University Press, 1964), pp. 341-52.

—b. Herman Ooms, *Tokugawa Ideology: Early Constructs, 1570-1680* (Princeton, NJ: Princeton University Press, 1985).

55a. Ryusaku Tsunoda, Wm. Theodore de Bary, and Donald Keene, *Sources of Japanese Tradition* (New York: Columbia University Press, 1958/64).

56a. Mary Evelyn Tucker, *Moral and Spiritual Cultivation in Japanese Neo-Confucianism: The Life and Thought of Kaibara Ekken (1630-1713)* (Albany, NY: SUNY Press, 1989).

—b. Olaf Graf, *Kaibara Ekken* (Leiden, Netherlands: E.J. Brill, 1942).

57a. Nishida Kitarō, *Intelligibility and the Philosophy of Nothingness,* trans. by R. Schinzinger (Tokyo: Muruzen, 1958), also in reprint: (Westport, Conn.: Greenwood Press, 1973).

—b. *—Last Writings: Nothingness and the Religious Worldview,* trans. by D.A. Dilworth (Honolulu, Hawaii: University of Hawaii Press, 1987).

—c. *—A Study of Good,* trans. by V.H. Viglielmo (Tokyo: Government Printing Bureau, 1960).

—d. *—Intuition and Reflection in Self-Consciousness,* trans. by V.H. Viglielmo, with Y. Takeuchi and J.S. O'Leary (Albany, NY: SUNY Press, 1987).

—e. *—Art and Morality,* trans. by D.A. Dilworth and V.H. Viglielmo (Honolulu, Hawaii, University of Hawaii Press, 1973).

—f. Robert E. Carter, *The Nothingness Beyond God: An Introduction to the Philosophy of Nishida Kitarō* (New York: Paragon House, 1989).

58a. Keiji Nishitani, *Religion and Nothingness*, trans. by Jan van Bragt (Berkeley, Calif.: University of California Press, 1982).

—b. —*The Self-Overcoming of Nihilism*, trans. by Graham Parkes and Setsuko Aihara (Albany, NY: SUNY Press, 1990).

—c. Donald Mitchell, *Spirituality and Emptiness: The Dynamics of Spiritual Life in Buddhism and Christianity* (New York: Paulist Press, 1991).

—d. Hans Waldenfels, *Absolute Nothingness: Foundations for a Buddhist-Christian Dialogue,* trans. by James W. Heisig (New York: Paulist Press, 1980).

Korea

59a. Chong-hong Pak, "Wonhyo's Philosophical Thought," *Assimilation of Buddhism in Korea: Religious Maturity and Innovation in the Silla Dynasty*, edited by Lewis R. Lancaster and C.S. Yu (Berkeley, Calif.: Asian Humanities Press, 1991), pp. 47-103.

—b. Sung-bae Park, *Wonhyo's Commentaries on the "Awakening of Faith in Mahaāyāna."* Ph.D. dissertation (Berkeley, Calif.: University of California, 1979).

—c. Young B. Oh, *Wonhyo's Theory of Harmonization.* Ph.D. Dissertation (New York: New York University, 1988).

—d. Peter H. Lee, ed. *Sourcebook of Korean Civilization* (New York: Columbia University Press, 1993).

60a. Robert E. Buswell Jr., trans. and ed. *The Korean Approach to Zen: The Collected Works of Chinul* (Honolulu, Hawaii: University of Hawaii Press, 1983).

—b. Hee Sung Keel, *Chinul: The Founder of the Korean Son* [Zen] *Tradition*. Ph.D. dissertation (Cambridge, Mass.: Harvard University, 1977).

61a. Hyujong, *Choson sidae p'yon. Han'guk Pulgyo chonso* [Comprehensive Collection of Korean Buddhism], Vol. 7, (Seoul: Tongguk Taehakkyo Ch'ulp'anbu, 1990), in classical Chinese.

62a. Min-Hong Choi, *A Modern History of Korean Philosophy* (Seoul: Seong Moon Sa, 1983).

—b. Shin-yong Chun, ed. *Korean Thought* (Seoul: The Si-sa-yong-o-sa Publishers, Inc., 1982).

63a. Peter H. Lee, ed. *The Silence of Love: Twentieth Century Korean Poetry* (Honolulu, Hawaii: The University Press of Hawaii, 1980).

—b. Beongcheon *Yu, Han Yong-un and Yi Kwang-su* (Detroit: Wayne State University, 1992).

—c. Robert E. Buswell Jr., *The Zen Monastic Experience* (Princeton, NJ: Princeton University Press, 1992).

—d. Uch'ang Kim, "Han Yong-un: The Poet in Time of Need," *Korea Journal*. Vol. 19, No. 12 (December 1979), pp. 4-12.

22
Life from Holy Life: Make Today Count

1. Courtney Tower, "Mother Teresa's Work of Grace," in *Reader's Digest*, December 1987, p. 248.

2. *Ibid.*, p. 166.

3. A.C. Bhaktivedanta Swami Prabhupada, *Śrimad-Bhāgavatam* (New York: The Bhaktivedanta Book Trust, 1978).

4. Hafiz, trans. by Daniel Ladinsky, *The Gift* (New York: Arkana, Penguin Group, 1999), p. 325.

5. Dag Hammarskjöld, *Markings*, trans. from the Swedish by Leif Sjöberg & W.H. Auden (New York: Ballantine Books, 1993), p. 11.

6. *Ibid.*, p. 107.

7. Satya Sai Baba, *Teachings of Sri Satya Sai Baba*, first compiled by N. Kasturi, and published in India. This edited version is by Roy Eugene Davis (Lakemont, Georgia: CSA Press, 1974), pp. 88-9, 10.

8. Meher Baba, *God to Man, and Man to God*, ed. by C.B. Purdom (Myrtle Beach, SC: Sheriar Press, Inc., 1975), pp. 23-4.

9. Meister Eckhart, Introduction and Commentaries by Matthew Fox, O.P. *Breakthrough: Meister Eckhart's Creation Spirituality in New Translation* (New York: Doubleday, 1980), p. 118.

10. Aldous Huxley, *The Perennial Philosophy* (New York: Meridian Books, 1968), p. 22.

11. Julian Huxley, *Aldous Huxley 1894-1963: A Memorial Tribute* (London: Chatto and Windus; New York: Harper & Row, 1974), p. 174.

12. Satya Sai Baba, *Teachings of Sri Satya Sai Baba*, first compiled by N. Kasturi, and published in India. This edited version is by Roy Eugene Davis (Lakemont, Georgia: CSA Press, 1974), p. 23.

13. Walter M. Abbott and Geoffrey Chapman, eds., *The Documents of Vatican II*, with notes by Protestant and Orthodox authorities, 1966, p. 223.

14. Meher Baba, *God to Man, and Man to God*, ed. by C.B. Purdom (Myrtle Beach, SC: Sheriar Press, Inc., 1975), pp. 16-17.

15. Ken Wilber, *Quantum Questions* (London: New Science Library, 1984), p.110.

16. *Ibid.*, p. 111.

23
Beyond the Evolutionary Adventure—
Beyond Creation

1. Robert B. Downs, *Books That Changed the World* (New York: The New American Library, 1956), p. 169.

2. Orest Bedrij, "Scale Invariance, Unifying Principle, Order and Sequence of Physical Quantities and Fundamental Constants," *Ukrainian Mathematical Journal,* A trans. of the Proc. of the Nat. Acad. of Sci. of Ukraine (New York: Allerton Press, 1994), N. 4, pp. 67-73).

3. Orest Bedrij, "Revelation and Verification of Ultimate Reality and Meaning Through Direct Experience and the Laws of Physics." *Ultimate Reality and Meaning* (Toronto: University of Toronto Press, 2000), Vol. 23:1, pp. 49-50.

4. St. Irenaeus, *Adversus Haereses,* Book V, ch. (28, 4), in *The Ante-Nicene Fathers,* Vol. 1, A. Roberts and J. Donaldson, Eds. (Grand Rapids: Eerdmans, 1958), p. 557.

5. St. Athanasius, *De Incarnatione Verbi,* p. 5, 192B.

6. Ricky Alan Mayotte, *The Complete Jesus* (South Royalton, Vermont: Steerforth Press, 1997), p. 174.

7. H.G. Raverty, *Selections from the Poetry of the Afghans* (London, 1892), p. 75. Also, Annemarie Schimmel, *Mystical Dimensions of Islam* (Chapel Hill: The University of North Carolina Press, 1975), p. 399.

8. Guru Arjan (*Adi Granth, Rag Gauri,* M. 5, p. 176) in *Teachings of the Saints* by Maharaj Charan Singh (Punjab, India: Radha Soami Satsang Beas, 1987), p. 6.

9. Hafiz, trans. by Daniel Ladinsky, *The Gift* (New York: Arkana, Penguin Group, 1999), p. 320.

10. Jalal al-Din Rūmi, *Teachings of Rumi the Masnavi,* trans. and abridged by E. H. Whinfield (New York: E.P. Dutton & Co., 1975), p. 159; also quoted in Aldous Huxley, *The Perennial Philosophy* (New York: Meridian Books, 1968), p. 213.

11. Charlene Leslie-Chaden, *A Compendium of the Teachings of Sathya Sai Baba* (Prasanthi Nilayam: Sai Towers Publishing, 1997), p. 181.

12. Alice A. Bailey, *The Consciousness of the Atom* (New York: Lucis Publishing Company, 1922), pp. 21-22.

13. *Encyclopaedia Britannica* (Chicago: Helen Hemingway Benton, 1975), Vol. 15, p. 410.

14. Swami Muktananda, *Guru* (New York: Harper & Row Publishers, 1971), p. 8.

15. Christopher Key Chapple, "Mahāvīra," In: Ian P. McGreal, ed. *Great Thinkers of the Eastern World* (New York: Harper Collins Publishers, 1995), p. 168.

16. Piere Teilhard de Chardin, "The Evolution of Chastity," In: *Toward the Future* (New York: Harcourt Brace Jovanovich, 1975), p. 87.

24
Your Future Is Very Bright

1. Aldous Huxley, *The Perennial Philosophy* (New York: Meridian Books, 1968), p. 207.

2. Zuzuki, D.T. *Studies in Zen Buddhism* (London, 1927).

3. Orest Bedrij, ed., "Union Without Ceasing," In: *Yes, It's Love: Your Life Can Be A Miracle* (New York: Pyramid Publications, 1974), p. 32.

4. Swami Muktananda, *Kundalini: The Secret of Life* (South Fallsburg, NY: SYDA Foundation, 1987), pp. 47-8.

5. The description of the illumination experience, cited from *The Proceedings and Transactions of the Royal Society of Canada*, 1872, Series II, Vol. 12, pp. 159-196.

6. George Moreby Acklom "The Man and the Book" in Maurice R. Bucke, *Cosmic Consciousness: A Study in the Evolution of the Human Mind* (New York: E.P. Dutton & Co., 1901 and 1975), p.VI.

7. *Ibid.*, p. VIII.

8. Maurice R. Bucke, *Cosmic Consciousness: A Study in the Evolution of the Human Mind* (New York: E.P. Dutton & Co., 1901 and 1975), p. 66.

9. Narayan Champawat, "Rabindranath Tagore" in Ian P. McGreal, ed., *Great Thinkers of the Eastern World* (New York: Harper Collins Publishers, 1995), p. 261.

10. *Ibid.*, p. 263.

11 Meister Eckhart, *Works*, trans. by C. B. Evans (London, 1924); also quoted in Aldous Huxley, *The Perennial Philosophy* (New York: Meridian Books, 1968), p. 76.

12. Ralph Waldo Emerson, *The Works of Ralph Waldo Emerson* (Roslyn, NY: Black's Readers Service, 2000), p. 109.

13. de Chardin, Pierre Teilhard, *The Future of Man* (New York: Harper & Row, 1959).

14. *Ibid.*, pp. 319, 322.

15. Quoted in Tony Rothman, *Discover,* May 1987, p. 96.

25
Loosening of the Knots of Bondage:
You Make the Call

1. Orest Bedrij, "Revelation and Verification of Ultimate Reality and Meaning Through Direct Experience and the Laws of Physics." *Ultimate Reality and Meaning* (Toronto: University of Toronto Press, 2000), Vol. 23:1, pp. 56-59; also, "Scale Invariance, Unifying Principle, Order and Sequence of Physical Quantities and Fundamental Constants," *Dopovidi* (Kyiv: National Academy of Sciences of Ukraine, April 1993), #4, pp. 67-74.

2. Bhagavan Das, *The Essential Unity of All Religions* (Wheaton, Ill: The Theosophical Publishing House, 1973), p. 159.

3. Sri Aurobindo, *The Light Divine* (New York: the Sri Aurobindo Library, Inc.,1949); idem, *The Future Evolution of Man* (Wheaton, Ill.: The Theosophical Publishing House, 1974).

    C.K. Barrett, *From First Adam to Last: A Study in Pauline Theology* (New York: Scribner, 1962).

    A.C. Bhaktivedanta Swami Prabhupada, *Bhagavad Gita As It Is* (Los Angeles: Macmillan Publishing, 1973).

    Jacob Boehme, *The Incarnation of Jesus Christ*, trans. by J.R. Earle (London: Constable, 1934).

    Lucien Cerfaux, *Christ in the Theology of St. Paul* (New York: Harper & Row, 1959).

    Lecomte DuNouy, *Human Destiny* (New York: Longmans, Green & Co., 1947).

    Allan D. Galloway, *The Cosmic Christ* (New York: Harper Brothers, 1951).

    G.H.C. MacGregor, *St. John's Gospel* (London: Hodder & Stoughton, 1936).

    G. Montague, *Growth in Christ* (Kirkwood, MO: Maryhurst Press, 1961).

    L.H. Taylor, *The New Creation* (New York: Pageant Press, 1958).

    A.Wilkenhause, *Pauline Mysticism* (Freiburg: Herder, 1956).

4. Orest Bedrij, "The Principle of the One-and-the-Many" in *Ultimate Reality and Meaning* (Toronto: University of Toronto Press, 2000), Vol. 23:1, pp. 59-61.

5. Sheldon Cheney, *Men Who Have Walked with God* (New York: Alfred A. Knopf, 1945), p. 57.

6. Sri Aurobindo, *The Mind Light* (New York: E.P. Dutton & Co., 1953).

7. Patanjali, *The Yoga Sutras*, trans. by Shri Ramamurti (Monroe, NY: ICSA Press), p. 11.

8. Swami Rama, *The Book of Wisdom* (Kanpur, India: Himalayan International Institute of Yoga, Science and Philosophy, 1972), p. 109.

9. Maurice R. Bucke, *Cosmic Consciousness: A Study in the Evolution of the Human Mind* (New York: E.P. Dutton & Co., 1901 and 1975).

10. Quoted in Geoffrey Hodson, *The Hidden Wisdom in the Holy Bible* (Wheaton, Ill.: The Theosophical Publishing House, 1978), p. 42.

11. Maurice Nicoll, *The New Man* (Baltimore: Penguin Books, 1972), p. 20.

12. John C. Haughey, *The Conspiracy of God* (Garden City, NY: Image Books, 1976), p. 24.

13. Dwight Goddard, ed., *A Buddhist Bible* (Boston: Beacon Press, 1994), p. 216.

14. Jetsun Milarepa, *One Hundred Thousand Songs of Milarepa,* trans. and annotated by Garma C. C. Chang (Boulder: Shambala, 1977), Vol. 2, p. 499.

15. Ken Carey, *Vision* (Kansas City, MO: Uni Sun, 1985), p. 87.

16. Aldous Huxley, *The Perennial Philosophy* (New York: Meridian Books, 1968), p. 15.

17. Walter J. Burghardt, *The Image of God in Man According to Cyril of Alexandria* (Washington, D.C.: The Catholic University of America, 1957).

   A. Kerrigan, *St. Cyril of Alexandria: Interpreter of the Old Testament* (Rome: 1952).

   John Lawson, *The Biblical Theology of Saint Irenaeus* (London: Epworth Press, 1948).

   J. Lebreton, *History of the Dogma of the Trinity from its Origins to the Council of Nicaea* (London: Burns, Oates, and Washbourne, 1939).

   Emile Mersch, *The Whole Christ* (Milwaukee: Bruce, 1938).

   E.F. Osborne, *The Philosophy of Clement of Alexandria* (Cambridge: Cambridge University Press, 1957).

   R.B. Tollinton, *Clement of Alexandria,* 2 vols. (London: Williams and Norgate, 1914).

18. Quoted in Joseph James, *The Way of Mysticism* (London: Jonathan Cape, 1950), p. 178.

19. Aldous Huxley, *The Perennial Philosophy* (New York: Meridian Books, 1968), p. 12.

20. *Ibid.,* p. 11.

21. *Ibid.,* p. 14.

22. Jelaluddin Rumi, *The Essential Rumi,* trans. by Coleman Barks with John Moyne, A.J. Arberry, Reynold Nicholson (New York: Quality Paperback Book Club, 1998), p.13.

23. Bhagavan Das, *The Essential Unity of All Religions* (Wheaton, Ill.: The Theosophical Publishing House, Quest Book Edition, 1973), p. 109.

24. Mechtchild of Magdeburg, *Das Flieszende Licht der Gottheit von Mechtchild von Magdeburg* (The Flowing Light of the Godhead) (Berlin, 1909).

25. Gerald Tranter, *The Mystery Teachings and Christianity* (Wheaton, Ill.: The Theosophical Publishing House, 1969), p. 70.

26. D.T. Suzuki, *Essays in Zen Buddhism* (New York: Grove Weidenfeld, 1961), p.336.

27. Swami Muktananda, *Guru* (New York: Harper & Row Publishers, 1971), p. 43.

28. Annie Besant's birthday message of 1923 in "Stewardship of the World" by Carin Citroen, *The Theosophist* (Adyar, Chennai, India: The Theosophical Society, June 2003), p. 342.

29. Peter Roche de Coppens, *The Nature and the Use of Ritual for Spiritual Attainment* (St. Paul, MN: Llewellyn Publications, 1986), p. 73.

30. Charlene Leslie-Chaden, *A Compendium of the Teachings of Sathya Sai Baba* (Prasanthi Nilayam: Sai Towers Publishing, 1997), p. 214.

26
Is Anybody Here Apart from God?

1. Aldous Huxley, *The Perennial Philosophy* (New York: Meridian Books, 1968).

2. Gustav Teres, S. J. *The Bible and Astronomy. The Magi and the Star in the Gospel.* (Budapest: Springer Orvosi Kiado Kft., 2000), p. 251.

3. Annie Besant, *Thought Power* (Wheaton, Il.: Theosophical Publishing House, 1988).

4. St. John of the Cross, *The Collected Works of St. John of the Cross,* trans. by Kieran Kavanaugh and Otilio Rodriguez (Washington, D.C.: Institute of Carmelite Studies, 1973).

5. P. J. and A.E. Dobel, *The Poetical Works of Thomas Traherne*, n.d.

6. Maurice R. Bucke, *Cosmic Consciousness: A Study in the Evolution of the Human Mind* (New York: E.P. Dutton & Co., 1901 and 1975), pp.215-236.

7. Walt Whitman, "Song of the Open Road," Verse 5, *Leaves of Grass* (New York: Quality Paperback Book Club, 1992), p. 113.

8. His Holiness Pope Paul VI, *Ecclisiam Suam* (New York: Paulist Press, 1965), p. 30.

9. Sri Aurobindo, *Essays on the Gita* (Pondicherry: Sri Aurobindo Ashram Press, 1950); idem, *The Ideal of Human Unity* (New York: Dutton, 1950); idem, *The Life Divine, Vol. 3 of the Sri Aurobindo Center of Education Collection* (Pondicherry: Sri Aurobindo Ashram Press, 1960).

   Beatrice Bruteau, *Evolution Toward Divinity: Teilhard de Chardin and the Hindu Traditions* (Wheaton, Ill.: The Theosophical Publishing House, 1974).

   Lao Tzu, *Tao te Ching*, trans. by D.C. Lau (Baltimore: Penguin Books, 1963).

Pantanjali, *How To Know God: The Yoga Aphorisms of Pantanjali,* trans. by Swami

Praghavanda and Christopher Isherwood (New York: Mentor Books, 1969).

S. Radhakrishnan, *The Principal Upanishads* (London: Allen & Unwin, 1953).

Rabindranath Tagore, *The Religion of Man* (London: Allen & Unwin, 1931).

Pierre Teilhard de Chardin, *Activation of Energy* (New York: Harcourt Brace Jovanovich, 1971); idem, *The Appearance of Man* (New York: Harper & Row, 1956); idem, *Building the Earth* (Wilkes-Barre, PA: Dimension Books, 1965); idem, *Christianity and Evolution* (New York: Harcourt Brace Jovanovich, 1971); *The Divine Milieu* (New York: Harper & Row, 1956); idem, *The Future of Man* (New York: Harper & Row, 1964); idem, *Human Energy* (New York: Harcourt Brace Jovanovich, 1960); idem, *Hymn of the Universe* (New York: Harper & Row, 1965); idem, *The Making of a Mind* (New York: Harper & Row, 1956).

Oliver Reiser, *Cosmic Humanism* (Schenkman, 1966).

Preston Harold and Winifred Babcock, *Cosmic Humanism and World Unity* (New York: Dodd, Mead, 1971).

10. Bhagavan Das, *The Essential Unity of All Religions* (Wheaton, Ill.: The Theosophical Publishing House, Quest Book Edition, 1973), p. 388.

11. *Ibid.,* p. 388

Part 2

BREAKTHROUGH TO THE THEORY OF EVERYTHING

1
Toward the Foundation of Nature: The Stakes Have Never Been Higher

1. Nick Herbert, *Quantum Reality: Beyond the New Physics* (New York: Doubleday, 1985), p. xi.

2. Roman Inquisition (1542-1908) organ of papal government.

3. St. Thomas Aquinas, "Summa Theologica," *The Great Books of the Western World* (Chicago: Encyclopaedia Britannica, Inc., 1971), Vol. 19.

4. Steven Weinberg, *Dreams of a Final Theory* (New York: Pantheon Books, 1992), p. 233.

5. Eugene P. Wigner, "The Limits of Science," *Proceedings of the American Philosophical Society* 94, 1950, p. 422.

6. Stephen W. Hawking, *A Brief History of Time: From the Big Bang to Black Holes* (New York: Bantam Books, 1988), pp. 165-6.

7. Karl R. Popper, *Objective Knowledge: An Evolutionary Approach* (Oxford: Clarendon Press, 1972), p. 195.

8. Murray Gell-Mann, Lectures on weak interactions of strongly interacting particles. Bombay, Tata Institute of Fundamental Research, 1961.

9. Robert Muller, *A Planet of Hope* (Warwick, NY: Amity House, 1985), p. 59.

10. Thomas Merton, Edited by Patrick Hart and Jonathan Montaldo, *The Intimate Merton* (New York: Harper Collins Publishers, 1999), p. x.

11. James M. Robinson, "The Gospel According to Thomas" in *The Nag Hammadi Library in English*, Gen. Ed., Coptic Text Established and Translated by A. Guillaumont et al. (San Francisco: Harper & Row, 1988), p. 126.

12. Robert Ernest Hume, trans. from the Sanskrit, *The Thirteen Principal Upanishads* (London: Oxford University Press, 1971), p. 261, (Chandogya Upanishad 7.25.1).

13. D.J. Thomas, "The Gospel of Thomas." *The Nag Hammandi Library in English* (San Francisco: Harper & Row, 1988), p. 135.

14. Maulānā Abdurrahmān Jāmī, *Lawā'ih* (Tehran, 1342 sh./1963), chap. 21; see the English translation by Edward Henry Whinfield and Mirza Muhammad Kazwini (London, 1914); also, Annemarie Schimmel, *Mystical Dimensions of Islam* (Chapel Hill: The University of North Carolina Press, 1975), p. 283.

15. Meister Eckhart, *Meister Eckhart: A Modern Translation,* trans. by Raymond Bernard Blankney (New York: Harper Torchbook, 1941), p. 129.

16. A.C. Bhaktivedanta Swami Prabhupada, *Bhagavad Gita As It Is* (Los Angeles: Macmillan Publishing, 1973), p. 432.

17. Acts 17:28.

18. Bhagavan Das, *The Essential Unity of All Religions* (Wheaton, Ill.: The Theosophical Publishing House, Quest Book Edition, 1973), p. 176.

19. Psalms 139:7.

20. Charlene Leslie-Chaden, *A Compendium of the Teachings of Sathya Sai Baba* (Prasanthi Nilayam: Sai Towers Publishing, 1997), p. 36.

21. Digha Nikaya, *Thus Have I Heard: The Long Discourses of the Buddha,* trans. by Maurice Walsh (London: Wisdom Publications, 1987), pp. 19, 43.

22. Charlene Leslie-Chaden, *A Compendium of the Teachings of Sathya Sai Baba* (Prasanthi Nilayam: Sai Towers Publishing, 1997), p. 37.

23. Galileo Galilei, *Opere Il Saggiatore,* p. 171.

2
Precision Science:
Agreement at Every Point of the Universe

1. Steven Weinberg, *Dreams of a Final Theory* (New York: Pantheon Books, 1992), pp. 235, 231, 6.

2. Stephen W. Hawking, *A Brief History of Time: From the Big Bang to Black Holes* (New York: Bantam Books, 1988), pp. 165-6.

3. John Archibald Wheeler, *At Home in the Universe* (Woodbury, NY: American Institute of Physics, 1994), p. 310.

4. Patricia Barnes-Svarney, Editorial Director, *Science Desk Reference* (New York: Macmillan, 1995), p. 2.

5. Steven Weinberg, *Dreams of a Final Theory* (New York: Pantheon Books, 1992).

6. Sir Arthur Stanley Eddington, *The Nature of the Physical World* (New York: Macmillan, 1929), p. 282.

7. Arthur Eddington, *Science and the Unseen World* (New York: Macmillan, 1929).

8. Albert Einstein, in *The New York Post,* November 18, 1972.

9. Table 1, Major Scientist, Astronomers, and Mathematicians before 1600: Muhammad Abu'l-Wafa al Buzjani (940-97/8); Anaxagoras of Clazomenae (499-428 BC); Anaximander of Miletus (611-547 BC); Anaximenes (545 BC); Archimedes (287-212 BC); Aristarchus of Samos (310-230 BC); Aristotle (384-322 BC); Brahmagupta (598-665); Chu Shih-Chieh (1280-1303); Conon of Samos (245 BC); Democritus (460-370 BC); Diophantus (250); Eratosthenes (276-194 BC); Euclid of Alexandria (330-260 BC); Leonardo Fibonacci (1170-1250); Hero of Alexandria (AD first century); Hypatia (370-415); Leucippus (fifth century BC); Plato (428/427-348/347 BC); Thales of Miletus (624-546 BC); Ptolemy (Claudius Ptolemaeus, 127-145); Pythagoras (580-500 BC); Zeno (of Elea, 490430).

10. Table 2, Major Scientists, Astronomers, and Mathematicians after 1600: Niels Henrik Abel (1802-1829); Walter Sydney Adams Jr. (1876-1956); George Biddell Airy (1801-1892); Robert Grant Aitken (1864-1951); Luis W. Alvarez (1911-1988); André-Marie Ampère (1775-1836); Stefan Banach (1892-1945); Isaac Barrow (1630-1677); Daniel Bernoulli (1700-1782); Hans Albrecht Bethe (1906-2005); David Bohm (1917-1992); Harald August Bohr (1887-1951); Niels Bohr (Henrik David) (1885-1962); Max Born (1882-1970); Louis-Victor de Broglie (1892-1987); Georg Cantor (1845-1918); Baron Augustin Louis Cauchy (1789-1857); Chandrasekhar Subrahmanyan (1910-1995); Arthur

Compton (1892-1962); Charles-Augustin Coulomb (1736-1806); Marie Sklodowska Curie (1867-1934); Paul Adrien Maurice Dirac (1902-1984); Sir Arthur Stanley Eddington (1882-1944); Albert Einstein (1879-1955); Leonhard Euler (1707-1783); Michael Faraday (1791-1867); Pierre de Fermat (1601-1665); Enrico Fermi (1901-1954); Jean Baptiste Joseph Fourier (1768-1830); Friedrich Ludwig Gottlob Frege (1848-1925); Galileo Galilei (1564-1642); Luigi Galvani (1737-1798); Carl Friedrich Gauss (1777-1855); Murray Gell-Mann (1929-present); Sheldon Lee Glashow (1932-present); Kurt Gödel (1906-1978); Hermann Gunther Grassmann (1809-1877); George Green (1793-1841); Otto Hahn (1979-1968); Werner Karl Heisenberg (1901-1976); Heinrich Hertz (1857-1894); Gustav Ludwig Hertz (1887-1975); Sir James Hopwood Jeans (1877-1946); Sir William Rowan Hamilton (1805-1865); Godfrey Harold Hardy (1877-1947); Thomas Hariot (1560-1621); Karl Gustav Jacobi (1804-1851); Ernst Pascual Jordan (1902-1980); Johannes Kepler (1571-1630); Joseph-Louis Lagrange (1736-1813); Sir Horace Lamb (1849-1934); Johan Heinrich Lambert (1728-1777); Pierre-Simon Laplace (1749-1827); Adrien-Marie Legendre (1752-1833); Gottfried Wilhelm Leibniz (1646-1716); Hendrik Antoon Lorentz (1853-1928); Ernst Mach (1838-1916); Guglielmo Marconi (1874-1937); James Clerk Maxwell (1831-1879); Gregor Mendel (1822-1884); Albert Abraham Michelson (1852-1931); Robert Andrews Millikan (1868-1953); Hermann Minkowski (1864-1909); John Napier (1550-1617); John von Neumann (1903-1957); Sir Isaac Newton (1643-1727); Mykhailo Vasyl'ovych Ostrohrads'kyi (1801-1861); Wilhelm Friedrich Ostwald (1853-1932); Blaise Pascal (1623-1662); Wolfgang Pauli (1900-1958); Linus Carl Pauling (1901-1994); Roger Penrose (1931-present); Max Karl Ernst Ludwig Planck (1858-1947); Jules Henri Poincaré (1854-1912); Ilya Prigogine (1917-2003); Isidor Isaac Rabi (1898-1988); Sir Chandrasekhara Venkata Raman (1888-1970); Bernhard Georg Friedrich Riemann (1826-1866); Wilhelm Conrad Röntgen (1845-1923); Bertrand Russell (1872-1970); Lord Ernest Rutherford (1871-1937); Abdus Salam (1926-1996); Erwin Schrödinger (1887-1961); Edward Teller (1908-2003); Nikola Tesla (1879-1948); Sir Joseph John Thomson (1856-1940); Alessandro Giuseppe Volta (1745-1827); Steven Weinberg (1933-present); Eugene Paul Wigner (1902-1995); Chen Ning Yang (1922-present); Hideki Yukawa (1907-1981).

11. S. Saunders and H.R. Brown, eds. *The Philosophy of Vacuum*. (Oxford: Oxford University Press, 1991).

12. Psalms 139:7.

13. Freeman Dyson, *Infinite in All Directions* (New York: Harper & Row, 1988), p. 45.

14. Paul Davies, *Superforce* (New York: Simon & Schuster, 1984), p. 5.
15. Alfred North Whitehead, "On Mathematical Method," from *An Introduction to Mathematics* (London: Oxford University Press, 1948).
16. Paul Davies, *Superforce* (New York: Simon & Schuster, 1984), pp. 5, 10.

3
Physical Quantities: A Means to Ultimacy

1. Karl R. Popper, *Objective Knowledge: An Evolutionary Approach* (Oxford: Clarendon Press, 1972), p. 195.
2. E. Amaldi, "The Unity of Physics," in *Physics Today*, September 1973, pp. 23-29.

   D. Bohm, *Wholeness*; idem, *The Special Theory of Relativity* (New York: W.A. Benjamin, 1965).

   N. Bohr, *Atomic Theory and the Description of Nature* (Cambridge: Cambridge University Press, 1934).

   Max Born, *Atomic Physics* (London: Black & Son Ltd., 1969).

   D. A. Bromley, ed., "The Unity of Physics," in *Physics in Perspective* (Washington, D.C.: National Academy of Sciences, 1972), pp. 333-5.

   T. E. Clark, T. K. Kuo, N. Nakagawa, "An SO(10) Supersymmetric Grand Unified Theory," Dept. of Physics, Purdue Univ., West Lafayette, IN, August 1982.

   M. Dine, W. Fischler, "Supersymmetric Gut," Inst. for Advanced Study, Princeton, NJ, *Nucl Phys. B. Part. Phys.* (Netherlands), Vol. B204, no. 3-346-64.20. Sep. 1982.

   H. P. Durr, "Radical Unification," Max Planck Inst. Fur Phys. und Astrophysics, Munchen, Germany; P. Breitenlohner and H.P. Durr, eds. *Unified Theories of Elementary Particles: Critical Assessment and Prospects. Proceedings of the Heisenberg Symposium, 36-60, 1982.*

   Albert Einstein, "Prinzipielles zur Allgemeinen Relativitaetstheorie" (Principles Concerning the General Theory of Relativity), *Ann d. Physik*, 55 (1918), pp. 241-4; idem, "Generalization of Gravitation Theory," a reprint of Appendix II from the fourth edition of *The Meaning of Relativity* (Princeton: Princeton University Press, 1953).

   J. Ellis, M.K. Gaillard, D.V. Nanopoulos, Serge Rudaz, "Grand Unification, The Neutron Electric Dipole Moment and Galaxy Formation," Cern, Geneva, Switzerland; *Nature* (GB), Vol. 293, no. 5827, 41-3, 3-9, September 1981.

   J. Ellis, M.K. Gaillard, B. Zumino, "Superunification," Cern, Switzerland, ACTA Phys. Pol. B (Poland), Vol. B13, no. 4, 253-83, April 1982.

   E. Farhi, L. Suskind, "Grand Unified Theory with Heavy Color," Stanford

Linear Accelerator Center, Stanford Univ., Stanford, CA., *Phys. Rev. D,* Vol. 20, no. 12, 3404-11, 15 December 1979.

R. P. Feynman et al., *The Feynman Lectures on Physics* (Addison-Wesley, 1963-1965).

Y. Fujimoto, "SO (18) Unification," International Center for Theoretical Physics, Trieste, Italy, *Phys. Rev. D,* Vol. 26, no. 11318-94, 1 December 1982.

M. K. Gaillard, "Guts, Susy Guts and Super Guts," Dept. of Phys., Univ. of California, Berkeley, CA, *AIP Conf. Proc.* (USA), no. 93, 291-304, 1982.

H. Georgi, "The Case for and against New Directions in Grand Unification," Lyman Lab. for Phys. (Cambridge, MA: Harvard Univ., 1982).

John C. Grave, *Conceptual Foundations of Contemporary Relativity Theory* (Cambridge: MIT Press, 1971).

Werner Heisenberg, *Across the Frontiers* (New York: Harper & Row,1974).

Werner Heisenberg, *Physics and Philosophy* (London: Allen & Unwin, 1958).

W. M. Honig, "Preface to a GUT (Grand Unified Theory)," School of Phys. Sci., Western Australian Inst. of Technol., Perth, Australia, *Speculations Sci. and Technol.* (Switzerland), Vol. 5, no. 4, 395-411, October 1982,

J. E. Kim, "Supersymmetric Grand Unification in SO(14)," Dept. of Phys., Seoul Nat. Univ., Seoul, Korea, *Phys. Rev. D* (USA), Vol. 26, no. 3, 674-901, August 1982.

M. Konuma and T. Maskawa, eds., *Grand Unified Theories and Related Topics.* Proceedings of the 4th Kyoto Summer Institute 109-41 1981.

D. V. Nanopoulos, "Tales of the Gut Age," Cern, Geneva, Switzerland.

R. E. Peierls, *The Laws of Nature* (London: George Allen: 1955).

T. G. Rizzo and G. Senjanovic, "Grand Unification and Parity Restoration at Low Energies II," *Unification Constraints,* Brookhaven Nat. Lab., Upton, NY, USA, *Phys. Rev. D* (USA), Vol. 25, no. 1, 2335-47, 1 January 1982.

M. A. Tonnelat, *Einstein's Unified Field Theory* (New York: Gordon and Breach, Inc., 1966).

Edwin F. Taylor and John A. Wheeler, *Space Time Physics* (San Francisco: W. H. Freeman and Co., 1966).

C. F. von Weizsacker, *The Unity of Physics in Quantum Theory and Beyond,* ed. by Ted Bastin (Cambridge: Cambridge University Press, 1971); idem, *The Unity of Nature,* trans. Francis J. Zucker (New York: Farrar, Strauss, Giroux, 1980).

3. David Halliday and Robert Resnick, *Physics for Students of Science and Engineering* (New York: John Wiley & Sons, Inc., 1966), p. 2.

4. Charles Seife, *Zero: The Biography of a Dangerous* Idea (New York: The Penguin Group, 2000), p. 25.

5. Acharya Debendranath, *Ultimate Reality of Hinduism* (Calcutta: Indranil Basu, Basu Mandir', 2000).

6. Bhagavan Das, *The Essential Unity of All Religions* (Wheaton, Ill.: The Theosophical Publishing House, Quest Book Edition, 1973).

7. Acharya Debendranath, *Ultimate Reality of Hinduism* (Calcutta: Indranil Basu, Basu Mandir', 2000), p. 118.

4
The Golden Alphabet: From Zero to Infinity

1. A.N. Wilson, *God's Funeral* (New York: W.W. Norton & Company, 1999); as well, Karen Armstrong, *A History of God* (New York: Ballantine Books, 1993), p. 378: "Those of us who have had a difficult time with religion in the past find it liberating to be rid of the God who terrorized our childhood. It is wonderful not to have to cower before a vengeful deity, who threatens us with eternal damnation if we do not abide by his rules. We have a new intellectual freedom and can boldly follow up our own ideas without pussyfooting around difficult articles of faith, feeling all the while a sinking loss of integrity. We imagine that the hideous deity we have experienced is the authentic God of Jews, Christians and Muslims and do not always realize that it is merely an unfortunate aberration." Also read, in *A History of God*, pp. 377-399: "Does God Have a Future?"

2. William W. Meissner, S.J., "Freud and the Bible." *The Oxford Companion to the Bible*, ed. by Bruce M. Metzger and Michael D. Coogan (New York: Oxford University Press, 1993), pp. 232, 234.

2. Steven Weinberg, *Dreams of a Final Theory* (New York: Pantheon Books, 1992), pp. 251, 256.

4. *Ibid.*, p. 6.

5. John Archibald Wheeler, *At Home in the Universe* (Woodbury, NY: American Institute of Physics, 1994), p. 302.

6. Steven Weinberg, *Dreams of a Final Theory* (New York: Pantheon Books, 1992), p. 212.

7. Charles Seife, *Zero: The Biography of a Dangerous Idea* (New York: The Penguin Group, 2000), pp. 196, 194.

8. Amir D. Aczel, *The Mystery of the Aleph* (New York: Four Walls Eight Windows, 2000), p. 11.

9. Steven Weinberg, *Dreams of a Final Theory* (New York: Pantheon Books, 1992), p. 207.

10. Georg Cantor, *Gesammelte Abhandlungen*; also in Rudy Rucker, *Infinity and the Mind* (New York: Bantam Books, 1983), p 42.

11. George Boole, *An Investigation of the Laws of Thought on Which are Founded the Mathematical Theories of Logic and Probabilities* (1854).

12. Amir D. Aczel, *The Mystery of the Aleph* (New York: Four Walls Eight Windows, 2000), p. 155.

13. G. Holton, *Thematic Origins of Scientific Thought* (Cambridge, MA: Harvard University Press, 1973).

14. On a report by Sullivan and Kingsley on a meteorite shower which fell in Weston, CT, in 1807. Physics Bulletin July 1968, 19 225. Also, in H.H. Nininger, *Our Stone-pelted Planet* (Boston, MA: Houghton Miflin, 1933).

15. John Davidson, *The Secret of the Creative Vacuum* (Saffron Walden: The C.W. Daniel Company Limited, 1989).

16. Quoted by John Davidson in *The Secret of the Creative Vacuum* (Saffron Walden: The C.W. Daniel Company Limited, 1989), p. 171.

17. *Ibid.,* p. 171.

18 Quoted in *Network: The Scientific and Medical Network Review* (Moreton-in-Marsh: The Scientific & Medical Network, 2001), No. 76, p. 2.

19. Amir D. Aczel, *The Mystery of the Aleph* (New York: Four Walls Eight Windows, 2000), p.155.

20. Ibid., pp. 201, 204.

21 Werner Heisenberg, quoted in *Quantum Questions*, Ken Wilber, ed. (Boulder & London: Shambhala, 1984), pp. 59-60.

5
'1' via the One and the Many Principle

1. One and the Many, *The Great Books of the Western World* (Chicago: Encyclopaedia Britannica, Inc. 1971), Vol. 3, pp. 282-9.

2. *Ibid.,* pp. 290-302.

3. Aristotle, "Topics" [Bk iv, Ch 1], *The Great Books of the Western World* (Chicago: Encyclopaedia Britannica, Inc. 1971), Vol. 8, pp. 176, 7.

4. Benedict de Spinoza, *The Great Books of the Western World* (Chicago: Encyclopaedia Britannica, Inc. 1971), Vol. 31, p. 359.

5. Benedict de Spinoza: *Ethics, Short Treatise on God, Man and his Well-Being,* the *Treatise on the Improvement of Understanding, Descartes' Principles of Philosophy Geometrically Demonstrated* with appended *Metaphysical Thoughts* what in due course turned into the *Ethics.*

6. Maurice R. Bucke, *Cosmic Consciousness: A Study into Evolution of the Human Mind* (New York: E. P. Dutton & Co., 1901 and 1975), pp. 276-282.

7.   *The New Encyclopaedia Britannica* (Chicago: Helen Hemingway Benton, 1973-4), Vol. 2, p. 101.

8.   Orest Bedrij, "New Relationships and Measurements for Gravity Physics." Proc. of the Fourth Inter. Conf. Symmetry in Nonlinear Mathematical Physics, *Proc. of Institute of Mathematics of National Academy of Sciences of Ukraine*, 2002, Vol. 43, Part 2, pp. 589-601.

9.   Orest Bedrij, "Revelation and Verification of Ultimate Reality and Meaning Through Direct Experience and the Laws of Physics." *Ultimate Reality and Meaning* (Toronto: University of Toronto Press, 2000), Vol. 23:1, pp. 59-61.

10. Orest Bedrij, "The Principle of the One-and-the-Many" in "New Relationships and Measurements for Gravity Physics," Proc. of the Fourth Inter. Conf. Symmetry in Nonlinear Mathematical Physics, *Proc. of Institute of Mathematics of National Acad. of Sci. of Ukraine*, 2002, Vol. 43, Part 2, pp. 591-593.

Table 3. '1' and the One/Many through the Laws of Physics

q_k: Individual Quantity	Q_k: Group Quantity
Wavelength λ_c	Number of waves n (= $1/\lambda_c$), where $\lambda_c n = 1$.
Period of harmonic motion T	Frequency f (= $1/T$), where $Tf = 1$.
Conductance G	Resistance R (= $1/G$), where $GR = 1$.
Inductance L	Reluctance r (= $1/L$), where $Lr = 1$.
Resistivity ρ	Conductivity σ (= $1/\rho$), where $\rho\sigma = 1$.
Magnetic flux quantum $\Phi_0 = h/2e^*$	Josephson constant $2e/h$, where $(\Phi_0)(2e/h) = 1$.
Quantized Hall conductance e^2/h	von Klitzing const. $R_K = h/e^2$, where $(e^2/h)(R_K) = 1$.

* h is Planck's constant; e is electric charge.

Where the individual phenomenon q_k is an *inverted* group phenomena Q_k. Thus,

$$(1) \qquad 1 = Q_k q_k,$$

and q_k is either equal to or less than ($\leq$) 1, or 1 is equal less than ($\leq$) Q_k, so that,

$$(2) \qquad q_k \leq 1 \leq Q_k.$$

The q_k and Q_k values are determined by fundamental physical constants.

11. Orest Bedrij, "Scale Invariance, Unifying Principle, Order and Sequence of Physical Quantities and Fundamental Constants," *Ukrainian Mathematical Journal,* a transl. of the Proc. of the Nat. Acad. of Sci. of Ukraine (New York: Allerton Press, 1994), N. 4, pp. 67-73.

12. John Archibald Wheeler, *At Home in the Universe* (Woodbury, NY: American Institute of Physics, 1994), p. 302.

13. K.S. Guthrie, *The Pythagorean Sourcebook and Library* (Grand Rapids, MI.: Phanes Press, 1987), p. 26.

14. Orest Bedrij, "Scale Invariance, Unifying Principle, Order and Sequence of Physical Quantities and Fundamental Constants," *Dopovidi* (Kyiv: *Proc. of the Nat. Acad. Of Sci. of Ukr.*, April 1993), p. 68.

15. David Bohm, *Wholeness and the Implicate Order* (London: Ark Paperbacks, 1983), p. 177.

16. Orest Bedrij, "New Relationships and Measurements for Gravity Physics," Proc. of the Fourth Inter. Conf. Symmetry in Nonlinear Mathematical Physics" (Kyiv: Proc. of Institute of Mathematics, Nat. Acad. of Sci. of Ukraine, 2002), Vol. 43, Part 2, pp. 589-601.

17. Orest Bedrij, "Revelation and Verification of Ultimate Reality and Meaning Through Direct Experience and the Laws of Physics." *Ultimate Reality and Meaning* (Toronto: University of Toronto Press, 2000), Vol. 23:1, p. 74.

18. Orest Bedrij, "Fundamental Physical Constants," *Dopovidi* (Kyiv: Proc. of the Nat. Acad. of Sci. of Ukraine, March 1993), N3; also, "Fundamental Constants of Nucleon-Meson Dynamics." *Dopovidi* (Kyiv: Proc. of the Nat. Acad. of Sci. of Ukr. May 1993), N 5, pp. 62-65.

19. John D. Barrow, *The Book of Nothing* (New York: Pantheon Books, 2000), p. 37.

20. Orest Bedrij, "Scale Invariance, Unifying Principle, Order and Sequence of Physical Quantities and Fundamental Constants," *Dopovidi* (Kyiv: *Proc. of the Nat. Acad. of Sci. of Ukr.*, April 1993), p. 70.

21. Albert Einstein, *Über den Äther* (Schweizerische Naturforschende Gesellschaft Verhanflungen, 1924), 105:85-93. For translation see S. Saunders and H.R. Brown 1991, p. 13 (Ref. 24 below).

22. Albert Einstein, message conveyed at Leyden, Holland, 1953, for the honor of the one hundredth anniversary of the birth of Lorentz. Published in *Mein Weltbild* (Zurich: Europa Verlag, 1953).

23. Leonardo da Vinci, *The Notebook,* translated and edited by E. Macurdy (London, 1954), p. 61.

24. S. Saunders and H.R. Brown, ed. 1991. *The Philosophy of Vacuum.* (Oxford: Oxford University Press, 1991), p. 17.

25. Basil Hiley, "Vacuum or Holomovement." *The Philosophy of Vacuum.* (Oxford: Oxford University Press, 1991), p. 3.

26. I. J. R. Aitchison, "Nothing's Plenty: The Vacuum in Modern Quantum Field Theory," (*Contem. Phys.*, 1985), pp. 333-91.

27. J. Ambjorn & S. Wolfram, "Properties of the Vacuum. 1. Mechanical and Thermodynamic" (*Ann. Phys.*, 1983), 147: 1-32; also, "Properties of the Vacuum, 2. Electrodynamic" (*Ann. Phys.*, 1983), 147: 33-56.

28. Michael Atiyah, "Topology of the Vacuum." *The Philosophy of Vacuum.* (Oxford: Oxford University Press, 1991).

29. S. Coleman, "The Invariance of the Vacuum is the Invariance of the World" (*J. Math. Phys.*, 1966), 7:787.

30. G.N. Fleming, *The Vacuum on Null Planes.* Presented to the 1987 Oxford University Symposium on the Vacuum in Quantum Field Theory; Gell-Mann, M. February 1999. "Observant Readers Take the Measure of Novel Approaches to Quantum Theory." *Physics Today* (College Park, MD: American Institute of Physics).

31. R. Weingart, "Making Everything Out of Nothing." *The Philosophy of Vacuum.* (Oxford: Oxford University Press, 1991).

32. Finkelstein, "Theory of Vacuum." *The Philosophy of Vacuum.* (Oxford: Oxford University Press, 1991), p. 251.

33. John Davidson, *The Secret of the Creative Vacuum* (Saffron Walden: The C.W. Daniel Company Limited, 1989), p. 117.

34. Mahamudra, 1986. *Mahamudra: The Quintessence of Mind and Meditation.* (Takpo Tashi Namgyal), trans. and Annotated by Lobsang P. Lhalungpa (Boston: Shambhala Publications, Inc., 1986), p. 7.

35. Jetsun Milarepa, *The Hundred Thousand Songs of Milarepa* (*Milagrubum*), trans. and annotated by Garmac C. Chang (Boulder Co.: Shambhala Publications, Inc., 1977), Vol. I, p. 135.

36. I.K. Taimni, *Man, God and the Universe* (Wheaton, Ill.: The Theosophical Publishing House, 1969), p. 69.

37. K. Rinpoche, *Gently Whispered: Oral Teachings.* Compiled, ed. and annotated by E. Selandia. (Tarrytown, NY: Station Hill Press, Inc.), p. 153.

38. *Ibid.*, p. 13.

39. Robert D. Richardson Jr., *Emerson* (Berkeley: University of California Press, 1995), p. 155.

40. Max Planck, at a lecture given in Florence, Italy, quoted in John Davidson, *The Secret of the Creative Vacuum* (Saffron Walden: The C.W. Daniel Company Limited, 1989), p. 128.

6
'1': The Theory of Everything

1. Steven Weinberg, *Dreams of a Final Theory.* (New York: Pantheon Books, 1992), pp. 17-18.

2. Max Planck, "Vom Relativen zum Absoluten" (Guest lecture at the University of Munich, 1 Dec. 1924), *VE*, pp. 169-82.

3. Max Planck, "Positivismus und reale Aussenwelt" (Public address at Harnack House of the Kaiser-Wilhelm-Society for the Advancement of the Sciences, Berlin, 12 Nov. 1930), *VE*, pp. 228-45.

4. M. Friedman, ed., *Martin Buber's Life and Work: The Early Years 1878-1923* (New York: E.P. Dutton, 1981).

5. John D. Barrow, *The Universe That Discovered Itself* (New York: Oxford University Press, 2000), p. 215.

6. Orest Bedrij, "Scale Invariance, Unifying Principle, Order and Sequence of Physical Quantities and Fundamental Constants." *Dopovidi* (Kyiv: Proc. of the Nat. Acad. of Sci. of Ukr., April 1993), pp. 67-73.

7. Orest Bedrij, "New Relationships and Measurements for Gravity Physics." *Proc. of the Fourth Inter. Conf. Symmetry in Nonlinear Mathematical Physics"* (Kyiv: Proc. of Institute of Mathematics, National Acad. of Sci. of Ukraine, 2002), Vol. 43, Part 2, pp. 589-601.

8. The Book of Angelus Silesius, trans. by F. Franck (New York: Vintage Books, 1976), p. 45.

9. Deut 4:39; 10:14; 33:27.

10. Ps 139:7-9

11. 1 Kgs 8:27.

12. 23:23-24.

13. 14:2, 10.

14. In *Georgics* iv. 220; and *Aeneid* iv 721.

15. In *Allegories,* at the beginning of Book I.

16. A.C. Bhaktivedanta Swami Prabhupada, *Bhagavad Gita As It Is* (Los Angeles: Macmillan Publishing, 1973), p. 432.

17. H. Poincaré, *Revue de metaphysique et de morale*, 1912, 20: 486.

18. Orest Bedrij, "Revelation and Verification of Ultimate Reality and Meaning Through Direct Experience and the Laws of Physics." *Ultimate Reality and Meaning* (Toronto: University of Toronto Press, 2000), Vol. 23:1, p. 74.

19. *Ibid.*, pp. 68-75.

20. Orest Bedrij, "Connection of π with the Fine Structure Constant." Dopovidi (Kyiv: Proc. of the Nat. Acad. of Sci. of Ukr., 1994), N 10, pp. 63-66.

21. Orest Bedrij, "Fundamental Constants of Nucleon-Meson Dynamics." *Dopovidi* (Kyiv: Proc. of the Nat. Acad. of Sci. of Ukr, 1993), N 5, pp. 62-65.

22. Stephen W. Hawking, *A Brief History of Time: From the Big Bang to Black Holes.* (New York: Bantam Books, 1988), p. 159.

23. See the One and the Many Principle, part 2, chapter 5, and the Nature of Time, part 2, chapter 6.

24. See Note 10, part 2, chapter 5.

25. See Note 11, part 2, chapter 5.

7
The Same Essence in Different Containers

1. Bertrand Russell, *Introduction to Mathematical Philosophy* (New York: The MacMillan Co. and George Allen & Unwin Ltd., 1919), ch. 2.

8
The Grand Hierarchical Stairway

1. Orest Bedrij, "Revelation and Verification of Ultimate Reality and Meaning Through Direct Experience and the Laws of Physics." *Ultimate Reality and Meaning* (Toronto: University of Toronto Press, 2000), Vol. 23:1, pp. 56-9.

2. Orest Bedrij, "New Relationships and Measurements for Gravity Physics." *Proc. of the Fourth Inter. Conf. Symmetry in Nonlinear Mathematical Physics* (Kyiv: Proc. of Institute of Mathematics of National Acad. of Sci. of Ukraine, 2002), Vol. 43, Part 2, pp. 589-601.

3. Orest Bedrij, "Scale Invariance, Unifying Principle, Order and Sequence of Physical Quantities and Fundamental Constants." *Dopovidi* (Kyiv: Proc. of the Nat. Acad. of Sci. of Ukr., April 1993), p. 70.

4. *Ibid.,* pp. 69-70 shows a more complete list and the relationships of Fundamental Constants of Quantum Electrodynamics.

5. Kalu Rinpoche, *Gently Whispered: Oral Teachings.* Compiled, ed. and annotated by E. Selandia (Tarrytown, NY: Station Hill Press, Inc., 1994), p.164.

6. Orest Bedrij, "Grand Unification of the Science of Physics through the Cosmolog." *Abstracts.* Amer. Assoc. for the Adv. of Sci., Annual Meeting (1990).

7. Orest Bedrij, *You* (Warwick, NY: Amity House, 1988), p. 155.

8. Institute of Mathematical Physics, "Landmark Breakthrough in Physics." *Physics Today* (College Park, MD: American Institute of Physics, Oct. 1994), p. 29, Prod. advert.

9. O. Trylis, "Cosmolog: Slide Rule That Knows Physics" (in Ukrainian). *Physics* (Kyiv: Schkilnyj Swit, Dec 2001; Feb 2002), No. 36 (120) p. 9; No. 4 (124) pp. 3-4, 9.

10. Orest Bedrij, "New Relationships and Measurements for Gravity Physics." *Proc. of the Fourth Inter. Conf. Symmetry in Nonlinear Mathematical Physics* (Kyiv: Proc. of Institute of Mathematics of National Acad. of Sci. of Ukraine, 2002), Vol. 43, Part 2, pp. 589-601.

9
All People Are Members of Your Immediate Family

1. Albert Einstein, *Mein Weltbild* (Amstterdam: Querido Verlag, 1934)
2. A.C. Bhaktivedanta Swami Prabhupada, *Bhagavad Gita As It Is,* (Los Angeles: Macmillan Publishing, 1973), p. 261.
3. Johann Wolfgang von Goethe, Versuch die Metamorphose der Pflanzen zu Erklären (1790).
4. Robert D. Richardson Jr., *Emerson* (Berkeley: University of California Press, 1995), p. 317.
5. [Sir] Arthur Eddington quoted in Werner Heisenberg's *The Physicist's Conception of Nature* (New York: Harcourt and Brace, 1955).
6. Lk 22:19.

10
Winning Options: Comprehend the Incomprehensible

1. The Nuremberg (1945-46) indictments from *Nazi Conspiracy and Aggression, Official Record of the International Military Tribunal at Nuremberg* (8 Vol. 1946):

Item: There were mass shootings to the accompaniment of music played by interned prisoners.

Item: Concentration-camp officials and guards bleached human skulls for souvenirs and used the skin of prisoners to make lampshades, handbags, and gloves.

Item: Prisoners still alive were thrown indiscriminately into carts loaded with dead taken to the crematory.

Item: Bodies of the dead were sent to barbers, who removed the hair, and to the dentists, who extracted gold from the teeth before cremation.

Item: Prisoners who refused to talk were placed in heated asbestos cells until they were cooked beyond endurance.

2. Sri Aurobindo, *The Future Evolution of Man: The Divine Life upon Earth.* Compiled with a summary and notes by P. B. Saint-Hilaire (Wheaton, Ill.: The Theosophical Publishing House, 1974), p. 51.

3. Bruce C. Murray, *Navigating the Future* (New York: Harper & Row, Publishers, 1975), pp. 40-1.

4. Albert Einstein, "Education for Independent Thought" (New York: New York Times, October 5, 1952).

5. Angela Hynes, "Spiritual Circuitry: Some technologies enhance spiritual growth and may one day promote cultural evolution," *Science & Spirit* (Radnor, PA: Templeton Foundation Press, Nov. 2001), p. 12.

6. Robert A. F. Thurman quoted by Tom Morgan, ed., *A Simple Monk: Writings On His Holiness the Dalai Lama* (Novato, CA: New World Library, 2001), p. 127.

7. David Bohm, *Wholeness and the Implicate Order* (London: Ark Paperbacks, 1983), p. xi.

8. Milton Friedman, *Capitalism & Freedom* (Chicago: The University of Chicago Press, 1975), p. 12.

9. L. R. Sharma, "Fundamentalism is Foreign to Indian Thought," *The Theosophist* (Adyar, India: The Theosophical Publishing House, May 2001), Vol. 123 No. 8, pp. 312-13.

10. Robert Muller, *A Planet of Hope* (Warwick, NY: Amity House, 1985), pp. 78, 101.

11. Robert Muller, *New Genesis: Shaping a Global Spirituality* (Garden City, NY: Image Books, 1984), p. 9.

12. Oliver Wendell Holmes, quoted by John P. Bradley, in *The International Dictionary of Thoughts* (Chicago: J.G. Ferguson Publishing Company, 1975), p. 648.

13. Gandhi, Mohandas K. *The Way to God* [The original title of this work is *Pathway to God*] (Berkeley, CA: Berkeley Hills Books, 1999), p. 53.

14. Introduced by N. Bohr to overcome the doubt by Einstein, quoted in John Archibald Wheeler, *At Home in the Universe* (Woodbury, NY: American Institute of Physics, 1994), pp. 290, 439.

15. John Archibald Wheeler, *At Home in the Universe* (Woodbury, NY: American Institute of Physics, 1994), p. 292, ref. 119, and p. 350.

16. Robert Ernest Hume, trans. from the Sanskrit, *The Thirteen Principal Upanishads* (London: Oxford University Press, 1971), p. 341.

17. Alice A. Bailey, *The Externalisation of Hierarchy* (London: Lucis Press Ltd., 1957), p. 26.

18. Charlene Leslie-Chaden, *A Compendium of the Teachings of Sathya Sai Baba* (Prasanthi Nilayam: Sai Towers Publishing, 1997), p. 86.

19. John Archibald Wheeler, *At Home in the Universe* (Woodbury, NY: American Institute of Physics, 1994), p. 251.

20. Abraham Lincoln. Quoted by William Lee Miller, *Lincoln's Virtues: An Ethical Biography* (New York: Alfred A. Knopf, 2002), p. 291.

SELECT BIBLIOGRAPHY

Abbott, Walter M. and Chapman, Geoffrey, eds. *The Documents of Vatican II*, with Notes by Protestant and Orthodox authorities, 1966.

Acklom, George Moreby. "The Man and the Book," in Maurice R. Bucke, *Cosmic Consciousness: A Study in the Evolution of the Human Mind*. New York, NY: E. P. Dutton & Co., 1901 and 1975.

Aczel, Amir D. *The Mystery of the Aleph*. New York, NY: Four Walls Eight Windows, 2000.

Adler, M. J., editor-in-chief. *The Great Ideas: A Syntopicon of Great Books of the Western World*. Chicago: Encyclopaedia Britannica, Inc. 1971.

Affifi, Abū'l-'Alā. *The Mystical Philosophy of Muhyid'Dīn Ibnul-'Arabī*. Cambridge, 1936.

Afterman, Allen. *Kabbalah and Consciousness*. Riverdale, NY: Sheep Meadow Press, 1992.

Aitchison, I. J. R. "Nothing's Plenty: The Vacuum in Modern Quantum Field Theory." *Contem. Phys.*, 1985.

Albert, D.Z. *Quantum Mechanics and Experience*. Cambridge, Massachusetts: Harvard University Press, 1992.

Amaldi, E. "The Unity of Physics." *Physics Today*. September 1973.

Ambjorn, J. and Wolfram, S. "Properties of the Vacuum. 1. Mechanical and Thermodynamic." *Ann. Phys.*, 1983. 147:1-32;

_____. "Properties of the Vacuum. 2. Electrodynamic." *Ann. Phys.*, 1983, 147:33-56.

Andrews, Allan A. *The Teachings Essential for Rebirth: A Study of Genshin's Ōjōyōshu*. Tokyo: Sophia University Press, 1973.

Anesaki, Masaharu. *Nichiren, the Buddhist Prophet*. Cambridge, Mass.: Harvard University Press, 1916.

Ansari, Muhammad Abdul-Haq. *Sufism and Shari'ah: A Study of Shaykh Ahmad Sirhindi's Effort to Reform Sufism*. Leicester, England: The Islamic Foundation, 1986.

Aquinas, St. Thomas. *On Being and Essence*, translated with introduction by Armand Maurer. Toronto: The Pontifical Institute of Medieval Studies, 1949.

_____. "Summa Theologica," *The Great Books of the Western World*. Chicago: Encyclopaedia Britannica, Inc. Vol. 19. 1971.

Aristotle. "Topics," bk. 4, ch. 1, *The Great Books of the Western World*. Chicago: Encyclopaedia Britannica, Inc. Vol. 8. 1971.

Armstrong, Karen. *A History of God*. New York, NY: Ballantine Books, 1993.

Ashvagosha. *The Awakening of Faith*, trans. by D. T. Suzuki. Chicago: Open Court, 1900.

Aspect, A., Dalibard, J., Roger, R. 1982. "Experimental Test of Bell's Inequalities Using Time-Varying Analyzers." *Physical Review Letters* 49 1804.

Assagioli, Roberto. *La Vie dello Spirito*. Rome: G. Filipponio, 1974.

Athenagoras. "A Plea for the Christians," trans. by Rev. B. P. Pratten, *Fathers of the Second Century*. Peabody, Mass: Hendrickson Publishers, 1999. Vol. 2.

Atiyah, Michael. "Topology of the Vacuum." *The Philosophy of Vacuum*. Oxford: Oxford University Press, 1991.

Attar, Fariduddin. *Muslim Saints and Mystics*, trans. by A. J. Arberry. London: Routledge and Kegan Paul, 1966.

Augustine, Saint, 1952. "The City of God." *Great Books of the Western World*. Chicago: Encyclopaedia Britannica, Inc. 1952. Vol. 18.

_____. *On the Gospel of St. John*. Grand Rapids: Wm B. Eerdmans Publishing Co. 1987.

Aurobindo, Sri. *The Light Divine*. New York, NY: The Sri Aurobindo Library, Inc., 1949.

_____. *Essays on the Gita*. Pondicherry: Sri Aurobindo Ashram Press, 1950.

_____. *The Ideal of Human Unity*. New York, NY: E. P. Dutton & Co., 1950.

_____. *The Mind Light*. New York, NY: E. P. Dutton & Co., 1953.

_____. *The Life Divine*. Pondicherry: Sri Aurobindo Ashram Press, 1960.

_____. *Birth Centenary Library*. 30-vol. set. Pondicherry, India: Sri Aurobindo Ashram Press, 1972.

_____. *The Future Evolution of Man*. Wheaton, Ill.: The Theosophical Publishing House, 1974.

Baba, Meher. *God to Man and Man to God*. Edited by C. B. Purdom. Myrtle Beach, SC: Sheriar Press, 975.

_____. *Sparks from Meher Baba*. Myrtle Beach, SC: Sheriar Press, 1962.

Baba, Satya Sai. *Teachings of Sri Satya Sai Baba*, first compiled by N. Kasturi, and published in India. This edited version is by Roy Eugene Davis. Lakemont, Georgia: CSA Press, 1974.

Bailey, Alice A. *The Consciousness of the Atom*. New York, NY: Lucis Publishing Company, 1922.

_____. *The Soul and Its Mechanism*. London: Lucis Trust, 1971.

_____. *From Intellect to Intuition*. London: Lucis Trust, 1971.

Bandera, Cesareo. *The Sacred Game: The Role of the Sacred in the Genesis of Modern Literary Fiction.* Penn. State Studies in Romance Literatures.

Barnstone, Willis, ed. *The Other Bible,* "The Gospel of Thomas." San Francisco: HarperCollins Publishers, 1984.

Barrett, C. K. *From First Adam to Last, A Study in Pauline Theology.* New York, NY: Scribner, 1962.

Barrow, John D. *Theories of Everything.* London: Oxford University Press, 1990.

_____. *Pi in the Sky: Counting, Thinking, and Being.* New York, NY: Oxford University Press, 1992.

_____. *The Book of Nothing.* New York, NY: Pantheon Books, 2000.

_____. *The Universe That Discovered Itself.* New York, NY: Oxford University Press, 2000.

Barrow, J., and Tipler, F. *The Antropic Cosmological Principle.* Oxford: Oxford University Press, 1986.

Basler, Roy P., and others *The Collected Works of Abraham Lincoln* (8 vols., plus index) New Brunswick: Rutgers University Press, 1953.

Bedrij, Orest. "Carry-Select Adder." *IRE Transactions on Electronic Computers.* Vol. EC-11, no. 3, June 1962.

_____. *Selecting Adder* (Filed Jan. 6, 1960, Patented Aug. 13, 1963, U.S. Patent 3100,835).

Also, *Electronic Binary Parallel Adder* (International Classification: G 06 f, London: The Patent Office, no. 963,429).

_____, ed. *Yes, It's Love: Your Life Can Be A Miracle.* New York, NY: Pyramid Publications, 1974.

_____. *One.* San Francisco: Strawberry Hill Press, 1977, 1978.

_____. *You.* Warwick, NY: Amity House, 1988

_____. "Grand Unification of the Science of Physics through the Cosmolog." *Abstracts: Amer. Assoc. for the Adv. of Sci.* Annual Meeting, 1990.

_____. "Fundamental Constants in Quantum Electrodynamics." *Dopovidi: Proceedings of the National Academy of Sciences of Ukraine,* March 1993. no. 3.

_____. "Scale Invariance, Unifying Principle, Order and Sequence of Physical Quantities and Fundamental Constants." *Dopovidi: Proc. of the Nat. Acad. of Sci. of Ukr.* April 1993. no. 4.

_____. "Connection of π with the Fine Structure Constant." *Dopovidi: Proc. of the Nat. Acad. of Sci. of Ukr.* 1994. N 10.

_____. "Revelation and Verification of Ultimate Reality and Meaning through Direct Experience and the Laws of Physics." *Ultimate Reality and Meaning,* Toronto: University of Toronto Press, 2000. Vol. 23:1.

_____. *La Preuve Scientifique de L'Existence de Dieu*. Montreal: Courteau Louise Ed., 2000.

_____. "New Relationships and Measurements for Gravity Physics." *Proc. of the Fourth Inter. Conf. Symmetry in Nonlinear Mathematical Physics, Proc. of Nat. Acad. of Sci. of Ukr. Institute of Mathematics* 2002. Vol. 43, pt. 2.

Bedrij, O., Fushchych, W. I. "On the Electromagnetic Structure of Elementary Particles' Masses," in Russian. *Doklady, Ukr. SSR Academy of Sciences*, Feb. 1991. N 2.

_____. "Fundamental Constants of Nucleon-Meson Dynamics." *Dopovidi: Proc. of the Nat. Acad. of Sci. of Ukr.* 1993. N 5.

_____. "Planck's Constant Is Not Constant in Different Quantum Phenomena." *Dopovidi: Proc. of the Nat. Acad. of Sci. of Ukr.* 1995. N 12.

Bell, J. S. "On the Einstein-Podolsky-Rosen Paradox." *Physics*, 1964. *1*, 195.

_____. "On the Problem of Hidden Variables in Quantum Mechanic." *Reviews of Modern Physics*, 1966. *38*, 447.

_____. *Speakable and Unspeakable in Quantum Mechanics*. Cambridge: Cambridge University Press, 1987.

_____. *Collected Papers in Quantum Mechanics*. Cambridge U. K.: Cambridge University Press, 1987.

Benardete, José. *Infinity*. Oxford: Clarendon Press, 1964.

Benacerraf, P. and H. Putnam, eds. *Philosophy of Mathematics*. Englewood Cliffs, NJ: Prentice-Hall, 1964.

Besant, Annie. *The Self and Its Sheaths*. Adyar, Madras, India: The Theosophical Publishing House (TPH), 1948.

_____. *An Autobiography*, TPH: Adyar, Chennai, 1984.

_____. *Esoteric Christianity*, Preface, Adyar, Chennai: TPH, 1989.

_____. *Thought Power*. Wheaton, Il.: TPH, 1988.

Bhagavad-Gita, The in Sanskrit. Many English translations are available, among them that of Swami Prabhavananda and Christopher Isherwood, a Mentor Paperback, 1954; that of Ann Stanford, New York, NY: Herder & Herder, 1971; that of P. Lal, Calcutta: Writers Workshop, 1965; and that of Swami Nikhilanada, New York, NY: Ramakrishna-Vivekananda Center, 1952. Also a complete edition with original Sanskrit text by His Divine Grace A. C. Bhaktivedanta Swami Prabhupada.

Bhatnagar, R. S. *Dimensions of Classical Sufi Thought*. Delhi: Motilal Banarsidass, 1984.

Bible, Holy: From the Ancient Eastern Text. George M. Lamsa's Translation from the Aramaic of the Peshitta. Philadelphia: A.J.Holman Co., a division of B. Lippincott Co., 1933.

Bible, The Holy: New International Version. Grand Rapids, MI: Zondervan Bible Publishers, 1978.

Bible, The Holy. New Revised Standard Version. London: Collins Publishers, 1989.

Bible, The New American. Translated from the Original Languages with Critical Use of All the Ancient Sources. Washington, D.C.: Confraternity of Christine Doctrine, 1970.

Blake, William. *The Complete Writings of William Blake*, ed. Geoffrey Keynes. Oxford: Oxford University Press, 1969.

Blavatsky, H. P. *The Theosophical Glossary*. Los Angeles: The Theosophy Co., 1930.

_____. *Collected Writings*, 15 vols., Wheaton, Il; Adyar, Chennai, India: Theosophical Publishing House, 1966-91

_____. *The Secret Doctrine*. Adyar, Madras, India: Theosophical Publishing, 1987.

Boehme, Jacob. *The Incarnation of Jesus Christ*, trans. by J. R. Earle. London: Constable, 1934.

Bohm, David. *Quantum Theory*. New York, NY: Prentice-Hall, 1951.

_____. *The Special Theory of Relativity*. New York, NY: W. A. Benjamin, 1965.

_____. *Wholeness and the Implicate Order*. Boston: Routledge & Kegan Paul Ltd., 1980. Reprint. London: Associated Book Publishers Ltd.; Ark Paperbacks Ltd., 1983.

Bohm, D. and Hiley, B. *The Undivided Universe: An Ontological Interpretation of Quantum Theory*. London: Routledge, 1993.

Bohr, N. *Atomic Theory and the Description of Nature*. Cambridge, England: Cambridge University Press, 1934.

_____. *Essays 1958-1962 on Atomic Physics and Human Knowledge*. New York, NY: Wiley-Interscience, 1963.

Bokser, Rabbi Ben Zion, ed. and trans. *The Essential Writings of Abraham Isaac Kook*. Warwick, NY: Amity House, 1988.

Bolzano, Bernard. *Paradoxes of the Infinite*. New Haven, Conn.: Yale University Press, 1950.

Boole, George. *An Investigation of the Laws of Thought on Which Are Founded the Mathematical Theories of Logic and Probabilities* (1854).

Born, Max. *Atomic Physics*. London: Black & Son Ltd., 1969.

_____. (ed.), *The Born-Einstein Letters*. London: Macmillan, 1971.

Bromley, D. A., ed. "The Unity of Physics." *Physics in Perspective*. Washington, D.C.: National Academy of Sciences, 1972.

Brugel, J. W. "The Crime of Genocide." *Central European Observer*. xxiv. October 17, 1947.

Bruno, Giordano. *On the Infinite Universe and Worlds*. trans. by Dorothy Singer. New York: Greenwood Press, 1968.

Brunton, Paul. *The Hidden Teaching Beyond Yoga*. New York, NY: Samuel Weiser, 1972.

Bruteau, Beatrice. *Worthy Is the World: The Hindu Philosophy of Sri Aurobindo*. Rutherford, NJ: Fairleigh Dickinson University Press, 1971.

_____. *Evolution Toward Divinity: Teilhard de Chardin and the Hindu Traditions*. Wheaton, Ill.: The Theosophical Publishing House, 1974.

Brzezinski, Zbigniew K. *The Permanent Purge*. Cambridge: Harvard University Press, 1956.

_____. *Out of Control: Global Turmoil on the Eve of the Twenty-First Century*. New York, NY: Scribner, 1993.

Bub, Jeffrey. *Interpreting the Quantum World*. Cambridge: Cambridge University Press, 1997.

Buber, Martin, *Hasidism*. New York, NY: Philosophical Library, 19?

Bucke, Maurice R. *Cosmic Consciousness: A Study into Evolution of the Human Mind*. New York, NY: E. P. Dutton & Co., 1901 and 1975.

Burghardt, Walter J. *The Image of God in Man according to Cyril of Alexandria*. Washington, D.C.: Catholic University of America, 1957.

Buswell, Robert E. Jr., trans. and ed. *The Korean Approach to Zen: The Collected Works of Chinul*. Honolulu, Hawaii: University of Hawaii Press, 1983.

_____. *The Zen Monastic Experience*. Princeton, NJ: Princeton University Press, 1992.

Cantor, Georg. *Contributions to the Founding of the Theory of Transfinite Numbers*, trans. by Philip E. B. Jourdain. La Salle, IL: Open Court, 1952.

Capra, Fritjof. *The Tao of Physics*. Boston: Shambhala, 1975; third, updated edition: 1991.

_____. *The Turning Point*. New York, NY: Simon & Schuster, 1982.

Capra, Fritjof and Steindl-Rast, David with Matus, Thomas. *Belonging to the Universe: Explorations on the Frontiers of Science and Spirituality*. San Francisco: Harper Collins Publishers, 1991.

Carey, Ken. *Vision*. Kansas City, MO: Uni Sun, 1985.

_____. *Starseed: The Third Millennium*. San Francisco: HarperCollins Publishers, 1991.

Carpenter, Edward. *The Drama of Love and Death*. London: George Allen & Unwin Ltd.

Carter, Robert E. *The Nothingness beyond God: An Introduction to the Philosophy of Nishida Kitaro*. New York, NY: Paragon House, 1989.

Catherine of Genoa, Saint. *Vita Mirabile e Dottnna Celeste de Santa Catherina de Genova*. Insieme Col Trattato del Purgatorio e col Dialogo Della Santa. 1743.

Catherine of Siena, Saint. *The Divine Dialogue of Saint Catherine of Siena*, trans. Alger Thorold, 2nd ed. London, 1926.

Chaden, Charlene Leslie-. *A Compendium of the Teachings of Sathya Sai Baba*. Prasanthi Nilayam: Sai Towers Publishing, 1997.

Champawat, Narayan. "Rabindranath Tagore," in Ian P. McGreal, ed., *Great Thinkers of the Eastern World*. New York, NY: HarperCollins Publishers, 1995.

Chan, Wing-Tsit, ed. and trans. *The Platform Scripture*. New York, NY: St. John's University Press, 1963. An unabridged translation of the Tun-huang (Dunhuang) manuscript, found in a cave in Dunhuang, northwest China, in 1900.

_____. trans. and comp. *A Source Book in Chinese Philosophy*. Princeton, NJ: Princeton University Press. 1963. Chapter 28 discusses Chou and gives a variety of selections from his books.

Chang, Garma C. C. *The Buddhist Teaching of Totality: The Philosophy of Hwa Yen Buddhism*. University Park, Pa.: Penn State Press, 1971.

Chapple, Christopher Key and Yogi Ananda Viraj (Eugene P. Kelly Jr.), trans. *The Yoga Sutras of Patanjali: An Analysis of the Sanskrit with Accompanying English Translation*. Delhi: Sri Satguru Publications, 1990.

_____. "Mahavira," in Ian P. McGreal, ed. *Great Thinkers of the Eastern World*. Harper Collins Publishers, 1995.

Chardin, Pierre Teilhard de. *The Appearance of Man*. New York, NY: Harper & Row, 1956.

_____. *The Divine Milieu*. New York, NY: Harper & Row, 1956.

_____. *The Making of a Mind*. New York, NY: Harper & Row, 1956.

_____. *The Phenomenon of Man*, trans. by Bernard Wall. London: Collins, 1959.

_____. *The Future of Man*. New York, NY: Harper & Row, 1959.

_____. *Building the Earth*. Wilkes-Barre, PA: Dimension Books, 1965.

_____. *Hymn of the Universe*. New York, NY: Harper & Row, 1965.

_____. *Activation of Energy*. New York, NY: Harcourt Brace Jovanovich, 1971.

_____. *Christianity and Evolution*. New York, NY: Harcourt Brace Jovanovich, 1971.

_____. "The Evolution of Chastity," *Toward the Future*. New York, NY: Harcourt Brace Jovanovich, 1975.

Cheney, Sheldon, *Men Who Have Walked With God*. New York, NY: Alfred A. Knopf, 1945.

Chertov, A. G. *Units of Measurement of Physical Quantities*. New York, NY: Hayden Book Company, Inc., 1964.

Chittick, William C. *The Sufi Path of Knowledge*. Albany: State University of New York Press, 1989.

Chuang Tzu. *The Book of Chuang Tzu*, trans. Martin Palmer with Elizabeth Breuilly. London: Arkana, 1996.

Chuang-Tzu. *Musings of a Chinese Mystic*. London, 1920.

Chung, Bruya. *Zhuangzi Speaks!* Princeton, NJ: Princeton University Press, 1992.

Chu Ta-kao, trans. *Tao-Te Ching*. Boston, MA: Mandala Books, 1982.

Cidade Calelixnese manuscript, found in Oxyrynchus, Egypt. Located in the British Library, Department of Manuscripts, London.

Clark, Kenneth. *Civilization: A Personal View*. New York, NY: Harper & Row, 1969.

Clauser, J. F. and Shimony, A. "Bell's Theorem: Experimental Tests and Implications." *Reports on Progress in Physics*. 1978. *41*, 1881.

Cleary, Thomas. *The Dhammapada: The Sayings of Buddha*. New York, NY: Bantam Books, 1994.

Clement of Alexandria, "The Stromata, or Miscellanies," *Ante-Nicene Fathers*. Peabody, Mass: Hendrickson Publishers, 1999. Vol. 2.

_____, in Eusebius, *Ecclesiastical History* 6.14.7.

Cohen, E. R., and Taylor, B. N. "The Fundamental Physical Constants." *Physics Today*. 1998. Vol. 51, no. 8, pt. 2, BG 7-11.

Cohen, Paul J. *Set Theory and the Continuum Hypothesis*. New York, NY: Benjamin, 1966.

Coleman, S. "The Invariance of the Vacuum Is the Invariance of the World." *J. Math. Phys.*, 1966. 7:787.

Collie, David, trans. and ed. *The Chinese Classical Works Commonly Called "The Four Books."* Gainesville, Fla.: Scholars' Facsimiles and Reprints, 1970, from the Mission Press 1828 edition.

Confraternity of Christian Doctrine. The New American Bible. New York, NY: Catholic Book Publishing Co., 1986.

Conquest, Robert. *The Great Terror: Stalin's Purge of the Thirties*. New York, NY: The Macmillan Co., 1969.

Conze, Edward, ed. and trans. *Buddhist Wisdom Books: The Diamond Sūtra and Heart Sūtra*. London: George Allen & Unwin, 1958.

_____. *Buddhist Scriptures*. Harmondsworth: Penguin Books Ltd., 1959.

Cooper, M. *Beethoven: The Last Decade 1817-1827*. London: Oxford University Press, 1970.

Corbin, Henri. "Imagination créatrice et prière créatrice dans le soufisme d'Ibn 'Arabi." *Eranos-Jahrbuch* 25, 1956.

_____. *Creative Imagination in the Sufism of Ibn 'Arabi*. Princeton: Princeton University Press, 1969.

Danielou, Jean, and Herbert Musurrillo, *From Glory to Glory: Texts from Gregory of Nyssa's Mystical Writings*. London, 1961.

Das, Bhagavan, *The Essential Unity of All Religions*. Wheaton, Ill.: The Theosophical Publishing House, Quest Book Edition, 1973.

Datta, Dhirenda Mohan. *The Philosophy of Mahatma Gandhi*. Madison, WI: The University of Wisconsin Press, 1972.

_____. *Six Ways of Knowing*. Calcutta: University of Calcutta, 1972.

Dauben, Joseph W. *Georg Cantor, His Mathematics and Philosophy of the Infinite*. Cambridge, Mass.: Harvard University Press, 1979.

Davies, Paul. *Other Worlds*. New York, NY: Simon & Schuster, 1980.

_____. *Superforce*. New York, NY: Simon & Schuster, 1984.

Davidson, H. "Avicenna's Proof of the Existence of God as a Necessarily Existent Being," in *Islamic Philosophical Theology*, edited by P. Morewedge. Albany, NY: SUNY Press, 1979.

Davidson, John. *The Secret of the Creative Vacuum*. Saffron Walden: The C. W. Daniel Company Limited, 1989.

Descartes, Rene. "Rules for the Direction of the Mind," trans. by Elizabeth S. Haldane and G. R. T. Ross. *The Great Books of the Western World*. Chicago: Encyclopaedia Britannica, Inc., 1971. Vol. 31.

Deussen, Paul. *The Philosophy of the Upanishads*. Edinburgh: T&T Clark, 1906.

Dhammapada. *Dhammapada: Wisdom of the Buddha*, trans. by Harischandra Kaviratna. Pasadena, Ca.: Theosophical University Press. 1889.

_____. *The Dhammapada: With Introductory Essays, Pali Text, English Translation and Notes*, trans. by S. Radakrishnan. London: Oxford University Press, 1966.

Digha Nikaya. *Thus Have I Heard: The Long Discourses of the Buddha*, trans. by Maurice Walshe. London: Wisdom Publications. 1987.

Dirac, P. A. M. *Quantum Mechanics*, 4th ed. Oxford: Clarendon Press, 1958.

_____. *Directions in Physics*. New York, NY: John Wiley and Sons, 1978.

Donald, David Herbert. *We Are Lincoln Men: Abraham Lincoln and His Friends*. New York: Simon & Schuster, 2003.

Dossey, Larry, MD. *Space, Time & Medicine*. Boston and London: New Science Library, Shambhala, 1985.

Downs, Robert B. *Books That Changed the World*. New York, NY: The New American Library, Inc., 1956.

Dundas, Paul. *The Jainas*. London: Routledge, 1992.

DuNouy, Lecomte, *Human Destiny*, New York, NY: Longmans, Green & Co., 1947.

Dyson, Freeman J. *Infinite in All Directions*. New York, NY: Harper & Row, 1988.

Eckhart, Meister. *Meister Eckhart: A Modern Translation*, trans. Raymond Bernard Blankney. New York, NY: Harper Torchbook, 1941.

_____. *Works*, trans. by C. B. Evans. London, 1924.

Eddington, Sir Arthur Stanley. *The Mathematical Theory of Relativity*. Cambridge, MA: Cambridge University Press, 1923.

_____. *The Nature of the Physical World*. New York, NY: Macmillan, 1929.

_____. *Science and the Unseen World*. New York, NY: Macmillan, 1929.

_____. *Fundamental Theory*. Cambridge, England: Cambridge University Press, 1946.

_____. *Space, Time and Gravitation*. New York, NY: Harper Torchbooks, 1959.

Ehrman, Bart D. *Lost Scriptures: Books that Did Not Make It into the New Testament*. Oxford: Oxford University Press, 2003.

_____. *Lost Christianities: The Battles for Scripture and the Faiths We Never Knew*. Oxford: Oxford University Press, 2003.

Einstein, Albert. "Prinzipielles rur Allgemeinen Relativitaetstheorie" (Principles Concerning the General Theory of Relativity). *Ann d. Physik* 55, 1918.

_____. *Über den Äther*. Schweizerische Naturforschende Gesellschaft Verhanflungen, 1924. 105:85-93. For translation, see S. Saunders and H. R. Brown 1991, below.

_____. "Religion and Science," *New York, NY Times Magazine*, November 9, 1930, pp. 1-4. The German text was published in *The Berliner Tageblatt*, November 11, 1930.

_____. *Mein Weltbild*. Amstterdam: Querido Verlag, 1934.

_____. Address at Albany, NY, on the occasion of the celebration of the tercentenary of higher education in America, October 15, 1936. Published in *Out of My Later Years*. New York, NY: Philosophical Library, 1950.

_____. "Education for Independent Thought." New York, NY: *New York Times*, October 5, 1952.

_____. "Generalization of Gravitation Theory." A reprint of Appendix 2 from the fourth edition of *The Meaning of Relativity*. Princeton, NJ: Princeton University Press, 1953.

_____. Message conveyed at Leyden, Holland, 1953, for the honor of the one hundredth anniversary of the birth of Lorentz. Published in *Mein Weltbild*. Zurich: Europa Verlag, 1953.

_____. *The New York Post*, November 18, 1972.

Einstein, A., B. Podolsky & N. Rosen, 1935. *Phys. Rev.* 45: 777.

Eliot, T. S. *Four Quarters*. London: Faber and Faber, 1944.

_____. *Collected Poems*. London: Faber and Faber, 1963.

Emerson, Ralph Waldo. *The Works of Ralph Waldo Emerson*. Roslyn, NY: Black's Readers Service, 2000.

_____. *The Journals and Miscellaneous Notebooks of Ralph Waldo Emerson*. ed. William H. Gilman et al. 16 vols. Cambridge: Harvard University Press. 1960-1982.

Encyclopaedia Britannica, The New. Chicago: Helen Hemingway Benton, 1973-4; 1987.

Erkes, Eduard. *Ho-shang Kung's Commentary on Lao-tse*. Ascona, Switzerland: Artibus Asiae, 1958. d'Espagnat, Bernard. *Conceptual Foundations of Quantum Mechanics* (second edition). Reading, Mass: W. A. Benjamin, 1976.

_____. "The Quantum Theory and Reality." *Scientific American*, pp. 158-181, November, 1979.

_____. *Veiled Reality*. Reading, Mass.: Addison-Wesley, 1995. d'Estaing, Giscard. *U.S. News and World Report*. March 3, 1975.

Evans-Wentz, W. Y., ed. *Tibet's Great Yogi Milarepa*. London: Oxford University Press, 1951.

_____. *The Tibetan Book of the Great Liberation*. London: Oxford University Press, 1954.

_____. *Tibetan Yoga and Secret Doctrines*. London: Oxford University Press, 1958.

Fakhruddin Iraqi: Divine Flashes," trans. Peter Lamborn Wilson. New York, NY: Paulist Press, 1982.

Fehrenbacher, Don, ed. *Abraham Lincoln: Speeches and Writings 1832-58*, and *Abraham Lincoln: Speeches and Writings 1859-65*. Library of America, two-volume set, as well as the one-volume edition: New York, NY: Vintage, 1965.

Feng, English. *Chuang Tsu: The Inner Chapters*. NY: Vintage Books, 1974.

Ferguson, Marilyn. *The Brain Revolution*. New York, NY: Taplinger Publishing Company, 1973.

Fermi, Enrico. *Thermodynamics*. New York, NY: Dover Publications, Inc., 1956.

Feuerstein, Georg. *Yoga-Sūtra of Patanjali: A New Translation and Commentary*. Folkenstone, Kent, England: Dawson, 1979.

Feynman, Richard. *QED*. Princeton, NJ: Princeton University Press, 1985.

_____. "The Distinction of Past and Future," in *The Character of Physical Law*. Cambridge, MA: MIT Press, 1965.

_____. "The Distinction of Past and Future," in *The World Treasury of Physics, Astronomy, and Mathematics*. ed. Timothy Ferris. Boston: Little, Brown and Company, 1991.

Feynman, R. P. et al. *The Feynman Lectures on Physics*. Addison-Wesley, 1963-65.

Feynman, R. and Weinberg, S. *Elementary Particles and the Laws of Physics*. Cambridge: Cambridge University Press, 1999.

_____. Finegan, Jack. *Light from the Ancient Past*. Princeton: Princeton University Press, 1946.

Finkelstein, D. "Theory of Vacuum." *The Philosophy of Vacuum*. Oxford: Oxford University Press, 1991.

Fleming, G. N. *The Vacuum on Null Planes*. Presented to the 1987 Oxford University Symposium on the Vacuum in Quantum Field Theory.

Foard, James Harlan. *Ippen and Popular Buddhism in Kamakura Japan*. PhD dissertation, Stanford University, 1977. Ann Arbor, Mich.: Xerox University Microfilms.

Fox, Emmet. *The Sermon on the Mount: A General Introduction to Scientific Christianity in the Form of a Spiritual Key to Matthew V, VI, and VII*. New York, NY: Harper & Row, Publishers, 1938.

Freire, Paulo. Pedagogy of the Oppressed. New York, NY: Herder and Herder, 1972.

Fremantle, Anne. *Woman's Way to God*. New York, NY: St. Martin's Press, 1977.

Friedman, Milton. *Capitalism and Freedom*. Chicago: The University of Chicago Press, 1975.

Friedman, M., ed. *Martin Buber's Life and Work: The Early Years 1878-1923*. New York: E. P. Dutton, 1981.

Friedmann, Yohanan. *Shaykh Ahmad Sirhindī*. Montreal: McGill University, 1971.

Fujimoto, Y. "SO(18) Unification." International Center for Theoretical Phys., Trieste, Italy. *Phys. Rev.* (USA). Vol. 26, no. 11318-94, 1 December 1982.

Fung, Yu-lan, trans. *Chuang Tzu, A New Selected Translation with an Exposition of the Philosophy of Kuo Hsing*. Shanghai: Commercial Press, 1933.

_____. *A History of Chinese Philosophy*. 2 vols., trans. by Derk Bodde. Princeton, NJ: Princeton University Press, 1953.

_____. *A Taoist Classic: Chuang Tzu*. Beijing: Foreign Language Press, 1989.

Gabor, Dennis. *Inventing the Future*. Harmondsworth, England: Penguin, 1964.

Galilei, Galileo. *Two New Sciences*, trans. by Henry Crew and Alfonso De Salvio. New York: Macmillan, 1914.

_____. *The Achievement of Galileo*, edited with notes by James Brophy and Henry Paolucci. Smyrna, DE: Griffon House Publications, 2001.

Galloway, Allan D. *The Cosmic Christ*. New York, NY: Harper Brothers, 1951.

Gandhi, Mohandas K. *The Way to God*. (The original title of this work is *Pathway to God*). Berkeley, CA: Berkeley Hills Books, 1999.

Garriga, Jaume and Vilenkin. "Many Worlds in One." *Physical Review*, Vol. D64, No. 043511; July 26, 2001. Available online at arXiv.org/abs/gr-qc/0102010

Gell-Mann, Murray. "Observant Readers Take the Measure of Novel Approaches to Quantum Theory." *Physics Today*. College Park, MD: American Institute of Physics, Feb. 1999.

Gell-Mann, Murray, and Ne'eman, Yuval. *The Eightfold Way*. New York, NY: W. A. Benjamin, Inc., 1964.

Georgi, H. "The Case for and against New Directions in Grand Unification" Lyman Lab. for Phys., Harvard University, Cambridge, MA. Edited by M. Konuma and T. Maskawa. *Grand Unified Theories and Related Topics.* Proceedings of the 4th Kyoto Summer Institute 109-41, 1981.

Gill, Pritam Singh. *The Doctrine of Guru Nānak.* Jullundher: New Book Company, 1969.

Gilson, Etienne. *The Mystical Doctrine of Saint Bernard.* London and New York, NY, 1940.

Girard, Rene. *Deceit, Desire & the Novel.* Baltimore: The John Hopkins University Press, 1961.

_____. *Things Hidden Since the Foundation of the World.* Stanford, CA: Stanford University Press, 1978.

Glasberg, R. 1999. "Internal and External Perspectives on Immediate and Ultimate Reality: Toward the Unity of Knowledge." *Ultimate Reality and Meaning,* Toronto: University of Toronto Press, 1999. 22:2-142.

Gödel Kurt. *The Consistency of the Continuum Hypothesis.* Princeton, NJ: Princeton University Press, 1940.

—. *Collected Works.* Vols. I (II) Feferman, Solomon, et al., eds. New York, NY: Oxford University Press, 1986 (1990).

—. *On Formally Undecidable Propositions of Prtincipia Mathematica and Related Systems,* trans. by B. Meltzer. New York, NY: Dover, 1992.

Goddard, Dwight, ed. *A Buddhist Bible.* Boston: Beacon Press, 1994.

Goethe, Johann Wolfgang von. *Versuch die Metamorphose der Pflanzen zu erklären.* 1790.

Goldstein, S. March. "Quantum Theory without Observers—Part One." *Physics Today.* College Park, MD: American Institute of Physics, 1998.

Gollancz, Victor, *Man and God.* Boston: Houghton Mifflin Company, 1951.

Good News for Modern Man. New York, NY: American Bible Society, 1970.

Gopal, Sarvelli. *Radhakrishnan, A Biography.* London: Unwin Hyman Ltd. 1989.

Gospel according to Thomas, The. Coptic Text established and translated by A. Guillaumont et al. San Francisco: Harper & Row, 1959.

Gospel of Thomas, The. York, England: The Ebor Press, 1987.

Gospel of Thomas Comes of Age, The. Harrisburg, PA: Trinity Press International, 1998.

Goswami, Amit. *The Self-Aware Universe.* New York, NY: Tarcher, 1993

Graham, A. C. *Later Mohist Logic, Ethics and Science.* Hong Kong: The Chinese University Press, 1978.

_____. *Chuang-tzu: The Inner Chapters.* London: George Allen & Unwin, 1981.

_____, trans. *The Book of Lieh-tzu: A Classic of Tao.* New York, NY: Columbia University Press, 1990.

Great Treasures of Ancient Teachings. Berkeley, CA: Dharma Publishing, 1983-93. 627 vols.

Greenberger, Dadiel M. and Zeilinger, ed. *Fundamental Problems in Quantum Theory: A Conference Held in Honor of Professor John A. Wheeler*. New York, NY: The New York Academy of Sciences, Vol. 755, 1995.

Greene, Brian. *The Elegant Universe: Superstrings, Hidden Dimensions, and the Quest for the Ultimate Theory*. New York: Vintage Books, 2003.

—————The *Fabric of the Cosmos: Space, Time, and the Texture of Reality*. New York: Vintage Books, 2004.

Gregory of Nyssa, *The Life of Moses*. Trans. by Abraham J. Malherbe and Everett Ferguson. New York, NY: Paulist Press, 1978.

Griffiths, Bede. *Return to the Center*. London: Collins Fontana, 1978.

—————. *River of Compassion*. Warwick, NY: Amity House, 1987.

Guthrie, Kenneth Sylvan. Comp. and trans., *The Pythagorean Sourcebook and Library*. Grand Rapids, Michigan: Phanes Press, 1987.

Gutierrez, Gustavo. *A Theology of Liberation*. Maryknoll, NY: Orbis Books, 1972.

Hafiz. *The Gift*, trans. Daniel Ladinsky, New York, NY: Arkana, Penguin Group, 1999.

Haich, Elizabeth. *Sexual Energy and Yoga*. London: George Allen & Unwin Ltd.

Hakeda, Yoshito, trans. *Kūkai: Major Works*. New York, NY: Columbia University Press, 1972.

Halliday, David and Resnick, Robert. *Physics for Students of Science and Engineering*. New York, NY: John Wiley & Sons, 1966.

Hammarskjöld, Dag. *Markings*, trans. from Swedish by Leif Sjöberg and W. H. Auden. New York, NY: Ballantine Books, 1993.

Hardy, G. H. *Orders of Infinity, the 'Infinitärcalcul' of Paul DuBois Reymond*. Cambridge, England: Cambridge University Press, 1910.

Harman, W. Willis. "Business as a Component of the Global Economy," *Noetic Sciences Review*, Nov. 1971.

Harman, Willis and Hormann, John. *Creative Work: The Constructive Role of Business in a Transforming Society*. Indianapolis, In: Knowledge Systems, 1990.

Harman, Willis and Rheingold, Howard. *Higher Creativity: Liberating the Unconscious for Breakthrough Insights*. Los Angeles, CA: Jeremy P. Tarcher, Inc., 1984.

Harold, Preston, and Babcock, Winifred. *Cosmic Humanism and World Unity*. New York: Dodd, Mead, 1971.

Haughey, John C. *The Conspiracy of God*. Garden City, NY: Image Books, 1976.

Hawking, Stephen. Singularities in the Universe, *Physical Review Letters* 17.

—————. *A Brief History of Time*. New York, NY: Bantam Books, 1988.

Hawking, S. W. and Ellis, G. F. R. *The Large Scale Structure of Space-Time*. Cambridge, England: Cambridge University Press, 1973.

Hawkins, Donald J., ed. *Famous Statements, Speeches and Stories of Abraham Lincoln.* Scarsdale, NY: Heathcote Publications, 1981.

Heath, Sir Thomas L., trans., "The Thirteen Books of Euclid's Elements." *The Great Books of the Western World.* Chicago: Encyclopaedia Britannica, Inc., 1952. Vol. 11.

Heidegger, M. *The Basic Problems of Phenomenology*, trans. by Albert Hofstadter. Indianapolis: Indiana University Press, 1998.

Heisenberg, Werner. *The Physical Principles of the Quantum Theory.* New York, NY: Dover Publications, Inc., 1930.

_____. *The Physicist's Conception of Nature.* New York, NY: Harcourt and Brace, 1955.

_____. *Physics and Philosophy: The Revolution in Modern Science.* New York, NY: Harper & Row, 1958.

_____. *Across the Frontiers.* New York, NY: Harper & Row, 1974.

Herbert, Nick. *Quantum Reality: Beyond the New Physics.* New York, NY: Doubleday, 1985.

Heschel, Abraham Joshua Heschel. *The Prophets.* New York, NY: HarperCollins, 1969

_____. *I Asked for Wonder: A Spiritual Anthology*, edited by Samuel H. Dresner. New York, NY: Crossroad, 2000.

Hilbert, David. *The Foundations of Geometry.* Chicago: Open Court, 1902.

Hiley, Basil. "Vacuum or Holomovement." *The Philosophy of Vacuum.* Oxford: Oxford University Press, 1991.

Hirtenstein, S., ed. *Journal of the Muhyiddin Ibn 'Arabi Association.* Oxford: 1981.

Hodson, Geoffrey. *The Hidden Wisdom in the Holy Bible.* (An examination of the idea that the contents of the Bible are partly allegorical.) 3 vols. Wheaton, Ill: The Theosophical Publishing House, 1955.

_____.Lecture Notes from *The School of Wisdom.* Vol. 2, Adyar, Madras, India: The Theosophical Publishing House, 1955.

_____.*The Christ Life from Nativity to Ascension.* London: The Theosophical Publishing House, 1975.

_____.*The Brotherhood of Angels and Men.* Wheaton, Ill.: The Theosophical Publishing House, 1983.

Holton, G. *Thematic Origins of Scientific Thought.* Cambridge, MA: Harvard University Press, 1973.

Horvath, T. "A Study of Man's Horizon-Creation: A Perspective for Cultural Anthropology." *The Concept and Dynamic of Culture*, edited by B. Bernardi. The Hague: Mouton Publishers, 1976.

_____. "Methods and Systematic Reflections: The Structure of Scientific Discovery and Man's Ultimate Reality and Meaning." *Ultimate Reality and Meaning*, Toronto: University of Toronto Press, 1980, 3:2-161.

_____. "John Neumann's Idea of Ultimate Reality and Meaning." *Ultimate Reality and Meaning*, 1997, 20:134-7.

Huffines, LaUna. *Bridge of Light: Tools of Light for Spiritual Transformation*. New York: H. J. Kramer Inc., Pub., 1993.

_____. *Healing Yourself with Light: How to Connect with the Angelic Healers*. New York, NY:

H. J. Kramer Inc., Pub., 1995.

Hughes, David. *The Star of Bethlehem Mystery. An Astronomer's Confirmation*. New York: Walter & Co., and London: Dent & Sons, 1979.

Hume, Robert Ernest. *The Thirteen Principal Upanishads*, trans. from Sanskrit, with an outline of the philosophy of the Upanishads. London: Oxford University Press, 1971.

Humes, James C. *The Wit and Wisdom of Abraham Lincoln*. New York, NY: Gramercy Books, 1999.

Huxley, Aldous. *The Perennial Philosophy*. New York, NY: Meridian Books, 1968.

Huxley, Julian, *Aldous Huxley 1894-1963; A Memorial Tribute*. London: Chato and Windus; New York, NY: Harper & Row.

Hyujong. *Choson sidae p'yon. Han'guk Pulgyo chonso* [*Comprehensive Collection of Korean Buddhism*]. Vol. 7. Seoul: Tongguk Taehakkyo Ch'ulp'anbu, 1990, in classical Chinese.

Ibn 'Arabī. "Bezels of Wisdom." *Classics of Western Spirituality*, trans. by Ralph Austin. New York, NY: Paulist Press, 1980.

_____. *The Seven Days of the Heart*, trans. Pablo Beneito and Stephen Hirtenstein. Oxford: Anqua Publishing, 2000.

Inada, Kenneth. *Nāgārjuna: A Translation of his Mūla-madhyamaka-kārikā with an Introductory Essay*. Tokyo: Hokuseido Press, 1970.

Irenaeus, Saint. *Adversus Haereses*. Book 5, ch. 28, 4. *The Ante-Nicene Fathers*. Vol. 1. Edited by A. Roberts and J. Donaldson. Grand Rapids, MI: Eerdmans, 1958.

_____, of Lyons, *Libros quinque adversus haereses*, ed. W. W. Harvey (2 vols.) Cambridge, 1857.

Jaeger, W., *Two Rediscovered Works of Ancient Christian Literature: Gregory of Nyssa and Macarius*. Leiden, 1954.

Jahn, R. G. and Dunne, B. J. *Margins of Reality: Role of Consciousness in the Physical World*. San Diego: Harcourt, Brace, Jovanovish, 1988.

Jaini, Padmanabh S. *The Jaina Path of Purification*. Berkeley, Calif.: University of California Press, 1979.

Jammer, Max. *The Conceptual Development of Quantum Mechanics*. New York, NY: McGraw-Hill, 1966.

_____. *The Philosophy of Quantum Mechanics*. New York, NY: John Wiley, 1974.

_____. *Concepts of Space: The History of Theories of Space in Physics*. New York, NY: Dover Publications, 1993.

James, Joseph. *The Way to Mysticism*. London: Jonathan Cape, 1950.

James, William. *The Varieties of Religious Experience*. London: Longmans Green, 1919.

_____. *William James: The Essential Writings*. Bruce W. Wilshire, ed. Albany: State University of New York, 1984.

_____. *A Pluralistic Universe*. Lincoln: University of Nebraska, 1996.

_____. *William James: The Essential Writings*. Bruce W. Wilshire, ed. Albany: State University of New York, 1984.

Jami, Maulana Abdurrahman, *Lawa'ih*. Tehran, 1342 sh./1963.

_____. *Diwan-I kamil*, ed. Hashim Riza. Tehran, 1341 sh./1962.

Jeans, Sir James. *The Mysterious Universe*. Cambridge:Cambridge University Press, 1931.

John of the Cross, Saint. *Dark Night of the Soul*. New York, NY: Doubleday, 1959.

_____. *The Collected Works of St. John of the Cross*, trans. by Kieran Kavanaugh and Otilio Rodriguez. Washington, D.C.: Institute of Carmelite Studies, 1973.

_____. *Flame of Love, Spiritual Canticle*. Classics of Western Spirituality. New York, NY: Paulist Press, 1984.

John Paul II. Encyclical Letter of John Paul II to The Catholic Bishops of the World on the Relationship Between Faith and Reason. Rome: L'Osservatore Romano, 1998.

Kalupahana, David J. *Nāgārjuna: The Philosophy of the Middle Way*. Albany, NY: SUNY Press, 1986.

Kanamori, Akihiro. *The Higher Infinite*. Berlin: Springer-Verlag, 1997.

Kawai, Hayao. *The Buddhist Priest Myōe: A Life of Dreams*, trans. by Mark Unno. Venice, Calif.: Lapis Press, 1992.

Keating, Thomas. *Open Mind, Open Heart*. Warwicck, NY: Amity House, 1986.

Keel, Hee Sung. *Chinul: The Founder of the Korean Son [Zen] Tradition*. PhD dissertation. Cambridge, Mass.: Harvard University, 1977.

Kempis, Thomas à. *Imitation of Christ*. New York, NY: Doubleday, 1955.

Kerner, Fred (ed.). *A Treasury of Lincoln Quotations*. New York, NY: Doubleday & Co., 1965.

Kerrigan, A. *St. Cyril of Alexandria: Interpreter of the Old Testament*. Rome, 1952.

Keynes, Geoffrey, ed. *The Writings of William Blake*, (3 vols.). London, 1925.

Khrushchev, Nikita. *Secret Report to the Twentieth Party Congress K.P.S.S. v Rezolyutsiakh*. Moscow: Marx-Engels-Lenin Institute, 1953.

Kieffer, Gene, ed. *Kundalini for the New Age: Selected Writings by Gopi Krishna*. New York: Bantam Books, 1988.

King, Martin Luther Jr. *Stride Toward Freedom*. New York, NY: Harper & Row, 1958.

Kitaro, Nishida. *Intelligibility and the Philosophy of Nothingness*, trans. by R. Schinzinger. Tokyo: Muruzen, 1958; also reprint, Westport, Conn.: Greenwood Press, 1973.

Kiyota, Minoru. *Shingon Buddhism: Theory and Practice*. Los Angeles: Buddhist Books International, 1978.

_____. *Last Writings: Nothingness and the Religious Worldview*, trans. by D. A. Dilworth. Honolulu, Hawaii: University of Hawaii Press, 1987.

Klotz, Neil Douglas. *The Hidden Gospel*. Wheaton, Illinois: Quest Books, 1999.

Kochumuttom, Thomas. *A Buddhist Doctrine of Experience: A New Translation and Interpretation of the Works of Vasubandhu the Yogācārin*. Delhi: Motilal Banarsidass, 1982.

Kodlubovsky, E. and Palmer, G.E.H. *Early Fathers from the Philokalia*. London: Faber and Faber Limited, 1954.

Koestler, Arthur. *The Act of Creation*. New York, NY: Dell, 1964.

Krishna, Gopi. *Kundalini: The Evolutionary Energy in Man*. Berkeley, 1970.

_____. *The Biological Basis of Religion and Genius*. New York, NY: Harper & Row, 1972.

_____. *Higher Consciousness: The Evolutionary Thrust of Kundalini*. New York, NY: The Julian Press, 1974.

_____. *The Awakening of Kundalini*. New York, NY: Dutton, 1975.

La Fleur, William R., ed. *Dōgen Studies*. Honolulu, Hawaii: University of Hawaii Press, 1985.

Landry, Tom, with Greg Lewis. *Tom Landry: An Autobiography*. New York, NY: Harper Collins, 1990.

Lao Tzu. *Tao Te Ching*, trans. by D. C. Lau, Baltimore: Penguin Books, 1963.

_____. *The Tao Teh King: Sayings of Lao Tzu*, trans. with Commentary by C. Spurgeon Medhurst. Wheaton, Ill: The Theosophical Publishing House, 1972.

_____. *Lao Tsu: Tao Te Ching*, trans. by Gia-Fu Feng and Jane English. New York, NY: Vintage, 1972.

_____. *Lao-Tzu: Te-Tao Ching: A New Translation Based on the Recently Discovered Ma-wang-tui Texts*, trans. by Robert G. Henricks. New York, NY: Ballantine, 1989.

Lavine, Shaughan. *Understanding the Infinite*. Cambridge, MA: Harvard University Press, 1994.

Lawson, John. *The Biblical Theology of Saint Irenaeus*. London: Epworth Press, 1948.

Leadbeater, C. *The Chakras*. Wheaton, Ill: The Theosophical Publishing House, 1969.

_____. *The Hidden Side of Things*. Wheaton, Ill.: Theosophical Publishing House, 1974.

_____. *The Science of the Sacraments.* Adyar, India: Theosophical Publishing House, 1974

_____. *The Christian Gnosis,* Ojai, CA: St. Alban's Pres, 1983.

Lebreton, J. *History of the Dogma of the Trinity from its Origins to the Council of Nicaea.* London: Burns, Oates, and Washbourne, 1939.

Lee, Peter H., ed. *The Silence of Love: Twentieth Century Korean Poetry.* Honolulu, Hawaii: The University Press of Hawaii, 1980.

_____, ed. *Sourcebook of Korean Civilization.* New York, NY: Columbia University Press, 1993.

Legge, James, trans. and ed. *The Life and Work of Mencius.* Oxford: Clarendon Press, 1895.

Lenin, Vladimir I. *V. I. Lenin: Selected Works* (Essential Aspects of Lenin's Contributions to Revolutionary Marxism). New York, NY: International Publishers Co. Inc, 1976.

Levy, A. *Basic Set Theory.* Berlin: Springer-Verlag, 1979.

Lewis, Gilbert N. *The Anatomy of Science.* New Haven: Yale University Press, 1926.

Liu, Ming-wood. *The Teaching of Fa-Tsang: An Examination of Buddhist Metaphysics.* Ann Arbor, Mich.: University Microfilms International, 1979.

Logan, Alastair H. B. *Gnostic Truth and Christian Heresy: A Study in the History of Gnosticism.* Edinburgh, Scotland: Hendrickson Publishers, 1996.

Lombardi, Vince, with Heinz, W. C. *Run to Daylight.* Englewood Cliffs, NJ: Prentice Hall, 1963.

Lopez, Donald S., and Steven C. Rockefeller (eds.), *Christ and the Bodhisattva.* Albany: State University of New York Press, 1987.

Lorimer, David, ed. *The Spirit of Science: From Experiment to Experience.* New York, NY: Continuum, 1999.

Lovejoy, Arthur. *The Great Chain of Being.* Cambridge, MA: Harvard University Press, 1953.

MacGregor, G. H. C. *St. John's Gospel.* London: Hodder & Stoughton, 1936.

Mackay, Alan L. *A Dictionary of Scientific Quotations.* Bristol and Philadelphia: Institute of Physics Publishing, 1992.

Maffie, James. "'Like a Painting, We Will Be Erased; Like a Flower, We Will Dry Here on Earth': Ultimate Reality and Meaning according to Nahua Philosophy in the Age of Conquest." *Ultimate Reality and Meaning.* Toronto: University of Toronto Press, 2000. Vol. 23:4.

Mahamudra. *Mahamudra: The Quintessence of Mind and Meditation,* translated and annotated by Lobsang P. Lhalungpa. Boston: Shambhala Publications, Inc., 1986

Maimonides, Moses. *The Guide for the Perplexed,* trans. by M. Friedlander. New York, NY Dover Publications, 1956.

Manaka, Fujiko. *Jichin Kashō oyobi shūgyokushū no kenkyū* [*Master Jien and the Collection of Gleaned Jewels*]. Kawasaki, Japan: Mitsuru Bunko, 1974.

Mandino, Og. *The Greatest Salesman in the World.* New York, NY: Frederick Fell Publishers, 1973.

Margenau, Henry. *The Nature of Physical Reality.* New York, NY: McGraw-Hill, 1950.

Margenau, Watson, and Montgomery. *Physics Principles and Applications.* New York, NY:

McGraw-Hill Book Company, 1953.

Marx, Karl. "The German Ideology, Vol. 1" Extracts in *The Portable Karl Marx* ed. by Eugene Kamenka. New York, NY: Penguin Books, 1981.

_____. *Selected Writings in Sociology and Social Philosophy*, ed. T. Bottomore and Rubel. London, 1956.

Mason, S.F. *A History of the Sciences.* London: Routledge, 1953.

Matt, Daniel C. *Zohar: The Book of Enlightenment.* Mahwah, NJ: Paulist Press, 1983.

_____. *The Essential Kabbalah.* San Francisco: Harper San Francisco, 1996.

Maurice, Nicoll. *The New Man.* Baltimore: Penguin Books, 1972.

Mayotte, Ricky Alan. *The Complete Jesus.* South Royalton, Vermont: Steerforth Press, 1997.

McGreal, Ian P., ed. *Great Thinkers of the Eastern World.* HarperCollins Publishers, 1995.

McKenzie, Clancy D., MD, & Lance S. Wright, MD. *Delayed Post-traumatic Stress Disorders from Infancy and the Two Trauma Mechanism: Clinical Examples.* Bala Cynwyd, PA: American Health Association, 1990.

McLellan, David. *Karl Marx: His Life and Thought.* Norwalk, Connecticut: The Easton Press, 1973.

Mearns, David (ed). *Lincoln Papers* (2 vols.). *New York, NY: Doubleday & Co.*, 1948.

Mechtchild of Magdeburg. *Das Flieszende Licht der Gottheit von Mechtchild von Magdeburg* (*The Flowing Light of the Godhead*). Berlin, 1909.

Mei, Yi-Pao. *The Ethical and Political Works of Motse.* Westport, Conn.: Hyperion Press, 1973.

Mersch, Emile. *The Whole Christ.* Milwaukee: Bruce & Bruce, 1938.

Merton, Thomas. *New Seeds of Contemplation.* New York, NY: New Directions Books, 1961.

_____. *The Asian Journal of Thomas Merton.* Edited by Naomi Burton, Brother Patrick Hart, and James Laughlin. New York, NY: New Directions Press, 1973.

_____. *The Way of Chuang Tzu.* New York, NY: Norton Co., 1975.

_____. *The Intimate Merton.* Edited by Patrick Hart and Jonathan Montaldo. New York, NY: HarperCollins Publishers, 1999.

Milarepa, Jetsun. *One Hundred Thousand Songs of Milarepa*, translated and annotated by Garma C. C. Chang. Boulder: Shambala, 1977, 2 vols.

Miller, William Lee. *Lincoln's Virtues: An Ethical Biography*. New York, NY: Alfred A. Knopf, 2002.

Miller, W. R. *Nonviolence: A Christian Interpretation*. New York, NY: Schocken, 1966.

Misner, C. W., Thorne, K. S., and Wheeler, J. A. *Gravitation*. San Francisco: Freeman, 1973.

Mitchell, Donald. *Spirituality and Emptiness: The Dynamics of Spiritual Life in Buddhism and Christianity*. New York, NY: Paulist Press, 1991.

Mitchel, Stephen. *The Enlightened Mind*. New York, NY: Harper Perennial, 1993.

Montague, G. *Growth in Christ*. Kirkwood, MO: Maryhurst Press, 1961.

Moore, Gregory H. *Zermelo's Axiom of Choice: Its Origins, Developments, and Influence*. New York, NY: Springer-Verlag, 1982.

Morgan, Tom, ed. *A Simple Monk*. Novato, CA: New World Library, 2001.

Morris, James. *Introduction to Wisdom of the Throne*, trans. of Mulla Sadra's *al-Hikmat al-'arshiyyah*. Princeton, NJ: Princeton University Press, 1981.

Muktananda, S. P. *Guru*. New York, NY: Harper & Row, Publishers. 1971.

_____. *Kundalini: The Secret of Life*. South Fallsburg, NY: SYDA Foundation, 1979.

_____. *Play of Consciousness*. New York, NY: Harper & Row, 1980.

Muller, Robert. *New Genesis: Shaping a Global Spirituality*. Garden City, NY: Image Books, 1984.

_____. *What War Taught Me about Peace*. New York, NY: Doubleday, 1985.

_____. *A Planet of Hope*. Warwick, NY: Amity House, 1985.

Murray, Bruce C. *Navigating the Future*. New York, NY: Harper & Row, Publishers, 1975.

Namgyal, Takpo Tashi, translated and annotated by Lobsang P. Lhalungpa. *Mahamudra: The Quintessence of Mind and Meditation*. Boston: Shambhala Publications, Inc., 1986.

Nanopoulos, D. V. "Tales of the Gut Age." CERN, Geneva, Switzerland. *Grand Unified Theories and Related Topics*. Edited by M. Konuma and T. Maskawa. Proceedings of the 4th Kyoto Summer Institute 5-63, 1981.

Nasr, Seyyed Hossein. *Three Muslim Sages*. New York, NY: Carvan Books, 1969.

_____. *Sadr al-Dīn Shīrāzī and His Transcendental Theosophy*. Tehran: Iranian Academy of Philosophy, 1978.

Needleman, Jacob. *Lost Christianity*. New York, NY: Bantam Books, 1980.

Neumann, J. von. *The Mathematical Foundations of Quantum Mechanics*, trans. from the German edition by R. T. Beyer, Princeton, NJ: Princeton University Press, 1955.

_____. *Collected Works*. A. H. Taub, ed. Oxford: Pergamon, 1961.

Neumann, J. von and Morgenstern, Oskar. *The Theory of Games and Economic Behavior*. Princeton, NJ: Princeton University Press, 1959.

_____. *Theory of Self-Reproducing Automata*. Urbana, Ill.: University of Illinois Press, 1966.

New American Bible, The. Translated from the Original Languages with Critical Use of All the Ancient Sources. Washington, D.C.: Confraternity of Christine Doctrine, 1970.

Newton, I. "Mathematical Principles of Natural Philosophy." *Great Books of the Western World*. Chicago: Encyclopaedia Britannica, Inc., 1971. Vol. 34.

Nicolaevsky, Boris, ed. *The Crimes of the Stalin Era*. New York, NY: The New Leader, 1962.

Nicoll, Maurice. *The New Man*. Baltimore: Penguin Books, 1972.

Nietzsche, Friedrich. *The Will to Power*. New York, NY: Vintage Books, 1969.

Nikaya, Digha. *Thus Have I Heard: The Long Discourses of the Buddha*, trans. by Maurice Walshe. London: Wisdom Publications, 1987.

Nikilananda, Swami. The Upanishads. New York, NY: Harper & Brothers, 1959. 4 vols.

Nishitani, Keiji. *Religion and Nothingness*, trans. by Jan van Bragt. Berkeley, Calif.: University of California Press, 1982.

Novak, Philip. *The World's Wisdom: Sacred Texts of the World's Religions*. New York, NY: HarperCollins Publishers, 1994.

Novikov, I. D. *The River of Time*. Cambridge: Cambridge University Press, 1998.

Nyingma Edition of the Tibetan Buddhist Canon. Berkeley, CA: Dharma Publishing, 1981. 120 vols.

O'Leary, Brian. *Miracle in the Void*. Kihei, Hawaii: Kamapua'a Press, 1996.

Ooms, Herman. *Tokugawa Ideology: Early Constructs, 1570-1680*. Princeton, NJ: Princeton University Press, 1985.

O'Reilly, Bill. *Who's Looking Out for You*. New York, NY: Broadway Books, 2003.

Orlov, Alexander. *The Secret History of Stalin's Crimes*. New York, NY: Random House, 1953.

Origen, *Origenes Werke*. Leipzig, 1899-1925. 8 vols.

Osborne, E. F. *The Philosophy of Clement of Alexandria*. Cambridge: Cambridge University Press, 1957.

Osbourne, Arthur. *Ramana Maharshi and the Path of Self-Knowledge*. New York, NY: Samuel Weiser, 1973.

Pagels, Elaine. *The Gnostic Gospels*. New York, NY: Random House, 1980.

Pagels, Heinz. *The Cosmic Code*. London: Penguin Books, 1994.

Pak, Chong-hong. "Wonhyo's Philosophical Thought," *Assimilation of Buddhism in Korea: Religious Maturity and Innovation in the Silla Dynasty*, edited by Lewis R. Lancaster and C. S. Yu. Berkeley, Calif.: Asian Humanities Press, 1991.

Pantanjali. *How to Know God: The Yoga Aphorisms of Pantanjali*, trans. by Swami Pascal, Blaise. *Pensees and Other Writings*, trans. by Honor Levi. Oxford: Oxford University Press, 1995.

Paul VI, His Holiness, Pope. *Ecclesiam Suam*. New York, NY: Paulist Press, 1965.

Pauling, Linus. *The Nature of the Chemical Bond*. New York, NY: Cornell University Press, 1960.

Peebles, P. J. E. *Principles of Physical Cosmology*. Princeton: Princeton University Press, 1993.

Peierls, R. E. *The Laws of Nature*. George Allen, 1955.

Pelikan, Jaroslav. *The Idea of the University: A Reexamination*. New Haven, CT: Yale University Press, 1992.

Penrose, Roger. "Gravitational Collapse and Space-Time Singularities." *Physical Review Letters*, 1965.

_____. *Cosmology*. London: BBC Publications, 1974.

_____. "Singularities in Cosmology," *Confrontation of Cosmological Theories with Observational Data*. Longair, M. S. (ed.). Boston: D. Reidel.

_____. "Singularities and Time-asymmetry." *General Relativity: An Einstein Centenary Survey*, ed. by Stephen Hawking and W. Israel. Cambridge: Cambridge University Press, 1979.

_____. *Shadows of the Mind*. Oxford: Oxford University Press, 1994.

_____. *The Large, the Small and the Human Mind*, Cambridge: Cambridge University Press, 1997.

Petley, B. *The Fundamental Physical Constants and the Frontier of Measurement*, Bristol and Boston: Adam Hilger Ltd., 1985.

Phillips, Donald T. *Run to Win: Vince Lombardi on Coaching and Leadership*. New York: St. Martin's Press, 2001.

Planck, Max. *Where Is Science Going?* New York, NY: Norton, 1932.

Plato. "Dialogues of Plato: Parmenides." *Great Books of the Western World*. Chicago: Encyclopaedia Britannica, Inc., 1971.

_____. "Timaeus." *Great Books of the Western World* Chicago: Encyclopaedia Britannica, Inc., 1952. Vol. 7.

Plotinus. "*The Six Enneads*." *Great Books of the Western World*. Chicago: Encyclopaedia Britannica, Inc., 1952. Vol. 17.

_____. *Works*, trans. A. H. Armstrong. London: Heinemann, 1996-1984.

Plzak, Richard F. Jr. *Paradox East and West*. Senior Dissertation. Cambridge: MIT, 1973.

Poincare, H. *La Valeur de la Science*. Paris: Flammarion. 1904.

———. *Revue de métaphysique et de morale* 20, 486. 1912.

Popper, Karl Raimund. *The Logic of Scientific Discovery*. London: Hutchison, 1959.

———. *Conjectures and Refutations: The Growth of Scientific Knowledge*. New York, NY: Basic Books, 1963.

———. *Objective Knowledge: An Evolutionary Approach*. Oxford: Clarendon Press, 1972.

Prabhupada, A. C. Bhaktivedanta Swami. *Bhagavad-Gita as It Is*. Los Angeles: Macmillan Publishing, 1973.

———. *Sri Isopanisad*. Los Angeles: The Bhaktivedanta Book Trust, 1995.

Preston, Harold. *Cosmic Humanism and World Unity*. New York, NY: Dodd, Mead, 1971.

Prigogine, I. *From Being to Becoming*. San Francisco: Freeman, 1980.

Quine, W. V. O. *Set Theory and Its Logic*. Cambridge, MA: Harvard University Press, 1963. al-Qushayri. *Principles of Sufism*, trans. from Arabic by B. R. Von Schlegel. Berkeley, Calif.: Mizan Press, 1990.

Radhakrishnan, Sarvepalli. *The Bhagavadgita*. London: Allen and Unwin, 1948.

———. *The Principal Upsanishads*. New York, NY: Harper & Brothers, 1953.

Radhakrishnan, Sarvepalli, and Moore, Charles. *A Sourcebook in Indian Philosophy*. Princeton, NJ: Princeton University Press, 1957.

Radin, D. I. *The Conscious Universe*. San Francisco: Harper Edge, 1997.

Rahula, Walpola. *What the Buddha Taught*. New York, NY: Grove Press, 1974.

Rama, Swami, *The Book of Wisdom*. Kanpur, India: Himalayan International Institute of Yoga, Science & Philosophy, 1972.

Ramakrishna. *Ramakrishna: Prophet of New India*, trans. by Swami Nikhilananda. New York, NY: Harper & Brothers, n.d.

Randall, J. C. *Mr. Lincoln* (4 vols.). New York, NY: Dodd Mead, 1945.

Rayfield, Donald. *Stalin and His Hangmen*. New York, NY: Random House, 2004.

Reichenbach, Hans. *Experience and Prediction*. Chicago: University of Chicago Press, 1938.

———. *Philosophic Foundations of Quantum Mechanics*. Berkeley: University of California Press, 1946.

———. *The Direction of Time*. Berkeley: University of California Press, 1956.

Reischauer, A. K. "Genshin's Ōjō Yōshu: Collected Essays on Birth into Paradise." *Transactions of the Asiatic Society of Japan*. 2nd ser., vol. 7, 1930, pp. 16-97.

Reiser, Oliver. *Cosmic Humanism*. London: Schenkman, 1966.

Rele, Vasant. *The Mysterious Kundalini*. India: D. B. Taraporevala Sons & Company.

Renan, Ernest. *The Life of Jesus*, trans. by C. E. Wilbur. New York, NY: Everyman's Library, E. P. Dutton, 1987.

Resnick, Robert, David Halliday, Kenneth S. Krane. *Physics*. 2 vols. 4th edition. New York: John Wiley & Sons, 1992.

Ribera, Francisco de, *Vida de S. Teresa de Jesus*. Barcelona: Nuova ed., 1908. (First published in 1590.)

Richards, I. A. *Mencius on the Mind*. London: Kegan Paul, Trench, Trubner & Company, 1932.

Richardson, Robert D. Jr. *Emerson*. Berkeley: University of California Press, 1995.

Rinpoche, K. *Gently Whispered: Oral Teachings*. Compiled, edited and annotated, E. Selandia. Tarrytown, NY: Station Hill Press, Inc.

Roberts, Alexander, DD, and James Donaldson, LLD, ed., *Ante-Nicene Fathers*. Peabody, Mass: Hendrickson Publishers, 1999. Vols. 1-10—the writings of the Fathers down to CE 325.

Robinson, James M., Gen. Ed., *The Nag Hammadi Library in English*. San Francisco: Harper & Row, 1988.

_____. "The Gospel according to Thomas." *The Nag Hammadi Library in English*. San Francisco: Harper & Row, 1988.

Roche de Coppens, Peter. *Spiritual Man in the Modern World*. Washington: University Press of America, 1976.

_____. *Spiritual Perspective II: The Spiritual Dimension and Implications of Love, Sex, and Marriage*. Washington, D.C.: University Press of America, 1981.

_____. *The Nature and Use of Ritual for Spiritual Attainment*. St. Paul, MN: Llewellyn Publications, 1985.

_____. *Apocalypse Now*. St Paul: Llewellyn, 1988.

_____. *The Art of Joyful Living*. Rockport, Mass.: Element, 1992.

_____. *Divine Light and Fire: Experiencing Esoteric Christianity*. Rockport, MA: Element, 1992.

Rodd, Laurel Rasplica. *Nichiren: Selected Writings*. Honolulu, Hawaii: University Press of Hawaii, 1980.

Rotman, Brian. *Signifying Nothing*. Stanford, CA: Stanford University Press, 1987.

Rucker, Rudy. *Infinity and the Mind*. New York, NY: Bantam Books, 1983.

Rumi, Jalal al-Din. *The Discourses of Rumi*, trans. A. J. Arberry. London: Murray, 1961.

_____. *Teachings of Rumi the Masnavi*, translated and abridged E. H. Whinfield. New York, NY: E. P. Dutton & Co., 1975.

_____. *Light upon Light*, trans. Andrew Harvey. Berkeley: North Atlantic Books, 1996.

_____. *The Essential Rumi*, trans. by Coleman Barks with John Moyne, A. J. Arberry, Reynold Nicholson. New York, NY: Quality Paperback Book Club, 1998.

Rump, Ariane. *Commentary on the Lao Tzu by Wang Pi*. Honolulu, Hawaii: University of Hawaii Press, 1979.

Russell, Bertrand. *Introduction to Mathematical Philosophy*. New York, NY: The MacMillan Company and George Allen & Unwin Ltd., 1919.

_____. *Mysticism and Logic*. Totowa, NJ: Barnes & Noble Books, [1917], 1981.

_____. *Human Knowledge, Its Scope and Limits*. New York, NY: Simon and Schuster, 1948.

_____. *The Analysis of Mind*. London: George Allen and Unwin, Ltd., 1956.

_____. *Wisdom of the West*. New York, NY: Doubleday and Company, Inc., 1959

Russell, Bertrand, and Whitehead, Alfred North. *Principia Mathematica*. 2nd ed., 3 vols. London: Cambridge University Press, 1935.

Russell, Peter. *The Global Brain: Speculations on the Evolutionary Leap to Planetary Consciousness*. Los Angeles, CA: J. P. Tarcher, Inc., 1983.

Sahn, S. *The Compass of Zen*. Boston: Shambhala Publications, Inc., 1997.

Sandburg, Carl. *Abraham Lincoln*. (6 vols.). New York, NY: Charles Scribner & Sons, 1943.

_____. *Abraham Lincoln*. Norwalk, Conn.: The Easton Press, 1954.

Sanella, Lee, MD. *Kundalini—Psychosis or Transcendence?* San Francisco: Sannela, 1976.

Sanford, John A. *The Kingdom Within*. New York, NY: Harper & Row, 1987.

Santayana, George. *Reason in Common Sense*. New York, NY: Charles Scribner and Sons, 1927.

Sartre, Jean-Paul. *Being and Nothingness*, trans. Hazel Barnes. New York, NY: Philosophical Library, 1956.

Sastri, S. S. and Raja, C. K., trans. and eds. *The Bhāmāti of Vācaspati*. Madras, India: The Theosophical Publishing House, 1933.

Satprakashanada, Swami. *Methods of Knowledge*. Calcutta: Advaita Ashrama, 1974.

Saunders, S. and Brown, H. R., ed. *The Philosophy of Vacuum*. Oxford: Oxford University Press, 1991.

\, Philip, ed., *Nicene and Post-Nicene Fathers*. Peabody, Mass: Hendrickson Publishers, 1999. Vols. 1-28—a select library of the Christian Church.

_____. *History of the Christian Church* (Peabody, Massachusetts: Hendrickson Publishers, Inc., 2002), 8 vols.

Schilpp, Paul A, ed. *The Philosophy of Sarvepalli Radhakrishnan*. Library of Living Philosophers, New York, NY: Tudor Publishing Company, 1952.

Schimmel, Annemarie. *Mystical Dimensions of Islam*. Chapel Hill: The University of North Carolina Press, 1975.

Schrödinger, Erwin. *What Is Life?* Cambridge: The MacMillan Company, 1946.

Schuhmacher, Stephan. *The Encyclopedia of Eastern Philosophy and Religion.* Boston: Shambhala, 1994.

Schure, Edouard, *The Great Initiates,* trans. from French by Gloria Rasberry. San Francisco: Harper & Row, 1980.

Seife, Charles. *Zero: The Biography of a Dangerous Idea.* New York, NY: The Penguin Group, 2000.

Sells, Michael A. "Foundations of Islamic Mysticism." *Classics of Western Spirituality.* New York, NY: Paulist Press, 1994.

Sharma, B. N. K. *The Brahmasūtras and their Principal Commentaries: A Critical Exposition.* Bombay: Bharatiya Vidya Bhavan. 3 vols: vol. 1, 1971; vol. 2, 1974; vol. 3. 1978.

Sheldrake, R. *A New Science of Life: The Hypothesis of Formative Causation.* London: Blond & Briggs, 1981.

Shipov, Gennady. *A Theory of Physical Vacuum: A New Paradigm.* Moscow: Russian Academy of Natural Sciences, 1998.

Simonetti, Manlio. *Biblical Interpretation in the Early Church: An Historical Introduction to the Patristic Exegesis,* trans. John A. Hughes. Edinburgh: T&T Clark, 1994.

Singh, Gopal Singh, trans. and ed. *Sri Guru Granth Sahib: An Anthology.* Calcutta: M. P. Birla Foundations, 1989.

Singh, Maharay Charan. *Light on Saint John.* Punjab, India: Radha Soami Satsang Beas, 1985.

Skolimowski, Henry. "Global Philosophy as the Canvas for Human Unity." *The American Theosophist.* May 1983.

Skovorodá, Hryhorij Savych. *Hryhory Skovorodá: Works in Two Volumes,* trans. M. Kashuba and W. Shewchuk. Cambridge-Kyiv: Ukr. Research Institute of Harvard University, Shevchenko Inst. of Literature, Nat. Academy of Sciences of Ukraine, 1994.

Sky Dancer: The Secret Life and Songs of the Lady Yeshe Tsogyel, trans. by Keith Dowman. London: Routledge & Kegan Paul, 1984.

Smith, Margaret. *Rabi'a the Mystic.* Cambridge: Cambridge University Press, 1928, 1984.

SODEPAX. *Peace: The Desperate Imperative.* Geneva: Committee on Society, Development and Peace, 1969.

Solzhenitsyn, Aleksandr. *The Gulag Archipelago Two.* New York, NY: Harper & Row, 1975.

Sorokin, Pitirim. *The Ways and Power of Love.* Boston: Beacon Press, 1950.

Srinivasa, K. R. *Sri Aurobindo: A Biography and a History,* 2 vols. Pondicherry, India: Sri Aurobindo Centre of Education, 1972.

Stein, Edith. *Finite and Eternal Being: An Attempt at an Ascent to the Meaning of Being.* Trans. K. F. Reinhardt. Washington, D.C.: ICS Publications, 2002.

_____. *Edith Stein Gesamtausgabe* (ESGA, The Complete Edition of Works of Edith Stein), when completed, it will comprise twenty-four volumes. ESGA Eds, M. Linssen, O. C. D. and H. B. Gerl-Falkovitz. Wien: Herder, 2000.

Stulman, Julius. *Evolving Mankind's Future.* Philadelphia: J. B. Lippincott, 1967.

Sullivan, Lawrence E. *Icanchu's Drum: An Orientation to Meaning in South American Religions.* New York, NY: Macmillan Publishing Company, 1988.

Suzuki, D. T. *An Introduction to Zen Buddhism.* New York, NY: Grove Press, 1964.

_____. *The Field of Zen.* New York, NY: Harper & Row 1970.

_____. *Mysticism: Christian and Buddhist.* Westport, Conn.: Greenwood, 1976.

Svarney, Patricia Barnes. Editorial Director, *Science Desk Reference.* New York, NY: Macmillan, 1995.

Swan, Laura. *The Forgotten Desert Mothers.* New York, NY: Paulist Press, 2001.

Symeon the New Theologian, St., *Hymns of Divine Love*, trans. by George A. Maloney, SJ. Denville, NJ: Dimension Books, 1968.

Tagore, Rabindranath. *The Religion of Man.* London: Allen & Unwin, 1931.

_____. *Gitanjali.* New York, NY: Macmillan Publishing Co., Inc. 1973.

Taimni, I. K. *Man, God and the Universe.* Wheaton, Ill.: The Theosophical Publishing House, 1969.

Talbot, George Robert. *Electronic Thermodynamics.* Los Angeles: Pacific State University Press, 1973.

_____. *Philosophy and Unified Science.* 2 vols. Madras, India: Ganesh & Company, 1977.

Tarada, Tōru, and Yaoko, Mizuno, eds. *Dōgen.* 2 vols. Tokyo: Iwanami, 1971.

Tarski, Alfred. *Introduction to Logic.* London: Oxford University Press, Inc, 1941

Tatia, Nathmal. *Studies in Jaina Philosophy.* Banares, India: Jaina Cultural Research Society, 1951.

Tauler, Johan. *Theologia Germanica*, trans. by Winkworth. London, 1937.

Taylor, Edwin F., and Wheeler, John A. *Space Time Physics.* San Francisco: W.H. Freeman and Co., 1966.

Taylor, L. H. *The New Creation.* New York, NY: Pageant Press, 1958.

Tehrani, Kazem. *Mystical Symbolism in Four Treatises of Suhrawardi.* PhD dissertation, Columbia University, 1974.

Teller, P. "Relativity, Wholeness, and Quantum Mechanics." *British Journal for the Philosophy of Science*, 1986, 37, 71-81.

Templeton, John Marks. *The Humble Approach: Scientists Discover God.* New York, NY: Continuum, 1995.

Teres, Gustav, SJ. *The Bible and Astronomy: The Magi and the Star in the Gospel.* Budapest: Springer Orvosi Kiado Kft., 2000.

Teresa, Mother. *A Simple Path,* compiled by Lucinda Vardey. New York, NY: Ballantine Books, 1995.

_____. *The Joy in Loving.* New York, NY: Viking Penguin, 1997.

Teresa of Avila, Saint. *The Interior Castle,* translated and edited by E. Allison Peers. Garden City, NY: Image Books, 1944.

Thackston, W. M. *Mystical and Visionary Treatise of Suhrawardi.* London: The Octagon Press, 1982.

Theophilus of Antioch. "Thoeophilus to Autolycus," trans. by Marcus Dods, A. M., *Fathers of the Second Century.* Peabody, Mass: Hendrickson Publishers. Vol. 2.

Thibaut, George, trans. "The *Vedānta Sūtras* with the Commentary of Rāmānuja," in *The Sacred Books of the East.* Vol. 48. Oxford: The Clarendon Press, 1904.

Thomas, D. J. "The Gospel of Thomas." *The Nag Hammandi Library in English.* San Francisco: Harper & Row, Publishers, 1988.

Thomson, E. J. *Rabindranath Tagore: Poet and Dramatist.* London: Oxford University Press, 1948.

Tiller, William A. *Science and Human Transformation: Subtle Energies, Intentionality and Consciousness.* Walnut Creek, CA: Pavior Publishing, 1997.

Tiller, William A., Dibble, Walter E. Jr., and Kohane, Michael J. *Conscious Acts of Creation: The Emergence of a New Physics.* Walnut Creek, CA: Pavior Publishing, 2001.

Tirtha, Swami Mahjaraj Vishnu. *Devatma Shakti,* India.

Tishby, Isaiah, and Lachower, Fischel. *The Wisdom of the Zohar.* New York, NY: Oxford University Press, 1989.

Tollinton, R. B. *Clement of Alexandria.* Vols. 1 and 2. London: Williams and Norgate, 1914.

Tolstoy, Leo. *Tolstoy's Writings on Civil Disobedience and Nonviolence.* New York, NY: New American Library, 1968.

Tower, Courtney. "Mother Theresa's Work of Grace." *Reader's Digest.* December 1987.

Toynbee, Arnold, and Ikeda, Daisaku. *Choose Life: A Dialogue.* London: Oxford University Press, 1976.

Tranter, Gerald. *The Mystery Teachings and Christianity.* Wheaton, Ill: The Theosophical Publishing House, 1969.

Trump, Ernest. *The Adi Granth, or the Holy Scriptures of the Sikhs.* New Delhi: Munshiram Manoharlal, 1970.

Trungpa, Chögyam. *Orderly Chaos: The Mandala Principle.* Boston: Shambhala, 1991.

Trylis, O. "Cosmolog: Slide Rule That Knows Physics" *Physics* (in Ukrainian) (Kyiv: Schkilnyj Swit, Dec 2001; Feb 2002), no. 36 (120) p. 9; no. 4 (124) pp. 3-4, 9. Also, Institute of Mathematical Physics. "Landmark Breakthrough in Physics." *Physics Today*. College Park, MD: American Institute of Physics. Oct. 1994.

Tseu, Augustinus A. *The Moral Philosophy of Mo-tzu.* Taiwan: Fu Jen Catholic University Press, 1965.

Tyler, Royall, trans. *Selected Writings of Suzuki Shōsan*. Cornell University East Asia Papers, no. 13. Ithaca, NY: China-Japan Program, Cornell University, 1977.

Udanavarga. *The Dhammapada with the Udanavarga*, ed. by Raghavan Iyer. The Pythagorean Sangha, 1986.

Ueda, Yoshifumi, and Hirota, Dennis. *Shinran: An Introduction to His Thought*. Kyoto: Hongwanji International Center, 1989.

Underhill, Evelyn. *Mysticism: A Study in the Nature and Development of Man's Spiritual Consciousness*. New York, NY: E. P. Dutton & Co., Inc., 1961 (first published in 1911). Amongst her other excellent works are: *The Mystic Way* (1913); *Practical Mysticism* (1915); *The Essentials of Mysticism* (1920); *The Life of the Spirit and the Life of Today* (1922); *Concerning the Inner Life* (1926); *Man and the Supernatural* (1927); and *The House of the Soul* (1929).

Upanishads, The. *The Thirteen Principal Upanishads*. translated from Sanskrit by Robert Ernest Hume. London: Oxford University Press, 1971.

Utke, A. "The Cosmic Holism Concept: An Interdisciplinary Tool in the Quest for Ultimate Reality and Meaning." *Ultimate Reality and Meaning*, Toronto: University of Toronto Press, 1986. 9:134-55.

U.S. Congress House Committee on Un-American Activities. *The Crimes of Khrushchev: Hearings*. Washington, D.C.: Government Printing Office, 1959.

U.S. Congress Senate Committee on Foreign Relations. *The Genocide Convention: Hearings before a Subcommittee*, January 23 to February 9, 1950, on Executive Order. Washington, D.C.: Government Printing Office, 1950.

U.S. Congress Senate Committee on Judiciary. *Soviet Empire: Prison House of Nations and Races*. Washington, D.C.: Government Printing Office, 1958.

_____. *Soviet Empire: A Study in Genocide, Discrimination and Abuse of Power*. Washington, D.C.: Government Printing Office, 1958.

Vatican II, The Documents of, with notes by Protestant and Orthodox authorities. Edited by Walter M. Abbot, Geoffrey Chapman, 1966.

Verster, F. "Silence, Subjective Absence and the Idea of Ultimate Reality and Meaning in Beethoven's Last Piano Sonata, Op. 111." *Ultimate Reality and Meaning*, 1999. 22:4-23.

Vivekananda. *Living at the Source*. Boston: Shambhala, 1993. da Vinci, Leonardo. *The Notebook*, trans. and ed. by E. Macurdy. London, 1954.

Vishnu Tirtha, Swami Maharaj. *Devarma Shakti*. India.

Waldenfels, Hans. *Absolute Nothingness: Foundations for a Buddhist-Christian Dialogue*, trans. James W. Heisig. New York, NY: Paulist Press, 1980.

Waley, Arthur. *The Way and Its Power: A Study of the Tao Te Ching and Its Place in Chinese Thought*. New York, NY: Evergreen, 1958.

Warder, A. K. *Indian Buddhism*. Delhi: Motilal Banarsidass, 1980.

Watson, Burton. *Chuang Tzu: Basic Writings*. New York, NY: Columbia University Press, 1964.

_____. *Basic Writings of Mo Tzu, Hsun Tzu, and Han Fei Tzu*. New York, NY: Columbia University Press, 1967.

_____. *Complete Writings of Chuang Tzu*. New York, NY: Columbia University Press, 1968.

Watts, Alan. *The Book: On the Taboo against Knowing Who You Are*. New York, NY: Random House, 1972.

Weber, Max. *Protestant Ethic and the Spirit of Capitalism*. New York, NY: Charles Scribner's Sons, 1976.

Weinberg, Steven. *Gravitation and Cosmology: Principles and Applications of the General Theory of Relativity*. New York, NY: John Wiley, 1972.

_____. *The First Three Minutes: A Modern View of the Origin of the Universe*. New York, NY: Basic Books, 1976.

_____. *Dreams of a Final Theory*. New York, NY: Pantheon Books, 1992.

Weingart, R. "Making Everything Out of Nothing." *The Philosophy of Vacuum*. Oxford: Oxford University Press, 1991.

Weizsacker, C. F. von. *The Unity of Nature*, trans. by Francis J. Zucker. New York, NY: Farrar, Strauss, Giroux, 1980.

_____. *The Unity of Physics in Quantum Theory and Beyond*. Edited by Ted Bastin. Cambridge: Cambridge University Press, 1971.

Weyl, Hermann. *Philosophy of Mathematics and Natural Science*. Revised and augmented English edition. Princeton, NJ: Princeton University Press, 1949.

_____. *Theory of Groups and Quantum Mechanics*, trans. by H. P. Robertson. New York, NY: Dover, 1950.

_____. *Space Time Matter*, trans. by H. L. Brose. New York, NY: Methuen, 1922; repr. Mineola, NY: Dover Publications, Inc., 1950.

_____. *The Continuum: A Critical Examination of the Foundation of Analysis*. New York, NY: Dover Publications, Inc., 1987.

Wheeler, John Archibald. *Frontiers of Time*. Amsterdam: North Holland, 1979.

_____. *At Home in the Universe*. Woodbury, NY: American Institute of Physics, 1994.

Wheeler, J. A. and Zurek, W. H. (eds.) *Quantum Theory and Measurement*. Princeton: Princeton University Press, 1983.

White, John, ed. *The Highest State of Consciousness*. New York, NY: Doubleday, 1972.

———. *Kundalini, Evolution and Enlightenment*. New York, NY: Anchor Books/ Doubleday, 1978.

———. *Theory and Beyond*. Edited by Ted Bastin. Cambridge: Cambridge University Press, 1971.

———. *What Is Enlightenment*. Los Angeles: Jeremy P. Tarcher, Inc., 1984.

Whitehead, Alfred North. *Process and Reality*. New York, NY: The Macmillan Company, 1929.

———. *Adventure of Ideas*. New York, NY: Macmillan Company, 1933.

———. *Essays in Science and Philosophy*. New York, NY: Philosophical Library, 1947.

———. *An Introduction to Mathematics*. London: Oxford University Press, 1984.

Whitehead, Alfred North and Bertrand Russell. *Principia Mathematica*. Cambridge, UK: Cambridge University Press. Vol. 1, 1910; vol. 2, 1912; vol. 3, 1913.

Whitman, Walt. *Leaves of Grass*. New York, NY: Quality Paperback Book Club, 1992.

Whitrow, G. J. *What Is Time?* London: Thames and Hudson, 1972.

———. *The Natural Philosophy of Time*. Oxford: Oxford University Press, 1980.

———. *Time in History*. Oxford: Oxford University Press, 1989.

Wick, David. *The Infamous Boundary: Seven Decades of Controversy in Quantum Physics*. Boston: Birkhäuser, 1995.

Wigner, Eugene P. "The Limits of Science," *Proceedings of the American Philosophical Society* 94, 1950.

Wilbur, Ken. *The Atman Project*. Wheaton, Ill.: The Theosophical Publishing House, 1980.

———. *Quantum Questions*. London: New Science Library, 1984.

———. *Sex, Ecology and Spirituality*. Boulder, CO: Shambhala, 1995.

Wilhelm, M. *Education: The Healing Art*. Houston, Tx: Paideia Press, 1995.

Wilkenhause, A. *Pauline Mysticism*. Freiburg: Herder, 1956.

Williams, R. *Jaina Yoga: A Survey of the Mediaeval Sravkacaras*. London: Oxford University Press, 1963.

Wingate. *Tilling the Soul*. Santa Fe, NM: Aurora Press, 1984.

Yampolsky, Philip, ed. and trans. *The Platform Sūtra of the Sixth Patriarch: The Text of the Tunhuang Manuscript*. New York, NY: Columbia University Press, 1967.

Yogananda, Paramahansa. *Men's Eternal Quest*. Los Angeles: Self-Realization Fellowship, 1982.

Yusuf 'Ali, 'Abdullah. *The Meaning of the Holy Qur'an*. Beltsville, MD: Amana Publications, 1994.

Zaehner, R. C. *Matter and Spirit: Their Convergence in Eastern Religions, Marx, and Teilhard de Chardin*. New York, NY: Harper & Row, 1963.

_____. *The Bhagavad Gītā, with Commentary Based on Original Sources*. London: Oxford University Press, 1969.

Zohar, The. Edited by Soncino. III, 1528. Vol. 5, p. 211. A good edition of this book of *The Zohar* is that by Christian Knorr von Rosenroth, with Jewish commentaries (Schulzbach, 1684). Reprints contain additional index (Amsterdam 1714, 1728, 1722, 1805, 3 vols.). Later editions of *The Zohar* were published at Breslau (1866, 3 vols., Livorno (1877-78, in 7 parts), and Wilna (1882, 3 vols., 1882-83 in 10 parts).

Zuzuki, Daisetz Teitaro. *Studies in Zen Buddhism* (London, 1927).

_____. *Collected Writings on Shin Buddhism*. Kyoto: Shinshu Otaniha, 1973.

Index

G

J

M

About the Author

Orest Bedrij is a scientist, businessman, and the author of books. In 1962, at the age of twenty-nine, he was IBM's technical director at the California Institute of Technology Jet Propulsion Laboratory, responsible for the development and integration of a computer complex that controlled the first soft-landing on the moon. For the past 37 years Bedrij has been doing research into the unity of nature and into the physics and philosophy of ultimate reality and meaning known as the nature of God in religion, or the "theory of everything" and the "final law" in physics, which he presents in this book.

Dr. Bedrij is a founder of several high technology companies in computers, semiconductors, communication, finance, and human resource development and the author of books including: *Yes It's Love Your Life Can Be A Miracle, One, You, Science Proves Existence of God* (in French), and *Seeing God Face to Face*. He is married and the father of three children.

95711475R00380

Made in the USA
Columbia, SC
14 May 2018